APR 1 5 1995 DATE			

Mass Media and the Constitution

An Encyclopedia of Supreme Court Decisions

American Law and Society
Series editor: John W. Johnson
VOL. 1

Garland Reference Library
of Social Science
VOL. 421

Mass Media and the Constitution

An Encyclopedia of
Supreme Court Decisions

Richard F. Hixson

Garland Publishing, Inc.
New York & London   1989

Library of Congress Cataloging-in-Publication Data

Hixson, Richard F.
  Mass media and the Constitution : an encyclopedia of Supreme Court
decisions / Richard F. Hixson.
    p.   cm.—(Garland reference library of social science ; vol.
421. American law and society : vol. 1)
    Includes indexes.
    ISBN 0-8240-7947-7 (alk. paper)
    1. Mass media—Law and legislation—United States—Cases.
I. Title. II. Series: Garland reference library of social science ;
v. 421. III. Series: Garland reference library of social science.
American law and society ; vol. 1.
KF2750.A7H58   1989
343.73'0994—dc19   88-25069
[347.303994]

For
Joan and Sam and Mary Lou
and Ben
and Cynthia,
our friend for all time.

Contents

Foreword

The formal law, its practitioners, and the culture it has engendered pervade the United States. The brilliant nineteenth-century French traveler and writer Alexis de Tocqueville maintained in *Democracy in America* that in this country virtually every political question sooner or later leads to a legal decision. Garland Publishing's American Law and Society series encyclopedias, of which *Mass Media and the Constitution: An Encyclopedia of Supreme Court Decisions* is a part, goes Tocqueville one better. Those of us involved in this project believe that the prism of the law gathers, refracts, reflects, and (not infrequently) blurs American life. At its best, law provides a framework that enables us to make sense out of our physical and intellectual surroundings. At its worst, it confuses, frustrates, and impedes progress. Law has affected and continues to affect virtually everything we do or think about: giving birth, rearing and educating children, marriage, work, travel, business transactions, what we read and see, and, of course, how we get along with one another.

Although studying law in its social context might be a valuable approach to use in grappling with any country's history, it is particularly appropriate for the United States. This is, after all, the country with more statutes and published case law than any in the world. D. H. Lawrence, the great British writer and critic, once referred to America as a nation of "Thou Shalt Nots." The United States now has about 25 times as many lawyers per capita as Japan. Yet Americans are not totally comfortable with the law and those who perform what the legal philosopher Karl Llewellyn once called the "law jobs." For example, the first lawyer who arrived in the Pilgrim colony of Plymouth in the 1620s was quickly driven out of town for being too disputatious. This may have spawned the first American lawyer joke. Perhaps the residents of Plymouth were saying that law is too important to be left to the lawyers.

Professor Richard Hixson's *Mass Media and the Constitution* provides over 200 entries treating Supreme Court decisions on communication law, an area of vital interest to attorneys and law students. But that is not all. As he states in his preface, this volume can be profitably used by journalists, historians, political scientists, sociologists, and "untold and unidentified others." With its fine indexes and careful organizational plan, the volume is a valuable reference tool. It also makes good reading; open it anywhere and dip into the rich case literature on such subjects as privacy, censorship, and fair trial. But be prepared to spend some time and to do some thinking. As these case entries indicate, the media have enriched and complicated our lives. Over a generation ago the Canadian educator Marshall McLuhan pointed out that the media "extended" human nature. Professor Hixson's comprehensive volume measures, qualifies, and probes the nature of that extension. Each of the other volumes planned for the American Law and Society series will have an editor who will harness the work of numerous individual contributors. *Mass Media and the Constitution*, the first contribution to this series, is unique in that Professor Hixson wrote every entry himself.

Richard Hixson is Professor of Communication Law and Journalism History at Rutgers University in New Brunswick, New Jersey, where he has been a faculty member since 1960. Before beginning his academic career, he worked in advertising, in public relations, and as a reporter and newspaper editor. Among his numerous publications are *Privacy in a Public Society: Human Rights in Conflict* (1987), *Mass Media: A Casebook* (1973), and *Isaac Collins: A Quaker Printer in 18th Century America* (1968). He is currently at work on a study of the Supreme Court's decisions on pornography in their social, economic, and political contexts.

JOHN W. JOHNSON
Series Editor
University of Northern Iowa

Preface

This encyclopedia is a ready reference, nothing more nor less, the first stop for an almost unlimited number of researchers: the historian who needs to know the nuances of federalism; the political scientist who wants to understand the Constitution; the sociologist who suspects a connection between mores and jurisprudence; the attorney who requires a quick refresher on the chronology of communication law; the journalist who wants to avoid being sued; the law student who is stymied by a case study; or the teacher in search of lecture material. Each, plus untold and unidentified others, was in mind during the book's preparation. It was written for the layperson as well as the specialist.

Although the more than 200 entries under 12 generic categories of communication law are incomplete—that is, not definitive—the volume taken as a whole is indeed complete. Routinely summarized are major Supreme Court cases identified as coming under either the free speech clause or the free press subclause of the First Amendment. But each entry also lists, with abbreviated rationale, all prior decisions used by the Court. Thus, in this broad sense, the volume is definitive. All cases, major and minor, are listed in the index, which is perhaps the most important part of the book. Like most such encyclopedic efforts, this is a book to be read backward.

Depending on the reason for consulting the book, of course, the reader might wisely start with the table of contents to see if he or she has the right book. The next step is to go either directly to the appropriate section or to the index to see where a particular case is mentioned. Each entry is brief, depending on the significance and/or length of the decision as originally written. Within a matter of minutes, a case can be reviewed: first, from its full title and the various citations in major federal case reporters; second, from the dates the case was argued before, and decided by, the Court; third, from a summary of the law made; fourth, from the factual circumstances; fifth, from the opinion, including excerpts from the majority, concurring, and dissenting views; sixth, from the referenced cases, or prior decisions, briefly annotated; and seventh, from further reading in law journals and reviews. Upon leaving this exercise, the researcher should have a firm grasp of the decision and the law it generated.

In those decisions that were reversed and remanded for further proceedings, the Court may note in its opinion the lower court to which it returned its findings. If such is not mentioned, the case was remanded to the court which generated the appeal to the Supreme Court. The final outcome is seldom dealt with in the present volume, however, for that information is beyond the purpose and scope of the book. The reader should also note that with *per curiam* "by the court" decisions, where no "Argued" date appears it is because with these cases no oral argument took place.

The decisions are summarized chronologically under each section. Each decision has an individual citation reflecting the name of the case reporter in which the decision may be found, the volume of that reporter, and the page on which the case begins. For example, the official government citation for *Beauharnais v. Illinois*, an early libel decision, is 343 U.S. 250 (1952). The number 343 refers to the specific volume of the *United States Reports* where the full decision may be found. The second number, 250, is the page, and 1952 is the year. The same format is used for citations in the other unofficial case reporters noted at the beginning of each decision and for the works listed in "Further Reading." A few early decisions in the book are cited by the name of the reporter, such as 1 Dall. 319 (1796) for Dallas, 4 Wheat. 316 (1819) for Wheaton, and 19 Wall. 178 (1874) for Wallace. Prior to 1817, the *United States Reports* was published by private reporters, and since then by official reporters. The first 90 volumes, from Dallas, beginning in 1789, through Wallace, in 1874, were later numbered consecutively. Beginning with volume 91 (1875), this numbering system was adopted and continues to this day.

In addition, at the end of each section there is a selected bibliography of other scholarly articles that address more generic issues over time and cite author(s), title, date, and publication information. They were gleaned from a number of sources, the main ones being *Journalism Quarterly*'s "A Selected Annotated Bibliography," which appears in every edition, published by the Association for Education in Journalism and Mass Communication (AEJMC), and *Media Law Notes*, published quarterly by the Law Division of the AEJMC.

There are actually two indexes, the first of cases, the second of names, terms, and concepts. The first is designed for the specialist who may be interested in going immediately to a specific case or cases to discover "the law," the precedents, and the ground on which certain justices based their opinions. Major decisions appear in bold. This researcher may also want to read further from the list of contemporaneous scholarly articles at the end of each entry, as well as consult the selected bibliography at the end of each category of decisions.

The second, more general, index is designed for the less knowing but equally serious reader whose initial interest may be in the evolutionary development of the First Amendment. This researcher will discover that Supreme Court justices are neither always nor seldom witty or wise, rational or irrational, conservative or liberal, constructionist or deconstructionist, activist or pacifist. They usually, but not always, defy such reductionist labels. Some have been more predictable than others, like William O. Douglas, who rarely wrote lengthy opinions, or Felix Frankfurter, who seldom wrote briefly on First Amendment law. The opinions of Oliver Wendell Holmes continue to dazzle with simple eloquence. William J. Brennan, Jr.'s efforts at balancing and William H. Rehnquist's uncompromising conservatism remind us of the worth of constitutional debate. And the risk-taking of Earl Warren and Harry A. Blackmun points to the volatile nature of the Court when it tackles social issues. Preparing the book was a learning experience for the author, as it should be for users as well.

Consulted were both primary and secondary sources. The primary are: *United States Reports* ("U.S."), the official government publication of Supreme Court decisions; *United States Court Reports, Lawyers' Edition* ("L.Ed." and "L.Ed.2d"), issued by the Lawyers' Cooperative Publishing Co.; *Supreme Court Reporter* ("S.Ct."), published by West Publishing Co.; *Media Law Reporter* ("Med.L.Rptr."), a specialized commercial reporting service published weekly by the Bureau of National Affairs; *American Law Reports* ("A.L.R."), a Lawyers' Cooperative publication of selected state and federal cases; *United States Law Week* ("U.S.L.W."), issued by the Bureau of National Affairs; *United States Patent Quarterly* ("U.S.P.Q."), also issued by the Bureau of National Affairs; and, finally, *Digest of United States Supreme Court Reports, Lawyers' Edition*, another Lawyers' Cooperative publication.

Of the many secondary sources available, the following were relied on heavily for composite verification of the author's own assessment of each case: Norman Dorsen, Paul Bender, and Burt Neuborne, *Emerson, Haber, and Dorsen's Political and Civil Rights in the United States, Law School Edition*, 4th ed., vol. 1 (Boston: Little, Brown, 1976); Donald M. Gillmor and Jerome A. Barron, *Mass Communication Law: Cases and Comment*, 3d ed. (St. Paul: West Publishing, 1979); Kent R. Middleton and Bill F. Chamberlin, *The Law of Public Communication* (New York: Longman, 1988); Don R. Pember, *Mass Media Law*, 4th ed. (Dubuque: Wm. C. Brown, 1987); William E. Francois, *Mass Media Law and Regulation*, 4th ed. (New York: John Wiley & Sons, 1986); Ralph L. Holsinger, *Media Law* (New York: Random House, 1987); Harold L. Nelson and Dwight L. Teeter, Jr., *Law of Mass Communications: Freedom and Control of Print and Broadcast Media*, 4th ed. (Mineola: The Foundation Press, 1982); T. Barton Carter, Marc A. Franklin, and Jay B. Wright, *The First Amendment and the Fourth Estate: The Law of Mass Media*, 3d ed. (Westbury: The Foundation Press, 1985); Kenneth S. Devol, ed., *Mass Media and the Supreme Court: The Legacy of the Warren Years* (New York: Hastings House, 1982); Christopher G. Wren and Jill Robinson Wren, *The Legal Research Manual*, 2d ed. (Madison: A-R Editions, 1986); and Justin D. Franklin and Robert E. Bourchard, comps. and eds., *Guidebook to the Freedom of Information and Privacy Acts*, 2d ed. (New York: Clark Boardman, 1986).

For further reading under each case, relied on exclusively was the *Index to Legal Periodicals*, first issued as *An Index to Legal Periodical Literature* by Charles C. Soule, Boston, in 1888 and issued under its present title since 1909 by H. W. Wilson Co. for the American Association of Law Librarians.

What remains to explain are the criteria used to select the decisions summarized. First, however, the reader should know that only U.S. Supreme Court decisions were considered; state and lower federal decisions were not, mainly to make the volume manageable, but also in the interest of portraying the highest degree of constitutional law. This was somewhat problematic in Broadcasting, a category that has had a number of significant lower court decisions; many important FCC cases have not reached the Supreme Court.

In each category except Free Speech, the guiding influence on selection was popular media, including radio, television, motion pictures, books, newspapers, and magazines. Where these were central to the decision, that is, circumstantial to the outcome, they were included. With those cases not affecting the media directly, persuasive were later decisions affected by these nonmedia rulings. But in most instances media were involved directly. The Free Speech section, which appears in alphabetical sequence, should probably have appeared first in the book, since it includes decisions, many with no apparent media connection, that contributed substantially to First Amendment theory. The Privacy section has few fully summarized decisions, the result of few cases of media invasion having reached the Court. If other such ambiguities appear, they may be explained by the above rationale. For example, many cases could have been assigned to more than one category, since communication law has never been easily compartmentalized. A category was chosen on the basis of what seemed the primary focus of a case—when, for example, both privacy and libel or obscenity and censorship were involved. When in doubt, the researcher is advised to consult the index.

It is appropriate at this juncture to acknowledge my indebtedness to these authors and the countless others who have inspired and taught me over the years, especially those whom I am privileged to have as valued friends. Bill Chamberlin of the University of Florida, truly an eminent scholar, has encouraged and scolded me with affection, as have many other colleagues around the country and abroad at various places of learning—cafés, homes, taverns, inns, dormitories. At Rutgers University, my home base for many years, there are Jerome Aumente, Richard Budd, Todd Hunt, Brent Ruben, David Sachsman, and Dania Stager-Snow, all colleagues in the School of Communication, Information and Library Studies. Dr. Stager-Snow is a special friend for all seasons. They, and the university's administration, allowed for my sabbatical absence to finish the book. Albert P. Blaustein of the Rutgers Law School in Camden responded patiently to my naive questions on copyright. Near the completion of the writing, I had the pleasure of guest lecturing on two occasions to Sylvia Sirlin's journalism students at Ft. Hamilton High School, Brooklyn. I thank them, as well as my Rutgers students, for their tough questions and enthusiastic support.

A number of librarians have been helpful, especially Nona Spooner of the law library at the Hunterdon County Courthouse, who was patient with me throughout the project. Unsung assistance also came from staff members at the Rutgers Alexander Library, the New Jersey State Law Library, the Rutgers Law Library in Newark, and the Biddle Law Library at the University of Pennsylvania.

I would be remiss if I did not confess my gratitude to another scholar, Robert V. Hudson, whose Garland reference book, *Mass Media: A Chronological Encyclopedia of Television, Radio, Motion Pictures, Magazines, Newspapers, and Books in the United States* (1987), finally provoked me into this similar but more specialized project. While reading Hudson's work in manuscript, I conceived my own encyclopedia, which Gary Kuris at Garland immediately accepted enthusiastically. Hudson's inclusion of several important Supreme Court decisions suggested the need for a separate volume on that aspect of American media chronology. I had not informed Hudson, a longtime colleague, before this writing, but now do so gladly. When the manuscript reached Garland, John W. Johnson of the University of Northern Iowa, the series editor, offered valuable advice and agreed to write the Foreword. At Garland the manuscript was edited with great care by Kennie Lyman and Julia Zafferano. I wish to thank them, as well as Paula Ladenburg, for their attention to every detail.

Closer to hearth are family members who graciously distanced themselves during the writing. They include Todd, Sommer, Tracy, and especially Cynthia, who did not live to see the completion of yet another project she encouraged me to start. Our many friends now guide me in her stead. I thank each of them from the heart. But, though my family and friends share in the excitement of authorship, I alone wrote the book and am responsible for its shortcomings.

RICHARD F. HIXSON
New Brunswick, New Jersey
May 1988

Broadcasting

1930   *Federal Radio Commission v. General Electric Co. et al.,* **281 U.S. 464, 74 L.Ed. 969, 50 S.Ct. 389**

Argued: Jan. 17, 20, 1930.

Decided: May 19, 1930.

Summary: Held that the Court is without jurisdiction to review a court of appeals determination on an order of the FRC refusing renewal of an existing broadcast license.

Circumstances: General Electric owned and operated a radio station in Schenectady when the Radio Act of 1927 went into effect, under which it obtained successive licenses. The last had been issued Nov. 1, 1927, for that month, and prolonged by short extensions to Nov. 11, 1928. On Oct. 12, 1928, the FRC said it would not issue a license under the existing terms but that it would issue a license with other terms less advantageous to the company and the communities it served. The Court of Appeals for the District of Columbia ruled that public convenience, interest, and necessity would be served by renewing the existing license without change in terms. The FRC was directed to issue the license. The Supreme Court granted certiorari on petition of the commission.

Opinion: Justice Willis Van Devanter wrote for the unanimous Court. Chief Justice Charles E. Hughes did not participate. Van Devanter, joined by Justices Oliver Wendell Holmes, Louis D. Brandeis, George Sutherland, James C. McReynolds, Pierce Butler, and Harlan F. Stone, concluded that the proceeding in the Court of Appeals for the District of Columbia was not a case or controversy in the sense of the judiciary article. Instead, he said, it was an administrative proceeding and, therefore, not reviewable by the Supreme

Court. "We think it plain ... that the powers confided to the commission respecting the granting and renewal of station licenses are purely administrative and that the provision for appeals to the court of appeals does no more than make that court a superior and revising agency in the same field." He noted that under the judiciary article of the Constitution, the courts of the District of Columbia are legislative courts, not solely judiciary in purpose. The Supreme Court, on the other hand, had been "brought into being" by the judiciary article and cannot give decisions that are merely advisory, nor can it exercise or participate in the exercise of functions that are essentially legislative or administrative.

Referenced Cases: *Butterworth v. U.S.*, 112 U.S. 50 (1884), *Postum Cereal Co. v. Calif. Fig Nut Co.*, 272 U.S. 693 (1927), and *Keller v. Potomac Electric Power Co.*, 261 U.S. 428 (1923), on relevance of patent appeals and public utilities appeals; *Liberty Warehouse Co. v. Grannis*, 273 U.S. 70 (1927), *Willing v. Chicago Auditorium Asso.*, 277 U.S. 274 (1928), and *Ex parte Bakelite Corp.*, 279 U.S. 438 (1929), on essentially legislative or administrative functions; *Old Colony Trust Co. v. Commissioner of Internal Revenue*, 279 U.S. 716 (1929), regarding judicial power as defined in the judiciary article of the Constitution.

Further Reading:
1 *J. Air L.* 353, 416 (July 1930).
1 *J. Radio L.* 128 (April 1931).
8 *NYU L.Q. Rev.* 149 (Summer 1930).

1933   *Federal Radio Commission v. Nelson Bros. Bond & Mortgage Co. (Station WIBO), FRC v. North Shore Church (Station WPCC), FRC and Johnson-Kennedy Radio Corp. (Station WJKS) v. Nelson Bros., and FRC and Johnson-Kennedy Radio Corp. v. North Shore Church,* **289 U.S. 266, 77 L.Ed. 1166, 53 S.Ct. 627, 89 A.L.R. 406**

Argued: April 11, 1933.

Decided: May 8, 1933.

Summary: State lines do not divide radio waves; national regulation of broadcasting is not only appropriate but also essential to the efficient use of radio facilities.

Circumstances: The Court of Appeals for the District of Columbia reversed a decision of the FRC granting an application to broadcast with unlimited time on a certain frequency and terminating existing licenses of interfering stations. The Supreme Court reversed. The Johnson-Kennedy Radio Corp., owner of station WJKS in Gary, Indiana, applied to the FRC for modification of its license to permit unlimited operation time on a frequency then assigned to WIBO, owned by Nelson Bros., and WPCC, owned by the North Shore Church, both stations in Chicago. The FRC granted the application and terminated licenses held by WIBO and WPCC. The court of appeals determined the FRC's actions arbitrary and capricious. The licenses for the stations had been issued temporarily and conditioned on the commission's review of the WJKS application. Its ultimate decision was based on the fact that the deletion of WIBO and WPCC would not deprive the service area of "any type of programs not now received from other stations."

Opinion: Chief Justice Charles E. Hughes wrote the unanimous decision, joined by Justices Willis Van Devanter, James C. McReynolds, Louis D. Brandeis, George Sutherland, Pierce Butler, Harlan F. Stone, Owen J. Roberts, and Benjamin N. Cardozo. First, on the matter of jurisdiction, Hughes said that questions of law are the appropriate subject of judicial determinations. Second, on the matter of regional allocation of licenses, he said that the FRC, in making its "fair and equitable allocations," was entitled to consider all the broadcasting facilities assigned to respective states. The commission's broad authority under the law "plainly extended to the deletion of existing stations if that course was found to be necessary to produce an equitable result," so long as the agency did not act arbitrarily or capriciously. "The concern of the Congress was with the interests of the people—that they might have a reasonable equality of opportunity in radio transmission and reception, and this involved an equitable distribution not only as between zones but as between States as well." The Court supported the commission's authority.

Referenced Cases: *FRC v. General Electric Co.*, 281 U.S. 464 (1930), *Keller v. Potomac Electric Power Co.*, 261 U.S. 428 (1923), and *Postum Cereal Co. v. Calif. Fig Nut Co.*, 272 U.S. 693 (1927), on administrative or legislative versus judicial functions of courts; *Interstate Commerce Commission v. Illinois C. R. Co.*, 215 U.S. 452 (1910), *Akron C. & Y. R. Co. v. U.S.*, 261 U.S. 184 (1923), *Baltimore & O. R. Co. v. U.S.*, 264 U.S. 258 (1924), *Silberschein v. U.S.*, 266 U.S. 221 (1924), *Ma-King Products Co. v. Blair*, 271 U.S. 479 (1926), *FTC v. Klesner*, 280 U.S. 19 (1929), *Tagg Bros. & Moorhead v. U.S.*, 280 U.S. 420 (1930), *FTC v. Raladam Co.*, 283 U.S. 643 (1931), and *Crowell v. Benson*, 285 U.S. 22 (1932), all on questions of law, the finding of fact, and judiciary; *FTC v. Eastman Kodak Co.*, 274 U.S. 619 (1927), and *Old Colony Trust Co. v. Commissioner of Internal Revenue*, 279 U.S. 716 (1929), on the substance and intent of proceedings; *Union Bridge Co. v. U.S.*, 204 U.S. 364 (1907), *Philadelphia Co. v. Stimson*, 223 U.S. 605 (1912), *Philadelphia B. & W. R. Co. v. Schubert*, 224 U.S. 603 (1912), *Greenleaf-Johnson Lumber Co. v. Garrison*, 237 U.S. 251 (1915), *Continental Ins. Co. v. U.S.*, 259 U.S. 156 (1922), *Sproles v. Binford*, 286 U.S. 374 (1932), and *Stephenson v. Binford*, 287 U.S. 251 (1932), on the power of Congress to regulate interstate commerce; *New York Cent. Securities Corp. v. U.S.*, 287 U.S. 12 (1932), on agency standards conferring limited power.

Further Reading:
33 *Columbia L. Rev.* 921 (May 1933).
28 *Illinois L. Rev.* 409 (Nov. 1933).
18 *Minnesota L. Rev.* 209 (Jan. 1934).
42 *Yale L. J.* 1274 (June 1933).

1940 *Federal Communications Commission v. Pottsville Broadcasting Co.*, 309 U.S. 134, 84 L.Ed. 656, 60 S.Ct. 437

Argued: Jan. 11, 1940.

Decided: Jan. 29, 1940.

Summary: Ascertained and enforced the FCC's sphere of authority over radio station licensing through the standard of "public convenience, interest, or necessity" as determined by Congress in the Communications Act of 1934 and amended in 1937.

Circumstances: In May 1936 the Pottsville Broadcasting Co. sought from the FCC a permit to construct a broadcasting station in that city. The commission denied the application on the grounds that the company was financially unqualified and that the applicant did not sufficiently represent local interests in the community. The company went to court. The court of appeals withheld judgment on the second point, but said that the first was based on an erroneous interpretation of Pennsylvania law. It reversed the FCC's decision and ordered the commission to reconsider the application. Instead of granting the original application, the FCC decided to hear arguments along with two rival applications for the same facilities. At this stage, Pottsville Broadcasting obtained a writ of mandamus ordering the commission to set aside its comparative hearing and reconsider the original application. The court of appeals said that a lower court is bound to respect the mandate of an appellate tribunal, viewing the FCC, in this instance, the same as a lower court. On appeal, the Supreme Court noted the "deeper issue" that a mandate from court to court is different from one from a court to an administrative agency. Congress has distinguished between its power to regulate commerce and the reviewing power it has conferred on the courts under Article III of the Constitution.

Opinion: Justice Felix Frankfurter wrote the unanimous decision. In question was a writ of mandamus issued by the Court of Appeals for the District of Columbia forbidding the FCC from allocating a radio station construction permit application on a comparative basis. Endorsing the commission's authority, Frankfurter said that Congress provided for a system of permits and licenses to avoid the "widespread fear that in the absence of governmental control the public interest might be subordinated to monopolistic domination in the broadcasting field." In granting or withholding permits for the construction of stations and their operation, "public convenience, interest, or necessity" was the touchstone for the exercise of the commission's authority. "The Communications Act is not designed primarily as a new code for the adjustment of conflicting private rights through adjudication. Rather it expresses a desire on the part of Congress to maintain, through appropriate administrative control, a grip on the dynamic aspects of radio transmission." Although courts may correct errors of law in reviewing agency decisions, such does not foreclose the administrative unit, upon correcting its error, from enforcing the legislative policy "committed to its charge." The fact that the FCC, in this case, had committed a legal error did not create rights of priority for the station. "Only Congress could confer such a priority. It has not done so."

Referenced Cases: *In re Sanford Fork & Tool Co.*, 160 U.S. 247 (1895), *U.S. v. Morgan*, 307 U.S. 183 (1939), and *Sprague v. Ticonic Bank*, 307 U.S. 161 (1939), on binding nature of appellate mandates; *Interstate Commerce Commission v. Baird*, 194 U.S. 25 (1904), and *New England Divisions Case*, 261 U.S. 184 (1923), on power and authority of administrative agencies; *Federal Radio Comm'n v. General Electric Co.*, 281 U.S. 464 (1930), and *FRC v. Nelson Bros. Co.*, 289 U.S. 266 (1933), regarding the Court of Appeals as a superior and revising agency; *Federal Power Comm'n v. Pacific Co.*, 307 U.S. 156 (1939), and *Ford Motor Co. v. Labor Board*, 305 U.S. 364 (1939), on agency errors of law and remands for corrections; *Missouri K. & T. Ry. Co. v. May*, 194 U.S. 267 (1904), on legislatures as guardians of liberties and welfare in as great a degree as the courts.

Further Reading:
28 *Illinois Bar J.* 362 (June 1940).
1 *Washington & Lee L. Rev.* 253 (Spring 1940).

1940   *Federal Communications Commission v. Columbia Broadcasting System of California, Inc. and FCC v. Associated*

Broadcasters, Inc., 311 U.S. 132, 85 L.Ed. 87, 61 S.Ct. 152

Argued: Nov. 15, 1940.

Decided: Nov. 25, 1940.

Summary: On the matter of judicial authority under the Communications Act of 1934, the Court upheld the FCC's refusal to consent to an assignment of a radio station's license.

Circumstances: Acting under Section 310 of the Communications Act, the FCC refused consent to an assignment to CBS of California of a radio station license held by the Associated Broadcasters, which sought a court of appeals review of the commission's denial of consent. The court of appeals, with one dissent, denied the motions and entertained jurisdiction. The Supreme Court reversed.

Opinion: Justice Felix Frankfurter, writing for the unanimous Court, said that the Communications Act of 1934 "bifurcates access to the lower federal courts according to the nature of the subject matter before the Commission." Excepted from jurisdiction of the district courts is, in the words of the act, "any order of the Commission granting or refusing an application for a construction permit for a radio station, or for a radio station license, or for renewal of an existing radio station license, or for modification of an existing radio station license, or suspending a radio operator's license." The crux of the controversy, Frankfurter opined, is whether an order of the FCC denying consent to an assignment of a radio station license is the same as an order refusing application for a station license. The Court reversed a review of the denial of consent by the Court of Appeals for the District of Columbia. That court had denied the FCC's move to dismiss the appeal for want of jurisdiction.

Referenced Cases: None referred to in the text of the opinion, but in oral arguments the following were cited: *Washington Market Co. v. Hoffman*, 101 U.S. 112 (1879), *FRC v. Nelson Bros. Bond & Mortg. Co.*, 289 U.S. 266 (1933), and *FCC v.*

Sanders Bros. Radio Station, 309 U.S. 470 (1940), on transfer of license and the granting of a new one; *Latimer v. U.S.*, 223 U.S. 501 (1912), *U.S. v. Raynor*, 302 U.S. 540 (1938), *U.S. V. Ryan*, 284 U.S. 167 (1931), and *Ohio Bell Teleph. Co. v. Public Utilities Commission*, 301 U.S. 292 (1937), regarding congressional intent on the matter of judicial review; *Wright v. Vinton Mountain Trust Bank*, 300 U.S. 440 (1937), and *Federal Trade Commission v. Raladam Co.*, 283 U.S. 643 (1931), on jurisdiction of the Court of Appeals for the District of Columbia; *Sessions v. Romadka*, 145 U.S. 29 (1892), and *Hecht v. Malley*, 265 U.S. 144 (1924), on judicial rejection of the *Pote Case*, writ of certiorari denied in 290 U.S. 680 (1933).

Further Reading:
12 *Air L. Rev.* 82 (Jan. 1941).
29 *Georgia L. J.* 342 (Dec. 1940).

1943   *National Broadcasting Co., Inc. and Stromberg-Carlson Telephone Manufacturing Co. v. U.S. Federal Communications Commission, and Mutual Broadcasting System Inc. and Columbia Broadcasting System Inc. v. U.S. et al.*, 319 U.S. 190, 87 L.Ed. 1344, 63 S.Ct. 997; 1 Med.L.Rptr. 1965

Argued: Feb. 10, 11, 1943.

Decided: May 10, 1943.

Summary: FCC's overall regulatory powers, specifically its chain broadcasting regulations in the "public interest," and its authority to withhold licenses for violation of antitrust laws upheld by the Court.

Circumstances: On Oct. 30, 1941, the two networks sought to enjoin enforcement of the FCC's chain broadcasting regulations, which were adopted as the result of the commission's investigation and subsequent hearings. The FCC found that at the end of 1938 there were 660 commercial stations in the United States and that 341 of them were affiliated with national networks—135 exclusively with NBC and 102 with CBS. Stations affiliated with the networks, including Mutual, utilized more than 97 percent of the total nighttime broadcasting power of all stations in the country. NBC and CBS controlled more than 85 percent of the total nighttime wattage. The FCC noted several network abuses: hindering growth of new networks through exclusive affiliations that prevented stations from broadcasting programs of other networks; depriving audiences of program variety through the binding of networks not to sell to competing area stations; constraining future station and community needs through five-year contracts between networks and stations; hindering the development of local programming through network "option time"; burdening stations unduly with having to justify their option to reject network programs; controlling competition through ownership of stations; and controlling finances through the networks' control of station advertising rates. The FCC's new regulations were designed to correct these abuses. The District Court for the Southern District of New York disposed of the cases upon the pleadings and the record made before the commission without trial de novo. The Supreme Court affirmed.

Opinion: Justice Felix Frankfurter wrote the Court's 5-to-2 opinion, joined by Chief Justice Harlan F. Stone and Justices Stanley F. Reed, William O. Douglas, and Robert H. Jackson. Dissenting were Frank Murphy and Owen J. Roberts. Hugo L. Black and Wiley B. Rutledge did not participate. Frankfurter, in supporting the FCC's right to enforce its chain broadcasting regulations, traced the history of government supervision of broadcasting and stated that regulation was as vital to the development of radio "as traffic control was to the development of the automobile." In enacting the Radio Act of 1927, which was replaced by the Communications Act of 1934, Congress "acted upon the knowledge that if the potentialities of radio were not to be wasted, regulation was essential." In essence, Frankfurter said, the chain broadcasting regulations represent "a particularization of the Commission's conception of the 'public interest' sought to be safeguarded by Congress in enacting the Communications Act of 1934." He concluded, therefore, that the law authorized the FCC to promulgate regulations designed to correct abuses in chain broadcasting, defined in the act as the "simultaneous broadcasting of an identical program by two or more connected stations." He also asserted that the regulations did not violate the First Amendment, nor was their enforcement capricious and arbitrary. Addressing the free-speech issue, Frankfurter wrote: "Freedom of utterance is abridged to many who wish to sue the limited facilities of radio. Unlike other modes of expression, radio inherently is not available to all. That is its unique characteristic, and that is why . . . it is subject to government regulation. Because it cannot be used by all, some who wish to use it must be denied."

Justice Murphy, in dissent, pointed out that radio "may be a weapon of authority and misrepresentation instead of a means of entertainment and enlightenment." He accused the Court of exceeding its competence in bestowing on an agency power that he said Congress had not granted. He said the Communications Act of 1934 did not give the FCC power to regulate contractual relations between stations and the networks. He underscored the gravity of permitting the exercise of comprehensive control of broadcasting by government without explicit statutory authority, as Congress had made clear in other fields of regulation.

Referenced Cases: *Columbia System v. U.S.*, 316 U.S. 407 (1942), and *National Broadcasting Co. v. U.S.*, 316 U.S. 447 (1942), on the reach of the Communications Act of 1934; *FCC v. Pottsville Broadcasting Co.*, 309 U.S. 134 (1940), on Congress' desire to formulate a unified and comprehensive regulatory system for the industry; *New York Central Securities Co. v. U.S.*, 287 U.S. 12 (1932), and *FRC v. Nelson Bros. Co.*, 289 U.S. 266 (1933), on limited power interpreted within the context of the nature of radio; *FCC v. Sanders Radio Station*, 309 U.S. 470 (1940), on rendering community service; *Board of Trade v. U.S.*, 314 U.S. 534 (1942), on the Court's inability to deal with technical competence; *Tagg Bros. v. U.S.*, 280 U.S. 420 (1930), and *Acker v. U.S.*, 298 U.S. 426 (1936), on the procedure for judicial review.

Further Reading:
41 *Michigan L. Rev.* 1195 (June 1943).

1943   *Federal Communications Commission*
         v. National Broadcasting Co., Inc.
         (KOA), **319 U.S. 239, 87 L.Ed. 1374, 63**
         S.Ct. 1035

Argued: April 8, 9, 1943.

Decided: May 17, 1943.

Summary: The owner of a station, whose license specified frequency, power, and a clear nighttime channel, is entitled to
participate in the granting of an application of another station on
the same frequency to increase its power and have the right to
operate at night.

Circumstances: Two radio stations, KOA in Denver
and WHDH in Boston, were licensed to operate on the same frequency, 850 kilocycles, but WHDH only permitted daytime broadcasting. On Oct. 25, 1938, WHDH applied to the FCC for an increase in power and for unlimited operation. The commission set
hearings to decide whether the interests of any other stations would
be adversely affected by interference and to determine if public interest, convenience, or necessity would be served by authorizing
WHDH's request. This meant modifying rules that precluded the
operation of a second station on KOA's frequency. KOA's petition
to intervene was denied by the FCC, as was its petition to dismiss
WHDH's application for failure to conform to rules and regulations.
Hearings were held on two days in January 1939, but KOA was not
permitted to appear or participate. Three of five commissioners
voted to modify the regulations to grant the application. KOA's
second petition to intervene was also denied. In early April the FCC
amended Section 3.25 of its rules and granted the application, two
commissioners dissenting. Still a third petition was denied KOA,
which then went to the Court of Appeals for the District of Columbia, which concluded that the FCC's actions affected modification
of KOA's license and that the Communications Act entitled the
station to be a participant in the process. The Supreme Court agreed.

Opinion: Justice Owen J. Roberts wrote the Court's 4-to-
2 opinion, joined by Chief Justice Harlan F. Stone and Justices

Stanley F. Reed and Robert H. Jackson. Felix Frankfurter and William O. Douglas wrote separate dissents. Not participating were Hugo L. Black, Frank Murphy, and Wiley B. Rutledge. Roberts said that, under the terms of the Communications Act of 1934, station KOA in Denver was entitled to participate in the FCC's proceedings to hear the application of station WHDH in Boston, operating on the same frequency, to increase its power and have the right to unlimited operation. "If, within the intent of the statute, the interests of KOA would be adversely affected, or if KOA would be aggrieved by granting the application of WHDH, then the statute grants KOA a right of appeal."

In dissent, Justice Frankfurter argued that the "vitality of the administrative process" required that the procedural powers given to such agencies not be confined within the conventional modes by which business is done in the courts. He said the Court's decision "imposes a hampering restriction upon the functioning of the administrative process." Whereas the Court held that the FCC was required by law to grant KOA's petition to intervene in the WHDH hearing, Frankfurter believed the law precluded such a construction. "The Commission has exercised the authority given it by Congress to formulate its administrative procedure." He added that KOA failed to show that its interests were substantially impaired by the application grant. Douglas, in substantial agreement with Frankfurter, said that if Congress meant to endow private litigants with such appeal power over FCC decisions, then the Court must be "exceedingly scrupulous" to see to it that the private party's interest in the matter is substantial and immediate.

Referenced Cases: *FCC v. Sanders Bros. Radio Station,* 309 U.S. 470 (1940), in which the Court ruled that Sanders had standing to appeal under the Communications Act; *FCC v. Pottsville Broadcasting Co.,* 309 U.S. 134 (1940), on FCC's licensing authority; *Scripps-Howard Radio v. FCC,* 316 U.S. 4 (1941), on judicial review of FCC actions; *Muskrat v. U.S.,* 219 U.S. 346 (1911), and *FRC v. General Electric Co.,* 281 U.S. 464 (1930), on the constitutionality of a statutory scheme that allowed someone who showed no invasion of a private right to call on the courts to review an order of the FCC; *U.S. v. Alaska S. S. Co.,* 253 U.S. 113 (1920), and *Massachusetts v. Mellon,* 262 U.S. 447 (1923), regarding "direct and substantial" injury.

Further Reading:
42 *Michigan L. Rev.* 329 (Oct. 1943).
52 *Yale L. J.* 671 (June 1943).

1951   *Radio Corporation of America, National Broadcasting Company Inc., RCA Victor Distributing Corp., et al. v. U.S., Federal Communications Commission, and Columbia Broadcasting System Inc., 341 U.S. 412, 95 L.Ed. 1962, 71 S.Ct. 806*

Argued: March 26, 27, 1951.

Decided: May 28, 1951.

Summary: Sustained the FCC's power to prescibe standards for transmission of color television.

Circumstances: RCA and two of its subsidiaries brought action in a three-judge District Court for the Northern District of Illinois, Eastern Division, to enjoin and set aside an order of the FCC prescribing color television transmission standards. Following a hearing and oral arguments, the court entered summary judgment sustaining the FCC, one judge dissenting. RCA contended that the district court failed to review the record as a whole. RCA also argued that the standard for color broadcasting should have been postponed until a more perfect system was developed, and it contended that it was on the verge of discovering a system compatible with receivers in public use. The Supreme Court rejected these claims primarily on the ground that the FCC had not acted capriciously in allowing television viewers the immediate opportunity to receive color transmission if they so desired.

Opinion: Justice Hugo L. Black wrote the Court's 8-to-1 decision, joined by Chief Justice Fred M. Vinson and Justices Stanley F. Reed, William O. Douglas, Robert H. Jackson, Harold H.

Burton, Sherman Minton, and Tom C. Clark. Felix Frankfurter, dissenting, expressed doubts about the case. Black said that the effect of the FCC's challenged order was to reject a color system proposed by RCA and to accept one proposed by CBS. The Court rejected the view, held by RCA, that no system had yet been proved worthy of acceptance for public use and that commercial color broadcasting should have been postponed to await inventions that would achieve "more nearly perfect results." While recognizing the desirability of a "compatible" color system, Black noted the correctness of the FCC's position, that further delay in making color available was too high a price to pay for possible compatibility in the future. On the matter of questionable administrative and judicial procedure, Black wrote: "Whether the Commission should have reopened its proceedings to permit RCA to offer proof of new discoveries for its system was a question within the discretion of the Commission which we find was not abused."

Justice Frankfurter, though "no friend of judicial intrusion into the administrative process," said that so long as Congress had deemed it right to subject FCC orders to Court review, "the duty of analyzing the essential issues of an order cannot be escaped by too easy reliance on the conclusions of a district court or on the indisputable formula that an exercise of discretion by the Commission is not to be displaced by a contrary exercise of judicial discretion." Comparing the broadcasting industry's uncertainty on color television systems with the rapid change of opinion among physicists on the use of the cyclotron, Frankfurter concluded: "One need not have the insight of a great scientific investigator, nor the rashness of the untutored, to be confident that the prognostications now made in regard to the feasibility of a 'compatible' color television system will be falsified in the very near future."

Referenced Cases: *Universal Camera Corp. v. NLRB*, 340 U.S. 474 (1951), on relying on a first reviewing court's conclusion regarding the sufficiency of evidence to support an administrative order; *NBC v. U.S.*, 319 U.S. 190 (1943), on the broad powers of the FCC; *Stark v. Wickard*, 321 U.S. 288 (1944), regarding Congress' power to withdraw court review procedure; *FCC v. NBC*, 319 U.S. 239 (1943), on FCC freedom to act in spite of judicial review; *Telephone Cases*, 126 U.S. 1 (1888), *McCormick v. Whitmer*, 129 U.S. 1 (1889), *Corona Cord Tire Co. v. Dovan Chemical Corp.*, 276 U.S. 358 (1928), *DeForest Radio Co. v. General Electric Co.*,

283 U.S. 664 (1931), *RCA v. Radio Engineering Laboratories*, 293 U.S. 1 (1934), *Marconi Wireless Tel. Co. v. U.S.*, 320 U.S. 1 (1943), and *Universal Oil Products Co. v. Globe Oil & Ref. Co.*, 322 U.S. 471 (1944), all cases related the Court's experience with complicated scientific and technical issues.

Further Reading:
37 *ABA J.* 768 (Oct. 1951).
14 *Georgia Bar J.* 88 (Aug. 1951).
1 *J. Public L.* 198 (Spring 1952).
18 *Univ. Chicago L. Rev.* 802 (1951–52).

1953   *Federal Communications Commission v. RCA Communications Inc. and Mackay Radio & Telegraph Co. Inc. v. RCA Communications Inc.*, **346 U.S. 86, 97 L.Ed. 1470, 73 S.Ct. 998**

Argued: April 29, 30, 1953.

Decided: June 8, 1953.

Summary: "Reasonably feasible" competition not the single or controlling factor in determining and safeguarding the "public interest" in radiotelegraphy.

Circumstances: Mackay provided radiotelegraph service between the United States and several foreign countries. Over the opposition of RCA, which provided similar service through 65 circuits including ones to Portugal and the Netherlands, the FCC authorized Mackay to open circuits to those countries. The FCC determined that competition would not impair the ability of the existing carrier, RCA, to provide adequate service. In seeking a review, RCA was successful in the Court of Appeals for the District of Columbia Circuit on its claim that an applicant must show that tangible benefit to the public would be derived from the authorization. The Supreme Court vacated the judgment and remanded the case, first to the court of appeals, then to the FCC.

Opinion: Justice Felix Frankfurter delivered the Court's 5-to-2 decision, joined by Chief Justice Fred M. Vinson and Justices Harold H. Burton, Tom C. Clark, and Sherman Minton. Hugo L. Black and William O. Douglas dissented. Stanley F. Reed and Robert H. Jackson did not participate. RCA had argued that it was not "in the public interest" for Mackay to be allowed to duplicate radiotelegraph service to the Netherlands and Portugal already provided by RCA. In this, the first case on duplicate radiotelegraph circuits to come before the Court, Frankfurter opined that Congress did not purport to transfer its legislative power to the "unbounded discretion" of the FCC. Since the commission had made its decision largely on the basis of "reasonably feasible" competition, the justice noted that in the past the Court had not held that competition is an absolute. He said that the Communications Act of 1934 prohibited competition by those whose entry into the field did not satisfy the "public interest" standard. This restriction was based on the limited availability of international communication facilities. But the FCC was not precluded from drawing on competition for complementary or auxiliary support. "There can be no doubt that competition is a relevant factor in weighing the public interest." Frankfurter accused the FCC of abdicating its responsibility to determine the public interest beyond competition that is merely "reasonably feasible." He wrote: "Merely to assume that competition is bound to be of advantage, in an industry so regulated and so largely closed as is this one, is not enough." Justice Black was of the opinion that the FCC's findings were sufficient to support its order. Justice Douglas dissented from the majority's call for a remand. He said the commission acted without authority. "This is a field where without the proposed service there is active competition and an excess of facilities to meet present or expected needs."

Referenced Cases: *NBC v. U.S.*, 319 U.S. 190 (1943), on early radio regulation; *New York Central Securities Corp. v. U.S.*, 287 U.S. 12 (1932), on the fair enforcement of "public interest, convenience, or necessity"; *FCC v. Pottsville Broadcasting Co.*, 309 U.S. 134 (1940), on discretion and imaginative interpretation of statute; *FRC v. Nelson Bros. Co.*, 289 U.S. 266 (1933), regarding the Court's role in determining the "governing principle" of the statute; *Chicago Board of Trade v. U.S.*, 246 U.S. 231 (1918), holding that competition is not an absolute; *U.S. v. Trans-Missouri Freight Assn.,* 166 U.S. 290 (1897), and *U.S. v. Joint Traffic Assn.,* 171 U.S. 505 (1898), on rigors and restraints of competition in railroad industry; *McLean Trucking Co. v. U.S.,* 321 U.S. 67 (1944), on the relevance of competition to public interest; *Texas & Pac. R. Co. v. Gulf, C. & S. F. R. Co.,* 270 U.S. 266 (1926), on FCC judgment vis-à-vis congressional judgment; *Far East Conf. v. U.S.,* 342 U.S. 570 (1952), and *NLRB v. Seven-Up Co.,* 344 U.S. 344 (1953), regarding the need for FCC latitude in weighing intangibles wherever competition is involved.

Further Reading:
39 *ABA J.* 910 (Oct. 1953).
41 *Georgia L. J.* 243 (Jan. 1953).

1954 *Federal Communications Commission v. American Broadcasting Co., Inc., FCC v. National Broadcasting Co., Inc., and FCC v. Columbia Broadcasting System, Inc.,* 347 U.S. 284, 98 L.Ed. 699, 74 S.Ct. 593

Argued: Feb. 1, 1954.

Decided: April 5, 1954.

Summary: The FCC's denial of licenses to stations broadcasting "give-away" programs ruled invalid and beyond the scope of its regulatory power.

Circumstances: The national broadcasting companies appealed directly from a decision of a three-judge District Court for the Southern District of New York, enjoining the FCC from enforcing certain provisions in its rules relating to the broadcast of so-called give-away programs. Examples were ABC's "Stop the Music," NBC's "What's My Name," and CBS's "Sing It Again," contestants for which are in the studio audience or at home.

Opinion: Chief Justice Earl Warren wrote the Court's 8-to-0 decision, joined by Justices Hugo L. Black, Stanley F. Reed, Felix Frankfurter, Robert H. Jackson, Harold H. Burton, Tom C. Clark, and Sherman Minton. William O. Douglas did not participate. At issue was Section 1304 of the U.S. Criminal Code, formerly Section 316 of the Communications Act of 1934, which prohibits the broadcast of "any lottery, gift enterprise, or similar scheme, offering prizes dependent in whole or in part upon lot or chance." Although the Court endorsed the FCC's power to apply and enforce Section 1304, it held that these giveaway game shows were not lotteries. "We believe that it would be stretching the statute to the breaking point to give it an interpretation that would make such programs a crime." To qualify as a lottery, a contest must have three elements: a prize for the winner; the prize awarded on the basis wholly or partly by chance; and winners must provide something of value, a "consideration," to participate in the game. The third element was missing from the musical game shows, because tickets to the shows are always free. The FCC, in believing these programs to be the "old lottery evil under a new guise," had overstepped the boundaries of interpretation, Warren said, and hence exceeded its rule-making power. "Regardless of the doubts held by the Commission and others as to the social value of the programs . . . such administrative expansion of Section 1304 does not provide the remedy."

Referenced Cases: None. The Court observed: "We find no decisions precisely in point on the facts of the cases before us."

Further Reading:
40 *ABA J.* 515 (June 1954).
68 *Harvard L. Rev.* 174 (Nov. 1954).
39 *Iowa L. Rev.* 372 (Winter 1954).

1956   *U.S. and Federal Communications Commission v. Storer Broadcasting Co.,* 351 U.S. 192, 95 L.Ed. 1081, 76 S.Ct. 763

Argued: Feb. 28, 29, 1956.

Decided: May 21, 1956.

Summary: The FCC was within its statutory power to withhold a license from a television station if applicant had an interest in more than five other stations.

Circumstances: On Aug. 19, 1948, the FCC issued a notice of proposed rule-making under the authority of 47 USC, Sections 303, 311, 313, and 314 of the amended Communications Act of 1934. Relating to multiple ownership of standard, FM, and television stations, the rules provided that licenses would not be granted if the applicant had an interest in more than five other stations. Storer, licensee of a number of radio and television stations, objected on the grounds that such limitations might cause financial damage to owners of standard stations if an obsolescent standard station could not be augmented by FM and television facilities. At the time Storer owned seven standard radio, five FM radio, and five television stations. The FCC denied Storer's application for an additional television station in Miami on the basis of the rules. The Court of Appeals for the District of Columbia Circuit granted Storer relief and directed the commission to allow a full hearing on the question of public interest, convenience, or necessity. On writ of certiorari, the Supreme Court reversed.

Opinion: Justice Stanley F. Reed wrote the opinion, joined by Chief Justice Earl Warren and Justices Hugo L. Black, Harold H. Burton, Tom C. Clark, and Sherman Minton. William O. Douglas concurred separately. John M. Harlan concurred on the merits but dissented on the station's standing to seek review of the FCC order. Felix Frankfurter dissented on the jurisdictional issues. On the question of jurisdiction, Reed said Storer Broadcasting had standing to sue, the process of rule-making having been completed at the time. Next, the Court held that the FCC's multiple ownership rules were reconcilable with the Communications Act as a whole. Harlan said he would remand the case to the court of appeals with directions to dismiss the petition for lack of jurisdiction. Frankfurter, like Harlan, said that Storer was not a "party aggrieved" under the law.

Referenced Cases: *FCC v. NBC*, 319 U.S. 239 (1943), on the right to appeal; *FCC v. Sanders Bros. Radio Station*, 309 U.S. 470 (1940), *CBS v. U.S.*, 316 U.S. 407 (1942), and *FCC v. ABC*, 347 U.S. 284 (1954), on jurisdictional standing; *Scripps-Howard Radio v. FCC*, 316 U.S. 4 (1941), regarding the public interest; *NBC v. U.S.*, 319 U.S. 190 (1943), on the FCC's authority to regulate chain broadcasting; *FCC v. CBS*, 311 U.S. 132 (1940), on reviewing FCC orders by direct appeal; *United Public Workers v. Mitchell*, 330 U.S. 75 (1947), regarding declaratory relief; *L. Singer & Sons v. Union Pacific R. Co.*, 311 U.S. 295 (1940), on "party aggrieved" or "party in interest"; *Ashwander v. Tennessee Valley Authority*, 297 U.S. 288 (1936), on threshold objections of procedure and jurisdiction.

Further Reading:

42 *ABA J.* 656 (July 1956).
44 *Calif. L. Rev.* 938 (Dec. 1956).
43 *Georgia L. J.* 671 (June 1955).
46 *Georgia L. J.* 166 (Fall 1957).
70 *Harvard L. Rev.* 158 (Nov. 1956).

1959   *Farmers' Educational and Cooperative Union of America, North Dakota Division, a Corporation v. WDAY Inc., 360 U.S. 525, 3 L.Ed.2d 1407, 79 S.Ct. 1302*

Argued: March 23, 1959.

Decided: June 29, 1959.

Summary: Federal Communications Act bars censorship of political speech and grants station immunity from libelous political statements.

Circumstances: In 1956, A. C. Townley, a candidate for the U.S. Senate in North Dakota, broadcast a speech in which he accused his opponents and the Farmers' Educational and Cooperative Union of conspiring to "establish a Communist Farmers'

Union Soviet right here in North Dakota." The Union sued Townley and WDAY for libel in a North Dakota state district court, which dismissed the complaint on the ground that Section 315 rendered the station immune from liability. The state supreme court affirmed. On certiorari, the U.S. Supreme Court also affirmed the judgment.

Opinion: Justice Hugo L. Black wrote the 5-to-4 opinion, joined by Chief Justice Earl Warren and Justices William O. Douglas, Tom C. Clark, and William J. Brennan, Jr. Felix Frankfurter dissented, joined by John M. Harlan, Charles E. Whittaker, and Potter Stewart. At issue was Section 315 of the Communications Act, which contains the equal opportunities or equal time rule: "(a) If any licensee shall permit any person who is a legally qualified candidate for any public office to use a broadcasting station, he shall afford equal opportunities to all other such candidates for that office in the use of such broadcasting station: *Provided*, That such licensee shall have no power of censorship over the material broadcast under the provisions of this section. No obligation is imposed upon any licensee to allow the use of its station by any such candidate." Thus, the Court held that since broadcasters are not allowed to censor the remarks of a candidate, they are immune from libel suits based on those remarks. Black said that permitting a station to censor allegedly libelous remarks would undermine the basic purpose of Section 315—full and unrestricted discussion of political issues by legally qualified candidates. Otherwise, a station might censor all remarks, even those "faintly objectionable . . . out of an excess of caution." The candidate, however, can still be sued; lawsuits must be directed at the candidate, not the station. Justice Frankfurter, in dissent, agreed that Section 315 bars censorship by stations, but he said that the federal statute does not grant immunity from liability under state libel laws. "Section 315 has left to the States the power to determine the nature and extent of the liability, if any, of broadcasters to third persons."

Referenced Cases: None in the text.

Further Reading:
45 *ABA J.* 1304 (Dec. 1959).
9 *American Univ. L. Rev.* 150 (June 1960).

37 *Dicta* 196 (May–June 1960).

73 *Harvard L. Rev.* 234 (Nov. 1959).

42 *Marquette L. Rev.* 417 (Winter 1959).

19 *Maryland L. Rev.* 345 (Fall 1959).

44 *Minnesota L. Rev.* 787 (March 1960).

35 *No. Dakota L. Rev.* 80 (Jan. 1959).

35 *NYU L. Rev.* 903 (April 1960).

12 *Oklahoma L. Rev.* 297 (May 1959).

32 *Rocky Mtn. L. Rev.* 254 (Fall 1960).

34 *St. John's L. Rev.* 140 (Dec. 1959).

12 *So. Carolina L. Q.* 475 (Spring 1960).

4 *So. Dakota L. Rev.* 173 (Spring 1959).

32 *So. Calif. L. Rev.* 71 (Fall 1958).

11 *Syracuse L. Rev.* 117 (Fall 1959).

37 *Texas L. Rev.* 114 (Nov. 1958).

107 *Univ. Pa. L. Rev.* 280 (Dec. 1958).

13 *Vanderbilt L. Rev.* 423 (Dec. 1959).

11 *Western Reserve L. Rev.* 305 (March 1960).

1968 *U.S. and Federal Communications Commission v. Southwestern Cable Co. and Midwest Television Inc. et al. v. Southwestern Cable Co.*, 392 U.S. 157, 20 L.Ed.2d 1001, 88 S.Ct. 1994, 1 Med.L.Rptr. 2247

Argued: March 12, 13, 1968.

Decided: June 10, 1968.

Summary: FCC can regulate cable television (CATV) to the extent "reasonably ancillary to the effective performance of the commission's various responsibilities for the regulation of television broadcasting."

Circumstances: Midwest Television averred that Southwestern's CATV systems transmitted signals from Los Angeles stations into the San Diego area and adversely affected

Midwest's station in that city. The FCC therefore restricted Southwestern's service. On petitions for review, the Court of Appeals for the Ninth Circuit held that the commission lacked authority under the Communications Act of 1934 to issue such an order. The Supreme Court granted certiorari "to consider this important question of regulatory authority" and reversed.

Opinion: Justice John M. Harlan wrote the 7-to-0 opinion, joined by Chief Justice Earl Warren and Justices Hugo L. Black, William J. Brennan, Jr., Potter Stewart, and Abe Fortas. Byron R. White concurred separately. William O. Douglas and Thurgood Marshall did not participate. The Court held that the FCC's authority over "all interstate communication by wire or radio" permitted the regulation of CATV systems. The Court also ruled that the commission had the authority to limit further expansion of such systems pending hearings on complaints against expansion. Because it was an early CATV case, the opinion reviewed the history of the relatively new industry and its relationship to the federal regulatory agency. Not at issue was the validity of the FCC's rules for regulating CATV. Instead, two issues were addressed: whether the FCC had authority under the Communications Act to regulate such systems, and, if so, whether it had the authority to issue the prohibitory order. The Court recognized both, "restricted to that reasonably ancillary to the effective performance of the Commission's various responsibilities for the regulation of television broadcasting." Whereas Harlan found Section 152(a) as the authority for the FCC's prohibition against a CATV system interfering with a local television station, White looked to Sections 301 and 303 of the act, which gave the commission broad authority over broadcasting, including the right to prevent interference between stations and to establish zones served by any station.

Referenced Cases: *FCC v. Pottsville Broadcasting Co.*, 309 U.S. 134 (1940), on Congress' formulation of a "unified and comprehensive regulatory system for the [broadcasting] industry"; *FRC v. Nelson Bros. Co.*, 289 U.S. 266 (1933), on interstate communication; *Wong Yang Sung v. McGrath*, 339 U.S. 33 (1950), on recognizing the need for administrative agencies to seek congressional clarification of statutes; *Rainwater v. U.S.*, 356 U.S. 590 (1958), *U.S. v. Price*, 361 U.S. 304 (1960), and *Haynes v. U.S.*, 390

U.S. 85 (1968), on the "very little, if any, significance" of congressional statutory history; *NBC v. U.S.*, 319 U.S. 190 (1943), on Congress' "comprehensive mandate" to the FCC; *Permian Basin Area Rate Cases*, 390 U.S. 747 (1968), and *American Trucking Assns. v. U.S.*, 344 U.S. 298 (1953), on prohibiting administrative action without compelling congressional evidence.

Further Reading:
54 *ABA J.* 912 (Sept. 1968).

1969   *Red Lion Broadcasting Co. Inc., etc., et al. v. Federal Communications Commission and U.S. et al. v. Radio Television News Directors' Association, 395 U.S. 367, 23 L.Ed.2d 371, 89 S.Ct. 1794, 1 Med.L.Rptr. 2053*

Argued: April 2, 3, 1969.

Decided: June 9, 1969.

Summary: Ruled constitutional the FCC's fairness doctrine and its personal-attack and political-editorializing rules. Also held the FCC within its statutory authority, encouraged the commission to support controversial issues, and defined scarcity as a matter of spectrum space.

Circumstances: In *Red Lion*, a Pennsylvania radio station, WGCB, carried a 15-minute broadcast on Nov. 27, 1964, by the Reverend Billy James Hargis as part of his "Christian Crusade" series. While discussing a book by Fred J. Cook entitled *Goldwater—Extremist on the Right*, Hargis accused the author of working for a communist-affiliated publication and of having defended Alger Hiss. Now, Hargis said, Cook had written a "book to smear and destroy Barry Goldwater." Cook said he had been personally attacked and demanded free reply time. The station refused. Following an exchange of letters among Cook, the Red Lion Broadcasting Co., and the FCC, the commission concluded that the broadcast amounted to a personal attack and that the station had failed to meet its obligation under the fairness doctrine. The Court of Appeals for the District of Columbia Circuit upheld as constitutional the FCC's position. Meanwhile, in the second case, the RTNDA challenged the FCC's political-editorializing rules. Shortly after *Red Lion* litigation had begun, the commission issued a Notice of Proposed Rulemaking with an eye to making the personal-attack aspect of the fairness doctrine more precise and more readily enforceable. The rules were held unconstitutional by the Court of Appeals for the Seventh Circuit as abridging freedoms of speech and press. On writs of certiorari, the Supreme Court affirmed the *Red Lion* judgment and reversed *RTNDA*.

Opinion: Justice Byron R. White wrote the Court's 8-to-0 opinion, joined by Chief Justice Earl Warren and Justices Hugo L. Black, John M. Harlan, William J. Brennan, Jr., Potter Stewart, Abe Fortas, and Thurgood Marshall. William O. Douglas did not participate. In *Red Lion*, the Court ruled that the station had not met its obligation under the FCC's fairness doctrine. In *U.S. v. RTNDA*, the Court held that the personal-attack aspect of the doctrine did not abridge the freedoms of speech and press. White noted first that the FCC had for many years imposed on radio and television broadcasters the requirement that they present discussion of public issues and that each side of an issue be given fair coverage. Known as the fairness doctrine, it is an "obligation whose content has been defined in a long series of FCC rulings in particular cases, and which is distinct from the statutory requirement of Section 315 of the Communications Act that equal time be allotted all qualified candidates for public office." The justice then traced the history of broadcasting regulation from before 1927, when private-sector allocation of frequencies resulted in chaos. "In light of the fact that the 'public interest' in broadcasting clearly encompasses the presentation of vigorous debate of controversial issues of importance and concern to the public . . . we think the fairness doctrine and its component personal attack and political editorializing regulations are a legitimate exercise of congressionally delegated authority." In response to the broadcaster's "conventional" defense, White said: "It would be strange if the First Amendment, aimed at protecting and furthering communications, prevented the Government from making radio communication possible by requiring licensees to broadcast and by limiting the number of licenses so as not to overcrowd the spectrum. A license permits broadcasting, but the licensee has no constitutional right to be the one who holds the license or to monopolize a radio frequency to the exclusion of his fellow citizens." He added: "Licenses to broadcast do not confer ownership of designated frequencies, but only the temporary privilege of using them."

Referenced Cases: *NBC v. U.S.*, 319 U.S. 190 (1943), *FCC v. Pottsville*, 309 U.S. 134 (1940), *FCC v. RCA Communications Inc.*, 346 U.S. 86 (1953), and *FRC v. Nelson Bros.*, 289 U.S. 266 (1933), on FCC's broad mandate, "not niggardly but expansive," to assure public interest broadcasting; *U.S. v. Paramount Pictures*, 334 U.S. 131 (1948), *Burstyn v. Wilson*, 343 U.S. 495 (1952), *Kovacs v. Cooper*, 336 U.S. 77 (1949), and *Associated Press v. U.S.*, 326 U.S. 1 (1945), regarding limitations on speech of broadcasters justified by different technologies; *FCC v. Sanders Bros. Radio Station*, 309 U.S. 470 (1940), and *FCC v. Allentown Broadcasting Corp.*, 349 U.S. 358 (1955), on paramount right of viewers and listeners; *New York Times v. Sullivan*, 376 U.S. 254 (1964), *Abrams v. U.S.*, 250 U.S. 616 (1919), and *Garrison v. Louisiana*, 379 U.S. 64 (1964), on First Amendment protection of uninhibited marketplace of ideas; *Farmers' Educ. & Coop. Union v. WDAY*, 360 U.S. 525 (1959), on insulating broadcasters from defamation liability.

Further Reading:
23 *Fed. Communications Bar J.* 75 (1969).
37 *Federal Communications L. J.* 113 (1985).
56 *Georgetown L. J.* 547 (Jan. 1968).
5 *Harvard Civil Rights L. Rev.* 89 (Jan. 1970).
53 *Journalism Quarterly* 429 (1976).
3 *Loyola Univ.-LA L. Rev.* 451 (April 1970).
44 *Notre Dame Lawyer* 447 (Feb. 1969).
47 *Notre Dame Lawyer* 550 (1972).
15 *So. Dakota L. Rev.* 172 (Winter 1970).
37 *Tenn. L. Rev.* 383 (Winter 1970).
37 *Univ. Cincinnati L. Rev.* 550 (Summer 1968).
29 *Univ. Pittsburgh L. Rev.* 691 (June 1968).
61 *Virginia L. Rev.* 579 (1975).

1972   *U.S. et al. v. Midwest Video Corporation* (*Midwest Video I*), 406 U.S. 649, 32 L.Ed.2d 390, 92 S.Ct. 1869, 46 U.S. L.W. 2447

Argued: April 19, 1972.

Decided: June 7, 1972.

Summary: Upheld FCC rule that cable television (CATV) systems with more than 3,500 subscribers must operate "to a significant extent as a local outlet by originating cablecasting."

Circumstances: Shortly after the Court's decision in *U.S. v. Southwestern Cable Co.* (1968), the FCC began "to explore the broad question of how best to obtain, consistent with the public interest standard of the Communications Act, the full benefits of developing communications technology for the public, with particular immediate reference to CATV technology." On Oct. 24, 1969, the commission adopted the rule that "no CATV system having 3,500 or more subscribers shall carry the signal of any television broadcast station unless the system also operates to a significant extent as a local outlet by cablecasting and has available facilities for local production and presentation of programs other than automated services." Midwest Video petitioned for review in the Court of Appeals for the Eighth Circuit, which set aside the FCC's order.

Opinion: Although the Court could not agree on an opinion, five justices agreed by plurality that the FCC's regulation "preserves and enhances the integrity of broadcast signals and therefore is 'reasonably ancillary' to the effective performance of the commission's various responsibilities for the regulation of television broadcasting." Justice William J. Brennan, Jr., announced the judgment of the Court, joined by Byron R. White, Thurgood Marshall, and Harry A. Blackmun. Chief Justice Warren E. Burger concurred and expressed the separate view that, though the FCC's position strained the outer limits of its jurisdiction, it should be permitted wide latitude. In a strong dissent, Justice William O. Douglas argued, as did the CATV operator, that the FCC was forcing them into the broadcasting business when they did not want to be licensed for that business. "CATV is simply a carrier having no more control over the message content than does a telephone company. A carrier may, of course, seek a broadcaster's license; but there is not the slightest suggestion in the Act or in its history that a carrier can be bludgeoned into becoming a broadcaster while all other broadcasters live under more lenient rules. There is not the slightest clue in the Act that CATV carriers can be compulsorily converted into broadcasters." Douglas was joined by Justices Potter Stewart, Lewis F. Powell, Jr., and William H. Rehnquist. The plurality opinion had argued, in endorsing programming far beyond the simple automated services offered by cable operators, that the regulation was to assure that in the retransmission of broadcast signals viewers were provided diversified programming—the same objective underlying regulations sustained in *NBC v. U.S.* (1943) as well as the local-carriage rule reviewed in *Southwestern*.

Referenced Cases: *U.S. v. Southwestern Cable Co.*, 392 U.S. 157 (1968), on the FCC's jurisdiction to regulate the CATV industry; *FCC v. Pottsville Broadcasting Co.*, 309 U.S. 134 (1940), and *NBC v. U.S.*, 319 U.S. 190 (1943), regarding the commission's "unified jurisdiction," "broad authority," "comprehensive mandate," and "not niggardly but expansive powers"; *FRC v. Nelson Bros. Co.*, 289 U.S. 266 (1933), on CATV systems enhancing as well as impairing broadcast services; *U.S. v. Storer Broadcasting Co.*, 351 U.S. 192 (1956), on the Court's role in furthering or retarding the "public interest"; *Fortnightly Corp. v. United Artists Television*, 392 U.S. 390 (1968), a copyright case, marking the difference between communication and origination.

Further Reading:
58 *ABA J.* 1310 (Dec. 1972).
22 *Catholic Univ. L. Rev.* 708 (Spring 1973).
22 *DePaul L. Rev.* 461 (Winter 1972).
22 *J. Public L.* 301 (1973).
4 *Rutgers Camden L. J.* 391 (Spring 1973).
41 *Univ. Cincinnati L. Rev.* 983 (1972).

1973 *Columbia Broadcasting System, Inc. v. Democratic National Committee; Federal Communications Commission et al. v. Business Executives' Move for Vietnam Peace et al.; Post-Newsweek Stations, Capital Area, Inc. v. Business Executives' Move for Vietnam Peace; and American Broadcasting Companies, Inc. v. Democratic National Committee, 412 U.S. 94, 36 L.Ed.2d 772, 93 S.Ct. 2080, 1 Med.L.Rptr. 1855*

Argued: Oct. 16, 1972.

Decided: May 29, 1973.

Summary: Broadcasters have the absolute right to refuse to sell time to individuals or groups for advertisements dealing with political campaigns and controversial public issues if their general policy is to refuse such advertisements.

Circumstances: In Jan. 1970, the Business Executives' Move for Vietnam Peace (BEM) filed a complaint with the FCC charging that radio station WTOP in Washington, D.C., had refused to sell time for a series of one-minute spot announcements. WTOP was following its policy, common among some broadcasters, of refusing to sell time to individuals and groups who wished to expound their views on controversial issues. The station said it had aired criticism of U.S. policy on Vietnam. The BEM challenged the fairness of WTOP's coverage. In May 1970, the Democratic National Committee (DNC) filed with the FCC a request for a declaratory ruling, claiming that broadcasters may not refuse to sell time per the First Amendment and the Communications Act. In separate opinions, the FCC rejected each respondent's demand. A majority of the Court of Appeals for the District of Columbia Circuit reversed the commission, holding that "a flat ban on paid public issue announcements is in violation of the First Amendment, at least when other sorts of paid announcements are accepted." On certiorari, the Supreme Court reversed.

Opinion: Chief Justice Warren E. Burger wrote the 7-to-2 opinion, joined by Justices Potter Stewart (Parts I, II, III), Byron R. White, Harry A. Blackmun, Lewis F. Powell, Jr. (Parts I, II, IV), and William H. Rehnquist (Part II). William O. Douglas concurred separately. Parts I, II, and IV constituted the opinion of the Court. Dissenting were William J. Brennan, Jr. and Thurgood Marshall. In Part I, Burger deferred to the decisions of Congress and the experience of the FCC in evaluating First Amendment claims of the DNC and the BEM. In Part II, the chief justice noted that Congress intended private broadcasting to develop with the widest journalistic freedom consistent with its public obligations, banning censorship and denying common carrier status for stations. "Only when the interests of the public are found to outweigh the private journalistic interests of the broadcasters will government power be asserted within the framework of the [1934] Act." In Part III, Burger said that a broadcaster's policy against accepting editorial advertisements cannot be examined in the abstract. "[The] role of the Government as an 'overseer' and ultimate arbiter and guardian of the public interest and the role of the licensee as a journalistic 'free agent' call for a delicate balancing of competing interests." He concluded that the policies complained of did not constitute violations of the First Amendment. In Part IV, the chief justice said that the FCC was justified in concluding that the public interest in providing access to the marketplace of "ideas and experiences" would scarcely be served by a system so heavily weighted in favor of the financially affluent, or those with access to wealth. Even under a first-come-first-served system, proposed by dissenting FCC commissioner Nicholas Johnson, "the views of the affluent could well prevail over those of others, since they would have it within their power to purchase time more frequently," according to Burger. Even if the fairness doctrine or Cullman standard were applied to editorial advertising, the affluent could still determine in large part the issues to be discussed because of their power to initiate such speech. (In what has become known as the Cullman Doctrine, the FCC has said that if one side of a controversial issue is presented during a sponsored program, the broadcaster may have to provide contrasting views in unsponsored programming. An otherwise acceptable reply cannot be rejected because proponents of an opposing view lack funds. See Cullman Broadcasting Co., 25 P. & F. Radio Reg. 895 [1963].) Burger also opined that the fairness doctrine might be jeopardized because the broadcaster might experience financial hardship from having to make regular programming time available to those holding a view different from that expressed in an editorial advertisement. "The result would be a further erosion of the journalistic discretion of broadcasters in the coverage of public issues, and a transfer of control over the treatment of public issues from the licensees who are accountable for broadcast performance to private individuals who are not." He concluded that Congress or the FCC—"or the broadcasters"—may devise some kind of limited access that is both practicable and desirable, noting the then ongoing commission inquiry into various aspects of the fairness doctrine.

Justice Stewart, who concurred in Parts I, II, and III, added that, since broadcasters as part of the press were protected by the First Amendment, it would be improper to hold that the amendment's protection required the government to impose controls to protect First Amendment "values." He said: "The First Amendment protects the press *from* governmental interference; it confers no analogous protection *on* the Government. To hold that broadcaster action is governmental action would thus simply strip broadcasters of their own First Amendment rights. They would be obligated to grant the demands of all citizens to be heard over the air, subject only to reasonable regulations as to 'time, place and manner.'"

Justice White noted in his concurrence in Parts I, II, and IV that broadcasters possess the freedom and discretion to make up their own programs and choose their method of compliance with the fairness doctrine. Justices Blackmun and Powell said it was not necessary to decide the governmental action issue of Part IV. Justice Douglas concurred on the ground that broadcasters "stand in the same protected position under the First Amendment as do newspapers and magazines." In one of his longer and more quotable opinions, Douglas took issue with FCC commissioner Johnson, who said in his own "powerful dissent" that "for any given forum of speech the First Amendment *demands* rules permitting as many to speak and be heard as possible." Douglas, in reply: "But the prospect of putting government in a position of control over publishers is to me an appalling one, even to the extent of the Fairness Doctrine. The struggle for liberty has been a struggle against Government. The essential scheme of our Constitution and Bill of Rights was to take government off the backs of people.

And it is anathema to the First Amendment to allow Government any role of censorship over newspapers, magazines, books, art, music, TV, radio, or any other aspect of the press."

Justices Brennan and Marshall, in dissent, said that the public nature of the airwaves required governmental action and that the fairness doctrine was not sufficient to guarantee the uninhibited exchange of views on public issues. "I can only conclude that the exclusionary policy upheld today can serve only to inhibit, rather than to further, our 'profound national commitment to the principle that debate on public issues should be uninhibited, robust, and wide open,'" Brennan said, quoting from his majority opinion in *New York Times v. Sullivan* (1964). "I can only conclude that there is simply no overriding First Amendment interest of broadcasters that can justify the *absolute* exclusion of virtually all of our citizens from the most effective 'marketplace of ideas' ever devised. . . . A society already so saturated with commercialism can well afford another outlet for speech on public issues. All that we may lose is some of our apathy."

Referenced Cases: *Red Lion Broadcasting Co. v. FCC*, 395 U.S. 367 (1969), cited by the DNC as establishing limited constitutional right of access to the airwaves, and for a summary of the development and nature of the fairness doctrine; *U.S. v. Paramount Pictures*, 334 U.S. 131 (1948), on right of viewers and listeners as paramount; *NBC v. U.S.*, 319 U.S. 190 (1943), *FCC v. Sanders Brothers Radio Station*, 309 U.S. 470 (1940), and *FCC v. Pottsville Broadcasting*, 309 U.S. 134 (1940), on origins of the modern system of broadcast regulation; *Farmers' Union v. WDAY*, 360 U.S. 525 (1959), on striking a balance between private and public control; *New York Times v. Sullivan*, 376 U.S. 254 (1964), Justice Brennan on "profound national commitment that debate on public issues should be uninhibited, robust, and wide-open"; *Public Utilities Comm'n v. Pollak*, 343 U.S. 451 (1952), on First Amendment restraint on government action, not on that of private persons; *Burton v. Wilmington Parking Authority*, 365 U.S. 715 (1961), and *Moose Lodge No. 107 v. Irvis*, 407 U.S. 163 (1972), regarding the need to analyze government involvement in particular acts; *Fowler v. Rhode Island*, 345 U.S. 67 (1953), and *Niemotko v. Maryland*, 340 U.S. 268 (1951), on the risk of an enlargement of government control over content of broadcast discussion of public issues; *Kovacs v. Cooper*, 336 U.S. 77 (1949), on "captive audience" aspect of broadcasting; *Cox v. Louisiana,* 379 U.S. 536 (1965), *Grayned v. City of Rockford,* 408 U.S. 104 (1972), and *Police Dept. of Chicago v. Mosley,* 408 U.S. 92 (1972), regarding unconstitutional city ordinances that permitted "peaceful picketing"; *American Commercial Lines Inc. v. Louisville & N. R. Co.,* 392 U.S. 571 (1968), on the search for reasonable regulation; *Amalgamated Food Employees v. Logan Valley Plaza,* 391 U.S. 308 (1968), Marsh v. Alabama, 326 U.S. 501 (1946), and *Lloyd Corp. v. Tanner* 407 U.S. 551 (1972), on applicability of the First Amendment where private parties control public forums; *Poulos v. New Hampshire,* 345 U.S. 395 (1953), and *Cox v. New Hampshire,* 312 U.S. 569 (1941), on time, place, and manner restrictions; *Garner v. Louisiana,* 368 U.S. 157 (1961), *Lombard v. Louisiana,* 373 U.S. 267 (1963), and *Plessy v. Ferguson,* 163 U.S. 537 (1896), on governmental control or supervision of private activities; *Associated Press v. U.S.,* 326 U.S. 1 (1945), regarding antitrust laws as not inconsistent with the First Amendment; *Roth v. U.S.,* 354 U.S. 476 (1957), and *Malloy v. Hogan,* 378 U.S. 1 (1964), on vigor of the First Amendment at the state level; *Lovell v. Griffin,* 303 U.S. 444 (1938), and *Hague v. CIO,* 307 U.S. 496 (1939), on parks as public domain not under government censorship; *Memoirs v. Massachusetts,* 383 U.S. 413 (1966), and *Ginzburg v. U.S.,* 383 U.S. 463 (1966), as applied to obscene conversations on a telephone talk show; *EPA v. Mink,* 410 U.S. 73 (1973), on Court approval of "secret" and "top secret" classifications in Freedom of Information Act cases; *Mills v. Alabama,* 384 U.S. 214 (1966), regarding Justice Hugo L. Black's Court opinion on constitutionally guaranteed press freedom; *Evans v. Newton,* 382 U.S. 296 (1966), on constitutional limitations on private speech entwined with governmental policies; *Reitman v. Mulkey,* 387 U.S. 369 (1967), and *Kotch v. Pilot Comm'rs,* 330 U.S. 552 (1947), on attempts at infallible test for determining private or governmental speech; *Turner v. City of Memphis,* 369 U.S. 350 (1962), regarding speech on privately owned property; *American Communications Assn. v. Douds,* 339 U.S. 382 (1950), on further indicia of governmental involvement; *Abrams v. U.S.,* 250 U.S. 616 (1919), *Whitney v. California,* 274 U.S. 357 (1927), and *Gitlow v. New York,* 268 U.S. 652 (1925), regarding Justice Oliver Wendell Holmes and the First Amendment; *Garrison v. Louisiana,* 379 U.S. 64 (1964), *Thomas v. Collins,* 323 U.S. 516 (1945), and *NAACP v. Button,* 371 U.S. 415 (1963), on the right of individuals to hear and participate in public debate; *Breard v. Alexandria,* 341 U.S. 622

(1951), and *Valentine v. Chrestensen*, 316 U.S. 52 (1942), on commercial speech enjoying less protection than political speech.

Further Reading:
54 *Cornell L. Rev.* 294 (1969).
1973 *Duke L. J.* 89 (1973).
13 *FCC* 1246 (1949).
39 *George Washington L. Rev.* 532 (1971).
80 *Harvard L. Rev.* 1641 (1967).
85 *Harvard L. Rev.* 768 (1972).
1970 *Law and Social Order* 424 (1970).
17 *UCLA L. Rev.* 868 (1970).
19 *UCLA L. Rev.* 723 (1972).
5 *Univ. Michigan J. L. Reform* 193 (1972).
57 *Virginia L. Rev.* 574, 636 (1971).

1978 *Federal Communications Commission v. Pacifica Foundation*, 438 U.S. 726, 57 L.Ed.2d 1073, 98 S.Ct. 3026, 2 Med.L.Rptr. 1465

Argued: April 18, 19, 1978.

Decided: July 3, 1978.

Summary: Ruled not violative of the First Amendment
an FCC declaratory order holding that radio station WBAI could
have been the subject of administrative sanctions for broadcasting
an indecent program.

Circumstances: At about 2 P.M. on Oct. 30, 1973, a
New York radio station, WBAI, owned by the Pacifica Foundation,
broadcast George Carlin's "Filthy Words" monologue. A few weeks
later a man, who said he heard the program while driving with his
young son, wrote a complaint to the FCC, which was forwarded to
the station for comment. On Feb. 21, 1975, the commission issued a
declaratory order granting the complaint and holding that Pacifica
"could have been the subject of administrative sanctions." Instead,

the FCC said the order would become part of the station's license file. The commission said: "We therefore hold that the language as broadcast was indecent and prohibited by 18 U.S.C. [Section] 1464." The FCC's decision was reversed by the Court of Appeals for the District of Columbia but reinstated by the Supreme Court. Each of the appellate judges wrote separately. Judge Tamm concluded that the order represented censorship and was prohibited by the Communications Act, Section 326. Judge Bazelon rested his view on the Constitution. Judge Leventhal, in dissent, emphasized the interest in protecting children and said that the FCC had correctly condemned the daytime broadcast as indecent. The Supreme Court granted the FCC's petition for certiorari.

Opinion: Justice John Paul Stevens wrote the Court's 5-to-4 plurality opinion, joined by Chief Justice Warren E. Burger and Justices William H. Rehnquist, Harry A. Blackmun, and Lewis F. Powell, Jr. Dissenting were William J. Brennan, Jr., Potter Stewart, Bryon R. White, and Thurgood Marshall. In Part I, Stevens said that the Court's review was limited to the FCC's determination that the George Carlin monologue, entitled "Filthy Words," was indecent as broadcast within the meaning of 18 U.S.C. Section 1464, which bars the broadcast of "any obscene, indecent, or profane language." In Part II, addressing the Communications Act's prohibition of program censorship (47 U.S.C. Section 326), the justice said the FCC is barred from editing in advance a proposed broadcast, but that the law had never been construed to deny the commission the power to review the content of completed broadcasts in the performance of its regulatory duties. In Part III, Stevens found the content of the monologue to be vulgar, offensive, and shocking. In Part IV, the justice argued that the commission's order was not constitutional under the First Amendment, either because of being overbroad or because the monologue was not obscene. On the question of whether a broadcast of patently offensive words dealing with sex and excretion may be regulated because of its content, Stevens said that case law showed that obscene materials had been denied protection because their content is "so offensive to contemporary moral standards." He noted that, because of its unique characteristics, broadcasting had traditionally received the least First Amendment protection of all media. "Patently offensive, indecent material presented over the airwaves confronts the citizen, not only in public, but also in the privacy of the home, where the individual's right to be left alone plainly outweighs the First Amendment rights of an intruder. The ease with which children may obtain access to broadcast material . . . amply justifies special treatment of indecent broadcasting." He concluded: "We simply hold that when the Commission finds that a pig has entered the parlor, the exercise of its regulatory power does not depend on proof that the pig is obscene." (Justice George Sutherland had written that "[a] nuisance may be merely a right thing in the wrong place—like a pig in the parlor instead of the barnyard." *Euclid v. Ambler Realty Co.*, 272 U.S. 365 [1926].)

Separately, Justice Powell, joined by Blackmun, concurred but disagreed with Stevens that Supreme Court justices were free to decide on the basis of content which protected speech was deserving of more or less protection. "The result turns instead on the unique characteristics of the broadcast media, combined with society's right to protect its children from speech generally agreed to be inappropriate for their years, and with the interest of unwilling adults in not being assaulted by such offensive speech in their homes."

In dissent, Justice Brennan, joined by Marshall, believed that such factors—intrusiveness and children in the audience—"simply do not support even the professedly moderate degree of governmental homogenization of radio communications—if, indeed, such homogenization can ever be moderate given the pre-eminent status of the right of free speech in our constitutional scheme— that the Court today permits." Also dissenting, Justice Stewart, joined by Brennan, White, and Marshall, expressed the view that, since the monologue was not obscene, the FCC lacked statutory authority to ban it.

Referenced Cases: *Black v. Cutter Laboratories*, 351 U.S. 292 (1956), *Rescue Army v. Municipal Court*, 331 U.S. 549 (1947), and *Herb v. Pitcairn*, 324 U.S. 117 (1945), on Court reviews based on judgments, not statements in opinions; *Tidewater Oil Co. v. U.S.*, 409 U.S. 151 (1972), *Miller v. California*, 413 U.S. 15 (1973), *Hamling v. U.S.*, 418 U.S. 87 (1974), and *Manual Enterprises Inc. v. Day*, 370 U.S. 478 (1962), on definition of "indecent" and "obscene"; *Red Lion Broadcasting v. FCC*, 395 U.S. 367 (1969), on vague regulations defining the fairness doctrine; *Bates v. State Bar of Arizona*, 433 U.S. 350 (1977), *Young v. American Mini Theatres*, 427 U.S. 50 (1976), and *Broadrick v. Oklahoma*, 413 U.S. 601 (1973), regarding self-censorship and the overbreadth doctrine; *Schenck v. U.S.*, 249 U.S. 47 (1919), Justice Oliver Wendell Holmes on "falsely shouting fire in a theatre and causing a panic"; *Chaplinsky v. New Hampshire*, 315 U.S. 568 (1942), and *Gertz v. Robert Welch*, 418 U.S. 323 (1974), on unprotected speech; *Roth v. U.S.*, 354 U.S. 476 (1957), on contemporary moral standards; *Cohen v. California*, 403 U.S. 15 (1971), regarding the paraphrase of Justice John Harlan's "one occasion's lyric is another's vulgarity"; *Joseph Burstyn v. Wilson*, 343 U.S. 495 (1952), on how each medium of expression presents special First Amendment problems; *Miami Herald Publishing Co. V. Tornillo*, 418 U.S. 241 (1974), on newspaper protection against right-of-reply; *Rowan v. Post Office Dept.*, 397 U.S. 728 (1970), contrasting the right to be left alone to the rights of an intruder; *Ginsburg v. New York*, 390 U.S. 629 (1968), that youth well-being justifies regulation of otherwise protected speech; *Ashwander v. TVA*, 297 U.S. 288 (1936), on the Court's practice of not deciding constitutional issues unnecessarily; *Lewis v. New Orleans*, 415 U.S. 130 (1974), *Hess v. Indiana*, 414 U.S. 105 (1973), *Papish v. Univ. of Missouri Curators*, 410 U.S. 667 (1973), *Eaton v. Tulsa*, 415 U.S. 697 (1974), and *Brown v. Oklahoma*, 408 U.S. 914 (1972), all on cases and contexts of protected speech; *Erznoznik v. Jacksonville*, 422 U.S. 205 (1975), and *Jacobellis v. Ohio*, 378 U.S. 184 (1964), on society's right to "adopt more stringent controls on communicative materials available to youths than on those available to adults"; *CBS v. Democratic National Committee*, 412 U.S. 94 (1973), and *Capital Broadcasting Co. v. Acting Attorney General*, 405 U.S. 1000 (1972), regarding different First Amendment treatment for broadcast media; *Rosenfeld v. New Jersey*, 408 U.S. 901 (1972), on differing captivity between home and elsewhere; *Butler v. Michigan*, 352 U.S. 380 (1957), on "reduc[ing] the adult population . . . to [hearing] only what is fit for children"; *U.S. v. 12 200-ft. Reels of Film*, 413 U.S. 123 (1973), on the term "indecent" prohibiting only obscene speech; *Lehman v. Shaker Heights*, 418 U.S. 298 (1974), on point that, unlike other intrusive modes, "the radio can be turned off"; *Wisconsin v. Yoder*, 406 U.S. 205 (1972), and *Pierce v. Society of Sisters*, 268 U.S. 510 (1925), regarding parental right to bring up children; *Towne v. Eisner*, 245 U.S. 418 (1918), on Justice Holmes' comment, "A word is not a crystal, transparent and unchanged, it is the skin of a living thought and may vary greatly in color and content according to the circumstances and the time in which it is used."

Further Reading:

27 *Cleve. St. L. Rev.* 465 (1978).

9 *Communication & Law* 41 (Feb. 1987).

28 *Drake L. Rev.* 745 (1978–79).

7 *Hofstra L. Rev.* 781 (Spring 1979).

16 *Houston L. Rev.* 551 (1979).

67 *Kentucky L. J.* 947 (1978–79).

25 *New York L. School L. J.* 347 (1979).

40 *Ohio St. L. J.* 155 (1979).

31 *So. Carolina L. Rev.* 377 (Jan. 1980).

57 *Univ. Detroit J. Urban L.* 95 (Fall 1979).

1979 *Univ. Illinois L. Forum* 969 (1979).

34 *Univ. Miami L. Rev.* 147 (Nov. 1979).

41 *Univ. Pittsburgh L. Rev.* 321 (Winter 1980).

32 *Vanderbilt L. Rev.* 1377 (Nov. 1979).

61 *Virginia L. Rev.* 579 (1975).

6 *Western State Univ. L. Rev.* 281 (Spring 1979).

1979 *Federal Communications Commission v. Midwest Video Corp. et al., American Civil Liberties Union v. FCC, and National Black Media Coalition et al. v. Midwest Video Corp. (Midwest Video II), 440 U.S. 689, 59 L.Ed.2d 692, 99 S.Ct. 1435, 4 Med.L.Rptr. 2345*

Argued: Jan. 10, 1979.

Decided: April 2, 1979.

Summary: The promulgation of cable television access rules held to be not within FCC's authority.

Circumstances: In 1976 the FCC required large cable operators to develop a minimum 20-channel capacity by 1986, to set aside certain channels for public access, and to provide equipment and facilities for access purposes. Under the rules, cable operators were deprived of all discretion regarding who might exploit their access channels and what may be transmitted. System operators were enjoined from exercising any control over the content of access programming except the adoption of rules proscribing the transmission of lottery information and commercial matter. The Court of Appeals for the Eighth Circuit set aside the FCC's access, channel capacity, and facilities rules as being beyond its jurisdiction. The Supreme Court affirmed.

Opinion: Justice Bryon R. White wrote the Court's 6-to-3 opinion, joined by Chief Justice Warren E. Burger and Justices Potter Stewart, Harry A. Blackmun, Lewis F. Powell, Jr., and William H. Rehnquist. John Paul Stevens dissented, joined by William J. Brennan, Jr., and Thurgood Marshall. Unlike in *Midwest Video I* (1972), the Court said this time that the FCC had gone beyond its statutory authority. Previous regulations had fostered the goals of broadcasting as determined by Congress, White said, but the access rules deprived cable operators of the ability to determine what kind of programming to provide. The justice noted that the Court could not ignore that Congress had strongly disapproved of infringements on the editorial discretion "enjoyed by broadcasters and cable operators alike." White noted that, although the Court in *Midwest Video I* had sustained the FCC's authority to regulate cable television, the origination requirement did not abrogate the cable operators' control over the composition of their programming, "as do the access rules." He said that the access rules transferred control of the content of access channels from operators to the public. "Effectively, the Commission has relegated cable systems, pro tanto, to common-carrier status." In conclusion, the FCC may not regulate cable systems as common carriers, White wrote, just as it may not impose such obligations on television broadcasters. "We think authority to compel cable operators to provide common carriage of public-originated transmissions must come specifically from Congress." Justice Stevens, in dissent, believed the access rules to be within the commission's statutory authority, "since Congress has not seen fit to modify the scope of the statute as construed in *Midwest Video.*"

Referenced Cases: *U.S. v. Southwestern Cable Co.,* 392 U.S. 157 (1968), on FCC rules as "reasonably ancillary" to the commission's performance; *FCC v. Pottsville Broadcasting Co.,* 309 U.S. 134 (1940), and *U.S. v. Midwest Video Corp.,* 406 U.S. 649

(1972), regarding the FCC's "circumscribed range of power" to regulate cable television; *CBS v. Democratic National Committee*, 412 U.S. 94 (1973), on relevance of Section 3(h) to common-carrier status.

Further Reading:

65 *ABA J.* 961 (June 1979).

13 *Creighton L. Rev.* 1023 (Spring 1980).

16 *Idaho L. Rev.* 123 (Fall 1979).

7 *Pepperdine L. Rev.* 469 (Winter 1980).

1979 *Wisconsin L. Rev.* 962 (1979).

1981   *Federal Communications Commission et al. v. WNCN Listeners' Guild et al., Insilco Broadcasting Corp. et al. v. WNCN Listeners' Guild et al., American Broadcasting Companies Inc. et al. v. WNCN Listeners' Guild et al., and National Association of Broadcasters et al. v. WNCN Listeners' Guild et al., 450 U.S. 582, 67 L.Ed.2d, 101 S.Ct. 1266*

Argued: Nov. 3, 1980.

Decided: March 24, 1981.

Summary: Upheld FCC's preference of relying on market forces rather than "its own attempt to oversee format changes at the behest of disaffected listeners" in promoting diversity in entertainment format and programming.

Circumstances: In a 1976 Policy Statement, the FCC concluded that "the public interest, convenience, and necessity" is best served by promoting diversity in entertainment formats through market forces and competition among broadcasters. It said that a change in entertainment programming is therefore not a material factor in ruling on a license renewal or transfer. A

number of citizen groups interested in preserving particular programming formats petitioned for review in the Court of Appeals
for the District of Columbia. That court held that the FCC's
statement violated the Communications Act, rejecting the position that the choice of entertainment formats should be left to the
licensee. The court concluded that the market only imperfectly
reflects listener preferences and that the FCC was statutorily
obligated to review format changes whenever there is "strong
prima facie evidence that the market has in fact broken down." On
certiorari, the Supreme Court reversed and remanded to the court
of appeals.

Opinion: Justice Bryon R. White wrote the Court's 7-to-
2 opinion, joined by Chief Justice Warren E. Burger and Justices
Potter Stewart, Harry A. Blackmun, Lewis F. Powell, Jr., William H.
Rehnquist, and John Paul Stevens. Dissenting was Thurgood Marshall, joined by William J. Brennan, Jr. White said that the commission's policy statement, which advanced reliance on the
market rather than on government intervention, was in harmony
with prior cases recognizing that the Communications Act seeks
to preserve journalistic discretion while promoting the interests
of the listening public. Radio broadcasters are not required to seek
permission to make format changes, he said. The FCC is vested
with broad discretion in determining how much weight should be
given to its goal of promoting diversity in programming and what
policies should be pursued in promoting it. White warned the
agency, however, to be alert to the consequences of its policies
and said that it "should stand ready to alter its rule if necessary to
serve the public interest more fully." The Court found the policy
not inconsistent with the Communications Act and a constitutionally permissible way of implementing the law's public interest
standard within the meaning of the First Amendment. In dissent,
Justice Marshall, with Brennan, said that the FCC's policy statement lacked the flexibility "we have required of such general
regulations and policies." He said the statement should be vacated
because it did not contain a "safety valve" procedure to allow the
agency to consider applications for exemptions based on special
circumstances.

Referenced Cases: *NBC v. U.S.*, 319 U.S. 190 (1943),
on securing the maximum benefits of radio to all the people; *FCC*

v. Sanders Bros. Radio Station, 309 U.S. 470 (1940), on Congress' intention "to leave competition in the business of broadcasting where it found it"; *FCC v. Pottsville Broadcasting Co.*, 309 U.S. 134 (1940), defining the public-interest standard of the Communications Act as "a supple instrument for the exercise of discretion by the expert body which Congress has charged to carry out its legislative policy"; *FCC v. National Citizens' Committee for Broadcasting*, 436 U.S. 775 (1978), on diverse sources being consistent with public interest and the First Amendment; *FCC v. Midwest Video Corp.*, 440 U.S. 689 (1979), regarding the commission's goal of promoting diversity; *Red Lion Broadcasting v. FCC*, 395 U.S. 397 (1969), on fairness doctrine as consistent with public-interest standard; *E. I. du Pont de Nemours & Co. v. Train*, 430 U.S. 112 (1977), *Permian Basin Area Rate Cases*, 390 U.S. 747 (1968), *FPC v. Texaco*, 377 U.S. 33 (1964), and *U.S. v. Storer Broadcasting*, 351 U.S. 192 (1956), on "safety valve" for exemptions based on special circumstances.

Further Reading:

27 *Loyola L. Rev.* 1250 (Fall 1981).
55 *Notre Dame Lawyer* 848 (June 1980).
53 *Temple L. Q.* 362 (1980).
22 *William & Mary L. Rev.* 281 (Winter 1980).

1981   *CBS, Inc. v. Federal Communications Commission et al.; American Broadcasting Companies, Inc. v. FCC et al.; and National Broadcasting Co., Inc. v. FCC et al.*, 453 U.S. 367, 69 L.Ed.2d 706, 101 S.Ct. 2813, 5 Med.L.Rptr. 2649, 7 Med.L.Rptr. 1563

Argued: March 3, 1981.

Decided: July 1, 1981.

Summary: Upheld the FCC's "reasonable access" order to the broadcast media for legally qualified candidates for federal office. Broadcasters could not institute an across-the-board policy rejecting all requests from candidates for airtime.

Circumstances: On Oct. 11, 1979, the Carter-Mondale Presidential Committee requested each of the three major television networks to provide time for a 30-minute program between 8 and 10:30 P.M. on one of four days in December, approximately eleven months before the 1980 election and eight months before the Democratic National Convention. The committee intended to present a documentary on President Carter's administration in conjunction with his formal announcement of his candidacy. The networks declined the request. CBS emphasized the large number of candidates from both parties and the potential disruption of regular programming to allow for equal time for each; however, it did offer to sell two five-minute segments. ABC said it had not yet decided when to begin selling political time for the 1980 campaign, but later said sales would begin in January. NBC said it was not prepared to sell time to candidates as early as December 1979. Later in October the Carter-Mondale Presidential Committee filed a complaint with the FCC, charging violation of Section 312(a) (7). The commission determined that a national campaign was underway and stressed, among other points, that the national print media had given campaign activities prominent coverage for almost two months. The Court of Appeals for the District of Columbia affirmed the commission orders regarding the networks' statutory obligations. On certiorari, the Supreme Court affirmed.

Opinion: Chief Justice Warren E. Burger wrote the Court's 6-to-3 opinion, joined by Justices William J. Brennan, Jr., Potter Stewart, Thurgood Marshall, Harry A. Blackmun, and Lewis F. Powell, Jr. Dissenting were Byron R. White, William H. Rehnquist, and John Paul Stevens. Burger wrote: "Broadcasters are free to deny the sale of airtime prior to the commencement of a campaign, but once a campaign has begun, they must give reasonable and good-faith attention to access requests from 'legally qualified' candidates for federal elective office. Such requests must be considered on an individualized basis, and broadcasters are required to tailor their responses to accommodate, as much as reasonably possible, a candidate's stated purposes in seeking airtime. In responding to access requests, however, broadcasters may also give weight to such factors as the amount of time previously sold to the candidate, the disruptive impact on regular programming, and the likelihood of requests for time by rival candidates under the equal opportunities provision of Section 315(a). These considerations may not be invoked as pretexts for denying access; to justify a negative response, broadcasters must cite a realistic danger of substantial program disruption—perhaps caused by insufficient notice to allow adjustments in the schedule—or of an excessive number of equal time requests." Burger concluded that Section 312(a) (7) represents an effort by Congress to ensure that an important resource—the airwaves—will be used in the public interest, and that the statutory right of access "properly balances the First Amendment rights of federal candidates, the public, and broadcasters."

In dissent, Justice White, joined by Rehnquist and Stevens, asserted that the FCC "seriously misconstrued the statute when it assumed that it had been given authority to insist on its own views as to reasonable access even though this entailed rejection of media judgments representing different but nevertheless reasonable reactions to access requests." White said that the regulation of the broadcast media has been marked by a clearly defined legislative desire to preserve values of private journalism. Separately, Stevens said that the question of whether a broadcaster has violated the Communications Act must be answered in the context of an entire political campaign, rather than by focusing solely on particular requests or the particular needs of individual candidates.

Referenced Cases: *Reiter v. Sonotone Corp.*, 442 U.S. 330 (1979), on the starting point in cases involving statutory construction depending on the language employed by Congress; *Farmers' Educational & Cooperative Union v. WDAY*, 360 U.S. 525 (1959), on distinctions among federal, state, and local elections; *Red Lion Broadcasting v. FCC*, 395 U.S. 367 (1969), *CBS v. Democratic National Committee*, 412 U.S. 94 (1973), and *U.S. v. Rutherford*, 442 U.S. 544 (1979), on executing a statute that is compellingly wrong; *Zemel v. Rusk*, 381 U.S. 1 (1965), regarding congressional intention in failing to repeal or revise a statute; *FCC v. WOKO*, 329 U.S. 223 (1946), and *RCA v. U.S.*, 341 U.S. 412 (1951), on judicial review discretion; *FCC v. National Citizens Comm. for Broadcasting*, 436 U.S. 775 (1978), on requiring licensees to share frequencies with others; *FCC v. Midwest Video Corp.*, 440 U.S. 689 (1979), and *Miami Herald Publishing Co. v. Tornillo*, 418 U.S. 241 (1974), on absence of *general* right of access to the media; *Citizens to Preserve Overton Park v. Volpe*, 401 U.S. 402 (1971), on "clear error of judgment"; *Udall v. Tallman*, 380 U.S. 1 (1965), on discretion in hands of broadcaster, not candidates.

Further Reading:
16 *Akron L. Rev.* 171 (Summer 1982).
35 *Arkansas L. Rev.* 637 (1983).
48 *Brooklyn L. Rev.* 355 (Winter 1982).
1981 *Sup. Ct. Rev.* 223 (1981).

1984   *Capital Cities Cable, Inc., et al. v. Richard A. Crisp, Director, Oklahoma Alcoholic Beverage Control Board, 467 U.S. 691, 81 L.Ed.2d 580, 104 S.Ct. 2694*

Argued: Feb. 21, 1984.

Decided: June 18, 1984.

Summary: Overturned a state law prohibiting cable systems from carrying advertising for wine and liquor; found the ban preempted by FCC regulations and federal copyright law.

Circumstances: Although Oklahoma did not prohibit the sale and consumption of alcoholic beverages within the state, it prohibited the advertising of such products except by on-premises signs. In 1980, the state attorney general determined that the advertising ban prohibited cable television systems in the state from retransmitting out-of-state signals containing alcoholic beverage commercials, particularly wine advertisements. The law required cable operators to edit wine and liquor commercials out of network programming distributed within Oklahoma. The District Court for the Western District of Oklahoma granted summary judgment and a permanent injunction for the cable operators, holding that the operators were prohibited by federal law from altering or modifying out-of state signals and had no feasible means for deleting wine commercials. It also ruled that the ban was an unconstitutional restriction on protected commercial speech. The Court of Appeals for the Tenth Circuit reversed. On certiorari, the Supreme Court reversed that ruling.

Opinion: Justice William J. Brennan, Jr., for a unanimous Court, said that the FCC had authority under the Communications Act to regulate cable signal carriage. "Although the FCC has recently relaxed its regulation of importation of distant broadcast signals to permit greater access to this source of programming for cable subscribers, it has by no means forsaken its regulatory power in this area." He said the Oklahoma advertising ban "plainly reaches beyond the regulatory authority reserved to local authorities by the Commission's rules, and trespasses into the exclusive domain of the FCC." The Court said that the federal laws preempted conflicting state and local laws. Moreover, Brennan said, if the state ban were enforced, cable operators would be compelled to abandon altogether both distant signals and specialized non-broadcast services. "As a consequence, the public may very well be deprived of the wide variety of programming options that cable systems make possible." And, he added, such is wholly at odds with the regulatory goals contemplated by the FCC. Finally, Brennan said that the 21st Amendment did not make the regulation safe from preemption.

Referenced Cases: *Central Hudson Gas & Electric Corp. v. Public Service Comm'n.*, 447 U.S. 557 (1980), on the test for determining protected commercial speech; *California v. Taylor*, 353 U.S. 553 (1957), *Youakim v. Miller*, 425 U.S. 231 (1976), and *Blonder-Tongue Laboratories Inc. v. University of Illinois Foundation*, 402 U.S. 313 (1971), on considering questions not specifically passed upon by a lower court; *California Retail Liquor Dealers' Assn. v. Midcal Aluminum Inc.*, 445 U.S. 97 (1980), regarding a state wine-pricing program found violative of the Sherman Act despite reliance on the 21st Amendment; *Fidelity Federal Savings and Loan Assn. v. De la Cuesta*, 458 U.S. 141 (1982), on federal regulations no less preemptive than federal statutes; *FCC v. Midwest Video Corp.*, 440 U.S. 689 (1979), and *U.S. v. Midwest Video Corp.*, 406 U.S. 649 (1972), on the FCC's authority over all regulatory actions necessary to ensure its statutory responsibilities; *U.S. v. Southwestern Cable Co.,* 392 U.S. 157 (1968), confirming the FCC's authority to regulate cable television systems; *Himes v. Davidowitz,* 312 U.S. 52 (1941), and *Farmers' Union v. WDAY Inc.,* 360 U.S. 525 (1959), on the state as an obstacle to the federal regulatory scheme; *Teleprompter Corp. v. Columbia Broadcasting System Inc.,* 415 U.S. 394 (1974), *Fortnightly Corp. v. United Artists Television Inc.,* 392 U.S. 390 (1968), *Twentieth Century Music Corp. v. Aiken,* 422 U.S. 151 (1975), and *Sony Corp. v. Universal City Studios Inc.,* 464 U.S. 417 (1984), on the relationship of the Copyright Act to cable television and television generally.

Further Reading:
34 *American Univ. L. Rev.* 557 (Winter 1985).
19 *Univ. Richmond L. Rev.* 177 (Fall 1984).
17 *Urban Lawyer* 277 (Spring 1985).

1984 *Federal Communications Commission v. League of Women Voters of California et al.,* 468 U.S. 364, 82 L.Ed.2d 278, 104 S.Ct. 3106, 10 Med. L. Rppr. 1937

Argued: Jan. 16, 1984.

Decided: July 2, 1984.

Summary: Held unconstitutional a statute banning editorials by federally funded public broadcasting stations.

Circumstances: Pacifica Foundation, which owns several noncommercial educational stations in five major metropolitan areas, had received grants from the Corporation for Public Broadcasting (CPB) and was therefore prohibited from editorializing by the terms of Section 399 of the Public Broadcasting Act of 1967. In April 1979, Pacifica, the League of Women Voters of California, and Congressman Henry Waxman, a regular listener and viewer of public broadcasting, challenged the law's constitutionality in the District Court for the Central District of California. According to Justice Stevens: "Pacifica wants to broadcast its views to Waxman via its radio stations; Waxman wants to listen to those views on his radio; and the League of Women Voters wants a chance to convince Pacifica to take positions its members favor in its radio broadcasts." The court granted summary judgment, holding that the statute violated the First Amendment. On direct appeal, the Supreme Court affirmed.

Opinion: Justice William J. Brennan, Jr., wrote the Court's 5-to-4 decision, joined by Thurgood Marshall, Harry A. Blackmun, Lewis F. Powell, Jr., and Sandra Day O'Connor. Dissenting were Chief Justice Warren E. Burger and Justices William H. Rehnquist, Byron R. White, and John Paul Stevens. At issue was Section 399 of the Public Broadcasting Act of 1967 forbidding any noncommercial educational station that receives money from CPB to "engage in editorializing." Brennan noted that Section 399 appeared to restrict precisely that form of speech that the framers of the Bill of Rights were most anxious to protect: speech that is "indispensable to the discovery and spread of political truth." He reiterated that, because of spectrum scarcity, those who are awarded a broadcast license can be required to provide programming that serves the public interest. In Footnote 11, Brennan recognized that the "prevailing rationale for broadcast regulation based on spectrum scarcity" had come under increasing criticism in recent years. Critics charge that, with the advent of cable and satellite television technology, communities now have access to such a wide variety of stations that the scarcity doctrine is obsolete. He added, however, that the Court was not prepared to reconsider its long-standing approach without some signal from Congress or the FCC that technology had advanced so far "that some revision of the system of broadcast regulation may be required." In Footnote 12, the justice noted that, were it to be shown that the fairness doctrine reduces rather than enhances speech, the Court would then be forced to reconsider the constitutionality of the doctrine. Meanwhile, given the fact that there are hundreds of public radio and television stations throughout the country, "it seems reasonable to infer that the editorial voices of these stations will prove to be as distinctive, varied, and idiosyncratic as the various communities they represent. Accordingly, absent some showing by the Government to the contrary, the risk that local editorializing will place all of public broadcasting in jeopardy is not sufficiently pressing to warrant Section 399's broad suppression of speech."

In dissent, Justice Rehnquist, joined by Burger and White, said that Congress had not violated the First Amendment when it decided that public funds shall not be used to subsidize noncommercial, educational broadcasting stations that engage in editorializing or endorse or oppose any political candidate. Because it is impossible to separate programming expenses from other expenditures, Rehnquist said that the only effective means for preventing the use of public moneys to subsidize the airing of management's views is for Congress to ban a subsidized station from all on-the-air editorializing. Justice Stevens, in a separate dissent, said that the statute was proper because of the overriding interest in forestalling creation of propaganda organs for the government. "One need not have heard the raucous voice of Adolf Hitler over Radio Berlin to appreciate the importance of that concern." He agreed with White's brief comment appended to the Rehnquist dissent, that the statutory prohibitions against editorializing and candidate endorsement rest on the same foundation. "The quality of the interest in maintaining government neutrality in the free market of ideas—of avoiding subtle forms of censorship and propaganda— out-weighs the impact on expression that results from this statute. Indeed, by simply terminating or reducing funding, Congress could curtail much more expression with no risk whatever of a constitutional transgression."

Referenced Cases: *Minnesota Star & Tribune Co. v. Minnesota Commissioner of Revenue*, 460 U.S. 575 (1983), *First National Bank of Boston v. Bellotti*, 435 U.S. 765 (1978), *Buckley v. Valeo*, 424 U.S. 1 (1976), *Thornhill v. Alabama*, 310 U.S. 88 (1940), and *Mills v. Alabama*, 384 U.S. 214 (1966), on First Amendment protection of editorial opinion; *Miami Herald Publishing Co. v. Tornillo*, 418 U.S. 241 (1974), *Red Lion Broadcasting v. FCC*, 395 U.S. 367 (1969), and *CBS v. Democratic National Committee*, 412 U.S. 94 (1973), on different rules for different media; *CBS v. FCC*, 453 U.S. 367 (1981), and *FCC v. Midwest Video Corp.* 440 U.S. 689 (1979), on broadcasters entitled to the "widest journalistic freedom"; *FCC v. Pacifica Foundation*, 438 U.S. 726 (1978), on determinations in the light of the particular circumstances of each case; *NAACP v. Claiborne Hardware Co.*, 458 U.S. 886 (1982), regarding "expression on public issues 'has always rested on the highest rung of the hierarchy of First Amendment values'"; *New York Times v. Sullivan*, 376 U.S. 254 (1964), on Justice Brennan's statement that "debate on public issues should be uninhibited, robust, and wide-open"; *Whitney v. California*, 274 U.S. 357 (1927), on weighing interests against restrictions; *Consolidated Edison v. Public Service Comm'n*, 447 U.S. 530 (1980), Justice Stevens on abridgment of speech by curtailing a particular point of view; *Regan v. Taxation With Representation of Washington*, 461 U.S. 540 (1983), regarding Congress' spending power; *Oklahoma v. CSC*, 330 U.S. 127 (1947), *CSC v. Letter Carriers*, 413 U.S. 548 (1973), and *United Public Workers v. Mitchell*, 330 U.S. 75 (1947), on banning local or state employees from political activities; *Cammarano v. U.S.*, 358 U.S. 498 (1959), *Speiser v. Randall*, 357 U.S. 513 (1958), and *American Communications Assn. v. Douds*, 339 U.S. 382 (1950), on the point that government funds should not be aimed at the suppression of dangerous ideas.

Further Reading:

70 *ABA J.* 163 (Oct. 1984).
71 *Cornell L. Rev.* 453 (Jan. 1986).
8 *George Mason Univ. L. Rev.* 419 (Spring 1986).
98 *Harvard L. Rev.* 205 (Nov. 1984).
17 *J. of Broadcasting* 363 (1973).
12 *J. of Legislation* 104 (Winter 1985).
69 *L. Ed. 2d* 1110 (1982).
12 *Pepperdine L. Rev.* 699 (March 1985).
60 *Texas L. Rev.* 207 (1982).
39 *Vanderbilt L. Rev.* 323 (March 1986).
31 *Wayne L. Rev.* 1103 (March 1986).

1986   *City of Los Angeles and Department of Water and Power v. Preferred Communications, Inc.*, **476 U.S. 488, 90 L.Ed.2d 480, 106 S.Ct. 2034; 12 Med.L.Rptr. 2244**

Argued: April 29, 1986.

Decided: June 2, 1986.

Summary: A city's refusal to permit competitive cable television service in violation of the First Amendment. The Court compared cable systems more to newspapers than to broadcasting stations.

Circumstances: Preferred Communications, a cable operator, sued Los Angeles and its Department of Water and Power (DWP) for refusing to grant it a cable franchise and access to the DWP's utility poles and underground conduits. The company was turned down by the DWP and Pacific Telephone and Telegraph until it first obtained a franchise from the city, application for which the city refused because the company had failed to participate in an auction that was to award a single franchise to the area. The District Court for the Central District of California dismissed the complaint for failure to state a claim on which relief could be granted. The Court of Appeals for the Ninth Circuit affirmed the antitrust allegation but reversed the First Amendment claim. On certiorari, the Supreme Court affirmed the court of appeals' judgment and remanded to the district court.

Opinion: Justice William H. Rehnquist wrote for the unanimous Court. Harry A. Blackmun, with Thurgood Marshall and Sandra Day O'Connor, wrote a separate concurrence. In a case the Court said "plainly implicate[s] First Amendment interests," a California cable television operator challenged the right of Los Angeles to limit which company could and could not wire the city when it failed to acquire a franchise for a section of the city. Rehnquist said : "Cable television partakes of some of the aspects of speech and the communication of ideas as do the traditional enterprises of newspaper and book publishers, public speakers and pamphleteers." The Court made no ruling on the constitutionality of the city's franchising authority, but remanded for construction of a better factual record at a trial. Blackmun, with Marshall and O'Connor, agreed with the opinion on the understanding that it left open the question of the proper standard for judging First Amendment challenges to a municipality's restriction of access to cable facilities. "Different communications media are treated differently for First Amendment purposes."

Referenced Cases: *Parker v. Brown,* 317 U.S. 341 (1963), on antitrust immunity under state-action doctrine; *Miami*

Herald Publishing Co. v. Tornillo, 418 U.S. 241 (1974), *Red Lion Broadcasting Co. v. FCC*, and *Members of City Council v. Taxpayers for Vincent*, 466 U.S. 789 (1984), on relevant access doctrine; *Kugler v. Helfant*, 421 U.S. 117 (1975), on truth of allegations for the purpose of dismissal; *FCC v. Midwest Video Corp.*, 440 U.S. 689 (1979), on cable editorial discretion; *Cornelius v. NAACP Legal Defense & Educational Fund*, 473 U.S. 788 (1985), holding that "even protected speech is not equally permissible in all places and at all times"; *U.S. Railroad Retirement Board v. Fritz*, 449 U.S. 166 (1980), and *Schweiker v. Wilson*, 450 U.S. 221 (1981), on Fifth Amendment equal protection challenges; *Ohralik v. Ohio State Bar Ass'n*, 436 U.S. 447 (1978), and *Landmark Communications v. Virginia*, 435 U.S. 829 (1978), on sustaining legislation against constitutional challenges.

Further Reading:
24 *American Business L. Rev.* 541 (Winter 1987).
35 *Catholic Univ. L. Rev.* 851 (Spring 1986).
8 *Comm/Ent L. J.* 535 (Spring/Summer 1986).
11 *Oklahoma City Univ. L. Rev.* 525 (Summer 1986).
7 *Pace L. Rev.* 1 (Fall 1986).
53 *Tennessee L. Rev.* 179 (Fall 1985).
61 *Washington L. Rev.* 665 (April 1986).

Selected Bibliography

Albert, James A., "Constitutional Regulation of Televised Violence," 64 *Virginia L. Rev.* 1299 (Dec. 1978).

Bals, B., "The Growing Pains of Cable Television," 7 *Campbell L. Rev.* 175 (1984).

Barron, Jerome A., "The Federal Communications Commission's Fairness Doctrine: An Evaluation," 30 *George Washington L. Rev.* 1 (1961).

Bazelon, David L., "FCC Regulation of the Telecommunications Press," 1975 *Duke L. J.* 213 (1975).

Botein, Michael, "Access to Cable Television," 57 *Cornell L. Rev.* 419 (1972).

"Broadcasting Obscene Language," 43 *Arizona State L. J.* 457 (1974).

Cahn, Edmond, "Law in the Consumer Perspective," 112 *Univ. Pa. L. Rev.* 1 (1963).

Canby, William J., Jr., "Programming in Response to the Community: The Broadcast Consumer and the First Amendment," 55 *Texas L. Rev.* 67 (1977).

"CATV Regulation: A Jumble of Jurisdiction," 45 *NYU L. Rev.* 816 (1970).

Chamberlin, Bill F., "Lessons in Regulating Information Flow: The FCC's Weak Track Record in Interpreting the Public Interest Standard," 60 *North Carolina L. Rev.* 1067 (1982).

———, "The FCC and the First Principle of the Fairness Doctrine: A History of Neglect and Distortion," 31 *Fed. Communications L. J.* 113 (1985).

"The Darkened Channels: UHF Television and the FCC," 75 *Harvard L. Rev.* 1578 (1962).

Evans, Anne C., "An Examination of the Theories Justifying Content Regulation of the Electronic Media," 30 *Syracuse L. Rev.* 871 (Summer 1979).

"Expanding the Scarcity Rationale: The Constitutionality of Public Access Requirements in Cable Franchise Agreements," 20 *Univ. Michigan J. L. Reform* 305 (Fall 1986).

"FCC Comparative Renewal Hearings: The Role of the Commission and the Role of the Court," 21 *Boston College L. Rev.* 421 (1980).

Fogarty, Joseph R., and Marcia Spielholz, "FCC Cable Jurisdiction: From Zero to Plenary in Twenty-Five Years," 37 *Fed. Communications L. J.* 113 (1985).

Fowler, Mark S., and Daniel L. Brenner, "A Marketplace Approach to Broadcast Regulation," 60 *Texas L. Rev.* 207 (1982).

Fowler, Mark S., et al., "50th Anniversary of the Communications Act: Special Supplement," 37 *Fed. Comunications L. J.* 71 (1985).

Friedenthal, Jack H., and Richard J. Medalie, "The Impact of Federal Regulation of Political Broadcasting: Section 315 of the Communications Act," 72 *Harvard L. Rev.* 445 (1959).

"The Future of the Radio Format Change Controversy: The Case for the Competitive Marketplace," 22 *William & Mary L. Rev.* 281 (1980).

Goddard, Richard P., "Home Box Office and the FCC's Reasonably Ancillary Jurisdiction," 35 *Washington & Lee L. Rev.* 197 (Winter 1978).

Hanna, Mitchell J., "Controlling 'Pirate' Broadcasting," 15 *San Diego L. Rev.* 547 (April 1978).

Hillman, N. L., "The Fair Use of Free Broadcast Television: The Betamax Case and the Distinction Between Marketable and Disposable Software," 15 *Seton Hall L. Rev.* 52 (1984).

Houser, Thomas J., "The Fairness Doctrine: An Historical Perspective," 47 *Notre Dame Lawyer* 550 (1972).

Jaffe, Louis L., "The Editorial Responsibility of the Broadcaster," 85 *Harvard L. Rev.* 768 (1972).

Johnson, Timothy P., "Regulating CATV: Local Government and the Franchising Process," 19 *So. Dakota L. Rev.* 143 (1974).

Krattenmaker, T. G., and L. A. Power, Jr., "The Fairness Doctrine Today: A Constitutional Curiosity and an Impossible Dream," 1985 *Duke L. J.* 151 (1985).

McKenna, R., "Preemption under the Communications Act," 37 *Fed. Communications L. J.* 1 (1985).

Meyer, Karl E., "Television's Trying Times," *Saturday Review* (Sept. 16, 1978).

Meyerson, Michael, "The Cable Communications Policy Act of 1984: A Balancing Act on the Coaxial Wires," 19 *Georgia L. Rev.* 543 (1985).

Noto, Thomas A., "FCC Regulation of Cable Television Content," 31 *Rutgers L. Rev.* 238 (July 1978).

"Redefining 'Common Carrier': The FCC's Attempt at Deregulation by Redefinition," 1987 *Duke L. J.* 501 (June 1987).

"Regulation of Program Content by the FCC," 77 *Harvard L. Rev.* 701 (1963).

Riggs, R. E., "Regulation of Indecency on Cable Television," 59 *Florida Bar J.* 9 (1985).

Robbins, Vicky H., "Indecency on Cable Television—A Barren Battleground for Regulation of Programming Content," 15 *St. Mary's L. J.* 417 (1984).

Robinson, Glen O., "The FCC and the First Amendment: Observations on 40 Years of Radio and Television Regulation," 52 *Minnesota L. Rev.* 67 (1967).

Simmons, Steven J., "The Problem of 'Issue' in the Administration of the Fairness Doctrine," 65 *California L. Rev.* 546 (1977).

Simon, Jules F., "The Collapse of Consensus: Effects of the Deregulation of Cable Television," 81 *Columbia L. Rev.* 612 (1981).

"The Supreme Court Strikes Down the Public Broadcasting Editorial Ban: Federal Communications Commission v. League of Women Voters," 12 *Pepperdine L. Rev.* 699 (1985).

Topinka, Ralph, "FCC v. Midwest Video Corp.," 1979 *Wisconsin L. Rev.* 962 (1979).

"The TRAC to Fairness: Teletext and the Political Broadcasting Regulations," 39 *Hastings L. J.* 165 (Nov. 1987).

Wall, T. H., "Program Evaluation by Federal Communications Commission: An Unconstitutional Abridgment of Free Speech?" 40 *Georgia L. J.* 1 (Nov. 1951).

Witt, J. W., "Cable Television Content Regulation After Crisp," 17 *Urban L.* 277 (1985).

Yasser, Raymond L., "Federal Communications Commission v. National Citizens Committee for Broadcasting: The Ultimate Media Hype," 67 *Kentucky L. J.* 903 (1978–79).

Business

1936 *Alice Lee Grosjean, Supervisor of Public Accounts for the State of Louisiana v. American Press Co.,* 297 U.S. 233, 80 L.Ed. 660, 56 S.Ct. 444, 1 Med.L.Rptr. 2685

Argued: Jan. 14, 1936.

Decided: Feb. 10, 1936.

Summary: A license tax on advertisements, "single in kind," held unfair, discriminatory, and an unconstitutional restraint on the press.

Circumstances: Huey P. Long, governor of Louisiana and then senator, is said to have been bothered by the frequent newspaper attacks on his political machine. To retaliate, the state legislature enacted a special 2 percent tax on the gross advertising income of publications with a circulation of more than 20,000 per week. Of the state's 163 newspapers, only 13 had more than 20,000 subscribers, and 12 of them frequently opposed Long. Nine publishers, who owned the 13 newspapers, succeeded in getting a decree from the District Court for the Eastern District of Louisiana enjoining enforcement of the tax statute. The Supreme Court, on appeal, affirmed.

Opinion: Justice George Sutherland, writing for the unanimous Court, said that "the act imposing the tax . . . is unconstitutional under the due process of law clause because it abridges the freedom of the press." The Court struck down a state statute imposing a license tax on the business of publishing advertising in publications with a circulation of more than 20,000 copies a week. Sutherland wrote that the 2 percent tax on gross receipts from newspaper advertisements operates as a restraint in a double sense: it curtails the amount of revenue realized and it restricts circulation.

Such "taxes on knowledge," as they were called in colonial times, had the effect of curtailing newspaper circulation among the masses of people. Sutherland said the tax was bad because, "in the light of its history and of its present setting, it is seen to be a deliberate and calculated device in the guise of a tax to limit the circulation of information to which the public is entitled in virtue of the constitutional guarantees." He thus hinted at the background, explained above, and went on to note that the tax had "the plain purpose of penalizing the circulation of a selected group of newspapers." Joining Sutherland were Chief Justice Charles E. Hughes and Justices Willis Van Devanter, James C. McReynolds, Louis D. Brandeis, Pierce Butler, Harlan F. Stone, Owen J. Roberts, and Benjamin N. Cardozo.

Referenced Cases: *The Rio Grande v. Otis*, 19 Wall. 178 (1874), and *Gibson v. Shufeldt*, 122 U.S. 27 (1887), regarding dismissal on jurisdictional grounds; *Ohio Oil Co. v. Conway*, 279 U.S. 813 (1929), *Davis v. Wakelee*, 156 U.S. 680 (1895), and *Union P. R. Co. v. Weld County*, 247 U.S. 282 (1918), on equitable relief; *Hurtado v. California*, 110 U.S. 516 (1884), and *Powell V. Alabama*, 287 U.S. 45 (1932), on relationship of grand jury presentment or indictment to "due process of law" clause; *Gitlow v. New York*, 268 U.S. 652 (1925), and *Near v. Minnesota*, 283 U.S. 697 (1931), on fundamental rights of free speech and press as safeguarded by due process of law clause of 14th Amendment; *Allgeyer v. Louisiana*, 165 U.S. 578 (1897), on freedom from physical restraint and right to enjoyment of all faculties; *Paul v. Virginia*, 8 Wall. 168 (1869), *Covington v. L. Turnp. Road Co. v. Sandford*, 164 U.S. 578 (1896), and *Smyth v. Ames*, 169 U.S. 466 (1898), regarding a corporation as "citizen" and "person" within equal protection and due process; *A. Magnano Co. v. Hamilton*, 292 U.S. 40 (1934), *Hebert v. Louisiana*, 272 U.S. 312 (1926), and *Twining v. New Jersey*, 211 U.S. 78 (1908), on validity of the tax; *Continental Illinois Nat. Bank & T. Co. v. Chicago, R. I. & P. R. Co.*, 294 U.S. 648 (1935), *Murray v. Hoboken Land & Improv. Co.*, 18 How. 272 (1855), and *Waring v. Clarke*, 5 How. 441 (1846), on applicability of the common law.

Further Reading:
16 *Boston Univ. L. Rev.* 919 (Nov. 1936).
5 *Brooklyn L. Rev.* 328 (March 1936).
24 *Georgia L. J.* 1015 (May 1936).

49 *Harvard L. Rev.* 998 (April 1936).

4 *J. of Bar Assoc., Kansas* 326 (May 1936).

20 *Minnesota L. Rev.* 671 (May 1936).

1937   *The Associated Press v. National Labor Relations Board*, **301 U.S. 103, 81 L.Ed. 953, 57 S.Ct. 650; 1 Med.L.Rptr. 2689**

Argued: Feb. 9, 10, 1937.

Decided: April 12, 1937.

Summary: In denying the press constitutional protection from economic regulations (that is, the National Labor Relations Act), the Court held that the business of the Associated Press (AP) is not immune just because it is an agency of the press and that no special immunity exists under the First Amendment from general laws, including antitrust laws.

Circumstances: In Oct. 1935, the AP discharged an employee of its New York office, Morris Watson. The American Newspaper Guild, a labor union, filed a charge with the National Labor Relations Board (NLRB) alleging that Watson's discharge was in violation of Section 7 of the National Labor Relations Act, which allows employees to organize, form, join, or assist labor organizations to bargain collectively. The NLRB charged the AP with unfair labor practices. A trial examiner, following a hearing, recommended that an order be entered against the AP. The NLRB, in turn, ordered the AP to cease and desist from discouraging membership in the guild and enjoined the AP to reinstate Watson to his former position. When the AP refused to comply, the NLRB petitioned the Circuit Court of Appeals for the Second Circuit, which issued a decree enforcing the board's order. On writ of certiorari, the Supreme Court affirmed the judgment.

Opinion: Justice Owen J. Roberts, writing for the five-man majority, said, "The business of the Associated Press is not immune from regulation because it is an agency of the press. The publisher of a newspaper has no special immunity from the application of general laws. He has no special privileges to invade the rights and liberties of others. He must answer for libel. He may be punished for contempt of court. He is subject to the anti-trust laws. Like others he must pay equitable and non-discriminatory taxes on his business. The regulation here in question has no relation whatever to the impartial distribution of news." Roberts was joined by Chief Justice Charles F. Hughes and Justices Harlan F. Stone, Louis D. Brandeis, and Benjamin N. Cardozo. Dissenting were Justices George Sutherland, Willis Van Devanter, James C. McReynolds, and Pierce Butler. In response to the AP's contention that the National Labor Relations Act's protection of union activities violates freedom of the press, Roberts called that view an "unsound generalization," for it ignores the fact that the statute does not compel employment or retention of an incompetent or biased editor. "The act permits a discharge for any reason other than union activity or agitation for collective bargaining with employees." Justice Sutherland, writing for the dissenters, noted, however, that the constitutional immunity of the press does not permit any legislative restriction of the authority of the publisher to discharge anyone engaged in the editorial service. "For the saddest epitaph which can be carved in memory of a vanished liberty is that it was lost because its possessors failed to stretch forth a saving hand while yet there was time."

Referenced Cases: *Virginian R. Co. v. System Federation,* 300 U.S. 515 (1937), on the efficacy of legislation preventing strikes and obviating interference with interstate commerce; *Texas & N. O. R. Co. v. Brotherhood of R. & S. S. Clerks,* 281 U.S. 548 (1930), and *American Steel Foundries v. Tri-City Cent. Trades Council,* 257 U.S. 184 (1921), regarding rights of collective bargaining; *National Labor Relations Bd. v. Jones & L. Steel Corp.,* 301 U.S. 1 (1937), on regulating intrastate and interstate commerce; *De Jonge v. Oregon,* 299 U.S. 353 (1937), *Grosjean v. American Press Co.,* 297 U.S. 233 (1936), *Near v. Minnesota,* 283 U.S. 697 (1931), and *Pierce v. Society of Sisters,* 268 U.S. 510 (1925), on guaranteed First Amendment liberties; *Louisville & N. R. Co. v. Mottley,* 219 U.S. 467 (1911), on liberty guaranty of the Fifth Amendment; *Boyd v. U.S.,* 116 U.S. 616 (1886), and *Olmstead v. U.S.,* 277 U.S. 471 (1928), on protecting liberty when a government is beneficent.

Further Reading:
17 *Boston Univ. L. Rev.* 710 (June 1937).
25 *California L. Rev.* 593 (July 1937).
51 *Harvard L. Rev.* 163 (Nov. 1937).
25 *Illinois Bar J.* 376 (June 1937).
32 *Illinois L. Rev.* 196 (June 1937).

1945   *Associated Press, Paul Bellamy, George Francis Booth et al. v. U.S.; Tribune Co. and Robert Rutherford McCormick v. U.S.; and U.S. v. Associated Press, Paul Bellamy, George Francis Booth, et al.,* **326 U.S. 1, 89 L.Ed. 2013, 65 S.Ct. 1416, 1 Med.L.Rptr. 2269**

Argued: Dec. 5, 6, 1944.

Decided: June 18, 1945.

Summary: In this, the first time the Sherman Act was used as a vehicle for affirmative government intervention in the realm of dissemination of information, the Associated Press (AP) bylaws were held to be an "unreasonable" restraint of trade and commerce.

Circumstances: The United States filed a bill in the District Court for the Southern District of New York for an injunction against the AP and others, charging that they had violated the Sherman Anti-Trust Act of July 2, 1890, by a combination and conspiracy in restraint of trade and commerce in news among the states and for attempting to monopolize part of that trade. The government alleged that the AP's bylaws prohibited all members from selling news to nonmembers and granted powers to block its nonmember competitors from membership in the AP. The government's motion for summary judgment, under Rule 56 of Civil Procedure, was granted and its prayer for relief was granted in part and denied in part for an injunction against alleged violations of the act. The three-judge district court panel held that the bylaws unlawfully restricted admission to AP membership and violated the act insofar as the bylaws "clothed a member with powers to impose or dispense with conditions upon the admission of his business competitor." Continued observance of the bylaws was enjoined. Both sides brought the case on direct appeal to the Supreme Court, which affirmed the ruling.

Opinion: Justice Hugo L. Black wrote the opinion of the 5-to-3 Court, joined by Stanley F. Reed, Wiley B. Rutledge, William O. Douglas, and Felix Frankfurter. Douglas and Frankfurter also wrote separately. Owen J. Roberts, joined by Chief Justice Harlan F. Stone, and Frank Murphy wrote separate dissents. Robert H. Jackson did not participate. Black, in dealing with the AP as a business rather than strictly a press enterprise, said: "Member publishers of AP are engaged in business for profit exactly as are other business men who sell food, steel, aluminum, or anything else people need or want. All are alike covered by the Sherman Act." He said that the inability to buy news from the agency could seriously affect a publication and endanger its ability to function successfully. "The joint effect of these By-Laws is to block all newspaper non-members from any opportunity to buy news from AP or any of its publisher members." Then, in a memorable defense of freedom of the press, Black wrote: "The First Amendment . . . rests on the assumption that the widest possible dissemination of information from diverse and antagonistic sources is essential to the welfare of the public, that a free press is a condition of a free society. Surely a command that the government itself shall not impede the free flow of ideas does not afford non-governmental combinations a refuge if they impose restraints upon that constitutionally guaranteed freedom. Freedom to publish means freedom for all and not for some. Freedom to publish is guaranteed by the Constitution, but freedom to combine to keep others from publishing is not. Freedom of the press from governmental interference under the First Amendment does not sanction repression of that freedom by private interests. The First Amendment affords not the slightest support for the contention that a combination to restrain trade in news and views has any constitutional immunity."

Justice Douglas added that such an "exclusive arrangement" might result in the growth of a monopoly in the furnishing of news, in the access to news, or in the gathering and distribution of news. Justice Frankfurter likened the AP's monopoly to that of a public utility, with a relation to the public interest unlike that of any other enterprise pursued for profit. "The interest of the public is to have the flow of news not trammeled by the combined self-interest of those who enjoy a unique constitutional position precisely because of the public dependence on a free press."

In dissent, Justice Roberts noted that what is being denied nonmembers is "access to AP news, not . . . to news. *In limine*, it should be remembered that newspaper proprietors who are members of AP are not, as publishers, in the trade of buying or selling news. Their business is the publishing of newspapers." Finally, Roberts, finding no Sherman Act application, said that he preferred to entrust regulatory legislation of commerce to the elected representatives of the people instead of "freezing it in the decrees of courts less responsive to the public will." Justice Murphy, also in dissent, said that the evidence falls short of proving that the AP members were trying to hamper or destroy competition, and that they were entirely within their legal rights to form a collective organization. "Certainly the Sherman Act was not designed to discourage men from combining their talents and resources in order to outdo their rivals by producing better goods and services."

Referenced Cases: *Sartor v. Arkansas Natural Gas Corp.*, 321 U.S. 620 (1944), on need for trial when facts are in dispute; *International News Service v. Associated Press*, 248 U.S. 215 (1918), on the business aspect of news; *Bridges v. California*, 314 U.S. 252 (1941), regarding the "clear and present danger" doctrine; *Associated Press v. NLRB*, 301 U.S. 103 (1937), and *American Medical Assoc. v. U.S.*, 317 U.S. 519 (1943), on news trade as interstate commerce and cooperatives as businesses; *Standard Oil Co. v. U.S.*, 221 U.S. 1 (1911), on "reasonable" trade restraints; *U.S. v. Bausch & L. Co.*, 321 U.S. 707 (1944), and *Fashion Originators' Guild v. FTC*, 312 U.S. 457 (1941), on the obstructive nature of contracts or combinations; *W. W. Montague & Co. v. Lowry*, 193 U.S. 38 (1904), *Eastern States Retail Lumber Dealers' Assoc. v. U.S.*, 234 U.S. 600 (1914), *U.S. v. Crescent Amusement Co.*, 323 U.S. 173 (1944), *Addyston Pipe & Steel Co. v. U.S.*, 175 U.S. 211 (1899), and *Anderson v. Shipowners' Assoc.*, 272 U.S. 359 (1926), on products other than news within realm of Sherman Act; *Indiana Farmer's Guide Pub. Co. v. Prairie*

Farmer Pub. Co., 293 U.S. 268 (1934), on Sherman Act as an abridgment of press freedom; *Ethyl Gasoline Corp. v. U.S.*, 309 U.S. 436 (1940), on restraint of trade as part of larger illegal arrangement; *U.S. v. Terminal R. Assoc.*, 224 U.S. 383 (1912), on equality as alternative to dissolving illegal combinations.

Further Reading:
14 *George Washington L. Rev.* 461 (April 1946).
21 *Indiana L. J.* 221 (Jan. 1946).
31 *Iowa L. Rev.* 432 (March 1946).
44 *Michigan L. Rev.* 677 (Feb. 1946).
31 *Virginia L. Rev.* 954 (Sept. 1945).
55 *Yale L. J.* 428 (Feb. 1946).

1946　　*Courtney M. Mabee, Charles K. Barnum, Edward G. Tompkins et al. v. White Plains Publishing Co., Inc.*, 327 U.S. 178, 90 L.Ed. 607, 66 S.Ct. 511

Argued: Dec. 5, 1945.

Decided: Feb. 11, 1946.

Summary: Newspapers are not excluded from economic regulation, in this instance the Fair Labor Standards Act of June 25, 1938, the application of which does not violate the First Amendment.

Circumstances: Employees of the newspaper publishing firm brought an unfair labor practice suit in New York courts to recover overtime pay, damages, and legal fees pursuant to the federal Fair Labor Standards Act. The employees argued that the business of receiving, transmitting, and exchanging news and advertising through interstate communications and agencies constituted interstate commerce and, thus, was within the meaning of the act. The publisher argued that newspaper publishing is peculiarly local, whether or not its circulation crosses state lines, and, thus, is exempt from the act. The Supreme Court, Westchester County, ruled for the employees, but the Appellate Division of the Supreme Court, Second Department, reversed, a judgment affirmed by the New York State Court of Appeals. On writ of certiorari, the U.S. Supreme Court reversed and remanded to the state appellate courts to determine the applicability of the Fair Labor Standards Act to the employees.

Opinion: Justice William O. Douglas wrote the 7-to-1 opinion, joined by Chief Justice Harlan F. Stone and Justices Hugo L. Black, Stanley F. Reed, Felix Frankfurter, Wiley B. Rutledge, and Harold H. Burton. Frank Murphy dissented, and Robert H. Jackson did not participate. Douglas said that the newspaper should not be excluded from the Fair Labor Standards Act, which regulates labor disputes affecting commerce. He noted that the act's exemptions are for weekly or semiweekly newspapers with circulations of less than 3,000, but he added that no such exemptions were granted dailies no matter the amount of out-of-state circulation. "The choice Congress made was not the exemption of newspapers with small out-of-state circulations but the exemption of certain types of small newspapers." Because the press has business aspects, it has no special immunity from laws applicable to business in general, Douglas said. At issue was the small number of papers shipped out of state, one criterion for judging interstate commerce. In Justice Murphy's opinion in dissent, "a company that produces 99½% of its products for local commerce is essentially and realistically a local business . . . , which we have said Congress plainly excluded from this Act."

Referenced Cases: *National Labor Relations Bd. v. Fainblatt*, 306 U.S. 601 (1939), *Walling v. Jacksonville Paper Co.*, 317 U.S. 564 (1943), and *Skidmore v. Swift & Co.*, 323 U.S. 134 (1944), on provisions of the Fair Labor Standards Act affecting labor disputes; *U.S. v. Darby*, 312 U.S. 100 (1941), and *Warren-Bradshaw Drilling Co. v. Hall*, 317 U.S. 88 (1942), on volume or amount of shipments affecting suppression of competition; *Grosjean v. American Press Co.*, 297 U.S. 233 (1936), regarding discrimination against dailies; *Associated Press v. NLRB*, 301 U.S. 103 (1937), on laws applicable to business generally; *Steward Mach. Co. v. Davis*, 301 U.S. 548 (1937), and *Currin v. Wallace*, 306 U.S. 1 (1939), regarding Congress' power to restrict legislative policy to less than the entire field; *Phillips Co. v. Walling*, 324 U.S.

490 (1945), on local wage and hour problems being a matter for state regulation.

Further Reading:
9 *Georgia Bar J.* 104 (Aug. 1946).
22 *Indiana L. J.* 127 (Jan. 1947).
See also under *Oklahoma Press Publishing Co. v. Walling*, 32 U.S. 186 (1946), decided the same day.

1946   *Oklahoma Press Publishing Co. v. L. Metcalfe Walling, Administrator of the Wage and Hour Division, U.S. Department of Labor and News Printing Co., Inc. v. L. Metcalfe Walling, 327 U.S. 186, 90 L.Ed. 614, 66 S.Ct. 494*

Argued: Oct. 17, 18, 1945.

Decided: Feb. 11, 1946.

Summary: Newspapers are not exempt from the regulation of business in general, in this instance the Fair Labor Standards Act of June 25, 1938, the application of which does not violate the First Amendment.

Circumstances: The Oklahoma newspaper sought relief from an order requiring compliance with a subpoena duces tecum issued by the wage hour administrator in the course of an investigation into the applicability and violation of the Fair Labor Standards Act. The News Printing Co. of Paterson, New Jersey, sought show cause regarding compliance with a subpoena issued by the administrator in the course of a similar investigation. The Circuit Court of Appeals for the Tenth Circuit affirmed an order of the District Court for the Eastern District of Oklahoma requiring compliance with the order directing access to the records and documents specified. The Circuit Court of Appeals for the Third Circuit dismissed an order of the District Court for the District of New Jersey to show cause why an order should not be issued requiring compliance with the subpoena. The district court had denied enforcement of the order for want of a showing of cause. But the court of appeals said that requiring the administrator "to make proof of coverage would be to turn the proceeding into a suit to decide a question which must be determined by the Administrator in the course of his investigation." The Supreme Court affirmed both judgments of both circuits.

Opinion: Justice Wiley B. Rutledge wrote the 7-to-1 opinion, joined by Chief Justice Harlan F. Stone and Justices Hugo L. Black, William O. Douglas, Stanley F. Reed, Felix Frankfurter, and Harold H. Burton. Frank Murphy dissented, and Robert H. Jackson did not participate. Rutledge said that the First Amendment does not preclude application of the Fair Labor Standards Act to the business of newspaper publishing. "If Congress can remove obstructions to commerce by requiring publishers to bargain collectively with employees and refrain from interfering with their rights of self-organization, matters closely related to eliminating low wages and long hours, Congress likewise may strike directly at those evils when they adversely affect commerce." In these cases, decided together, the Court disagreed with the publishers' contention that by requiring the submission of specified books, records, and papers for examination by the Department of Labor, the government could perforce conduct a general "fishing expedition." Rutledge said that the publishers seek a total immunity from the act rather than an unlawful search and seizure. The Court thus rejected all First, Fourth, and Fifth Amendment claims. "All the records sought were relevant to the authorized inquiry, the purpose of which was to determine two issues, whether petitioners were subject to the Act and, if so, whether they were violating it."

Justice Murphy, in dissent, objected to the use of non-judicial subpoenas by administrative agents. "To allow a non-judicial officer, unarmed with judicial process, to demand the books and papers of an individual is an open invitation to abuse of that power. Liberty is too priceless to be forfeited through the zeal of an administrative agent." Attending the growth in administrative law "in the past few years" should be a broader sense of responsibility on the part of administrative agencies and officials, Murphy concluded.

Referenced Cases: *Endicott Johnson Corp. v. Perkins,* 317 U.S. 501 (1943), on the government's proof of coverage requirement in the course of investigation; *Associated Press v. NLRB*, 301 U.S. 103 (1937), *Associated Press v. U.S.*, 326 U.S. 1 (1945), and *Mabee v. White Plains Pub. Co.*, 327 U.S. 178 (1946), on violating the First Amendment; *U.S. v. Darby*, 312 U.S. 100 (1941), on evils that adversely affect commerce; *Buck v. Bell*, 274 U.S. 200 (1927), on statutory exemptions to Fair Labor Standards Act; *Grosjean v. American Press Co.*, 297 U.S. 233 (1936), on the unconstitutionality of special taxation of newspapers; *Boyd v. U.S.*, 116 U.S. 616 (1886), and *Wilson v. U.S.*, 221 U.S. 361 (1911), on self-incrimination; *Blair v. U.S.*, 250 U.S. 273 (1919), and *Hale v. Henkel*, 201 U.S. 43 (1906), regarding the act's limitations vis-à-vis probable results of investigations.

Further Reading:

34 California L. Rev. 428 (June 1946).
14 *George Washington L. Rev.* 602 (June 1946).
22 *Indiana L. J.* 148 (Jan. 1947).
20 *So. Calif. L. Rev.* 66 (Dec. 1946).
9 *Univ. Detroit L. J.* 210 (May 1946).
14 *Univ. Kansas City L. Rev.* 116 (April–June 1946).
56 *Yale L. J.* 162 (Nov. 1946).

1948   *U.S. v. Paramount Pictures, Inc., Paramount Film Distributing Corp., Loew's, Inc., et al.; Loew's, Inc., Radio-Keith-Orpheum Corp., RKO Radio Pictures, Inc., et al. v. U.S.; Paramount Pictures, Inc., and Paramount Film Distributing Corp. v. U.S.; Columbia Pictures Corp. and Columbia Pictures of Louisiana, Inc. v. U.S.; United Artists Corp. v. U.S.; Universal Pictures Co., Inc., Universal Film Exchanges, Inc. and Big U. Film Exchange, Inc. v. U.S.; American Theatres Assoc., Inc., Southern California Theatre Owners*

Assoc., Joseph Moritz et al. v. U.S., Paramount Pictures, Inc., Paramount Film Distributing Corp. et al.; and W. C. Allred, Charles E. Beach and Elizabeth L. Beach et al. v. U.S., Paramount Pictures, Inc., Paramount Film Distributing Corp. et al., 334 U.S. 131, 92 L.Ed. 1260, 68 S.Ct. 915

Argued: Feb. 9, 10, 11, 1948.

Decided: May 3, 1948.

Summary: In one of the most protracted and complicated media decisions ever, the Court declared the following practices of major film studios in violation of the Sherman Anti-Trust Act: fixing of minimum admission price, joint ownership of theaters, theater pooling agreements, formula deals, master agreements and franchises, block-booking, and discrimination between distributors.

Circumstances: The eight cases reached the Court on appeal from a judgment of a three-judge panel of the District Court for the Southern District of New York holding that the defendants had violated Sections 1 and 2 of the Sherman Act and granting an injunction and other relief. One group of defendants included those who produced, distributed, and exhibited films. The second group produced and distributed films. The third was engaged only in distribution. The Supreme Court affirmed in part and reversed in part and remanded to the district court.

Opinion: Justice William O. Douglas wrote the long 7-to-1 ruling, joined by Chief Justice Fred M. Vinson and Justices Hugo L. Black, Stanley F. Reed, Frank Murphy, Wiley B. Rutledge, and Harold H. Burton. Felix Frankfurter dissented in part, and Robert H. Jackson did not participate. On the lower court finding, that two price-fixing conspiracies existed—a horizontal one between all defendants and a vertical one between each distributor-defendant and its licensees—the Court used the premise that a price-fixing arrangement was illegal per se. Douglas noted that such price structuring suppresses competition, for "a copyright may no more be used than a patent to deter competition between rivals in the exploitation of their licenses." On clearances, designed to protect a particular run of a film against subsequent runs, the Court found that the defendants restrained trade by imposing unreasonable clearances. "Clearances have been used along with price fixing to suppress competition with the theatres of the exhibitor-defendants and with other favored exhibitors." On the pooling and joint ownership agreements, whereby two or more theaters, normally competitive, operated as a unit, the Court called such practices "bald efforts" to substitute monopoly for competition. "Clearer restraints of trade are difficult to imagine," Douglas wrote. However, the Court did not ban all joint ownership, especially those where neither monopoly nor unreasonable restraint of trade would result. On formula deals in which a theater's license fee is measured by a specified percentage of a feature film's national gross, such deals, as well as other master agreements, effectuate a restraint of trade and monopolistic practice. The Court set aside the lower court's findings on franchises, some of which it said may be discriminatory, in order for the court to examine the problem further.

On block-booking (the practice of licensing one or more features on condition that the exhibitor will license other features released during a given period), all but United Artists engaged in the practice. "Block-booking prevents competitors from bidding for single features on their individual merits," Douglas said. The Court approved the lower court's restriction. "We do not suggest that films may not be sold in blocks or groups, when there is no requirement, express or implied, for the purchase of more than one film." The Court also found discriminatory the practice of favoring large affiliated and unaffiliated circuits over small independent exhibitors through various special contract provisions. Even competitive bidding, which the Court noted was "at first blush" commendable, was believed of questionable value.

Finally, on the issues of monopoly, theater expansion, and divestiture, Douglas responded to the suggestion that the hold the defendants had on the industry was so great as to raise a First Amendment problem: "We have no doubt that moving pictures, like newspaper and radio, are included in the press whose freedom is guaranteed by the First Amendment." Although the production of motion pictures was not at issue in these cases—the chief issues were monopoly of and restraints on exhibition—the statement is important as the first instance of constitutional protection given the medium of film.

Justice Frankfurter dissented in part on the ground that the framing of the lower court's decree should be "a matter peculiarly" for that court and that review should be limited to whether the district court abused its discretion, which the justice thought not the case.

Referenced Cases: *Interstate Circuit v. U.S.*, 306 U.S. 208 (1939), and *U.S. v. Masonite Corp.*, 316 U.S. 265 (1942), on determining conspiracy; *U.S. v. General Electric Co.*, 272 U.S. 476 (1926), on applicability of Copyright Act of March 4, 1909, and patent statutes; *U.S. v. Socony-Vacuum Oil Co.*, 310 U.S. 150 (1940), on price-fixing as illegal per se; *U.S. v. U.S. Gypsum Co.*, 333 U.S. 364 (1948), regarding the extent of patents; *U.S. v. Bausch & L. Optical Co.*, 321 U.S. 707 (1944), and *U.S. v. Crescent Amusement Co.*, 323 U.S. 173 (1944), on the power of equity to uproot all parts of an illegal scheme; *Schine Chain Theatres v. U.S.*, 334 U.S. 110 (1948), and *U.S. v. Griffith*, 334 U.S. 101 (1948), on acquisitions sufficient to warrant divestiture; *Ethyl Gasoline Corp. v. U.S.*, 309 U.S. 436 (1940), *Morton Salt Co. v. G. S. Suppiger Co.*, 314 U.S. 488 (1942), and *Mercoid Corp. v. Mid-Continent Invest. Co.*, 320 U.S. 661 (1944), on conditioning the use of a patent on purchase and use of patented or unpatented materials; *Fox Film Corp. v. Doyal*, 286 U.S. 123 (1932), on copyright monopoly; *Associated Press v. U.S.*, 326 U.S. 1 (1945), regarding First Amendment protection; *U.S. v. Reading Co.*, 253 U.S. 26 (1920), and *U.S. v. Lehigh Valley R. Co.*, 254 U.S. 255 (1920), on the Sherman Act's view of a vertically integrated enterprise; *U.S. v. Terminal R. Assoc.*, 236 U.S. 194 (1915), on competitive bidding affecting prejudice.

Further Reading:
17 *George Washington L. Rev.* 59 (Dec. 1948).
24 *Notre Dame Lawyer* 114 (Fall 1948).
20 *So. Calif. L. Rev.* 1 (Dec. 1946).
95 *Univ. Pa. L. Rev.* 662 (May 1947).
97 *Univ. Pa. L. Rev.* 234 (Dec. 1948).

1951   *Lorain Journal Co., Samuel A. Horvitz,*
          Isadore Horvitz et al. v. U.S., 342 U.S.
          143, 96 L.Ed. 162, 72 S.Ct. 181, 1
          Med.L.Rptr. 2697

Argued: Oct. 17, 1951.

Decided: Dec. 11, 1951.

Summary: Held in violation of the Sherman Act a
newspaper's refusal to accept advertising from businesses that
also used a local radio station; in addition, held that an injunction
against the paper did not infringe the First Amendment.

Circumstances: The Lorain Journal Co. had published the *Journal* in Lorain, Ohio, since 1932, the year it purchased the *Times-Herald*, its lone competitor. Their combined
circulation reached 99 percent of Lorain families, with the only
print competition the *Sunday News.* In 1948 the Elyria-Lorain
Broadcasting Co., independent of the newspaper publisher, was
licensed as WEOL to operate in nearby Elyria. Shortly afterward
the publisher refused to accept local advertisements in the *Journal*
from any Lorain County business that advertised over WEOL. The
District Court for the Northern District of Ohio found that the
newspaper's purpose was to destroy the broadcasting company,
characterizing the plan as "bold, relentless, and predatory commercial behavior," and enjoined the publisher from violating the Sherman Anti-Trust Act. The Supreme Court affirmed.

Opinion: Justice Harold H. Burton, writing for a unanimous Court, wrote that a single newspaper, already enjoying a
substantial monopoly in its area, violates the "attempt to monopolize" of the Sherman Act when it uses its monopoly to destroy
threatened competition. The publisher's claimed right to select its
customers and to refuse advertisements from whomever it pleases
is neither absolute nor exempt from regulation, Burton said. In
response to the publisher's suggestion that the court decree
amounted to a prior restraint, he said the First Amendment afforded the paper no special protection: "The injunction applies to
a publisher what the law applies to others." Joining Burton were

Chief Justice Fred M. Vinson and Justices Hugo L. Black, Stanley F. Reed, Felix Frankfurter, William O. Douglas, and Robert H. Jackson. Tom C. Clark and Sherman Minton did not participate.

Referenced Cases: *Associated Press v. U.S.*, 326 U.S. 1 (1945), *Associated Press v. NLRB*, 301 U.S. 103 (1937), on news agencies as part of interstate commerce; *Blumenstock Bros. Adv. Agency v. Curtis Pub. Co.*, 252 U.S. 436 (1920), on advertising contracts; *Paul v. Virginia*, 8 Wall. 168 (1868), *New York Life Ins. Co. v. Deer Lodge County*, 231 U.S. 495 (1913), *U.S. v. South-Eastern Underwriters' Asso.*, 322 U.S. 533 (1944), *North American Co. v. Securities & Exchange Comm.*, 327 U.S. 686 (1946), and *Indiana Farmer's Guide Pub. Co. v. Prairie Farmer Pub. Co.*, 293 U.S. 268 (1934), on what constitutes interstate commerce; *Binderup v. Pathe Exchange*, 263 U.S. 291 (1923), *Stafford v. Wallace*, 258 U.S. 495 (1922), *Illinois Cent. R. Co. v. Defuentes*, 236 U.S. 157 (1915), and *Swift & Co. v. U.S.*, 196 U.S. 375 (1905), on distribution of news and advertisements being an inseparable part of the flow of interstate commerce and the public's protection through competition; *American Tobacco Co. v. U.S.*, 328 U.S. 781 (1946), on Sherman Act's protection against "dangerous probability" of monopoly as well as against completed result; *Standard Oil Co. v. U.S.*, 221 U.S. 1 (1911), on Sherman Act's second section; *Fashion Originators' Guild v. FTC*, 312 U.S. 457 (1941), *FTC v. Beech-Nut Packing Co.*, 257 U.S. 441 (1922), and *Loewe v. Lawlor*, 208 U.S. 274 (1908), on violating Sections 1 and 2 of the Sherman Act; *U.S. v. Colgate & Co.*, 250 U.S. 300 (1919), and *U.S. v. Bausch & L. Optical Co.*, 321 U.S. 707 (1944), regarding private business rights in the absence of creating and maintaining a monopoly; *Oklahoma Press Pub. Co. v. Walling*, 327 U.S. 186 (1946), and *Mabee v. White Plains Pub. Co.*, 327 U.S. 186 (1946), on injunctive relief under the Sherman Act as appropriate against newspapers as it is against others.

Further Reading:

3 *Alabama L. Rev.* 376 (Spring 1951).
66 *Harvard L. Rev.* 137 (Nov. 1952).
1952 *Intramural L. Rev., UCLA* 25 (June 1952).
27 *Notre Dame Lawyer* 472 (Spring 1952).
61 *Yale L. J.* 948 (1952).

1953   *Times-Picayune Publishing Co. v. U.S.*
            and *U.S. v. Times-Picayune Publishing*
            ***Co.*, 345 U.S. 594, 97 L.Ed. 1277, 73 S.Ct.**
            872, 1 Med.L.Rptr. 2697

Argued: March 11, 1953.

Decided: May 25, 1953.

Summary: Held that "forced combination" advertising
in two newspapers owned by the same company did not violate
the Sherman Anti-Trust Act.

Circumstances: The Times-Picayune Co. of New Orleans, publisher of the morning *Times-Picayune* and the evening
States, required advertisers who wanted to purchase space in
either paper to purchase space in both. In an action under the
Sherman Anti-Trust Act, the government challenged such unit-
rate contracts as violating the prohibition against unreasonable
restraints of trade included in Section 1 of the act and the prohibition against attempts to monopolize interstate commerce included in Section 2. The District Court for the Eastern District of
Louisiana enjoined the publisher from continuing the advertising
practices. On appeal from both the publisher and the government,
the former on the merits of the decision and the latter for broader
relief, the Supreme Court reversed.

Opinion: In the 5-to-4 ruling, Justice Tom C. Clark said
that the advertising-rate combination, or "tying" arrangement, was
not in violation of the antitrust law, despite the possibility that
such a scheme could hurt competition. Clark said that such an
arrangement was illegal only if a business with a dominant position
in the market coerced its customers into buying an unwanted inferior product along with the desired product. In this case, the government had argued that the morning *Times-Picayune* was the
dominant and desired product and the evening *States*, owned by the
same company, was the unwanted and inferior product advertisers
were forced to buy. But the majority believed that the *Times-
Picayune* was not dominant nor the *States* really inferior. "Here . . .
two newspapers under single ownership at the same place, time, and

terms sell indistinguishable products to advertisers; no dominant 'tying' product exists . . . no leverage in one market excludes sellers in the second, because for present purposes the products are identical and the market the same." Clark also noted that local display advertising in the competing *New Orleans Item* had actually increased substantially and, therefore, there was not evidence to show a deleterious effect on competition. Clark was joined by Chief Justice Fred M. Vinson and Justices Stanley F. Reed, Felix Frankfurter, and Robert H. Jackson. In dissent, Harold H. Burton was joined by Hugo L. Black, William O. Douglas, and Sherman Minton. Burton wrote that, though the *Times-Picayune* may not enjoy a "dominant position," it uses its "complete monopoly of access to the morning newspaper readers in the New Orleans area" to restrain unreasonably competition between its evening newspaper and the independent *Item*. This violates the Sherman Act, he said.

Referenced Cases: *Associated Press v. U.S.*, 326 U.S. 1 (1945), *Wieman v. Updegraff*, 344 U.S. 183 (1952), *Joseph Burstyn Inc. v. Wilson*, 343 U.S. 495 (1952), *Grosjean v. American Press Co.*, 297 U.S. 233 (1936), and *Near v. Minnesota*, 283 U.S. 697 (1931), on the press as chief source of democratic expression and controversy in a free society; *Standard Oil Co. v. U.S.*, 337 U.S. 293 (1949), *FTC v. Gratz*, 253 U.S. 421 (1920), *United Shoe Machinery Corp. v. U.S.*, 258 U.S. 451 (1922), *FTC v. Sinclair Refining Co.*, 261 U.S. 463 (1923), *Pick Mfg. Co. v. General Motors Corp.*, 299 U.S. 3 (1936), *IBM v. U.S.*, 298 U.S. 131 (1936), and *International Salt Co. v. U.S.*, 332 U.S. 392 (1947), on tying arrangements as suppressive of competition; *U.S. v. Paramount Pictures*, 334 U.S. 131 (1948), and *U.S. v. Griffith*, 334 U.S. 100 (1948), regarding "block-booking" films and monopoly power; *FTC v. Motion Picture Advertising Service Co.*, 344 U.S. 392 (1953), *FTC v. Cement Institute*, 333 U.S. 683 (1948), and *Fashion Originators' Guild v. FTC*, 312 U.S. 457 (1941), on Clayton and Sherman acts; *Lorain Journal Co. v. U.S.*, 342 U.S. 143 (1951), and *Indiana Farmer's Guide Pub. Co. v. Prairie Farmer Pub. Co.*, 293 U.S. 268 (1934), on dominance in advertising market versus dominance in readership; *U.S. v. Socony-Vacuum Oil Co.*, 310 U.S. 150 (1940), and *U.S. v. Trenton Potteries Co.*, 273 U.S. 392 (1927), on nascent and accomplished restraints of trade; *Kiefer-Stewart Co. v. Joseph E. Seagram & Sons, Inc.*, 340 U.S. 211 (1951), and *U.S. v. Colgate & Co.*, 250 U.S. 300 (1919), the first of several cases on right to refuse to sell.

Further Reading:

23 *Cincinnnati L. Rev.* 118 (1954).

53 *Columbia L. Rev.* 1011 (Nov. 1953).

39 *Cornel L. Q.* 102 (Fall 1953).

67 *Harvard L. Rev.* 128 (Nov. 1953).

25 *Mississippi L. J.* 74 (Dec. 1953).

33 *Oregon L. Rev.* 169 (Fall 1954).

32 *Texas L. Rev.* 618 (May 1954).

28 *Tulane L. Rev.* 149 (Dec. 1953).

102 *Univ. Pa. L Rev.* 125 (Nov. 1953).

1954 *Washington Univ. L. Q.* 233 (April 1954).

63 *Yale L. J.* 389 (Jan. 1954).

1962   *Lou Poller v. Columbia Broadcasting System, Inc., et al.,* **368 U.S. 464, 7 L.Ed.2d 458, 82 S.Ct. 486**

Argued: Nov. 13, 14, 1961.

Decided: Feb. 19, 1962.

Summary: A summary judgment of dismissal held improperly entered in damage action based on alleged violations of the restraint of trade and monopoly sections of the Sherman Act.

Circumstances: Poller, assignee of the Midwest Broadcasting Co., owner in 1954 of WCAN, an ultrahigh frequency (UHF) station in Milwaukee, charged CBS with conspiracy to eliminate WCAN. According to Poller, CBS sought FCC permission to purchase a competing UHF station, WOKY. If granted permission, it was said that the network would cancel its affiliation agreement with Poller's station and move the affiliation to WOKY, leaving WCAN in the precarious position of competing with the two major national networks with stations in Milwaukee. Further, Poller alleged that CBS not only would acquire WCAN at the network's price but that Midwest Broadcasting would be obliged to buy WOKY at an exorbitant price. Subsequently, CBS discontinued UHF broadcasting in 1959 when it became affiliated with a Milwaukee very high frequency (VHF) station. The District Court for the District of Columbia granted CBS's motion for summary judgment on the ground that the cancellation of the affiliation agreement was merely the legal exercise of the network's right to select the outlet for its product. The Court of Appeals for the D.C. Circuit affirmed. The Supreme Court reversed.

Opinion: Justice Tom C. Clark wrote the 5-to-4 decision, joined by Chief Justice Earl Warren and Justices Hugo L. Black, William O. Douglas, William J. Brennan, Jr., and Arthur J. Goldberg. John M. Harlan dissented, joined by Felix Frankfurter, Charles E. Whittaker, and Potter Stewart. Clark, noting that the trial judge's summary judgment was not in order, said that such a dismissal should be entered only when the pleadings, depositions, affidavits, and admissions filed in the case show that there is no genuine issue as to material facts. CBS, attempting to acquire a Milwaukee UHF television station by entering into an "unlawful conspiracy" to eliminate a competing station, had argued that the only issue was the legality of its cancellation of an affiliation agreement with the competing station. Poller, however, maintained that the right of cancellation was merely one of the means used to effectuate the conspiracy. The Court found the record unclear on the various claims, including CBS's assertion that the monopolization charges were frivolous, and remanded for a trial on the merits. "It may well be that in a trial appropriate allegations and proof can be adduced showing violations [of the law]."

Justice Harlan said that the antitrust laws did not fit the case and that the courts were correct in holding that CBS was entitled to summary judgment. He said that there was no evidence that the purpose of the business transactions was to restrain or monopolize trade. "It must be obvious that the cancellation of an affiliation agreement by one network, not acting in concert with any other, does not alone give rise to a cause of action under the antitrust laws." Finally, Harlan accused the Court of doing disservice to the healthy observance of the laws by encouraging this sort of antitrust "enforcement."

Referenced Cases: *Sartor v. Arkansas Natural Gas Corp.*, 321 U.S. 620 (1944), on rules governing summary judgment; *Times-Picayune Pub. Co. v. U.S.*, 345 U.S. 594 (1953), and *Eastman Kodak Co. v. Southern Photo Materials Co.*, 273 U.S. 359 (1927), on running afoul of the Sherman Act; *Klor's Inc. v. Broadway-Hale Stores Inc.*, 359 U.S. 207 (1959), on the "public will" being served; *International Boxing Club v. U.S.*, 358 U.S. 242 (1959), and *U.S. v. E. I. Du Pont de Nemours & Co.*, 353 U.S. 586 (1957), on trials to establish allegations and proof regarding alleged violations; *U.S. v. Paramount Pictures Inc.*, 334 U.S. 131 (1948), and *U.S. v. Columbia Steel Co.*, 334 U.S. 495 (1948), on vertical expansion and the Sherman Act.

Further Reading:
48 *ABA J.* 375 (April 1962).
21 *Maryland L. Rev.* 276 (Summer 1961).

1962   *U.S. v. Loew's Inc., Loew's Inc. v. U.S., and C & C Super Corp. v. U.S.*, 371 U.S. 38, 9 L.Ed.2d 11, 83 S.Ct. 97

Argued: Oct. 16, 1962.

Decided: Nov. 5, 1962.

Summary: Block-booking of copyrighted feature television films to television stations held in violation of the Sherman Act.

Circumstances: The United States brought separate civil antitrust actions in the District Court for the Southern District of New York in 1957 against six major distributors of pre-1948 copyrighted motion picture feature films for television exhibition, alleging that each defendant had engaged in block-booking in violation of Section 1 of the Sherman Act. The judge found each in violation of the act. On direct appeal, the Supreme Court vacated and remanded to the district court.

Opinion: Justice Arthur J. Goldberg wrote the Court's 7-to-2 decision, joined by Chief Justice Earl Warren and Justices Hugo L. Black, Tom C. Clark, William O. Douglas, William J. Brennan, Jr., and Byron R. White. John M. Harlan and Potter Stewart concurred in part and dissented in part. The three separate cases, involving six major distributors of pre-1948 films, were decided as one. Goldberg said that "tying" arrangements, or block-booking, were illegal. (Block-booking is described as conditioning the license or sale of the right to exhibit one or more feature films on acceptance by each television station of a package or block of films containing one or more unwanted or inferior films.) Goldberg noted that the Court has recognized in the past that tying agreements serve "hardly any purpose beyond the suppression of competition." They may force buyers into giving up the purchase of substitutes for the tied product, Goldberg said, and they may destroy the free access of competing suppliers of the tied product to the consuming market. Drawing on *Paramount Pictures* (1948), the justice said: "A copyrighted feature film does not lose its legal or economic uniqueness because it is shown on a television rather than a movie screen." By both their "inherent nature" and their "effect," tying deals injuriously restrain trade. Justice Harlan, joined by Stewart, thought much of the Court's decision "trivial remedial glosses" on the lower court's decree. He said that the high court should exercise revisory power over the terms of anti-trust relief only in instances where things have manifestly gone awry. "This is not such a case."

Referenced Cases: *U.S. v. Paramount Pictures*, 334 U.S. 131 (1948), applying the principle of patent law to copyrighted feature films; *Standard Oil Co. of California v. U.S.*, 337 U.S. 293 (1949), *Times-Picayune Pub. Co. v. U.S.*, 345 U.S. 594 (1953), *International Salt Co. v. U.S.*, 332 U.S. 392 (1947), and *Northern Pacific R. Co. v. U.S.*, 356 U.S. 1 (1958), on economic power of tying products; *U.S. v. American Tobacco Co.*, 221 U.S. 106 (1911), on tying arrangements restraining trade; *U.S. v. U.S. Gypsum Co.*, 340 U.S. 76 (1950), on Court's duty to review trial decree; *Ethyl Gasoline Corp. v. U.S.*, 309 U.S. 436 (1940), *U.S. v. Bausch & Lomb Optical Co.*, 321 U.S. 707 (1944), and *Hartford-Empire Co. v. U.S.*, 323 U.S. 386 (1945), holding that otherwise permissable practices connected with illegal acts may be enjoined in the process; *Motion Picture Patents Co. v. Universal Film Mfg. Co.*, 243 U.S. 502 (1917), *Carbice Corp. v. American Patents Dev. Corp.*, 283 U.S. 27 (1931), *Leitch Mfg. Co. v. Barber Co.*, 302 U.S. 458 (1938), *Morton Salt Co. v. G. S. Suppiger Co.*, 314 U.S. 488 (1942), and *Mercoid Corp. v. Mid-Continent Investment Co.*, 320

U.S. 661 (1944), a series of patent cases eventuating the doctrine that patentee who uses tying agreements would be denied relief against infringements.

Further Reading:
49 *ABA J.* 93 (Jan. 1963).
4 *Boston College Industrial & Commercial L. Rev.* 405 (Winter 1963).
31 *Fordham L. Rev.* 807 (April 1963).
1963 *Sup. Ct. Rev.* 152 (1963).

1968 *Lester J. Albrecht v. Herald Co, Globe-Democrat Publishing Co.*, 371 U.S. 38, 9 L.Ed.2d 11, 83 S.Ct. 97

Argued: Nov. 9, 1967.

Decided: March 4, 1968.

Summary: Ruled a restraint of trade a newspaper publisher's requirement that a carrier conform to the advertised retail price of the home-delivered paper.

Circumstances: Albrecht, newspaper carrier for the *Globe-Democrat*, a morning paper in St. Louis, Missouri, adhered to the paper's suggested retail price, but in 1961 raised the price to customers. After repeated warnings, the paper wrote to subscribers that the paper itself would deliver to those who wanted it at the lower price. It also hired a circulation sales company to solicit residents on Albrecht's old route. About 300 of the 1,200 customers switched. Meanwhile, the paper continued to sell papers to Albrecht, but set up a new route of 314 customers, taken over by another carrier. Later the *Globe-Democrat* told Albrecht he could have his old route back as long as he charged the suggested price. When Albrecht brought suit, the publisher fired him. He sold the route for more than he had paid for it but less than he could have gotten if he had 1,200 instead of 900 customers. The jury found for the newspaper and the Court of Appeals for the Eighth Circuit affirmed. On writ of certiorari, the Supreme Court reversed and remanded to the court of appeals.

Opinion: Justice Byron R. White delivered the Court's 7-to-2 opinion, joined by Chief Justice Earl Warren and Justices Hugo L. Black, William O. Douglas, Tom C. Clark, William J. Brennan, Jr., and Abe Fortas. Douglas also wrote a separate opinion. John M. Harlan and Potter Stewart dissented, each writing separately and Harlan joining Stewart's opinion. White said the newspaper combined with two other carriers to force Albrecht, a carrier, to conform to the advertised retail price. He noted that resale price fixing is a per se violation of the Sherman Act. White compared the case to *Kiefer-Stewart Co. v. Seagram & Sons* (1951), in which the Court held a restraint of trade the setting of maximum liquor prices. Douglas added, "A fixing of prices for resale is conspicuously unreasonable because of the great leverage that price has over the market." Justice Harlan faulted his brethren for rendering economically equivalent the practice of setting genuine price ceilings and that of fixing minimum prices. The latter states a Sherman Act cause of action, he said. Justice Stewart, even more poignantly, wrote: "The Court in this case does more . . . than simply depart from the rule of reason. The Court today stands the Sherman Act on its head."

Referenced Cases: *U.S. v. Parke, Davis & Co.*, 362 U.S. 29 (1960), on determining a combination or conspiracy under the law to fix resale prices; *U.S. v. Trenton Potteries Co.*, 273 U.S. 392 (1927), *U.S. v. Socony-Vacuum Oil Co.*, 310 U.S. 150 (1940), *Kiefer-Stewart Co. v. Seagram & Sons*, 340 U.S. 211 (1951), and *U.S. v. McKesson & Robbins Inc.*, 351 U.S. 305 (1956), on Sherman Act cases related to per se violation; *Standard Oil Co. v. U.S.*, 221 U.S. 1 (1911), a "rule of reason" case; *White Motor Co. v. U.S.*, 372 U.S. 253 (1963), on finding the actual impact of such arrangements on competition.

Further Reading:
54 *ABA J.* 493 (May 1968).
10 *Boston College Industrial & Commercial L. Rev.* 208 (Fall 1968).
57 *California L. Rev.* 262 (Jan. 1969).
82 *Harvard L. Rev.* 254 (Nov. 1968).
63 *Northwestern Univ. L. Rev.* 862 (Jan.–Feb. 1969).
37 *Univ. Cincinnati L. Rev.* 411 (Spring 1968).

1969   *Citizen Publishing Co. et al. v. U.S.*, **394**
U.S. 131, 22 L.Ed.2d 148, 89 S.Ct. 927, 1
Med.L.Rptr. 2704

Argued: Jan. 15, 1969.

Decided: March 10, 1969.

Summary: A joint operating agreement between competing newspapers held in violation of the Sherman Act because
of price fixing, pooling of profits, and a "division of the field."

Circumstances: In Tucson, Arizona, and 22 other cities by the mid-1960s, agreements had been made between competing newspapers to establish certain joint operations. In Tucson
prior to 1940 the *Star* and the *Citizen* competed with each other,
but in that year, because of the latter's financial losses, the two
companies reached a joint operating agreement to run for 25 years.
They formed Tucson Newspapers Inc. (TNI) to manage all departments except the news and editorial units. The agreement ended
all commercial rivalry between the papers. In 1965 the *Citizen*
bought the *Star*, but they continued to run independent editorial
departments. At that point the Department of Justice filed a
complaint in district court charging unreasonable restraint of
trade in violation of Section 1 of the Sherman Act and monopoly
in violation of Section 7 of the Clayton Act. The District Court
for the District of Arizona granted the government summary
judgment on the Section 1 allegation. A trial on the other charges
resulted in a finding that the operating agreement monopolized
Tucson's only newspaper business and that the *Citizen*'s acquisition of the *Star* continued in more permanent form a lessening of
competition in violation of the Clayton Act. The court's decree
called for a divestiture plan, reestablishment of the *Star*'s independence, and elimination of price-fixing, market control, and
profit-pooling. The Supreme Court, on direct appeal, affirmed.

Opinion: Justice William O. Douglas wrote the 7-to-1
decision, joined by Chief Justice Earl Warren and Justices Hugo L.
Black, John M. Harlan, William J. Brennan, Jr., Byron R. White,
and Thurgood Marshall. Harlan wrote a separate concurring opin-

ion, and Potter Stewart dissented. Abe Fortas took no part in the decision. Douglas, in affirming the lower court, said that the Sherman Act violations are "plain beyond peradventure." The affirmed decree required the newspaper publisher to submit a plan for divestiture of one of the joint-operating papers and its reestablishment as an independent competitor and to eliminate price-fixing, market control, and profit-pooling from the joint operating agreement. "Neither news gathering nor news dissemination is being regulated by the present decree," Douglas said, because it deals only with restraints on certain business or commercial practices. The First Amendment is not affected. The Court also found the "failing newspaper" defense—a judicially created doctrine—inapplicable, "unless it is established that the company that acquires the failing company or brings it under dominion is the only available purchaser." Harlan found it unnecessary to define the circumstances in which a declining newspaper may properly act to ensure its future independence as a news medium by entering into a joint operating agreement. Stewart, in disagreement, noted that proof of unsuccessful efforts to sell the company is not, "as a logical, evidentiary matter," the only possible conclusive proof that it was not marketable. He said whether the newspaper was a failing company had not yet been determined and recommended remanding for an answer to that question.

Referenced Cases: *U.S. v. Masonite*, 316 U.S. 265 (1942), *Northern Securities Co. v. U.S.*, 193 U.S. 197 (1904), *Timken Co. v. U.S.*, 341 U.S. 593 (1951), and *Northern Pac. R. Co. v. U.S.*, 356 U.S. 1 (1958), on price-fixing, division of fields, and summary judgment in antitrust field; *International Shoe Co. v. FTC*, 280 U.S. 291 (1930), regarding the "failing company" defense; *U.S. v. Diebold Inc.*, 369 U.S. 654 (1962), on conditions of failing company doctrine; *Associated Press v. U.S.*, 326 U.S. 1 (1945), on relevance of First Amendment; *U.S. v. Crescent Amusement Co.*, 323 U.S. 173 (1944), on divestiture and abuse of judicial discretion.

Further Reading:
55 *ABA J.* 675 (July 1969).
11 *Arizona L. Rev.* 531 (Fall 1969).
7 *Duquesne L. Rev.* 571 (Summer 1969).

1977   *National Geographic Society v.*
          California Board of Equalization,
          430 U.S. 551, 51 L.Ed.2d 631, 97 S.Ct. 1386

Argued: Feb. 23, 1977.

Decided: April 4, 1977.

Summary: Affirmed a state court holding that a "use tax" on retailers doing business in the state was constitutional because the retailer, though headquartered in the District of Columbia, maintained two offices in California.

Circumstances: The National Geographic Society, a nonprofit scientific and educational corporation of the District of Columbia, maintained two offices in California to solicit advertising for the society's monthly magazine. The offices have nothing to do with the society's mail-order business. Such orders go directly to its Washington headquarters. California tax law required every retailer engaged in business in the state to collect from each purchaser a use tax in lieu of the sales tax imposed on local merchants. The California Supreme Court found the imposition of the tax on the society valid. The U.S. Supreme Court, on direct appeal, affirmed.

Opinion: Justice William J. Brennan, Jr. wrote the 7-to-0 opinion, joined by Justices Potter Stewart, Byron R. White, Thurgood Marshall, Lewis F. Powell, Jr., John Paul Stevens, and Harry A. Blackmun, who also wrote separately. Chief Justice Warren E. Burger and Justice William H. Rehnquist did not participate. The Court found sufficient nexus between the out-of-state seller, the society, and the state as required by the due process clause of the 14th Amendment and the commerce clause to support the imposition of a use-tax-collection liability. Brennan disagreed with the society's contention that there must exist a nexus of relationship between the seller and the taxing state, but also between the seller's general activity and its activity within the state. The society had argued that its contacts with customers in California related solely to mail-order sales through a common carrier and that its two California offices were not part of that activity. Brennan, however, noted that the society's "continuous presence" in the state that solicits advertising for its magazine provided a "sufficient nexus." Justice Blackmun simply added his agreement, though he found some inconsistency with earlier decisions.

Referenced Cases: *Henneford v. Silas Mason Co.*, 300 U.S. 577 (1937), and *Monamotor Oil Co. v. Johnson*, 292 U.S. 86 (1934), on settled law regarding use tax in addition to a sales tax; *Nelson v. Sears, Roebuck & Co.*, 312 U.S. 359 (1941), on due process problems in the extension of a sales tax to interstate commerce; *Miller Bros. Co. v. Maryland*, 347 U.S. 340 (1954), on collection being the burden of the out-of-state seller; *Felt & Tarrant Co. v. Gallagher*, 306 U.S. 62 (1939), *General Trading Co. v. Tax Comm'n*, 322 U.S. 335 (1944), and *Scripto Inc. v. Carson*, 362 U.S. 207 (1960), on the requisite nexus; *Standard Pressed Steel Co. v. Washington Rev. Dept.*, 419 U.S. 560 (1975), on what constitutes "a sufficient relation to activities within the state" to support imposition of a tax; *General Motors Corp. v. Washington*, 377 U.S. 436 (1964), *Northwestern Cement Co. v. Minnesota*, 358 U.S. 450 (1959), *Memphis Gas Co. v. Stone*, 335 U.S. 80 (1948), and *Wisconsin v. J. C. Penney Co.*, 311 U.S. 435 (1940), cases sustaining fairly apportioned, nondiscriminatory direct taxes; *McLeod v. Dilworth Co.*, 322 U.S. 327 (1944), on collection of such taxes; *National Bellas Hess Inc. v. Illinois Rev. Dept.*, 386 U.S. 753 (1967), on the customer connection being common carrier or mail.

Further Reading:
63 *ABA J.* 1620 (Nov. 1977).
7 *Capital Univ. L. Rev.* 143 (1977).
91 *Harvard L. Rev.* 72 (Nov. 1977).
21 *Howard L. J.* 245 (1978).
47 *J. Taxation* 44 (July 1977).
64 *Virginia L. Rev.* 145 (Feb. 1978).

1978 Federal Communications Commission v. National Citizens Committee for Broadcasting (NCCB), Channel Two

Television Co. v. NCCB, National Association of Broadcasters v. FCC, American Newspaper Publishers Assn. v. NCCB, Illinois Broadcasting Co. Inc. v. NCCB, and Post Co. v. NCCB, 436 U.S. 775, 56 L.Ed.2d 697, 98 S.Ct. 2096, 3 Med.L.Rptr. 2409

Argued: Jan. 10, 1978.

Decided: June 12, 1978.

Summary: Upheld the FCC's prospective licensing ban on "co-located" newspaper-broadcast combinations, a regulation designed to promote media diversification, but did not endorse the agency's decision to limit divestiture to "egregious cases" of "effective" monopoly.

Circumstances: At issue were FCC regulations governing the permissibility of common ownership of a radio or television station and a daily newspaper located in the same community: *Rules Relating to Multiple Ownership of Standard, FM, and Television Broadcast Stations, Second Report and Order, 50 F.C.C.2d 1046* (1975). The rules barred formation or transfer of co-located newspaper-broadcast combinations, but permitted existing combinations to continue to operate. However, in places where common ownership of the only daily and the only station existed, divestiture of either property was required within five years, unless waived on demonstrated grounds. Various parties—including the NCCB, the National Association of Broadcasters (NAB), the American Newspaper Publishers' Association (ANPA), and several broadcast licensees subject to divestiture—petitioned for review of the regulations in the Court of Appeals for the District of Columbia Circuit. The NAB, ANPA, and licensees argued that the regulations went too far in restricting cross-ownership. The NCCB and Justice Department contended that the regulations did not go far enough and that the FCC inadequately justified its decision not to order divestiture on a more widespread basis. The court of appeals affirmed the prospective ban on new licensing of co-located newspaper-broadcast combinations, but vacated the limited divestiture rules, ordering the FCC to adopt regulations requiring dissolution of existing combinations that did not qualify for waiver. On writ of certiorari, the Supreme Court affirmed in part and reversed in part.

Opinion: Justice Thurgood Marshall wrote the Court's 8-to-0 decision, joined by all other members except William J. Brennan, Jr., who did not participate. Marshall said that the FCC had not acted arbitrarily or capriciously in requiring divestiture in only "egregious" cases. The Court viewed favorably the commission's determination that forced divestiture of all cross-owned combinations would cause industry disruption and might lead to a decline of local media ownership. "We believe that the limited divestiture requirement reflects a rational weighing of competing policies," Marshall wrote. The Court did not rule out challenges to cross-owned monopolies by means of comparative hearings and petitions. To arguments advanced by broadcasters and publishers that their First Amendment rights were being violated by forced divestiture, Marshall cited precedents, such as *Red Lion Broadcasting Co. v. FCC*, 395 U.S. 367 (1969), *Miami Herald Broadcasting Co. v. Tornillo*, 418 U.S. 241 (1974), and *Columbia Broadcasting System v. Democratic National Committee*, 412 U.S. 94 (1973), to point out that broadcast and print media have different characteristics and, therefore, warrant different First Amendment consideration or application. Marshall added that the FCC's regulations at issue in the case were based on "permissible public-interest goals" that fall within the general rule-making authority of the agency.

Referenced Cases: See under "Opinion" above. Also: *Associated Press v. U.S.*, 326 U.S. 1 (1945), on ownership as the power to select, edit, and choose the methods, manner, and emphasis of presentation; *U.S. v. Storer Broadcasting Co.*, 351 U.S. 192 (1956), and *National Broadcasting Co. v. U.S.*, 319 U.S. 190 (1943), on FCC's public-interest licensing standards; *U.S. v. Midwest Video Corp.*, 406 U.S. 649 (1972), and *U.S. v. Radio Corp. of America*, 358 U.S. 334 (1959), on First Amendment goal; *FCC v. RCA Communications Inc.*, 346 U.S. 86 (1953), on difficulty of documenting abuses by common owners; *FCC v. Pottsville Broadcasting Co.*, 309 U.S. 134 (1940), on rules relating to changed industry circumstances; *Federal Radio Commission v. Nelson*

Bros. Bond & Mortgage Co., 289 U.S. 266 (1933), relating government regulation to physical scarcity of frequencies; *Speiser v. Randall*, 357 U.S. 513 (1958), and *Elrod v. Burns*, 427 U.S. 347 (1976), regarding a broadcast license conditioned on forfeiture of right to publish a newspaper; *Grosjean v. American Press Co.*, 297 U.S. 233 (1936), on singling out newspapers for special treatment; *FCC v. Sanders Bros. Radio Station*, 309 U.S. 470 (1940), on effects of divestiture.

Further Reading:
22 *Howard L. J.* 527 (1979).
67 *Kentucky L. J.* 903 (1978–79).
1978 *Sup. Ct. Rev.* 1 (1978).

1983   ***Minneapolis Star & Tribune Co. v. Minnesota Commissioner of Revenue,* 460 U.S. 575, 75 L.Ed.2d 295, 103 S.Ct. 1365, 9 Med.L.Rptr. 1369**

Argued: Jan. 12, 1983.

Decided: March 29, 1983.

Summary: Ruled invalid, discriminatory, and unconstitutional a special state "use tax" on ink and paper that applied only to larger users of the products. Court held the tax in violation of the First Amendment.

Circumstances: While exempting periodic publications from its general sales and use tax, Minnesota imposed a "use tax" on the price of paper and ink consumed, but exempted the first $100,000 worth of these products in any calendar year. The newspaper publisher brought an action seeking a refund of the use taxes it had paid during certain years, contending that the tax violates, inter alia, the First Amendment. In 1974 the Star & Tribune Co., publisher of morning and afternoon newspapers at the time, incurred roughly two-thirds of the total revenue raised by the tax, there being 11 publishers producing 14 of the state's

388 paid circulation newspapers. The Minnesota Supreme Court upheld the tax against the federal constitutional challenge. On direct appeal, the U.S. Supreme Court reversed.

Opinion: Justice Sandra Day O'Connor wrote the opinion, joined by Chief Justice Warren E. Burger and Justices William J. Brennan, Jr., Thurgood Marshall, and Lewis F. Powell, Jr. John Paul Stevens, Byron R. White, and Harry A. Blackmun joined in part. White filed a separate opinion, concurring in part and dissenting in part. William H. Rehnquist dissented. O'Connor described the tax as a "special tax that applies only to certain publications protected by the First Amendment." She said, "A power to tax differentially, as opposed to a power to tax generally, gives a government a powerful weapon against the taxpayer selected." Such a tax, as struck down in *Grosjean v. American Press Co.* (1936), could be used to censor the press, a clear violation of the First Amendment. The law was also found deficient in that it results in taxing only a few of the newspapers in the state. "Whatever the move of the legislature in this case, we think that recognizing a power in the State not only to single out the press but also to tailor the tax so [as] to single out a few members of the press presents such a potential for abuse that no interest suggested by Minnesota can justify the scheme." The Court was willing to permit a special tax on newspapers if the state could meet its heavy constitutional burden of justification.

Justice White concurred in the judgment, but he doubted that the Court's decision rested on the fear that the government might use the tax to achieve a censorial purpose. "Since it is plainly evident that *Minneapolis Star* is not disadvantaged and is almost certainly benefited by a use tax vis-à-vis a sales tax, I cannot agree that the First Amendment forbids a State to choose one method of taxation over another."

Justice Rehnquist, in dissent, could not accept the proposition that a state runs afoul of the First Amendment proscription of laws abridging the freedom of speech, or of the press, where the state structures its taxing system to the advantage of newspapers. "This seems very much akin to protecting something so overzealously that in the end it is smothered." He called the decision "a hollow victory" for newspapers, since, in Rehnquist's view, the ruling subjects newspapers to millions of additional dollars in sales tax liability. The sales tax scheme, as compared to the special use tax on ink and paper, was found constitutional because it does not distinguish between the press and other businesses.

Referenced Cases: *U.S. v. O'Brien*, 391 U.S. 367 (1968), *Houchins v. KQED Inc.*, 438 U.S. 1 (1978), and *Pittsburgh Press Co. v. Pittsburgh Comm'n on Human Relations*, 413 U.S. 376 (1973), on relevancy and irrelevancy of *Grosjean v. American Press Co.*, 297 U.S. 233 (1936), to subsequent decisions; *Citizen Publishing Co. v. U.S.*, 394 U.S. 131 (1969), *Lorain Journal Co. v. U.S.*, 342 U.S. 143 (1951), *Breard v. Alexandria*, 341 U.S. 622 (1951), *Oklahoma Press Publishing Co. v. Walling*, 327 U.S. 186 (1946), *Mabee v. White Plains Publishing Co.*, 327 U.S. 178 (1946), *Associated Press v. U.S.*, 326 U.S. 1 (1945), and *Associated Press v. NLRB*, 301 U.S. 103 (1937), on antitrust laws and door-to-door solicitation; *National Geographic Society v. Calif. Board of Equalization*, 430 U.S. 551 (1977), on use tax on out-of-state purchases; *Railway Express Agency Inc. v. New York*, 336 U.S. 106 (1949), *Police Dept. of Chicago v. Mosley*, 408 U.S. 92 (1972), and *Brown v. Hartlage*, 456 U.S. 45 (1982), on "differential treatment" in taxation; *NAACP v. Button*, 371 U.S. 415 (1963), on the government's ability to achieve censorship with threat of sanctions as potently as with actual sanctions; *NAACP v. Alabama ex rel. Patterson*, 357 U.S. 449 (1958), *Lovell v. Griffin*, 303 U.S. 444 (1938), and *Schneider v. State*, 308 U.S. 147 (1939), on the Court's recognition that even regulations aimed at proper governmental concerns can be restrictive; *U.S. v. County of Fresno*, 429 U.S. 452 (1977), and *U.S. v. Detroit*, 355 U.S. 466 (1958), on comparative burden of different taxes; *Henneford v. Silas Mason Co.*, 300 U.S. 577 (1937), on taxes vis-à-vis interstate commerce; *Moorman Mfg. Co. v. Bair*, 437 U.S. 267 (1978), and *Hans Rees' Sons Inc. v. North Carolina*, 283 U.S. 123 (1931), regarding the amount of in-state business to violate due process; *Allied Stores of Ohio Inc. v. Bowers*, 358 U.S. 522 (1959), *Kahn v. Shevin*, 416 U.S. 351 (1974), *Independent Warehouses Inc. v. Scheele*, 331 U.S. 70 (1947), *Madden v. Kentucky*, 309 U.S. 83 (1940), *Fox v. Standard Oil Co. of New Jersey*, 294 U.S. 87 (1935), and *New York Rapid Transit Corp. v. City of New York*, 303 U.S. 573 (1938), on deferring to states in devising their taxing schemes; *Massachusetts Board of Retirement v. Murgia*, 427 U.S. 307 (1976), *Calif. Medical Assn. v. Federal Election Commission*, 453 U.S. 182 (1981), *Maher v. Roe*, 432 U.S. 464

(1977), *Storer v. Brown*, 415 U.S. 724 (1974), *American Party of Texas v. White*, 415 U.S. 767 (1974), and *San Antonio Independent School District v. Rodriguez*, 411 U.S. 1 (1973), on requiring states to justify tax classifications where infringement is at issue; *Branzburg v. Hayes*, 408 U.S. 665 (1972), on infringement and the First Amendment.

Further Reading:

38 *Columbia L. Rev.* 49 (1938).
89 *Dickinson L. Rev.* 261 (Fall 1984).
39 *Fed. Communications L. J.* 1 (May 1987).
97 *Harvard L. Rev.* 172 (Nov. 1983).
69 *Iowa L. Rev.* 1103 (May 1984).
21 *Wake Forest L. Rev.* 59 (Spring 1985).
11 *William Mitchell L. Rev.* 294 (1985).

Selected Bibliography

"Alcoholic Beverage Advertising on the Airwaves: Alternatives to a Ban or Counteradvertising," 94 *UCLA L. Rev.* 1139 (April 1987).

Ames, O. K., "Evidentiary Aspects of Relevant Product Market Proof in Monopolization Cases," 26 *De Paul L. Rev.* 530 (1977).

Barber, Richard J., "Newspaper Monopoly in New Orleans: The Lessons of Antitrust Policy," 24 *Louisiana L. Rev.* 503 (1964).

Bezanson, R. P., "Political Agnosticism, Editorial Freedom, and Government Neutrality Toward the Press: Observations on Minneapolis Star & Tribune Co. v. Minnesota Commissioner of Revenue," 72 *Iowa L. Rev.* 1359 (July 1987).

Coulson, David C., "Antitrust Law and the Media: Making the Newspaper Safe for Democracy," 57 *Journalism Quarterly* 79 (Spring 1980).

Howard, Herbert H., "Ownership Trends in Cable Television: 1972–1979," 58 *Journalism Quarterly* 288 (Summer 1981).

Lee, William E., "Antitrust Enforcement, Freedom of the Press, and the 'Open Market': The Supreme Court on the Structure and Conduct of Mass Media," 32 *Vanderbilt L. Rev.* 1249 (Nov. 1979).

Murphy, Mary Pat, "The United States v. the AP," *Montana Journalism Rev.* 40 (1974).

"The Newspaper Preservation Act," 32 *Univ. Pittsburgh L. Rev.* 347 (1971).

Ovelman, Richard J., Samuel A. Terilli, and Dan Paul, "Newsracks: Permits, Taxes, Regulations and the First Amendment," 2 *Communications Law Practising Law Institute* 7 (1987).

"Press Associations and Restraint of Trade," 55 *Yale L. J.* 428 (1946).

Roach, Catherine B., "Media Conglomerates, Anti-Trust Laws, and Marketplace of Ideas," 9 *Memphis State Univ. L. Rev.* 257 (Winter 1979).

Roberts, K., "Antitrust Problems in the Newspaper Industry," *Harvard L. Rev.* 319 (1968).

Rosen, Leslie Brooks, "Media Cross-Ownership, Effective Enforcement of the Anti-Trust Laws, and the FTC," 32 *Federal Communications Law* 105 (1980).

Shumadine, Conrad M., and Walter D. Kelley, Jr., "Antitrust and the Media," 1 *Communications Law Practising Law Institute* 441 (1987).

Censorship

1907   ***Thomas M. Patterson v. Colorado*, 205
U.S. 454, 51 L.Ed. 879, 27 S.Ct. 556**

Argued: March 5, 6, 1907.

Decided: April 15, 1907.

Summary: Upholding contempt of court by the press,
the Court noted "premature . . . interference with the course of
justice." Truthful criticism immaterial in constructive contempt.

Circumstances: The case involved a conviction for
contempt of the Colorado Supreme Court through publication of
articles and a cartoon questioning the motives of the high court
and the manner in which two of its judges had been seated.
Publication was found to have reflected upon the motives and
conduct of the court in pending cases. The Denver newspaper
editor and publisher claimed they had a right under the federal
Constitution to prove the truth of the material in question.

Opinion: Justice Oliver Wendell Holmes wrote for the 7-
to-2 Court, joined by Chief Justice Melville W. Fuller, Edward D.
White, Rufus W. Peckham, Joseph McKenna, William R. Day, and
William H. Moody. Dissenting were John M. Harlan and David J.
Brewer. Holmes said that the 14th Amendment did not forbid a
state from punishing contemptible conduct. He wrote that the main
purpose of such constitutional provisions is to prevent all such
previous restraints on publications, and they do not prevent the
subsequent punishment of "such as may be deemed contrary to the
public welfare." The newspaper comments were inappropriate,
Holmes said, because the case criticized was still under consideration by the court. "When a case is finished, courts are subject to the
same criticism as other people, but the propriety and necessity of

preventing interference with the course of justice by premature statement, argument or intimidation hardly can be denied." Justice Harlan, in dissent, believed that the 14th Amendment prohibited the states from impairing or abridging the constitutional rights to free speech and a free press. Justice Brewer disagreed with the Court's determination that it did not have jurisdiction.

Referenced Cases: *French v. Taylor*, 199 U.S. 274 (1905), *Rawlins v. Georgia*, 201 U.S. 638 (1906), *Burt v. Smith*, 203 U.S. 129 (1906), and *Ex parte Wall.*, 107 U.S. 265 (1883), on subjecting state decisions to revision by the Supreme Court; *Virginia v. Rives*, 100 U.S. 313 (1880), and *Missouri v. Dockery*, 191 U.S. 165 (1903), on the power of the state vis-à-vis the 14th Amendment; *Respublica v. Oswald*, 1 Dall. 319 (1796), regarding "previous restraints" on publications; *Ex parte Terry*, 128 U.S. 289 (1888), on preventing interference with the course of justice; *U.S. v. Shipp*, 203 U.S. 563 (1906), on the impersonal grounds of contempt; *Civil Rights Cases*, 109 U.S. 1 (1883), on 13th Amendment prohibitions.

Further Reading:
16 *Harvard L. Rev.* 55 (1902).
23 *Harvard L. Rev.* 415 (1910).
13 *Law Notes* 21 (1909).

1911   *Kalem Co. v. Harper Brothers, Marc Klaw, Abraham Erlanger, and Henry L. Wallace,* **222 U.S. 55, 56 L.Ed. 92, 32 S.Ct. 20**

Argued: Oct. 31, Nov. 1, 1911.

Decided: Nov. 13, 1911.

Summary: Copyright of a book infringed by the public exhibition of moving pictures of its incidents.

Circumstances: Kalem, makers of films, made a motion picture called *Ben Hur*, with photos presenting "almost the illusion of reality." The firm employed a person to read from the novel and write the scenarios, "giving enough of the story to be identified with ease." Kalem advertised the film and sold copies for public exhibition. The Circuit Court of Appeals for the Second Circuit affirmed a restraining order by the Circuit Court for the Southern District of New York. The Supreme Court affirmed.

Opinion: Justice Oliver Wendell Holmes wrote for a unanimous Court. He said that the unauthorized movie "dramatization" of the late Lew Wallace's book *Ben Hur* constituted infringement. Holmes noted that, according to the Copyright Act, as amended March 3, 1891, authors have the exclusive right to dramatize any of their works. "[I]f . . . moving pictures may be used for dramatizing a novel, when the photographs are used in that way, they are used to infringe a right which the statute reserves." Holmes went on: "It is suggested that to extend copyright to a case like this is to extend it to the ideas, as distinguished from the words in which those ideas are clothed. But there is no attempt to make a monopoly of the ideas expressed. The law confines itself to a particular, cognate, and well-known form of reproduction."

Referenced Cases: *Holmes v. Hurst*, 174 U.S. 82 (1899), *White-Smith Music Pub. Co. v. Apollo Co.*, 209 U.S. 1 (1908), *Baker v. Selden*, 101 U.S. 99 (1880), *Ferris v. Hexamer*, 99 U.S. 674 (1879), and *Bobbs-Merrill Co. v. Straus*, 210 U.S. 339 (1908), on copyright coverage of the form of expression, not the intellectual conception; *Bleistein v. Donaldson Lithographing Co.*, 188 U.S. 239 (1903), on pictures as "the personal reaction of an individual upon nature"; *Burrows-Giles v. Savrony*, 111 U.S. 53 (1884), *Higgins v. Keuffel*, 140 U.S. 428 (1891), and *American Tobacco Co. v. Werckmeister*, 207 U.S. 291 (1907), on the unconstitutional aspects of prohibiting the making and exhibiting of motion pictures.

Further Reading:
None indexed.

1913   *Lewis Publishing Co. v. Edward M. Morgan, as Postmaster of the U.S.A. in*

and for New York City, Borough of
Manhattan, and Journal of Commerce
& Commercial Bulletin v. Albert S.
Burleson, as Postmaster General of the
U.S., James C. McReynolds, as Attorney
General of the U.S., et al., 229 U.S. 288,
57 L.Ed. 1190, 33 S.Ct. 867

Argued: Dec. 2, 3, 1912.

Decided: June 10, 1913.

Summary: Found constitutional provisions of the Post Office Appropriation Act of 1912 that required disclosure of the ownership of publications having second-class mailing privileges, the average circulation of dailies, names of certain staff members, and a report on owners and security holders of all kinds.

Circumstances: Two New York newspaper publishers complained that the provisions of the Postal Act abridged freedom of the press protected by the First Amendment and the due process of law guaranteed by the Fifth. They filed bills against designated U.S. officials to prevent enforcement of the disclosure provision. The District Court for the Southern District of New York dismissed the bills for want of equity. On direct appeal, the Supreme Court affirmed.

Opinion: Chief Justice Edward D. White wrote the unanimous opinion. White responded to the newspaper publishers' allegations that the "newspaper law" was designed to "regulate journalism" and enforce "censorship of the press," and that the disclosure provision was "inquisitorial." He said that it was always conceived not only that Congress might so exert its power as to favor the circulation of newspapers, but that it also possessed the authority to fix a general standard to which "publishers seeking to obtain the proffered privileges" must conform in order to obtain them. He said publishers were accorded "exceptional privileges," especially the "high privilege" of the second-class mail permit. "For instance," White wrote, "the postage on a newspaper coming under the second-class rate when mailed by an individual is higher than is the rate of postage exacted for the mailing of the same newspaper by publishers or news agents." The Court agreed with the government's contention that publishers had no *right* to the lower rates but merely the *privilege* of enjoying them after meeting the conditions. Rather than infringe the First Amendment or discriminate against newspapers, the law actually discriminated against the public and in favor of newspapers, periodicals, and their publishers, White opined. For many years, he said, the legislation has favored the press by discriminating so as to secure to it "great pecuniary and other concessions, and a wider circulation and consequently a greater sphere of influence."

Referenced Cases: *Chicago M. & St. P. R. Co. v. Minnesota*, 134 U.S. 418 (1890), *Smyth v. Ames*, 169 U.S. 466 (1898), and *Munn v. Illinois*, 94 U.S. 113 (1877), on the profitable and free use of property; *U.S. v. Fox*, 95 U.S. 670 (1877), *U.S. v. Reese*, 92 U.S. 214 (1876), and *Dent v. West Virginia*, 129 U.S. 114 (1889), on congressional powers impliedly condemned by the Constitution; *Mugler v. Kansas*, 123 U.S. 623 (1887), on private rights, personal freedom, and private property; *Allegeyer v. Louisiana*, 165 U.S. 578 (1897), and *Booth v. Illinois*, 184 U.S. 425 (1902), on freedom in the conduct and pursuit of lawful business; *Plessy v. Ferguson*, 163 U.S. 537 (1896), on police power as moderate and reasonable; *U.S. v. Press Pub. Co.*, 219 U.S. 1 (1911), on the pertinent nature of a statute; *Trade Mark Cases*, 100 U.S. 82 (1879), *U.S. v. Harris*, 106 U.S. 629 (1883), *Civil Rights Cases*, 109 U.S. 3 (1883), and *Income Tax Cases*, 157 U.S. 429 (1894), on federal enactments that have been adjudged unconstitutional; *Lochner v. New York*, 198 U.S. 45 (1905), and *Union Bridge Co. v. U.S.*, 204 U.S. 364 (1907), on the authority of courts to interfere to protect rights injuriously affected by illegal governmental action; *Francis v. U.S.*, 188 U.S. 375 (1903), *France v. U.S.*, 164 U.S. 676 (1897), *Re Rapier*, 143 U.S. 110 (1892), and *Patterson v. Colorado*, 205 U.S. 454 (1907), on statutes affecting freedom of the press.

Further Reading:
72 *Central L. J.* 29 (1911).
23 *Yale L. J.* 559 (May 14, 1914).

1915 *Mutual Film Corp. v. Industrial Commission of Ohio*, 236 U.S. 230, 59 L.Ed. 552, 35 S.Ct. 387

Argued: Jan. 6, 7, 1915.

Decided: Feb. 23, 1915.

Summary: Affirmed a state court decree refusing to restrain the enforcement of a statute for the censorship of motion picture films.

Circumstances: Two suits were involved. In the first, Mutual sought an interlocutory injunction against enforcement of an Ohio law passed in April 1913 that created a board of film censors under the state Industrial Commission and that required film distributors to submit their products for review. Mutual sold films in Ohio and leased or rented films there and to distributors in Michigan. The second suit involved Mutual's similar operations in Virginia, the records being nearly identical and the Court rendering one opinion to cover both. Both cases were on appeal from the District Court for the Northern District of Ohio. On the same day the Supreme Court also upheld a similar statute in Kansas, ruling that both the Ohio and Kansas state statutes are "valid exercises of the police power of the states, and are not amenable to the objections urged against them—that is, do not interfere with interstate commerce nor abridge the liberty of opinion; nor are they delegations of legislative power to administrative officers." *Mutual Film Corp. of Missouri v. Hodges et al.*, 236 U.S. 246 (1915).

Opinion: Justice Joseph McKenna wrote the unanimous opinion upholding a state's right to censor motion pictures. The Ohio statute stipulated, in part: "Only such films as are, in the judgment and discretion of the board of censors, of a moral, educational, or amusing and harmless character shall be passed and approved by such board." In response to the contention that the statute violated freedom of speech and publication guaranteed by the Ohio Constitution, McKenna pointed out that the statute was enacted to prevent the showing of films "used for evil," not those with "moral" character. Rather than comparing films to the traditional press, the Court likened them to the theater, the circus, and "all other shows and spectacles." McKenna said that the "judicial sense supporting the common sense of the country" was against the argument that extends the guaranties of free opinion and speech to the "multitudinous shows which are advertised on the billboards of our cities and towns, and which regards them as emblems of public safety . . . and which seeks to bring motion pictures and other spectacles into practical and legal similitude to a free press and liberty of opinion." He went on to say that the exhibition of moving pictures was a business, originated and conducted for profit, "not to be regarded, nor intended to be regarded by the Ohio Constitution . . . as part of the press of the country, or as organs of public opinion. They are mere representations of events, of ideas and sentiments published and known; vivid, useful, and entertaining, no doubt, but . . . capable of evil, having power for it, the greater because of their attractiveness and manner of exhibition."

Referenced Cases: *Gundling v. Chicago,* 177 U.S. 183 (1900), *Red "C" Oil Mfg. Co. v. Board of Agriculture,* 222 U.S. 380 (1912), *Monongahela Bridge Co. v. U.S.,* 216 U.S. 177 (1910), *Buttfield v. Stranahan,* 192 U.S. 470 (1904), and *Waters-Pierce Oil Co. v. Texas,* 212 U.S. 86 (1909), analogous cases in support of judgments derived at by common sense and proper government utility; *Savage v. Jones,* 225 U.S. 501 (1912), *Collins v. New Hampshire,* 171 U.S. 30 (1898), *Caldwell v. North Carolina,* 187 U.S. 622 (1903), and *Crenshaw v. Arkansas,* 227 U.S. 389 (1913), on the constitutional guaranty of freedom of publication; *Robertson v. Baldwin,* 165 U.S. 275 (1897), on allowable restraint in matters of morality, "having no legitimate connection with criticism of men or government"; *Kalem Co. v. Harper Bros.,* 222 U.S. 60 (1911), on protecting property in copyrights.

Further Reading:
9 *Illinois L. Rev.* 130 (June 14, 1914).
2 *Virginia L. Rev.* 216 (Dec. 14, 1914).

1921   *U.S.A. ex rel. Milwaukee Social Democratic Publishing Co. v. Albert S.*

Burleson, Postmaster General of the U.S., 255 U.S. 407, 65 L.Ed. 704, 41 S.Ct. 352

Argued: Jan. 18, 19, 1921.

Decided: March 7, 1921.

Summary: Upheld the postmaster general's administrative order revoking a newspaper's second-class mail privilege because of published articles that violated the Espionage Act of June 15, 1917.

Circumstances: Following a hearing on Sept. 22, 1917, the second-class mail privilege granted the Milwaukee *Leader* in 1911 was revoked. The postmaster general, on appeal, upheld the administrative order. Petition to the Supreme Court of the District of Columbia was dismissed, and the court of appeals affirmed the judgment. On writ of error, the U.S. Supreme Court affirmed.

Opinion: Justice John H. Clarke wrote the 7-to-2 decision, joined by Chief Justice Edward D. White and Justices Mahlon Pitney, James C. McReynolds, Willis Van Devanter, Joseph McKenna, and William R. Day. Dissenting were Louis D. Brandeis and Oliver Wendell Holmes. Clarke based the decision on the high privilege nature of the second-class rate, the overriding of the First Amendment by expanding postal power, and the finality of the postmaster general's findings. The National Defense Laws, one of which was known as the Espionage Act, declared violative publications nonmailable, thus making the postmaster general a law enforcement agent. Clarke said the purpose of the law was to prevent disloyalty and disunion "among our people of many origins" and to present a united front. The Espionage Act stipulated "severe punishment" for any person who, "when the United States is at war," made or conveyed false reports or false statements with intent to interfere with military operations or advance the enemy's cause. As for the newspaper articles at issue, Clarke said they conveyed false reports and false statements "with the intent to promote the success of the enemies of the United States, and . . . constituted a willful attempt to cause disloyalty and refusal of duty in the military and naval forces, and to obstruct the recruiting and enlistment service of the United States. Freedom of the press may protect criticism and agitation for modification or repeal of laws, but it does not extend to protection of him who counsels and encourages the violation of the law as it exists."

Justice Brandeis, in dissent, said he could not find congressional authorization for denial of second-class rates in the Espionage Act, though outright denial of use of the mail was authorized by the statutes. By removing the mailing privilege, the postmaster general became a censor in that future matter not yet offered for transportation was excluded. Postal laws and regulations, he continued, gave no jurisdiction over content to the postmaster. It seemed to him that the second-class rate was more a right than a privilege, since the payment of postal deficits came from taxes. Both dissenters believed that the Bill of Rights limited postal power. Justice Holmes, who agreed in substance with Brandeis, added: "The United States may give up the Postoffice when it sees fit; but while it carries it on, the use of the mails is almost as much a part of free speech as the right to use our tongues; and it would take very strong language to convince me that Congress ever intended to give such a practically despotic power to any one man."

Referenced Cases: *Smith v. Hitchcock*, 226 U.S. 53 (1912), *Bates & G. Co. v. Payne*, 194 U.S. 106 (1904), *Public Clearing House v. Coyne*, 194 U.S. 497 (1904), and *Lewis Pub. Co. v. Morgan*, 229 U.S. 288 (1913), on a hearing satisfying requirements of due process; *Schenck v. U.S.*, 249 U.S. 47 (1919), *Frohwerk v. U.S.*, 249 U.S. 204 (1919), *Debs. v. U.S.*, 249 U.S. 211 (1919), and *Abrams v. U.S.*, 250 U.S. 616 (1919), on the Espionage Act as a valid constitutional law; *Burton v. U.S.*, 202 U.S. 344 (1906), and *Adair v. U.S.*, 208 U.S. 161 (1908), on government power subject to the limitations of the Bill of Rights.

Further Reading:
29 *American Legal News* 21 (1918).
49 *Chicago Legal News* 238 (1917).
32 *Harvard L. Rev.* 932 (1919).
10 *J. Criminal L.* 71 (1919).
17 *Michigan L. Rev.* 621 (1919).
2 *Minnesota L. Rev.* 239 (1918).
62 *Ohio L. Bulletin* 1 (1917).
65 *Univ. Pa. L. Rev.* 170 (1917).

1938   *Lovell v. Griffin,* **303 U.S. 444, 82 L.Ed. 949, 58 S.Ct. 666**

Argued: Feb. 4, 1938.

Decided: March 28, 1938.

Summary: An ordinance banning pamphleteering or leafletting without permission held in violation of First Amendment, that the "struggle for freedom of the press was primarily directed against the power of the licensor."

Circumstances: Alma Lovell, a Jehovah's Witness, was convicted in Recorder's Court of Griffin, Georgia, for distributing religious tracts without required permission. She was sentenced to 50 days in jail for failure to pay a $50 fine. The Superior Court refused sanction of a petition for review, which judgment was confirmed by the state court of appeals. The Georgia Supreme Court denied certiorari. The U.S. Supreme Court reversed and remanded to the Georgia Court of Appeals.

Opinion: Chief Justice Charles E. Hughes, for the unanimous Court, said that the First Amendment was not confined to protection of newspapers and magazines, but included pamphlets and leaflets as well, "every sort of publication which affords a vehicle of information and opinion." Hughes was joined by Justices James C. McReynolds, Louis D. Brandeis, George Sutherland, Pierce Butler, Harlan F. Stone, Owen J. Roberts, and Hugo L. Black. Benjamin N. Cardozo did not participate. Hughes said that the ordinance, which was not limited to "literature" that was obscene or that advocated unlawful conduct, "strikes at the very foundation of the freedom of the press by subjecting it to license and censorship." Nor could the ordinance be saved because it related to distribution and not to publishing, Hughes said; indeed, without circulation, publication would be of little value.

Referenced Cases: *Gitlow v. New York,* 268 U.S. 652 (1925), *Stromberg v. California,* 283 U.S. 359 (1931), *Near v. Minnesota,* 283 U.S. 697 (1931), *Grosjean v. American Press Co.,* 297 U.S. 233 (1936), *De Jonge v. Oregon,* 299 U.S. 353 (1937), and *Palko v.*

Connecticut, 302 U.S. 319 (1937), on First Amendment rights protected from state invasion by the 14th Amendment; *Raymond v. Chicago Union Traction Co.*, 207 U.S. 20 (1907), *Home Teleph. & Teleg. Co. v. Los Angeles*, 227 U.S. 278 (1913), and *Cuyahoga River Power Co. v. Akron*, 240 U.S. 462 (1916), on municipal ordinances within prohibition of the 14th Amendment; *Ex parte Jackson*, 96 U.S. 727 (1878), on the liberty to circulate as well as publish.

Further Reading:

14 *Indiana L. J.* 454 (June 1939).
3 *Legal Notes on Local Gov.* 351 (May 1938).
5 *Ohio State L. J.* 89 (Dec. 1938).
12 *So. Calif. L. Rev.* 466 (June 1939).
13 *St. John's L. Rev.* 141 (Nov. 1938).
5 *Univ. Chicago L. Rev.* 675 (June 1938).
25 *Virginia L. Rev.* 96 (Nov. 1938).

1940 *Jesse Cantwell, Newton Cantwell, and Russell Cantwell v. Connecticut*, 310 U.S. 296, 84 L.Ed. 1213, 60 S.Ct. 900, 128 A.L.R. 1352

Argued: March 29, 1940.

Decided: May 20, 1940.

Summary: Reversed the conviction of a Jehovah's Witness for inciting a breach of the peace and found constitutionally invalid a state law authorizing government officials to determine a religious cause as a "bona fide object of charity."

Circumstances: Newton Cantwell and his sons, Jesse and Russell, Jehovah's Witnesses, were arrested in New Haven for violating a state law that prohibited the solicitation of money by a religious group without first getting approval from the local official who had the authority to first determine whether the religious cause was a "bona fide object of charity" and whether it conformed to "reasonable standards of efficiency and integrity." On the day of their arrest, the Cantwells were going from house to house on a street where about 90 percent of the residents were Roman Catholic. Among their wares were phonograph records, one of which, in describing a book entitled *Enemies*, included an attack on the Catholic religion. What supported Jesse Cantwell's break of the peace conviction was a street encounter with two Catholic men, who, upon hearing the *Enemies* record, "were tempted to strike Cantwell unless he went away," which he promptly did. He was convicted of inciting others to breach of the peace. The Connecticut Supreme Court of Errors affirmed their Common Pleas Court convictions. The U.S. Supreme Court reversed and remanded to the State Supreme Court.

Opinion: Justice Owen J. Roberts wrote for the unanimous Court. He said that, although the defendant's communications were "couched in terms which naturally would offend . . . all others who respect the honestly held religious faith of their fellows," they "raised no . . . clear and present menace to public peace and order," nor had the state legislature determined that the type of utterance constituted a clear and present danger. Roberts said, however, that the state had the right to protect its citizens from fraudulent solicitations by requiring strangers in the community to identify themselves as representatives of a particular cause before permitting solicitation. He said the state could pass reasonable regulations on the time of day solicitations could be made. "But to condition the solicitation of aid for the perpetuation of religious views or systems upon a license, the grant of which rests in the exercise of a determination by state authority as to what is a religious cause, is to lay a burden upon the exercise of liberty protected by the Constitution." First, Roberts said that the statute deprived the defendants of liberty without due process of law in contravention of the 14th Amendment, which embraces the liberties of the First Amendment, especially the "establishment of religion." Also, a statute authorizing prior restraint on the exercise of the guaranteed freedom by judicial decision after trial is as obnoxious to the Constitution as one providing for like restraint by administrative action. Second, Roberts said that Jesse Cantwell's conduct, "considered apart from the effect of his communication upon his hearers," did not amount to a breach of the peace.

Referenced Cases: *Schneider v. State*, 308 U.S. 147 (1939), that the concept of liberty in the 14th Amendment embraces liberties guaranteed by the First; *Reynolds v. U.S.*, 98 U.S. 145 (1878), on conduct being subject to regulation for the protection of society; *Near v. Minnesota*, 283 U.S. 697 (1931), on previous and absolute restraint; *Lewis Publishing Co. v. Morgan*, 229 U.S. 288 (1913), and *New York ex rel. Bryant v. Zimmerman*, 278 U.S. 63 (1928), on a state's right to protect citizens against fraudulent solicitation; *Gitlow v. New York*, 268 U.S. 652 (1925), and *Thornhill v. Alabama*, 310 U.S. 88 (1940), similar cases involving narrowly drawn statutes to prevent a supposed evil; *Schenck v. U.S.*, 249 U.S. 47 (1919), and *Herndon v. Lowry*, 301 U.S. 242 (1937), on the clear-and-present-danger test.

Further Reading:
1 *Bill of Rights Rev.* 134 (Winter 1941).
15 *Calif. State Bar J.* 161 (June 1940).
40 *Columbia L. Rev.* 1067 (June 1940).
3 *Georgia Bar J.* 68 (Nov. 1940).
26 *Iowa L. Rev.* 126 (Nov. 1940).
14 *So. Calif. L. Rev.* 56 (Nov. 1940).
15 *St. John's L. Rev.* (Nov. 1940).
89 *Univ. Pa. L. Rev.* 515 (Feb. 1941).

1943   *Daisy Largent v. Texas*, 318 U.S. 418, 87 L.Ed. 873, 63 S.Ct. 667

Argued: Feb. 12, 1943.

Decided: March 8, 1943.

Summary: A city ordinance forbidding distribution of publications without a permit held an abridgment of freedom of religion, speech, and press guaranteed by the 14th Amendment.

Circumstances: Mrs. Largent, a member of the Jehovah's Witnesses, was convicted in the Corporation Court of Paris,

Texas, for unlawfully soliciting and selling books, wares, or merchandise without first filing an application and obtaining a permit. The mayor had the power to issue the permit "after investigation." Mrs. Largent appealed to the Lamar County Court, where a trial de novo was conducted. After the hearing, the judge found her guilty and fined her $100. The Supreme Court reversed.

Opinion: Justice Stanley F. Reed delivered the Court's 8-to-0 opinion. Wiley B. Rutledge did not participate. Reed, calling the case "administrative censorship in an extreme form," said the appeal was governed by recent decisions involving ordinances that left the granting or withholding of permits for the distribution of religious publications to the discretion of municipal officers.

Referenced Cases: *Bandini Co. v. Superior Court*, 284 U.S. 8 (1931), and *Bryant v. Zimmerman*, 278 U.S. 63 (1928), on judicial jurisdiction; *Lovell v. Griffin*, 303 U.S. 444 (1938), *Schneider v. State*, 308 U.S. 147 (1939), and *Cantwell v. Connecticut*, 310 U.S. 296 (1940), on ordinances requiring distribution permits; *Chaplinsky v. New Hampshire*, 315 U.S. 568 (1942), and *Gitlow v. New York*, 268 U.S. 652 (1925), on 14th Amendment protections.

Further Reading:
None indexed.

1948   *Murray Winters v. New York,* **333 U.S. 507, 92 L.Ed. 840, 68 S.Ct. 665**

Reargued: Nov. 19, 1946; Nov. 10, 1947.

Decided: March 29, 1948.

Summary: State statute held too vague and indefinite in prohibiting publications devoted to "criminal news, police reports, or accounts of criminal deeds or pictures or stories of deeds of bloodshed, lust or crime."

Circumstances: A New York City book-dealer was convicted for having in his possession with intent to sell certain magazines prohibited by the New York Penal Law, a section of which banned publications of criminal news, police reports, or accounts of criminal deeds, or pictures or stories of deeds of bloodshed, lust, or crime. Persons involved were guilty of a misdemeanor. On appeal from the Court of Special Sessions, the trial court, his conviction was upheld by the Appellate Division of the New York Supreme Court, whose judgment was later upheld by the New York Court of Appeals, the state's highest court. The appeal was first argued before the U.S. Supreme Court in the October 1945 term, then reargued before a full bench in the October 1946 term. It was again reargued in the October 1948 term. In effect, the Court distinguished between obscenity and bloodshed, choosing not to prohibit publications about the latter.

Opinion: Justice Stanley F. Reed wrote the Court's 6-to-3 opinion, joined by Chief Justice Fred M. Vinson and Justices Hugo L. Black, William O. Douglas, Frank Murphy, and Wiley B. Rutledge. Dissenting were Felix Frankfurter, Robert H. Jackson, and Harold H. Burton. Reed said that, when a legislative body concludes that the mores of the community call for an extension of the impermissible limits for accepted standards of conduct, an enactment aimed at the evil is plainly within its power, "if it does not transgress the boundaries fixed by the Constitution for freedom of expression." However, the standards of certainty in statutes punishing for offenses is higher than in those depending primarily on civil sanctions for enforcement. Quoting from *Cantwell v. Connecticut*, 310 U.S. 296 (1940), Reed said the crime "must be defined with appropriate definiteness." New York's vague statute involved the circulation of only vulgar magazines. "The next may call for decision as to free expression of political views in the light of a statute intended to punish subversive activities," Reed wrote, and noted that the law as construed did not limit punishment to the indecent and obscene. "When stories of deeds of bloodshed . . . are massed so as to incite violent crimes, the statute is violated," but, according to the majority, "massed" tales was simply too broad a category to be prohibited without injury to the innocent. Justice Frankfurter, with Jackson and Burton, dissented, saying that the Court's decision 'gave publications that have "nothing of any possible value to society" constitutional protection because of the "indefiniteness" of the statute, but denied to the states the power to prevent "the grave evils to which, in their rational judgment, such publications give rise."

Referenced Cases: *Gitlow v. New York,* 268 U.S. 652 (1925), and *Pennekamp v. Florida,* 328 U.S. 331 (1946), regarding freedom of speech and press protected against state interference by 14th Amendment; *Lovell v. Griffin,* 303 U.S. 444 (1938), on the principle of a free press covering distribution as well as publication; *Stromberg v. California,* 283 U.S. 359 (1931), and *Herndon v. Lowry,* 301 U.S. 242 (1937), on vague and indefinite language; *Fox v. Washington,* 236 U.S. 273 (1915), on prohibiting speech because of its tendency to lead to crime; *Hannegan v. Esquire,* 327 U.S. 146 (1946), *Ex parte Jackson,* 96 U.S. 727 (1877), and *Chaplinsky v. New Hampshire,* 315 U.S. 568 (1942), on protecting literature and controlling lewd, indecent, obscene, or profane publications; *Edwards v. California,* 314 U.S. 160 (1941), a similar state statute "lain dormant for decades."

Further Reading:
61 *Harvard L. Rev.* 1208 (July 1948).
23 *Indiana L. J.* 272 (April 1948).
17 *J. Bar Assoc. Kansas* 247 (Nov. 1948).
23 *Notre Dame Lawyer* 602 (May 1948).
9 *Ohio State L. J.* 346 (Spring 1948).
20 *Rocky Mt. L. Rev.* 366 (June 1948).
22 *So. Calif. L. Rev.* 298 (April 1949).
96 *Univ. Pa. L. Rev.* 889 (June 1948).

1951   *Irving Feiner v. New York,* 340 U.S. 315, 95 L.Ed. 295, 71 S.Ct. 303

Argued: Oct. 17, 1950.

Decided: Jan. 15, 1951.

Summary: With a "clear danger of disorder" threatened by defendant's speech, the Court ruled that free expression gave way to preservation of peace and order.

Circumstances: On the evening of March 8, 1949, Feiner, a college student, was addressing an open-air rally at a street corner in Syracuse, inviting the gathering crowd to a meeting later that night, but also criticizing President Truman, the American Legion, and the city mayor and other officials. The speaker also urged "Negroes," many of whom were in the crowd, to rise up in arms and fight for equal rights. Police, upon assessing the situation, which included some pedestrians being forced to walk on the street to avoid the crowd, finally "stepped in to prevent it [the situation] from resulting in a fight." When Feiner refused to stop speaking or leave the box, he was arrested and charged with violating the state penal law. Feiner was convicted of disorderly conduct, a misdemeanor, in the Court of Special Sessions of Syracuse and sentenced to 30 days in the county penitentiary. The conviction was affirmed by the Onondaga County Court and the New York Court of Appeals. On certiorari, the U.S. Supreme Court upheld the judgment. Feiner had claimed that his conviction was in violation of the right of free speech under the 14th Amendment.

Opinion: Chief Justice Fred M. Vinson wrote for the Court in the 6-to-3 decision, joined by Justices Stanley F. Reed, Robert H. Jackson, Harold H. Burton, and Tom C. Clark. Felix Frankfurter concurred separately. Dissenting were Hugo L. Black, William O. Douglas, and Sherman Minton. Vinson wrote: "It is one thing to say that the police cannot be used as an instrument for the oppression of unpopular views, and another to say that, when as here the speaker passes the bounds of argument or persuasion and undertakes incitement to riot, they are powerless to prevent a breach of the peace. The findings of the state courts as to the existing situation and the imminence of greater disorder coupled with petitioner's deliberate defiance of the police officers convince us that we should not reverse this conviction in the name of free speech." Justice Frankfurter agreed on the basis of his concurrence in *Niemotko v. Maryland*, decided the same day, along with a third, *Kunz v. New York* (see below). He said the cases presented three variations on a theme of great importance: claims of the right to disseminate ideas in public places as against claims of an effective power in government to keep the peace and to protect other interests in a civilized community. After reviewing cases dealing with the inevitable conflict between free speech and other interests, Frankfurter concluded in *Feiner* that police power was used only when the officers "apprehended imminence of violence." In *Niemotko*, on the other hand, neither danger to public peace nor consideration of time and convenience to the public appeared to have entered into denial of the permit, the justice reasoned.

Justice Black, in dissent, averred that the defendant, a young college student, had been sentenced to the penitentiary for his unpopular views. He said the conviction made a mockery of the free speech guarantees of the First and 14th Amendments. "I will have no part or parcel of this holding which I view as a long step toward totalitarian authority. Hereafter . . . the policeman's club can take heavy toll of a current administration's public critics." Despite majority efforts in *Kunz* and *Niemotko* safeguarding freedom of speech, "The three cases read together mean that while previous restraints probably cannot be imposed on an unpopular speaker, the police have discretion to silence him as soon as the customary hostility to his views develops." Also in dissent, Justice Douglas, joined by Minton, said that the record showed only an unsympathetic audience and the threat of one man hauling the speaker from the stage, but not a clear and present danger of riot. "It is against that kind of threat that speakers need police protection."

Referenced Cases: *Cantwell v. Connecticut*, 310 U.S. 296 (1940), on a breach of the peace and clear and present danger of riot; *Schneider v. State*, 308 U.S. 147 (1939), and *Kovacs v. Cooper*, 336 U.S. 77 (1949), on the interest of the community in maintaining peace and order on its streets; *Kunz v. New York*, 340 U.S. 290 (1951), and *Niemotko v. Maryland*, 340 U.S. 268 (1951), decided the same day as *Feiner*, on a theoretical safeguard for freedom of speech; *Chaplinsky v. New Hampshire*, 315 U.S. 568 (1942), on inciting riot and breach of peace with "fighting words"; *Lovell v. Griffin*, 303 U.S. 444 (1938), *Hague v. C.I.O.*, 307 U.S. 496 (1939), *Murdock v. Pennsylvania*, 319 U.S. 105 (1943), and *Saia v. New York*, 334 U.S. 558 (1948), on striking down police censorship, in Justice Douglas's dissent.

Further Reading:
1 *Buffalo L. Rev.* 68 (Spring 1951).
39 *Georgetown L. J.* 488 (March 1951).

2 *Hastings L. J.* 64 (Spring 1951).
6 *Loyola L. Rev.* 70 (1951).
49 *Michigan L. Rev.* 896 (April 1951).
5 *Rutgers L. Rev.* 556 (Spring 1951).
2 *Syracuse L. Rev.* 171 (Fall 1951).
See also under *Kunz v. New York*, 340 U.S. 290 (1951), and *Niemotko v. Maryland*, 340 U.S. 268 (1951), decided the same day.

1951 *Daniel Niemotko v. Maryland* and *Neil W. Kelley v. Maryland*, 340 U.S. 268, 95 L.Ed. 267, 71 S.Ct. 325

Argued: Oct. 17, 1950.

Decided: Jan. 15, 1951.

Summary: A standardless permit system regulating use of a public park ruled in violation of constitutional rights of speech and religion. Interest in clean streets not justification for requiring permit to leaflet.

Circumstances: Members of the Jehovah's Witnesses had requested of the city of Havre de Grace, Maryland, use of the city park on four consecutive Sundays in June and July 1949. Although there was no ordinance regulating park use, it was customary for groups or individuals to obtain a permit from the park commissioner. Permission was denied. When the Witnesses learned of a Flag Day ceremony for the first Sunday, they filed a written request for the other days. The commissioner denied the request. While awaiting the city council's decision after a requested review of the denial, the group proceeded to hold a meeting on the third Sunday. Two speakers, Niemotko and Kelley, were quickly arrested, tried, and convicted, each fined $25. Because under Maryland judicial procedure the jury is the judge of the law as well as the facts, the state court of appeals declined to review the decision of the Circuit Court of Harford County. The U.S. Supreme Court, noting probable jurisdiction because of the substantial constitutional issues involved, reversed.

Opinion: Chief Justice Fred M. Vinson, for the unanimous Court, wrote that the lack of standards in the license-issuing "practice" rendered that "practice" a prior restraint in contravention of the 14th Amendment. He also noted that the completely arbitrary and discriminatory refusal to grant the permits was a denial of equal protection. Justice Hugo L. Black concurred separately without opinion, but see his dissent above in *Feiner v. New York*, decided the same day. Justice Felix Frankfurter, separately, said: "To allow expression of religious views by some and deny the same privilege to others merely because they or their views are unpopular, even deeply so, is a denial of equal protection of the law forbidden by the Fourteenth Amendment." (For more on his opinion, see under *Feiner* above, the last of the three speech cases decided on Jan. 15, 1951.)

Referenced Cases: *Kunz v. New York*, 340 U.S. 290 (1951), *Saia v. New York*, 334 U.S. 558 (1948), *Hague v. C.I.O.*, 307 U.S. 496 (1939), and *Lovell v. Griffin*, 303 U.S. 444 (1938), on licensing systems whereby local bodies regulate use of parks and public places; *Near v. Minnesota*, 283 U.S. 697 (1931), *Grosjean v. American Press Co.*, 297 U.S. 233 (1936), and *Hughes v. Superior Court*, 339 U.S. 460 (1950), on historic experience with prior restraints and economic and social interests; *Cantwell v. Connecticut*, 310 U.S. 296 (1940), *Largent v. Texas*, 318 U.S. 418 (1943), *Marsh v. Alabama*, 326 U.S. 501 (1946), and *Thomas v. Collins*, 323 U.S. 516 (1945), on similar instances of efforts to control community solicitation; *Jones v. Opelika*, 319 U.S. 103 (1943), *Murdock v. Pennsylvania*, 319 U.S. 105 (1943), and *Follett v. McCormick*, 321 U.S. 573 (1944), on nondiscriminatory taxes or a flat tax on solicitation; *Martin v. Struthers*, 319 U.S. 141 (1943), on an ordinance to prevent crime and assure privacy; *Prince v. Massachusetts*, 321 U.S. 158 (1944), on protecting children; *Davis v. Massachusetts*, 167 U.S. 433 (1897), the pioneer case concerning speaking in parks and streets, upholding an ordinance requiring a permit; *Cox v. New Hampshire*, 312 U.S. 569 (1941), holding that the Constitution does not deny licensing if discretion is "appropriately confined"; *Kovacs v. Cooper*, 336 U.S. 77 (1949), on a conviction for operation of a "loud and raucous" sound truck; *Schenck v. U.S.*, 249 U.S. 47 (1919), on the clear-and-present-danger test; *Terminiello v. Chicago*, 337 U.S. 1 (1949), on breach of peace in a private building.

Further Reading:

11 *Jurist* 333 (April 1951).

37 *Virginia L. Rev.* 449 (April 1951).

See also under *Kunz v. New York*, 340 U.S. 290 (1951), and *Feiner v. New York*, 340 U.S. 315 (1951), decided the same day.

1951 *Carl Jacob Kunz v. New York*, 340 U.S. 290, 95 L.Ed. 280, 71 S.Ct. 312

Argued: Oct. 17, 1950.

Decided: Jan. 15, 1951.

Summary: Invalidated a standardless permit system regulating religious meetings on public streets.

Circumstances: Kunz, a Baptist minister who spoke under the auspices of the "Outdoor Gospel Work," was arrested on Sept. 11, 1948, for speaking at Columbus Circle, New York City, without a permit. The police commissioner had denied his request for a 1948 permit on the ground that one had been revoked previously for disorderly conduct, "stirring strife and threatening violence" by ridiculing and denouncing other religious beliefs. The conviction and $10 fine, imposed by the magistrate's court, were affirmed by the Appellate Part of the Court of Special Sessions and by the New York Court of Appeals, three judges dissenting. On appeal, the U.S. Supreme Court reversed.

Opinion: Chief Justice Fred M. Vinson wrote for the Court in the 8-to-1 decision. Hugo L. Black concurred separately but without opinion, and Felix Frankfurter concurred separately on the ground that the ordinance contained no standards to preclude discriminatory or arbitrary action. Robert H. Jackson dissented, saying that the Constitution did not preclude regulating speech on public streets that tended to incite an immediate breach of peace. Vinson wrote for the Court in the trio of First Amendment free speech cases decided in sequence the same day, the others being *Niemotko v. Maryland* and *Feiner v. New York* (see above). As in the other opinions, Vinson here said that, although the Court has recognized that a statute may be enacted that prevents serious interference with normal usage of streets, as in *Feiner*, and parks, as in *Niemotko*, as well as in *Hague v. C.I.O.*, 307 U.S. 496 (1939), and *Cox v. New Hampshire*, 312 U.S. 569 (1941), "we have consistently condemned licensing systems which vest in an administrative official discretion to grant or withhold a permit upon broad criteria unrelated to proper regulation of public places." The Court said that New York, or, by extension, any other state, could not vest restraining control over the right to speak on religious subjects in an administrative official where there are no appropriate standards to guide his actions. Justice Frankfurter agreed on the basis of his concurrence in *Niemotko*. Justice Jackson, in dissent, distinguished between private and public speech, saying that Kunz, a street preacher, took advantage of people's presence on the street to impose his message on a captive audience. On the other hand, a church meeting on private property is made up of an audience that volunteered to listen. "The question . . . is not whether New York could, if it tried, silence Kunz, but whether it must place its streets at his service to hurl insults at the passerby."

Referenced Cases: See under "Opinion" above.

Further Reading:
37 *ABA J.* 221 (March 1951).
19 *George Washington L. Rev.* 637 (June 1951).
14 *Georgia Bar J.* 191 (Nov. 1951).
39 *Illinois Bar J.* 610 (June 1951).
22 *Mississippi L. J.* 241 (May 1951).
26 *Notre Dame Lawyer* 531 (Spring 1951).
See also under *Niemotko v. Maryland*, 340 U.S. 268 (1951), and *Feiner v. New York*, 340 U.S. 315 (1951), decided the same day.

1961 *Times Film Corp. v. Chicago*, 365 U.S. 43, 5 L.Ed.2d 403, 81 S.Ct. 391

Argued: Oct. 19, 20, 1960.

Decided: Jan. 23, 1961.

Summary: An ordinance requiring the submission of motion pictures to a censor held not void on its face, the Court affirming denial of injunctive relief.

Circumstances: In an action in the District Court for the Northern District of Illinois, Times Film Corp. challenged the validity of that part of the Chicago Municipal Code which required submission of all motion pictures for examination prior to public exhibition. The company had applied for a permit to show the film *Don Juan* and paid the fee, but it refused to submit the film to the board of censors. The court dismissed the complaint and the Court of Appeals for the Seventh Circuit affirmed. The Supreme Court affirmed the judgment, ruling that there was no complete and absolute freedom to exhibit, even once, any and every kind of motion picture.

Opinion: Justice Tom C. Clark wrote for the Court in the 5-to-4 opinion, joined by Justices Felix Frankfurter, John M. Harlan, Charles E. Whittaker, and Potter Stewart. Dissenting were Chief Justice Earl Warren and Justices Hugo L. Black, William O. Douglas, and William J. Brennan, Jr. Clark said: "[T]he broad justiciable issue is . . . whether the ambit of constitutional protection includes complete and absolute freedom to exhibit, at least once, any and every kind of motion picture. It is that question alone which we decide. We have concluded that . . . Chicago's ordinance requiring submission of films prior to their public exhibition is not . . . void on its face [as a previous restraint on freedom of speech]. The claim of absolute privilege against prior restraint under the First Amendment [is] a claim without sanction in our cases. As to what may be decided when a concrete case involving a specific standard provided by this ordinance is presented, we intimate no opinion."

Chief Justice Warren, joined by Black, Douglas, and Brennan, said that the constitutional guaranty of freedom of speech prohibited unlimited censorship of films before exhibition through a system of administrative licensing. His dissent is one of the most comprehensive on the subject, with quotations from a number of sources, including John Milton's *Areopagitica*: "If he [the censor] be of such worth as behoovs him, there cannot be more tedious and unpleasing Journey-work, a greater loss of time levied upon his head, then to be made the perpetuall reader of unchosen books

and pamphlets . . . we may easily forsee what kind of licensers we
are to expect hereafter, either ignorant, imperious, and remisse, or
basely pecuniary." Warren went on to illustrate the tendency of
censorship to engulf everything, which in Chicago alone included
newsreels of policemen shooting at labor pickets, films criticizing
Nazi Germany, the movie "Anatomy of a Murder" because it
contained the words "rape" and "contraceptive," and a scene from
Walt Disney's "Vanishing Prairie" showing the birth of a buffalo.
And he noted cases in other cities; for instance, the one-man board
of censors in Memphis banned all of Ingrid Bergman's movies
because the censor judged her soul "black as the soot of hell."
Warren concluded succinctly: "The censor's sword pierces deeply
into the heart of free expression."

In another separate dissent, Justice Douglas, with Warren
and Black joining, simply noted that censorship of movies is
unconstitutional. (The decision was distinguished four years later
in a ruling dealing primarily with obscenity, *Freedman v. Maryland*, 380 U.S. 51 [1965]. A revised version of the Chicago censorship ordinance came before the Court three years after *Freedman*,
in *Teitel Film Corp. v. Cusack*, 390 U.S. 139 [1968].)

Referenced Cases: *Gitlow v. New York*, 268 U.S. 652
(1925), the first in a series of such cases in which the Court
reserved for future decisions on First Amendment vis-à-vis neces-
sities of public welfare; *Near v. Minnesota*, 283 U.S. 697 (1931), on
previous restraint not absolutely unlimited; *Chaplinsky v. New
Hampshire*, 315 U.S. 568 (1942), on well-defined, narrowly limited
classes of speech; *Joseph Burstyn Inc. v. Wilson*, 343 U.S. 495
(1952), on motion pictures within guarantees of First and 14th
Amendments but not absolutely; *Roth v. U.S.*, 354 U.S. 476 (1957),
holding that the First Amendment was not intended to protect
every utterance; *Kingsley Books Inc. v. Brown*, 354 U.S. 436 (1957),
on liberty of speech, and of the press, not being an absolute right;
Smith v. California, 361 U.S. 147 (1959), on states' power to prevent distribution of obscene matter; *Grosjean v. American Press
Co.*, 297 U.S. 233 (1936), *Lovell v. Griffin*, 303 U.S. 444 (1938),
Schneider v. State, 308 U.S. 147 (1939), and *Cantwell v. Connecticut*, 310 U.S. 296 (1940), on abuses in the system of licensing;
Niemotko v. Maryland, 340 U.S. 268 (1951), and *Kunz v. New
York*, 340 U.S. 290 (1951), on conflict between speech and laws
imposing punishment; *Largent v. Texas*, 318 U.S. 418 (1943),

Thomas v. Collins, 323 U.S. 516 (1945), and *Kovacs v. Cooper,* 336 U.S. 77 (1949), dealing with ordinances inhibiting speech through permits.

Further Reading:

30 *Cincinnati L. Rev.* 386 (Summer 1961).
75 *Harvard L. Rev.* 51 (Nov. 1961).
50 *Illinois Bar J.* 248 (Nov. 1961).
47 *Iowa L. Rev.* 162 (Fall 1961).
21 *L. in Transition* 235 (Winter 1962).
21 *Louisiana L. Rev.* 807 (June 1961).
33 *Rocky Mt. L. Rev.* 421 (April 1961).
12 *Syracuse L. Rev.* 3981 (Spring 1961).
1961 *Univ. Pittsburgh L. Rev.* 229 (Oct. 1961).
14 *Vanderbilt L. Rev.* 1525 (Oct. 1961).
6 *Villanova L. Rev.* 567 (Summer 1961).
7 *Wayne L. Rev.* 589 (Summer 1961).
1961 *Wisconsin L. Rev.* 659 (July 1961).

1962   *Manual Enterprises, Inc., et al. v. J. Edward Day, Postmaster General of the U.S.,* **370 U.S. 478, 8 L.Ed.2d 639, 82 S.Ct. 1432**

Argued: Feb. 26, 27, 1962.

Decided: June 25, 1962.

Summary: The Post Office could not bar a magazine from the mails without proof of the publisher's knowledge that the advertisements inside promoted obscene merchandise.

Circumstances: Petitioners were three companies publishing magazines consisting largely of photos of nude, or near-nude, male models, their names and the names of the photographer, with their addresses. The magazines also contained advertisements by photographers offering nudist pictures for sale. In March 1960, six parcels containing more than 400 copies of the three magazines were detained by the Alexandria, Virginia, postmaster, pending a ruling from his superiors in Washington on whether the magazines were "nonmailable." The Post Office judicial officer found them "obscene" under 18 U.S.C. Section 1461 and that the magazines provided information on how to obtain obscene material. The publishers' petition for injunctive relief was dismissed without opinion by the District Court for the District of Columbia, affirmed by the court of appeals. The Supreme Court reversed.

Opinion: The Court could not agree on an opinion, but six justices concurred that 18 U.S.C. Section 1461, known as the Comstock Act, did not authorize the postmaster general to exclude matter from the mails on his own determination of what's obscene, therefore unmailable. Justice John M. Harlan, joined by Potter Stewart, said the magazines were not patently offensive and that the government had failed to show that the publishers knew that advertisers were offering obscene matter for sale. Justice William J. Brennan, Jr., joined by Chief Justice Earl Warren and Justice William O. Douglas, said that the postmaster general was not authorized by law to determine obscenity. Hugo L. Black concurred without opinion. Tom C. Clark dissented. Felix Frankfurter and Byron R. White did not participate. The decision is also important because of the Court's effort to define "hard-core" and its attempt to reinforce its "national standard of decency," which was implied but left dangling in *Roth-Alberts* (1957). "Patent offensiveness," "self-demonstrating indecency," and "obnoxiously debasing portrayals of sex" were used to describe obscene material that would appeal to "prurient interest." Harlan, who wrote the central opinion, found the magazines "dismally unpleasant, uncouth and tawdry," appealing only "to the unfortunate persons whose patronage they were aimed at capturing," but he could not label them "obscene." Here, the "merchandise" was pictures of nearly nude male models.

Referenced Cases: *Roth v. U.S.*, 354 U.S. 476 (1957), and *Smith v. California*, 361 U.S. 147 (1959), on principles for determining obscene matter; *Butler v. Michigan*, 352 U.S. 380 (1957), on prevailing community standards of decency; *Sunshine Book Co. v. Summerfield*, 355 U.S. 372 (1958), and *Mounce v. U.S.*, 355 U.S. 180 (1957), on the portrayal of male and female nudity;

Marcus v. Search Warrant of Property, 367 U.S. 717 (1961), and *Kingsley Books Inc. v. Brown*, 354 U.S. 436 (1957), on the methods for condemning and the standards for judging obscenity; *Hannegan v. Esquire*, 327 U.S. 146 (1946), and *Kent v. Dulles*, 357 U.S. 116 (1958), on the constitutional aspect of administrative censorship; *U.S. ex rel. Milwaukee S. D. Pub. Co. v. Burleson*, 255 U.S. 407 (1921), Justice Oliver Wendell Holmes on "despotic power of any one man"; *Swearingen v. U.S.*, 161 U.S. 446 (1896), on revising the statute to apply only to immorality related to sexual impurity.

Further Reading:
48 *ABA J.* 1073 (Nov. 1962).
27 *Albany L. Rev.* 127 (Jan. 1963).
29 *Brooklyn L. Rev.* 325 (April 1963).
31 *Fordham L. Rev.* 570 (Feb. 1963).
76 *Harvard L. Rev.* 125 (Nov. 1962).
24 *Montana L. Rev.* 65 (Fall 1962).
17 *Rutgers L. Rev.* 213 (Fall 1962).
30 *Tenn. L. Rev.* 291 (Winter 1963).
16 *Vanderbilt L. Rev.* 251 (Dec. 1962).

1963 *Bantam Books, Inc., et al. v. Sullivan et al.*, 372 U.S. 58, 9 L.Ed.2d 584, 83 S.Ct. 631, 1 Med.L.Rptr. 1116

Argued: Dec. 3, 4, 1962.

Decided: Feb. 18, 1963.

Summary: The 14th Amendment violated by the Rhode Island Commission to Encourage Morality in Youth, whose informal sanctions to limit distribution of publications deemed "objectionable" for display or sale to minors constituted prior restraint.

Circumstances: The Rhode Island legislature created the "Rhode Island Commission to Encourage Morality in Youth" and gave the body inter alia "the duty . . . to educate the public concerning any book, picture, pamphlet, ballad, printed paper or other thing containing obscene, indecent or impure language, or manifestly tending to the corruption of the youth." The practice was for the commission to notify a distributor on official commission stationery that certain books or magazines handled by him had been declared objectionable by a majority of the body for sale or display to youths under age 18. Max Silverstein & Sons, exclusive wholesaler of books by Bantam throughout most of Rhode Island, had received at least 35 such notices. Upon receiving a notice, Silverstein stopped further circulation of the listed publications. Despite such cooperation, "rather than face the possibility of some sort of a court action against ourselves, as well as the people that we supply," four out-of-state publishers in the Superior Court of Rhode Island sued for injunctive relief and a declaratory judgment that the law and the practices were unconstitutional. The publishers argued that the commission's practices amounted to a scheme of government censorship. The court declined to declare the law creating the commission unconstitutional on its face but granted an injunction against the acts and practices of the commission. The state supreme court affirmed the superior court on the constitutional question but reversed the injunction. The U.S. Supreme Court reversed and remanded to the Rhode Island Superior Court.

Opinion: Justice William J. Brennan, Jr., wrote for the Court in the 8-to-1 decision, joined by Chief Justice Earl Warren and Justices Potter Stewart, Bryon R. White, and Arthur J. Goldberg. Hugo L. Black, William O. Douglas, and Tom C. Clark concurred separately. John M. Harlan was the lone dissenter. Brennan said that "informal censorship" may sufficiently inhibit the circulation of publications to warrant injunctive relief because the acts and practices of the members and executive secretary of the commission, performed "under the color of state law," directly and designedly stopped circulation of publications in many parts of the state. Although book dealers were "free" to ignore the commission's notices, Brennan wrote: "It would be naive to credit the State's assertion that these blacklists are in the nature of mere legal advice, when they plainly serve as instruments of regulation independent of laws against obscenity. What Rhode Island has done, in fact, has been to subject the distribution of publications to a system of prior administrative restraints, since the Commission is not a judicial body and its decisions to list particular publications as objectionable do not follow judicial determinations that such publications may lawfully be banned." Justice Douglas, concurring, added that he adhered to his views expressed in *Roth-Alberts* (1957), an obscenity case, respecting the very narrow scope of governmental authority to suppress publications on the grounds of obscenity.

Justice Clark, though concurring in the result, said that the Court, in condemning the commission's overzealous efforts to implement obscenity laws, "as if shearing a hog, comes up with little wool," owes Rhode Island the duty of articulating standards that must be met, lest the state supreme court be left at sea as to the appropriate disposition on remand. "In my view the Court should simply direct the Commission to abandon its delusions of grandeur and leave the issuance of 'orders' to enforcement officials and 'the State's criminal regulation of obscenity' to the prosecutors, who can substitute prosecution for 'thinly veiled threats' in appropriate cases."

Justice Harlan, in dissent, said: "It could not well be suggested, as I think the Court concedes, that a prosecutor's announcement that he intended to enforce strictly the obscenity laws or that he would proceed against a particular publication unless withdrawn from circulation amountd to an unconstitutional restraint upon freedom of expression, still less that such a restraint would occur from the mere existence of a criminal obscenity statute."

Referenced Cases: *Roth v. U.S.*, 354 U.S. 476 (1957), on obscenity not within the area of constitutionally protected speech, therefore subject to state regulation; *Smith v. California*, 361 U.S. 147 (1959), *Marcus v. Search Warrant*, 367 U.S. 717 (1961), *Thornhill v. Alabama*, 310 U.S. 88 (1940), *Winters v. New York*, 333 U.S. 507 (1948), *NAACP v. Button*, 371 U.S. 415 (1963), and *Speiser v. Randall*, 357 U.S. 513 (1958), that freedoms of expression must be ringed about with adequate bulwarks and that the separation of legitimate from illegitimate speech calls for sensitive tools; *Ex parte Young*, 209 U.S. 123 (1908), and *Terry v. Adams*, 345 U.S. 461 (1953), on acts "under color of state law" constituting acts of the state and thus within the 14th Amendment; *Joint-AntiFacist Refugee Committee v. McGrath*, 341 U.S. 123 (1951), on blacklists as instruments of regulation independent of laws; *Near v. Minnesota*, 283 U.S. 697 (1931), *Lovell v. Griffin*, 303 U.S. 444 (1938), *Schneider v. State*, 308 U.S. 147 (1939), *Cantwell v. Connecticut*, 310 U.S. 296 (1940), *Niemotko v. Maryland*, 340 U.S. 268 (1951), *Kunz v. New York*, 340 U.S. 290 (1951), and *Staub v. Baxley*, 355 U.S. 313 (1958), on any system of prior restraints of expression bearing heavy presumption against its constitutional validity; *Kingsley Books Inc. v. Brown*, 354 U.S. 436 (1957), on a tolerable system under judicial superintendence and immediate determination of validity.

Further Reading:

49 *ABA J.* 495 (May 1963).
12 *American Univ. L. Rev.* 211 (June 1963).
51 *California L. Rev.* 620 (Aug. 1963).
77 *Harvard L. Rev.* 124 (Nov. 1963).
49 *Iowa L. Rev.* 161 (Fall 1963).
9 *NY L. Forum* 385 (Aug. 1963).

1965   *Corliss Lamont, Doing Business as Basic Pamphlets v. Postmaster General of the U.S. and John F. Fixa, Individually and as Postmaster, San Francisco, et al. v. Leif Heilberg*, 381 U.S. 301, 14 L.Ed.2d 398, 85 S.Ct. 1493

Argued: April 26, 1965.

Decided: May 24, 1965.

Summary: Invalidating requirement of affirmative request for mail delivery of "communist political propaganda," Court recognized a right to know. The First Amendment protects those who want to receive information and ideas as well as those who want to communicate with others.

Circumstances: Two challenges to the Postal Service and Federal Employees Salary Act of 1962, which provides that mail matter, except sealed letters, that originates in a foreign country and that the secretary of the treasury believes to be "communist political propaganda" will only be delivered upon the request of the addressee. The Lamont case arose out of the detention in 1963 of a copy of the *Peking Review*, addressed to Dr. Lamont, a publisher and distributor of pamphlets. Instead of responding to the Post Office's notice, Lamont sued to enjoin enforcement of the statute, an action that the Post Office interpreted as his desire to receive the publication. He thus amended his suit. The three-judge District Court for the Southern District of New York dismissed the complaint as moot. Heilberg, like Lamont, refused to return the reply card and filed a complaint in the District Court for the Northern District of California. The Post Office reacted the same way, but the court declined to hold that his suit was moot and unanimously held that the statute was unconstitutional. On appeals, the Supreme Court reversed the judgment in *Lamont* and affirmed that in *Heilberg*.

Opinion: Justice William O. Douglas wrote for five members in the unanimous decision. William J. Brennan, Jr., joined by Arthur J. Goldberg, concurred separately, as did John M. Harlan without opinion. Byron R. White did not participate. The Court held that a Post Office regulation requiring that addressees of communist political propaganda from abroad affirmatively request its delivery violated the First Amendment. Douglas noted that the unconstitutional nature of the regulation stemmed from the fact that it required an official act, namely, returning the reply card, as a limitation on the "unfettered exercise of the addressee's First Amendment rights." He quoted Justice Oliver Wendell Holmes, who said in dissent in *Milwaukee Pub. Co. v. Burleson*, 255 U.S. 407 (1921), "The United States may give up the Post Office when it sees fit, but while it carries it on the use of the mails is almost as much a part of free speech as the right to use our tongues." Brennan, in his concurring opinion, stated: "I think the right to receive publications is . . . a fundamental right. The dissemination of ideas can accomplish nothing if otherwise willing addressees are not free to receive and consider them. It would be a barren marketplace of ideas that had only sellers and no buyers." (Later that year, in *Griswold v. Connecticut*, 381 U.S. 479, Douglas went further in saying, for the majority, that the right to know was within the penumbra of the First Amendment. "The right of freedom of speech and press includes not only the right to utter or to print, but the right to distribute, the right to receive, the right to read.")

Referenced Cases: *Murdock v. Pennsylvania*, 319 U.S. 105 (1943), on striking down a flat license tax on exercise of First Amendment rights; *Thomas v. Collins*, 323 U.S. 516 (1945), *Lovell v. Griffin*, 303 U.S. 444 (1938), and *Harman v. Forssenius*, 380 U.S. 528 (1965), regarding other attempts by states to impose burdens on constitutional rights; *New York Times v. Sullivan*, 376 U.S. 254 (1964), on "uninhibited, robust, and wide-open" debate; *Dombrowski v. Pfister*, 380 U.S. 479 (1965), *Johnson v. Eisentrager*, 339 U.S. 479 (1950), and *Martin v. Struthers*, 319 U.S. 141 (1943), on the First Amendment protecting the right to receive material; *NAACP v. Alabama*, 357 U.S. 449 (1958), *Kent v. Dulles*, 357 U.S. 116 (1958), *Aptheker v. Secretary of State*, 378 U.S. 500 (1964), and *Zemel v. Rusk*, 381 U.S. 1 (1965), on personal rights necessary to make express guarantees fully meaningful.

Further Reading:
51 *ABA J.* 871 (Sept. 1965).
15 *American Univ. L. Rev.* 114 (Dec. 1965).
79 *Harvard L. Rev.* 154 (1965).
37 *Mississippi L. J.* 159 (Dec. 1965).
17 *So. Carolina L. Rev.* 616 (1965).
40 *St. John's L. Rev.* 274 (May 1966).
18 *Vanderbilt L. Rev.* 2043 (Oct. 1965).

1968   *Tietel Film Corp. et al. v. John F. Cusack et al.*, 390 U.S. 139, 19 L.Ed.2d 966, 88 S.Ct. 754

Decided: Jan. 29, 1968.

Summary: Held that Chicago film censorship procedures violate the Constitution and judicial safeguards against the dangers of a censorship system.

Circumstances: Proceeding under the Chicago Motion Picture Censorship Ordinance, the Circuit Court of Cook County enjoined the defendants from showing the films, "Rent-A-Girl" and "Body of a Female." The Illinois Supreme Court affirmed, holding that no constitutional rights had been violated. The U.S. Supreme Court reversed.

Opinion: In a per curiam opinion, expressing the views of seven members, the Court held, relying on *Freedman v. Maryland*, 380 U.S. 51 (1965), that the ordinance violated the constitutional rights of the defendants by its failure to ensure that the censor would, within a specified period, either issue a license or go to court to restrain showing the film. Nor did the ordinance provide for a prompt final judicial decision. Justices Hugo L. Black and William O. Douglas based their reversal as well on *Redrup v. New York*, 386 U.S. 767 (1967), in which the Court reversed judgments affirming an obscenity conviction on the ground that the distribution of books and magazines was protected by the First and 14th Amendments from government suppression. Justice Potter Stewart based his concurrence solely on *Redrup*. Justice John M. Harlan concurred without separate notation.

Referenced Cases: See under "Opinion" above.

Further Reading:
17 *De Paul L. Rev.* 597 (Summer 1968).

1969 *John F. Tinker and Mary Beth Tinker, Minors, etc., et al. v. Des Moines Independent Community School District et al.,* **393 U.S. 503, 21 L.Ed.2d 731, 89 S.Ct. 733**

Argued: Nov. 12, 1968.

Decided: Feb. 24, 1969.

Summary: First Amendment protection accorded "symbolic speech" in holding that students had a right to wear black armbands as an antiwar protest, provided the activity presented no immediate danger to normal school operations.

Circumstances: In a double protest, three students, backed by others and adults, wore black armbands to school as a protest against the hostilities in Vietnam and also as a gesture against the school's recently adopted policy banning such activity. The students were sent home and suspended until they removed the armbands. The students, through their fathers, filed a complaint in the District Court for the Southern District of Iowa, which dismissed the complaint on the ground that the school's action was reasonable to prevent disruption. The Court of Appeals for the Eighth Circuit affirmed without opinion. The Supreme Court reversed and remanded.

Opinion: Justice Abe Fortas wrote the opinion of the 7-to-2 Court, joined by Chief Justice Earl Warren and Justices William O. Douglas, William J. Brennan, Jr., Thurgood Marshall, Potter Stewart, and Byron R. White. Stewart and White also wrote separately. Hugo L. Black and John M. Harlan dissented. Fortas likened the wearing of armbands to "pure speech." He said, "It can hardly be argued that either students or teachers shed their constitutional rights to freedom of speech or expression at the schoolhouse gate." Fortas also noted that similar symbolic acts were not prohibited, such as political buttons and, in some cases, the Iron Cross. Instead, a particular symbol—black armbands worn to exhibit opposition to U.S. involvement in Vietnam—was singled out for prohibition. Justice Stewart, though in basic agreement, said that he did not share the Court's uncritical assumption that, school discipline aside, the First Amendment rights of children are co-extensive with those of adults.

Justice Black, in dissent, said, "It is a myth that any person has a constitutional right to say what he pleases, where he pleases, and when he pleases. Uncontrolled and uncontrollable liberty is an enemy of domestic peace. We cannot close our eyes to the fact that some of the country's greatest problems are crimes committed by the youth, too many of school age." He chastised the students for "crisply and summarily" refusing to obey a school order. Justice Harlan, also in dissent, said he could find nothing in the record that impugned the good faith of the school officials in promulgating the armband regulation.

Referenced Cases: *West Virginia v. Barnette*, 319 U.S. 624 (1943), *Stromberg v. California*, 283 U.S. 359 (1931), *Thornhill v. Alabama*, 310 U.S. 88 (1940), *Edwards v. South Carolina*, 372 U.S. 229 (1963), and *Brown v. Louisiana*, 383 U.S. 131 (1966), on symbolic acts within the free speech clause of the First Amendment; *Cox v. Louisiana*, 379 U.S. 536 (1965), and *Adderly v. Florida*, 385 U.S. 39 (1966), on "pure speech" being comprehensively protected by the First Amendment; *Meyer v. Nebraska*, 262 U.S. 390 (1923), *Bartels v. Iowa*, 262 U.S. 404 (1923), *Pierce v. Society of Sisters*, 268 U.S. 510 (1925), *McCollum v. Board of Education*, 333 U.S. 203 (1948), *Wieman v. Updegraff*, 344 U.S. 183 (1952), *Sweezy v. New Hampshire*, 354 U.S. 234 (1957), *Shelton v. Tucker*, 364 U.S. 479 (1960), *Engle v. Vitale*, 370 U.S. 421 (1962), *Keyishian v. Board of Regents*, 385 U.S. 589 (1967), and *Epperson v. Arkansas*, 393 U.S. 97 (1968), the litany of "school environment" cases over 50 years; *Terminiello v. Chicago*, 337 U.S. 1 (1949), on "hazardous freedom" as basis of national strength; *Ginsberg v. New York*, 390 U.S. 629 (1968), that children do not have speech rights co-extensive with adults.

Further Reading:

55 *ABA J.* 583 (June 1969).
38 *Fordham L. Rev.* 35 (Oct. 1969).
3 *Gonzaga L. Rev.* 227 (Spring 1968).
5 *Harvard Civil Rights L. Rev.* 278 (April 1970).
83 *Harvard L. Rev.* 154 (Nov. 1969).
57 *Illinois Bar J.* 848 (June 1969).
16 *Loyola L. Rev.* 165 (1969–70).
52 *Marquette L. Rev.* 608 (Winter 1969).
20 *Mercer L. Rev.* 505 (Summer 1969).
54 *Minnesota L. Rev.* 721 (Jan. 1970).
23 *Southwestern L. J.* 929 (Dec. 1969).
4 *Suffolk Univ. L. Rev.* 169 (Fall 1969).
22 *Univ. Florida L. Rev.* 168 (Summer 1969).
11 *William & Mary L. Rev.* 275 (Fall 1969).

1980   *PruneYard Shopping Center and Fred
Sahadi v. Michael Robins et al.,* **447 U.S.
74, 64 L.Ed.2d 741, 100 S.Ct. 2035, 6
Med.L.Rptr. 1311**

Argued: March 18, 1980.

Decided: June 9, 1980.

Summary: Access to shopping center for expression
and petitioning not violative of owner's constitutional rights. A
state is free to adopt constitutional liberties more expansive than
those of the federal constitution.

Circumstances: In 1974 in Campbell, California, a
group of high school students took a card table, some leaflets, and
unsigned petitions to the large PruneYard Shopping Center. The
students had been angered by a recent anti-Israel United Nations'
resolution and sought to pass out literature and collect signatures
on petitions to send to the president and Congress. The shopping
center did not permit such activity, and the students were told to
leave the property by a security guard. Their activity was peaceful
and orderly and PruneYard patrons did not object to their presence.
The students sought to enjoin the center from denying them access
to circulate their petitions in the Superior Court of Santa Clara
County. The court said they were not entitled under either state or
federal constitutions to exercise their rights on shopping center property. The California Court of Appeals affirmed, but the state supreme court reversed. The U.S. Supreme Court affirmed that reversal.

Opinion: Justice William H. Rehnquist, for six members,
said that the state could go further in the protection of personal
liberties than the federal government. The Court upheld the California Supreme Court's interpretation of the state constitution,
which entitles citizens to exercise free expression and petition
rights on the property of a privately owned shopping center to
which the public is invited. It said this does not violate the shopping center owner's property rights under the Fifth and 14th
Amendments nor his free speech rights under the First and 14th.
Rehnquist was joined by Chief Justice Warren E. Burger and Jus-

tices William J. Brennan, Jr., Potter Stewart, Thurgood Marshall, and John Paul Stevens. Joining the judgment but differing on some points were Justices Byron R. White, Lewis F. Powell, Jr., and Harry A. Blackmun. The Court said that prohibiting such activity did not "unreasonably impair" the value or use of the shopping center. But it agreed with the California Supreme Court, that the center may restrict expressive activity by adopting time, place, and manner regulations to minimize interference with commercial functions. As for the owner being identified with a particular message, the Court said the center could have posted signs near the speakers or handbillers disclaiming any sponsorship of the message. Powell, with White, added that the decision was not necessarily applicable to all shopping centers because serious First Amendment issues arise when privately owned property is transformed perforce into a forum for expression of the public's views.

Referenced Cases: *Torcaso v. Watkins,* 367 U.S. 488 (1961), *Adamson v. California,* 332 U.S. 46 (1947), and *Railway Express Agency v. Virginia,* 282 U.S. 440 (1931), on a state constitution qualifying as a "statute"; *Lloyd Corp. v. Tanner,* 407 U.S. 551 (1972), applying the federal constitution to restrict expressive behavior at a privately owned shopping center; *Food Employees v. Logan Valley Plaza,* 391 U.S. 308 (1968), and *Hudgens v. NLRB,* 424 U.S. 507 (1976), on the private character of stores clustered with other stores; *Cooper v. California,* 386 U.S. 58 (1967), on a state's sovereign right to adopt liberties more expansive than those of the federal constitution; *Euclid v. Ambler Realty Co.,* 272 U.S. 365 (1926), and *Young v. American Mini Theatres Inc.,* 427 U.S. 50 (1976), on reasonable restrictions on private property; *Kaiser Aetna v. U.S.,* 444 U.S. 164 (1979), on the right to exclude others; *Pennsylvania Coal Co. v. Mahon,* 260 U.S. 393 (1922), holding that when regulation goes too far it amounts to a taking; *Chicago, B. & O. R. Co. v. Chicago,* 166 U.S. 226 (1897), regarding the just compensation clause of the Fifth Amendment; *Nebbia v. New York,* 291 U.S. 502 (1934), on denying property without due process of law; *Wooley v. Maynard,* 430 U.S. 705 (1977), a state may not require an individual to participate in the dissemination of a message by displaying it on his private property; *West Virginia State Board of Education v. Barnette,* 319 U.S. 624 (1943), and *Miami Herald Pub. Co. v. Tornillo,* 418 U.S. 241 (1974), on compelling recitation of a message.

Further Reading:
64 *Marquette L. Rev.* 507 (Spring 1981).
21 *Santa Clara L. Rev.* 801 (Summer 1981).
11 *Stetson L. Rev.* 145 (Fall 1981).
15 *Univ. Richmond L. Rev.* 699 (Spring 1981).

1982   *Board of Education, Island Trees Union Free School District No. 26 et al. v. Steven A. Pico, by his next friend, Frances Pico et al.*, 457 U.S. 853, 73 L.Ed.2d 435, 102 S.Ct. 2799, 8 Med.L.Rptr. 1721

Argued: March 2, 1982.

Decided: June 25, 1982.

Summary: A local school board violated the First Amendment when it removed a number of books from the school library, characterizing them as "anti-American, anti-Christian, anti-Semitic, and just plain filthy."

Circumstances: School board president Richard Ahrens, board vice president Frank Martin, and board member Patrick Hughes attended a conference sponsored by Parents of New York United (PONYU), a politically conservative group of parents concerned about education legislation in New York state. There the trio distributed lists of books described by Ahrens as "objectionable" and by Martin as "improper fare for school students." At a meeting in Feb. 1976 between the superintendent and principals of the high school and junior high, the board had unofficially directed that certain books be removed from the library. Later, the board's appointed Book Review Committee read the volumes and determined that five be retained in the library and that two others be removed. The board rejected the report, deciding that only one of the books should be returned to the high school library and that the remaining nine "be removed from elementary and secondary libraries and [from] use in the curriculum." Several students at the high school and the junior high brought action in the District Court for the Eastern District of New York, which granted the board summary judgment. The Court of Appeals for the Second Circuit reversed and remanded for a trial on the students' allegations, with each of the three judges filing a separate opinion. Judge Sifton, for the court, said that the case involved "an unusual and irregular intervention in the school libraries' operations by persons not routinely concerned with such matters" and concluded that the board was obliged to demonstrate a reasonable basis for interfering with the students, this to ensure that the actions were not simply pretexts for the suppression of free speech. A plurality of the Supreme Court affirmed, agreeing that a material issue of fact precluded summary judgment in favor of the school board.

Opinion: Justice William J. Brennan, Jr., wrote for the plurality in the 5-to-4 decision, joined by Justices Thurgood Marshall, John Paul Stevens, and, in part, Harry A. Blackmun. Byron R. White concurred separately, as did Blackmun. Dissenting were Chief Justice Warren E. Burger and Justices Lewis F. Powell, Jr., William H. Rehnquist, and Sandra Day O'Connor. The ruling means that high school students are protected from school boards that would arbitrarily remove library books vaguely described as "inappropriate." Brennan first pointed out that the case did not involve the school board's discretion to prescribe the curricula. "On the contrary, the only books at issue . . . are *library* books, books that by their nature are optional rather than required reading." He went on to cite cases requiring states and school boards to exercise educational discretion "in a manner that comports with the transcendent imperatives of the First Amendment." In keeping with the Court's evolving "right to know" doctrine, Brennan said that "the right to receive ideas is a necessary predicate to the *recipient's* meaningful exercise of his own rights of speech, press, and political freedom." On student rights in the light of the special characteristics of the school environment, Brennan said that the school library was especially appropriate for the recognition of the First Amendment rights of students. The majority concluded that school boards could not remove books from school libraries simply because they disliked the ideas contained in them, seeking to prescribe orthodoxy in politics, nationalism, religion, or other matters of opinion. Justice Blackmun, concurring in part and in the judgment, added that school officials must still be allowed, in a politically neutral way, to select one book over another without outside interference. Justice White, separately, said that the majority need not have issued a dissertation on the extent to which the First Amendment limited school boards, since the underlying reasons cited by this board, as the "material issue of fact," were enough to preclude summary judgment.

In dissent, Chief Justice Burger, joined by Powell, Rehnquist, and O'Connor, said that, since such matters were normally left to the states, the plurality of the Court was wrong in subjecting the local judgment to federal review. If school board decisions are to be subject to federal court review, Burger said, the Court would come perilously close to becoming a "super censor" of school board library decisions. "I categorically reject [the] notion that the Constitution dictates that judges, rather than parents, teachers, and local school boards, must determine how the standards of morality and vulgarity are to be treated in the classroom." Justice Powell, in dissent separately, believed that local school boards should have the responsibility for determining educational policy. Justice Rehnquist, joined by Burger and Powell, added that actions by the government as educator did not raise the same First Amendment problems as actions by the government as sovereign. Responding to Brennan's view of schools as preparatory to citizenship and the preservation of societal values, Rehnquist said: "The idea that . . . students have a right to access, *in the school*, to information other than that thought by their educators to be necessary is contrary to the very nature of an inculcative education." Justice O'Connor, in a brief separate dissent, wrote: "If the school board can set the curriculum, select teachers, and determine initially what books to purchase for the school library, it surely can decide which books to discontinue or remove from the school library so long as it does not also interfere with the right of students to read the material and to discuss it. As Justice Rehnquist persuasively argues, the plurality's analysis overlooks the fact that in this case the government is acting in its special role as educator." (Among the books found inappropriate were Eldridge Cleaver's *Soul on Ice*, Alice Childress' *A Hero Ain't Nothing But a Sandwich*, Kurt Vonnegut's *Slaughterhouse Five*, Langston Hughes' *The Best Short Stories by Negro Writers*, Oliver La Farge's

Laughing Boy, Desmond Morris's *The Naked Ape*, and Richard Wright's *Black Boy*.)

Referenced Cases: *Meyer v. Nebraska*, 262 U.S. 390 (1923), and *Epperson v. Arkansas*, 393 U.S. 97 (1968), on limits on states to control curriculum and classroom; *Adickes v. S. H. Kress & Co.*, 398 U.S. 144 (1970), on the issue of material fact; *Tinker v. Des Moines School Dist.*, 393 U.S. 503 (1969), and *Ambach v. Norwick*, 441 U.S. 68 (1979), on the authority of states and school boards in the preparation of future citizens; *West Virginia Board of Education v. Barnette*, 319 U.S. 624 (1943), a major decision affecting schools relative to the imperatives of the First Amendment; *Terminiello v. Chicago*, 337 U.S. 1 (1949), on the value, as well as the risk, of openness; *First National Bank of Boston v. Bellotti*, 435 U.S. 765 (1978), on public access to discussion, debate, and dissemination of information and ideas; *Griswold v. Connecticut*, 381 U.S. 479 (1965), against contracting the spectrum of available knowledge; *Stanley v. Georgia*, 394 U.S. 557 (1969), *Kleindienst v. Mandel*, 408 U.S. 753 (1972), *Martin v. Struthers*, 319 U.S. 141 (1943), and *Lamont v. Postmaster General*, 381 U.S. 301 (1965), on the right to receive, as well as distribute, information and ideas; *Brown v. Louisiana*, 383 U.S. 131 (1966), and *Keyishian v. Board of Regents*, 385 U.S. 589 (1967), on the library as "a place dedicated to quiet, to knowledge, and to beauty," where students are free to inquire, study, and evaluate; *Brown v. Board of Education*, 347 U.S. 483 (1954), on awakening the child to cultural values; *FCC v. Pacifica Foundation*, 438 U.S. 726 (1978), and *Pierce v. Society of Sisters*, 268 U.S. 510 (1925), on offensive language and ideas "manifestly inimical to the public welfare."

Further Reading:

17 *Akron L. Rev.* 483 (Winter 1984).
36 *Arkansas L. Rev.* 551 (1983).
21 *Duquesne L. Rev.* 1055 (Summer 1983).
7 *J. Juvenile L.* 40 (1983).
18 *Land & Water L. Rev.* 837 (1983).
68 *Minnesota L. Rev.* 213 (1983).
14 *No. Carolina Central L. J.* 255 (1983).
10 *Ohio Northern Univ. L. Rev.* 395 (Spring 1983).
44 *Ohio State L. J.* 1103 (1983).

35 *Stanford L. Rev.* 497 (Feb. 1983).

62 *Texas L. Rev.* 197 (Oct. 1983).

14 *Univ. Toledo L. Rev.* 1329 (Summer 1983).

25 *Washington Univ. J. Urban & Contemporary L.* 385 (1983).

1988   *Hazelwood School District et al. v. Cathy Kuhlmeier et al.,* 484 U.S. ___, 98 L.Ed.2d 592, 108 S.Ct. 562

Argued: Oct. 13, 1987.

Decided: Jan. 13, 1988.

Summary: Public school officials possess broad power to censor school newspapers, plays, and other "school-sponsored expressive activities" that are "part of the school curriculum" and appear to carry the school's imprimatur.

Circumstances: In May 1983, a high school principal in Missouri deleted two pages from the student newspaper, which was published as part of the journalism curriculum. He considered two articles on divorce and student pregnancy inappropriate. Three staff members challenged the censorship as a violation of their First Amendment right of free speech in the District Court for the Eastern District of Missouri, which denied an injunction and said that the principal's actions were reasonable. The Court of Appeals for the Eighth Circuit reversed, holding that the paper was a public forum and that school officials were entitled to censor the articles only if publication could have resulted in tort liability to the school. On certiorari, the Supreme Court reversed.

Opinion: Justice Byron R. White wrote the 5-to-3 opinion, joined by Chief Justice William H. Rehnquist and Justices John Paul Stevens, Sandra Day O'Connor, and Antonin Scalia. Dissenting was William J. Brennan, Jr., joined by Thurgood Marshall and Harry A. Blackmun. The seat held by retired justice Lewis F. Powell, Jr., was still vacant. White said that there had been no violation of the First Amendment, noting that public school officials may restrict student speech in school more than government may restrict speech generally. The opinion extended the Court's earlier reasoning that a school need not tolerate student speech inconsistent with its "basic educational mission" even though "government could not censor similar speech outside the school." White reaffirmed the Court's statement in *Tinker v. Des Moines Independent Community School Dist.*, 393 U.S. 503 (1969), that students in public schools do not "shed their constitutional rights to freedom of expression at the schoolhouse gate." But, the justice said that the *Tinker* rules limit only "educators' ability to silence a student's personal expression that happens to occur on the school premises" and not speech that occurs in the school curriculum. A school has broad power to "refuse to lend its name and resources to the dissemination of student expression" that it believes inappropriate. White wrote: "A school must be able to set high standards for the student speech that is disseminated under its auspices—standards that may be higher than those demanded by some newspaper publishers or theatrical producers in the 'real' world—and may refuse to disseminate student speech that does not meet those standards. In addition, a school must be able to take into account the emotional maturity of the intended audience in determining whether to disseminate student speech on potentially sensitive topics. . . . A school must also retain the authority to refuse to sponsor student speech that might reasonably be perceived to advocate drug or alcohol use, irresponsible sex, or conduct otherwise inconsistent with the shared values of a civilized social order."

In dissent with Justices Marshall and Blackmun, Brennan said the principal and the Court's majority decision "violated the First Amendment's prohibition against censorship of any student expression that neither disrupts classwork nor invades the rights of others." He said the decision "denudes high school students of much of the First Amendment protection that *Tinker* itself prescribed" instead of teaching youths "to respect the diversity of ideas that is fundamental to the American system."

Referenced Cases: *Bethel School District No. 403 v. Fraser*, 478 U.S. 675 (1986), recognizing that student First Amendment rights are not automatically co-extensive with the rights of adults in other settings; *Hague v. CIO*, 307 U.S. 496 (1939), *Widmar v. Vincent*, 454 U.S. 263 (1981), *Perry Education Assn. v.*

Perry Local Educators' Assn., 460 U.S. 37 (1983), and *Cornelius v. NAACP Legal Defense & Educational Fund Inc.*, 473 U.S. 788 (1985), defining public forums of expression; *Board of Education of Hendrick Hudson Central School Dist. v. Rowley*, 458 U.S. 176 (1982), *Wood v. Strickland*, 420 U.S. 308 (1975), and *Epperson v. Arkansas*, 393 U.S. 97 (1968), on the "oft-expressed view" that education is primarily the responsibility of parents, teachers, and state and local school officials, not federal judges; *Brown v. Board of Education*, 347 U.S. 483 (1954), *Ambach v. Norwick*, 441 U.S. 68 (1979), and *Board of Education v. Pico*, 457 U.S. 853 (1982), that schools prepare youth for citizenship, teaching fundamental democratic and community values; *West Virginia Board of Education v. Barnette*, 319 U.S. 624 (1943), and *Meyer v. Nebraska*, 262 U.S. 390 (1923), on certain unconstitutional education laws; *Keyishian v. Board of Regents*, 385 U.S. 589 (1967), and *Thomas v. Collins*, 323 U.S. 516 (1945), on the "pall of orthodoxy over the classroom" and Orwellian "guardianship of the public mind"; *Shuttlesworth v. Birmingham*, 394 U.S. 147 (1969), *Cox v. Louisiana*, 379 U.S. 536 (1965), and *Staub v. Baxley*, 355 U.S. 313 (1958), on licensing speech from a particular forum.

Further Reading:
18 *Cumberland L. Rev.* 181 (1987/88).
14 *Hastings Const. L. Q.* 889 (Summer 1987).
65 *Washington Univ. L. Q.* 243 (Dec. 1987).

Selected Bibliography

Coggins, T. L., "Book Removals from School Libraries and Students' First Amendment Rights," 17 *School L. Bull.* 17 (Summer 1986).

"The Eighth Circuit Extends First Amendment Protections for High School Students Working on School-Sponsored Newspapers: Kuhlmeier v. Hazelwood School District," 65 *Washington Univ. L. Q.* 243 (1987).

"The Founding Fathers and Political Speech: The First Amendment, the Press and the Sedition Act of 1798," 6 *Univ. St. Louis Public L. Rev.* 395 (1987).

Haiman, Franklyn S., "The Rhetoric of the Streets: Some Legal and Ethical Considerations," 53 *Quarterly J. Speech* 99 (April 1977).

———, "Nonverbal Communication and the First Amendment: The Rhetoric of the Streets Revisited," 68 *Quarterly J. Speech* 371 (Nov. 1982).

Linde, Hans A., "Courts and Censorship," 66 *Minnesota L. Rev.* 171 (Nov. 1981).

Marks, Richard D., "Broadcasting and Censorship: First Amendment Theory After Red Lion," 38 *George Washington L. Rev.* 974 (1970).

Nichols, John E., "The Pre-Tinker History of Freedom of Student Press and Speech," 56 *Journalism Quarterly* 727 (Winter 1979).

Orentlicher, Diane F., "Snepp v. United States: The CIA Secrecy Agreement and the First Amendment," 81 *Columbia L. Rev.* 662 (April 1981).

Sayer, J., "Art and Politics, Dissent and Repression: The Masses Magazine versus the Government, 1917–1918," 32 *American J. Legal History* 42 (Jan. 1988).

Trager, Robert, and Donna L. Dickerson, "Prior Restraint in High School: Law, Attitudes and Practice," 57 *Journalism Quarterly* 135 (Spring 1980).

"What Are the Limits to a School Board's Authority to Remove Books from School Library Shelves?" 1982 *Wisconsin L. Rev.* 417 (1982).

Commercial Speech

1942 *Lewis J. Valentine, Individually and as*
Police Commissioner of the City of
New York, v. F. J. Chrestensen, **316 U.S.**
52, 86 L.Ed. 1262, 62 S.Ct. 920, 1
Med.L.Rptr. 1907

Argued: March 31, 1942.

Decided: April 13, 1942.

Summary: Enunciating for the first time its "commercial speech doctrine," the Court held that the Constitution imposes no restraint on government regulation of "purely commercial advertising."

Circumstances: F. J. Chrestensen, a Floridian who moored his former Navy submarine at a state-owned pier in the East River, distributed handbills in the city streets advertising tours of his boat for a stated fee. When the police commissioner advised him to stop distributing the flyers because the activity violated the city's sanitary code, but that he might freely distribute handbills solely devoted to "information or a public protest," Chrestensen prepared a double-faced handbill. One side contained the advertisement, with the admission fee deleted, and the other a protest against the Dock Department's refusal of wharfage for his submarine. Police told Chrestensen that a protest flyer was acceptable, but that distribution of the double-faced bill was prohibited. Upon being restrained by the police, Chrestensen sought an injunction barring police interference with distribution of the newly printed advertisements. The District Court for the Southern District of New York granted an interlocutory injunction, and the Second Circuit Court of Appeals, in a divided vote, affirmed. On writ of certiorari, the Supreme Court reversed.

Opinion: Justice Owen J. Roberts, who wrote the unanimous four-page decision, said that New York City officials could stop distribution of handbills advertising tours of Chrestensen's moored submarine without violating the First Amendment. Joining in the opinion were Chief Justice Harlan F. Stone and Justices Hugo L. Black, Stanley F. Reed, Felix Frankfurter, William O. Douglas, Frank Murphy, James F. Byrnes, and Robert H. Jackson. Roberts said that the application of the city's Sanitary Code, which prohibited the distribution of "commercial and business advertising," was not an unconstitutional abridgment of the freedom of the press and of speech. The Court drew a distinction between freedom to express political views, which is protected by the First Amendment, and the freedom to advertise a commercial enterprise, which is not. The former is of public interest and the latter is for private profit. In response to Chrestensen having added a political protest to the back of his flyers to gain protection, Roberts averred that this second effort to distribute the advertisements was for the purpose of evading the prohibition of the ordinance. "If that evasion were successful, every merchant who desires to broadcast advertising leaflets in the streets need only append a civic appeal, or a moral platitude, to achieve immunity from the law's command."

Referenced Cases: *Fifth Ave. Coach Co. v. New York*, 221 U.S. 467 (1911), *Packer Corp. v. Utah*, 285 U.S. 105 (1932), *Lewis Pub. Co. v. Morgan*, 229 U.S. 288 (1913), and *Mutual Film Corp. v. Industrial Commission*, 236 U.S. 230 (1915), on distinction between commercial advertisements and protest or opinion literature respecting constitutional guaranty; *Grosjean v. American Press Co.*, 297 U.S. 233 (1936), *Thornhill v. Alabama*, 310 U.S. 88 (1940), and *Carlson v. California*, 310 U.S. 106 (1940), regarding the constitutional concept of freedom of the press; *Lovell v. Griffin*, 303 U.S. 444 (1938), *Hague v. Committee for Industrial Organization*, 307 U.S. 496 (1939), and *Schneider v. Irvington*, 308 U.S. 147 (1939), on unrestricted distribution of commercial advertisements not essential to maintaining freedom of the press; *Matson Nav. Co. v. State Bd. of Equalization*, 297 U.S. 441 (1936), and *J. E. Raley & Bros. v. Richardson*, 264 U.S. 157 (1924), regarding distinction between commercial advertisements and opinion or protest literature dictated by federal and state constitutional guaranties of press freedom; *Lawton v. Steele*, 152

U.S. 133 (1894), on courts' control of police power; *Meyer v. Nebraska*, 262 U.S. 390 (1923), *Louis K. Liggett Co. v. Baldridge*, 278 U.S. 105 (1928), *Allgeyer v. Louisiana*, 165 U.S. 578 (1897), and *New State Ice Co. v. Liebmann*, 285 U.S. 262 (1932), on discrimination against small businesses.

Further Reading:

2 *Bill of Rights Rev.* 222 (Spring 1942).
30 *Calif. L. Rev.* 655 (Sept. 1942).
11 *Int'l Juridical Assoc. Bull.* 29 (Sept. 1942).
26 *Minnesota L. Rev.* 895 (June 1942).
8 *Ohio St. L. J.* 331 (June 1942).

1943 *Mrs. Ella Jamison v. Texas*, 318 U.S. 413, 87 L.Ed. 869, 63 S.Ct. 669

Argued: Feb. 12, 1943.

Decided: March 8, 1943.

Summary: Reversed the conviction of a member of the Jehovah's Witnesses for violating an ordinance prohibiting the distribution of handbills on the street. *Valentine v. Chrestensen* (1942) held inapplicable to certain kinds of commercial religious solicitations.

Circumstances: Mrs. Jamison, a member of the Jehovah's Witnesses, was charged with distributing handbills on the streets of Dallas in violation of an ordinance prohibiting their distribution. She was convicted in the Corporation Court of Dallas and appealed to the county criminal court, where, after a trial de novo, she was again convicted and fined $5 and costs. Under Texas law she could appeal no higher, but, since the judgment upheld a municipal ordinance, the validity of which under the U.S. Constitution was challenged, the Supreme Court took jurisdiction under the Judicial Code, Section 237(a). It reversed the conviction.

Opinion: Justice Hugo L. Black wrote the opinion for the unanimous Court. He was joined by Chief Justice Harlan F. Stone and Justices Owen J. Roberts, who wrote the *Valentine v. Chrestensen* decision, Stanley F. Reed, William O. Douglas, Frank Murphy, and Robert H. Jackson. Justice Felix Frankfurter acquiesced in the Court's refusal to reconsider *King Mfg. Co. v. Augusta* (1928) because he thought that case erroneously decided, but otherwise agreed with the *Jamison* opinion. Justice Wiley B. Rutledge did not participate. Black said the Dallas ordinance denied Mrs. Jamison the freedom of press and of religion guaranteed to her by the First and 14th Amendments. "The mere presence of an advertisement of a religious work on a handbill of the sort distributed here may not subject the distribution of the handbill to prohibition." Black added that states can prohibit the use of the streets for the distribution of purely commercial leaflets, even though they may contain "a civic appeal, or a moral platitude," but they may not prohibit the distribution of handbills "in the pursuit of a clearly religious activity merely because the handbills invite the purchase of books for the improved understanding of the religion or because the handbills seek in a lawful fashion to promote the raising of funds for religious purposes."

Referenced Cases: *King Manufacturing Co. v. Augusta*, 277 U.S. 100 (1928), under which the Supreme Court takes jurisdiction on appeal from judgments sustaining the validity of municipal ordinances; *Davis v. Massachusetts*, 167 U.S. 43 (1897) and *Hague v. CIO*, 307 U.S. 496 (1939), on the power of cities to prohibit use of streets for communication of ideas; *Cox v. New Hampshire*, 312 U.S. 569 (1941), and *Chaplinsky v. New Hampshire*, 315 U.S. 568 (1942), on safety control of streets and conduct in violation of valid law; *Schneider v. Irvington*, 308 U.S. 147 (1939), on the rightful use of streets for communicating ideas; *Lovell v. Griffin*, 303 U.S. 444 (1938), regarding circumstances governing distribution of handbills on religious topics; *Cantwell v. Connecticut*, 310 U.S. 296 (1940), on unreasonably obstructing or delaying collection of funds for religious purposes; *Valentine v. Chrestensen*, 316 U.S. 52 (1942), regarding adding "civic appeal or a moral platitude" to otherwise commercial leaflets.

Further Reading:
5 *Georgia Bar J.* 70 (May 1943).

1943   ***Robert Murdock v. Pennsylvania (City of Jeannette), 319 U.S. 105, 87 L.Ed. 1292, 63 S.Ct. 870, 146 A.L.R. 81***

Argued: March 10, 11, 1943.

Decided: May 3, 1943.

Summary: Invalidated a tax on the door-to-door distribution of religious literature in the first of three separate but related rulings, decided the same day, affecting the Jehovah's Witnesses in particular and commercial speech in general.

Circumstances: Robert Murdock and seven other Jehovah's Witnesses were convicted and fined for violating a city ordinance prohibiting canvassing or soliciting for the sale of merchandise without a license for which a fee was charged. The eight, who had not obtained licenses, went door-to-door distributing religious literature and soliciting "contributions" of 25 cents for books and 5 cents for pamphlets. Each judgment was sustained by the Superior Court of Pennsylvania and their appeals were denied by the Pennsylvania Supreme Court. The state courts rejected their contention that the ordinance deprived them of freedom of speech, press, and religion guaranteed by the First Amendment. On separate writs of certiorari, the U.S. Supreme Court reversed all eight convictions together.

Opinion: Justice William O. Douglas wrote the opinion of the 5-to-4 Court, joined by Chief Justice Harlan F. Stone and Justices Hugo L. Black, Frank Murphy, and Wiley B. Rutledge. In dissent were Justices Stanley F. Reed, Owen J. Roberts, Felix Frankfurter, and Robert H. Jackson. Douglas found the case to be governed by *Jamison v. Texas* (1943) rather than *Valentine v. Chrestensen* (1942). "The constitutional rights of those spreading their religious beliefs through the spoken and printed word are not to be gauged by standards governing retailers or wholesalers of books," he wrote. "[I]t plainly cannot be said that petitioners were engaged in a commercial rather than a religious venture." Douglas noted that an itinerant evangelist, however misguided or intolerant he may be, does not become a mere book agent by selling the

Bible or religious tracts to help defray his expenses or sustain him. "The taxes imposed by this ordinance can hardly help but be as severe and telling in their impact on the freedom of the press and religion as the 'taxes on knowledge' at which the First Amendment was partly aimed."

Justice Reed, in a dissent joined by Roberts, Frankfurter, and Jackson, said that neither the church nor the press is completely free from the financial burdens of government. The affixation of a price for the religious articles turns the evangelist into a book agent, he noted. "The rites which are protected by the First Amendment are in essence spiritual—prayer, mass, sermons, sacraments—not sales of religious goods." Justice Frankfurter, separately, noted that no claim had been made that the tax restricted religious propaganda activities. He objected to the Witnesses' insistence on absolute immunity from any kind of monetary "exaction" for their occupation. "There is nothing in the Constitution which exempts persons engaged in religious activities from sharing equally in the costs of benefits to all, including themselves, provided by government." Justice Jackson joined Frankfurter's dissent.

Referenced Cases: *Reynolds v. U.S.*, 98 U.S. 145 (1878), and *Davis v. Beason*, 133 U.S. 333 (1890), regarding the sincerity of religious beliefs in constitutional law; *Chaplinsky v. New Hampshire*, 315 U.S. 568 (1942), *Cox v. New Hampshire*, 312 U.S. 569 (1941), and *Schneider v. State*, 308 U.S. 147 (1939), on states' rights to regulate special problems; *Jones v. Opelika*, 319 U.S. 103 (1943), on determining whether activity is religious or purely commercial; *Valentine v. Chrestensen*, 316 U.S. 52 (1942), and *Jamison v. Texas*, 318 U.S. 413 (1943), early commercial speech cases; *Magnano Co. v. Hamilton*, 292 U.S. 40 (1934), *Lovell v. Griffin*, 303 U.S. 444 (1938), *Largent v. Texas*, 318 U.S. 418 (1943), and *Panhandle Oil Co. v. Knox*, 277 U.S. 218 (1928), on repressive and censorial nature of taxes; *Gitlow v. New York*, 268 U.S. 652 (1925), and *Near v. Minnesota*, 283 U.S. 697 (1931), on the relationship of the 14th Amendment to the First; *Gibbons v. District of Columbia*, 116 U.S. 404 (1886), holding that religious tax exemptions depend on state constitutions or general statutes, not on federal constitution.

Further Reading:

18 *Indiana L. J.* 314 (July 1943).
41 *Michigan L. Rev.* 1197 (June 1943).

42 *Michigan L. Rev.* 163 (Aug. 1943).
28 *Minnesota L. Rev.* 133 (Jan. 1944).
22 *Texas L. Rev.* 230 (Feb. 1944).
11 *Univ. Kansas City L. Rev.* 230 (June 1943).
See also under *Martin v. Struthers,* 319 U.S. 141 (1943), and *Douglas v. City of Jeannette,* 319 U.S. 157 (1943), decided the same day.

1943 *Thelma Martin v. City of Struthers,* **319 U.S. 141, 87 L.Ed. 1313, 63 S.Ct. 862**

Argued: March 11, 1943.

Decided: May 3, 1943.

Summary: Recognizing a constitutional right to receive information, the Court struck down an ordinance banning the door-to-door distribution of literature as it applied to a Jehovah's Witness advertising a religious meeting.

Circumstances: Ms. Martin, a Jehovah's Witness, went to the homes of strangers, knocked on doors, and rang doorbells in order to distribute leaflets advertising a religious meeting. She was convicted in the mayor's court and fined $10 for violating an ordinance prohibiting such activity. The Ohio Supreme Court dismissed her appeal on the ground that "no debatable constitutional question is involved." The U.S. Supreme Court at first dismissed the appeal, thinking that the state high court meant that no constitutional question had been properly raised in accordance with Ohio procedure. On reconsideration, the Court concluded that, since a constitutional question was presented, the Ohio decision may be construed as based on the constitutional question. The Court then reversed the decision.

Opinion: Justice Hugo L. Black, joined by Chief Justice Harlan F. Stone and Justices Frank Murphy, William O. Douglas, and Wiley B. Rutledge, wrote the 5-to-4 opinion. Dissenting were Justices Stanley F. Reed, Owen J. Roberts, Felix Frankfurter, and

Robert H. Jackson. Also decided the same day were *Murdock v. Pennsylvania* and *Douglas v. City of Jeannette,* both of which concerned Jehovah's Witnesses distributing religious materials. The Court said that the ordinance infringed on the rights of individual householders to decide whether to receive information as well as on the rights of the distributor. Black wrote: "The authors of the First Amendment knew that novel and unconventional ideas might disturb the complacent, but they chose to encourage a freedom which they believed essential if vigorous enlightenment was ever to triumph over slothful ignorance." The ordinance, he said, submits the distributor to criminal punishment for annoying the person on whom he calls, "even though the recipient of the literature . . . is in fact glad to receive it." Although door-to-door distribution can be regulated, it cannot be altogether banned. It is a valuable and useful way for poorly financed groups to disseminate their ideas. But the Struthers ordinance was overbroad, and the city's objective could be realized by a law making it illegal for any person to ring the doorbell of a houseowner who had, through a sign or other means, indicated that she or he did not want to be disturbed. Justice Murphy, joined by Douglas and Rutledge, wrote separately that the right given by the First and 14th Amendments freely to practice and proclaim one's religious convictions extends to the "aggressive and disputatious as well as to the meek and acquiescent."

Justice Frankfurter, in dissent, said the Court's opinion was presumptuous. "I myself cannot say that those in whose keeping is the peace of the City of Struthers and the right of privacy of its home dwellers could not single out, in circumstances of which they have knowledge and I certainly have not, this class of canvassers as the particular source of mischief." Justice Reed, joined by Roberts and Jackson, said he could not find in "this trivial town police regulation" a violation of the First Amendment. "No ideas are being suppressed. No censorship is involved. The freedom to, teach or preach by word or book is unabridged, save only the right to call a householder to the door of his house to receive the summoner's message. The ordinance seems a fair adjustment of the privilege of distributors and the rights of householders."

Referenced Cases: *Lovell v. Griffin,* 303 U.S. 444 (1938), and *Schneider v. State,* 308 U.S. 147 (1939), on the right to distribute literature; *Jones v. Opelika,* 319 U.S. 584 (1943), and

Cantwell v. Connecticut, 310 U.S. 296 (1940), on the right to proclaim religious convictions; *Goldman v. U.S.*, 316 U.S. 129 (1942), regarding "a man's home is his castle"; *Jamison v. Texas*, 318 U.S. 413 (1943), *Largent v. Texas*, 318 U.S. 418 (1943), and *Murdock v. Pennsylvania*, 319 U.S. 105 (1943), on street distribution and a paid license; *Thornhill v. Alabama*, 310 U.S. 88 (1940), regarding narrowly drawn statutes; *Near v. Minnesota*, 283 U.S. 697 (1931), *Schenck v. U.S.*, 249 U.S. 47 (1919), and *Chaplinsky v. New Hampshire*, 315 U.S. 568 (1942), on reasonable regulation of obscenity, disloyalty, and provocatives.

Further Reading:
32 *Illinois Bar J.* 276 (March 1944).
18 *St. John's L. Rev.* 64 (Nov. 1943).
See also under *Murdock v. Pennsylvania*, 319 U.S. 105 (1943), and *Douglas v. City of Jeannette*, 319 U.S. 157 (1943), decided the same day.

1943   *Robert L. Douglas v. City of Jeannette,* 319 U.S. 157, 87 L.Ed. 1324, 63 S.Ct. 877

Argued: March 10, 11, 1943.

Decided: May 3, 1943.

Summary: Held unconstitutional a city ordinance prohibiting the solicitation of merchandise orders without a license in the last of three separate decisions affecting the Jehovah's Witnesses in particular and commercial speech in general.

Circumstances: Douglas and colleagues, Jehovah's Witnesses, brought suit in the District Court for Western Pennsylvania to restrain threatened criminal prosecution in state courts by the city of Jeannette and its mayor for violation of an ordinance prohibiting the solicitation of orders for merchandise without first acquiring a license and paying a license tax. In April 1939 the Witnesses were arrested and prosecuted. No preliminary or interlocutory injunction was granted, but the district court, following trial, held the ordinance invalid. The Third Circuit Court of Appeals sustained the jurisdiction of the district court but reversed on the merits. On writ of certiorari, the Supreme Court affirmed the judgment of the circuit court and directed the bill be dismissed.

Opinion: Chief Justice Harlan F. Stone delivered the Court's unanimous opinion. Justices Robert H. Jackson, Stanley F. Reed, and Felix Frankfurter, who had dissented in the other cases decided the same day—*Murdock v. Pennsylvania* and *Martin v. Struthers*—concurred. Justice Owen J. Roberts who had also dissented in the others, joined the Court without a separate concurrence. Justices Hugo L. Black, William O. Douglas, Frank Murphy, and Wiley B. Rutledge joined Stone in the Court's opinion in all three cases. Stone applied *Murdock* in finding the ordinance an unconstitutional abridgment of free speech, press, and religion. Therefore, "we find no ground for supposing that the intervention of a federal court, in order to secure petitioners' constitutional rights, will be either necessary or appropriate." Justice Jackson, in his lengthy agreement in *Douglas*, explained as well his dissents in *Murdock* and *Martin*, based largely on the facts in each situation. "Only the *Douglas* record gives a comprehensive story of the broad plan of campaign employed by Jehovah's Witnesses and its full impact on a living community. But the facts of this case are passed over as irrelevant to the theory on which the Court would decide its particular issue."

Referenced Cases: *Hague v. CIO*, 307 U.S. 496 (1939), on jurisdiction of U.S. district courts; *Schneider v. State*, 308 U.S. 147 (1939), and *Jamison v. Texas*, 318 U.S. 413 (1943), on guaranties of First Amendment made applicable to states by the 14th; *DiGiovanni v. Camden Ins. Assn.*, 296 U.S. 64 (1935), *Pennsylvania v. Williams*, 294 U.S. 176 (1935), and *Twist v. Prairie Oil Co.*, 274 U.S. 684 (1927), on want of equity jurisdiction; *Davis & Farnum Mfg. Co. v. Los Angeles*, 189 U.S. 207 (1903), and *Fenner v. Boykin*, 271 U.S. 240 (1926), regarding courts of equity in criminal prosecutions; *Spielman Motor Co. v. Dodge*, 295 U.S. 89 (1935), *Beal v. Missouri Pacific R. Corp.*, 312 U.S. 45 (1941), *Watson v. Buck*, 313 U.S. 387 (1941), and *Williams v. Miller*, 317 U.S. 599 (1942), on determinations of criminal liability under state law by federal court of equity based on "great and immediate" injury.

Further Reading:
See under *Murdock v. Pennsylvania*, 319 U.S. 105 (1943), and *Martin v. Struthers*, 319 U.S. 141 (1943), decided the same day.

1973 *Pittsburgh Press Company v. The Pittsburgh Commission on Human Relations*, **413 U.S. 376, 37 L.Ed.2d. 669, 93 S.Ct. 2553, 1 Med.L.Rptr. 1908**

Argued: March 20, 1973.

Decided: June 21, 1973.

Summary: Held that help-wanted ads in a newspaper were commercial speech and that an ordinance prohibiting illegal gender-designated advertising columns did not violate the newspaper's First Amendment rights.

Circumstances: The Pittsburgh Commission on Human Relations found that the Pittsburgh *Press* had violated the city's Human Relations Ordinance by placing help-wanted ads in columns captioned "Jobs—Male Interest," "Jobs—Female Interest," and "Male-Female." The commission ordered compliance and the use of a system without reference to gender. The Court of Common Pleas, Allegheny County, affirmed, and the Commonwealth Court of Pennsylvania affirmed the order as modified to allow the paper to carry ads in gender-designated columns for jobs exempt from the ordinance. The Pennsylvania Supreme Court denied review. On certiorari, the U.S. Supreme Court affirmed.

Opinion: Justice Lewis F. Powell, Jr., wrote the 5-to-4 opinion, joined by William J. Brennan, Jr., Byron R. White, Thurgood Marshall, and William F. Rehnquist. Powell said that the advertisements at issue resembled *Valentine v. Chrestensen* (1942) rather than *New York Times Co. v. Sullivan* (1964), the former a classic commercial speech and the latter a political statement traditionally protected by the Constitution. The want ads in the Pittsburgh *Press* did not comment on, as a matter of social policy, the propriety of gender preferences in employment nor did the paper criticize the enforcement practices of the Human Relations Commission, a governmental agency. The ads were merely proposals of job opportunities and thus considered "classic examples of commercial speech." The Court rejected the *Press's* contention that commercial speech should be accorded a higher level of protection than *Chrestensen* and its progeny suggest. Insisting that the exchange of information is as important in the commercial realm as in any other, the paper wanted the Court to abrogate the distinction between commercial and other speech. "Whatever the merits, however, they are unpersuasive," Powell said, because discrimination in employment is not only commercial activity but is also illegal commercial activity under the ordinance. "We have no doubt that a newspaper constitutionally could be forbidden to publish a want ad proposing a sale of narcotics or soliciting prostitutes. The illegality in this case may be less overt, but we see no difference in principle here."

In dissent, Chief Justice Warren E. Burger said that, despite the Court's efforts to decide only the narrow question, he found the holding a disturbing enlargement of the "commercial speech doctrine" begun in *Chrestensen* and a serious encroachment on press freedom. He saw the Human Relations Commission's order enforcing the ordinance as "impermissible prior restraint" and noted that protected journalism includes the right to arrange all content of the newspaper, whether news, editorials, or advertisements. Further, the paper was not blatantly involved in a criminal transaction. Justice William O. Douglas, also in a separate dissent, said commercial speech is protected by the First Amendment as is all expression unless an integral part of action. Justice Potter Stewart, joined by Douglas, said that no government agency can tell a newspaper in advance what it can print, even on its advertising pages. Justice Harry A. Blackmun dissented on essentially the same grounds. Stewart averred that so long as members of the Court see the First Amendment as no more than a set of "values" to be balanced against other "values," the First Amendment will remain in "grave jeopardy."

Referenced Cases: *New York Times Co. v. U.S.,* 403 U.S. 713 (1971), and *Grosjean v. American Press Co.,* 297 U.S. 233 (1936), on the press as essential to self-government; *Associated Press v. NLRB,* 301 U.S. 103 (1937), *Mabee v. White Plains Publish-*

ing Co., 327 U.S. 178 (1946), *Oklahoma Press Publishing Co. v. Walling*, 327 U.S. 186 (1946), *Associated Press v. U.S.*, 326 U.S. 1 (1945), *Citizen Publishing Co. v. U.S.*, 394 U.S. 131 (1969), *Branzburg v. Hayes*, 408 U.S. 665 (1972), *Lovell v. Griffin*, 303 U.S. 444 (1938), and *Martin v. Struthers*, 319 U.S. 141 (1943), on regulatory legislation from which newspapers have no special immunity; *Valentine v. Chrestensen*, 316 U.S. 52 (1942), which started the Court's commercial speech doctrine; *New York Times Co. v. Sullivan*, 376 U.S. 254 (1964), on speech not rendered commercial by mere fact that it relates to an ad; *Capital Broadcasting Co. v. Kleindienst*, 405 U.S. 1000 (1972), on prohibiting electronic media from carrying cigarette advertisements; *Near v. Minnesota*, 283 U.S. 697 (1931), and *Lorain Journal Co. v. U.S.*, 342 U.S. 143 (1951), regarding permissibility of injunctions against a newspaper; *Schenck v. U.S.*, 249 U.S. 47 (1919), on the relationship of speech to action; *Columbia Broadcasting System Inc. v. Democratic National Committee*, 412 U.S. 94 (1974), on balancing of "the competing First Amendment interests."

Further Reading:

59 *ABA J.* 1042 (Sept. 1973).

38 *Albany L. Rev.* 847 (1974).

23 *DePaul L. Rev.* 1258 (Spring 1974).

12 *Duquesne L. Rev.* 1000 (Summer 1974).

87 *Harvard L. Rev.* 153 (Nov. 1973).

48 *Tulane L. Rev.* 426 (Feb. 1974).

8 *Univ. Richmond L. Rev.* 292 (Winter 1974).

1975   *Jeffrey Cole Bigelow v. Virginia*, **421 U.S. 809, 44 L.Ed.2d 600, 95 S.Ct. 2222, 1 Med.L.Rptr. 1919**

Argued: Dec. 18, 1974.

Decided: June 16, 1975.

Summary: Held that a state antiabortion statute unconstitutionally infringed on a newspaper editor's First Amendment rights of free speech and press because a commercial advertisement was involved and conveyed information of potential interest and value to a diverse audience.

Circumstances: Bigelow, a director and managing editor of *The Virginia Weekly* of Charlottesville, was convicted in 1971 for violating a Virginia statute that made it a misdemeanor, by the sale or circulation of any publication, to encourage or prompt the procuring of an abortion, which was illegal in the state at the time. The advertisement in question announced that the Women's Pavilion in New York City would help women with unwanted pregnancies to obtain abortions, which were legal in New York. Bigelow was convicted in the Albemarle County Court. He appealed to the county circuit court and on trial de novo was again convicted. The Virginia Supreme Court affirmed on the ground that the ad was strictly commercial and not protected by the First Amendment, particularly since the ad related to the medical field. Bigelow also claimed to be the victim of overbreadth, but the Virginia court said he had no standing to rely on the hypothetical rights of those in the noncommercial zone. The U.S. Supreme Court vacated the judgment of conviction and remanded for further consideration in the light of its intervening rulings on the constitutionality of state abortion laws, 413 U.S. 909 (1973). Virginia's high court again affirmed the conviction. On second appeal to the U.S. Supreme Court, the Court reversed.

Opinion: Justice Harry A. Blackmun wrote the 7-to-2 opinion, joined by Chief Justice Warren E. Burger and Justices William O. Douglas, William J. Brennan, Jr., Potter Stewart, Thurgood Marshall, and Lewis F. Powell, Jr. Blackmun said that the advertisement for abortions in New York was more than simply one proposing a commercial transaction. "Viewed in its entirety, the advertisement conveyed information of potential interest and value to a diverse audience—not only to readers possibly in need of the services offered, but also to those with a general curiosity about, or genuine interest in, the subject matter or the law of another State and its development, and to readers seeking reform in Virginia." Moreover, Blackmun noted, the services advertised were legally available in New York. At that time abortions were not legal in Virginia. The Court chose not to decide the "precise extent to which the First Amendment permits regulation of advertising that is related to activities the state may legitimately regulate or even prohibit. Unlike the original submarine flyer in *Valentine v. Chrestensen*, 316 U.S. 52 (1942), and the help-wanted ads in *Pittsburgh Press Co. v. Human Relations Comm'n* (1973), the ad for the abortion referral service contained factual material similar to the political content of news columns and editorials. In dissent, Justice William H. Rehnquist, joined by Byron R. White, said the advertisement was directed toward the exchange of services and not the exchange of ideas, and was thereby deserving of little constitutional protection. He also thought that Virginia had a legitimate interest in regulating such advertisement to help prevent the commercial exploitation of the health needs of its citizens.

Referenced Cases: *Roe v. Wade*, 410 U.S. 113 (1973), and *Doe v. Bolton*, 410 U.S. 179 (1973), the Court's abortion decisions; *Dombrowski v. Pfister*, 380 U.S. 479 (1965), *Grayned v. City of Rockford*, 408 U.S. 104 (1972), *Gooding v. Wilson*, 405 U.S. 518 (1972), *Coates v. City of Cincinnati*, 402 U.S. 611 (1971), *NAACP v. Button*, 371 U.S. 415 (1963), and *Thornhill v. Alabama*, 310 U.S. 88 (1940), regarding the Court's First Amendment overbreadth doctrine; *Laird v. Tatum*, 408 U.S. 1 (1972), *Moose Lodge No. 107 v. Irvis*, 407 U.S. 163 (1972), *Breard v. Alexandria*, 341 U.S. 622 (1951), and *Broadrick v. Oklahoma*, 413 U.S. 601 (1973), on the individual's standing regarding the application of the overbreadth doctrine; *Pittsburgh Press Co. v. Human Relations Comm'n*, 413 U.S. 376 (1973), and *New York Times Co. v. Sullivan*, 376 U.S. 254 (1964), on First Amendment protection of commercial advertisements; *Murdock v. Pennsylvania*, 319 U.S. 105 (1943), *Thomas v. Collins*, 323 U.S. 516 (1945), and *Ginzburg v. U.S.*, 383 U.S. 463 (1966), on commercial activity alone not lessening protection; *Chaplinsky v. New Hampshire*, 315 U.S. 568 (1942), *Roth v. U.S.*, 354 U.S. 476 (1957), *Miller v. California*, 413 U.S. 15 (1973), *Gertz v. Robert Welch Inc.*, 418 U.S. 323 (1974), and *Brandenburg v. Ohio*, 395 U.S. 444 (1969), on categories of speech unprotected; *Lehman v. City of Shaker Heights*, 418 U.S. 298 (1974), *Barsky v. Board of Regents*, 347 U.S. 442 (1954), and *Packer Corp. v. Utah*, 285 U.S. 105 (1932), on states' legitimate interest in regulating commercial advertising; *Semler v. Dental Examiners*, 294 U.S. 608 (1935), *Williamson v. Lee Optical Co.*, 348 U.S. 483 (1955), and *North Dakota Pharmacy Bd. v. Snyder's Stores*, 414 U.S. 156 (1973), on the prevention of commercial advertising in health field to protect against unscrupulous practices.

Further Reading:

61 *ABA J.* 971 (Aug. 1975).
1975 *Brigham Young Univ. L. Rev.* 797 (1975).
61 *Cornell L. Rev.* 640 (April 1976).
24 *Emory L. J.* 1165 (Fall 1975).
78 *Harvard L. Rev.* 1191 (1965).
80 *Harvard L. Rev.* 1005 (1967).
83 *Harvard L. Rev.* 844 (1970).
89 *Harvard L. Rev.* 111 (Nov. 1975).
8 *Indiana L. Rev.* 890 (1975).
54 *No. Carolina L. Rev.* 468 (Feb. 1976).
42 *Tenn. L. Rev.* 573 (Spring 1975).
44 *Univ. Cincinnati L. Rev.* 852 (1975).
10 *Univ. Richmond L. Rev.* 427 (Winter 1976).

1976 *Virginia State Board of Pharmacy v. Virginia Citizens' Consumer Council, Inc.,* 425 U.S. 748, 48 L.Ed.2d 346, 96 S.Ct. 1817, 1 Med.L.Rptr. 1930

Argued: Nov. 11, 1975.

Decided: May 24, 1976.

Summary: Held truthful commercial speech protected by the First Amendment. The Court for the first time extended constitutional protections to a purely commercial advertisement.

Circumstances: A Virginia resident who was required to take prescription drugs daily and two nonprofit organizations challenged a state statute prohibiting a licensed pharmacist from advertising or promoting the prices of prescription drugs. A three-judge District Court for the Eastern District of Virginia declared that part of the law void and enjoined the pharmacy board from enforcing it. On direct appeal, the Supreme Court affirmed.

Opinion: Justice Harry A. Blackmun delivered the 7-to-1 opinion. He was joined by Chief Justice Warren E. Burger and Justices William J. Brennan, Jr., Potter Stewart, Byron R. White, Thurgood Marshall, and Lewis F. Powell, Jr. William H. Rehnquist dissented, and John Paul Stevens did not participate. The Court struck down a Virginia statute prohibiting licensed pharmacists from advertising the prices of prescription drugs. Blackmun pointed out that, although the Court in *Valentine v. Chrestensen* (1942) said "purely commercial advertising" is not protected, later decisions had tempered this view to the point that First Amendment interests in the free flow of price information could be found to outweigh the countervailing interests of the state. "If there is a kind of commercial speech that lacks all First Amendment protection . . . it must be distinguished by its content." He said that the "consumer's interest in the free flow of commercial information" may be as keen, if not keener, than his interest in the day's most urgent political debate. An advertisement, though entirely commercial, may be of general public interest. Some regulation is permissible, however, such as curbs on false or misleading advertisements or illegal advertising, as in *Pittsburgh Press Co. v. Human Relations Comm'n* (1973). Blackmun said that the free flow of information is indispensable to our predominantly free enterprise system. Chief Justice Burger, in a separate opinion, said that the Court's decision dealt largely with the state's power to prohibit pharmacists from advertising the retail price of prepackaged drugs and that different factors might govern a law regulating or prohibiting advertising by the medical or legal professions. Justice Stewart separately noted that the decision did not preclude state and federal regulation of false or deceptive advertising. Justice Rehnquist's principal objection concerned truthful advertising for products that are potentially harmful. "Current prohibitions on television advertising of liquor and cigarettes are prominent in this category."

Referenced Cases: *Valentine v. Chrestensen*, 316 U.S. 52 (1942), establishing the Court's early commercial speech doctrine; *Head v. New Mexico Board*, 374 U.S. 424 (1963), *Williamson v. Lee Optical Co.*, 348 U.S. 483 (1955), and *Semler v. Dental Examiners*, 294 U.S. 608 (1935), on advertisements of prices for various medical services; *Lamont v. Postmaster General*, 381 U.S. 301 (1965), *Kleindienst v. Mandel*, 408 U.S. 753 (1972),

Procunier v. Martinez, 416 U.S. 396 (1974), *Red Lion Broadcasting Co. v. FCC*, 395 U.S. 367 (1969), *Stanley v. Georgia*, 394 U.S. 557 (1969), *Griswold v. Connecticut*, 381 U.S. 479 (1965), *Marsh v. Alabama*, 326 U.S. 501 (1946), *Thomas v. Collins*, 323 U.S. 516 (1945), and *Martin v. Struthers*, 319 U.S. 141 (1943), on the right to receive information; *Breard v. Alexandria*, 341 U.S. 622 (1951), regarding support for a "commercial speech" exception to the First Amendment; *New York Times Co. v. Sullivan*, 376 U.S. 254 (1964), *Murdock v. Pennsylvania*, 319 U.S. 105 (1943), and *Jamison v. Texas*, 318 U.S. 413 (1943), on protection given for speech not purely commercial; *Pittsburg Press Co. v. Human Relations Comm'n*, 413 U.S. 376 (1973), regarding permissible restrictions on illegal advertisements; *Bigelow v. Virginia*, 421 U.S. 809 (1975), in which the notion of unprotected commercial speech "all but passed from the scene"; *Buckley v. Valeo*, 424 U.S. 1 (1976), *Smith v. California*, 361 U.S. 147 (1959), *Joseph Burstyn Inc. v. Wilson*, 343 U.S. 495 (1952), *NAACP v. Button*, 371 U.S. 415 (1963), *Jamison v. Texas*, 318 U.S. 413 (1943), and *Cantwell v. Connecticut*, 310 U.S. 296 (1940), regarding speech protected even though sold for profit; *NLRB v. Gissel Packing Co.*, 395 U.S. 575 (1969), *NLRB v. Virginia Electric & Power Co.*, 314 U.S. 469 (1941), and *AFL v. Swing*, 312 U.S. 321 (1941), on protection for both employer and employee in matters of dispute; *Dun & Bradstreet v. Grove*, 404 U.S. 898 (1971), and *FTC v. Procter & Gamble Co.*, 386 U.S. 568 (1967), on free flow of commercial information; *Gertz v. Robert Welch Inc.*, 418 U.S. 323 (1974), and *Konigsberg v. State Bar*, 366 U.S. 36 (1961), on untruthful speech never protected for its own sake; *Goldfarb v. Virginia State Bar*, 421 U.S. 773 (1975), *Cohen v. Hurley*, 366 U.S. 117 (1961), and *U.S. v. Oregon Medical Society*, 343 U.S. 326 (1952), on regulating lawyers and doctors; *Cammarano v. U.S.*, 358 U.S. 498 (1959), in which Justice Douglas called *Valentine v. Chrestensen* "casual, almost offhand."

Further Reading:
37 *Brooklyn L. Rev.* 617 (1971).
23 *DePaul L. Rev.* 1258 (1974).
52 *George Washington L. Rev.* 127 (1983).
80 *Harvard L. Rev.* 1005 (1967).
24 *Washington & Lee L. Rev.* 299 (1967).

1977 *Linmark Associates Inc. and William Mellman v. Township of Willingboro and Gerald Daly,* **431 U.S. 85, 52 L.Ed.2d 155, 97 S.Ct. 1614**

Argued: March 2, 1977.

Decided: May 2, 1977

Summary: An ordinance forbidding "For Sale" or "Sold" signs on private homes held in violation of the First Amendment.

Circumstances: Linmark, a New Jersey corporation, listed a piece of realty with Mellman, a real estate agent, who wanted to place a "For Sale" sign on the lawn. Prevented from doing so by the ordinance, the owner and the agent sought declaratory and injunctive relief in the District Court for the District of New Jersey, which held the ordinance unconstitutional. A divided Court of Appeals for the Third Circuit reversed, noting that Willingboro was experiencing "incipient" panic selling and that a "fear psychology" had developed. The Supreme Court reversed the Court of Appeals decision.

Opinion: Justice Thurgood Marshall, writing for the 8-to-0 Court, said: "If the Willingboro law is to be treated differently from those invalidate in *Bigelow* [1975] and *Virginia Pharmacy Bd.* [1976], it cannot be because the speakers—or listeners—have a lesser First Amendment interest in the subject matter of the speech that is regulated here. Persons desiring to sell their homes are just as interested in communicating that fact as are sellers of other goods and services." The municipality had sought to stop what it perceived as the flight of white homeowners from the racially integrated community. Although laws regulating time, place, or manner of speech are treated differently from those prohibiting speech altogether, Marshall said that the ordinance prohibited the basic marketing option available to sellers. Besides, the ordinance was not needed to assure that Willingboro remained integrated. Marshall pointed out that the town was still free to continue "the process of education" it had begun. It could give publicity, through "Not for Sale" signs, to the number of whites staying in the community, and it could create inducements to retain individuals who were thinking of selling their homes. Marshall was joined by Chief Justice Warren E. Burger and Justices William J. Brennan, Jr., Potter Stewart, Byron R. White, Harry A. Blackmun, Lewis F. Powell, Jr., and John Paul Stevens. William H. Rehnquist did not participate.

Referenced Cases: *Bigelow v. Virginia*, 421 U.S. 809 (1975), in which the Court expressed dissatisfaction with resolving First Amendment claims simply by categorizing the speech as "commercial"; *Virginia Pharmacy Bd. v. Virginia Citizens' Consumer Council*, 425 U.S. 748 (1976), that commercial speech is not wholly outside First Amendment protection; *Kovacs v. Cooper*, 36 U.S. 77 (1949), *Adderley v. Florida*, 385 U.S. 39 (1966), and *Grayned v. City of Rockford*, 408 U.S. 104 (1972), on time, place, or manner regulations on speech; *Martin v. City of Struthers*, 319 U.S. 141 (1943), *U.S. v. O'Brien*, 391 U.S. 367 (1968), and *Cohen v. California*, 403 U.S. 15 (1971), on effective marketing alternatives; *Erznoznik v. City of Jacksonville*, 422 U.S. 205 (1975), *Young v. American Mini Theatres*, 427 U.S. 50 (1976), *Police Department of Chicago v. Mosley* 408 U.S. 92 (1972), and *Tinker v. Des Moines School Dist.*, 393 U.S. 503 (1969), regarding regulating content of speech as opposed to regulating the form; *Whitney v. California*, 274 U.S. 357 (1927), on Justice Brandeis's assertion that more speech, not enforced silence, is the best remedy for the misuse of information; *Pittsburgh Press Co. v. Human Relations Comm'n*, 413 U.S. 376 (1973), on speech that is no more than a commercial transaction.

Further Reading:
63 *ABA J.* 851 (June 1977).
19 *Boston College L. Rev.* 329 (Jan. 1978).
7 *Capital Univ. L. Rev.* 271 (1977).
10 *Connecticut L. Rev.* 980 (Summer 1978).
26 *Emory L. J.* 913 (Fall 1977).
23 *Loyola L. Rev.* 1038 (Fall 1977).
24 *NY L. School L. Rev.* 225 (1978).
29 *Syracuse L. Rev.* 941 (Summer 1978).
7 *Univ. Baltimore L. Rev.* 73 (Fall 1977).
46 *Univ. Cincinnati L. Rev.* 883 (1977).
1978 *Washington Univ. L. Q.* 258 (Winter 1978).

1977 *Hugh Carey v. Population Services*
International, **431 U.S. 678, 52 L.Ed.2d**
675, 97 S.Ct. 2010, 2 Med.L.Rptr. 1935

Argued: Jan. 10, 1977.

Decided: June 9, 1977.

Summary: Held unconstitutional a state statute making it a crime to sell or distribute contraceptives to minors under age 16, for anyone other than licensed pharmacists to distribute contraceptives to persons over age 15, and for anyone to advertise or display contraceptives.

Circumstances: Population Planning Associates, Inc. (PPA), a North Carolina mail-order retailer of nonmedical contraceptives, challenged a New York statute making it a crime to sell or distribute contraceptives to minors under age 16, for anyone other than licensed pharmacists to distribute such devices to minors, and for anyone, including pharmacists, to advertise or display contraceptives. Neither its advertisements, which appeared in New York publications, nor the accompanying order forms limited its products to individuals of a certain age. When threatened with prosecution, PPA sought relief in the District Court for the Southern District of New York, where a three-judge panel held the statute unconstitutional under the First and 14th Amendments. On direct appeal, the Supreme Court affirmed, determining all provisions of the New York statute unconstitutional.

Opinion: Justice William J. Brennan, Jr., wrote the opinion, joined by Justices Potter Stewart, Thurgood Marshall, and Harry A. Blackmun and, in part, by Byron R. White, Lewis F. Powell, Jr., and John Paul Stevens. Chief Justice Warren E. Burger and Justice William H. Rehnquist dissented. The Court could not agree on the prohibition of distribution of contraceptives to minors under age 16, but seven brethren agreed that such was unconstitutional under the 14th Amendment's due process clause guaranteeing right of privacy. Brennan said that limiting the distribution of nonprescription contraceptives to licensed pharmacists "clearly imposes a significant burden on the right of the individuals to use contraceptives if they choose to do so." The justice pointed out that the right of privacy in connection with decisions affecting procreation extends to minors as well as to adults. Moreover, he said, there is substantial reason to doubt that limiting access to contraceptives will in fact substantially discourage early sexual behavior. On the First Amendment issue, Brennan noted that, where obscenity is not involved, the Court has consistently held that the fact that protected speech may be offensive to some does not justify its suppression. Justice White concurred in the result, but added that the opinion should not be regarded as declaring unconstitutional any state law forbidding extramarital sexual relations. Justice Powell added in a separate opinion that he believed that the Court's "compelling state interest" standard required of state legislation was too exacting and too severe in matters of sexual freedom. There should be more room for state regulation in this area than seems permissible under the plurality's decision, according to Powell, who added that the possibility of sexual promiscuity is no justification for a complete ban on advertising, though "carefully tailored" restrictions on commercial advertising for the young could serve legitimate state concerns. Justice Stevens, who concurred in the judgment, said separately that New York's prohibition against the distribution of contraceptives to minors denied them liberty without due process and that the prohibition of all contraceptive advertising violated the First Amendment. But he would not deny all power to minimize offensive speech. Justice Rehnquist, in dissent, said that the state could properly use its police powers to regulate the public morality of unmarried minors and that the state's restrictions of the advertising and sale of contraceptives did not significantly impair access to birth control devices of people intent on procuring them.

Referenced Cases: *Craig v. Boren*, 429 U.S. 190 (1976), *Eisenstadt v. Baird*, 405 U.S. 438 (1972), *Sullivan v. Little Hunting Park*, 396 U.S. 229 (1969), and *Barrows v. Jackson*, 346 U.S. 249 (1953), on gender-based discrimination and third-party advocacy; *Roe v. Wade*, 410 U.S. 113 (1973), *Whalen v. Roe*, 429 U.S. 589 (1977), *Loving v. Virginia*, 338 U.S. 1 (1967), *Skinner v. Oklahoma*, 316 U.S. 535 (1942), *Prince v. Massachusetts*, 321 U.S. 158 (1944), *Pierce v. Society of Sisters*, 268 U.S. 510 (1925),

Meyer v. Nebraska, 262 U.S. 390 (1923), Cleveland Board of Education v. LaFleur, 414 U.S. 632 (1974), and Planned Parenthood of Central Missouri v. Danforth, 428 U.S. 52 (1976), a cluster of constitutionally protected private choices; Poe v. Ullman, 367 U.S. 497 (1961), and Bigelow v. Virginia, 421 U.S. 809 (1975), on effects of limiting access to birth control devices; Morrissey v. Brewer, 408 U.S. 471 (1972), and Goldberg v. Kelly, 397 U.S. 254 (1970), regarding administrative inconvenience not justification for invasion of fundamental rights; In re Gault, 387 U.S. 1 (1967), Ginsberg v. New York, 390 U.S. 629 (1968), and McKeiver v. Pennsylvania, 403 U.S. 528 (1971), on state's power to regulate conduct of minors; Virginia Pharmacy Bd. v. Virginia Consumer Council, 425 U.S. 748 (1976), and Pittsburgh Press Co. v. Human Relations Comm'n, 413 U.S. 376 (1973), on protection of lawful commercial speech; Cohen v. California, 403 U.S. 15 (1971), and Brandenburg v. Ohio, 395 U.S. 444 (1969), on suppressing offensive speech and speech producing "imminent lawless action."

Further Reading:

63 ABA J. 1131 (Aug. 1977).
44 Brooklyn L. Rev. 565 (Spring 1978).
77 Columbia L. Rev. 1216 (Dec. 1977).
88 Harvard L. Rev. 1001 (1975).
16 J. Family L. 639 (April 1978).
24 Loyola L. Rev. 149 (Winter 1978).
23 NY L. School L. Rev. 777 (1978).
48 NYU L. Rev. 670 (1973).
5 Ohio Northern L. Rev. 167 (Jan. 1978).
7 Univ. California, Davis, L. Rev. 270 (1974).
29 Univ. Florida L. Rev. 1019 (Fall 1977).
126 Univ. Pa. L. Rev. 1135 (May 1978).

1977 John R. Bates and Van O'Steen v. State Bar of Arizona, 433 U.S. 350, 53 L.Ed.2d 810, 97 S.Ct. 2691, 2 Med.L.Rptr. 2097

Argued: Jan. 18, 1977.

Decided: June 27, 1977.

Summary: Extended constitutional protection to price advertising by attorneys, ruling that a state bar association's ban on truthful advertising of "routine legal services" violated the First Amendment.

Circumstances: Bates and O'Steen, licensed to practice law in Arizona, opened a legal clinic in Phoenix in 1974 specializing in routine matters for which costs could be kept low with the use of paralegals, automatic typing equipment, and standardized forms and office procedures. Two years later, in order to attract clients, they advertised in the *Arizona Republican* and listed fees for certain services. A three-member disciplinary board of the state bar suspended the lawyers for one week. On review, the Arizona Supreme Court held that the regulation was shielded from the Sherman Act and that the commercial advertising was not protected by the First Amendment. The U.S. Supreme Court reversed on the second point, concluding "that it has not been demonstrated that the advertisement at issue could be suppressed."

Opinion: Justice Harry A. Blackmun, joined by Justices William J. Brennan, Jr., Byron R. White, Thurgood Marshall, and John Paul Stevens, wrote the 5-to-4 opinion. The Court, in allowing publicity for routine services, said that attorneys may advertise their prices for such services as uncontested divorces, adoptions, simple wills, and uncontested bankruptcies. It did not recognize a right to advertise complex services, such as complicated divorces and estate settlements. First, the five-member majority affirmed the Arizona Supreme Court's determination that the Sherman Act claim by the appellant lawyers, Bates and O'Steen, did not apply to this case. Some state actions imposing price restraints may be exempt from the Sherman Act. Second, the majority reversed the Arizona high court's rejection of the appellants' First Amendment claim. Justice Lewis F. Powell, Jr., joined by Potter Stewart, concurred with the majority on the Sherman Act exemption, but dissented in the First Amendment holding. "I am apprehensive, despite the Court's expressed intent to proceed cautiously, that today's holding will be viewed by tens of thousands of lawyers as an invitation—by the public-spirited and the selfish lawyers alike—to engage in competitive advertising on an escalating basis." Chief Justice Warren E. Burger concurred and dissented along the same lines, calling the Court's opinion a "draconian solution." Justice William H. Rehnquist, too, agreed that certain state action is exempted from the Sherman Act, but he added "that the First Amendment speech provision, long a sanctuary for expressions of public importance or intellectual interest, is demeaned by invocation to protect advertisements of goods and services." He said he was unwilling to take even one step down "the slippery slope" away from *Valentine v. Chrestensen*, 315 U.S. 52 (1942).

Referenced Cases: *Williamson v. Lee Optical Co.*, 348 U.S. 483 (1955), *Semler v. Dental Examiners*, 294 U.S. 608 (1935), *Virginia Pharmacy Board v. Virginia Consumer Council*, 425 U.S. 748 (1976), and *Bigelow v. Virginia*, 421 U.S. 809 (1975), on professional advertising restrictions versus constitutional protections; *Parker v. Brown*, 317 U.S. 341 (1943), *Olsen v. Smith*, 195 U.S. 332 (1904), *Goldfarb v. Virginia State Bar*, 421 U.S. 773 (1975), and *Cantor v. Detroit Edison Co.*, 428 U.S. 579 (1976), on application of federal Sherman Act to state trade restrictions; *Cohen v. Hurlwey*, 366 U.S. 117 (1961), on regulating lawyers because they are officers of the court; *Buckley v. Valeo*, 424 U.S. 1 (1976), *New York Times Co. v. Sullivan*, 376 U.S. 254 (1964), *Smith v. California*, 361 U.S. 147 (1959), *Murdock v. Pennsylvania*, 319 U.S. 105 (1943), *Cantwell v. Connecticut*, 310 U.S. 296 (1940), *NLRB v. Gissel Packing Co.*, 395 U.S. 575 (1969), *Thornhill v. Alabama*, 310 U.S. 88 (1940), and *FTC v. Procter & Gamble Co.*, 386 U.S. 568 (1967), regarding protected commercial speech; *Broadrick v. Oklahoma*, 413 U.S. 601 (1973), *U.S. v. Raines*, 362 U.S. 17 (1960), *NAACP v. Button*, 371 U.S. 415 (1963), and *Ashwander v. TVA*, 297 U.S. 288 (1936), regarding First Amendment overbreadth doctrine; *Faretta v. California*, 422 U.S. 806 (1975), holding that most legal services may be performed legally by the citizen for himself.

Further Reading:

61 *ABA J.* 586 (1975).
20 *Arizona L. Rev.* 427 (1978).
30 *Baylor L. Rev.* 585 (Fall 1978).
77 *Columbia L. Rev.* 898 (Oct. 1977).
11 *Creighton L. Rev.* 577 (Dec. 1977).
55 *Denver L. J.* 103 (1978).
12 *Family L. Q.* 275 (Winter 1979).

21 *Howard L. J.* 903 (1978).
37 *Maryland L. Rev.* 350 (1977).
20 *New England L. Rev.* 215 (1984–85).
54 *No. Dakota L. Rev.* 253 (1977).
23 *NY L. School L. Rev.* 763 (1978).
18 *Santa Clara L. Rev.* 818 (Summer 1978).
9 *Texas Tech. L. Rev.* 295 (Winter 1977–78).
52 *Tulane L. Rev.* 414 (Fall 1978).
22 *UCLA L. Rev.* 483 (1974).
46 *Univ. Cincinnati L. Rev.* 1029 (1978).
30 *Univ. Florida L. Rev.* 479 (Winter 1978).
62 *Virginia L. Rev.* 1135 (1976).
14 *Wake Forest L. Rev.* 160 (Fall 1978).
21 1978 *Wisconsin L. Rev.* 297 (1978).

1978   *First National Bank of Boston v. Francis X. Bellotti,* **435 U.S. 765, 55 L.Ed.2d 707, 98 S.Ct. 1407, 3 Med.L.Rptr. 2105**

Argued: Nov. 9, 1977.

Decided: April 26, 1978.

Summary: Held unconstitutional a state law prohibiting corporations from spending money to influence votes on referenda except when they "materially affect" the corporation's business or assets. The Court recognized that nonmedia corporations have First Amendment rights.

Circumstances: In upholding a state criminal statute forbidding certain expenditures by banks and business corporations to influence the public vote on referenda questions, the Massachusetts Supreme Judicial Court ruled that the First Amendment rights of a corporation are limited to issues that directly and materially affect its business, property, or assets. The court rejected the constitutional claim that the statute abridged freedom of speech protected by the First and 14th Amendments. On appeal, the U.S. Supreme Court reversed, holding that the

Massachusetts statute was unconstitutional because it suppressed valuable political speech.

Opinion: Justice Lewis F. Powell, Jr. wrote the 5-to-4 opinion, joined by Chief Justice Warren E. Burger and Justices Potter Stewart, Harry A. Blackmun, and John Paul Stevens. Burger also wrote a separate concurring opinion. Justice Byron R. White, joined by William J. Brennan, Jr., and Thurgood Marshall, dissented, as did William H. Rehnquist separately. Powell said that the referendum issue before Massachusetts voters, a proposed constitutional amendment to allow the legislature to impose a graduated personal income tax, was of sufficient public concern to be "at the heart of the First Amendment's protection. It is the type of speech indispensable to decisionmaking in a democracy, and this is no less true because the speech comes from a corporation rather than an individual." Powell noted that the First Amendment includes not only the right to speak and publish, but also the right to receive information. The statute's "materially affecting" requirement amounted to an impermissible legislative prohibition of speech "based on the identity of the interests that spokesmen may represent in public debate over controversial issues and a requirement that the speaker have a sufficiently great interest in the subject to justify communication." Chief Justice Burger added that the Court had yet to resolve whether the press clause of the First Amendment confers upon the "institutional press" any freedom from government restraint not enjoyed by all others. Burger said the First Amendment does not "belong" to any definable category of persons or entities. "It belongs to all who exercise its freedoms." Justice White, in strong dissent, said there is no reason to believe that wealthy corporations would not dominate the political process if their expenditures on information dissemination received First Amendment protection. Justice Rehnquist, also in dissent, said business corporations do not have a constitutionally protected liberty to engage in political activity on matters having no material effect on their business.

Referenced Cases: *Buckley v. Valeo*, 424 U.S. 1 (1976), on whether business corporations have rights co-existent with those of "natural persons"; *Southern Pacific Terminal Co. v. ICC*, 219 U.S. 498 (1911), *Weinstein v. Bradford*, 423 U.S. 147 (1975), *Nebraska Press Assn. v. Stuart*, 427 U.S. 539 (1976), and

Spomer v. Littleton, 414 U.S. 514 (1974), on the question of mootness; *Storer v. Brown*, 415 U.S. 724 (1974), *American Party of Texas v. White*, 415 U.S. 767 (1974), *Rosario v. Rockefeller*, 410 U.S. 752 (1973), and *Dunn v. Blumstein*, 405 U.S. 330 (1972), concerning corporate expenditures for ballot questions; *Thornhill v. Alabama*, 310 U.S. 88 (1940), and *Mills v. Alabama*, 384 U.S. 214 (1966), on the First Amendment and free discussion of governmental affairs; *Pierce v. Society of Sisters*, 268 U.S. 510 (1925), *Gitlow v. New York*, 268 U.S. 652 (1925), *NAACP v. Alabama ex rel. Patterson*, 357 U.S. 449 (1958), *Stromberg v. California*, 283 U.S. 359 (1931), *DeJonge v. Oregon*, 299 U.S. 353 (1937), *Times Film Corp. v. Chicago*, 365 U.S. 43 (1961), *Kingsley Int'l Pictures Corp. v. Regents*, 360 U.S. 684 (1959), *Grosjean v. American Press Co.*, 297 U.S. 233 (1936), and *Joseph Burstyn Inc. v. Wilson*, 343 U.S. 495 (1952), on First Amendment freedoms as components of the 14th Amendment's due process clause; *Red Lion Broadcasting Co. v. FCC*, 395 U.S. 367 (1969), *New York Times Co. v. Sullivan*, 376 U.S. 254 (1964), *Associated Press v. U.S.*, 326 U.S. 1 (1945), *Stanley v. Georgia*, 394 U.S. 557 (1969), *Time Inc. v. Hill*, 385 U.S. 374 (1967), and *Winters v. New York*, 333 U.S. 507 (1948), regarding other than press access to information and ideas and the expanse of the First Amendment; *Virginia State Bd. of Pharmacy v. Virginia Citizens' Consumer Council*, 425 U.S. 748 (1976), and *Linmark Associates Inc. v. Willingboro*, 431 U.S. 85 (1977), on constitutionally protected commercial speech; *Police Dept. of Chicago v. Mosley*, 408 U.S. 92 (1972), *Bates v. Little Rock*, 361 U.S. 516 (1960), *NAACP v. Button*, 371 U.S. 415 (1963), *Thomas v. Collins*, 323 U.S. 516 (1945), *Elrod v. Burns*, 427 U.S. 347 (1976), and *Shelton v. Tucker*, 364 U.S. 479 (1960), on legislature's role in restricting public speaking on public issues; *U.S. v. Automobile Workers*, 352 U.S. 567 (1957), *U.S. v. CIO*, 335 U.S. 106 (1948), *Burroughs v. U.S.*, 290 U.S. 534 (1934), *Wood v. Georgia*, 370 U.S. 375 (1962), and *CSC v. Letter Carriers*, 413 U.S. 548 (1973), on interests of high importance of maintaining democratic process and citizen confidence in system; *Miami Herald Publishing Co. v. Tornillo*, 418 U.S. 241 (1974), on media enterprises as extensive corporations with far-reaching ownership; *Lovell v. Griffin*, 303 U.S. 444 (1938), *Pennekamp v. Florida*, 328 U.S. 331 (1946), and *Branzburg v. Hayes*, 408 U.S. 665 (1972), on liberty encompassed by press clause.

Further Reading:

64 *ABA J.* 889 (June 1978).

28 *American Univ. L. Rev.* 149 (Winter 1979).

8 *Capital Univ. L. Rev.* 575 (1979).

9 *Cumberland L. Rev.* 881 (Winter 1979).

92 *Harvard L. Rev.* 163 (Nov. 1978).

16 *Houston L. Rev.* 195 (Oct. 1978).

4 *J. Corporation L.* 460 (Winter 1979).

67 *Kentucky L. J.* 75 (1978–79).

6 *Pepperdine L. Rev.* 529 (Spring 1979).

32 *Southwestern L. J.* 1359 (Fall 1979).

13 *Suffolk Univ. L. Rev.* 124 (Winter 1979).

10 *Texas Tech L. Rev.* 315 (Winter 1978).

47 *Univ. Cincinnati L. Rev.* 661 (1979).

1979 *Utah L. Rev.* 95 (1979).

18 *Washburn L. J.* 373 (Winter 1979).

1980   *Consolidated Edison Company of New York, Inc. v. Public Service Commission of New York,* **447 U.S. 530, 65 L.Ed.2d 319, 100 S.Ct. 2326, 6 Med.L.Rptr. 1518**

Argued: March 17, 1980.

Decided: June 20, 1980.

Summary: Held in violation of the First Amendment a state public utilities order barring utilities from including inserts on controversial public issues in billing envelopes mailed to customers.

Circumstances: Consolidated Edison Company (Con Ed) inserted material, "Independence Is Still a Goal, and Nuclear Power Is Needed to Win the Battle," in its Jan. 1976 billing envelope. The insert stated Con Ed's opinion that "the benefits of nuclear power" outweigh potential risk and that nu-

clear power plants are safe, economical, and clean. In March the
Natural Resources Defense Council (NRDC) requested to enclose
a rebuttal in Con Ed's next billing. When Con Ed refused, the
NRDC asked the Public Service Commission to open the billing
envelopes to contrasting views on controversial issues of public
importance. Although it denied the request, the commission prohibited utilities from using bill inserts to discuss political issues,
drawing on its Statement of Policy on Advertising and Promotional Practices of Public Utilities issued in Feb. 1977. The Supreme Court of New York, Special Term, held the order unconstitutional, but the appellate division reversed and the state court of
appeals affirmed, finding the order a valid time, place, and manner
regulation designed to protect the privacy of a utility's customers.
On appeal, the U.S. Supreme Court reversed.

Opinion: Justice Lewis F. Powell, Jr., issued the Court's
7-to-2 opinion, joined by Chief Justice Warren E. Burger and Justices William J. Brennan, Jr., Potter Stewart, Byron R. White, and
Thurgood Marshall. Justices Marshall and John Paul Stevens also
wrote separate concurrences. In dissent was Harry A. Blackmun,
joined in pertinent part by William H. Rehnquist. Powell said that
the First Amendment, as incorporated by the 14th Amendment,
was violated by an order of the Public Service Commission of the
State of New York that prohibited the inclusion in monthly electric bills of inserts discussing controversial issues of public policy.
"The First Amendment's hostility to content-based regulation extends not only to restrictions on particular viewpoints, but also to
prohibition of public discussion of an entire topic." The justice
said that the state action was not a valid time, place, or manner
restriction, nor a permissible subject-matter regulation, nor a narrowly drawn prohibition justified by a compelling state interest.
(See the Court's similar position in *Central Hudson Gas & Electric
Corp. v. Public Service Commission of New York*, handed down
the same day.) Justice Marshall, in a separate opinion, emphasized
that the decision did not address whether the commission could
exclude the costs of bill inserts from the rate base and did not
intimate any view of the appropriateness of any allocation of such
costs that the commission might choose to make. Justice Stevens,
separately, said the censorial regulation was based on a desire to
curtail expression of a particular point of view on controversial
issues of general interest and was thus unconstitutional. Justice

Blackmun, joined in part by Rehnquist, dissented out of concern for a utility taking advantage of its monopoly power to force customers to subsidize dissemination of the utility's political views.

Referenced Cases: *Joseph Burstyn Inc. v. Wilson*, 343 U.S. 495 (1952), *Whitney v. California*, 274 U.S. 357 (1927), *Abrams v. U.S.*, 250 U.S. 616 (1919), and *Cohen v. California*, 403 U.S. 15 (1971), on First and 14th Amendment guarantees; *Thornhill v. Alabama*, 310 U.S. 88 (1940), and *Mills v. Alabama*, 384 U.S. 214 (1966), on the liberty to discuss publicly and truthfully matters of public concern; *First National Bank of Boston v. Bellotti*, 435 U.S. 765 (1978), on speech restriction not of itself unconstitutional; *Linmark Associates Inc. v. Willingboro*, 431 U.S. 85 (1977), *Virginia Pharmacy Board v. Virginia Citizens' Consumer Council*, 425 U.S. 748 (1976), *Kovacs v. Cooper*, 336 U.S. 77 (1949), *Cox v. New Hampshire*, 312 U.S. 569 (1941), and *Grayned v. City of Rockford*, 408 U.S. 104 (1972), regarding permissible limitations on speech; *Niemotko v. Maryland*, 340 U.S. 268 (1951), *Erznoznik v. City of Jacksonville*, 422 U.S. 205 (1975), *Police Department of Chicago v. Mosley*, 408 U.S. 92 (1972), on the reasonableness of time, place, and manner regulations; *Greer v. Spock*, 424 U.S. 828 (1976), and *Lehman v. Shaker Heights*, 418 U.S. 298 (1974), regarding restrictions on a military base and public transit vehicles; *New Orleans v. Dukes*, 427 U.S. 297 (1976), on regulating private behavior in the public interest; *Young v. American Mini Theatres Inc.*, 427 U.S. 50 (1976), on curtailing a particular point of view; *Abood v. Detroit Board of Education*, 431 U.S. 209 (1977), *Wooley v. Maynard*, 430 U.S. 705 (1977), and *Buckley v. Valeo*, 424 U.S. 1 (1976), on costs of utility's speech expenses.

Further Reading:
39 *Albany L. Rev.* 707 (1975).
64 *Virginia L. Rev.* 921 (1978).
See also under *Central Hudson Gas & Electric Corp. v. Public Service Commission of New York*, 447 U.S. 557 (1980), decided the same day.

1980   *Central Hudson Gas & Electric Corp. v.*
Public Service Commission of New
York, **447 U.S. 557, 65 L.Ed.2d 341, 100**
S.Ct. 2343, 6 Med.L.Rptr. 1497

Argued: March 17, 1980.

Decided: June 20, 1980.

Summary: Held a state public utilities regulation banning advertising by electric utilities in violation of the First Amendment. An electric utility cannot be prohibited from promoting the sale and use of its product, electricity. Established a four-part commercial speech test for determining constitutionality of state restrictions.

Circumstances: During a fuel shortage, the Public Service Commission of New York State ordered electric utilities throughout the state to stop advertising the use of electricity because the state system did not have enough fuel in stock to supply all customers during the winter months. But when the shortage ebbed three years later, the commission proposed to continue the ban and sought public reaction. The commission extended the ban against "promotional" ads on the grounds of the state's interest in conserving energy. "Informational" advertising was permitted. The utility company challenged the order in state court, arguing restraint of commercial speech in violation of the First and 14th Amendments. The order was upheld by the trial court and at the appellate level. The New York Court of Appeals affirmed, finding little value to advertising in "the noncompetitive market in which electric corporations operate." On appeal, the U.S. Supreme Court reversed.

Opinion: Justice Lewis F. Powell, Jr., wrote the Court's 8-to-1 opinion, joined by Chief Justice Warren E. Burger and Justices Potter Stewart, Byron R. White, and Thurgood Marshall. Justice William J. Brennan, Jr., concurred but wrote a separate opinion, as did Harry A. Blackmun, joined by Brennan, and John Paul Stevens, also joined by Brennan. William H. Rehnquist dissented. Powell said that the First Amendment's concern for commercial speech is based on the informational function of advertising. "Consequently, there can be no constitutional objection to the suppression of commercial messages that do not accurately inform the public about lawful activity. If the communication is neither misleading nor related to unlawful activity, the government's power is more circumscribed." He noted that the utility commission's ban on discussion of a controversial issue "strikes at the heart of the freedom to speak." The Court rejected the argument that utility customers are a "captive audience," suggesting that a customer can avoid unwanted bill inserts by simply transferring them from the envelope to the wastebasket. The Court moved closer than ever before to defining the level of protection for commercial speech by establishing a four-part test for courts to determine whether commercial speech may be regulated. First, a court must decide if the expression is eligible for First Amendment protection, that is, lawful and not misleading. Second, it must ask if the asserted governmental interest is substantial enough to warrant regulation of the expression. Third, if both questions receive affirmative answers, a court must determine if the regulation directly advances the asserted governmental interest. Fourth, if so, a decision is made on whether the regulation is more extensive than is necessary to serve that interest. The Court recognized the state's interest in promoting energy conservation, but concluded that the commission's order suppressed speech that did not impair the state's interest in conservation. Justice Brennan added that there was no justification for the suppression of commercial speech in an effort to influence public conduct through the manipulation of the availability of information. Justice Blackmun averred that the majority's four-part test was not the proper one to be applied, and Justice Stevens did not believe that the case involved commercial speech. Justice Rehnquist, in dissent, said that the monopoly power of a utility justified a state's wideranging supervision, that such an advertising ban fell within the scope of permissible economic regulation.

Referenced Cases: *Virginia Pharmacy Board v. Virginia Citizens' Consumer Council*, 425 U.S. 748 (1976), *Bates v. State Bar of Arizona*, 433 U.S. 350 (1977), and *Linmark Associates Inc. v. Willingboro*, 431 U.S. 85 (1977), on unwarranted governmental regulation of commercial speech; *First National Bank of Boston v. Bellotti*, 435 U.S. 765 (1978), *Friedman v. Rogers*, 440

U.S. 1 (1979), *Ohralik v. Ohio State Bar Assn.*, 436 U.S. 447 (1978), and *Pittsburgh Press Co. v. Human Relations Comm'n*, 413 U.S. 376 (1973), on information function of accurate and lawful advertising; *In re Primus*, 436 U.S. 412 (1978), and *Carey v. Population Services International*, 431 U.S. 678 (1977), on the need for carefully drawn restrictions; *West Ohio Gas Co. v. Public Utilities Comm'n*, 294 U.S. 63 (1935), regarding existence of interfuel competition; *Tobacco Institute Inc. v. FCC*, 396 U.S. 842 (1969), on more limited speech regulation; *Whitney v. California*, 274 U.S. 357 (1927), on Justice Brandeis's remedy for falsehood and fallacies, "more speech, not enforced silence"; *Brandenburg v. Ohio*, 395 U.S. 444 (1969), regarding speech that incites "imminent lawless action"; *Valentine v. Chrestensen*, 315 U.S. 52 (1942), and *Breard v. Alexandria*, 341 U.S. 622 (1951), early commercial speech cases; *Cantor v. Detroit Edison Co.*, 428 U.S. 579 (1976), on state-created monopoly status of a utility necessitating public controls; *Chaplinsky v. New Hampshire*, 315 U.S. 568 (1942), *Beauharnais v. Illinois*, 343 U.S. 250 (1952), *Roth v. U.S.*, 354 U.S. 476 (1957), and *FCC v. Pacifica Foundation*, 438 U.S. 726 (1978), on speech outside the scope of First Amendment.

Further Reading:
39 *Albany L. Rev.* 707 (1975).
83 *Harvard L. Rev.* 844 (1970).
20 *New England L. Rev.* 215 (1984–85).
743 *Northwestern Univ. L. Rev.* 372 (1979).
25 *UCLA L. Rev.* 964 (1978).
44 *Univ. Chicago L. Rev.* 205 (1976).
1976 *Univ. Illinois L. Forum* 1080 (1976).
65 *Virginia L. Rev.* 1 (Feb. 1979).

1983   *William F. Bolger v. Youngs Drug Products Corp.*, 463 U.S. 60, 77 L.Ed.2d 469, 103 S.Ct. 2875

Argued: Jan. 12, 1983.

Decided: June 24, 1983.

Summary: A unanimous Court held unconstitutional a federal postal statute prohibiting the mailing of unsolicited advertisements for contraceptives.

Circumstances: In 1979 the Postal Service, hearing allegations of an unsolicited mailing of contraceptive advertisements, informed Youngs that the proposed mailings would violate a federal statute [39 USCS Section 3001 (e) (2)], that "any unsolicited advertisement of matter which is designed, adapted, or intended for preventing conception is nonmailable matter." The service rejected Youngs' legal argument that the statute was unconstitutional. Youngs sought declaratory and injunctive relief in the District Court for the District of Columbia and the court found for the drug company. On appeal, the Supreme Court affirmed.

Opinion: Justice Thurgood Marshall, writing for himself and Chief Justice Warren E. Burger and Justices Byron R. White, Harry A. Blackmun and Lewis F. Powell, Jr., said that the statute violates the First Amendment as applied to the proposed mailings, which included information on such important public issues as family planning and venereal disease, as well as promotional advertising for commercial products. Justice William H. Rehnquist, joined by Sandra Day O'Connor, concurred separately, as did John Paul Stevens. William J. Brennan, Jr., did not participate. Marshall said that the government's interests argued in support of the law were insufficient to warrant the "sweeping prohibition" against mailing the advertisements. He concluded that, because the proscribed information may bear on one of the most important decisions parents have a right to make, the restriction on the free flow of truthful information constitutes a basic constitutional defect regardless of the strength of the government's interest. Marshall asserted that the statute goes too far by "purging all mailboxes of unsolicited material that is entirely suitable for adults." Justice Rehnquist said that, though the restriction advances weighty governmental interests, it is more extensive than is necessary. Justice Stevens said that governmental suppression of a specific point of view strikes at the core of First Amendment values. "The statute . . . censors ideas, not style. It prohibits appellee from mailing any unsolicited advertisement of contraceptives, no matter how unobtrusive and tactful; yet it permits anyone to mail unsolicited advertisements of devices intended to facilitate conception, no matter how coarse or grotesque."

Referenced Cases: *Bigelow v. Virginia,* 421 U.S. 809 (1975), *Ohralik v. Ohio State Bar Assn.,* 436 U.S. 447 (1978), *Central Hudson Gas & Electric Corp. v. Public Service Comm'n of New York,* 447 U.S. 557 (1980), *Virginia Pharmacy Board v. Virginia Citizens' Consumer Council Inc.,* 425 U.S. 748 (1976), *Police Department of Chicago v. Mosley,* 408 U.S. 92 (1972), and *Consolidated Edison Co. v. Public Service Comm'n of New York,* 447 U.S. 530 (1980), *In re R.M.J.,* 455 U.S. 191 (1982), and *Friedman v. Rogers,* 440 U.S. 1 (1979), extending First Amendment protection to commercial speech and content-based regulation; *Ginzburg v. U.S.,* 383 U.S. 463 (1966), and *Thornhill v. Alabama,* 310 U.S. 88 (1940), on irrelevance of economic motivation to commercial speech designation; *Metromedia Inc. v. San Diego,* 453 U.S 490 (1981), but misleading information disguised as public-issue information unacceptable; *Rowan v. Post Office Department,* 397 U.S. 728 (1970), on right of addressees to stop mailings of erotic material; *Cohen v. California,* 403 U.S. 15 (1971), but recipients may avoid objectionable mailings by "averting their eyes"; *H. L. v. Matheson,* 450 U.S. 398 (1981), and *Bellotti v. Baird,* 443 U.S. 622 (1979), on parents' role in sex education; *Butler v. Michigan,* 352 U.S. 380 (1957), "The level of discourse reaching a mailbox simply cannot be limited to that which would be suitable for a sandbox"; *FCC v. Pacifica Foundation,* 438 U.S. 726 (1978), on protecting children from broadcast also heard by adults; *Blount v. Rizzi,* 400 U.S. 410 (1971), and *Milwaukee Social Democratic Publishing Co. v. Burleson,* 255 U.S. 407 (1921), on First Amendment right to use mails.

Further Reading:

69 *ABA J.* 1296 (Sept. 1983).
10 *American J. L. and Medicine* 203 (Summer 1984).
22 *J. Family L.* 368 (Jan. 1984).
74 *Northwestern Univ. L. Rev.* 372 (1979).
8 *UCLA L. Rev.* 44 (1961).
14 *Univ. Baltimore L. Rev.* 367 (Winter 1985).
46 *Univ. Chicago L. Rev.* 81 (1978).
32 *Univ. Kansas L. Rev.* 679 (Spring 1984).

1986   *Posadas de Puerto Rico Associates Doing Business as Condado Holiday Inn v. Tourism Co. of Puerto Rico, 478 U.S. 328, 92 L.Ed.2d 266, 106 S.Ct. 2968, 13 Med.L.Rptr. 1033*

Argued: April 28, 1986.

Decided: July 1, 1986.

Summary: Advertising restrictions on legal gambling casinos held not in violation of freedom of speech, due process, or equal protection. Truthful commercial speech may be banned even if it concerns a legal product or service.

Circumstances: In 1948 Puerto Rico legalized certain forms of casino gambling in an effort to encourage tourism. Although local residents were not banned from using the casinos, no casino was allowed to advertise to the public of the Commonwealth. If advertising were directed at tourists rather than residents, casinos might advertise within Puerto Rico. The hotel in question had been fined several times before eventually filing suit against the Tourism Co., which administered the statute, charging that the law suppressed commercial speech in violation of the Constitution. The Supreme Court of Puerto Rico upheld the lower court's determination that the restrictions were not unconstitutional. The U.S. Supreme Court affirmed.

Opinion: Justice William H. Rehnquist wrote the Court's 5-to-4 opinion, joined by Chief Justice Warren E. Burger and Justices Byron R. White, Lewis F. Powell, Jr., and Sandra Day O'Connor. Dissenting were William J. Brennan, Jr., Thurgood Marshall, Harry A. Blackmun, and John Paul Stevens. Noting that the case involved "pure commercial speech which does no more than propose a commercial transaction," Rehnquist applied the four-part test of *Central Hudson v. Public Service Commission*, 447 U.S. 557 (1980): first, the regulation concerned a lawful activity neither misleading nor fraudulent; second, the "reduction of demand for casino gambling by the residents of Puerto Rico" was a "substantial" government interest; third, the regulation "directly advanced" the government's stated interest; and fourth, the restrictions were "no more extensive than necessary to serve the government's interest." The Court disagreed with the casino's argument that the way to reduce demand for casino gambling by residents was to promulgate more speech, not less, designed to discourage gambling. "It would surely be a Pyrrhic victory for casino owners . . . to gain recognition of a First Amendment Right . . . only to thereby force the legislature into banning casino gambling by residents altogether."

Justice Brennan, joined by Marshall and Blackmun, said that none of the differences between commercial and other speech "justify protecting commercial speech less extensively where, as here, the government seeks to manipulate behavior by depriving citizens of truthful information concerning lawful activities." Regulation of speech based on "fear that recipients will act on the information provided . . . should be subject to strict judicial scrutiny." Even if substantial government interest had been shown, Brennan found no showing that the advertising regulation would meet concerns about corruption or organized crime. Justice Stevens, also in dissent and joined by Marshall and Blackmun, focused on the operation of the Puerto Rico regulatory scheme, which he found to discriminate between publications and involve aspects of prior restraint. To the dissenters, the First Amendment does not permit suppression of truthful speech as a way of manipulating economic behavior.

Referenced Cases: *Tumey v. Ohio*, 273 U.S. 510 (1927), on dismissal for want of a substantial constitutional question; *Virginia Pharmacy Board v. Virginia Citizens' Consumer Council Inc.*, 425 U.S. 748 (1976), on commercial speech proposing a commercial transaction; *Renton v. Playtime Theatres Inc.*, 475 U.S. 41 (1986), on a city's right to preserve its quality of life; *Carey v. Population Services Int'l*, 431 U.S. 678 (1977), and *Bigelow v. Virginia*, 421 U.S. 809 (1975), on advertisements for contraceptives and an abortion clinic; *Ohralik v. Ohio State Bar Assn.*, 436 U.S. 447 (1978), and *Bolger v. Youngs Drug Products Corp.*, 463 U.S. 60 (1983), on according less protection to commercial speech; *Capital Cities Cable Inc. v. Crisp*, 467 U.S. 691 (1984), and *Metromedia Inc. v. San Diego*, 453 U.S. 490 (1981), regarding limits on the substantiality of the interests that selective regulation asserts.

Further Reading:

10 *Communications & Law* 43 (Feb. 1988).
20 *Connecticut L. Rev.* 125 (Fall 1987).
72 *Minnesota L. Rev.* 289 (Dec. 1987).
40 *Rutgers L. Rev.* 241 (Fall 1987).

Selected Bibliography

Bowers, Gregory H., and Otis H. Stephens, Jr., "Attorney Advertising and the First Amendment: Development and Impact of a Constitutional Standard," 17 *Memphis State Univ. L. Rev.* 221 (Winter 1987).

"'Common Sense and Commercial Speech," 48 *Univ. Pittsburgh L. Rev.* 1121 (Summer 1987).

"The 'Common Sense' Distinction Between Commercial and Noncommercial Speech," 14 *Hastings Constitutional L. Q.* 869 (Summer 1987).

Devore, Cameron, and Marshall Nelson, "Commercial Speech and Paid Access to the Press," 26 *Hastings L. J.* 745 (1975).

Eckinger, Robert, "First Amendment Restrictions on the FTC's Regulation of Advertising," 31 *Vanderbilt L. Rev.* 349 (March 1978).

Farber, Daniel A., "Commercial Speech and First Amendment Theory," 74 *Northwestern L. Rev.* 372 (Oct. 1979).

"First Amendment Protection for Commercial Speech: An Optical Illusion?" 31 *Univ. Florida L. Rev.* 799 (Summer 1979).

Heller, Francis, "The End of the Commercial Speech Exception—Good Riddance or More Headaches for the Courts?" 67 *Kentucky L. J.* 927 (1978–79).

Jackson, Thomas H., and John C. Jeffries, "Commercial Speech: Economic Due Process and the First Amendment," 65 *Virginia L. Rev.* 1 (Feb. 1979).

Jones, Michael E., "Celebrity Endorsements: A Cause for Alarm and Concern for the Future," 15 *New England L. Rev.* 521 (1980).

Kushner, J. A., "Freedom to Hear: The First Amendment, Commercial Speech and Access to Information," 28 *Wayne L. Rev.* 137 (1981).

Langworthy, Elisabeth A., "Time, Place, or Manner Restrictions on Commercial Speech," 52 *George Washington L. Rev.* 127 (1983).

Lively, Donald E., "The Supreme Court and Commercial Speech: New Words With an Old Message," 72 *Minnesota L. Rev.* 289 (Dec. 1987).

Prentice, R. A., "Consolidated Edison and Bellotti: First Amendment Protection of Corporate Political Speech," 16 *Tulsa L. J.* 599 (1981).

Reich, Robert B., "Preventing Deception in Commercial Speech," 54 *NYU L. Rev.* 775 (Oct. 1979).

Roberts, Barry S., "Toward a General Theory of Commercial Speech and the First Amendment," 40 *Ohio State L. J.* 115 (1979).

Schuman, Gary, "False Advertising: A Discussion of a Competitor's Rights and Remedies," 15 *Loyola Univ.–Chicago L. School* 1 (1983).

"Symposium on Commercial Speech," 46 *Brooklyn L. Rev.* 389 (1980).

Trauth, Denise M., and John L. Huffman, "New U.S. Supreme Court Philosophy on Advertising Faces Opposition," 56 *Journalism Quarterly* 540 (Autumn 1979).

"Trends in First Amendment Protection of Commercial Speech," 41 *Vanderbilt L. Rev.* 173 (Jan. 1988).

Copyright

1834   *Henry Wheaton and Robert Donaldson v. Richard Peters and John Grigg, 33 U.S. 8 Pet. 591, 8 L.Ed. 1055*

Summary: Held that statutory law, rather than common law, protects copyright in the United States. Congress, by the Copyright Act of 1790, instead of sanctioning an existing perpetual right in an author in his works, created the right secured for a limited time by the provisions of the statute. The Court also ruled that judicial decisions are the property of the public and, thus, not the subject of a copyright. However, it allowed for a reporter of judicial decisions to secure a copyright for his headnotes, statements of facts, and arguments and notations.

Circumstances: The author of 12 volumes of the reports of cases decided by the U.S. Supreme Court, known as "Wheaton's Reports," covering the years 1816 to 1827, transferred his copyright in the first volume to Matthew Carey, a Philadelphia publisher. Eventually, Donaldson acquired the copyright, which included leftover copies of the first edition of the initial volume. In 1827 Donaldson published another edition of the first volume. Donaldson, for himself and for Wheaton, who maintained a contractual interest in the work, applied for a second 14-year copyright, as stipulated by the Copyright Act of 1790. Wheaton and Donaldson sought injunctive relief upon learning of the publication of the Peters and Grigg volume, "Condensed Reports of Cases in the Supreme Court of the United States," containing decisions of the Court from its organization to the start of "Peters's Reports" in 1827. They mainly charged infringement of copyright of the first volume of "Wheaton's Reports." A bill of complaint was dismissed by the Federal Circuit Court for the Eastern District of Pennsylvania. On appeal, the Supreme Court ruled in favor of Peters and Grigg on the questions of common law copyright and the nature of the material copyrighted, but remanded the case for a jury determination of the facts.

Opinion: Justice John McLean, writing for the Court, first challenged the traditional common law protection, which allowed for perpetual and exclusive property in the future publication of a work. "That every man is entitled to the fruits of his own labor must be admitted; but he can enjoy them only except by statutory provision under the rules of property, which regulate society, and which define the rights of things in general." Asserting that there can be no common law of the United States, McLean averred that such law could be made a part of the federal system only by legislative adoption. He noted Congress' right, empowered by the Constitution, to grant property rights for "limited times." With legislated protection the primary, if not only, secured right, the Court remanded the case to determine compliance with the federal law. The Court was unanimous in the opinion that no reporter has any copyright in the written opinion of courts, nor can judges confer any such right. Justices Smith Thompson and Henry Baldwin dissented. Thompson, in recognizing the common law right of authors, argued that the debate over common law versus legislated law misses the point. "Upon the whole, in whatever light this case is viewed, whether as a common law right or depending on the act of Congress, I think the appellants are entitled to the remedy sought by the bill." Justice Baldwin preferred the case to be decided solely on the basis of Wheaton's compliance with the federal law regarding renewal of his copyright.

Referenced Cases: *Baker v. Taylor*, 2 Blatchf. 82 (1848), establishing the principle that under copyright laws a title is not perfected without strict compliance to provisions of the statute; *Little v. Gould*, 2 Blatchf. 165 (1851), on judicial decisions as property of the public and not the subject of copyright; *Miller v. Taylor*, 4 Burr. 2303 (1769), regarding English common law governing "exclusive property"; Chief Justice John Marshall on framers of the Constitution referring to common law, 12 Wheat. 653; *Houston v. Moore*, 5 Wheat. 48 (1820), on common law rights as "enforced" by states and "secured" by federal government, concurrent power; *U.S. v. Worrall*, 1 Dall. 384 (1788), regarding common law in American colonies; *University v. Beyer*, 16 East. 316 (1812), and *Postmaster-General v. Early*, 12 Wheat. 136 (1827), on application of Copyright Act of 1802; *Butterworth v. Robinson*, 5 Vesey 709 (1801), regarding fair abridgment of copyright.

Further Reading:
Niles' Weekly Register 319–20 (July 2, 1831).
Westminster Review 187–97 (Jan. 1837).
Western L. J. 97–108 (Dec. 1847).
American L. Register 129–36 (Jan. 1855).
American L. Rev. 16–38 (Oct. 1875).
3 *Kansas L. J.* 242 (May 29, 1886).

1880 *William C. M. Baker v. Elizabeth Selden*, 101 U.S. 99, 25 L.Ed. 841

Argued: Dec. 2, 3, 1879.

Decided: Jan. 19, 1880.

Summary: In this early fair use case, the Court distinguished between facts and ideas, which are not the proper subject of copyright law, and their unique expression, which is copyrightable.

Circumstances: In 1859, Charles Selden secured copyright for his book, "Selden's Condensed Ledger, or Book-keeping Simplified," which explained a peculiar system of bookkeeping. He also obtained copyright in 1860 and 1861 for several other books on his system. A descendant, Elizabeth Selden, charged that Baker's account books, using substantially the same ruled lines and headings, violated Selden's exclusive right to the system. The legal question came down to this: whether the exclusive property in a system of book-keeping can be claimed, under the law of copyright, by means of a book in which that system is explained.

Opinion: In reversing the Circuit Court for the Southern District of Ohio, Justice Joseph P. Bradley, writing for the Court, ruled that the mere copyright of Charles Selden's published book on bookkeeping "did not confer upon him the exclusive right to make and use account-books, ruled and arranged as designated by him and described and illustrated in said book." Bradley said that "a system of ruling books in which accounts are kept" is not the subject of copyright. "It is a contribution to useful mechanical art, not to literature. It conveys no thought, gives no information, expresses no idea. It is a mechanical process of ruling, which any stationer's clerk could perform with simple pen and ruler." Although Selden's ruled lines were held not to be the subject of copyright, the Court said they may be protected as an invention under patent law. In its decision, the Court relied on the 1790 federal copyright statute, amended in 1802 and 1831, which states: "The literary property intended to be protected by the Act is not to be determined by the size, form or shape in which it makes its appearance, but by the subject-matter of the work." In establishing fair use as a limitation copyright, the Court said: "The very subject of publishing a book on science or the useful arts is to communicate to the world the useful knowledge which it contains. But this object would be frustrated if the knowledge could not be used without incurring the guilt of piracy of the book."

Referenced Cases: None in text.

Further Reading:
American L. Rev. 453–67 (April 1869).
Chicago Legal News 272 (April 24, 1880).
Niles' Weekly Register 188–89 (May 14, 1831).
Pittsburgh Legal J. 417–19 (June 29, 1881), 427–29 (July 6, 1881).
Publishers Weekly 43 (July 11, 1874).
Scribner's Monthly 897–99 (Oct. 1878).
68 *Univ. Pa. L. Rev.* 215 (1920).
4 *Virginia L. Rev.* 385 (1917).

Note: This case introduced the "idea-expression identity" exception to copyrightability. It denies copyright if there is literal, or substantial, identity between the idea and the manner of expression. The notion is that copyright should not create a monopoly on an idea. This mandate requires that if there is only one or a very limited number of ways to express an idea, copyright is denied in order to preserve the free use and exchange of ideas. The distinction between process and description (as well as the idea-expression identity theme) was first articulated by the Supreme Court in *Baker*. Although *Baker* has been criticized, it has had a lasting impact on standards of copyright and infringement. The case has been applied to instruction sets for games and contests. Copyright does not protect a method of play (process) but may protect the manner in which that method is described.

1903   *George Bleistein, John W. Bridgman, John A. Rudolph, Ansley Wilcox, Gerritt B. Lansing, and Edwin Fleming, Doing Business Under the Name of the Courier Company and the Courier Lithographing Company v. Donaldson Lithographing Company, 188 U.S. 239, 47 L.Ed. 460, 23 S.Ct. 298*

Argued: Jan, 13, 14, 1903.

Decided: Feb. 2, 1903.

Summary: Circus posters, though common and mundane, are copyrightable if original works.

Circumstances: The alleged copyright infringement consisted of copying in reduced size three chromolithographs prepared by employees of Courier Co. and Courier Lithographing Co. for advertising a circus. One depicted a ballet scene, the second a number of men and women performing on bicycles, and the third showed groups of men and women whitened to represent statues. Each had been properly copyrighted. The Circuit Court for the District of Kentucky ruled for the defendant on the ground that chromolithographs were not protected by copyright law. The Court of Appeals for the Sixth Circuit sustained the ruling. On writ of error, the Supreme Court reversed both judgments and remanded for a new trial to determine whether the pictures were copyrighted before publication.

Opinion: Justice Oliver Wendell Holmes, writing for the 7-to-2 Court, said: "A picture is none the less a picture, and none the less a subject of copyright, that it is used for an advertisement. And if pictures may be used to advertise soap, or the theatre, or monthly magazines, as they are, they may be used to advertise a circus." Courts have uniformly disclaimed the right to act as literary or art critic when applying copyright law. Holmes wrote: "It would be a dangerous undertaking for persons trained only to the law to constitute themselves final judges of the worth of pictorial illustrations, outside of the narrowest and most obvious limits." Holmes was joined by Chief Justice Melville W. Fuller and Justices David J. Brewer, Henry B. Brown, Edward D. White, Rufus W. Peckham, and William R. Day. In dissent, John M. Harlan, joined by Joseph McKenna, wrote: "The clause of the Constitution giving Congress power to promote the progress of science and useful arts . . . does not, as I think, embrace a mere advertisement of a circus."

Referenced Cases: *Burrow-Giles Lithographic Co. v. Sarony*, 111 U.S. 53 (1884), and *Trade-Mark Cases*, 100 U.S. 82 (1879), on the kinds of works covered by copyright law; *Higgins v. Kueffel*, 140 U.S. 428 (1891), regarding limitations on the right to copyright prints, cuts, or engravings; *Martinetti v. Maguire*, 1 U.S. Abb. 356 (1867), holding that copyright law does not protect what is "immoral in its tendency"; *Belford, C. & Co. v. Scribner*, 144 U.S. 488 (1892), on registering copyright.

Further Reading:
None indexed.

1918   *International News Service v.*
             Associated Press, **248 U.S. 215,**
             63 L.Ed. 211, 39 S.Ct. 68, 2 A.L.R. 293

Argued: May 2, 3, 1918.

Decided: Dec. 23, 1918.

Summary: Though an unfair competition case, the Court made mention of the fact that the news element of a literary production is not the creation of the writer but is a report of matters that ordinarily are publici juris—the history of the day. On the question of unfair competition, or misappropriation, the Court affirmed an injunction against taking the news collected by one news agency and transmitting it by another agency for commercial use.

Circumstances: The Associated Press (AP) accused the International News Service (INS), a rival news agency owned by William Randolph Hearst, of pirating news from its wire service for redistribution to its own customers. The AP charged that the INS had bribed AP employees to gain access to news before publication by AP member newspapers and that the INS had copied news from bulletin boards and from early editions of papers that carried AP dispatches. The INS admitted lifting AP stories from newspapers and from AP bulletin boards, but reasoned that it had no other way of obtaining news from allied nations during the early days of World War I since INS reporters had been barred from those countries because of pro-German news and editorials in Hearst-owned newspapers. In reviewing the District Court for the Southern District of New York's modified decree granting a preliminary injunction that allowed some relief for both parties, the Second Circuit Court of Appeals held that the AP was entitled to an injunction to restrain unfair competition. The Supreme Court affirmed.

Opinion: Justice Mahlon Pitney, in considering the general question of property in news matter, noted that it is necessary to recognize the dual character of news—between the substance of the information and the particular words in which the writer has communicated it. He said that the framers of the Constitution did not intend to confer upon one who might happen to be the first to report a historic event the exclusive right for any period to spread the knowledge of it. Beyond the copyright aspect, however, Pitney said the process used by the INS to acquire AP news accounts was "an unauthorized interference with the normal operation" of the AP's legitimate business "precisely at the point where the profit is to be reaped." As with the law of trusts, "he who has fairly paid the price should have the beneficial use of the property." The Court affirmed the court of appeals' review of the granting of the injunction by the district court. Justice John H. Clarke took no part in the 7-to-1 decision. Justice Oliver Wendell Holmes, in a separate opinion, defined "unfair trade" in the use of words as a competitor in business using the words in such a way as to convey a misrepresentation that materially injures the person who first used them, by appropriating credit of some kind that the first user has earned. "Fresh news is got only by enterprise and expense."

Justice Louis D. Brandeis, in dissent, disputed the notion that unfair competition was the applicable offense, since neither fraud nor breach of contract had been committed. "Such taking and gainful use of a product of another which, for reasons of public policy, the law has refused to endow with the attributes of property, does not become unlawful because the product happens to have been taken from a rival and is used in competition with him." He said courts are ill-equipped to determine limitations on any property right in news.

Referenced Cases: *Hitchman Coal & Coke Co. v. Mitchell*, 245 U.S. 229 (1917), on fair business practices; *In re Sawyer*, 124 U.S. 200 (1888), on the concerns of a court of equity; *Truax v. Raich*, 239 U.S. 33 (1915), regarding the rights to acquire and guard property; *Board of Trade v. Christie Grain & Stock Co.*, 198 U.S. 236 (1905), on the collection and confidential communication of price quotations and dealings; *Howe Scale Co. v. Wyckoff, Seamans & Benedict*, 198 U.S. 118 (1905), regarding the characteristics of unfair competition; *Hunt v. New York Cotton Exch.*, 205 U.S. 322 (1907), on general property right in price quotations; *Dr. Miles Medical Co. v. John D. Park & Sons Co.*, 220 U.S. 373 (1911), on trade secrets; *White-Smith Music Co. v. Apollo Co.*, 209 U.S. 1 (1908), and *Kalem Co. v. Harper Bros.*, 222 U.S. 55 (1911), on the form and sequence in which knowledge, truths, ideas, or emotions are expressed; *Hanover Star Milling Co. v. Metcalf*, 240 U.S. 403 (1916), regarding the fraudulent representation by word or act of another's goods; *Delaware & H. Canal Co. v. Clark*, 13 Wall. 311 (1872), and *Elgin Nat. Watch Co. v. Illinois Watch Co.*, 179 U.S. 665 (1901), "He who makes a city known through his product must submit to sharing the resultant trade with others who, perhaps for that reason, locate there later"; *Brown Chemical Co. v. Meyer*, 139 U.S. 540 (1891), *Donnell v. Herring-Hall-Marvin*

Safe Co., 208 U.S. 267 (1908), *Waterman Co. v. Modern Pen Co.*, 235 U.S. 88 (1914), and *Saxlehner v. Wagner*, 216 U.S. 375 (1910), holding that "One bearing a name made famous by another is permitted to enjoy the unearned benefit which necessarily flows from such use, even though the use proves harmful to him who gave the name value."

Further Reading:

4 *Cornell L. Q.* 223 (June 1919).
32 *Harvard L. Rev.* 566 (March 1919).
13 *Illinois L. Rev.* 708 (April 1919).
4 *Virginia L. Register* 847 (March 1919).
28 *Yale L. J.* 387 (Feb. 1919).

1954 *Emanuel L. Mazer and William Endicter, Doing Business as June Lamp Manufacturing Co. v. Benjamin Stein and Rena Stein, Doing Business as Reglor of California,* 347 U.S. 201, 98 L.Ed. 630, 74 S.Ct. 460

Argued: Dec. 3, 1953.

Decided: March 8, 1954.

Summary: In a decision that reviews the development of copyright coverage generally, the Court held that statuettes, though intended for practical use, are "works of art" as defined by the Copyright Act of 1870. The decision underscores the economic philosophy behind copyright law.

Circumstances: The Steins obtained copyrights for statuettes of male and female dancing figures, intended for use as bases for table lamps, with wiring, sockets, and shades. The statuettes were manufactured from original clay model sculpture, from which a mold for casting copies was made. The statuettes, which alone were registered as "works of art" with the Copyright Office, were sold both as lamp bases and as statuettes. Mazer and

Endicter, without authorization, copied the statuettes and embodied them in lamps for sale. On appeal, they questioned the validity of a copyright of a work of art for "mass" production—that is, industrial reproduction of the protected article. This case is the leading one in the copyrightable subject matter area called "utilitarian aspects of useful articles." With it, the Court constitutionalized that part of copyright law which draws a distinction between works of "applied art," protected by copyright, and "industrial designs," unprotected by copyright.

Opinion: Justice Stanley F. Reed, writing for seven members of the Court, affirmed the Fourth Circuit Court of Appeals' reversal of a dismissal by the Federal District Court for Maryland of a charge of copyright infringement. Reed said that the practice of the Copyright Office, under the 1870 and 1874 acts and before the 1909 act, was to allow registration "as works of the fine arts" of articles of the same character as those of the Steins. He quoted from the Copyright Regulations, which state that the law protects artistic efforts "notwithstanding they may afterwards be utilized for articles of manufacture." Further: "Unlike a patent, a copyright gives no exclusive right to the art disclosed; protection is given only to the expression of the idea—not the idea itself. Absent copying there can be no infringement of copyright." Reed emphasized that artistic articles are protected in "form but not their mechanical or utilitarian aspects." According to *U.S. v. Paramount Pictures* (1947), "The copyright law, like the patent statutes, makes reward to the owner a secondary consideration." Justice William O. Douglas, in a separate opinion joined by Hugo L. Black, urged reargument on the ground that it is still not clear, in the constitutional sense, whether articles such as statuettes are indeed "writings" within the meaning of the law.

Referenced Cases: *Burrow-Giles Lithographic Co. v. Sarony*, 111 U.S. 53 (1884), on the tangible expression of ideas; *Gorham Mfg. Co. v. White*, 14 Wall. 511 (1872), on patents as protection against monopoly; *Baker v. Selden*, 101 U.S. 99 (1880), on the limits of copyright protection; *U.S. v. Paramount Pictures*, 334 U.S. 131 (1947), regarding the secondary nature of the owner's reward in copyright and patent law; *Bleistein v. Donaldson Lithographing Co.*, 188 U.S. 239 (1903), on "pictorial illustrations"; and *F. W. Woolworth Co. v. Contemporary Arts Inc.*, 344 U.S. 228

(1952), regarding the constitutional range of meaning of "writings" in the field of art.

Further Reading:
43 *Calif. L. Rev.* 791 (Dec. 1955).
67 *Harvard L. Rev.* 1044 (April 1954).
98 *L. Ed.* 644 (1953).
52 *Michigan L. Rev.* 33 (Nov. 1958).
5 *Tax Law Rev.* 361 (March 1950).

1968   *Fortnightly Corp. v. United Artists Television, Inc.,* 392 U.S. 390, 20 L.Ed.2d 1176, 88 S.Ct. 2084

Argued: March 13, 1968.

Decided: June 17, 1968.

Summary: Because community antenna television (CATV) systems do not "perform" the programs they receive and retransmit to customers, the Court held that any such use of over-the-air copyrighted broadcasts did not constitute infringement by the CATV operator.

Circumstances: Fortnightly owned and operated CATV systems in West Virginia, where, because of hilly terrain, most residents could not receive broadcasts from distant stations by ordinary rooftop antennas. When the suit was filed in 1960, Fortnightly carried programs from five stations and charged a flat monthly rate regardless of the amount of television watched. United Artists, in its infringement suit, said it held copyrights on several motion pictures, some of which it had licensed the stations to air, Fortnightly not among them.

Opinion: The Court's 5-to-1 opinion, written by Justice Potter Stewart, joined by Chief Justice Earl Warren and Justices William J. Brennan, Jr., Hugo L. Black, and Byron R. White, held that CATV systems are akin to television viewers who simply receive performances from over-the-air broadcasts. "Broadcasters perform. Viewers do not perform." By such logic, the Court found nonapplicable Section 1 of the 1909 Copyright Act, which gave the copyright owner the exclusive right to control the "public performances" of his work. "The function of CATV systems has little in common with the function of broadcasters. Broadcasters select the programs to be viewed; CATV systems simply carry, without editing, whatever programs they receive." The Court declined an invitation from the Solicitor General to render a compromise designed to accommodate various competing considerations of copyright, communications, and antitrust policy. "That job is for Congress," Stewart said. "We take the Copyright Act of 1909 as we find it." The Court reversed the ruling in favor of the copyright holder by the District Court for the Southern District of New York and affirmed by the Court of Appeals for the Second Circuit.

Justice Abe Fortas dissented, saying the case "calls not for the judgment of Solomon but for the dexterity of Houdini" and suggesting that the majority had simplified a technical problem not foreseen by lawmakers who drafted the 1909 law. He argued that the Court had abandoned precedent in defining "perform" and that its holding may have disruptive consequences outside the area of CATV. Justices William O. Douglas, Thurgood Marshall, and John M. Harlan did not participate.

Referenced Cases: The decision was based on the Court's interpretation of the Copyright Act of 1909—Title 17 USC Section 1. Also: *White-Smith Music Publishing Co. v. Apollo Co.,* 209 U.S. 1 (1908), on defining "perform" in copyright law; *Buck v. Jewell-LaSalle Realty Co.,* 283 U.S. 191 (1931), on the "performed" test—"How much did the [petitioner] do to bring about the viewing and hearing of a copyrighted work?"

Further Reading:

18 *American Univ. L. Rev.* 644 (June 1969).
10 *Boston College Industrial & Commercial L. Rev.* 459 (Winter 1969).
16 *Bulletin Copyright Soc.* 157 (Feb. 1969).
1 *Connecticut L. Rev.* 401 (Dec. 1968).
36 *George Washington L. Rev.* 672 (March 1968).
80 *Harvard L. Rev.* 1514 (1967).

16 *Howard L. J.* 553 (Spring 1971).
47 *No. Carolina L. Rev.* 914 (June 1969).
52 *Virginia L. Rev.* 1505 (1966).

1973   *Donald Goldstein, Ruth Koven, and Donald Koven v. California,* **412 U.S. 546, 37 L.Ed.2d 163, 93 S.Ct. 2303**

Argued: Dec. 13, 1972.

Decided: June 18, 1973.

Summary: A state statute prohibiting the unauthorized duplication of sound recordings ("record piracy") held not in violation of the copyright and supremacy clauses of the U.S. Constitution.

Circumstances: Goldstein and the Kovens were charged with having copied, between April 1970 and March 1971, several musical performances from commercially sold recordings without the permission of the owner of the master record or tape. The pirated tapes, with labels stating the performance and the artists, were then distributed to retail outlets in competition with the original recordings. No payments were made to the artists nor to others responsible for producing the original recordings. The California statute forbids such activity, but copyright protection is provided solely for the specific expressions on the master record or tape. No limitation is placed on the use of the music, lyrics, or arrangement employed in making the master recording. A state court convicted and the Appellate Department of the Superior Court of California for the County of Los Angeles sustained the validity of the statute. On certiorari, the U.S. Supreme Court affirmed.

Opinion: Chief Justice Warren E. Burger, joined by Justices Potter Stewart, Byron R. White, Lewis F. Powell, Jr., and William H. Rehnquist, wrote for the Court that, since sound recordings were not part of the 1909 Copyright Act at the time

Goldstein et al. were accused of violating the California statute, states could protect those works not specifically noted in the federal law. (The 1976 act includes "sound recordings.") But even if Congress intended such an extension of protection, Burger noted, the copyright clause of the Constitution does not express or infer all power to grant copyright protection exclusively in the federal government. "Nor does the Constitution expressly provide that such power shall not be exercised by the States." In alluding to James Madison's call, in Federalist Paper No. 43, for a national system of law, Burger reasoned that, although the copyright clause recognizes the potential benefits of a national system, "it does not indicate that all writings are of national interest or that state legislation is, in all cases, unnecessary or precluded." The decision may be viewed as an affirmation of states' rights generally, for the chief justice noted that unprohibited tape piracy and record piracy "may adversely affect . . . a large industry in California."

In dissent, Justice William O. Douglas, joined by William J. Brennan, Jr., and Harry A. Blackmun, said that the constitutional provision authorizing Congress to pass such laws was to establish a uniform national system and that states should not be allowed to encroach on federal patent or copyright law. Also in dissent, Justice Thurgood Marshall, joined by Brennan and Blackmun, said that, in enacting copyright laws, Congress' failure to enumerate sound recordings meant that it believed that free competition should prevail in this area without any state regulation.

Referenced Cases: *Sears, Roebuck & Co. v. Stiffel Co.*, 376 U.S. 225 (1964), and *Compco Corp. v. Day-Brite Lighting*, 376 U.S. 234 (1964), on congressional intention regarding the establishment of a uniform national law to protect original writings; *Cooley v. Board of Wardens*, 12 How. 299 (1852), regarding congressional power to regulate commerce as "compatible with the existence of a similar power in the States"; *Hines v. Davidowitz*, 312 U.S. 52 (1941), on state laws as obstacles to the objectives of Congress; *Burrow-Giles Lithographic Co. v. Sarony*, 111 U.S. 53 (1884), on "author" as "originator," "he to whom anything owes its origin"; *Trade-Mark Cases*, 100 U.S. 82 (1879), on "writings" as "any physical rendering of the fruits of creative intellectual or aesthetic labor"; *White-Smith Music Publishing Co. v. Apollo Co.*, 209 U.S. 1 (1908), on "copies" of copyrighted compositions as infringement; *Rice v. Santa Fe Elevator Corp.*, 331 U.S. 218

(1947), on congressional occupation of the field of copyright protection to preempt all comparable state action; *Cleveland v. U.S.*, 329 U.S. 14 (1946), on congressional failure to act as inferring affirmative conclusions.

Further Reading:

74 *Columbia L. Rev.* 960 (June 1974).
23 *DePaul L. Rev.* 791 (Winter 1974).
25 *Hastings L. J.* 1196 (April 1974).
22 *UCLA L. Rev.* 1022 (June 1975).
1973 *Utah L. Rev.* 851 (Winter 1973).
31 *Washington & Lee L. Rev.* 604 (Fall 1974).

Note: Primarily at issue was Section 653(h) of the California Penal Code, which proscribed "record piracy" or "tape piracy" as violative of the Constitution's "Copyright Clause" (Art. I, Sec. 8, Cl. 8) and the federal Copyright Act of 1909 (17 USCS). The 1909 act did not include sound recordings, but amendments enacted in 1971 allowed for copyright protection of sound recordings "fixed, published and copyrighted" on and after Feb. 15, 1972, and before Jan. 1, 1975. The revisions were not to be applied retroactively nor to affect prosecutions under a state statute for piracy of recordings fixed prior to Feb. 15, 1972, the effective date of the 1971 amendments. Before *Goldstein*, state and federal courts generally had classified sound recordings as *unpublished* works on the belief that they were not copies of musical compositions. As unpublished works, they could be protected by state law or common law.

1974 *Teleprompter Corp. et al. v. Columbia Broadcasting System, Inc. et al. and CBS et al. v. Teleprompter et al., 415 U.S. 394, 39 L.Ed.2d 415, 94 S.Ct. 1129*

Argued: Jan. 7, 1974.

Decided: March 4, 1974.

Summary: The Court affirmed and extended its decision in *Fortnightly Corp. v. United Artists Television, Inc.* (1968), holding that irrespective of the distance from the broadcasting station, reception and transmission of its signals by a cable television (CATV) system does not constitute a "performance" of a copyrighted work.

Circumstances: Several creators and producers of copyrighted television programs claimed that Teleprompter and its subsidiary, Conley Electronics Corp., CATV owners and operators, infringed their copyrights by intercepting and rechanneling these programs to paying subscribers, especially the importation of distant signals. The district court dismissed the complaint on the ground that the cause of action was barred by the Supreme Court's ruling in *Fortnightly*. When the subsequent appellate decision, affirming in part and reversing in part, reached the Supreme Court on certiorari, Justice Potter Stewart made this final observation: "[These] shifts in current business and commercial relationships, while of significance with respect to the organization and growth of the communications industry, simply cannot be controlled by means of litigation based on copyright legislation enacted more than half a century ago, when neither broadcast television nor CATV was yet conceived. Detailed regulation of these relationships, and any ultimate resolution of the many sensitive and important problems in this field, must be left to Congress."

Opinion: Justice Potter Stewart wrote the Court's 6-to-3 opinion, joined by Justices William J. Brennan, Jr., Byron R. White, Thurgood Marshall, Lewis F. Powell, Jr., and William H. Rehnquist. Dissenting were Chief Justice Warren E. Burger and Justices William O. Douglas and Harry A. Blackmun. Stewart, who also wrote the Court's opinion in *Fortnightly*, said that a CATV system importing "distant" signals does not procure programs and propagate them to the public, since it is not engaged in converting the sights and sounds of an event or a program into electronic signals available to the public. "The electronic signals it receives and rechannels have already been 'released to the public' even though they may not be normally available to the specific segment of the public served by the CATV system." Stewart argued that by extending the range of viewability, CATV does not interfere in any traditional sense with the copyright holder's means of extracting recompense for his creativity or labor. The District Court for the Southern District of New York had dismissed the complaint brought by creators and producers of televised programs for CBS. The Court of Appeals for the Second Circuit affirmed in part and reversed in part. It determined that reception and retransmission of distant signals amounted to a "performance" and, thus, constituted copyright infringement. The Supreme Court reversed. It did not agree with CBS's contention that irrespective of the distance from the broadcasting station, the reception and retransmission of its signal constitute a performance. Further, the Court affirmed the appellate court judgment that, where the signal was already in the community and easily received, the CATV system merely enhanced the reception. Justice Blackmun would not have reversed the court of appeals. Justice Douglas, joined by Chief Justice Burger, believed that infringement takes place when CATV imports remote signals and that future interpretations of the Copyright Act relative to CATV should be left to Congress.

Referenced Cases: *Fortnightly Corp. v. United Artists Television Inc.*, 392 U.S. 390 (1968), regarding grounds for the district court's dismissal; *U.S. v. Southwestern Cable Co.*, 392 U.S. 157 (1968), on a description on CATV operations; *Fox Film Corp. v. Doyal*, 286 U.S. 123 (1932), on the benefits derived by the public from the labors of authors; *Buck v. Jewell-LaSalle Realty Co.*, 283 U.S. 191 (1931), on Justice Louis D. Brandeis's unanimous opinion for the rights of copyright holders; *Mazer v. Stein* 347 U.S. 201 (1954), regarding "encouragement" of copyright to the production of literary artistic works of lasting societal benefit; *U.S. v. Midwest Video Corp.*, 406 U.S. 649 (1972), on the need for the re-examination of statutes with CATV in mind.

Further Reading:
25 *Baylor L. Rev.* 637 (Fall 1973).
22 *Bulletin Copyright Soc.* 10 (Oct. 1974).
70 *Columbia L. Rev.* 837 (1970).
79 *Harvard L. Rev.* 366 (1965).
25 *Hastings L. J.* 1507 (May 1974).
35 *Ohio State L. J.* 974 (1974).
27 *Oklahoma L. Rev.* 39 (Winter 1974).
5 *Univ. Toledo L. Rev.* 133 (Fall 1973).

6 *Univ. W. Los Angeles L. Rev.* 152 (Winter 1974).
60 *Virginia L. Rev.* 137 (Jan. 1974).
14 *Washburn L. J.* 118 (Winter 1975).
33 *Yale L. J.* 554 (Jan. 1974).

1975   *Twentieth Century Music Corp. v. George Aiken*, 422 U.S. 151, 45 L.Ed.2d 84, 95 S.Ct. 2040

Argued: April 21, 1975.

Decided: June 17, 1975.

Summary: A restaurant owner's reception of radio broadcasts of copyrighted musical compositions, where the station has been licensed to perform the works publicly for profit, does not constitute a "performance" as delineated in federal copyright law and is thus not an infringement.

Circumstances: Aiken, owner and operator of a fast-food restaurant in downtown Pittsburgh, had four radio speakers in his establishment, receiving broadcasts of music and other normal fare. On March 11, 1972, customers and employees heard two copyrighted musical compositions, "The More I See You," owned by Twentieth Century, and "Me and My Shadow," owned by Mary Bourne. Both copyright holders were members of the American Society of Composers, Authors and Publishers (ASCAP), which licenses the performing rights of its members to their copyrighted works. The broadcasting station was properly licensed to broadcast the songs; Aiken did not hold a license, however. Twentieth Century Music and Ms. Bourne sued Aiken in the District Court for the Western District of Pennsylvania, which granted them statutory monetary awards for each infringement of copyright. The Court of Appeals for the Third Circuit reversed, holding that the claims were foreclosed by the Supreme Court's decisions in *Fortnightly Corp. v. United Artists Television, Inc.* (1968) and *Teleprompter Corp. v. CBS* (1974). On certiorari, the Supreme Court affirmed.

Opinion: Justice Potter Stewart, who also wrote the Court's opinions in the precedent cases, *Fortnightly* and *Teleprompter*, was joined by Justices William J. Brennan, Jr., Byron R. White, Thurgood Marshall, Lewis F. Powell, Jr., and William H. Rehnquist. Justice Harry A. Blackmun filed a separate concurring opinion, and Chief Justice Warren E. Burger, joined by Justice William O. Douglas, dissented. As he had opined in *Fortnightly*, Stewart said that if an unlicensed use of a copyrighted work does not conflict with an "exclusive" right conferred by the federal statute, it is no infringement of the holder's rights. "No license is required by the Copyright Act, for example, to sing a copyrighted lyric in the shower." Although the earlier cases involved television, not radio, and literary and dramatic works, not musical compositions, the court of appeals' observation was correct: "[I]f *Fortnightly*, with its elaborate CATV [cable television] plant and *Teleprompter* with its even more sophisticated and extended technological and programming facilities were not 'performing,' then logic dictates that no 'performance' resulted when the [respondent] merely activated his restaurant radio." To hold that Aiken "performed" the copyrighted works would not only require the Court to overturn the other decisions, Stewart said, but would result in a regime of copyright law that would be both wholly unenforceable and highly inequitable. Justice Blackmun added that the Court should overrule *Buck v. Jewell-LaSalle Realty Co.* (1931), holding that a hotel proprietor's use of a radio with loud-speakers for his guests constituted a "performance," rather than rule on the ground that the broadcaster there was not licensed to perform the compositions. Burger, in dissent, stated that the only satisfactory solution is for Congress to act upon proposals to amend the Copyright Act.

Referenced Cases: *Fortnightly Corp. v. United Artists*, 392 U.S. 390 (1968), and *Teleprompter Corp. v. CBS*, 415 U.S. 394 (1974), on most recent constitutional law in the area; *Fox Film Corp. v. Doyal*, 286 U.S. 123 (1932), on the benefits derived by the public from the labors of authors, also *Kendall v. Winsor*, 21 How. 322 (1858), and *Grant v. Raymond*, 6 Pet. 218 (1832); *Herbert v. Shanley Co.*, 242 U.S. 591 (1917), regarding radio reception as "performance" and "publicly for profit"; *Buck v. Jewell-LaSalle Realty Co.*, 283 U.S. 191 (1931), on licensed versus unlicensed broadcasters relative to "performance."

Further Reading:

25 *Buffalo L. Rev.* 607 (Winter 1976).

13 *Houston L. Rev.* 202 (Oct. 1975).

36 *Univ. Pittsburgh L. Rev.* 994 (Summer 1975).

1975 *Utah L. Rev.* 752 (Fall 1975).

1984   ***Sony Corporation of America v.
Universal City Studios, Inc.*, 465 U.S.
1112, 80 L.Ed.2d 1480, 104 S.Ct. 1619,
220 U.S.P.Q. 665, 52 U.S.L.W. 4090**

Reargued: Oct. 3, 1983.

Decided: Jan. 17, 1984.

Summary: The sale of videotape recorders (VTRs) to
the general public does not constitute contributory infringement
of copyright.

Circumstances: Several television production companies sued Sony, a manufacturer of home VTRs, charging that
VTR consumers were recording their copyrighted works and that
Sony was liable because of its marketing of the recorders. The
District Court for the Central District of California ruled that the
recording of material broadcast over the public airwaves was a fair
use of copyrighted works and that Sony could not be held liable as
a contributory infringer even if home use of VTRs were infringement. The Court of Appeals for the Ninth Circuit reversed, holding Sony liable for contributory infringement and ordered appropriate relief. The Supreme Court reversed.

Opinion: Justice John Paul Stevens delivered the Court's
opinion, joined by Chief Justice Warren E. Burger and Justices
William J. Brennan, Jr., Sandra Day O'Connor, and Byron R. White.
Harry A. Blackmun filed a dissent, joined by Thurgood Marshall,
Lewis F. Powell, Jr., and William H. Rehnquist. On the question of
"contributory infringement," Stevens noted that the Copyright
Act does not expressly render anyone liable for infringement

committed by another; thus, the manufacturer of the Betamax home recorder is not held accountable for how it may be used. Further, Stevens noted, taping television programs at home for viewing at a different time ("time-shifting") is a noncommercial, nonprofit activity. Sony had demonstrated a "significant likelihood" that substantial numbers of copyright holders who license their works for broadcast on free television would not object to having their programs time-shifted by private viewers. He also said that Universal Studios, Walt Disney Productions, and other plaintiffs in the suit had failed to demonstrate that "time-shifting would cause any likelihood of non-minimal harm to the potential market for, or the value of, their copyrighted works. The Betamax is, therefore, capable of substantial noninfringing uses."

In his dissent, Justice Blackmun contended that taping a copyrighted television program is an infringement unless permitted by the fair use exemption of the 1976 Copyright Act. The justice noted that video recording at home is an ordinary, rather than a productive, fair use of copyrighted works, not for "socially laudable purposes," as permitted by the fair use doctrine. Quoting from the district court finding for Sony, Blackmun said that "Betamax owners use the copy for the same purpose as the original. They add nothing of their own." He concluded: "It is my view that the Court's approach alters dramatically the doctrines of fair use and contributory infringement as they have been developed by Congress and the courts."

Referenced Cases: *Kalem Co. v. Harper Bros.*, 222 U.S. 55 (1911), regarding the producer of an unauthorized film of a copyrighted book held liable for his sale of the motion picture to jobbers; *Columbia Broadcasting System, Inc. v. Democratic National Committee*, 412 U.S. 94 (1973), on access to television programming as an interest "consistent with the First Amendment policy of providing the fullest possible access to information through the public airwaves"; *Fox Film Corp. v. Doyal*, 286 U.S. 123 (1932), and *U.S. v. Paramount Pictures*, 334 U.S. 131 (1947), holding that monopoly created by copyright rewards the author in order to benefit the public; *Wheaton v. Peters*, 33 U.S. 8 Peters 591 (1834), on the wholly statutory protection of copyright; *Thompson v. Hubbard*, 131 U.S. 123 (1889), on remedies for infringement prescribed by Congress; *Teleprompter Corp. v. CBS*, 415 U.S. 394 (1974), *Fortnightly Corp. United Artists*, 392 U.S. 390

(1968), *White-Smith Music Publishing Co. v. Apollo Co.*, 209 U.S. 1 (1908), and *Wilkens v. U.S.*, 429 U.S. 376 (1975), on the judiciary's reluctance to expand copyright protection without explicit legislative guidance; *Dawson Chemical Co. v. Rohm & Hass Co.*, 448 U.S. 176 (1980), holding that in contributory infringement decisions patent monopoly does not extend beyond the limits of a specific grant; *Twentieth Century Music Corp. v. Aiken*, 422 U.S. 151 (1975), holding that the unlicensed use of copyright is not infringement unless it conflicts with an exclusive right conferred by copyright statute; *Community Television of Southern California v. Gottfried*, 459 U.S. 498 (1983), regarding public interest in making television broadcasts more available but not an unlimited availability; *Buck v. Jewell-LaSalle Realty Co.*, 283 U.S. 191 (1931), holding that liability for copyright infringement can be imposed on persons other than those who actually carry out the infringing activity; *Bobbs-Merril Co. v. Straus*, 210 U.S. 339 (1908), holding that patent and copyright protections have not developed in a parallel fashion and that the Court has borrowed patent concepts in copyright cases sparingly.

Further Reading:

23 *American Business L. Rev.* 551 (Winter 1986).
36 *Baylor L. Rev.* 855 (Fall 1984).
33 *Buffalo L. Rev.* 269 (Spring 1984).
82 *Columbia L. Rev.* 1600 (1982).
20 *New England L. Rev.* 285 (1984/85).
11 *Ohio Northern Univ. L. Rev.* 333 (1984).
15 *Seton Hall L. Rev.* 52 (1984).
53 *Univ. Missouri-KC L. Rev.* 126 (Fall 1984).

1985 *Mills Music, Inc. v. Marie Snyder and Ted Snyder, Jr.*, 469 U.S. 153, 83 L.Ed.2d 556, 105 S.Ct. 638

Argued: Oct. 9, 1984.

Decided: Jan. 8, 1985.

Summary: In seeing the Copyright Act of 1976 as the culmination of a major legislative reexamination of copyright doctrine, the Court held that a music publisher was entitled to a share of the royalty income generated by derivative works of a copyrighted song after a copyright grant to the publisher had been terminated.

Circumstances: In a controversy over the 1923 song "Who's Sorry Now," involving the distribution of royalty income between the publisher and the composer's heirs, Ted Snyder had several years later assigned future interest in the copyright to his publisher in exchange for an advance on royalties and the publisher's agreement to pay a cash royalty on sheet music and 50 percent of all net proceeds received for mechanical reproductions. Synder's heirs subsequently terminated the grant and demanded that all royalties on the derivative works be remitted to them. The District Court for the Southern District of New York ruled for the publisher regarding the terms of all prior grants, but the Court of Appeals for the Second Circuit reversed and said that the law preserved only the grants from the publisher to the record companies, not the grant from the author to the publisher. On certiorari, the Supreme Court reversed, saying that the word "grant" in the statute encompassed the composer's grant as well.

Opinion: Justice John Paul Stevens wrote the 5-to-4 opinion, joined by Chief Justice Warren E. Burger and Justices Sandra Day O'Connor, Lewis F. Powell, Jr., and William H. Rehnquist. Adhering to the "Derivative Works Exception" to the 1976 Copyright Act, Stevens said that, under the terms of the grant in effect at the time of termination of the copyright, Mills is entitled to a share of the royalty income. Stevens likened a music publisher's license to a record company to a book publisher's license to a motion picture producer. Thus, "[W]e can see no reason why the Exception should not also limit the right of a composer, like Snyder, who made such a grant to a music publisher, like Mills, that preceded a series of licenses to record companies." In dissent, Justice Byron R. White, joined by Justices Harry A. Blackmun, William J. Brennan, Jr., and Thurgood Marshall, challenged the majority's reading of copyright legislative history, believing that Congress intended the law to compensate authors, not their grantees. Since Snyder and Mills had already benefited from their original bargain, now terminated by the composer's heirs, the so-called windfall conferred by Congress in the "Exception" should fall to the author, White said.

Referenced Cases: The decision was based on the Court's interpretation of the Copyright Act of 1976, Title 17 USC Sections 101–810 entitled "Copyrights." Also: *Fred Fisher Music Co. v. Witmark & Sons*, 318 U.S. 643 (1943), on an author's right to assign not only the initial term of the copyright in his work but also the renewal term.

Further Reading:
4 *Cardozo Arts & Entertainment L. J.* 1 (1985).
62 *Univ. Detroit L. Rev.* 181 (Winter 1985).
6 *Whittier L. Rev.* 923 (1984).

Note: Section 101 of the 1976 Copyright Act defines a "derivative work" as "a work based upon one or more preexisting works, such as a translation, musical arrangement, dramatization, fictionalization, motion picture version, sound recording, art reproduction, abridgment, condensation, or any other form in which a work may be recast, transformed, or adapted. A work consisting of editorial revisions, annotations, elaborations, or other modifications which, as a whole, represent an original work of authorship, is a 'derivative work.'" The Court's decision turned largely on Section 304(c)(6)(A), the "Derivative Works Exception," which states: "A derivative work prepared under authority of the grant before its termination may continue to be utilized under the terms of the grant after its termination, but this privilege does not extend to the preparation after the termination of other derivative works based upon the copyrighted work covered by the terminated grant."

1985   *Harper & Row, Publishers, Inc. and The Reader's Digest Association, Inc. v. Nation Enterprises and The Nation Associates, Inc.*, **471 U.S. 539, 88 L.Ed.2d 588, 105 S.Ct. 2218, 11 Med.L.Rptr. 1969**

Argued: Nov. 6, 1984.

Decided: May 20, 1985.

Summary: In addressing to what extent the "fair use" provision of the Copyright Revision Act of 1976 sanctions unauthorized use of quotations from a public figure's unpublished manuscript, the Court held that *The Nation*'s "clandestine publication" of parts of former President Ford's unpublished memoirs constituted copyright infringement.

Circumstances: In April 1979, *The Nation* published excerpts from former president Gerald R. Ford's not-yet-published memoirs, which Ford two years earlier had contracted to be issued by Harper & Row. (The Reader's Digest Association was co-owner of the copyright.) Near publication, the publisher negotiated a prepublication licensing agreement with *Time* magazine, under which *Time* would pay $25,000 ($12,500 in advance and the rest at publication) for the right to excerpt 7,500 words from Ford's account of his pardon of former president Richard Nixon. But before the article's scheduled release, *The Nation* acquired a copy of the unpublished book manuscript and produced a 2,250-word piece, including at least 300 words of direct quotes of copyrighted expression. Victor Navasky, editor, admitted at the bench trial that he intended to "scoop" the *Time* article. As a result, *Time* canceled its piece and refused to pay the remaining $12,500 to Harper & Row. The District Court for the Southern District of New York held that the memoirs were protected and that *The Nation's* unauthorized use constituted an infringement of the Copyright Act. The court awarded $12,500 in actual damages. The Court of Appeals for the Second Circuit reversed, holding that the identifiable words, though copyrightable expression, were sanctioned as a "fair use" of the material and also noted that the Ford disclosures were "politically significant" and legitimate news. The Supreme Court reversed, thus restoring the district court's finding of infringement.

Opinion: Justice Sandra Day O'Connor, writing for the majority, was joined by Chief Justice Warren E. Burger and Justices Harry A. Blackmun, Lewis F. Powell, Jr., William H. Rehnquist, and John Paul Stevens. O'Connor accused *The Nation* of "effectively arrogat[ing] to itself the right of first publication, an important marketable subsidiary right." She said that an author's right to choose when he will publish is deserving of protection, despite *The Nation*'s argument that public interest in news of public figures outweighs the right of the author to control its first publication. "Absent such protection, there would be little incentive to create or profit in financing such memoirs, and the public would be denied an important source of significant historical information." It is fundamentally at odds with the scheme of copyright, O'Connor said, to accord lesser rights to those works that are of greatest importance to the public. "We see no warrant for expanding the doctrine of fair use to create what amounts to a public figure exception to copyright." Most of the majority opinion is devoted to an examination of the four factors identified by Congress as especially relevant in determining whether the use was fair: the purpose and character of the use; the nature of the copyrighted work; the substantiality of the portion used in relation to the copyrighted work as a whole; and the effect on the potential market for or value of the copyrighted work. On the first, O'Connor said that *The Nation*'s use was *intended* to supplant the copyright holder's commercially valuable right of first publication. "The trial court found that *The Nation* knowingly exploited a purloined manuscript." Asserting that the scope of fair use is narrower with unpublished works, the justice concluded that this use clearly infringed confidentiality and creative control. On the third factor, "*The Nation* article is structured around the quoted excerpts which serve as its dramatic focal points." On the final factor, deemed the single most important element of fair use, the justice agreed with the trial court's finding not merely of a potential but of an actual effect on the market. In sum, the Court rejected the magazine's First Amendment defense of public interest in the subject matter. "We see no warrant for judicially imposing a 'compulsory license' permitting unfettered access to the unpublished copyrighted expression of public figures."

Justice William J. Brennan, Jr., joined by Justices Byron R. White and Thurgood Marshall, dissented, expressing the view that the Court had adopted an "exceedingly narrow approach" to fair use that permits Harper & Row to monopolize information. "The progress of arts and sciences and the robust public debate essential to an enlightened citizenry are ill served by this constricted reading of the fair use doctrine." The dissenters also took issue with the Court's reliance on the commercial nature of *The Nation*'s use. "To negate any argument favoring fair use based on news reporting or criticism because that reporting or criticism was published for profit is to render meaningless the congressional imprimatur placed on such uses."

Referenced Cases: *Twentieth Century Music Corp. v. Aiken*, 422 U.S. 151 (1975), on copyright assuring contributors to the "store of knowledge" a fair return for their labors; *Sony Corp v. Universal City Studios, Inc.*, 464 U.S. 417 (1984), regarding a limited period of exclusive control over creative activity; *Burrow-Giles Lithographic Co. v. Sarony*, 111 U.S. 53 (1884), on the originality of nonfiction work; *American Tobacco Co. v. Werckmeister*, 207 U.S. 284 (1907), on the common law doctrine of an author's absolute control until parting voluntarily with work; *Mills Music, Inc. v. Snyder*, 469 U.S. 153 (1985), on the Copyright Act as culmination of legislative reexamination of copyright doctrine; *New York Times Co. v. U.S.*, 403 U.S. 713 (1971), holding that copyright protects expression, not ideas expresed; *International News Service v. Associated Press*, 248 U.S. 215 (1918), on news element not being the creation of the writer but a report of matters publici juris—the history of the day; *Zacchini v. Scripps-Howard Broadcasting Co.*, 433 U.S. 562 (1977), on the right to market the "original expression" as just compensation; *Mazer v. Stein*, 347 U.S. 201 (1954), on point that marketable right supplies the economic incentive to create and disseminate ideas; *Wooley v. Maynard*, 430 U.S. 705 (1977), on the right to speak freely and the right to refrain from speaking at all; *Sheldon v. Metro-Goldwyn Pictures Corp.*, 309 U.S. 390 (1940), regarding profits in the commingling of infringing and noninfringing elements; *New York Times Co. v. Sullivan*, 376 U.S. 254 (1964), on "uninhibited, robust, and wide-open" debate; *Lee v. Runge*, 404 U.S. 887 (1971), on the inappropriateness of copyright for politicians and philosophers; *Garrison v. Louisiana*, 379 U.S. 64 (1964), on the breadth of information needed for self-governance.

Further Reading:
1986 *Brigham Young L. Rev.* 983 (1986).
70 *Columbia L. Rev.* 983 (1970).
35 *Emory L. J.* 163 (1986).
53 *Iowa L. Rev.* 832 (1968).

29 *J. Copyright Soc.* 560 (1982).
52 *Missouri L. Rev.* 175 (Winter 1987).
58 *St. John's L. Rev.* (1984).
59 *Tulane L. Rev.* 135 (1984).

Selected Bibliography

Abrams, Floyd, "Copyright and Preemption: Constitutional and Statutory Limits of State Law Protection," *Supreme Court Rev.* 509 (1984).

———, "First Amendment and Copyright: The Seventeenth Donald C. Brace Memorial Lecture," 35 *J. Copyright Society* 1 (Oct. 1987).

Apfelbaum, Marc J., "Copyright and the Right of Publicity: One Pea in Two Pods," 71 *Georgetown L. J.* 1567 (1983).

Banzhaf, John F. III, "Copyright Protection for Computer Programs," 64 *Columbia L. Rev.* 1274 (Nov. 1964).

Benway, Richard F., "Patents, Copyrights and Trademarks Compared and Distinguished," 3 *Portia L. J.* 17 (Fall 1967).

Cary, George D., "The Quiet Revolution in Copyright: The End of the 'Publication' Concept," 35 *George Washington L. Rev.* 652 (May 1967).

Collins, Janay, "Copyright and New Technology: Implications for Audiovisual Works," 64 *Journalism Quarterly* 94 (Spring 1987).

"The Copyright Act of 1976 Served on a Satellite Dish," 21 *Williamette L. Rev.* 79 (1985).

"Copyright Infringement and the First Amendment," 79 *Columbia L. Rev.* 320 (March 1979).

"Copyright Owners vs. Cable Television: The Evolution of a Copyright Liability Conflict," 33 *Syracuse L. Rev.* 693 (1982).

"Copyright Protection for the Structure and Sequence of Computer Programs," 21 *Loyola-LA L. Rev.* 255 (Nov. 1987).

Cullen, Mary Louise, "Literary Property—Common-Law Copyright—The Meaning and Effect of Publication," 14 *Univ. Detroit L. Rev.* 222 (May 1951).

Dana, Jane T., "Copyright and Privacy Protection of Unpublished Works—The Author's Dilemma," 13 *Columbia J. Law and Social Problems* 351 (1977).

Demeter, Thomas Paul, "Legal Perils of Parody and Burlesque," 17 *Cleveland Marshall L. Rev.* 242 (May 1968).

Dole, Richard F., Jr., et al., "A Symposium: Copyright Problems—Twenty-First Century Style," 53 *Iowa L. Rev.* 805 (Feb. 1968).

"The FCC's Deregulation of Cable Television: The Problem of Unfair Competition and the 1976 Copyright Act," 10 *Hofstra L. Rev.* 59 (1982).

Fletcher, Richard L., Jr., and Stephen P. Smith III, "Computers, the Copyright Law and Its Revision," 20 *Univ. Florida L. Rev.* 386 (Winter 1968).

Francois, William E., "Copyright Law and Videotaping of TV Programs for Classroom Use," 57 *Journalism Quarterly* 5 (Spring 1980).

Goldstein, Paul, "Copyright and the First Amendment," 70 *Columbia L. Rev.* 983 (1970).

Gorman, Robert, "An Overview of the Copyright Act of 1976," 126 *Univ. Pa. L. Rev.* 856 (April 1977).

Green, William, J., "'Copyright' Protection for Uncopyrightables: The Common-Law Doctrines," 108 *Univ. Pa. L. Rev.* 699 (March 1960).

Greene, S. C., "The Cable Provisions of the Revised Copyright Act," 27 *Catholic Univ. L. Rev.* 263 (1978).

"Harper & Row Publishers, Inc. v. Nation Enterprises: Pirating Unpublished Works: Does the Fair Use Doctrine Vindicate First Amendment Rights?" 19 *John Marshall L. Rev.* 501 (Winter 1986).

Hill, James, "Scope of Protection for Computer Programs Under the Copyright Act," 14 *DePaul L. Rev.* 360 (Spring–Summer 1965).

Hillman, N. L., "The Fair Use of Free Broadcast Television: The Betamax Case and the Distinction Between Marketable and Disposable Software," 15 *Seton Hall L. Rev.* 52 (1984).

Holbrook, Lanny R., "Copyright Infringement and Fair Use," 40 *Univ. Cincinnati L. Rev.* 534 (1971).

Litman, Jessica D., "Copyright, Compromise, and Legislative History," 72 *Cornell L. Rev.* 857 (July 1987).

Marks, Kevin, "An Assessment of the Copyright Model in Right of Publicity Cases," 70 *California L. Rev.* 786 (1982).

Mayer, David G., "The Transfer of Copyright Ownership to Periodicals," 46 *Fordham L. Rev.* 907 (1978).

Meyer, G., "The Feat of Houdini or How the New Act Disentangles the CATV Copyright Knot," 22 *New York Law School Rev.* 545 (1978).

Middleton, Kent R., "Copyright and the Journalist: New Powers for the Free-Lancer," 56 *Journalism Quarterly* 38 (Spring 1979).

Morrill, Stephen S., "Harper & Row Publishers v. Nation Enterprises: Emasculating the Fair Use Accommodation of Competing Copyright and First Amendment Interests," 79 *Northwestern Univ. L. Rev.* 587 (1984).

Nelson, Greg J., "The Copyrightability of Computer Programs," 7 *Arizona L. Rev.* 204 (Spring 1966).

Nimmer, Melville B., "The Nature of the Rights Protected by Copyright," 10 *UCLA L. Rev.* 60 (Nov. 1962).

———, "Does Copyright Abridge the First Amendment Guarantee of Free Speech and Press?" 17 *UCLA L. Rev.* 1180 (1970).

———, "Copyright Liability for Audio Home Recording: Dispelling the Betamax Myth," 68 *Virginia L. Rev.* 1505 (1982).

O'Meara, W., "'Works Made for Hire' Under the Copyright Act of 1976—Two Interpretations," 15 *Creighton L. Rev.* 523 (1982).

Patterson, L. R., "Private Copyright and Public Communication: Free Speech Endangered," 28 *Vanderbilt L. Rev.* 1161 (1975).

"Protecting Trade Secrets Through Copyright," 1981 *Duke L. J.* 981 (1981).

Schulman, John, "Fair Use and the Revision of the Copyright Act," 53 *Iowa L. Rev.* 832 (1968).

Schuster, Nancy, and Marc J. Bloch, "Mechanical Copying, Copyright Law, and the Teacher," 17 *Cleveland Marshall L. Rev.* 299 (May 1968).

See, H., "Copyright Ownership of Joint Works and Terminations of Transfers," 30 *Kansas L. Rev.* 517 (Summer 1982).

Walker, W. C., Jr., "Fair Use: The Adjustable Tool for Maintaining Copyright Equilibrium," 43 *Louisiana L. Rev.* 735 (Jan. 1983).

Wallahan, Franklin J., "Immorality, Obscenity and the Law of Copyright," 6 *South Dakota L. Rev.* 109 (Spring 1961).

Yankwich, Leon R., "What Is Fair Use?" 22 *Univ. Chicago L. Rev.* 203 (1954).

Fair Trial

1918 *Toledo Newspaper Co. and Negley D. Cochran v. U.S., 247 U.S. 402, 62 L.Ed. 1186, 38 S.Ct. 560*

Argued: March 7, 8, 1918.

Decided: June 10, 1918.

Summary: Upheld the conviction of a newspaper for summary contempt for its comments on a judge and on pending litigation.

Circumstances: During a major dispute over transit fares in Toledo, Ohio, and while a federal judge deliberated over the constitutionality of the change in the price of a streetcar ride, the *News-Bee* supported an ordinance temporarily freezing the old three-cent fare and criticized the judge for granting a preliminary injunction to restrain enforcement of the ordinance. After the judge found the fare charge unconstitutional, he ruled the paper in contempt and fined the managing editor, "not merely because of their intemperance" but also for creating disrespect for "any order which the court might render if it conflicted with the supposed rights of the city espoused by the publications." On one occasion the *News-Bee* published a cartoon representing the transit company as a moribund man in bed with his friends at the bedside, one of them saying, "Guess we'd better call in Doc Killits." The judge's name was Killits, who, sitting for the District Court for the Northern District of Ohio, found the defendants in contempt. The Circuit Court of Appeals for the Sixth Circuit affirmed the judgment, as did the Supreme Court.

Opinion: Chief Justice Edward D. White wrote for the Court in the 5-to-2 decision, joined by Justices Willis Van Devanter, Mahlon Pitney, James C. McReynolds, and Joseph McKenna. Dissenting were Justices Oliver Wendell Holmes and Louis D. Brandeis. Justices William R. Day and John H. Clarke did not participate. On judicial power to abridge freedom of the press, White said: "It suffices to say that, however complete is the right of the press to state public things and discuss them, that right, as every other right enjoyed in human society, is subject to the restraints which separate right from wrongdoing." The newspaper had argued that the judge lacked the authority to invoke such punishment, that summary contempt could only be used when an offense is committed in the presence of the court or "so near thereto" as to obstruct the administration of justice. The paper said that the 1831 federal contempt law placed a geographic limitation on the judge's use of summary punishment. But the chief justice wrote that, since the articles critical of the judge were related to the pending litigation, "so near thereto" meant "close relationship" to the administration of justice.

Justice Holmes, in a strong dissent joined by Brandeis, interpreting the phrase as "geographical," sought to discredit the summary power in favor of firm and steadfast judges not easily deflected from their sworn duty. After noting that the controversy had been brewing for nearly six months before the judge took action, Holmes concluded: "I would go as far as any man in favor of the sharpest and most summary enforcement of order in court and obedience to decrees, but when there is no need for immediate action contempts are like any other breach of law and should be dealt with as the law deals with other illegal acts. Action like the present . . . is wholly unwarranted by even color of law."

Referenced Cases: *Cary Mfg. Co. v. Acme Flexible Clasp Co.*, 187 U.S. 427 (1903), *O'Neal v. U.S.*, 190 U.S. 36 (1903), *Bessette v. W. B. Conkey Co.*, 194 U.S. 324 (1904), and *Gompers v. U.S.*, 233 U.S. 604 (1914), regarding summary contempt conviction as not within reviewing power of the Court; *Marshall v. Gordon*, 243 U.S. 521 (1917), on situation existing at time of adoption of the 1831 act, which limited the power of federal judges; *Gompers v. Buck's Stove & Range Co.*, 221 U.S. 418 (1911), on the lower court's determination of facts sustaining charges; *Ex parte Robinson*, 19 Wall. 505 (1873), on ensuring order and decorum.

Further Reading:
28 *Columbia L. Rev.* 401, 525 (1928).
1 *J. Criminal Law & Criminology* 849 (1911).
12 *Virginia L. Register* 25 (1926).

1946 *John D. Pennekamp and the Miami Herald Publishing Co. v. Florida,* 328 U.S. 331, 90 L.Ed. 1295, 66 S.Ct. 1029

Argued: Feb. 8, 1946.

Decided: June 3, 1946.

Summary: In a unanimous ruling, the Court said that the First Amendment protected the press against contempt citations meant to punish publications or broadcasts critical of court proceedings in general and judicial behavior in particular.

Circumstances: In two editorials, Nov. 2 and 7, 1944, which appeared in the Miami *Herald*, Pennekamp, the associate editor, accused judges of protecting criminals more than the public. Accompanying the first editorial was a cartoon, holding up the law to "public obloquy," depicting a judge tossing aside charges against the defendant, while an individual labeled "public interest" protests. The Circuit Court of Florida for Dade County found the newspaper and Pennekamp in contempt of court. The *Herald* was fined $1,000 and Pennekamp fined $250. The Supreme Court of Florida, with two judges dissenting, sustained the convictions. On writ of certiorari, the U.S. Supreme Court reversed.

Opinion: Justice Stanley F. Reed, joined by Chief Justice Harlan F. Stone and Justices Hugo L. Black, William O. Douglas, and Harold H. Burton, said that editorials containing "half-truths" and "misinformation" about rape cases still before a Florida court did not create a clear and present danger to the administration of justice. "Freedom of discussion should be given the widest range compatible with the essential requirement of the fair and orderly administration of justice." Reed said that discussion of a case only after its termination may be inadequate to emphasize the danger to public welfare of "supposedly wrongful judicial conduct." He concluded that the danger, in this case, to fair judicial administration "has not the clearness and immediacy necessary to close the door of permissible public comment. When that door is closed, it closes all doors behind it." Justice Felix Frankfurter, in a separate concurring opinion, noted that Justice Oliver Wendell Holmes, who created the literary phrase "a clear and present danger," did not mean "even remotely an absolutist test or had in mind a danger in the abstract." In its setting it served to indicate the importance of freedom of speech to a free society but also to emphasize that its exercise must be compatible with the preservation of other freedoms essential to a democracy and guaranteed by our Constitution." But criticism, he said, must not feel cramped, even criticism of the administration of criminal justice. Frankfurter pointed to the need for both the press and the judiciary to behave responsibly; however, the power to punish for contempt of court is a safeguard not for judges as persons but for the function that they exercise. "If men, including judges and journalists, were angels, there would be no problems of contempt of court."

Justice Frank Murphy, concurring separately, said that freedom of the press includes the right to criticize and disparage, "even though the terms be vitriolic, scurrilous or erroneous." Justice Wiley B. Rutledge, also concurring separately, said that he had no respect for a newspaper that is careless with facts, but that any standard requiring strict accuracy in reporting legal events factually or in commenting on them in the press "would be an impossible one. There must be some room for misstatement of fact, as well as for misjudgment, if the press and others are to function as critical agencies in our democracy concerning courts as for all other instruments of government." Justice Robert H. Jackson did not participate.

Referenced Cases: *Bridges v. California* and *Times-Mirror Co. v. Superior Court*, 314 U.S. 252 (1941), on limits on courts to punish those who criticize pending litigation; *Baumgartner v. U.S.*, 322 U.S. 665 (1944), and *Schneiderman v. U.S.*, 320 U.S. 118 (1943), regarding solidity of evidence to create a clear and present danger to judicial administration; *Near v. Minnesota*, 283 U.S. 697 (1937), on previous restraints not absolutely unlimited; *Schenck v. U.S.*, 249 U.S. 47 (1919), *Frohwerk v. U.S.*, 249 U.S. 204 (1919), and *Debs v. U.S.*, 249 U.S. 211 (1919), holding that the Constitution does not allow absolute freedom of expression; *Hyde v. U.S.*, 225 U.S. 347 (1912), on Justice Holmes's dissenting admonition against "encysted" legal phrases; *Schaefer v. U.S.*, 251 U.S. 466 (1920), on Justice Louis D. Brandeis's "permissible curtailment of free speech"; *Frank v. Mangum*, 237 U.S. 309 (1915), on atmosphere in courtroom subtly influenced from without; *Union P. R. Co. v. Public Service Commission*, 248 U.S. 67 (1918), *Ward v. Love County*, 253 U.S. 17 (1920), and *Davis v. Wechsler*, 263 U.S. 22 (1923), on court contempt power regarding "pending" cases.

Further Reading:

1 *Arkansas L. Rev.* 162 (Spring 1947).
32 *Cornell L. Q.* 413 (March 1947).
41 *Illinois L. Rev.* 690 (Jan.–Feb. 1947).
45 *Michigan L. Rev.* 513 (Feb. 1947).
31 *Minnesota L. Rev.* 97 (Dec. 1946).
22 *Notre Dame Lawyer* 231 (Jan. 1947).
16 *Revista Juridica de la Univ. de Puerto Rico* 417 (March–April 1947).
20 *Temple L. Q.* 369 (Dec. 1946).
25 *Texas L. Rev.* 173 (Dec. 1946).
95 *Univ. Pa. L. Rev.* 222 (Dec. 1946).

1952   *Fred Stroble v. California*, 343 U.S. 181, 96 L.Ed. 872, 72 S.Ct. 599, 1 Med.L.Rptr. 1169

Argued: March 6, 1952.

Decided: April 7, 1952.

Summary: Despite extensive newspaper pretrial coverage, the Court upheld a murder conviction, in part, on the ground of "no affirmative showing that any community prejudice ever

existed or in any way affected the deliberation of the jury." The
Court said Stroble had failed to show "actual prejudice."

Circumstances: Stroble, convicted of the first-degree
murder of a six-year-old girl and sentenced to death, asked the
Supreme Court to reverse his conviction, claiming that a fair trial
was impossible because of inflammatory newspaper accounts inspired by the district attorney. He also alleged he had been deprived of counsel in his sanity hearing, that there was an unnecessary delay in his arraignment, and that he was denied immediate
access to an attorney. At issue also was a questioning period of
approximately two hours, during which a confession was acquired
by the district attorney's office, portions of which were shared in a
press release, which was given prominent attention by newspapers. On appeal, the Supreme Court of California assumed that the
confession was the result of physical abuse or psychological tor-
ture, but affirmed the conviction that such defects could not have
influenced the fairness of the trial because Stroble made several
other confessions that were put into evidence. On writ of certiorari, the U.S. Supreme Court affirmed the conviction, overriding
various due process objections.

Opinion: Justice Tom C. Clark, joined by Chief Justice
Fred M. Vinson and Justices Sherman Minton, Harold H. Burton,
Robert H. Jackson, and Stanley F. Reed, ruled that a confession
acquired in the district attorney's office was voluntary and that
newspaper accounts of Stroble's arrest and confession were not so
inflammatory as to make a fair trial in the Los Angeles area
impossible. Clark pointed to the lapse of time, approximately six
weeks, between the day of Stroble's arrest and confession and the
beginning of the trial. He said that Stroble failed to show how the
publication of a portion of his confession four days before the
preliminary hearing, when it would have been available to the
press as "public property," prejudiced the jury in arriving at its
verdict two months later. However, the Court criticized the district attorney for releasing portions of the confession to the press
and announcing his belief that Stroble was guilty and sane.

Justice Felix Frankfurter, in dissent, wrote: "To have the
prosecutor himself feed the press with evidence that no self-
restrained press ought to publish in anticipation of a trial, is to
make the State itself . . . a conscious participant in trial by news-

paper. If guilt here is clear, the dignity of the law would be best enhanced by establishing that guilt wholly through the processes of law unaided by the infusion of extraneous passion." Frankfurter also believed that the Court had no authority to reexamine the state court's determination that the confession was involuntary; he believed that remand was in order. Justice William O. Douglas, joined by Hugo L. Black, dissented on the ground that all confessions obtained between the time of arrest and arraignment are illegal.

Referenced Cases: *Malinski v. New York,* 324 U.S. 401 (1945), and *Lyons v. Oklahoma,* 322 U.S. 596 (1944), on involuntary confessions related to jury verdicts; *Watts v. Indiana,* 338 U.S. 49 (1949), regarding Court's condemnation of the "pressure of unrelenting interrogation"; *Bridges v. California,* 314 U.S. 252 (1941), *Pennekamp v. Florida,* 328 U.S. 331 (1946), and *Craig v. Harney,* 331 U.S. 367 (1947), on press freedom to comment on the judiciary relative to proper functioning of the legal process; *Lisenba v. California,* 314 U.S. 219 (1941), on "fundamental fairness essential to the very concept of justice"; *Avery v. Alabama,* 308 U.S. 444 (1940), on the requirement of "zealous and earnest counsel"; *Gallegos v. Nebraska,* 342 U.S. 55 (1951), regarding the relevance of illegal acts of state officials; *Frank v. Mangum,* 237 U.S. 309 (1915), on courtroom atmosphere subtly influenced from without; *Turner v. Pennsylvania,* 338 U.S. 62 (1949), and *Harris v. South Carolina,* 338 U.S. 68 (1949), regarding Justice Douglas's views on illegality of confessions.

Further Reading:
38 *ABA J.* 851 (Oct. 1952).
66 *Harvard L. Rev.* 124 (Nov. 1952).
47 *Northwestern Univ. L. Rev.* 728 (Nov.–Dec. 1952).

1961   *Leslie Irvin v. A. F. Dowd, Warden,* **366 U.S. 717, 6 L.Ed.2d 751, 81 S.Ct. 1639, 1 Med.L.Rptr. 1178, 29 U.S.L.W. 4611**

Argued: Nov. 9, 1960.

Decided: June 5, 1961.

Summary: Noting a "pattern of deep and bitter prejudice" throughout the community, the Court ruled that the prisoner had been denied due process of law under the 14th Amendment because the trial jury was not impartial. It was not enough, the Court said, in modifying *Stroble v. California* (1952), that jurors believed they could render an impartial verdict despite exposure to prejudicial publicity.

Circumstances: Irvin was indicted for murder by a grand jury in Vanderburgh County, Indiana, and was granted a change of venue to adjoining Gibson County. After being denied a second change of venue, sought on the ground of local prejudice, he was convicted and sentenced to die. That verdict was confirmed by the Indiana Supreme Court. Next, claiming that he had been denied a fair trial as guaranteed by the 14th Amendment, Irvin sought a writ of habeas corpus in the District Court for the Northern District of Indiana. The court dismissed the proceeding on the ground that petitioner Irvin had failed to exhaust his state remedies, and the Court of Appeals for the Seventh Circuit affirmed. The U.S. Supreme Court granted certiorari and remanded the case to the court of appeals for decision on the merits or remand to the district court for consideration. The court of appeals retained jurisdiction and decided against Irvin. But, in reversing and remanding the case to the district court, the Supreme Court found a "pattern of prejudice" created by extensive press coverage dating from Irvin's arrest in April 1955, reporting, among other things, that "Mad Dog Irvin" had confessed to six murders. One story said he was "remorseless and without conscience," another reported a sheriff's promise "to devote his life" to be sure Irvin was executed. In many stories, Irvin was called the "confessed slayer of six," in addition to recalling his juvenile criminal record and his court-martial for going AWOL. (Some time after the Court's reversal and remand, Irvin was convicted in a second trial and sentenced to life imprisonment.)

Opinion: Justice Tom C. Clark, who had authored the *Stroble* decision nine years earlier, wrote the unanimous opinion, joined by Chief Justice Earl Warren and Justices Potter Stewart, Charles E. Whittaker, William J. Brennan, Jr., John M. Harlan, William O. Douglas, and Hugo L. Black. Felix Frankfurter concurred in a separate opinion. It is not required, Clark observed, that jurors be totally ignorant of the facts and issues involved in a case. "It is sufficient if the juror can lay aside his impression or opinion and render a verdict based on the evidence presented in court." But, in this case, "the build-up of prejudice is clear and convincing." Clark indicated that "a barrage of newspaper headlines, articles, cartoons and pictures was unleashed against him during the six or seven months preceding his trial." Of 430 prospective jurors, the trial judge excused 268 for having opinions as to guilt, or almost 90 percent with opinions ranging from mere suspicion of guilt to absolute certainty. A number admitted that if they were in Irvin's place and he in theirs on the jury they would not want him on the jury. Of the jurors finally seated, 8 out of the 12 said they thought he was guilty. "With such an opinion permeating their minds," Clark wrote, "it would be difficult to say that each could exclude this preconception of guilt from his deliberations." Yet all 12 told the judge they would be fair and impartial. Clark said the statements of impartiality could be given little weight where "so many, so many times, admitted of prejudice." With Irvin's life at stake, Clark said it is not requiring too much that he be tried in an atmosphere undisturbed by so huge a wave of public passion. Justice Frankfurter said it is impossible for fallible men and women to reach a disinterested verdict based exclusively on what they hear in court when, before they enter the jury box, their minds are saturated by press and radio with matter designed to establish guilt of the accused.

Referenced Cases: *Fay v. New York,* 332 U.S. 261 (1947), and *Palko v. Connecticut,* 302 U.S. 319 (1937), regarding the use of juries in a state's criminal procedure; *In re Oliver,* 333 U.S. 257 (1948), *Tumey v. Ohio,* 273 U.S. 510 (1927), and *In re Murchison,* 349 U.S. 133 (1955), on fair trial as basic requirement of due process; *Thompson v. Louisville,* 362 U.S. 199 (1960), and *Reynolds v. U.S.,* 98 U.S. 145 (1878), holding that opinionated jurors cannot be impartial; *Spies v. Illinois,* 123 U.S. 131 (1887), and *Holt v. U.S.,* 218 U.S. 245 (1910), holding that jurors *can* lay aside opinions and decide verdict on evidence; *Brown v. Allen,* 344 U.S. 443 (1953), on the adjudicative duty of a federal judge; *U.S. v. Wood,* 299 U.S. 123 (1936), on impartiality as a state of mind, not a technical concept; *Stroble v. California,* 343 U.S. 181 (1952), regarding the "pattern of deep and bitter prejudice"; *Shepherd v. Florida,* 341 U.S. 50 (1951), and *Moore v. Dempsey,*

261 U.S. 86 (1923), on petitioner's expectation of an undisturbed atmosphere; *Mahler v. Eby*, 264 U.S. 32 (1924), on court's power in a habeas corpus proceeding; *Chessman v. Teets*, 354 U.S. 156 (1957), *Dowd v. U.S.*, 340 U.S. 206 (1951), and *Tod v. Waldman*, 266 U.S. 113 (1924), on reasonable time in which to retry petitioner; *Maryland v. Baltimore Radio Show Inc.*, 338 U.S. 912 (1950), on extraneous influences forcing accused to forgo trial by jury.

Further Reading:
45 *ABA J.* 844 (Aug. 1959).
47 *ABA J.* 1208 (Dec. 1961).
73 *Harvard L. Rev.* 101 (Nov. 1959).
74 *Harvard L. Rev.* 1315 (May 1961).
22 *Law in Transition* 46 (Spring 1962).

1963   *Wilbert Rideau v. Louisiana*, 373 U.S. 723, 10 L.Ed.2d 663, 83 S.Ct. 1417, 1 Med.L.Rptr. 1183

Argued: April 29, 1963.

Decided: June 3, 1963.

Summary: The Court, in presuming prejudice, ruled that due process of law required a trial before a jury of community people who had not seen and heard the defendant's televised interview in jail with the sheriff.

Circumstances: In Feb. 1961, Rideau was arrested for bank robbery, kidnapping, and murder. While in the Calcasieu Parish jail in Lake Charles, Louisiana, a film was made of an "interview" between the prisoner and the sheriff, during which Rideau confessed to the reported crimes but without legal counsel present. Later the same day the film was televised to some 24,000 people in the community. The next day an estimated 53,000 people viewed the interview. The film was shown a third time, viewed by approximately 29,000 people. Calcasieu Parish was said to have a population of about 150,000 people. Two weeks later, Rideau was arraigned and two lawyers were appointed to represent him, and they promptly filed for a change of venue on the ground that no fair trial was possible in Calcasieu Parish after the three television broadcasts. The motion was denied. Three members of the jury that convicted him of murder said on voir dire that they had viewed the interview, and two others were local deputy sheriffs. The Supreme Court of Louisiana affirmed the judgment of conviction. On certiorari the U.S. Supreme Court reversed.

Opinion: Justice Potter Stewart, writing for the 7-to-2 Court and joined by Chief Justice Earl Warren and Justices Hugo L. Black, William O. Douglas, William J. Brennan, Jr., Byron R. White, and Arthur J. Goldberg, said that the state court had denied Rideau due process of law when it refused his request for a change of venue, after the people of Calcasieu Parish had been exposed "repeatedly and in depth" to the spectacle of the defendant personally confessing in detail to the crimes with which he was later charged. "For anyone who has ever watched television the conclusion cannot be avoided that this spectacle, to the tens of thousands of people who saw and heard it, in a very real sense *was* Rideau's trial—at which he pleaded guilty to murder. Any subsequent court proceedings in a community so pervasively exposed to such a spectacle could be but a hollow formality." Dissenting, Justice Tom C. Clark, joined by John M. Harlan, said that no nexus was established between the televised interview and the trial almost two months later. "Unless the adverse publicity is shown by the record to have fatally infected the trial, there is simply no basis for the Court's inference that the publicity, epitomized by the televised interview, called up some informal and illicit analogy to res judicata, making petitioner's trial a meaningless formality." Clark said he parted company with the Court not so much because it deviated from the principles established in *Irvin v. Dowd* (1961) but "because it applies no principles at all."

Referenced Cases: *Brown v. Mississippi*, 297 U.S. 278 (1936), and *White v. Texas*, 310 U.S. 530 (1940), on "free and voluntary confessions" acquired in jail without counsel and a state's judicial regulatory procedure; *Chambers v. Florida*, 309 U.S.

227 (1940), regarding due process of law in murder cases; *Marshall v. U.S.*, 360 U.S. 310 (1959), *Stein v. New York*, 346 U.S. 156 (1953), and *Brown v. Allen*, 344 U.S. 443 (1953), on the role of law enforcement officers in achievement of impartial justice and Supreme Court's supervisory reach; *Irvin v. Dowd*, 366 U.S. 717 (1961), regarding the impact of judicial environment on due process; *Beck v. Washington*, 369 U.S. 541 (1962), on the need to prove adverse publicity; *Cicenia v. Lagay*, 357 U.S. 504 (1958), and *Crooker v. California*, 357 U.S. 433 (1958), on right to counsel during interrogation; *Frazier v. U.S.*, 335 U.S. 497 (1948), and *U.S. v. Wood*, 299 U.S. 123 (1936), on juror qualifications; *In re Murchison*, 349 U.S. 133 (1955), on right to trial before a fair and impartial tribunal; *Adams v. U.S.*, 317 U.S. 269 (1942), on claimant's burden of showing unfairness.

Further Reading:
49 *ABA J.* 1119 (Nov. 1963).
10 *L. Ed. 2d* 1243 (1963).
18 *Rutgers L. Rev.* 686 (Winter 1964).

1965   *Billie Sol Estes v. Texas*, 381 U.S. 532; 14 L.Ed.2d 543, 85 S.Ct. 1628, 1 Med.L.Rptr. 1187

Argued: April 1, 1965.

Decided: June 7, 1965.

Summary: The Court held that, in view of the great notoriety of the trial, due process of law was denied the accused by the televising and broadcasting of the proceedings. Justice John M. Harlan, who provided the swing vote, concurred because of the trial's great notoriety, but would probably differ on one of a more or less routine nature.

Circumstances: Estes, a noted financier, was convicted in the District Court for the Seventh Judicial District of Texas of the crime of swindling: he had induced farmers to buy fertilizer tanks and property that did not exist. The trial was moved 500 miles from Reeves County, Texas, to Tyler to reduce the potential impact of pretrial publicity. However, the trial judge permitted broadcast coverage of the two-day pretrial hearing and part of the trial itself. A large television van was parked outside the courthouse and the second-floor courtroom was "a forest of equipment," one observer said. At least 12 television cameramen and still photographers were in the courtroom, which was so filled that 30 people stood in the aisles. Cables and wires were snaked across the floor, and microphones were on the judge's bench, the jury box, and the counsel table. Despite eventual adjustments to control the media's response, Estes appealed his conviction on the ground that he did not receive a fair trial because of the media coverage. After the Texas Court of Criminal Appeals affirmed his conviction, the U.S. Supreme Court, on certiorari, reversed.

Opinion: Justice Tom C. Clark wrote the 5-to-4 opinion, joined by Chief Justice Earl Warren and Justices William O. Douglas, Arthur J. Goldberg, and John M. Harlan. Clark said that careful safeguards had not yet been established to permit the televising and photographing of a criminal trial, "save in two States [Colorado and Texas at the time of the Estes trial] and there only under restrictions." Quoting from an article by Justice Douglas, Clark said that the nub of the question is not television's newness but, in Douglas's words, "the insidious influences which it puts to work in the administration of justice." (William O. Douglas, "The Public Trial and the Free Press," 33 *Rocky Mtn. L. Rev.* 1, 1960.) Referring to *Stroble v. California* (1952), *Irvin v. Dowd* (1961), and *Rideau v. Louisiana* (1963), where pretrial publicity occurred outside the courtroom and could not be effectively curtailed, Clark said that the rule of *probability* of unfairness clearly must be applied. "Television in its present state and by its very nature reaches into a variety of areas in which it may cause prejudice to an accused." Clark listed television's influences: (1) the potential impact on jurors, "the pressures of knowing that friends and neighbors have their eyes upon them"; (2) the impairment of the quality of testimony in criminal trials, the result of witnesses knowing they are being watched by a large audience; (3) the imposition of additional responsibilities on the judge, supervising television as well as the trial itself; and (4) the impact of courtroom cameras on the defendant, resembling, in Clark's words, "a police line-up or the third degree." Admittedly, the public may adjust eventually to the telecasting of trials, but Clark said a judgment must be made on the "facts as they are presented today."

In a separate concurring opinion, Chief Justice Warren, joined by Justices Douglas and Goldberg, said that it violates the Sixth Amendment for federal courts and the 14th Amendment for state courts to allow criminal trials to be televised to the public at large. "Broadcasting in the courtroom would give the television industry an awesome power to condition the public mind either for or against an accused." Justice Harlan, who agreed that in this case the accused had not received a fair trial, said in a separate opinion that cameras in the courtroom may not be unconstitutional in all cases, however. He noted that eventually television may become "so commonplace an affair in the daily life of the average person" as to dissipate likely damage to the judicial process. He did not want to stop the states from experimenting with cameras in the courtroom.

In dissent, Justice Potter Stewart, joined by Hugo L. Black, William J. Brennan, Jr., and Byron R. White, said that the televising of the trial did not violate any right guaranteed by the Constitution. "The idea of imposing upon any medium of communications the burden of justifying its presence is contrary to where I had always thought the presumption must lie in the area of First Amendment freedoms." White, in a separate dissent joined by Brennan, stated that it was premature "at the present time" to promulgate a flat constitutional ban on the use of cameras in the courtroom. As Harlan implied in his concurrence, White said that the Court's opinion precludes further opportunity for "intelligent assessment of the probable hazards imposed by the use of cameras at criminal trials." Brennan, in a separate memorandum, emphasized that only four of the majority viewed televised criminal trials as constitutionally infirm, whatever the circumstances. He said the decision is *not* a blanket prohibition against the televising of state criminal trials. "While I join the dissents of my Brothers Stewart and White, I do so on the understanding that their use of the expressions 'the Court's opinion' or 'the opinion of the Court' refers only to those views of our four Brethren which my Brother Harlan explicitly states he shares."

Referenced Cases: *Rideau v. Louisiana,* 373 U.S. 723 (1963), on the rule that televising confessions is inherently consti-

tutionally invalid; *In re Oliver*, 333 U.S. 257 (1948), on oppressive-
ness of secret tribunals; *Craig v. Harney*, 331 U.S. 367 (1947),
regarding the public's right to know what goes on in the courts;
Bridges v. California, 314 U.S. 252 (1941), and *Pennekamp v. Florida*, 328 U.S. 331 (1946), on media rights in open court occur-
rences; *In re Murchison*, 349 U.S. 133 (1955), on fairness in due
process and the probability of prejudice; *Offutt v. U.S.*, 348 U.S. 11
(1954), and *Tumey v. Ohio*, 273 U.S. 510 (1927), regarding the
"probability" of unfairness and "possible" temptation in due process of law; *Stroble v. California*, 343 U.S. 181 (1952), *Irvin v.
Dowd*, 366 U.S. 717 (1961), *Gideon v. Wainwright*, 373 U.S. 335
(1963), *White v. Maryland*, 373 U.S. 59 (1963), and *Turner v. Louisiana*, 379 U.S. 466 (1965), on "actual" versus "inherent" prejudice;
Patterson v. Colorado, 205 U.S. 454 (1907), on Justice Oliver Wendell Holmes's insistence on "evidence and argument in open court,
and not by any outside influence, whether of private talk or public
print"; *Cole v. Arkansas*, 333 U.S. 196 (1948), on the right to notice
of specific charges; *Pointer v. Texas*, 380 U.S. 400 (1965), and
Douglas v. Alabama, 380 U.S. 415 (1965), on the right to confrontation; *Moore v. Dempsey*, 261 U.S. 86 (1923), on the overwhelming
effect of a hostile courtroom atmosphere; *Lyons v. Oklahoma*, 322
U.S. 596 (1944), and *Payne v. Arkansas*, 356 U.S. 560 (1958), on
involuntary confessions; *Weems v. U.S.*, 217 U.S. 349 (1910), and
Brown v. Board of Education, 347 U.S. 483 (1954), on applying old
principles to new situations; *Hamilton v. Alabama*, 368 U.S. 52
(1961), regarding procedural protections at pretrial hearings as
well as at actual trial; *Mapp v. Ohio*, 367 U.S. 643 (1961), on the
constitutional conception of term "trial"; *Powell v. Alabama*, 287
U.S. 45 (1932), and *Betts v. Brady*, 316 U.S. 455 (1942), on distinctions between notorious and nonnotorious cases regarding the
issue of television; *Frank v. Mangum*, 237 U.S. 309 (1915), on
juries being "impregnated by the environing atmosphere";
Griffin v. California, 380 U.S. 609 (1965), *Tancil v. Woolls*, 379
U.S. 19 (1964), and *Avery v. Georgia*, 345 U.S. 559 (1953), regarding
the effects of one thing or another on human behavior; *Cox v.
Louisiana*, 379 U.S. 559 (1965), on the distracting aspect of "masses
of spectators" in the open courtroom; *Speiser v. Randall*, 357 U.S.
513 (1958), on the burden of media having to justify their presence; and *Jackson v. Denno*, 378 U.S. 368 (1964), on the showing of
specific prejudice.

Further Reading:

51 *ABA J.* 874 (Summer 1965).

30 *Albany L. Rev.* 158 (Jan. 1966).

34 *Fordham L. Rev.* 329 (Dec. 1965).

79 *Harvard L. Rev.* 146 (Nov. 1965).

37 *Mississippi L. J.* 168 (Dec. 1965).

11 *NY Law Forum* 533 (Fall 1965).

6 *Santa Clara Law* 109 (Fall 1965).

43 *Texas L. Rev.* 992 (July 1965).

38 *Univ. Colorado L. Rev.* 276 (Winter 1966).

27 *Univ. Pittsburgh L. Rev.* 141 (Oct. 1965).

18 *Vanderbilt L. Rev.* 2049 (Oct. 1965).

1966   *Samuel H. Sheppard v. E. L. Maxwell,* 384 U.S. 333, 16 L.Ed.2d 600, 86 S.Ct. 1507, 1 Med.L.Rptr. 1220

Argued: Feb. 28, 1966.

Decided: June 6, 1966.

Summary: Held that Dr. Sheppard was deprived of a fair trial in violation of the 14th Amendment because of the judge's failure to protect him sufficiently from the massive, pervasive, and prejudicial publicity that attended his prosecution.

Circumstances: On July 4, 1954, Marilyn Sheppard, Dr. Sheppard's pregnant wife, was bludgeoned to death in their lakeshore home in Bay Village, Ohio, a suburb of Cleveland. Dr. Sheppard was tried and convicted of second-degree murder before a jury in the Court of Common Pleas of Cuyahoga County. Before and during the celebrated trial, which started two weeks before an election in which the judge and the chief prosecutor were running for judgeships, Sheppard was the subject of extensive newspaper, radio, and television accounts, including revelations never presented in court. The judge denied requests by defense counsel for a continuance, change of venue, mistrial, and interrogation of the jurors about their exposure to the media.

During the nine-week trial, reporters sat at a press table inside the bar near the jury. Names and addresses of jurors were published and prospective witnesses were interviewed. Throughout, newspapers emphasized evidence tending to incriminate Sheppard and pointed out discrepancies in his statements to authorities. Sheppard himself made many public statements and wrote feature stories on his innocence. As observed later by the Ohio Supreme Court, "In this atmosphere of a 'Roman holiday' for the news media, Sam Sheppard stood trial for his life." The Court of Appeals of Cuyahoga County affirmed the conviction and the Ohio Supreme Court affirmed. The U.S. Supreme Court refused to review the case in 1956, but seven years later the Court held that convictions in state courts could be reviewed by federal district courts in habeas corpus proceedings, requiring prisoners to be brought before a judge along with information dealing with the reasons for their detention. If reasons are sufficient, the prisoner can be freed. Sheppard filed such a petition against the warden of Ohio State Penitentiary, E. L. Maxwell, and included several scrapbooks of newspaper clippings. The District Court for the Southern District of Ohio held that Sheppard had been denied a fair trial and was entitled to be released, but the Court of Appeals for the Sixth Circuit reversed in a divided vote. On certiorari, the Supreme Court reversed and directed that Sheppard be released unless the state tried him again within a reasonable time. (As reported by William E. Francois in *Mass Media Law and Regulation*, 4th ed. [New York: John Wiley, 1986]: "Concerning Sheppard's fate, the writ was issued and the state decided to try him again on the second-degree murder charge. The 16-day trial was marked by tight restrictions, with the number of reporters in the courtroom severely limited. A verdict of innocent was returned on November 16, 1966. Sheppard attempted to put his life together again. He remarried, returned to the practice of osteopathic medicine at a Youngstown, Ohio, hospital, but resigned shortly afterward when he was named in a malpractice suit after a patient died. He was divorced, set up an office in Columbus, turned briefly to professional wrestling, remarried, and on April 6, 1970, died—the end of a tragic personal story and one that casts a shadow across the news media" [p. 334].)

Opinion: Justice Tom C. Clark wrote the 8-to-1 opinion, joined by Chief Justice Earl Warren and Justices William O. Douglas, John M. Harlan, William J. Brennan, Jr., Potter Stewart, Byron R. White, and Abe Fortas. Justice Hugo L. Black dissented without opinion. Clark said that the trial judge had not adequately protected Sheppard's right to a trial by an impartial jury. "Given the pervasiveness of modern communication and the difficulty of effacing prejudicial publicity from the minds of the jurors, the trial courts must take strong measures to ensure that the balance is never weighed against the accused." He said the courts must take such steps by rule and regulation that will protect their processes from prejudicial outside interferences. The trial judge had failed to protect the defendant in three ways: (1) the press should have been limited, its representatives' conduct closely regulated, and reporters not permitted inside the bar; (2) the judge did not control the release of prejudicial information to the press during the trial; and (3) sequestration of the jury should have been raised sua sponte (without prompting) with counsel. "Neither prosecutors, counsel for defense, the accused, witnesses, court staff nor enforcement officers coming under the jurisdiction of the court should be permitted to frustrate its function. Collaboration between counsel and the press as to information affecting the fairness of a criminal trial is not only subject to regulation, but is highly censurable and worthy of disciplinary measures." Because justice cannot survive behind "walls of silence" and because the press guards against the "miscarriage of justice" by subjecting the police, prosecutors, and the judicial process to public scrutiny and criticism, the Court has been unwilling to place direct limitations on the reporting of public trials. But, he continued, no one ought to be punished for a crime without being "fairly tried in a public tribunal free of prejudice, passion, excitement, and tyrannical power."

Referenced Cases: In re Oliver, 333 U.S. 257 (1948), and Craig v. Harney, 331 U.S. 367 (1947), on distrust of secret trials and the courtroom as public property; Bridges v. California, 314 U.S. 252 (1941), on trials not to be won or lost like elections; Chambers v. Florida, 309 U.S. 227 (1940), Pennekamp v. Florida, 328 U.S. 331 (1946), Cox v. Louisiana, 379 U.S. 559 (1965), Marshall v. U.S., 360 U.S. 310 (1959), and Irvin v. Dowd, 366 U.S. 717 (1961), on the orderly administration of justice and information received in open court rather than through news accounts; Rideau v. Louisiana, 373 U.S. 723 (1963), Turner v. Louisiana, 379

U.S. 466 (1965), *Estes v. Texas*, 381 U.S. 532 (1965), and *In re Murchison*, 349 U.S. 133 (1955), regarding the probability of prejudice and unfairness; *Stroble v. California*, 343 U.S. 181 (1952), on prosecution and defense are both often to blame for prejudicial news.

Further Reading:

52 *ABA J.* 769 (Aug. 1966).
19 *Alabama L. Rev.* 150 (Fall 1966).
16 *DePaul L. Rev.* 203 (Autumn–Winter 1966).
80 *Harvard L. Rev.* 124 (Nov. 1966).
54 *Kentucky L. J.* 625 (Summer 1966).
26 *Louisiana L. Rev.* 818 (June 1966).
45 *Nebraska L. Rev.* 837 (July 1966).
45 *No. Carolina L. Rev.* 183 (Dec. 1966).
43 *No. Dakota L. Rev.* 1 (Fall 1966).
62 *Northwestern Univ. L. Rev.* 89 (March–April 1967).
41 *St. John's L. Rev.* 438 (Winter 1967).
1966 *Univ. Illinois L. Forum* 1063 (Winter 1966–67).
11 *Villanova L. Rev.* 737 (Summer 1966).
69 *West Virginia L. Rev.* 198 (Fall 1967).
8 *William & Mary L. Rev.* 143 (Fall 1966).

1975   *Jack Roland Murphy v. Florida*, 421 U.S. 794, 44 L.Ed.2d 589, 95 S.Ct. 2031

Argued: April 15, 1975.

Decided: June 16, 1975.

Summary: "In the totality of circumstances" presented in this case, the Court ruled failure to show that the setting of the trial was inherently prejudicial or that the jury selection process permitted an inference of actual prejudice. The fact that jurors know potentially prejudicial information does not necessarily mean that a defendant cannot receive a fair trial.

Circumstances: Jack Roland Murphy, known in the media as "Murph the Surf," had become notorious for his part in the 1964 theft of the Star of India sapphire, and his flamboyant lifestyle also attracted media attention. In 1968 he was arrested for robbery and assault at a Miami Beach home, but prior to being tried, he was convicted of murder and pleaded guilty to the interstate transportation of stolen securities. These events drew considerable media coverage. When Murphy was convicted in the Dade County, Florida, Criminal Court in 1970 of the 1968 charges of robbery and assault, he filed a petition for habeas corpus in the District Court for the Southern District of Florida. He alleged that his confinement was unlawful because the trial court had denied his effort to dismiss jurors and denied a change of venue. The grounds were that, through pretrial publicity, jurors were aware of his prior record and other facts about the crime charged. The district court denied relief and the Court of Appeals for the Fifth Circuit affirmed. On certiorari, the Supreme Court affirmed.

Opinion: Justice Thurgood Marshall, joined by Justices William O. Douglas, Potter Stewart, Byron R. White, Harry A. Blackmun, Lewis F. Powell, Jr., and William H. Rehnquist, said that the defendant had not been denied due process even though members of the jury knew from news accounts of a prior felony conviction and other facts about the crime with which he was charged. Marshall said that jurors need not be "totally ignorant of the facts and issues involved." He distinguished between "mere familiarity" with a defendant and a "predisposition against him." In *Rideau* (1963), *Estes* (1965), and *Sheppard* (1966), Marshall noted that the news media, either in the community at large or in the courtroom itself, pervaded the proceedings, but in *Murphy* the voir dire indicated no such hostility by the jurors to suggest a partiality that could not be laid aside. Most of the publicity was factual and published at least seven months before jury selection. None of the jurors betrayed any belief in the relevance of the past to the present case, and one juror volunteered that people who have been in trouble before are too often singled out for suspicion of each new crime—"a predisposition that could only operate in petitioner's favor." Only 20 of 78 persons questioned were excused, and neither the atmosphere in the community nor the courtroom was "sufficiently inflammatory." Chief Justice Warren E. Burger, concurring separately, said that, though the trial judge should have insulated prospective jurors from media coverage and prevented them from pretrial discussion of the case, the circumstances of the trial did not rise to the level of a violation of the due process clause of the 14th Amendment. Justice William J. Brennan, Jr., alone in dissent, said Murphy was denied a fair trial because of the widespread publicity regarding his criminal background known to all jurors. The denial of a change of venue was a prejudicial error, according to Brennan.

Referenced Cases: *Marshall v. U.S.*, 360 U.S. 310 (1959), on the Court's supervisory power over the enforcement of criminal law standards in federal courts; *Irvin v. Dowd*, 366 U.S. 717 (1961), *Rideau v. Louisiana*, 373 U.S. 723 (1963), *Estes v. Texas*, 381 U.S. 532 (1965), and *Sheppard v. Maxwell*, 384 U.S. 532 (1966), examples of trial atmosphere "utterly corrupted by press coverage"; *Beck v. Washington*, 369 U.S. 541 (1962), on factual nature of news articles.

Further Reading:
61 *ABA J.* 1123 (Sept. 1975).
13 *American Criminal L. Rev.* 285 (Fall 1975).

1976 *Nebraska Press Association v. Hugh Stuart, Judge, District Court of Lincoln County, Nebraska,* **427 U.S. 539, 49 L.Ed.2d 683, 96 S.Ct. 2791, 1 Med.L.Rptr. 1059**

Argued: April 19, 1976.

Decided: June 30, 1976.

Summary: Unanimously held that a restrictive order imposed on the news media relating to a sensational murder case violated the First Amendment and that barriers to prior restraints on the press remained high.

Circumstances: On the evening of Oct. 18, 1975, local police discovered the six members of the Henry Kellie family murdered in their home in Sutherland, Nebraska, a town of about 850 residents. Police released the description of a suspect, Erwin Charles Simants, to reporters who had hastened to the scene of the crime. Simants, who confessed, was arrested and arraigned in Lincoln County Court the next morning. Because the episode immediately attracted widespread media coverage, the county attorney and Simants's counsel asked the county court to enter a restrictive order relating to "matters that may or may not be publicly reported or disclosed to the public." In his "gag" order, the judge prohibited the publication of news obtained during pretrial proceedings and required members of the press to observe the Nebraska Bar-Press Guidelines. The district court upheld the order intended to suppress publication of the confession, statements Simants made to relatives, and results of medical tests related to a sexual assault. When the Nebraska Press Association appealed, the state supreme court upheld the key elements of the restrictive order. Five months after Simants was convicted of first-degree murder, a unanimous U.S. Supreme Court, on certiorari, reversed the judgment on grounds that the court order was unconstitutional.

Opinion: Chief Justice Warren E. Burger expressed the views of four other members of the Court, Byron R. White, Harry A. Blackmun, Lewis F. Powell, Jr., and William H. Rehnquist. White, Powell, and John Paul Stevens added separate concurring opinions. Justice William J. Brennan, Jr., joined by Potter Stewart and Thurgood Marshall, also concurred separately. Burger opined that prior restraints on speech and publication are the most serious and the least tolerable infringement on First Amendment rights. Burger reviewed a number of prior restraint cases, emphasizing the decision reached in the Pentagon Papers case (*New York Times Co. v. U.S.* [1971]), in which the Court reiterated prior restraint as "presumptively unconstitutional." But he also observed that because of the extraordinary protections afforded by the First Amendment, they "carry with them something in the nature of a fiduciary duty to exercise the protected rights responsibly—a duty widely acknowledged but not always observed by editors and publishers." However, Burger did not rule out the possibility that a prior restraint on the media might be constitutionally tolerated, as was noted in the Pentagon Papers decision. But before courts impose restrictive orders they must first exhaust other measures for ensuring a fair trial, such as those suggested in *Sheppard v. Maxwell* (1966). Moreover, he cited *Murphy v. Florida* (1975) in noting that pretrial publicity—even pervasive and adverse information—does not necessarily and inevitably lead to an unfair trial. "We reaffirm that the guarantees of freedom of expression are not an absolute prohibition under all circumstances, but the barriers to prior restraint remain high and the presumption against its use continues intact."

Justice White joined the Court's opinion but came close to an absolutist view when he added separately that "there is grave doubt in my mind whether orders with respect to the press as were entered in this case would ever be justifiable." He also urged the Court to announce at some point a more general rule and "avoid the interminable litigation that our failure to do so would necessarily entail." Justice Powell emphasized the unique burden that rests upon the party who undertakes to show the necessity for prior restraint on pretrial publicity. Justice Brennan, joined by Stewart and Marshall, held that resort to prior restraints on the freedom of the press is a "constitutionally impermissible" method for enforcing an accused's right to a fair trial by a jury. He applauded the Nebraska Bar-Press Guidelines as a commendable acknowledgment by the media that constitutional prerogatives bring enormous responsibilities. "However, the press may be arrogant, tyrannical, abusive, and sensationalist, just as it may be incisive, probing, and informative. But at least in the context of prior restraints on publication, the decision of what, when, and how to publish is for editors, not judges." Justice Stevens, also concurring in the judgment, said separately that, if ever required to face the issue squarely, he might well accept the ultimate conclusion reached by Brennan.

Referenced Cases: *New York Times Co. v. U.S.*, 403 U.S. 713 (1971), on the "heavy presumption against . . . constitutional validity" that a restraining order bears; *Indianapolis School Comm'rs. v. Jacobs*, 420 U.S. 128 (1975), and *Sosna v. Iowa*, 419 U.S. 393 (1975), regarding the Court's jurisdiction to actual cases and controversies; *Southern Pacific Terminal Co. v. ICC*, 219 U.S. 498 (1911), on jurisdiction relative to expired disputes; *Weinstein v. Bradford*, 423 U.S. 147 (1975), *Roe v. Wade*, 410 U.S. 113 (1973), *Moore v. Ogilvie*, 394 U.S. 814 (1969), and *Carroll v. Princess Anne*, 393 U.S. 175 (1968), on the repetitive aspect of otherwise moot cases; *Irvin v. Dowd*, 366 U.S. 717 (1961),

Rideau v. Louisiana, 373 U.S. 723 (1963), *Estes v. Texas,* 381 U.S. 532 (1965), and *Sheppard v. Maxwell,* 384 U.S. 532 (1966), examples of unfair trial atmosphere; *Stroble v. California,* 343 U.S. 181 (1952), *Murphy v. Florida,* 421 U.S. 794 (1975), and *Beck v. Washington,* 369 U.S. 541 (1962), examples of pretrial publicity not inevitably leading to an unfair trial; *Near v. Minnesota ex rel. Olson,* 283 U.S. 697 (1931), and *Grosjean v. American Press Co.,* 297 U.S. 233 (1936), regarding liberty of press and speech safeguarded by due process clause of 14th Amendment; *Patterson v. Colorado ex. rel. Attorney General,* 205 U.S. 454 (1907), *Organization for a Better Austin v. Keefe,* 402 U.S. 415 (1971), *Bantam Books Inc. v. Sullivan,* 372 U.S. 58 (1963), *Pittsburgh Press Co. v. Human Relations Comm'n,* 413 U.S. 376 (1973), and *New York Times Co. v. U.S.,* 403 U.S. 713 (1971), on prior restraint as the most serious and least tolerable First Amendment infringement; *Cox Broadcasting Corp. v. Cohn,* 420 U.S. 469 (1975), and *Craig v. Harney,* 331 U.S. 367 (1947), on special protection afforded truthful reports of public judicial proceedings; *Miami Herald Publishing Co. v. Tornillo,* 418 U.S. 241 (1974), and *Columbia Broadcasting v. Democratic Comm.,* 412 U.S. 94 (1973), on dangers of government insinuating itself into the editorial process; *Ex parte Milligan,* 4 Wall. 2 (1866), cautioning against suspending explicit guarantees, such as habeas corpus or trial by civilian courts; *Hanson v. Denckla,* 357 U.S. 235 (1958), and *Pennoyer v. Neff,* 95 U.S. 714 (1878), holding that concepts of sovereignty limit territorial jurisdiction of issuing court; *Hynes v. Mayor of Oradell,* 425 U.S. 610 (1976), *Buckley v. Valeo,* 424 U.S. 1 (1976), and *NAACP v. Button,* 371 U.S. 415 (1963), regarding scrutiny of restraints on First Amendment rights; *Roth v. U.S.,* 354 U.S. 476 (1957), and *Chaplinsky v. New Hampshire,* 315 U.S. 568 (1942), cases explaining "speech" not encompassed within the First Amendment; *Southeastern Promotions Ltc. v. Conrad,* 420 U.S. 546 (1975), *U.S. v. Thirty-seven Photographs,* 402 U.S. 363 (1971), *Freedman v. Maryland,* 380 U.S. 51 (1965), *Speiser v. Randall,* 357 U.S. 513 (1958), and *Kingsley Books Inc. v. Brown,* 354 U.S. 436 (1957), on protection of speech within the ambit of First Amendment; *Bridges v. California,* 314 U.S. 252 (1941), and *Pennekamp v. Florida,* 328 U.S. 331 (1946), on settled law on reporters' right to report whatever occurs in open court; *Ham v. South Carolina,* 409 U.S. 524 (1973), and *Swain v. Alabama,* 380 U.S. 202 (1965), on incriminating data heard or read by prospective jurors; *Times-*

Picayune Pub. Corp. v. Schulingkamp, 419 U.S. 1301 (1974), on whether the public interest in receiving information outweighs speculative impact on Sixth Amendment rights; *Ashwander v. TVA*, 297 U.S. 288 (1936), on judicial protections other than enjoining the press from publishing.

Further Reading:

9 *Creighton L. Rev.* 693 (June 1976).
26 *DePaul L. Rev.* 417 (Spring 1976).
90 *Harvard L. Rev.* 159 (Nov. 1976).
20 *Howard L. J.* 537 (1977).
25 *Kansas L. Rev.* 258 (Winter 1977).
22 *Loyola L. Rev.* 1095 (Fall 1976).
12 *New England L. Rev.* 763 (Winter 1977).
22 *NY L. School L. Rev.* 764 (1977).
29 *Stanford L. Rev.* 393, 431 (Feb. 1977).
8 *Texas Tech L. Rev.* 476 (Fall 1976).
45 *Univ. Missouri-KC L. Rev.* 311 (Winter 1976).
16 *Washburn L. J.* 523 (Winter 1977).
87 *Yale L. J.* 342 (Dec. 1977).

1979 *Gannett Co., Inc. v. Daniel A. DePasquale*, 443 U.S. 368, 61 L.Ed.2d 608, 99 S.Ct. 2898, 5 Med.L.Rptr. 1337, 46 U.S.L.W. 2330

Argued: Nov. 7, 1978.

Decided: July 2, 1979.

Summary: In upholding closure of a pretrial hearing, the Court said that the Constitution provides no affirmative right of access to a pretrial proceeding and that a defendant's right to a fair trial outweighs the interest of the press and the public.

Circumstances: The case resulted from the exclusion of the press, in this case a Gannett newspaper reporter, by Judge DePasquale of the Seneca County Court, New York, from a pretrial

suppression-of-evidence hearing in a second-degree murder case.
Defense counsel, arguing that an unabated buildup of adverse
publicity jeopardized the defendants' right to a fair trial, requested
the closure, and the district attorney did not oppose the motion. A
day later, a reporter for two Gannett newspapers in Rochester,
who had been in the courtroom when the motion was made but
did not object at the time, formally objected in a letter to the
judge, who responded that the hearing had concluded and that he
reserved the right to release the transcript. The judge next refused
to set aside the exclusionary order or to grant immediate access to
the transcript following a scheduled hearing on the motion. The
New York Supreme Court held that the exclusionary order trans-
gressed the public's vital interest in open judicial proceedings and
constituted an unlawful prior restraint in violation of the First
and 14th Amendments. The Court of Appeals for New York ruled
that the case was technically moot because the transcript of the
suppression hearing was available to the newspaper when the
defendants pleaded guilty to lesser charges. The court also upheld
the exclusion of the press and the public from the pretrial hearing.
On certiorari, the U.S. Supreme Court affirmed.

Opinion: Justice Potter Stewart wrote the 5-to-4 opinion, joined by Chief Justice Warren E. Burger and Justices Lewis F.
Powell, Jr., William H. Rehnquist, and John Paul Stevens. Stewart
said that the public has no constitutional right independent of an
accused's public-trial right under the Sixth and 14th Amendments
to insist upon access to a pretrial judicial proceeding in a criminal
case. "Publicity concerning pretrial suppression hearings . . . poses
special risks of unfairness. The whole purpose of such hearings is
to screen out unreliable or illegally obtained evidence and insure
that this evidence does not become known to the jury." Justice
Harry A. Blackmun, joined by William J. Brennan, Jr., Byron R.
White, and Thurgood Marshall, agreed with the majority that the
case was not moot, although a transcript of the hearing was made
available to the press prior to the trial of the defendants on lesser
charges. But Blackmun said that the facts of the case did not
justify the exclusion order, that no substantial probability existed
that an open proceeding would result in harm to the defendants'
right to a fair trial. Stewart went on to say that closure of pretrial
proceedings is often one of the most effective methods that a trial
judge can employ to attempt to ensure that the fairness of a trial

will not be jeopardized by the dissemination of such information throughout the community before the trial itself has begun. The history of the public-trial guarantee, Stewart wrote, demonstrates no more than a common law rule of open civil and criminal proceedings. Not many common law rules have been elevated to the status of constitutional rights, although the common law right to a jury trial is explicit in the Sixth and Seventh Amendments, he said. Nor does the Constitution explicitly reject these rules. Although there is no question that the Sixth Amendment "permits and even presumes open trials as a norm," Stewart said, it does not *require* that they be open to the public. The Sixth Amendment confers the right to a public trial only on a defendant and only in a criminal case, not on the public. Stewart, emphasizing the phrase "under the circumstances of this case," said that the trial judge had acted correctly in closing the suppression hearing because an open proceeding would have posed a "reasonable probability of prejudice to these defendants." Furthermore, any denial of access was not absolute but only temporary, for once the danger of prejudice dissipated, a transcript of the hearing was made available, at which time the press and the public had a full opportunity to scrutinize the process. Chief Justice Burger, in a separate brief opinion, emphasized that a hearing on a motion before trial to suppress evidence is not a trial; it is a pretrial hearing. "To make public the evidence developed in a motion to suppress evidence, would, so long as the exclusionary rule is not modified, introduce a new dimension to the problem of conducting fair trials." Justice Powell added separately that the news reporter's First Amendment right of access had been adequately respected by the trial judge, who, following oral argument challenging the closure order, determined that the newspaper had not presented any basis for changing the need for closure. He said the procedure followed by the trial court fully comported with that required by the Constitution. Justice Rehnquist wrote separately that, if the parties in a criminal case agree on a closed proceeding, the trial court is not required by the Sixth Amendment to advance any reason whatsoever for declining to open a pretrial hearing or trial to the public.

In the four-member dissent, Justice Blackmun said that the Sixth Amendment, when applied through the 14th Amendment, prohibits a state from conducting a pretrial suppression hearing in private, even at the request of the accused, unless fair and full consideration is first given to the public's interest in open trials. He quoted from the nineteenth-century British legal theorist Jeremy Bentham, who stressed that publicity was "the soul of justice," an important safeguard against judicial abuse, especially in criminal cases, and that it should not be dispensed with even at the request of the defendant.

Referenced Cases: *Nebraska Press Assn. v. Stuart*, 427 U.S. 539 (1976), *Southern Pacific Terminal Co. v. ICC*, 219 U.S. 498 (1911), and *Weinstein v. Bradford*, 423 U.S. 147 (1975), on determining mootness; *Sheppard v. Maxwell*, 384 U.S. 333 (1966), *Irvin v. Dowd*, 366 U.S. 717 (1961), *Marshall v. U.S.*, 360 U.S. 310 (1959), and *Estes v. Texas*, 381 U.S. 532 (1965), regarding the danger of adverse publicity; *Jackson v. Denno*, 378 U.S. 368 (1964), on excluding unreliable or illegally obtained evidence; *Rideau v. Louisiana*, 373 U.S. 723 (1963), regarding closure of pretrial proceedings as an effective way of ensuring fair trial; *Faretta v. California*, 422 U.S. 806 (1975), and *In re Oliver*, 333 U.S. 257 (1948), on the Sixth Amendment guarantees as personal to the accused; *Singer v. U.S.*, 380 U.S. 24 (1965), holding that the ability to waive a constitutional right does not ordinarily carry right to insist on the opposite of that right; *Barker v. Wingo*, 407 U.S. 514 (1972), and *Patton v. U.S.*, 281 U.S. 276 (1930), on public's interest in swift and fair justice and a jury trial in criminal cases; *Pell v. Procunier*, 417 U.S. 817 (1974), *Saxbe v. Washington Post Co.*, 417 U.S. 843 (1974), and *Houchins v. KQED Inc.*, 438 U.S. 1 (1978), on press access superior to that of public generally; *Branzburg v. Hayes*, 408 U.S. 665 (1972), on the flexible accommodation between First and Sixth Amendment rights; *Nixon v. Warner Communications Inc.*, 435 U.S. 589 (1978), and *Zemel v. Rusk*, 381 U.S. 1 (1965), regarding no First Amendment right of access to judicial or other governmental proceedings; *Times-Picayune Publishing Corp. v. Schulingkamp*, 419 U.S. 1301 (1974), on extent that the Constitution prohibits states from excluding members of the public from pretrial hearings; *Craig v. Harney*, 331 U.S. 367 (1947), *Levine v. U.S.*, 362 U.S. 610 (1960), and *Offutt v. U.S.*, 348 U.S. 11 (1954), on public trial as "public event" reflecting the "appearance of justice"; *Duncan v. Louisiana*, 391 U.S. 145 (1968), and *Argersinger v. Hamlin*, 407 U.S. 25 (1972), on 14th Amendment requiring public-trial provision of Sixth Amendment; *Klopfer v. North Carolina*, 386 U.S. 213 (1967), on history of common law view of the public trial;

Bivens v. Six Unknown Fed. Narcotics Agents, 403 U.S. 388 (1971), regarding the exclusion of relevant evidence; *Pinto v. Pierce,* 389 U.S. 31 (1967), on no federal requirement on states to conduct suppression hearings prior to trial; *Murphy v. Florida,* 421 U.S. 794 (1975), *Beck v. Washington,* 369 U.S. 541 (1962), and *Stroble v. California,* 343 U.S. 181 (1952), on factual publicity not always inconsistent with fair trial.

Further Reading:

65 *ABA J.* 1389 (Sept. 1979).
44 *Albany L. Rev.* 455 (Fall 1980).
55 *California State Bar J.* 18 (Jan. 1980).
1 *Communications & Law* 3 (Winter 1979).
7 *Florida State Univ. L. Rev.* 719 (Fall 1979).
93 *Harvard L. Rev.* 62 (Nov. 1979).
7 *Hastings Const. L. Q.* 339 (Winter 1980).
11 *Texas Tech L. Rev.* 159 (Fall 1979).
51 *Univ. Colorado L. Rev.* 425 (Spring 1980).

1980 *Richmond Newspapers, Inc. v. Virginia,* 448 U.S. 555, 65 L.Ed.2d 973, 100 S.Ct. 2814, 6 Med.L.Rptr. 1833

Argued: Feb. 19, 1980.

Decided: July 2, 1980.

Summary: Criminal trials are presumptively open to the public under the First Amendment. Specifically, the Court agreed that a court order closing a murder trial to the public and the press violated the right of access granted by the First and 14th Amendments.

Circumstances: A Virginia trial judge, who had presided over two of three previous trials of the defendant that ended in mistrials, excluded the public and press from a fourth trial on motion from the defense counsel. Prosecution had no objection, nor did the public or press object at the time. The judge said he relied on a state statute for the authority to close the trial. Later in the day, a newspaper and its two reporters sought a hearing on a motion to vacate the closure order, arguing that the court should first determine that the accused's right to a fair trial could be protected in no other way. The judge allowed the hearing but denied the motion to vacate. On appeal, the Virginia Supreme Court denied writs of mandamus and prohibition, upholding in effect the trial judge. On certiorari, the U.S. Supreme Court reversed.

Opinion: Chief Justice Warren E. Burger announced the 7-to-1 judgment of the Court, and in an opinion joined by Justices Byron R. White, and John Paul Stevens, Burger said that the First and 14th Amendments guarantee the public's right to attend criminal trials. Absent an overriding interest based on findings, a criminal trial must be open to the public. He added that the trial judge had made no findings to support closure, no inquiry into alternative measures to ensure fairness, and no recognition of any constitutional right for the public or the press to attend the trial. Burger noted that this marked the first time the Court had to distinguish between a right of access to *trials* and access to *pretrial* hearings, the Court having ruled no presumptive right to the latter in *Gannett Co. v. DePasquale*, decided exactly a year earlier. In reviewing the historical relationship between open trials and an open society, Burger said "we are bound to conclude that a presumption of openness adheres in the very nature of a criminal trial under our system of justice." Justice White, concurring separately, said that the case would have been unnecessary had the Court in *Gannett* construed the Sixth Amendment to forbid prohibiting the public from criminal proceedings except in narrowly drawn circumstances. Justice Stevens, also concurring separately, called it a watershed case and added: "Today, . . . for the first time, the Court unequivocally holds that an arbitrary interference with access to important information is an abridgment of the freedoms of speech and of the press protected by the First Amendment." Justice William J. Brennan, Jr., joined by Thurgood Marshall, suggested that trial closures should not be left to the unfettered discretion of the judge and parties. He said that the First Amendment, of its own force and as applied to the states through the 14th Amendment, secures the right of public access to trial proceedings independent of the Sixth Amendment. Justice

RICHMOND NEWSPAPERS v. VIRGINIA

Potter Stewart, concurring in the judgment, said the First and 14th Amendments "clearly give the press and the public a right to access to trials themselves, civil as well as criminal." Justice Harry A. Blackmun applauded the Court for relying upon legal history in determining the fundamental public character of the criminal trial and for washing away at least some of the "graffiti that married the prevailing opinions in Gannett." Alone in dissent, Justice William H. Rehnquist objected to his brethren overriding the federal judicial system by reviewing closure orders of state trial judges, who "are making the same effort as we to uphold the Constitution." Justice Lewis F. Powell, Jr., did not participate.

Referenced Cases: *Gannett Co. v. DePasquale,* 443 U.S. 368 (1979), *Nebraska Press Assn. v. Stuart,* 427 U.S. 539 (1976), and *Southern Pacific Terminal Co. v. ICC,* 219 U.S. 498 (1911), holding that a case is not moot if underlying dispute is "capable of repetition, yet evading review"; *Murphy v. Florida,* 421 U.S. 794 (1975), *Sheppard v. Maxwell,* 384 U.S. 333 (1966), and *Estes v. Texas,* 381 U.S. 532 (1965), on conflicts between publicity and fair trial; *Offutt v. U.S.,* 348 U.S. 11 (1954), on satisfying the "appearance of justice"; *First National Bank of Boston v. Bellotti,* 435 U.S. 765 (1978), and *Kleindienst v. Mandel,* 408 U.S. 753 (1972), regarding the freedom to listen; *Saxbe v. Washington Post Co.,* 417 U.S. 843 (1974), *Pell v. Procunier,* 417 U.S. 817 (1974), and *Branzburg v. Hayes,* 408 U.S. 665 (1972), on the right to gather information; *DeJonge v. Oregon,* 299 U.S. 353 (1937), on peaceable assembly cognate to and equally fundamental as free speech and press; *Cox v. New Hampshire,* 312 U.S. 569 (1941), and *Cox v. Louisiana,* 379 U.S. 559 (1965), on time, place, and manner restrictions; *Brown v. Glines,* 444 U.S. 348 (1980), *New York Times Co. v. U.S.,* 403 U.S. 713 (1971), and *Near v. Minnesota ex rel. Olson,* 283 U.S. 697 (1931), on freedom of expression made inviolate by First Amendment; *U.S. v. Carolene Products Co.,* 304 U.S. 144 (1938), *Grosjean v. American Press Co.,* 297 U.S. 233 (1936), *Stromberg v. California,* 283 U.S. 359 (1931), and *New York Times Co. v. Sullivan,* 376 U.S. 254 (1964), on First Amendment's structural role in fostering self-government; *In re Winship,* 397 U.S. 358 (1970), on the special force of public entree to proceedings or information; *In re Oliver,* 333 U.S. 257 (1948), regarding English common law heritage of public trial; *Landmark Communications Inc. v. Virginia,* 435 U.S. 829 (1978), holding that scrutiny of governmental body implicates

First Amendment; *Cox Broadcasting Corp. v. Cohn*, 420 U.S. 469 (1975), and *Time Inc. v. Firestone*, 424 U.S. 448 (1976), on prior restraint and the reporting of criminal proceedings and scrutiny of the administration of justice; *Shuttlesworth v. Birmingham*, 394 U.S. 147 (1969), holding that public and press presence in courtroom assures integrity; *Kovacs v. Cooper*, 336 U.S. 77 (1949), and *Illinois v. Allen*, 397 U.S. 337 (1970), on the need for courtroom to be quiet and orderly; *Brown v. Allen*, 344 U.S. 443 (1953), regarding Justice Robert H. Jackson's sense of the Court's power, "We are not final because we are infallible, but we are infallible only because we are final."

Further Reading:

66 *ABA J.* 999 (Aug. 1980).
33 *Baylor L. Rev.* 191 (Winter 1981).
22 *Boston College L. Rev.* 361 (Jan. 1981).
10 *Capital Univ. L. Rev.* 101 (Fall 1980).
14 *Creighton L. Rev.* 853 (1981).
16 *Harvard Civil Rights–Civil Liberties L. Rev.* 415 (1981).
94 *Harvard L. Rev.* 149 (Nov. 1980).
71 *J. Criminal L.* 547 (Winter 1980).
61 *Journalism Quarterly* 785 (Winter 1984).
61 *Journalism Quarterly* 615 (Autumn 1984).
60 *Nebraska L. Rev.* 169 (1981).
34 *Univ. Miami L. Rev.* 937 (July 1980).
110 *Univ. Pa. L. Rev.* 1 (1961).
26 *Villanova L. Rev.* 183 (Nov. 1980).
73 *Virginia L. Rev.* 1111 (1987).

1981 *Noel Chandler and Robert Granger v. Florida*, 449 U.S. 560, 66 L.Ed.2d 740, 101 S.Ct. 802, 7 Med.L.Rptr. 1041

Argued: Nov. 12, 1980.

Decided: Jan. 26, 1981.

Summary: Held constitutional a state program allowing radio, television, and photographic coverage of criminal proceedings. Use of such journalistic equipment does not by itself deprive the defendant of the right to a fair trial.

Circumstances: In Jan. 1976, Florida announced a one-year pilot program during which the electronic media were permitted to cover all judicial proceedings in the state without reference to the consent of participants but with strict standards to ensure fairness and decorum. Ten other states also started experiments. The Florida Supreme Court concluded "that on balance there [was] more to be gained than lost by permitting electronic media coverage of judicial proceedings subject to standards for such coverage. During Florida's experiment, a Dade County judge permitted limited television coverage of the criminal trial of two Miami Beach policemen—Chandler and Granger—charged with burglary. The trial court denied their motion to have declared unconstitutional a canon of the Florida Code of Judicial Conduct that permitted camera coverage of judicial proceedings in the appellate and trial courts of the state. After conviction, the two men alleged prejudice because of the television coverage but were denied a new trial. The Florida District Court of Appeals affirmed the convictions and the state supreme court denied review. On appeal, the U.S. Supreme Court affirmed.

Opinion: Chief Justice Warren E. Burger wrote for the Court in the 8-to-0 decision, joined by Justices William J. Brennan, Jr., Thurgood Marshall, Harry A. Blackmun, Lewis F. Powell, Jr., and William H. Rehnquist. Potter Stewart and Byron R. White concurred separately. John Paul Stevens did not participate. Burger wrote against the background of Judicial Canon 35, adopted in 1937 by the American Bar Association (ABA) House of Delegates to prohibit all photographic and broadcast coverage of courtroom proceedings. In Feb. 1978, the ABA's Committee on Fair Trial–Free Press proposed revised standards to permit controlled coverage. Although endorsed by two other ABA committees, it was rejected by the House of Delegates. Later that year, the Conference of State Chief Justices, by a vote of 44 to 1, resolved to allow the highest court in each state to promulgate standards and guidelines for regulating cameras in the courtroom.

In *Chandler*, Burger rejected the argument in *Estes v. Texas* (1965) that the televising of criminal trials is inherently a denial of due process, noting that only four justices had taken that position. John M. Harlan, who had provided the fifth vote in *Estes*, confined his view to the specific facts of the case and allowed that smaller, less obtrusive equipment might not interfere with a fair trial in the future. Thus, Burger said that the burden was on the petitioners to show that the trial had not been fair. "The risk of juror prejudice is present in any publication of a trial, but the appropriate safeguard . . . is the defendant's right to demonstrate that the media's coverage of his case—be it printed or broadcast—compromised the ability of the particular jury that heard the case to adjudicate fairly." In sum, Burger argued that, since the Court has no supervisory authority over state courts, the states must be free to experiment, so long as they do not violate either the Sixth Amendment's guarantee of trial by an impartial jury or the 14th's guarantee against the depriving of life, liberty, or property without due process of law. Justice Stewart, although concurring, said the Court should have simply overruled *Estes*, in which he dissented at the time. Justice White also said that *Estes* should have been overturned to affirm the *Chandler* judgment. "Although the Court's opinion today contends that it is consistent with Estes, I believe that it effectively eviscerates Estes."

Referenced Cases: *Nixon v. Warner Communications Inc.*, 435 U.S. 589 (1977), on the Sixth Amendment requirement of a public trial satisfied by allowing attendance and reportage; *Estes v. Texas*, 381 U.S. 532 (1965), on televising as inherent denial of due process; *Nebraska Press Association v. Stuart*, 427 U.S. 539 (1976), on the range of curative devices to prevent publicity about a trial from infecting jury deliberations; *New State Ice Co. v. Liebmann*, 285 U.S. 262 (1932), on Justice Louis D. Brandeis's dissenting admonition, that denial of a state's right to experiment may be "fraught with serious consequences"; *Furman v. Georgia*, 408 U.S. 238 (1972), on the randomness of humiliation evoking due process concerns; *Murphy v. Florida*, 421 U.S. 794 (1975), on the need to demonstrate prejudice in a specific case; *Sheppard v. Maxwell*, 384 U.S. 333 (1966), on unsequestered juries being exposed to sensational coverage.

Further Reading:
15 *Akron L. Rev.* 183 (Summer 1981).
9 *American J. Criminal L.* 113 (March 1981).
33 *Baylor L. Rev.* 679 (Summer 1981).

3 *Comm/Ent* 503 (Spring 1981).

9 *Florida St. Univ. L. Rev.* 315 (Spring 1981).

16 *Harvard Civil Rights L. Rev.* 405 (Fall 1981).

72 *J. Criminal L. & Criminology* 1393 (Winter 1981).

65 *Marquette L. Rev.* 166 (Fall 1981).

7 *Nat'l J. Criminal Defense* 445 (Fall 1981).

8 *Ohio Northern L. Rev.* 567 (July 1981).

9 *Pepperdine L. Rev.* 165 (Dec. 1981).

35 *Univ. Miami L. Rev.* 345 (Jan. 1981).

21 *Washburn L. J.* 419 (Winter 1982).

1982   *Globe Newspaper Co. v. Superior Court for the County of Norfolk,* 457 U.S. 596, 73 L.Ed.2d 248, 102 S.Ct. 2613, 8 Med.L.Rptr. 1689

Argued: March 29, 1982.

Decided: June 23, 1982.

Summary: A state statute requiring courtroom closure during testimony of minors in sex-offense cases held violative of First Amendment.

Circumstances: The Boston *Globe* unsuccessfully tried to gain access to a rape trial conducted in the Superior Court for the County of Norfolk. The defendant, an adult, had been charged with forcible rape and forced unnatural rape of three girls who were minors at the time of trial, two 16 and one 17. After the trial ended in acquittal, the Supreme Judicial Court of Massachusetts determined that the statute required, under all circumstances, the exclusion of the public and press. Interestingly, the defendant was an adult and only the witnesses were minors, suggesting that courts may still close proceedings where juveniles are on trial. On appeal, the U.S. Supreme Court reversed.

Opinion: Justice William J. Brennan, Jr., wrote for the Court in the 6-to-3 decision, joined by Justices Byron R. White,

Thurgood Marshall, Harry A. Blackmun, and Lewis F. Powell, Jr. Sandra Day O'Connor concurred separately. Dissenting were Chief Justice Warren E. Burger and Justices William H. Rehnquist and John Paul Stevens. A Massachusetts statute provided that a judge "shall exclude the general public from the courtroom" at a trial "of a complaint or indictment for rape, incest, carnal abuse or other crime involving sex" when the victim was less than 18 years old. While finding the state's interest in protecting young victims of sex crimes from further trauma compelling, Brennan emphasized that the right of access to criminal trials is secure historically. He noted that the right plays a particularly significant role in the functioning of the judicial process and the government as a whole. "Public scrutiny of a criminal trial enhances the quality and safeguards the integrity of the factfinding process, with benefits to both the defendant and to society as a whole," he wrote. However compelling the reasons for closure, they did not justify the mandatory closure required by state law. Rather, the need for closure must be made on a case-by-case basis, Brennan said, depending on the age of the minor, psychological maturity, nature of the crime, need for testimony, and the interests of close relatives. He added that the court should not be closed if the names of the minors were already in the public record or if the minors said they were willing to testify in the presence of the press. The Massachusetts law did not guarantee that the testimony would be kept secret, for in that state the press had access to court transcripts and other sources that provided the same information. In her concurring opinion, Justice O'Connor noted that the decision carried no implications outside the context of criminal trials and, in this case, the state had not demonstrated interest weighty enough to justify its bar to all cases. Chief Justice Burger, joined by Rehnquist, dissented vigorously against the Court undercutting state authority and duty to protect minor victims of crimes. Justice Stevens dissented on procedural grounds.

Referenced Cases: *Southern Pacific Terminal Co. v. ICC,* 219 U.S. 498 (1911), on mootness where issues are "significant and troublesome, and . . . capable of repetition yet evading review"; *Globe Newspaper Co. v. Superior Court,* 449 U.S. 894 (1980), where Court originally remanded in light of *Richmond Newspapers Inc. v. Virginia,* 448 U.S. 555 (1980), in which Court ruled criminal trials open under the First and 14th Amendments; *Nebraska Press Assn. v. Stuart,* 427 U.S. 539 (1976), on extending jurisdiction to actual cases or controversies; *Gannett Co. v. De-Pasquale,* 443 U.S. 368 (1979), upholding closure of a pretrial hearing; *NAACP v. Button,* 371 U.S. 415 (1963), eschewing "narrow, literal conception" of the First Amendment's terms; *Mills v. Alabama,* 384 U.S. 214 (1966), and *Thornhill v. Alabama,* 310 U.S. 88 (1940), on protecting the free discussion of governmental affairs; *In re Oliver,* 333 U.S. 257 (1948), on the solidly grounded presumption of openness; *Brown v. Hartlage,* 456 U.S. 45 (1982), and *Smith v. Daily Mail Publishing Co.,* 443 U.S. 97 (1979), basing denial of access on compelling governmental interest; *Pell v. Procunier,* 417 U.S. 817 (1974), *Saxbe v. Washington Post Co.,* 417 U.S. 843 (1974), and *Cox v. New Hampshire,* 312 U.S. 569 (1941), on Court's obligation to balance competing interests; *New State Ice Co. v. Liebmann,* 285 U.S. 262 (1932), *Chandler v. Florida,* 449 U.S. 560 (1981), *Reeves Inc. v. State,* 447 U.S. 429 (1980), and *Whalen v. Roe,* 429 U.S. 589 (1977), on the need to allow states to experiment without federal interference; *Bates v. State Bar of Arizona,* 433 U.S. 350 (1977), and *Young v. American Mini Theatres,* 427 U.S. 50 (1976), right of access plainly not co-extensive with right of expression.

Further Reading:

68 *ABA J.* 1301 (Oct. 1982).

47 *Albany L. Rev.* 408 (Winter 1983).

36 *Arkansas L. Rev.* 688 (1983).

24 *Boston College L. Rev.* 809 (May 1983).

11 *Florida St. Univ. L. Rev.* 487 (Summer 1983).

51 *George Washington L. Rev.* 269 (Jan. 1983).

11 *Hofstra L. Rev.* 1353 (Summer 1983).

73 *J. Criminal L. & Criminology* 1388 (Winter 1982).

81 *Michigan L. Rev.* 1540 (May 1983).

3 *Pace L. Rev.* 395 (Winter 1983).

23 *Santa Clara L. Rev.* 947 (Summer 1983).

6 *Univ. Arkansas, Little Rock, L. J.* 331 (1983).

4 *Univ. Bridgeport L. Rev.* 359 (1983).

19 *Wake Forest L. Rev.* 59 (Feb. 1983).

1984   ***Press-Enterprise Co. v. Superior Court***
          of California, Riverside County, 464
          U.S. 501, 78 L.Ed.2d 629, 104 S.Ct. 819,
          10 Med.L.Rptr. 1161

Argued: Oct. 12, 1983.

Decided: Jan. 18, 1984.

Summary: Unanimously held that the qualified First Amendment right to attend criminal trials covered proceedings for the voir dire examination of potential jurors.

Circumstances: Before the voir dire examination began in a rape-murder case, the newspaper had moved that the proceeding be open to the press and the public. The state, arguing against the motion, said that if the press were present the responses of prospective jurors to questions would lack the candor necessary for a fair trial to take place. The judge closed all but the "general voir dire," or three days of the six-week-long voir dire. After the jury was empaneled, the newspaper moved for release of the complete transcript of the voir dire. Both defense counsel and the prosecutor argued that release would violate the jurors' right of privacy, that jurors had answered questions under an implied promise of confidentiality. The newspaper then sought a writ of mandate from the California Court of Appeals to force the superior court to release the transcript and vacate the closure order. The petition was denied and the California Supreme Court denied the paper's request for a hearing. On certiorari, the U.S. Supreme Court vacated and remanded. (The California Supreme Court ruled on Dec. 31, 1984, that the U.S. high court's decision did not mandate repudiation of the earlier state court's determination that the First Amendment does not provide a right of access to pretrial proceedings. It reasoned that the Court's decision in *Press-Enterprise* and in *Globe Newspaper Co. v. Superior Court* (1982) concerned trials, not pretrials, and that in *Press-Enterprise* the Court had emphasized that fair trial remained the primary concern, not access to court proceedings. But the California court also noted that the state penal code had been amended to specify that preliminary hearings can only be closed if the trial court determines closure to be necessary to protect the accused's right to a fair and impartial trial. Open hearings are the rule rather than the exception, the California court noted.)

Opinion: Chief Justice Warren E. Burger wrote the opinion, joined by William J. Brennan, Jr., Byron R. White, Harry A. Blackmun, Lewis F. Powell, Jr., William H. Rehnquist, John Paul Stevens, and Sandra Day O'Connor. Thurgood Marshall concurred separately, and Blackmun and Stevens filed separate opinions. No right ranks higher than the right of the accused to a fair trial, Burger said, but the primacy of the accused's right is difficult to separate from the right of everyone in the community to attend the voir dire, which promotes fairness. Thus, the Court did not bother to make a distinction on whether the voir dire proceeding is part of a pretrial hearing or the trial itself. "The value of openness lies in the fact that people not actually attending trials can have confidence that standards of fairness are being observed." Burger pointed out, however, that the right of access is not absolute. The presumption of openness may be overcome only by an overriding interest based on findings that closure is essential to preserve higher values and is narrowly tailored to serve that interest, Burger said. On occasion privacy interests of a prospective juror may have to be dealt with by the judge in camera but with counsel present and on the record. "The privacy interests . . . must be balanced against the historic values . . . and the need for openness of the process." Yet, in this case, the judge provided no explanation why his broad closure order was not limited to information that was actually sensitive and deserving of privacy protection.

Justice Blackmun wrote to emphasize that the Court was not deciding prospective jurors' privacy rights and that the voir dire closing was overbroad. Justice Stevens added that the trial court had applied an impermissibly broad rule of secrecy, and he said that the right of access upheld by the Court is found in the First Amendment rather than in the public trial provision of the Sixth. Justice Marshall added that lengthy voir dire proceedings undermine public confidence in the courts and the legal profession. He said constitutionally protected access is not diminished by deeply personal revelations in voir dire. "In those cases where a closure order is imposed, the constitutionally preferable method for reconciling the First Amendment interests of the public and the

press with the legitimate privacy interests of jurors and the interests of defendants in fair trials is to redact transcripts in such a
way as to preserve the anonymity of jurors while disclosing the
substance of their responses."

Referenced Cases: *Richmond Newspapers v. Vir-
ginia*, 448 U.S. 555 (1980), on the essential nature of open criminal
trials; *U.S. v. Hasting*, 461 U.S. 499 (1983), and *Morris v. Slappy*,
461 U.S. 1 (1983), holding that openly selected juries enhance
public confidence in the criminal justice system; *Globe Newspaper Co. v. Superior Court*, 457 U.S. 596 (1982), on state justification in denying access must be weighty; *Nixon v. Administrator
of General Services*, 433 U.S. 425 (1977), regarding the legitimate
expectation of privacy in court proceedings.

Further Reading:
45 *So. Calif. L. Rev.* 51 (1972).
6 *Univ. Arkansas Little Rock L. J.* 331 (1983).

1986   *Press-Enterprise Co. v. Superior Court of California for the County of River- side*, 478 U.S. 1, 92 L.Ed.2d 1, 106 S.Ct. 2735, 13 Med.L.Rptr. 1001

Argued: Feb. 26, 1986.

Decided: June 30, 1986.

Summary: The qualified First Amendment right of access to criminal proceedings applies to preliminary hearings as
conducted in California.

Circumstances: On Dec. 23, 1981, California filed a
complaint in the Riverside County Municipal Court charging
Robert Diaz, a nurse, with 12 counts of murder. The complaint
alleged that Diaz had murdered 12 patients by giving them massive doses of the heart drug lidocaine. When the preliminary
hearing started on July 6, 1982, Diaz moved to exclude the public

in order to protect, under state law, his right to a fair and impartial trial. In granting the motion, the magistrate said that closure was necessary because the case had attracted national attention and "only one side may get reported in the media." At the end of the 41-day hearing, the newspaper asked that the transcript be released. The magistrate refused and sealed the record. On Jan. 21, 1983, the state moved in Superior Court to have the transcripts released, but the court found "a reasonable likelihood that release of all or any part of the transcript might prejudice defendant's right to a fair and impartial trial." The publisher's peremptory writ of mandate was denied. The Superior Court released the transcript when Diaz had waived a jury trial. But the California Supreme Court denied the writ of mandate, holding that there is no general First Amendment right of access to preliminary hearings. On certiorari, the U.S. Supreme Court reversed.

Opinion: Chief Justice Warren E. Burger wrote the opinion for the 7-to-2 Court, joined by Justices William J. Brennan, Jr., Byron R. White, Thurgood Marshall, Harry A. Blackmun, Lewis F. Powell, Jr., and Sandra Day O'Connor. Dissenting were John Paul Stevens and William H. Rehnquist. Burger also wrote the opinion in what is known as *Press-Enterprise I* (1984), in which the Court unanimously held that the qualified First Amendment right to attend criminal trials covered voir dire proceedings. In *Press-Enterprise II*, Burger said the First Amendment required that defendants seeking to close pretrial hearings must demonstrate a greater danger to their rights than a "reasonable likelihood," which the California Supreme Court had stipulated. Instead, the Court said, defendants must provide specific evidence that an open courtroom would have a "substantial probability" of endangering their rights to a fair trial. Echoing *Press-Enterprise I*, Burger said that judges must consider whether alternatives to closure could protect the rights of the defendants. The chief justice said that the same considerations that led the Court to apply the right of access to criminal trials in *Richmond Newspapers v. Virginia* (1980) and *Globe Newspaper Co. v. Superior Court* (1982) and the jury selection process in *Press-Enterprise I* applied in *Press-Enterprise II*. Preliminary hearings are enough like trials that the Court could conclude that public access is as essential to their success as it is for the success of trials. As in trials, preliminary hearings in California afford the accused the right to appear before a magis-

trate, to be represented by counsel, to cross-examine hostile witnesses, to present exculpatory evidence, and to exclude illegally
obtained evidence. "Because of its extensive scope, the preliminary hearing is often the final and most important step in the
criminal proceeding," Burger wrote. An open hearing becomes
even more important because of the absence of a jury, the "inesti-
mable safeguard against the corrupt or overzealous prosecutor and
against the compliant, biased, or eccentric judge," as the Court
averred in *Duncan v. Louisiana*, 391 U.S. 145 (1968).

Justice Stevens, with Rehnquist, said that the risk of prejudice was more significant in this case than the interest in publishing the transcript sooner rather than later. In addition, he noted
that the majority's reasoning on the "value of openness" was
flawed because it also applied to the traditionally secret grand
jury.

Referenced Cases: *Press-Enterprise Co. v. Superior
Court*, 464 U.S. 501 (1984), *Globe Newspaper Co. v. Superior
Court*, 457 U.S. 596 (1982), and *Gannett Co. v. DePasquale*, 443
U.S. 368 (1979), on the right to access to criminal proceedings;
Waller v. Georgia, 467 U.S. 39 (1984), on Sixth Amendment right
of the accused being no less protective of a public trial than the
First Amendment right of the press and public; *Richmond News-
papers v. Virginia*, 448 U.S. 555 (1980), on the "tradition of accessi-
bility"; *Douglas Oil Co. v. Petrol Stops Northwest*, 441 U.S. 211
(1979), holding that "the proper functioning of our grand jury
system depends upon the secrecy of grand jury proceedings";
Grosjean v. American Press Co., 297 U.S. 233 (1936), *Smith v.
Daily Mail Publishing*, 443 U.S. 97 (1979), *Landmark Communications v. Virginia*, 435 U.S. 829 (1978), *Oklahoma Publishing Co. v.
District Court*, 430 U.S. 308 (1977), *Nebraska Press Ass'n v. Stuart*,
427 U.S. 539 (1976), and *Cox Broadcasting v. Cohn*, 420 U.S. 469
(1975), on the core of the First Amendment and governmental
objectives of the "highest order" to overcome it; *Houchins v.
KQED*, 438 U.S. 1 (1978), on constitutional protection of information gathering; *Pell v. Procunier*, 417 U.S. 817 (1974), and *Saxbe v.
Washington Post*, 417 U.S. 843 (1974), on support of secrecy;
U.S. v. Procter & Gamble, 356 U.S. 677 (1958), *Branzburg v. Hayes*,
408 U.S. 665 (1972), and *U.S. v. Sells Engineering*, 463 U.S. 418
(1979), on secrecy of grand jury proceedings; *Seattle Times v.
Rhinehart*, 467 U.S. 230 (1984), on a newspaper not allowed to

publish information to which it was privy as a litigant in a civil action.

Further Reading:
24 *American Criminal L. Rev.* 379 (Fall 1986).
19 *Connecticut L. Rev.* 561 (Spring 1987).
56 *Mississippi L. J.* 417 (Aug. 1986).

Selected Bibliography

Apfel, Dov, "Gag Orders, Exclusionary Orders and Protective Orders: Expanding the Use of Preventive Remedies to Safeguard a Criminal Defendant's Right to a Fair Trial," 29 *American Univ. L. Rev.* 439 (1980).

Ares, C. E., "Chandler v. Florida: Television, Criminal Trials, and Due Process," 6 *Supreme Ct. Rev.* 157 (1981).

BeVier, Lillian R., "Like Mackerel in the Moonlight: Some Reflections on Richmond Newspapers," 10 *Hofstra L. Rev.* 311 (1982).

Block, I. J., "Cameras and Courtrooms: The Denial of Due Process," 52 *Florida Bar J.* 454 (June 1978).

"Cameras in the Courtroom and Due Process: A Proposal for a Qualitative Difference Test," 57 *Washington L. Rev.* 277 (1982).

Cohen, Susan D., "Reconciling Media Access with Confidentiality for the Individual in Juvenile Court," 20 *Santa Clara L. Rev.* 405 (1980).

"Constitutional Law—First Amendment Right of Access to Criminal Trials," 6 *Univ. Arkansas Little Rock L. J.* 331 (1983).

Day, Louise A., "Media Access to Juvenile Courts," 61 *Journalism Quarterly* 751 (Winter 1984).

"Evaluating Court Closures After Richmond Newspapers: Using the Sixth Amendment Standards to Enforce a First Amendment Right," 50 *George Washington L. Rev.* 304 (1982).

"Fair Trial and Free Press: A Symposium," 42 *Notre Dame Law* 857 (1967).

"First Amendment Protection of Criminal Defense Attorneys' Extrajudicial Statements in the Decade Since Nebraska Press Association v. Stuart," 8 *Whittier L. Rev.* 1021 (1987).

"First Amendment Right of Access to Pretrial Proceedings in Criminal Cases," 32 *Emory L. J.* 619 (Spring 1983).

"Freedom of the Press vs. Juvenile Anonymity: A Conflict Between Constitutional Priorities and Rehabilitation," 65 *Iowa L. Rev.* 1471 (1980).

Fulero, S. M., "The Role of Behavioral Research in the Free Press/Fair Trial Controversy: Another View," 11 *Law and Human Behavior* 259 (Sept. 1987).

Gerald, J. Edward, "Press-Bar Relationships: Progress Since Sheppard and Reardon," 47 *Journalism Quarterly* 223 (1970).

Gillmor, Donald M., "Free Press v. Fair Trial: A Continuing Dialogue—'Trial by Newspaper' and the Social Sciences," 41 *North Dakota L. Rev.* 156 (1965).

"Globe Newspapers: No Shield for the Child Witness," 15 *Univ. West LA L. Rev.* 109 (1983).

"Globe Newspaper Co. v. Superior Court: Fortifying the Right to Trial Access," 4 *Univ. Bridgeport L. Rev.* 359 (1983).

Greenberg, S. L., "Spotlight on the Jury: Trial Publicity and Juror Privacy," 6 *Comm/Ent* 369 (1984).

Hughes, R. L., "Chandler v. Florida: Cameras Get Probation in Courtrooms," 26 *J. Broadcasting* 431 (Winter 1982).

Jennings, James M. II, "Is Chandler a Final Rewrite of Estes?" 59 *Journalism Quarterly* 66 (Spring 1982).

Kline, Gerald, and Paul Jess, "Prejudicial Publicity: Its Effect on Law School Mock Juries," 43 *Journalism Quarterly* 113 (1966).

Leeper, Roy V., "Richmond Newspapers, Inc. v. Virginia and the Emerging Right of Access," 61 *Journalism Quarterly* 615 (Autumn 1984).

Lindsey, Richard P., "An Assessment of the Use of Cameras in State and Federal Courts," 18 *Georgia L. Rev.* 389 (1984).

Mason, Robert, "Commentary—The Supreme Court and Press Fashions," 22 *William & Mary L. Rev.* 259 (1980).

McLean, Deckle, "The Impact of Richmond Newspapers," 61 *Journalism Quarterly* 785 (Winter 1984).

Pember, Don R., "Does Pretrial Publicity Really Hurt?" *Columbia Journalism Review* 16 (Sept./Oct. 1984).

Pequignot, M., "From Estes to Chandler: Shifting the Constitutional Burden of Courtroom Cameras to the States," 9 *Florida State Univ. L. Rev.* 315 (1981).

Peskin, S. H., "Fair Trial/Free Press: A Novel Approach," 12 *Trial Lawyers Q.* 60 (Fall–Winter 1978).

Reardon, P. C., "Fair Trial–Free Press Controversy—Where We Have Been and Where We Should Be Going," 4 *San Diego L. Rev.* 255 (June 1967).

———, "Fair Trial–Free Press Standards," 54 *ABA J.* 343 (April 1968).

———, "Fair Trial–Free Press," 52 *Marquette L. Rev.* 547 (Winter 1969).

"Recognizing a Constitutional Right of Media Access to Evidentiary Records in Criminal Trials," 17 *Univ. Michigan J. L. Ref.* 121 (Feb. 1983).

Riley, Sam, "Pre-Trial Publicity: A Field Study," 50 *Journalism Quarterly* 17 (1973).

Simon, Rita, "Murders, Juries and the Press," *Transaction* 40 (May–June 1966).

———, "Does the Court's Decision in Nebraska Press Association Fit the Research Evidence on the Impact on Jurors of News Coverage?" 29 *Stanford L. Rev.* 515 (1977).

Stanga, J. E., Jr., "Judicial Protection of the Criminal Defendant Against Adverse Press Coverage," 13 *William & Mary L. Rev.* 1 (Fall 1971).

Tongue, T. H., "The Case Against Television in the Courtroom," 16 *Willamette L. Rev.* 777 (1980).

Warren, Robert S., and Jeffrey M. Abell, "Free Press–Fair Trial, the Gag Order: A California Aberration," 45 *So. Calif. L. Rev.* 51 (1972).

Freedom of Information Act (FOIA)

1973   *Environmental Protection Agency et al. v. Patsy T. Mink et al., 410 U.S. 73, 35 L.Ed.2d 119, 93 S.Ct. 827, 1 Med.L.Rptr. 2448*

Argued: Nov. 9, 1972.

Decided: Jan. 22, 1973.

Summary: Exemption 1 of the FOIA, as intended by Congress and interpreted by the Court, disallows court review of Executive Branch classification of records affecting national security and its determination on public access requests.

Circumstances: Congresswoman Mink and 32 of her colleagues brought their suit on the heels of a Washington newspaper article in late July 1971 that reported on President Nixon's receipt of conflicting recommendations on the advisability of the underground nuclear test scheduled for the autumn at Amchitka Island, Alaska. Mink sent the president a telegram requesting the "immediate release of recommendations and report by interdepartmental committee." When the request was denied, she and her colleagues sought access through the FOIA. Of the ten documents sought, one, an Environmental Impact Statement prepared by the Atomic Energy Commission (AEC), was publicly available and not in dispute. The others were said to be solely advisory to the president and involved highly sensitive matter vital to the national defense and foreign policy, according to an affidavit filed by the EPA, prepared by Under Secretary of State John N. Irwin II. The documents were classified Top Secret or Secret pursuant to Executive Order 10501. The District Court for the District of

Columbia granted the EPA summary judgment on the ground that each of the nine documents was exempted from compelled disclosure. The Court of Appeals for the District of Columbia Circuit reversed, holding: "If the nonsecret components [of such documents] are separable from the secret remainder and may be read separately without distortion of meaning, they . . . should be disclosed." The court also held that the intragovernment documents affected by Subsection (b)(5) should be examined in camera to determine if "factual data" could be separated out and disclosed "without impinging on the policymaking decisional processes intended to be protected by this exemption." The Supreme Court reversed.

Opinion: Justice Byron R. White wrote for five members in the 7-to-1 decision, joined by Chief Justice Warren E. Burger and Justices Harry A. Blackmun, Lewis F. Powell, Jr., and Potter Stewart, who also wrote a separate opinion. William J. Brennan, Jr., joined by Thurgood Marshall, concurred in part and dissented in part. William O. Douglas dissented. William H. Rehnquist did not participate. The Court held that Subsection (b)(1) of the FOIA does not compel disclosure of classified documents or in camera inspection to sift out "non-secret components." That part of the act exempts matters "specifically required by Executive order [No. 10501] to be kept secret in the interest of national defense or foreign policy." Seven members agreed that Subsection (b)(5), which prevents disclosure of certain inter-agency or intra-agency memoranda or letters, does not require that otherwise confidential documents undergo in camera viewing regardless of how little, if any, purely factual material they contain at risk to private matter in the intragovernment memoranda or letter. Instead of automatic inspection of purely factual material, defendants should have the opportunity to demonstrate, by oral or written testimony, that documents sought are clearly outside the range of material that would be available by law to a private party in litigation with a government agency. White found "wholly untenable" any claim that the FOIA was intended to subject the soundness of executive security classifications to judicial review at the insistence of any objecting citizen. But, he added, the burden is on the agency resisting disclosure, and if it fails to meet its burden without in camera inspection the district court may order such review.

Justice Stewart, in narrowing the issues, said that the case involved no constitutional claims, no challenge to "Executive privilege," nor an effort to invoke judicial power to reclassify documents. Only two exemptions were at issue. "[Congress] has built into the Freedom of Information Act an exemption that provides no means to question an Executive decision to stamp a document 'secret,' however cynical, myopic, or even corrupt that decision might have been." Quoting from the Court's decision, Stewart said Congress could require that the Executive Branch adopt new procedures, but in enacting Exemption 1, it chose, instead, to decree "blind acceptance of Executive fiat."

Justice Brennan, with Marshall, concurred in the Court's holdings on Subsection (b)(5) but dissented in its holdings on Subsection (b)(1), permitting, instead, disclosure of separable non-secret parts of otherwise classified documents. Justice Douglas, in dissent, said that the Court should trust federal district judges to inspect documents to separate out nonsecret and factual materials for disclosure. "Unless the District Court can do those things, the much-advertised Freedom of Information Act is on its way to becoming a shambles. Unless federal courts can be trusted, the Executive will hold complete sway and by *ipse dixit* make even the time of day 'Top Secret.'"

Referenced Cases: *U.S. v. Reynolds*, 345 U.S. 1 (1953), regarding congressional power over Executive Branch procedures and limitations imposed by executive privilege; *Gravel v. U.S.*, 408 U.S. 606 (1972), Justice Douglas on publisher's freedom to print classified documents without fear of retribution.

Further Reading:
52 *No. Carolina L. Rev.* 417 (Dec. 1973).
2 *Pepperdine L. Rev.* 8 (1974) [by Congresswoman Mink].
42 *Univ. Cincinnati L. Rev.* 529 (1973).
1975 *Utah L. Rev.* 943 (Winter 1975).

1976   *Department of the Air Force et al. v. Michael T. Rose et al.*, 425 U.S. 352, 48 L.Ed.2d 11, 96 S.Ct. 1592, 1 Med.L.Rptr. 2509

Argued: Oct. 8, 1975.

Decided: April 21, 1976.

Summary: In an important FOIA Exemption 2 case, the Court said the exemption "is not applicable to matters [of] genuine and significant public interest." Exemption 2 applies to matters "related solely to the internal personnel rules and practices of an agency."

Circumstances: Student editors and former editors of the *New York University Law Review* sought disclosure of Air Force Academy summaries of honors and ethics hearings, with identification of the participants deleted, for a law review article on disciplinary systems at military academies in general. They were denied access, despite the Academy practice of posting such summaries and distributing them to faculty and administrators at the school. The District Court for the Southern District of New York granted the Academy summary judgment without first requiring production of the summaries for inspection. It held that, although the information was not exempt under the FOIA's Exemption 6, the privacy exemption, the summaries were exempt under Exemption 2. The Court of Appeals for the Second Circuit reversed, holding that Exemption 2 was not applicable and that the summaries should be produced for in camera examination, with identifying data deleted to safeguard personal privacy. On certiorari, the Supreme Court affirmed.

Opinion: Justice William J. Brennan, Jr., writing for the majority in the 5-to-3 decision, said that where there is a "genuine and significant public interest" in the information sought under the FOIA, disclosure is compelled *except* "where disclosure may risk circumvention of agency regulations." Joining the judgment were Justices Potter Stewart, Byron R. White, Thurgood Marshall, and Lewis F. Powell, Jr. John Paul Stevens did not participate. Dissenting were Chief Justice Warren E. Burger and Justices Harry A. Blackmun and William H. Rehnquist. Brennan said the exemption was not designed to authorize withholding of all matters except otherwise secret law bearing directly on the propriety of actions of members of the public. "Rather, the general thrust of the exemption is simply to relieve agencies of the burden of assembling and maintaining for public inspection matter in which the public could not reasonably be expected to have an interest." The information sought—summaries of honors and ethics hearings at the Air Force Academy, edited to preserve anonymity— was not matter of merely internal significance, nor matter of a routine nature, nor administratively burdensome to provide, Brennan said. In sum, the justice averred that the files did not contain the "vast amounts of personal data" that under Exemption 2 constitute a personal file, thereby supporting Congress' intention "to open agency action to the light of public scrutiny." Referring to Exemption 6, Brennan said the Court found nothing in its wording to support the Air Force claim that Congress had created a blanket exemption for personnel files. Rather, Congress adopted a limited exemption, where privacy was threatened, for "clearly unwarranted" invasions. The case summaries named no names, except of cadets found guilty, were widely disseminated to cadets, contained only facts related to alleged violations of the honor or ethics codes, and were "justified by the Academy solely for their value as an educational and instructional tool the better to train military officers for discharge of their important and exacting functions."

Chief Justice Burger, in strong dissent, said, "If 'hard cases make bad law,' unusual cases surely have the potential to make even worse law." Even if the government must show that the summaries were subject to a "public interest" standard, Burger found it clear that disclosure constituted an invasion no matter what excision process is attempted by a federal judge. He called the Court's interpretation of congressional intent a "split-personality" reaction between a seeming passion for privacy and a comparable passion for needless invasions of privacy. Justice Blackmun dissented on the grounds that the summaries related solely to internal personnel practices and that their disclosure invaded individual privacy. Justice Rehnquist found Exemption 6 solely applicable.

Referenced Cases: *EPA v. Mink*, 410 U.S. 73 (1973), on the history of the FOIA, its legislative and judicial evolution; *Renegotiation Board v. Bannercraft Clothing Co.*, 415 U.S. 1 (1974), on congressional dissatisfaction with Exemption 2 and its legislative history; *Parker v. Levy*, 417 U.S. 733 (1974), and *Orloff v. Willoughby*, 345 U.S. 83 (1953), on opprobrium of allegations of dishonor among military officers and the stigma that follows; *Paul v. Davis*, 424 U.S. 693 (1976), on agency choosing to disseminate public records.

Further Reading:
62 *ABA J.* 897 (July 1976).
16 *Air Force L. Rev.* 54 (Spring 1974).
14 *California Western L. Rev.* 183 (1978).

1978 *National Labor Relations Board v. Robbins Tire and Rubber Co.,* 437 U.S. 214, 57 L.Ed.2d 159, 98 S.Ct. 2311

Argued: April 26, 1978.

Decided: June 15, 1978.

Summary: Upheld the NLRB's denial of records disclosure under FOIA Exemption 7, exempting "investigatory records compiled for law enforcement purposes" to the extent their production would "interfere with enforcement proceedings."

Circumstances: Following a contested representation election in a unit of the rubber company's employees, the regional office of the NLRB issued an unfair labor practice complaint. Prior to a scheduled hearing in April 1976, the company asked that the NLRB release copies of all potential witnesses' statements collected during the board's investigation. The board refused. The District Court for the Northern District of Alabama ruled that the exemption did not apply, and the Court of Appeals for the Fifth Circuit affirmed. On certiorari, the Supreme Court reversed.

Opinion: Justice Thurgood Marshall wrote the Court's decision, joined by Chief Justice Warren E. Burger and Justices Potter Stewart, Byron R. White, Harry A. Blackmun, William H. Rehnquist, and John Paul Stevens. Lewis F. Powell, Jr., with William J. Brennan, Jr., concurred in part and dissented in part. The

Court said that the NLRB was not required by the FOIA to disclose statements of potential witnesses in pending unfair labor practice proceedings, at least not until completion of the hearing. The NLRB said release of the records would have interfered with its investigation. The Court agreed, reasoning that disclosure might result in company intimidation of the witnesses. Reviewing Exemption 7's legislative history, Marshall pointed out that Congress recognized that law enforcement agencies have legitimate needs to keep certain records confidential lest the agencies be hindered in their investigations or placed at a disadvantage when it came time to present their case. But the Court pinned its decision here on the "danger of witness intimidation" and the fear of chilling cooperation with law enforcement if certain information were disclosed prematurely. In sum, Marshall said: "Since we are dealing here with the narrow question whether witnesses' statements must be released five days prior to an unfair labor practice hearing, we cannot see how [the] FOIA's purposes would be defeated by deferring disclosure until after the Government has presented its case in court." Justice Stevens, with Burger and Rehnquist, said simply that the Court's rationale applied equally to any enforcement proceedings. Justice Powell, with Brennan, said that the NLRB's rule of nondisclosure should only have applied to pre-hearing hostile statements by current employees, not statements by all witnesses.

Referenced Cases: *EPA v. Mink*, 410 U.S. 73 (1973), *Renegotiation Board v. Bannercraft Clothing Co.*, 415 U.S. 1 (1974), *NLRB v. Sears, Roebuck & Co.*, 421 U.S. 132 (1975), and *Dept. of the Air Force v. Rose*, 425 U.S. 352 (1976), on the history and purposes of the original FOIA of 1966; *NLRB v. Scrivener*, 405 U.S. 117 (1972), and *Nash v. Florida Industrial Comm'n*, 389 U.S. 235 (1967), regarding employees as witnesses and interference with witnesses in general.

Further Reading:
64 *ABA J.* 1762 (Nov. 1978).
47 *Fordham L. Rev.* 393 (Dec. 1978).
1974 *Washington Univ. L. Q.* 463 (1974).

1979 *Chrysler Corp. v. Harold Brown, Secretary of Defense, et al., 441 U.S. 281, 60 L.Ed.2d 208, 99 S.Ct. 1705*

Argued: Nov. 8, 1978.

Decided: April 18, 1979.

Summary: In an Exemption 4 case, the Court held that neither the FOIA nor the Trade Secrets Act afforded a private right of action to stop agency disclosure of documents submitted to a federal agency by a person or corporation.

Circumstances: Involved in a number of government contracts, Chrysler was required to provide information to the Department of Labor on its equal opportunity employment practices. The department's Office of Federal Contract Compliance Programs (OFCCP) is the designated compliance agency. The Defense Logistics Agency (DLA) is the Department of Defense's compliance agency. If inspection of information gathered furthers the public interest, the agencies may disclose matter voluntarily. The controversy began on May 14, 1975, when the DLA told Chrysler that third parties had requested affirmative action information on the company's Newark, Delaware, assembly plant. When the agency determined that the material was open to inspection, Chrysler sought to enjoin release in the District Court for the District of Delaware, which held that information relating to trade secrets fell within Exemption 4. The Court of Appeals for the Third Circuit vacated the judgment. The Supreme Court, on certiorari, vacated and remanded.

Opinion: Justice William H. Rehnquist wrote for the unanimous Court. Under the FOIA, third parties have been able to obtain government files containing information submitted by corporations and individuals who thought that the information would be held in confidence. Thus, Exemption 4 has spawned a peculiar species of FOIA litigation—a "reverse" FOIA suit. A person or corporation who is required by law to submit information to the government then seeks an injunction to prevent disclosure. The Court, agreeing with the Court of Appeals for the Third

Circuit, said that the FOIA is purely a disclosure statute and afforded Chrysler no private right of action to enjoin agency disclosure. But the Court disagreed on the conclusion that disclosure is "authorized by law." Rehnquist said that Congress did not limit an agency's discretion to disclose information, and thus the FOIA did not afford Chrysler any right to enjoin disclosure.

Referenced Cases: *Red Lion Broadcasting Co. v. FCC*, 395 U.S. 367 (1969), and *FHA v. The Darlington Inc.*, 358 U.S. 84 (1958), on congressional efforts over three decades to increase public access to government information; *Batterton v. Francis*, 432 U.S. 416 (1977), on the power and limitations of departments and agencies as imposed by Congress; *Morton v. Ruiz*, 415 U.S. 199 (1974), on "substantive rules" versus "interpretative rules," the former the binding "force of law"; *NLRB v. Wyman-Gordon Co.*, 394 U.S. 759 (1969), on ensuring fairness and mature consideration of rules of general application; *NBC v. U.S.*, 319 U.S. 190 (1943), regarding Justice Felix Frankfurter's conclusion that agency regulations had the force of law unless arbitrary or in violation of prescribed procedures; *Vermont Yankee Nuclear Power Corp. v. Natural Resources Defense Council Inc.*, 435 U.S. 519 (1978), holding that courts could only in "extraordinary circumstances" impose procedures beyond those specified in the Administrative Procedure Act.

Further Reading:
65 *ABA J.* 1092 (July 1979).
8 *Boston College Environmental Affairs L. Rev.* 299 (1979).
46 *Brooklyn L. Rev.* 269 (Winter 1980).
29 *Catholic Univ. L. Rev.* 159 (Fall 1979).
80 *Columbia L. Rev.* 109 (Jan. 1980).
4 *Corporation L. Rev.* 23, 43 (Winter 1981).
48 *Fordham L. Rev.* 185 (Nov. 1979).
56 *Indiana L. J.* 347 (Winter 1981).
13 *Loyola Univ., LA, L. Rev.* 133 (Dec. 1979).
49 *Univ. Cincinnati L. Rev.* 270 (1980).
57 *Univ. Detroit J. Urban L.* 445 (Winter 1980).

1979   *Federal Open Market Committee v. David R. Merrill*, 443 U.S. 340, 61 L.Ed.2d 587, 99 S.Ct. 2800

Argued: Dec. 6, 1978.

Decided: June 28, 1979.

Summary: In an FOIA Exemption 5 case, the Court held Federal Reserve policy directives to be intra-agency memoranda "that would not be available by law to a party other than another agency in litigation with the agency."

Circumstances: The Federal Open Market Committee of the Federal Reserve Board is allowed to withhold by law certain monetary policy directives during the month they are in effect. Afterward they are published in the Federal Register. Open market operations include the purchase and sale of government securities in the domestic securities market, considered the most important monetary policy instrument of the Federal Reserve System. A law student, who said he had "developed a strong interest in administrative law and the operation of agencies of the federal government," sought records of the committee. Denying the request, the committee said they were only available to the public on a delayed basis. The District Court for the District of Columbia granted the student summary judgment. The Court of Appeals for the District of Columbia Circuit affirmed. The Supreme Court, on certiorari, vacated and remanded to the district court to determine whether the directives, as confidential commercial information, would be privileged in civil discovery.

Opinion: Justice Harry A. Blackmun wrote for the Court in the 7-to-2 decision, joined by Chief Justice Warren E. Burger and Justices William J. Brennan, Jr., Byron R. White, Thurgood Marshall, Lewis F. Powell, Jr., and William H. Rehnquist. Dissenting was John Paul Stevens, joined by Potter Stewart. Exemption 5, sometimes called the "executive privilege" or "nondiscoverable documents" exemption, applies usually to working papers in the preparation of a legal suit, as well as to memoranda exchanged by government officials in making policy decisions. The exemption protects information acquired in an attorney-client relationship and is meant to shield "predecisional communications," but not "communications made after the decision and designed to explain it." Blackmun reiterated that the theory behind a privilege for confidential commercial information generated in the process of awarding a contract is not that the flow of advice may be hampered, but that the government will be placed at a competitive disadvantage or that the consummation of the contract may be endangered. Consequently, the rationale for protecting such information expires as soon as the contract is awarded or the offer withdrawn, he noted. As a nondiscoverable documents exemption, Congress did not intend for the FOIA to become a way of circumventing civil discovery rules.

In dissent, Justice Stevens, with Stewart, said that the FOIA does not provide any middle ground between "current" release and total exemption, that Exemption 5 does not protect commercial information, and that the directives are not exempt by any of the act's nine exemptions. He said the Court's newly created category invited substantial costs and burdens to overcome an agency's objection to immediate disclosure. "The imposition of such an obstacle to prompt disclosure is inconsistent with the overriding statutory policy of giving the ordinary citizen unfettered access to information about how his Government operates."

Referenced Cases: *EPA v. Mink*, 410 U.S. 73 (1973), and *NLRB v. Sears, Roebuck & Co.*, 421 U.S. 132 (1975), recognizing that one class of intra-agency memos shielded by Exemption 5 is agency reports and working papers subject to "executive" privilege for predecisional deliberations; *NLRB v. Robbins Tire & Rubber Co.*, 437 U.S. 214 (1978), and *Renegotiation Board v. Grumman Aircraft Corp.* 421 U.S. 168 (1975), on whether Exemption 5 incorporates every privilege in civil discovery; *E. I. Du Pont de Nemours Powder Co. v. Masland*, 244 U.S. 100 (1917), and *U.S. v. Procter & Gamble Co.*, 356 U.S. 677 (1958), on evidentiary privilege for trade secrets and other commercial information.

Further Reading:
65 *ABA J.* 1714 (Nov. 1979).
60 *Boston Univ. L. Rev.* 765 (July 1980).
1980 *Detroit College L. Rev.* 669 (Summer 1980).
25 *Villanova L. Rev.* 507 (March 1980).

1980   *Henry A. Kissinger v. Reporters'*
Committee for Freedom of the Press
et al. and Reporters' Committee for
Freedom of the Press et al. v. Henry A.
Kissinger, 445 U.S. 136, 63 L.Ed.2d 267,
100 S.Ct. 960, 6 Med.L.Rptr. 1001

Argued: Oct. 31, 1979.

Decided: March 3, 1980.

Summary: Under the FOIA provision for the production of "agency records improperly withheld," the Court ruled that notes neither possessed nor controlled by government agency cannot be "withheld" and that other notes may not be "agency records." An agency cannot be required to obtain documents that would be agency records if they were in the agency's possession.

Circumstances: While serving in the Nixon administration, first as assistant to the president for national security affairs, then as secretary of state, Kissinger kept in his personal files notes and transcripts of his telephone calls. After leaving office, he transferred the files to the New York estate of Nelson Rockefeller, then deeded the material to the Library of Congress, stipulating that he would control access to them for a specified period. Three separate FOIA requests provoked the litigation. The first was filed by William Safire, a *New York Times* columnist, who asked the State Department for certain transcripts of phone conversations. The department said the requested notes had been made while Kissinger was national security adviser and were thus not agency records subject to the FOIA. The second was filed by the Military Audit Project (MAP), which sought all phone notes while Kissinger was both secretary of state and national security adviser. The request was denied, first because the notes were deemed not agency records, and second because the notes had been deposited with the Library of Congress prior to the request, terminating State Department custody and control. The third request was filed by the Reporters' Committee for Freedom of the Press (RCFP), the American Historical Association, the American Political Science Association, and a number of other journalists.

The request was the same as MAP's and was denied for the same reasons. On Feb. 8, 1977, the RCFP requesters and Safire sought enforcement of their requests in the District Court for the District of Columbia, and on March 8 MAP filed a similar suit. The court ordered the Library of Congress to return the documents to the State Department, but denied requests for notes prepared while Kissinger was adviser to the president. The court of appeals affirmed and ordered those summaries made while Kissinger was secretary of state, but said that those made during his tenure as national security adviser need not be produced. Kissinger filed for certiorari, requesting the Supreme Court to review the court of appeals' determination that the State Department had improperly withheld agency records, thereby permitting their production from the Library of Congress. The RCFP requesters filed a cross-petition seeking review of that court's judgment denying production of the conversations transcribed while Kissinger served as national security adviser. The Supreme Court reversed the order compelling production of the phone manuscripts made by Kissinger while secretary of state and affirmed the order denying requests for transcripts while he was national security adviser.

Opinion: Justice William H. Rehnquist, joined by Chief Justice Warren E. Burger and Justices Potter Stewart, Byron R. White, and Lewis F. Powell, Jr., wrote the Court's opinion. William J. Brennan, Jr., and John Paul Stevens wrote separate opinions, concurring in part and dissenting in part. Thurgood Marshall and Harry A. Blackmun did not participate. Rehnquist said the FOIA only requires agencies to provide access to the records they have in their possession. Telephone conversation notes made while Kissinger was assistant to the president for national security affairs were not subject to the FOIA because the president and his close advisers are exempt from its terms. Other notes made when Kissinger was secretary of state had been transferred by him to the Library of Congress, which is not subject to the FOIA. Rehnquist pointed out that the FOIA does not require agencies to create or retain documents; it only obligates them to provide access to those which it in fact has created and retained. "If the agency is not required to create or to retain records under the FOIA, it is somewhat difficult to determine why the agency is nevertheless required to retrieve documents which have escaped its possession, but which it has not endeavored to recover." In Kissinger's case, he had first deeded his private papers, including the telephone summaries, to the Nelson Rockefeller estate, then to the Library of Congress, exclusive of the phone notes. "Under these circumstances, the State Department cannot be said to have had possession or control of the documents at the time the requests were made." Technically, it therefore did not withhold any agency records, an indispensable prerequisite to liability in a suit under the FOIA. On the request from William Safire, newspaper columnist, for certain notes of Kissinger's telephone conversations when he was national security adviser in the White House, Rehnquist concluded that these documents were not "agency records" within the meaning of the FOIA. The "Executive Office of the President" is an agency subject to the FOIA, but the president's immediate personal staff or units in the Executive Office whose sole function is to advise the president are not within the term "agency."

Justice Brennan concurred with the Court's view that the Federal Records and Records Disposal acts, which foster administrative interests, cannot be neatly interpolated into the FOIA, which is designed to serve the general public, but dissented on the conclusion that the FOIA did not reach records that have been removed from federal agency custody, as had Kissinger's Department of State phone records. Justice Stevens concurred with the view that an agency cannot "withhold" documents unless it has either custody or control of them, but dissented from the Court on the issue of "physical possession," urging instead "legal custody" of records. He said the Court's decision exempted documents that had been wrongfully removed from an agency's files and created an incentive for outgoing officials to remove potentially embarrassing documents from their files in order to frustrate future FOIA requests.

Referenced Cases: *NLRB v. Robbins Tire & Rubber Co.*, 437 U.S. 214 (1978), on the FOIA reaching "records and material in the possession of federal agencies"; *NLRB v. Sears, Roebuck & Co.*, 421 U.S. 132 (1975), and *Renegotiation Board v. Grumman Aircraft Engineering Corp.*, 421 U.S. 168 (1975), on the Federal Records Act.

Further Reading:

94 *Harvard L. Rev.* 232 (Nov. 1980).
18 *Houston L. Rev.* 641 (March 1981).

26 *Loyola L. Rev.* 706 (Summer 1980).
27 *Wayne L. Rev.* 1315 (Spring 1981).

1980   ***Peter H. Forsham et al. v. Patricia
Roberts Harris, Secretary, Dept. of
Health, Education, and Welfare, et al.,
445 U.S. 169, 63 L.Ed.2d 293, 100 S.Ct.
978, 5 Med.L.Rptr. 2473***

Argued: Oct. 31, 1979.

Decided: March 3, 1980.

Summary: In an FOIA Exemption 4 case, the Court held
that a government agency must physically possess documents for
them to be called "agency records" open to inspection.

Circumstances: In 1959 a group of private physicians
and scientists that specialized in the treatment of diabetes formed
the University Group Diabetes Program (UGDP) to study the effectiveness of various diabetes treatments with funding from the National Institute of Arthritis, Metabolism and Digestive Diseases, an
agency under HEW. The group kept the results of its study, although the Federal Food and Drug Administration used the study to
develop new drug labeling policies. The study indicated that the use
of certain drugs for the treatment of diabetes increased the risk of
heart disease. Some time later, the Committee on the Care of the
Diabetic (CCD), a national association of doctors involved in the
treatment of diabetics that had been critical of the UGDP study,
sought access to the raw data in order to review the UGDP's
findings. After both the UGDP and HEW denied the requests for
access, the CCD brought action in the District Court for the Dis-.
trict of Columbia. The court refused on the ground that the data
were not "agency records." The Court of Appeals for the District of
Columbia Circuit affirmed, as did the Supreme Court, on certiorari.

Opinion: Justice William H. Rehnquist wrote for the 7-
to-2 Court, joined by Chief Justice Warren E. Burger and Justices

Potter Stewart, Byron R. White, Harry A. Blackmun, Lewis F. Powell, Jr., and John Paul Stevens. Dissenting were William J. Brennan, Jr., and Thurgood Marshall. The decision was handed down the same day as *Kissinger v. Reporters' Committee for Freedom of the Press*, which also dealt with Exemption 4. In *Forsham*, the Court said a report about diabetes treatments, funded by a government agency and used to develop public policy, was not a record subject to the FOIA since it was generated, owned, and possessed by the consultant group of physicians and scientists. "Federal participation in the generation of the data by means of a grant from the Department of Health, Education, and Welfare (HEW) does not make the private organization a federal 'agency' within the terms of the Act. Nor does this federal funding in combination with a federal right of access render the data 'agency records' of HEW, which *is* a federal 'agency' under the terms of the Act." The decision was based largely on the supposition that Congress, though not defining "agency records" in the FOIA, did contemplate some relationship between an "agency" and the "record" requested under the act—that is, that the agency had created and/or obtained and possessed the document. Justice Brennan, with Marshall, said that where the nexus between an agency subject to the FOIA and information requested is close, the importance of the information to public understanding of the agency should determine "agency record." He feared that if important information is immune from public inspection, "then government by secrecy must surely return."

Referenced Cases: *U.S. v. Orleans*, 425 U.S. 807 (1976), in which the Court ruled that federal grants generally do not create a partnership or joint venture, nor turn a recipient's acts from private to governmental; *NLRB v. Sears, Roebuck & Co.*, 421 U.S. 132 (1975), holding that the FOIA imposes no duty on an agency to create records; *Kissinger v. Reporters' Committee for Freedom of the Press*, 445 U.S. 136 (1980), also on Exemption 4 and decided the same day.

Further Reading:
66 *ABA J.* 777 (June 1980).
94 *Harvard L. Rev.* 232 (Nov. 1980).
34 *Southwestern Univ. L. J.* 993 (Nov. 1980).

1980   *Consumer Product Safety Commission*
           et al. v. GTE Sylvania, Inc., et al., 447
           U.S. 102, 64 L.Ed.2d 766, 100 S.Ct. 2051

Argued: April 14, 1980.

Decided: June 9, 1980.

Summary: In an Exemption 3 case, the Court held that disclosure under the FOIA of product accident reports is governed by the Consumer Product Safety Act (CPSA) requiring that manufacturer be notified and allowed to defend product.

Circumstances: With enactment in 1972 of the CPSA, Congress created the Consumer Product Safety Commission, whose powers included the authority to collect and disseminate product safety information to help consumers evaluate the comparative safety of various products. Section 6 of the CPSA regulates the "public disclosure" of information, requiring the commission to notify the manufacturer at least 30 days prior to the release of information. The commission had received reports from manufacturers on television-related accidents, most of which were accompanied by claims of confidentiality. The reports were collected as part of the commission's plan to hold a public hearing on the hazards in the operation of television receivers and to consider safety standards. Upon receiving FOIA requests from two consumer groups, the Consumers Union and the Public Citizen's Health Research Group, the commission released even those reports claimed to be confidential. Lawsuits ensued. The District Court for the District of Delaware, where the several suits had been consolidated, granted the manufacturers' motion for summary judgment and permanently enjoined the commission from disclosing the accident reports. It ruled that the commission had failed to comply with the CPSA notification requirement. The Court of Appeals for the Third Circuit affirmed. On certiorari, the Supreme Court also affirmed.

Opinion: Justice William H. Rehnquist wrote the unanimous opinion. Exemption 3 allows federal agencies to withhold records that are "specifically exempted from discovery by statute," provided that the statute clearly "requires that the matters be withheld . . . in such a manner as to leave the agency no discretion . . . or establishes particular criteria for withholding." On this, the courts have been confronted with the job of weighing one law against another. Exemption 3, which also permits withholding on the basis of privacy, has been called the catch-all exemption. In this decision, the Court held that the CPSA, not the FOIA, governed the disclosure of records by the Consumer Product Safety Commission. The CPSA requires the commission to notify the manufacturer at least 30 days before the public disclosure of information pertaining to a consumer product, along with a summary of the information; this is to allow the manufacturer to respond to the information and the request. In an earlier related case, *GTE Sylvania Inc. v. Consumers Union* (1980), decided March 19, the Court upheld a Delaware court order forbidding the commission's release of product information on hazardous television sets, ruling only on the commission's proper obedience to the injunction and saying that it could not be charged with "improperly" withholding documents. With the present case, the Court answered the broader question, that the commission had not complied with the CPSA when it expressed its willingness to provide *Consumer Reports* with unfavorable information about television sets. In the first case, television manufacturers sought to restrain release of allegedly confidential reports; in the second, the commission sought clarification on conflicting law governing its behavior. The commission contended that being forced to comply with the CPSA requirement of notification in meeting FOIA requests would impose an insurmountable burden on its operations. But Rehnquist said the claim, entirely speculative, was more properly addressed to Congress than to the Court.

Referenced Cases: *GTE Sylvania Inc. v. Consumers Union*, 445 U.S. 375 (1980), on the relevant facts; *U.S. v. Philadelphia National Bank*, 374 U.S. 321 (1963), and *Chrysler Corp v. Brown*, 441 U.S. 281 (1979), on the warning that "the views of a subsequent Congress form a hazardous basis for inferring the intent of an earlier one"; *Skidmore v. Swift & Co.*, 323 U.S. 134 (1944), on conference committees as expressions of congressional will.

Further Reading:
66 *ABA J.* 1425 (Nov. 1980).
49 *Temple L. Q.* 238 (Fall 1975).

1982   *U.S. Department of State et al. v.*
Washington Post Co., **456 U.S. 595,**
72 L.Ed.2d 358, 102 S.Ct. 1957,
8 Med.L.Rptr. 1521

Argued: March 31, 1982.

Decided: May 17, 1982.

Summary: Citizenship information on foreign nationals qualifies as "similar files" under Exemption 6 of the FOIA.

Circumstances: The *Washington Post*, in Sept. 1979, filed a request with the Department of State, under the FOIA, 5 USC Section 552, for "documents indicating whether Dr. Ali Behzadnia and Dr. Ibrahim Yazdi . . . hold valid U.S passports." At the time, both men were Iranian nationals living in Iran. In denying the request, the State Department said that release of the information would be "a clearly unwarranted invasion of the personal privacy" of the individuals, quoting directly from the exemption. The department explained that both men were prominent figures in Iran's revolutionary government and that compliance with the request would threaten their safety because of the "intense anti-American sentiment in Iran." The District Court for the District of Columbia granted the newspaper's motion for summary judgment. The Court of Appeals for the District of Columbia affirmed, holding that the information sought was no less intimate than that normally contained in personnel and medical files, thus not part of Exemption 6. On certiorari, the Supreme Court unanimously reversed and remanded to the court of appeals to consider the effect of disclosure upon the privacy interests of Behzadnia and Yazdi.

Opinion: Justice William H. Rehnquist wrote for eight members in the 9-to-0 decision, joined by Chief Justice Warren E.

Burger and Justices William J. Brennan, Jr., Byron R. White, Thurgood Marshall, Harry A. Blackmun, Lewis F. Powell, Jr., and John Paul Stevens. Sandra Day O'Connor concurred without opinion. Exemption 6 is the FOIA's explicit privacy clause, excluding from public view "personnel and medical files and similar files, the disclosure of which would constitute a clearly unwarranted invasion of personal privacy." In seeking to find whether two Iranian officials were U.S. citizens, the *Washington Post* argued that the phrase "similar files" did not include all files that contain information about particular individuals, but instead was limited to those containing "intimate details" and "highly personal" information. Rehnquist said that Congress had not meant to limit Exemption 6 to a narrow class of files containing only discrete kinds of personal information. Instead, he said, the act's legislative history meant that the exemption was intended to cover detailed government records on an individual "which can be identified as applying to that individual." Therefore, the citizenship information sought satisfied the "similar files" requirement. Rehnquist said that a file does not have to contain intimate information to merit withholding. The kinds of files used as a benchmark in Exemption 6—personnel and medical files—contain much information that is not intimate.

Referenced Cases: *Department of Air Force v. Rose*, 425 U.S. 352 (1976), holding that "the primary concern of Congress in drafting Exemption 6 was to provide for the confidentiality of personal matters."

Further Reading:
68 *ABA J.* 850 (July 1982).
27 *Univ. Florida L. Rev.* 848 (Spring 1975).

1982　*Federal Bureau of Investigation et al. v. Howard S. Abramson*, 456 U.S. 615, 72 L.Ed.2d 376, 102 S.Ct. 2054

Argued: Jan. 11, 1982.

Decided: May 24, 1982.

Summary: FOIA Exemption 7, which protects investigatory materials, held to exempt information contained originally in law enforcement records but summarized in a new document not created for law enforcement purposes.

Circumstances: In the course of investigating allegations that President Nixon had used federal agencies for private political purposes, Abramson, an independent journalist, asked for a memo from J. Edgar Hoover to John Erlichman, plus approximately 63 pages of "name check" summaries, information culled from FBI files on 11 public figures. The FBI, in rejecting the requests, said that release would be an unwarranted invasion of privacy, as covered by both Exemption 6 and 7(c). Abramson had modified his request when the FBI, with his suit pending, provided him with 84 pages of information, from which certain names and facts had been stricken. The District Court for the District of Columbia found that the FBI had failed to show that the information had been compiled for "law enforcement" rather than political purposes, but ruled that Exemption 7(c) protected an "unwarranted invasion of personal privacy." The court granted the government's motion for summary judgment. In reversing, the Court of Appeals for the District of Columbia Circuit held that because the White House was not involved in law enforcement, the memorandum sought could not have been created for law enforcement purposes and, therefore, was not covered by Exemption 7. On certiorari, the Supreme Court reversed and remanded to the court of appeals to consider whether the information sought originated in a record protected by Exemption 7.

Opinion: Justice Byron R. White wrote for the 5-to-4 Court, joined by Chief Justice Warren E. Burger and Justices Lewis F. Powell, Jr., William H. Rehnquist, and John Paul Stevens. Dissenting were Harry A. Blackmun, William J. Brennan, Jr., Sandra Day O'Connor, and Thurgood Marshall. Exemption 7 shields "investigatory records compiled for law enforcement purposes," designed to control the flow of information that, if known publicly, might seriously harm ongoing proceedings of a civil, criminal, administrative, or judicial nature. When first applied, the exemption protected a wider than intended amount of information from the public. With the amended 1974 version, the government is required to show that the requested documents are truly investigatory and compiled specifically for law enforcement purposes. White noted that the sole question before the Court was whether information originally compiled for law enforcement purposes loses its FOIA exemption if summarized in a new document not created for law enforcement purposes. Emphasizing the FOIA's required assessment of harm created by disclosure, White said that, once it is established that information was compiled pursuant to a legitimate law enforcement investigation and that disclosure would lead to one of the six "categories of harm," the information is exempt. Congress thus created, in White's words, "a scheme of categorical exclusion." It did not invite judicial weighing of the benefits and evils of disclosure on a case-by-case basis, White said.

Justice Blackmun, joined by Brennan in dissent, said that Congress chose the term "records" rather than "information" advisedly in Exemption 7, contrary to the majority's view. The Court should not have deviated from the statutory language, Blackmun said. Also in dissent, Justice O'Connor, with Marshall, said the majority had redrafted the phrase "investigatory records compiled for law enforcement purposes" to fit records not compiled for such purposes.

Referenced Cases: *NLRB v. Robbins Tire & Rubber Co.*, 437 U.S. 214 (1978), and *EPA v. Mink*, 410 U.S. 73 (1973), on the FOIA's policy of broad disclosure of government documents "to ensure an informed citizenry"; *NLRB v. Sears, Roebuck & Co.*, 421 U.S. 132 (1975), on Exemption 5 protecting predecisional communications within an agency; *Dept. of Air Force v. Rose*, 425 U.S. 352 (1976), that FOIA exemptions are to be narrowly construed; *Forsham v. Harris*, U.S. 169 (1980), that the FOIA deals with "agency records," not information in the abstract; *Bread Political Action Committee v. FEC*, 455 U.S. 577 (1982), on statutory language being conclusive; *Consumer Product Safety Comm'n v. GTE Sylvania Inc.*, 447 U.S. 102 (1980), on the meaning of "clearly expressed legislative intention"; *U.S. v. Brown*, 333 U.S. 18 (1948), on "patently absurd consequences" not intended by Congress.

Further Reading:
68 *ABA J.* 1002 (Aug. 1982).
26 *Howard L. J.* 1614 (1983).
17 *Suffolk Univ. L. Rev.* 748 (Fall 1983).
57 *Tulane L. Rev.* 1564 (June 1983).
29 *Wayne L. Rev.* 1269 (Spring 1983)

1983 *Federal Trade Commission et al. v. Grolier Inc.*, 462 U.S. 19, 76 L.Ed.2d 387, 103 S.Ct. 2209, 9 Med.L.Rptr. 1737

Argued: March 29, 1983.

Decided: June 6, 1983.

Summary: FOIA Exemption 5, which protects the working papers of government lawyers, held to exempt agency attorney work product from mandatory disclosure without regard to status of litigation for which prepared.

Circumstances: The FTC had sued Grolier, charging that its sales representatives had used deception in the sale of its encyclopedias, but the lawsuit was dismissed with prejudice before reaching trial. Grolier then requested from the commission, under the FOIA, documents compiled by agency lawyers in preparation for trial. Grolier admitted that it wanted to know how much the FTC learned of its sales methods through surveillance of the sales representatives. The commission refused on the basis of Exemption 5. The District Court for the District of Columbia held that all the requested documents were exempt, but the Court of Appeals for the District of Columbia Circuit said that four documents must be disclosed unless the FTC could show that the possibility of future litigation existed. On certiorari, the Supreme Court reversed, holding, among other things, that Exemption 5 says nothing about the status of litigation.

Opinion: Justice Byron R. White wrote the opinion, joined by Chief Justice Warren E. Burger and Justices Thurgood Marshall, Lewis F. Powell, Jr., William H. Rehnquist, John Paul Stevens, and Sandra Day O'Connor. The Court ruled, in effect, that Exemption 5 protects the working papers of government attorneys at all times, even after specific litigation has ended. The Court rejected Grolier's contention that whenever work-product documents would be discoverable in any particular litigation, they must be disclosed to anyone under the FOIA. The Court construed Exemption 5 to exempt those documents, and only those documents, *normally* privileged in the civil discovery context. White wrote: "It is not difficult to imagine litigation in which one party's need for otherwise privileged documents would be sufficient to override the privilege, but that does not remove the documents from the category of normally privileged. Only by construing the Exemption to provide a categorical rule can the Act's purpose of expediting disclosure by means of workable rules be furthered." Justice Brennan, with Blackmun, joined the judgment but based his concurrence on the Federal Rule of Civil Procedure 26(b)(3), which protects materials prepared for *any* litigation or trial "as long as they were prepared by or for a party to the subsequent litigation." Brennan wrote: "If a document is a work product under the Rule, and if it is an 'inter-agency or intra-agency memoran-du[m] or lette[r]' under the Exemption, it is absolutely exempt."

Referenced Cases: *EPA v. Mink*, 410 U.S. 73 (1973), on the types of information the executive branch must have the option to keep confidential; *NLRB v. Sears, Roebuck & Co.*, 421 U.S. 132 (1975), on Exemption 5 in the context of civil litigation; *Renegotiation Board v. Grumman Aircraft Engineering Corp.*, 421 U.S. 168 (1975), on the Federal Records Act; *Hickman v. Taylor*, 329 U.S. 495 (1947), on the reasons for protecting work product from discovery; *Federal Open Market Committee v. Merrill*, 443 U.S. 340 (1979), on Exemption 5's exemption of documents normally privileged in the civil discovery context.

Further Reading:
69 *ABA J.* 1134 (Aug. 1983).

Other Cases Briefly Noted

U.S. v. Nixon, 418 U.S. 683 (1974). One of the most important contemporary decisions on executive privilege, and thus related to Exemption 5. The Court limited the boundaries of the privilege in its 8-to-0 decision, ruling that an absolute privilege can be asserted only when the material in question, or documents sought under the FOIA, consists of military or diplomatic secrets. When other kinds of information are involved, executive privilege must be balanced against other values—in this case, presidential privilege against the operation of the criminal justice system. Here, special Watergate prosecutor Leon Jaworski subpoenaed several of the White House tapes and other documents for use in criminal proceedings against Nixon aides. The president tried to quash the subpoena, claiming executive privilege. He argued that release of the material would damage the decision-making process and, if subjected to judicial review, undermine the separation of powers. "On the other hand," wrote Chief Justice Warren E. Burger for the Court, "the allowance of the privilege to withhold evidence that is demonstrably relevant in a criminal trial would cut deeply into the guarantee of due process of law and gravely impair the basic function of the courts. We conclude that when the ground for asserting privilege as to subpoenaed materials sought for use in a criminal trial is based only on the generalized interest in confidentiality, it cannot prevail over the fundamental demands of due process of law in the fair administration of criminal justice. The generalized assertion . . . must yield to the demonstrated, specific need for evidence in a pending criminal trial." This decision relates to the FOIA's Exemption 5 in that agencies claiming the exemption to deny access will have to submit the materials for court examination to determine the benefits of secrecy against those of disclosure. (See "Further Reading" below).

NLRB v. Sears, Roebuck & Co., 421 U.S. 132 (1975). Decided the same day as *Renegotiation Board v. Grumman Aircraft Engineering Corp.*, 421 U.S. 168 (1975), both under Exemption 5, which protects "inter-agency or intra-agency memoranda or letters which would not be available by law to a party other than an agency in litigation with the agency." In *NLRB*, the Court reasoned that disclosure of memoranda before the decision-making process was completed might diminish the quality of such deliberations (advisers might be less candid if their views were open to public scrutiny), but that disclosure after a decision has been made does not harm the process. Further, "the public is vitally concerned" with why government agencies adopt certain policies. In *Renegotiation Board*, the Court said that only the report of an agency that has the final authority for a decision is releasable. Memos, recommendations, opinions, and policy statements referred to in a report may be released because they form the basis for policy decisions, barring a claim under Exemption 7, which shields "investigatory records compiled for law enforcement purposes." If no material explains the final decision, an agency is not required to compile such information under the FOIA. In both decisions, the Court tried to distinguish between predecisional communications, which are exempt, and postdecisional information, which is not. In either event, facts are not shielded by Exemption 5 unless disclosure would jeopardize confidentiality or reduce the agency's chances of obtaining needed information in the future.

Administrator, FAA v. Robertson, 422 U.S. 255 (1975). Chief Justice Warren E. Burger, for the Court, said that the FAA reports on the operation and maintenance performance of commercial airlines was exempt by statute, Section 1104 of the Federal Aviation Act. The act allows the FAA to withhold information if disclosure is not in the public interest. The act, designed to ensure that the agency receive information, requires that the provider of the information be notified of material requested. Here, the Air Transport Association objected on the ground that without confidentiality the performance program would be jeopardized. Exemption 3 allows federal agencies to withhold records that are "specifically exempted from discovery by statute," provided the law clearly "requires that the matters be withheld ... in such a manner as to leave the agency no discretion ... or establishes particular criteria for withholding." Robertson won at district and appeals levels, but the Supreme Court reversed. Justice Potter Stewart, concurring separately, said that the only determination "in a district court's *de novo* inquiry is the factual existence of such a statute, regardless of how unwise, self-protective, or inadvertent the enactment might be."

Weinberger v. Catholic Action of Hawaii/Peace Education Project, 454 U.S. 139 (1981). In an Exemption 1 ruling, the Court reinstated the judgment of dismissal by the District Court of Hawaii, holding that the Navy was not required to file an environmental impact statement regarding the operation of a facility capable of storing nuclear weapons. The Court of Appeals for the Ninth Circuit reversed and held that the Environmental Policy Act of 1969 required the Navy to prepare and release a "Hypothetical Environmental Impact Statement" on such facilities. Exemption 1 of the FOIA is designed to prevent disclosure of properly classified records, the release of which could cause at least some "identifiable damage" to the national security, "specifically authorized under criteria established by an Executive order to be kept secret in the interest of national defense or foreign policy." In 1982, President Reagan exercised his power under the FOIA to set criteria for exempting information classified as secret and eliminated President Carter's order requiring officials to consider public interest in openness when deciding to classify documents. In *Weinberger*, the Court determined that the publication of an environmental impact statement would itself reveal confidential material and thus run afoul of Exemption 1.

U.S. v. Weber Aircraft Corp., 465 U.S. 792 (1984). In another Exemption 5 decision, the Court upheld the Air Force's refusal to release information obtained during the investigation of an aircraft accident. In the 1973 crash of an F-106B, the pilot was severely injured and, when he later sued the manufacturers of the craft's ejection mechanism, the firms sought access to the Air Force's investigatory files. The Air Force released all materials except the confidential parts. In the FOIA suit, a unanimous Supreme Court ruled that the testimony was unquestionably intra-agency communication shielded by the exemption. The Court said that confidential statements compiled by the safety investigators had been privileged in common law for more than 20 years in recognition of the need for "privilege when confidentiality is necessary to ensure frank and open discussion and hence efficient government operations."

CIA v. Sims, 471 U.S. 159 (1985). In another Exemption 3 decision, the Court held that the identities of researchers who had participated in a CIA-funded project were exempt from disclosure under the FOIA. In refusing to release information, the CIA relied on the National Security Act of 1947, which permits the agency to protect intelligence sources and methods from disclosure. A unanimous Court said that the statute referred to "particular types of matters" within the meaning of the exemption. The district court had ruled protection for researchers who had requested and received "express guarantees of confidentiality." But the Supreme Court, in reversing that part of the lower court's determination, said that Congress had vested in the CIA director "very broad authority to protect from disclosure all sources of intelligence information." Institutional affiliations were also exempt, the Court said, since disclosure of such could lead to exposure of the researchers themselves.

Further Reading:

Duke Univ. Law Journal, which since 1970 has published an annual review of the previous year's developments under the FOIA.

Among the number of scholarly articles generated by *U.S. v. Nixon* (1974), which deals with Exemption 5 on "executive privilege," the following are significant:

75 *Columbia L. Rev.* 603 (1975).

24 *Emory L. J.* 405 (Spring 1975).

8 *Georgia L. Rev.* 809 (1974).

88 *Harvard L. Rev.* 13, 281 (1974).

89 *Political Science Q.* 713 (Winter 1974–75).

27 *Stanford L. Rev.* 489 (1975).

22 *UCLA L. Rev.* 1 (1974).

83 *Yale L. J.* 1730 (1974).

On the FOIA in general:

20 *Administrative L. Rev.* 249, 445 (March 1968).

34 *Brooklyn L. Rev.* 72 (Fall 1967).

85 *Columbia L. R.* 611 (1985).

7 *Communication & the Law* 45 (April 1985).

36 *Fordham L. Rev.* 765 (May 1968).

56 *Georgetown L. J.* 18 (Nov. 1967).

38 *George Washington L. Rev.* 150 (Oct. 1969).

11 *Harvard Civil Rights–Civil Liberties L. R.* 596 (1976).

5 *Harvard Civil Rights L. Rev.* 1 (Jan. 1970).

54 *Iowa L. Rev.* 141 (Aug. 1968).

55 *Journalism Q.* 481, 526 (Autumn 1978).

62 *Journalism Q.* 465 (Autumn 1985).

43 *Military L. Rev.* 1 (Jan. 1969).

11 *New England L. R.* 463 (1976).

Selected Bibliography

Abrams, Floyd, "The New Effort to Control Information," *The New York Times Magazine* (Sept. 25, 1983).

Arnold, Marc, and Andrew Kisseloff, "An Introduction to the Federal Privacy Act of 1974 and Its Effect on the Freedom of Information Act," 11 *New England L. Rev.* 483 (Spring 1976).

"Comments on Proposed Amendments to Section 3 of the Administrative Procedure Act: The Freedom of Information Bill," 40 *Notre Dame Lawyer* 417 (1965).

"The Definition of 'Agency Records' Under the Freedom of Information Act," 31 *Stanford L. Rev.* 1093 (1979).

"Developments Under the Freedom of Information Act," a review of the previous year's litigation, published annually since 1970 by the Duke University *Law Journal.*

"The Freedom of Information Act's Privacy Exemption and the Privacy Act of 1974," 11 *Harvard Civil Rights–Civil Liberties L. Rev.* 596 (1976).

Furby, Tommy E., "The Freedom of Information Act: A Survey of Litigation Under the Exemptions," 48 *Mississippi L. J.* 784 (Sept. 1977).

Hehl, Stephen F., "Reverse FOIA Suits After Chrysler: A New Direction," 48 *Fordham L. Rev.* 185 (Nov. 1979).

Kielbowicz, Richard B., "The Freedom of Information Act and Government's Corporate Information Files," 55 *Journalism Quarterly* 481 (Autumn 1978).

Maxwell, Kimera, and Roger Reinsch, "The Freedom of Information Act Privacy Exemption: Who Does It Really Protect?" 7 *Communications and the Law* 45 (April 1985).

"National Security and the Public's Right to Know: A New Role for the Courts under the FOIA," 123 *Univ. Pa. L. Rev.* 1438 (1975).

"National Security Information Disclosure Under the FOIA: The Need for Effective Judicial Enforcement," 25 *Boston College L. Rev.* 614 (1984).

"The National Security Interest and Civil Liberties," 85 *Harvard L. Rev.* 1130 (1972).

O'Connell, Marie Veronica, "A Control Test for Determining 'Agency Record' Status Under the Freedom of Information Act," 85 *Columbia L. Rev.* 611 (1985).

O'Reilly, James T., "Regaining a Confidence: Protection of Business Confidential Data Through Reform of the Freedom of Information Act," 34 *Administrative L. Rev.* 263 (1982).

Pember, Don R., "The Burgeoning Scope of 'Access Privacy' and the Portent for a Free Press," 64 *Iowa L. Rev.* 1155 (1979).

Sporkin, S., "National Security, Law Enforcement, and Business Secrets Under the Freedom of Information Act," 38 *Business Law* 707 (1983).

Stevenson, Russell B., Jr., "Protecting Business Secrets Under the Freedom of Information Act: Managing Exemption 4," 34 *Administrative L. Rev.* 207 (1982).

Wald, Patricia M., "The Freedom of Information Act: A Short Case Study in the Perils and Paybacks of Legislating Democratic Values," 33 *Emory L. J.* 649 (Summer 1984).

Wright, Anne H., "The Definition of 'Agency' Under the Freedom of Information Act as Applied to Federal Consultants and Grantees," 69 *Georgetown L. J.* 1223 (1981).

Free Speech

1915   *Jay Fox v. State of Washington*, **236 U.S. 273, 59 L.Ed. 573, 35 S.Ct. 383**

Submitted: Jan. 19, 1915.

Decided: Feb. 23, 1915.

Summary: Upheld the constitutionality of a state law prohibiting speech that tends to lead to crime.

Circumstances: An article, "The Nude and the Prudes," reported that a community of "free spirits," called "Home," had been infiltrated by "prudes" who were responsible for the arrest of four persons for indecent exposure. "Home" was a nudist colony. The article encouraged a "boycott" of those who interfered with the freedom of "Home," thus indirectly inciting a breach of the state law against indecent exposure. Defense had argued that the statute violated the 14th Amendment. The state, however, argued as follows: "While all the agencies of government—executive, legislative, and judicial—cannot abridge the freedom of the press, the legislature may control, and the courts may punish, the licentiousness of the press."

Opinion: Justice Oliver Wendell Holmes wrote for the unanimous Court. The Washington statute stipulated that it was a "gross misdemeanor" for a person to willfully publish material "having a tendency to encourage or incite the commission of any crime, breach of the peace, or act of violence . . . or encourage or advocate disrespect of the law." Holmes reasoned that it was not likely that the statute would be construed to prevent publications merely because they tended to produce unfavorable opinions of a particular statute or of law in general. "In this present case the disrespect for law that was encouraged was disregard of it, an overt breach and technically criminal act. It would be in accord with the usages of English to interpret disrespect as manifested disrespect, as active disregard going beyond the line drawn by the law."

Referenced Cases: *Waters-Pierce Oil Co. v. Texas,* 212 U.S. 86 (1909), on state court's ruling that act was constitutionally valid; *U.S. ex rel. Atty. Gen. v. Delaware & H. Co.,* 213 U.S. 366 (1909), on construing state laws to conform to federal constitution; *Nash v. U.S.,* 229 U.S. 373 (1913), on limiting reach of state statutes.

Further Reading:
None indexed.

1919   *Charles T. Schenck v. U.S. and Elizabeth Baer v. U.S., 249 U.S. 47, 63 L.Ed. 470, 39 S.Ct. 247*

Argued: Jan. 9, 10, 1919.

Decided: March 3, 1919.

Summary: Replaced the bad-tendency test with the clear-and-present-danger test for determining punishable expression.

Circumstances: Schenck and Baer, members of the Socialist Party, were found guilty in the District Court for the Eastern District of Pennsylvania on three counts of violating the Espionage Act of 1917 and unlawful use of the mails to conspire against the United States. Schenck, general secretary of the party, had been in charge of sending antiwar circulars to men eligible for the draft during World War I. The circulars proclaimed that conscription for the war against Germany was an unconstitutional despotism. In "impassioned language," the leaflets urged draftees to "assert their rights." Although the government argued that Schenck only attempted to interefere with the war effort, the Court affirmed his conviction on the ground that the circulars presented a clear and present danger. Justice Oliver Wendell Holmes said the jury had acted reasonably when it determined that the circulars could persuade draftees to refuse induction. That possibility, rather than concrete evidence of interference, constituted a clear and present danger.

Opinion: Justice Holmes, who wrote the Court's unanimous opinion, said: "The question in every case is whether the words used are used in such circumstances and are of such a nature as to create a clear and present danger that they will bring about the substantive evils that Congress has a right to prevent. It is a question of proximity and degree." He also wrote: "The most stringent protection of free speech would not protect a man in falsely shouting fire in a theater, and causing a panic. It does not even protect a man from an injunction against uttering words that may have all the effect of force."

Referenced Cases: *Adams v. New York*, 192 U.S. 585 (1904), *Weeks v. U.S.*, 232 U.S. 383 (1914), *Johnson v. U.S.*, 228 U.S. 457 (1913), and *Holt v. U.S.*, 218 U.S. 245 (1910), on the admissibility of search warrant evidence and relevance of Fifth Amendment; *Patterson v. Colorado*, 205 U.S. 454 (1907), on previous restraints abridging freedom of speech; *Aikens v. Wisconsin*, 195 U.S. 194 (1904), holding that the character of every act depends on the circumstances; *Gompers v. Buck's Stove & Range Co.*, 221 U.S. 418 (1911), on uttering words that have the effect of force; *Goldman v. U.S.*, 245 U.S. 474 (1918), holding that success alone does not warrant making the act of speaking a crime.

Further Reading:
98 *J. American History* 24 (1971).
52 *Columbia L. Rev.* 313 (1952).
32 *Harvard L. Rev.* 932 (1919).
33 *Harvard L. Rev.* 442 (1920).
17 *Michigan L. Rev.* 621 (1919).
See under *Abrams v. U.S.*, 250 U.S. 616 (1919).

1919   ***Jacob Frohwerk v. U.S., 249 U.S. 204, 63 L.Ed. 561, 39 S.Ct. 249***

Argued: Jan. 27, 1919.

Decided: March 10, 1919.

Summary: In Justice Oliver Wendell Holmes's words, "the First Amendment, while prohibiting legislation against free speech as such, cannot have been, and obviously was not, intended to give immunity for every possible use of language."

Circumstances: Frohwerk and others were convicted in the District Court for the Western District of Missouri for conspiring to obstruct military recruiting in violation of the Espionage Act of 1917. Specifically, they had published 12 articles in the *Missouri Staats Zeitung* attacking the war and urging disaffection in the military. Frohwerk was found guilty on 12 of 13 counts and sentenced to ten years imprisonment. The Supreme Court affirmed.

Opinion: Justice Holmes, who wrote for the unanimous Court, said that, as the Court had determined in *Schenck v. U.S.* (1919), a person may be convicted of a conspiracy to obstruct recruiting by "words of persuasion." "We venture to believe that neither Hamilton nor Madison, nor any other competent person then or later, ever supposed that to make criminal the counseling of a murder within the jurisdiction of Congress would be an unconstitutional interference with free speech." Again, as with *Schenck*, the Court believed that the means of conspiracy were incidental to the fact that the parties intended to work for that common purpose. "That purpose could be accomplished or aided by persuasion as well as by false statements, and there was not need to allege that false reports were intended to be made or made."

Referenced Cases: *Schenck v. U.S.*, 249 U.S. 47 (1919), and *Robertson v. Baldwin*, 165 U.S. 275 (1897), holding that the First Amendment was not intended to provide absolute immunity; *Buckeye Powder Co. v. E. I. Du Pont de Nemours Powder Co.*, 248 U.S. 55 (1918), and *Joplin Mercantile Co. v. U.S.*, 236 U.S. 531 (1915), on conspiracy as a crime.

Further Reading:
See under *Abrams v. U.S.*, 250 U.S. 616 (1919).
See under *Schenck v. U.S.*, 249 U.S. 47 (1919).

1919 *Eugene V. Debs v. U.S.*, 249 U.S. 211, 63 L.Ed. 566, 39 S.Ct. 252

Argued: Jan. 27, 28, 1919.

Decided: March 10, 1919.

Summary: Found unprotected a speech "obstructing and attempting to obstruct the recruiting service of the United States."

Circumstances: Debs had made a speech on June 16, 1918, in Canton, Ohio, on the general theme of socialism and opposition to the war, in the course of which he had praised certain individuals who had been convicted for resisting the draft or causing insubordination in the armed forces. On the international socialist crusade, Debs interjected that "you need to know that you are fit for something better than slavery and cannon fodder." The District Court for the Northern District of Ohio found Debs guilty of violating the Espionage Act of 1917. The Supreme Court affirmed.

Opinion: On the same day as *Frohwerk v. U.S.*, Justice Oliver Wendell Holmes wrote for the unanimous Court. Using the same rationale as it had in *Schenck v. U.S.* (1919) and in *Frohwerk*, the Court held that the intended effect of the speech was to obstruct recruiting. "If that was intended, and if, in all the circumstances, that would be its probable effect, it would not be protected by reason of its being part of a general program and expression of a general and conscientious belief."

Referenced Cases: *Ruthenberg v. U.S.*, 245 U.S. 480 (1918), a case that sent three to prison for aiding and abetting another in failing to register for the draft; *Schenck v. U.S.*, 249 U.S. 47 (1919), and *Frohwerk v. U.S.*, 249 U.S. 204 (1919), on the First Amendment in previous cases.

Further Reading:
19 *New Republic* 13 (1919).
See under *Abrams v. U.S.*, 250 U.S. 616 (1919).
See also under *Schenck v. U.S.*, 249 U.S. 47 (1919).

1919   *Jacob Abrams et al. v. U.S.*, 250 U.S. 616, 63 L.Ed. 1173, 40 S.Ct. 17

Argued: Oct. 21, 22, 1919.

Decided: Nov. 10, 1919.

Summary: Ruled unprotected speech leaflets encouraging resistance to the U.S. war effort and attacking the American expeditionary force sent to Russia to defeat the Bolsheviks.

Circumstances: Abrams and four other Russian émigrés were convicted in the District Court for the Southern District of New York of conspiring to violate the Espionage Act. They had been indicted for publishing abusive language about the form of government, for publishing language intended to bring the form of government into contempt, for encouraging resistance to the United States in the war, and for inciting curtailment of production of war materials. The charges were based on two leaflets that the defendants had printed and distributed by throwing them out the window of a building. The first leaflet denounced President Wilson as a coward and hypocrite for sending troops to Russia. The second, addressed primarily to factory workers, declared, "you are producing bullets, bayonets, cannon, to murder not only the Germans, but also your dearest, best, who are in Russia and fighting for freedom." The Supreme Court affirmed the conviction.

Opinion: Justice John H. Clarke wrote the opinion of the 7-to-2 Court, joined by Chief Justice Edward D. White and Justices Joseph McKenna, William R. Day, Willis Van Devanter, Mahlon Pitney, and James C. McReynolds. Dissenting was Oliver Wendell Holmes, joined by Louis D. Brandeis. This was the only case to come before the Court that involved the May 16, 1918, amendments to the Espionage Act. The Court held that the publishing and distribution of the pamphlets during the war was not protected expression within the meaning of the First Amendment. Clarke wrote that "the plain purpose of their propaganda was to excite, at the supreme crisis of the war, disaffection, sedition, riots, and, as they hoped, revolution, in this country for the purpose of embarrassing and if possible defeating the military plans of the Government in Europe."

Justices Holmes and Brandeis dissented for the first time in a series of 1919 decisions. Holmes wrote: "I never have seen any reason to doubt that the questions of law that alone were before this court in the cases of Schenck, Frohwerk, and Debs, 249 U.S. 47, 204, 211, were rightly decided. I do not doubt for a moment that by the same reasoning that would justify punishing persuasion to murder, the United States constitutionally may punish speech that produces or is intended to produce a clear and imminent danger that will bring about forthwith certain substantive evils that the United States constitutionally may seek to prevent. The power undoubtedly is greater in time of war than in time of peace because war opens dangers that do not exist at other times. But, as against dangers peculiar to war, as against others, the principle of the right to free speech is always the same. It is only the present danger of immediate evil or an intent to bring it about that warrants Congress in setting a limit to the expression of opinion where private rights are not concerned. Congress certainly cannot forbid all effort to change the mind of the country. Now nobody can suppose that the surreptitious publishing of a silly leaflet by an unknown man, without more, would present any immediate danger that its opinions would hinder the success of the government arms or have any appreciable tendency to do so. Publishing those opinions for the very purpose of obstructing, however, might indicate a greater danger, and at any rate would have the quality of an attempt. So I assume that the second leaflet, if published for the purposes alleged in the fourth count, might be punishable. But it seems clear to me that nothing less than that would bring these papers within the scope of the law." Then, Holmes explained his famous "marketplace of ideas" concept: "[But] when men have realized that time has upset many fighting faiths, they may come to believe even more than they believe the very foundations of their own conduct that the ultimate good desired is better reached by free trade in ideas,—that the best test of truth is the power of the thought to get itself accepted in the competition of the market; and that truth is the only ground upon which their wishes safely can be carried out. It is an experiment, as all life is an experiment."

Referenced Cases: *Troxell v. Delaware L. & W. R. Co.*, 227 U.S. 434 (1913), *Lancaster v. Collins*, 115 U.S. 222 (1885), and *Chicago & N. W. R. Co. v. Ohle*, 117 U.S. 123 (1886), on the need for competent and substantial evidence before a jury tending to sustain a verdict; *Evans v. U.S.*, 153 U.S. 608 (1894), *Claasen v. U.S.*, 142 U.S. 140 (1891), and *Debs v. U.S.*, 249 U.S. 211 (1919), on sustaining a verdict if the evidence is sufficient to sustain any one of several counts; *Swift & Co. v. U.S.*, 196 U.S. 375 (1905), on the relationship between intent and actual attempt to commit crime.

Further Reading:
89 *Central L. J.* 443 (Dec. 19, 1919).
20 *Columbia L. Rev.* 90 (Jan. 1920).
3 *Docket* 2207 (Feb. 1920).
33 *Harvard L. Rev.* 442, 747 (Jan., April 1920).
14 *Illinois L. Rev.* 539 (March 1920).
18 *Michigan L. Rev.* 236 (Jan. 1920).
20 *Univ. Missouri Bull., Law Series* 75 (Nov. 1920).
5 *Virginia L. Register*, n.p. (Jan. 1920).
29 *Yale L. J.* 337 (Jan. 1920).

1920   *Peter Schaefer, Paul Vogel, Louis Werner, Martin Darkow, and Herman Lemke v. U.S.*, 251 U.S. 466, 64 L.Ed. 360, 40 S.Ct. 259

Argued: Oct. 21, 1919.

Decided: March 1, 1920.

Summary: Publication of a German-language newspaper with allegedly false accounts of the war found unprotected speech and in violation of the Espionage Act of 1917.

Circumstances: Schaefer, Vogel, Werner, Darkow, and Lemke were officers of the Philadelphia Tageblatt Assoc., publisher of the German-language newspapers, the *Tageblatt* and the *Sonntagsblatt*. The charges against them amounted to publishing false reports designed to interfere with U.S. military operations during the war, causing insubordination within the armed forces, and obstructing recruitment. Each defendant was found guilty on different counts in the nine-count indictment. Their trial was held in the District Court for the Eastern District of Pennsylvania. The Supreme Court affirmed the convictions of Werner, Darkow, and Lemke, who were, respectively, chief editor, managing editor, and business manager of the newspapers. The Court reversed the judgments against Schaefer and Vogel, president and treasurer, respectively, and remanded.

Opinion: Justice Joseph McKenna wrote for the 6-to-3 Court, joined by Chief Justice Edward D. White and Justices William R. Day, Willis Van Devanter, Mahlon Pitney, and James C. McReynolds. Dissenting were Oliver Wendell Holmes, Louis D. Brandeis, and John H. Clarke. McKenna said that, though the articles, published in German for a German-speaking audience, may have seemed coarse and vulgar to most people, to the primary readers they may have been "truly descriptive of American feebleness and inability to combat German prowess, and thereby chill and check the ardency of patriotism and make it despair of success, and, in hopelessness, relax energy both in preparation and action." He said the Court could not simply conclude that the pieces were mere expression of peevish discontent—aimless, vapid, and innocuous. "We must take them at their word, as the jury did, and ascribe to them a more active and sinister purpose. They were the publications of a newspaper, deliberately prepared, systematic, always of the same trend. . . . Their effect on the persons affected could not be shown, nor was it necessary. The tendency of the articles and their efficacy were enough for offense,—their 'intent' and 'attempt,' for those are the words of the law, and to have required more would have made the law useless."

Justice Brandeis, in a dissent joined by Holmes, referred to the "clear and present danger" test of *Schenck v. U.S.* (1919), a "rule of reason," he said. After noting that no jury "acting in calmness" could say the publications created a clear and present danger, Brandeis said that the nature and possible effect of a writing could not be determined by "culling here and there a sentence and presenting it separated from the context." He concluded that the articles could not have remotely or indirectly disrupted recruiting. "Convictions such as these, besides abridging freedom of speech, threaten freedom of thought and of belief."

Justice Clarke dissented on grounds of error in the conduct

of the trial. "To me it seems simply a case of flagrant mistrial, likely to result in disgrace and great injustice, probably in life imprisonment for two old men, because this court hesitates to exercise the power . . . to correct, in this calmer time, errors of law which would not have been committed but for the stress and strain of feeling prevailing in the early months of the late deplorable war."

Referenced Cases: *Sugarman v. U.S.*, 249 U.S. 182 (1919), and *Stilson v. U.S.*, 250 U.S. 583 (1919), on the constitutionality of the Espionage Act; *Capital Traction Co. v. Hof*, 174 U.S. 1 (1899), on duties of the court and the jury; *Schenck v. U.S.*, 249 U.S. 47 (1919), *Frohwerk v. U.S.*, 249 U.S. 204 (1919), *Debs v. U.S.*, 249 U.S. 211 (1919), and *Abrams v. U.S.*, 250 U.S. 616 (1919), on limits on freedom of speech.

Further Reading:
73 *Columbia L. Rev.* 929 (1973).
121 *Univ. Pa. L. Rev.* 189 (1972).

1920 *Clinton H. Pierce, Angelo Creo, Charles Z. Zeilman, and Charles Nelson v. U.S., 252 U.S. 239, 64 L.Ed. 542, 40 S.Ct. 205*

Argued: Nov. 18, 19, 1919.

Decided: March 8, 1920.

Summary: The Court upheld the convictions of socialists who had distributed pamphlets denouncing the war in violation of the Espionage Act of 1917.

Circumstances: Four members of the Albany local of the Socialist Party volunteered to distribute the leaflet, "The Price We Pay," sent from the national headquarters. They were arrested and indicted on six counts of violating the Espionage Act. The trial was held by the District Court for the Northern District of New York. The defendants had been charged with making false statements intended to interfere with military operations and to cause military insubordination. The Supreme Court affirmed, finding the words used were of such a nature as to create a clear and present danger to national security.

Opinion: Justice Mahlon Pitney wrote the 7-to-2 opinion, joined by Chief Justice Edward D. White and Justices Joseph McKenna, William R. Day, Willis Van Devanter, James C. McReynolds, and John H. Clarke. Dissenting were Oliver Wendell Holmes and Louis D. Brandeis. Pitney deduced, as had the jury, that, though the defendants had testified that their purpose was to gain converts to socialism, the real purpose of the pamphlet was to hamper the government war effort. He relied on the Court's decisions in *Schenck* (1919), *Frohwerk* (1919), and *Debs* (1919)—cases in which it was determined that the Espionage Act had been violated.

Justice Brandeis, in a dissent joined by Holmes, first noted that it was not out of the ordinary for the Socialist Party to seek to increase its membership. He then pointed out that the pamphlet in question, "The Price We Pay," had been written by Irwin St. John Tucker, an Episcopal clergyman and a person of sufficient prominence to have been included in the 1916–17 edition of *Who's Who in America*. The complete text of the leaflet was part of Brandeis's dissent. On the danger in attaching importance to a single cause of war, Brandeis wrote: "War is ordinarily the result of many co-operating causes, many different conditions, acts, and motives. One finds the determining cause of war in a great man, another in an idea, a belief, an economic necessity, a trade advantage, a sinister machination, or an accident. It is for this reason largely that men seek to interpret anew in each age, and often with each new generation, the important events in the world's history." Later he said: "The fundamental right of free men to strive for better conditions through new legislation and new institutions will not be preserved, if efforts to secure it by argument to fellow citizens may be construed as criminal incitement to disobey the existing law—merely because the argument presented seems to those exercising judicial power to be unfair in its portrayal of existing evils, mistaken in its assumptions, unsound in reasoning, or intemperate in language."

Referenced Cases: *Schenck v. U.S.*, 249 U.S. 47 (1919), *Frohwerk v. U.S.*, 249 U.S. 204 (1919), and *Debs v. U.S.*, 249

U.S. 211 (1919), on the constitutionality of the Selective Draft Act and the Espionage Act; *Brolan v. U.S.*, 236 U.S. 216 (1915), on Court's jurisdiction; *U.S. v. Britton*, 108 U.S. 199 (1883), *Joplin Mercantile Co. v. U.S.*, 236 U.S. 531 (1915), *U.S. v. Rabinowich*, 238 U.S. 78 (1915), and *Goldman v. U.S.*, 245 U.S. 474 (1918), on conspiracy; *Claasen v. U.S.*, 142 U.S. 140 (1891), *Evans v. U.S.*, 153 U.S. 584 (1894), *Putnam v. U.S.*, 162 U.S. 687 (1896), and *Abrams v. U.S.*, 250 U.S. 616 (1919), rulings on evidence and instructions given or not given to the jury.

Further Reading:
See under *Schaefer v. U.S.*, 251 U.S. 466 (1920).

1925   *Benjamin Gitlow v. New York*, 268 U.S. 652, 69 L.Ed. 1138, 45 S.Ct. 625

Reargued: Nov. 23, 1923.

Decided: June 8, 1925.

Summary: Applying the bad-tendency test, rather than the clear-and-present-danger test, the Court upheld a conviction under a state antisedition law, that government may punish for utterances inimical to public welfare, morals, and peace. But free expression found to be incorporated in 14th Amendment.

Circumstances: Gitlow, a member of the revolutionary, or left-wing, segment of the Socialist Party, was indicted for publishing a radical "manifesto" in violation of New York's criminal anarchy statute. The publication had urged mass strikes by the proletariat and accused moderate socialists of "introducing Socialism by means of legislative measures on the basis of the bourgeois state." The trial court found Gitlow and his associates guilty and the state appellate courts affirmed. The Supreme Court also affirmed, noting that constitutionality hinged on the question of whether there was a reasonable basis for the legislature to have enacted the statute. Gitlow and his associates served three years in prison before they were pardoned by Governor Al Smith.

Opinion: Justice Edward T. Sanford wrote for the 7-to-2 Court, joined by Chief Justice William H. Taft and Justices Joseph McKenna, Willis Van Devanter, James C. McReynolds, George Sutherland, and Pierce Butler. Dissenting was Oliver Wendell Holmes, joined by Louis D. Brandeis. In upholding the constitutionality of the New York State Criminal Anarchy Law, which banned oral or written advocacy of overthrowing the government by force or violence, the Court applied a loose standard that gave great weight to the legislative determination that there was "danger of substantive evil arising from utterances of a specific character." Sanford went on to say that "every presumption is to be indulged in favor of the validity of the statute." In what has since become settled law, the Court added: "For present purposes we may and do assume that freedom of speech and of the press— which are protected by the First Amendment from abridgment by Congress—are among the fundamental personal rights and 'liberties' protected by the due process clause of the Fourteenth Amendment from impairment by the States."

In dissent, Justice Holmes wrote: "Every idea is an incitement. It offers itself for belief and if believed it is acted on unless some other belief outweighs it or some failure of energy stifles the movement of its birth. The only difference between the expression of an opinion and an incitement in the narrower sense is the speaker's enthusiasm for the result. Eloquence may set fire to reason. If in the long run the beliefs expressed in a proletarian dictatorship are destined to be accepted by the dominant forces of the community, the only meaning of free speech is that they should be given their chance and have their way."

Referenced Cases: *Prudential Ins. Co. v. Cheek*, 259 U.S. 530 (1922), on the Court's disregarding the "incidental statement" that the 14th Amendment imposes no restrictions on states concerning freedom of speech; *Robertson v. Baldwin*, 165 U.S. 275 (1897), *Patterson v. Colorado*, 205 U.S. 454 (1907), *Fox v. Washington*, 236 U.S. 273 (1915), *Schenck v. U.S.*, 249 U.S. 47 (1919), *Frohwerk v. U.S.*, 249 U.S. 204 (1919), *Debs v. U.S.*, 249 U.S. 211 (1919), *Schaefer v. U.S.*, 251 U.S. 466 (1920), and *Gilbert v. Minnesota*, 254 U.S. 325 (1920), holding that the Constitution does not confer absolute right to speak or publish without responsibility and that states may punish those who abuse the right by tending to corrupt, incite, and disturb; *Mugler v. Kansas*, 123 U.S. 623

(1887), and *Great Northern R. Co. v. Minnesota*, 246 U.S. 434 (1918), on advocating the overthrow of organized government by force, violence, and unlawful means, inimical to general welfare.

Further Reading:

19 *Illinois L. Rev.* 124 (1924).
20 *Illinois L. Rev.* 809 (April 1926).
4 *Indiana L. J.* 445 (1929).
42 *Law Quarterly Rev.* 12 (Jan. 1926).
31 *West Virginia L. Q.* 273 (1925).
33 *West Virginia L. Q.* 29 (1926).

1927   *Charlotte Anita Whitney v. California,* 274 U.S. 357, 71 L.Ed. 1095, 47 S.Ct. 641

Reargued: March 18, 1926.

Decided: May 16, 1927.

Summary: Upheld the conviction of a member of the Communist Labor Party for violation of the California Criminal Syndicalism Act outlawing certain kinds of words deemed a danger to public peace and safety.

Circumstances: Miss Whitney, a 60-year-old California philanthropist and niece of Justice Stephen J. Field, who served on the Supreme Court from 1863 to 1897, joined the Socialist Party in the 1920s. A member of the Oakland branch of the party, she participated in the Chicago convention in 1919 during which the "radical" wing formed the Communist Labor Party. Whitney, who took an active part in the proceedings and then helped establish a California branch of the Communist Party, was convicted under that state's Criminal Syndicalism Act on the ground that the party was formed to teach criminal syndicalism. As a member of the party, she was deemed to have participated in the crime. Criminal syndicalism was defined "as any doctrine or precept advocating, teaching or aiding and abetting the commission of crime, sabotage . . . , or unlawful methods of terrorism as a means of accomplishing a change in industrial ownership or control, or effecting any political change." Whitney was tried and convicted in the Superior Court of Alameda County, and the judgment was affirmed by the state district court of appeal. The California Supreme Court refused to review. On first hearing before the U.S. Supreme Court, the writ of error was dismissed for want of jurisdiction, but later the Court granted a rehearing.

Opinion: Justice Edward T. Sanford wrote the majority opinion, with which Louis D. Brandeis, joined by Oliver Wendell Holmes, concurred separately. Sanford said the clear-and-present-danger test did not apply and that it was constitutional for the state legislature to outlaw certain kinds of utterances that it deemed "inimical to the public welfare, tending to incite to crime, disturb the public peace, or endanger the foundations of organized government and threaten its overthrow by unlawful means." The Court found no infringement of the First Amendment or of the due process clause of the 14th. "Every presumption is to be indulged in favor of the validity of the statute, and it may not be declared unconstitutional unless it is an arbitrary or unreasonable attempt to exercise the authority vested in the state in the public interest." Although Miss Whitney said she had not condoned violent acts, lower courts had determined the fact that a majority of her organization at the convention she attended had entertained such opinions. The Court upheld her conviction on the ground that concerted action involved a greater threat to the public order than isolated utterances and acts of individuals. Justices Brandeis and Holmes concurred, but only, Brandeis said, because the constitutional issue of freedom of expression had not been raised sufficiently at the trial to make it an issue in the appeal. Though he agreed with the Court's ruling, Brandeis disagreed pointedly with its view on the limits of free speech. The justice refined Holmes's clear-and-present-danger test. "To justify suppression of free speech there must be reasonable ground to fear that serious evil will result if free speech is practiced. There must be reasonable ground to believe that the danger apprehended is imminent. There must be reasonable ground to believe that the evil to be prevented is a serious one. Every denunciation of existing law tends in some measure to increase the probability that there will be a violation of it. Condonation of a breach enhances the probability. Expressions of approval add to the probability.

Propagation of the criminal state of mind by teaching syndicalism increases it. Advocacy of law-breaking heightens it further. But even advocacy of violation, however reprehensible morally, is not justification for denying free speech where the advocacy falls short of incitement, and there is nothing to indicate that the advocacy would be immediately acted on. The wide difference between advocacy and incitement, between preparation and attempt, between assembling and conspiracy, must be borne in mind. In order to support a finding of clear and present danger it must be shown either that immediate serious violence was to be expected or was advocated, or that the past conduct furnished reason to believe that such advocacy was then contemplated." Brandeis concluded that if there is time to expose through discussion the falsehood and fallacies, to avert the evil by the process of education, the remedy to be applied is more speech, not enforced silence.

Referenced Cases: *Crowell v. Randall*, 10 Pet. 368 (1836), *Mississippi & M. R. Co. v. Rock*, 4 Wall. 177 (1867), *California Powder Works v. Davis*, 151 U.S. 389 (1894), *Marvin v. Trout*, 199 U.S. 212 (1905), *Cincinnati, N. O. & T. P. R. Co. v. Slade*, 216 U.S. 78 (1910), *Consolidated Turnp. Co. v. Norfolk & O. V. R. Co.*, 228 U.S. 596 (1913), *Hiawassee River Power Co. v. Carolina-Tennessee Power Co.*, 252 U.S. 341 (1920), and *New York ex rel. Rosevale Realty Co. v. Kleinert*, 268 U.S. 646 (1925), on constituting appropriate ground for Supreme Court review; *First Nat. Bank v. Kentucky*, 10 Wall. 353 (1870), *Edwards v. Elliott*, 21 Wall. 532 (1875), *Dewey v. Des Moines*, 173 U.S. 193 (1899), *Keokuk & H. Bridge Co. v. Illinois*, 175 U.S. 626 (1900), *Capital City Dairy Co. v. Ohio*, 183 U.S. 238 (1902), *Montana ex rel. Haire v. Rice*, 204 U.S. 291 (1907), *Selover, B. & Co. v. Walsh*, 226 U.S. 112 (1912), and *Missouri P. R. & Co. v. McGrew Coal Co.*, 256 U.S. 134 (1921), on the constitutional question considered; *International Harvester Co. v. Kentucky*, 234 U.S. 216 (1914), and *U.S. v. L. Cohen Grocery Co.*, 255 U.S. 81 (1921), on statutes, unlike the Syndicalism Act, held void for uncertainty under the Fifth and 14th Amendments; *Connally v. General Constr. Co.*, 269 U.S. 385 (1926), and *U.S. v. Brewer*, 139 U.S. 278 (1891), on the essential requirement of due process being sufficient clear information; *Zucht v. King*, 260 U.S. 174 (1922), *James-Dickinson Farm Mortg. Co. v. Harry*, 273 U.S. 119 (1927), *Patsone v. Pennsylvania*, 232 U.S.

138 (1914), *Farmers & M. Bank v. Federal Reserve Bank*, 262 U.S. 649 (1923), *Keokee Consol. Coke Co. v. Taylor*, 234 U.S. 224 (1914), *Stebbins v. Riley*, 268 U.S. 137 (1925), and *Graves v. Minnesota*, 272 U.S. 425 (1926), on legislating against an existing evil without covering entire field of possible abuses; *Gitlow v. New York*, 268 U.S. 652 (1925), on constitutional limits on freedom of speech; *Mugler v. Kansas*, 123 U.S. 623 (1887), and *Great Northern R. Co. v. Clara City*, 246 U.S. 434 (1918), on presuming a statute to be valid unless arbitrary; *Meyer v. Nebraska*, 262 U.S. 390 (1923), *Pierce v. Society of Sisters*, 268 U.S. 510 (1925), *Farrington v. Tokushige*, 273 U.S. 284 (1927), and *Schenck v. U.S.*, 249 U.S. 47 (1919), on the fundamental rights of free speech, teaching, and assembly.

Further Reading:

22 *Illinois L. Rev.* 541 (Jan. 1928).
76 *Univ. Pa. L. Rev.* 198 (Dec. 1927).
14 *Virginia L. Rev.* 49 (Nov. 1927).

1931 *Yetta Stromberg v. California*, 283 U.S. 359, 75 L.Ed. 1117, 51 S.Ct. 532, 73 A.L.R. 1484

Argued: April 15, 1931.

Decided: May 18, 1931.

Summary: Struck down, on First Amendment grounds, a state "red flag law" because such emblems do not clearly advocate violence. This was an early "symbolic speech" ruling.

Circumstances: Miss Stromberg, a member of the Young Communist League, an international organization affiliated with the Communist Party, was convicted in the superior court of San Bernardino County for violating a section of the state penal code that prohibited the display of a "red flag, banner, or badge . . . in any public place . . . as a . . . symbol . . . of opposition to organized government." Stromberg had been a supervisor at a camp for children, where the daily ritual included raising "a camp-made reproduction of the flag of Soviet Russia." Stromberg's conviction was affirmed by the California state district court of appeal. The Supreme Court reversed.

Opinion: Chief Justice Charles E. Hughes wrote the 7-to-2 opinion, joined by Justices Oliver Wendell Holmes, Willis Van Devanter, Louis D. Brandeis, George Sutherland, Harlan F. Stone, and Owen J. Roberts. Dissenting were James C. McReynolds and Pierce Butler. The Court tackled the statute's three clauses, or purposes: the first related to the display of a flag or banner "as a sign, symbol or emblem of opposition to organized government"; the second described the display "as an invitation or stimulus to anarchistic action"; and the third said the display was "an aid to propaganda that is of a seditious character." But, because the jury was allowed to determine guilt on the basis of any one clause, Hughes noted that the Court could also base its review on such a single clause. Thus, the Court found the second and third clauses valid, as they related to incitements to violence, but allowed that the first could have included peaceful and orderly opposition to government by legal means and within constitutional limitations. "The maintenance of the opportunity for free political discussion to the end that government may be responsive to the will of the people and that changes may be obtained by lawful means, an opportunity essential to the security of the Republic, is a fundamental principle of our constitutional system. A statute which upon its face . . . is so vague and indefinite as to permit the punishment of the fair use of this opportunity is repugnant to the guaranty of liberty contained in the 14th Amendment."

In dissent, Justice McReynolds said that, since the petitioner had been charged with all of the statute's inhibitions, the conviction should have stood "even if one paragraph were invalid." Justice Butler, also in dissent, similarly said that the appellant had not been convicted for violation of the first clause and that the Court was thus not called upon to decide the constitutional issue of protected speech and press.

Referenced Cases: *Gitlow v. New York*, 268 U.S. 652 (1925), *Whitney v. California*, 274 U.S. 357 (1927), and *Fiske v. Kansas*, 274 U.S. 380 (1927), holding that the conception of liberty under the due process clause of the 14th Amendment embraces the right of free speech, but that the right is not absolute.

Further Reading:
2 *Detroit L. Rev.* 121 (March 1932).
2 *Idaho L. J.* 60 (Jan. 1932).
9 *NYU L. Q.* 64 (Sept. 1931).
5 *So. Calif. L. Rev.* 172 (Dec. 1931).

1931 *J. M. Near v. Minnesota ex rel. Floyd B. Olson, County Attorney of Hennepin County, Minnesota, 283 U.S. 697, 75 L.Ed. 1357, 51 S.Ct. 625, 1 Med.L.Rptr. 1001*

Argued: Jan. 30, 1931.

Decided: June 1, 1931.

Summary: Striking down a state law against "public nuisance" publications, the Court referred to the "general conception that liberty of the press . . . has meant, principally although not exclusively, immunity from previous restraints or censorship," but that government may restrain information affecting national security and private rights in judicial proceedings, as well as obscene publications.

Circumstances: Olson, the county attorney of Hennepin County (Minneapolis), brought an action under a Minnesota public nuisance statute to stop publication of a "malicious, scandalous, and defamatory newspaper, magazine, or other periodical," in this case *The Saturday Press*. Olson complained that Near and his co-publisher, Howard Guilford, had falsely accused city law enforcement agencies and officials of failing to expose and punish gambling, bootlegging, and racketeering, activities that the *Press* alleged were in control of a "Jewish gangster." The complaint asserted that on nine dates in Sept., Oct., and Nov. 1927 the newspaper had carried articles that were "largely . . . malicious, scandalous and defamatory." The state trial court found that the editors had violated the statute and the court "perpetually enjoined" Near and Guilford from conducting "said nuisance

under the title of *The Saturday Press* or any other name or title."
In 1928 the Minnesota Supreme Court upheld the constitutionality of the law, stating that under its broad police power the state
could regulate public nuisances, including scandalous and defamatory newspapers. The U.S. Supreme Court reversed, declaring
that the statute was not designed to redress wrongs to individuals
accused by the newspaper but, instead, was aimed at suppressing
The Saturday Press once and for all.

Opinion: Chief Justice Charles E. Hughes wrote the
Court's 5-to-4 opinion, joined by Justices Oliver Wendell Holmes,
Louis D. Brandeis, Harlan F. Stone, and Owen J. Roberts. Dissenting was Pierce Butler, joined by Willis Van Devanter, James C.
McReynolds, and George Sutherland. Hughes first noted the un-
usualness, if not uniqueness, of the statute, for the suppression as
a public nuisance of a newspaper or periodical. He said that the
Court, in passing upon constitutional questions, must regard substance and not mere matters of form, testing the statute by its
operation and effect. "The object of the statute is not punishment,
in the ordinary sense, but suppression of the offending newspaper
or periodical. This suppression is accomplished by enjoining publication and that restraint is the object and effect of the statute."
The statute also put the publisher under an effective censorship,
Hughes added. "[U]nless the owner or publisher is able and disposed to bring competent evidence to satisfy the judge that the
charges are true and are published with good motives and for
justifiable ends, his newspaper or periodical is suppressed and
further publication is made punishable as a contempt. This is the
essence of censorship." Hughes allowed, however, that public officers, whose character and conduct remained open to debate and
free discussion in the press, may find remedies for false accusa-
tions under libel laws, not in proceedings to restrain publication.
"Subsequent punishment for such abuses as may exist is the
appropriate remedy, consistent with constitutional privilege." In
sum, the chief justice said that the theory of the constitutional
guaranty of the First Amendment "is that even a more serious
public evil would be caused by authority to prevent publication."
    Justice Butler, who wrote the minority dissent, said that the
mere improbability of many of the published statements compelled a finding of falsity. "The articles themselves show malice."
He averred that the statute did not operate as a *previous* restraint,

since it did not authorize control in advance by licensers and censors. "The restraint authorized is only in respect of continuing to do what has been duly adjudged to constitute a nuisance."

Referenced Cases: *Gitlow v. New York*, 268 U.S. 652 (1925), *Whitney v. California*, 274 U.S. 357 (1927), *Fiske v. Kansas*, 274 U.S. 380 (1927), and *Stromberg v. California*, 283 U.S. 359 (1931), holding that liberty of speech and press is within liberty safeguarded by the due process clause of the 14th Amendment; *Railroad Commission Cases*, 116 U.S. 307 (1886), and *Northern P. R. Co. v. North Dakota*, 236 U.S. 585 (1915), on the essence of ownership being the owner's right to a fair return; *Tyson & Bro.- United Theatre Ticket Offices v. Banton*, 273 U.S. 418 (1927), *Ribnik v. McBride*, 277 U.S. 350 (1928), and *Adkins v. Children's Hospital*, 261 U.S. 525 (1923), on the limited power of the state to interfere with the fixing of prices and wages; *Henderson v. New York*, 92 U.S. 259 (1876), *Bailey v. Alabama*, 219 U.S. 219 (1911), *St. Louis S. W. R. Co. v. Arkansas*, 235 U.S. 350 (1914), and *Mountain Timber Co. v. Washington*, 243 U.S. 219 (1917), holding that on constitutional questions the Court regards substance as well as form, the operation as well as effect of statutes; *Patterson v. Colorado*, 205 U.S. 454 (1907), and *Toledo Newspaper Co. v. U.S.*, 247 U.S. 402 (1918), on the authority of courts to punish for contempt when publications tend to prevent discharge of judicial functions; *Schenck v. U.S.*, 249 U.S. 47 (1919), and *Gompers v. Bucks Stove & Range Co.*, 221 U.S. 418 (1911), holding that the protection against previous restraint is not absolutely unlimited; *Lindsley v. Natural Carbonic Gas Co.*, 220 U.S. 61 (1911), *Corporation Commission v. Lowe*, 281 U.S. 431 (1930), and *O'Gorman & Young v. Hartford F. Ins. Co.*, 282 U.S. 251 (1931), on laws designed to preserve the peace and good order of the state.

Further Reading:
12 *Boston Univ. L. Rev.* 261 (April 1932).
31 *Columbia L. Rev.* 1148 (Nov. 1931).
17 *Cornell L. Q.* 126 (Dec. 1931).
3 *Dakota L. Rev.* 431 (Dec. 1931).
22 *J. Criminal L.* 909 (March 1932).
35 *Law Notes* 155 (Nov. 1931).
30 *Michigan L. Rev.* 279 (Dec. 1931).
16 *Minnesota L. Rev.* 97 (Dec. 1931).

9 *NYU L. Q.* 64 (Sept. 1931).
1 *Univ. Detroit L. J.* 46 (Nov. 1931).
80 *Univ. Pa. L. Rev.* 130 (Nov. 1931).
41 *Yale L. Rev.* 262 (Dec. 1931).

1937   *Dirk De Jonge v. Oregon,* 299 U.S. 353, 81 L.Ed. 278, 57 S.Ct. 255

Argued: Dec. 9, 1936.

Decided: Jan. 4, 1937.

Summary: Conviction under a state criminal syndicalism statute reversed on general First Amendment grounds, that a "personal right of free speech" included peaceable assembly.

Circumstances: De Jonge was convicted in the Circuit Court, Multnomah County, under the Oregon Criminal Syndicalism law, which forbade a number of offenses "embracing the teaching of criminal syndicalism," defined as "the doctrine which advocates crime, physical violence, sabotage, or any unlawful acts or methods as a means of accomplishing or effecting industrial or political change or revolution." A member of the Communist Party, De Jonge had presided at a peaceful meeting of the organization protesting police brutality during a strike of longshoremen. The Oregon Supreme Court affirmed the conviction. The U.S. Supreme Court reversed.

Opinion: Chief Justice Charles E. Hughes wrote the 8-to-0 decision. Harlan F. Stone did not participate. Without specific reference to the clear-and-present-danger doctrine used in similar earlier cases, the Court said, however, that the rights embodied in the First and 14th Amendments may be abused by using speech or press or assembly in order to incite to violence and crime. "The people through their legislatures may protect themselves against that abuse. But the legislative intervention can find constitutional justification only by dealing with the abuse. The rights themselves must not be curtailed." Hughes concluded that the

Court had not been called upon to review the findings of the state court as to the objectives of the Communist Party. "Notwithstanding those objectives, the defendant still enjoyed his personal right of free speech and to take part in a peaceable assembly having a lawful purpose, although called by that party." The essence of De Jonge's guaranteed personal liberty was his right to discuss public issues of the day and, in a lawful manner, to seek redress of alleged grievances.

Referenced Cases: *Gitlow v. New York*, 268 U.S. 652 (1925), *Whitney v. California*, 274 U.S. 357 (1927), and *Burns v. U.S.*, 274 U.S. 328 (1927), in which statutes were upheld because they protected against violence and criminality; *Fiske v. Kansas*, 274 U.S. 380 (1927), and *Stromberg v. California*, 283 U.S. 359 (1931), in which statutes were struck down because unlawful methods were not shown to have been advocated; *Near v. Minnesota*, 283 U.S. 697 (1931), *Grosjean v. American Press Co.*, 297 U.S. 233 (1936), *U.S. v. Cruikshank*, 92 U.S. 542 (1875), *Herbert v. Louisiana*, 272 U.S. 312 (1926), and *Powell v. Alabama*, 287 U.S. 45 (1932), on redress of grievances and due process in the 14th Amendment.

Further Reading:
25 *California L. Rev.* 496 (May 1937).
37 *Columbia L. Rev.* 857 (May 1937).
25 *Georgetown L. J.* 736 (March 1937).
50 *Harvard L. Rev.* 689 (Feb. 1937).
16 *Oregon L. Rev.* 278 (April 1937).
85 *Univ. Pa. L. Rev.* 532 (March 1937).
3 *Univ. Pittsburgh L. Rev.* 229 (Feb. 1937).
15 *Texas L. Rev.* 373 (April 1937).
22 *Washington Univ. L. Q.* 427 (April 1937).

1942 *Chaplinsky v. New Hampshire*, 315 U.S. 568, 86 L.Ed. 1031, 62 S.Ct. 766

Argued: Feb. 5, 1942.

Decided: March 9, 1942.

Summary: "Fighting words," epithets "likely to provoke the average person to retaliation, and thereby cause a breach of the peace," declared outside First Amendment protection.

Circumstances: Chaplinsky, a Jehovah's Witness, was prosecuted under a state statute that forbade "addressing any offensive, derisive or annoying work" to another person in a public place. Citizens had complained to the city marshal of Rochester, New Hampshire, that Chaplinsky denounced all religion as a "racket," then subsequently derided the marshal as a "Goddamned racketeer and a damn Fascist." Chaplinsky was found guilty in municipal court, the judgment affirmed by a superior court jury and the state supreme court. The U.S. Supreme Court also affirmed.

Opinion: Justice Frank Murphy, for a unanimous Court, said that, although the city marshal had not struck Chaplinsky, the words used were likely to provoke the average person to physical retaliation. Therefore, Chaplinsky had no First Amendment right to call the marshal a racketeer or a fascist. Fighting words, Murphy said, are excluded from constitutional protection because, "by their very utterance," they "inflict injury or tend to incite an immediate breach of the peace." Such words are so offensive that "men of common intelligence would understand" that they are "likely to cause an average addressee to fight." Fighting words, like obscenity and false advertising, are "no essential part of any exposition of ideas, and are of such slight social value as a step to truth that any benefit that may be derived from them is clearly outweighed by the social interest in order and morality."

Referenced Cases: *Lovell v. Griffin*, 303 U.S. 444 (1938), and *Cantwell v. Connecticut*, 310 U.S. 296 (1940), on First Amendment shelter for freedom of speech, press, and religion; *Thornhill v. Alabama*, 310 U.S. 88 (1940), on punishing specific conduct in a public place likely to breach the peace; *Fox v. Washington*, 236 U.S. 273 (1915), regarding carefully drawn law that does not unduly impair liberty of expression.

Further Reading:
2 *Bill of Rights Rev.* 224 (Spring 1942).
22 *Boston Univ. L. Rev.* 446 (June 1942).

1949   ***Charles Kovacs v. Albert Cooper, Jr.,***
Judge of the First District Police Court
of Trenton, 336 U.S. 77, 93 L.Ed. 513, 69
S.Ct. 448

Argued: Oct. 11, 1948.

Decided: Jan. 31, 1949.

Summary: Held that sound trucks may broadcast political and commercial messages, but not in a loud and raucous
manner that disrupts residential areas. Time, place, and manner
regulations deemed reasonable.

Circumstances: At issue was the validity of a Trenton, New Jersey, ordinance making it unlawful to use sound am-
plifiers attached to trucks emitting "loud and raucous noises" on
city streets. Kovacs was found guilty of violating the ordinance,
but not necessarily of being loud and raucous, by a police judge.
His conviction was affirmed in the New Jersey appellate courts,
including the state supreme court. The U.S. Supreme Court also
affirmed.

Opinion: Justice Stanley F. Reed announced the judgment of the 5-to-4 Court, joined in the opinion by Chief Justice
Fred M. Vinson and Justice Harold H. Burton. Eight justices, ex-
cepting Frank Murphy, who dissented without opinion, agreed
that sound amplification in streets and public places may be
subjected to reasonable regulation and that an ordinance banning
"loud and raucous noises" did not go beyond such regulation. Two,
Felix Frankfurter and Robert H. Jackson, went further and said
that sound trucks in streets may be absolutely prohibited without
violating the constitutional right of free speech. Hugo L. Black,
joined by William O. Douglas and Wiley B. Rutledge, dissented on
the ground that no proof had been presented on the "noises" being
"loud and raucous." Reed said that the Court did not believe that
the Trenton ordinance abridged "the right of free speech . . . guaranteed every citizen [so] that he may reach the minds of willing
listeners and to do so there must be opportunity to win their
attention." He said the "preferred position of freedom of speech in

a society that cherishes liberty for all did not require legislators to be insensible to claims by citizens to comfort and convenience. "To enforce freedom of speech in disregard of the rights of others would be harsh and arbitrary in itself."

In his concurrence, Justice Frankfurter found the phrase "preferred position of freedom of speech" as having uncritically crept into recent Court decisions. "I deem it a mischievous phrase, if it carries the thought, which it may subtly imply, that any law touching communication is infected with presumptive invalidity," Frankfurter said. "So long as a legislature does not prescribe what ideas may be noisily expressed and what may not be, nor discriminate among those who would make inroads upon the public peace, it is not for us to supervise the limits the legislature may impose in safeguarding the steadily narrowing opportunities for serenity and reflection. Without such opportunities freedom of thought becomes a mocking phrase, and without freedom of thought there can be no free society." Justice Jackson said he did not agree that, if the Court sustained regulations or prohibitions of sound trucks, it would therefore be valid if applied to other methods of "communication of ideas." "Each, in my view, is a law unto itself, and all we are dealing with now is the sound truck."

Justice Black, in dissent with Douglas and Rutledge, feared "favoritism" among existing and future instruments of communication. "There are many people who have ideas that they wish to disseminate but who do not have enough money to own or control publishing plants, newspapers, radios, moving picture studios, or chains of show places. Yet everybody knows the vast reaches of these powerful channels of communication which from the very nature of our economic system must be under the control and guidance of comparatively few people."

Referenced Cases: *Winters v. New York*, 333 U.S. 507 (1948), on a statute so vague that a distributor of tales of war horrors could not know if in violation; *Saia v. New York*, 334 U.S. 558 (1948), on previous restraint without prescribed standards of discretion; *Schenck v. U.S.*, 249 U.S. 47 (1919), on unprotected speech, "words that may have all the effect of force"; *Martin v. Struthers*, 319 U.S. 141 (1943), the Court "never intimated that the visitor could insert a foot in the door or insist on a hearing"; *Palko v. Connecticut*, 302 U.S. 319 (1937), on the people's "concept of ordered liberty"; *Herndon v. Lowry*, 301 U.S. 242 (1937), *U.S. v.*

Carolene Products Co., 304 U.S. 144 (1938), *Thornhill v. Alabama*, 310 U.S. 88 (1940), *American Federation of Labor v. Swing*, 312 U.S. 321 (1941), *Schneider v. Irvington*, 308 U.S. 147 (1939), *Bridges v. California*, 314 U.S. 252 (1941), *Pennekamp v. Florida*, 328 U.S. 331 (1946), *Jones v. Opelika*, 316 U.S. 584 (1943), *Murdock v. Pennsylvania*, 319 U.S. 105 (1943), *Prince v. Massachusetts*, 321 U.S. 158 (1944), *Follett v. McCormick*, 321 U.S. 573 (1944), *Marsh v. Alabama*, 326 U.S. 501 (1946), *West Virginia State Bd. of Edu. v. Barnette*, 319 U.S. 624 (1943), and *Thomas v. Collins*, 323 U.S. 516 (1945), on the evolution of "preferred position" of First Amendment freedoms, first used by Chief Justice Harlan F. Stone in *Jones v. Opelika*.

Further Reading:

34 *Cornell L. Q.* 626 (Summer 1949).
17 *George Washington L. Rev.* 494 (June 1949).
62 *Harvard L. Rev.* 1228 (May 1949).
34 *Iowa L. Rev.* 681 (May 1949).
17 *J. Bar Assoc. Kansas* 491 (May 1949).
10 *Maryland L. Rev.* 355 (Fall 1949).
3 *Miami L. Q.* 452 (April 1949).
47 *Michigan L. Rev.* 1007 (May 1949).
14 *Missouri L. Rev.* 194 (April 1949).
28 *Nebraska L. Rev.* 618 (May 1949).
3 *Oklahoma L. Rev.* 219 (May 1950).
3 *Rutgers L. Rev.* 250 (June 1949).
22 *So. Calif. L. Rev.* 416 (July 1949).
18 *Univ. Cincinnati L. Rev.* 222 (March 1949).
2 *Univ. Florida L. Rev.* 257 (Summer 1949).
6 *Washington & Lee L. Rev.* 74 (1949).

1951   *Eugene Dennis, John B. Williamson, Jacob Stachel, Robert G. Thompson, Benjamin J. Davis, Jr., Henry Winston, John Gates, Irving Potash, Gilbert Green, Carl Winter and Gus Hall v. U.S.,* **341 U.S. 494, 95 L.Ed. 1137, 71 S.Ct. 857**

Argued: Dec. 4, 1950.

Decided: June 4, 1951.

Summary: Ad hoc balancing, a variation of the clear-and-present-danger test, used by the Court to uphold convictions under the federal sedition law, the Smith Act of 1940.

Circumstances: The Smith Act, the nation's second peacetime sedition law, was aimed at communism, making it a crime to advocate the violent overthrow of the government. In 1940 a federal grand jury indicted 12 of the country's leading communists. Eleven (one became ill and was excused temporarily) were found guilty by a jury on Oct. 14, 1949, following a nine-month trial, six months of which were devoted to the taking of evidence, resulting in a record of 16,000 pages. Judge Harold Medina, for the District Court for the Southern District of New York, instructed the jury that the law did not prohibit discussing the propriety of overthrowing the government by force or violence, but "the teaching and advocacy of action for the accomplishment of that purpose by language reasonably and ordinarily calculated to incite persons to such action." The Court of Appeals for the Second Circuit affirmed the convictions. The Supreme Court also affirmed.

Opinion: Chief Justice Fred M. Vinson wrote the Court's 6-to-2 ruling, joined by Justices Stanley F. Reed, Harold H. Burton, and Sherman Minton. Felix Frankfurter and Robert H. Jackson wrote separate concurring opinions. Dissenting were Hugo L. Black and William O. Douglas. Tom C. Clark did not participate. The Court upheld the convictions of leaders of the American Communist Party under the conspiracy provisions of the Smith Act. Vinson, following a formulation developed by Judge Learned Hand in the Second Circuit's affirmation, thus interpreted the clear-and-present-danger test created by Oliver Wendell Holmes in *Schenck v. U.S.* (1919): "In each case [courts] must ask whether the gravity of the evil, discounted by its improbability, justifies such invasion of free speech as is necessary to avoid the danger." This has been seen as an abandonment of the clear-and-present-danger test, dropping the requirement of "clear," subordinating "present," and overemphasizing the seriousness of "evil." Vinson explained that the "obvious purpose" of the Smith Act was to protect existing government, not from peaceable, lawful, and constitutional means, but from change by violence, revolution, and terrorism, and that the law was directed at advocacy, not discussion. "No one would conceive that it is not within the power of Congress to prohibit acts intended to overthrow the Government by force and violence." Vinson went on to note that the Court had never placed a unique emphasis on "certain utterances" protected by the First Amendment. And, despite earlier dissents by Oliver Wendell Holmes and Louis D. Brandeis in clear-and-present-danger decisions, Vinson said the dissenters doubted "the probable effectiveness of the puny efforts toward subversion." But, in *Dennis*, the petitioners had developed such a highly organized conspiracy with rigidly disciplined members subject to call, "coupled with the inflammable nature of world conditions," sufficient to convince the Court that the convictions were justified. "A claim of guilelessness ill becomes those with evil intent." The Court balanced "the gravity of the evil" against the free-speech interests of Dennis and his fellow communists, thereby reasoning that the evil of a communist takeover outweighed the right of free speech, despite the remoteness of the conspiratorial takeover.

Justice Frankfurter, in a lengthy concurrence, recalled what James Madison had written in *The Federalist No. 41*: "Security against foreign danger is one of the primitive objects of civil society." The justice added: "The most tragic experience in our history is a poignant reminder that the Nation's continued existence may be threatened from within." Frankfurter listed the values that had come out of an expressed attitude toward the judicial function: (1) free-speech cases had not been an exception to the principle that judges are not legislators, that reconciling competing interests is a legislative function unless the balance struck is unfair; (2) relevant decisions indicated, however, that there had been careful balancing of conflicting interests; and (3) not every type of speech occupied the same position on the scale of values. Frankfurter concluded: "While I think there was power in Congress to enact this statute and that, as applied in this case, it cannot be held unconstitutional, I add that I have little faith in the long-range effectiveness of this conviction to stop the rise of the Communist movement. Communism will not go to jail with these Communists. No decision by this Court can forestall revolution whenever the existing government fails to command the respect and loyalty of the people and sufficient distress and discontent is allowed to grow up among the masses." Justice Jackson concurred on the ground that a conviction for conspiring to advocate or teach the overthrow of the government did not violate the right of free speech, even if no clear and present danger existed.

Justice Black, in dissent, said that the indictments were a virulent form of prior censorship. "There is hope . . . that in calmer times, when present pressures, passions, and fears subside, this or some later Court will restore the First Amendment liberties to the high preferred place where they belong in a free society." Justice Douglas, also in dissent, said that illegality should not turn on intent, but on the nature of the act. Otherwise, people are punished *for what they thought*, convicted not for what they said but for the purpose with which they said it. It is dangerous to start probing minds for motive and purpose, he said.

Referenced Cases: *Williams v. U.S.*, 341 U.S. 97 (1951), and *Cramer v. U.S.*, 325 U.S. 1 (1945), on the essential element of proof of intent to overthrow the government by force and violence; *American Communications Asso. v. Douds*, 339 U.S. 382 (1950), on the existence of a mens rea—a guilty state of mind—as rule rather than exception in Anglo-American criminal jurisprudence; *Thornhill v. Alabama*, 310 U.S. 88 (1940), *Herndon v. Lowry*, 301 U.S. 242 (1937), and *De Jonge v. Oregon*, 299 U.S. 353 (1937), cases where interpretations of state laws held inconsistent with federal constitution; *Schenck v. U.S.*, 249 U.S. 47 (1919), the first important case involving free speech decided by the Court and the one in which Oliver Wendell Holmes introduced the clear-and-present-danger test; *Goldman v. U.S.*, 245 U.S. 474 (1918), on Holmes's own weakening of the test; *Frohwerk v. U.S.*, 249 U.S. 204 (1919), *Debs v. U.S.*, 249 U.S. 211 (1919), *Abrams v. U.S.*, 250 U.S. 616 (1920), *Schaefer v. U.S.*, 251 U.S. 466 (1920), and *Pierce v. U.S.*, 252 U.S. 239 (1920), cases reflecting uncertainty over application of the clear-and-present-danger test; *Whitney v. California*, 274 U.S. 357 (1927), on clear and present danger applied to syndicalism, concurred to by Holmes and Brandeis; *Schneider v. Irvington*, 308 U.S. 147 (1939), *Cantwell v. Connecticut*, 310 U.S. 296 (1940), *Martin v. Struthers*, 319 U.S. 141 (1943), *West Virginia State Board of Education v. Barnette*, 319 U.S. 624 (1943), *Thomas v. Collins*, 323 U.S. 516 (1945), *Marsh v.*

Alabama, 326 U.S. 501 (1946), *Prince v. Massachusetts,* 321 U.S. 158 (1944), and *Cox v. New Hampshire,* 312 U.S. 569 (1941), a category of cases involving insubstantial state interest to warrant speech restriction; *Pinkerton v. U.S.,* 328 U.S. 640 (1946), and *U.S. v. Rabinowich,* 238 U.S. 78 (1915), on the existence of conspiracy creating the danger; *Taylor v. Mississippi,* 319 U.S. 583 (1943), *Williams v. U.S.,* 341 U.S. 97 (1951), *Jordan v. De George,* 341 U.S. 223 (1951), and *Screws v. U.S.,* 325 U.S. 91 (1945), on the idea that guilelessness ill becomes those with evil intent; *U.S. v. Petrillo,* 332 U.S. 1 (1948), *U.S. v. Wurzbach,* 280 U.S. 396 (1930), and *Nash v. U.S.,* 229 U.S. 373 (1913), on indicating standards to those who advocate constitutionally prohibited conduct; *Patterson v. Colorado,* 205 U.S. 454 (1907), the Court's first decision on interference with the course of justice; *Craig v. Harney,* 331 U.S. 367 (1947), in which the Court said the 14th Amendment protected "strong," "intemperate," and "unfair" criticism of an elected judge; *Fox v. Washington,* 236 U.S. 273 (1915), the first time the Court considered conflict of interest between states prohibiting speech because of its tendency to lead to crime; *Schneiderman v. U.S.,* 320 U.S. 118 (1943), and *Bridges v. Wixon,* 326 U.S. 135 (1945), on limiting the effect of legislation on First Amendment interests; *Breard v. Alexandria,* 341 U.S. 622 (1951), decided the same day as *Dennis,* on regulating door-to-door selling; *Chaplinsky v. New Hampshire,* 315 U.S. 568 (1942), and *Niemotko v. Maryland,* 340 U.S. 268 (1951), on unprotected speech.

Further Reading:

37 *ABA J.* 920 (Dec. 1951).
3 *Alabama L. Rev.* 232 (Fall 1950).
31 *Boston Univ. L. Rev.* 544 (Nov. 1951).
39 *California L. Rev.* 475 (Dec. 1951).
56 *Dickinson L. Rev.* 343 (March 1952).
40 *Georgetown L. J.* 304 (Jan. 1952).
13 *Georgia Bar J.* 361 (Fall 1951).
26 *Indiana L. J.* 70 (Fall 1950).
4 *Miami L. Q.* 238 (Feb. 1950).
49 *Michigan L. Rev.* 130 (Nov. 1950).
50 *Michigan L. Rev.* 451 (Jan. 1952).
36 *Minnesota L. Rev.* 96 (Dec. 1951).
12 *Ohio St. L. J.* 123 (Winter 1951).

23 *So. Calif. L. Rev.* 640 (July 1950).
24 *Temple L. Q.* 241 (Oct. 1950).
5 *Vanderbilt L. Rev.* 141 (Feb. 1952).
37 *Virginia L. Rev.* 878 (Oct. 1951).
8 *Washington & Lee L. Rev.* 99 (1951).

1951   *Jack H. Breard v. City of Alexandria,*
341 U.S. 622, 95 L.Ed. 1233, 71 S.Ct. 920

Argued: March 7, 8, 1951.

Decided: June 4, 1951.

Summary: A nuisance ordinance against door-to-door solicitation upheld on ground that commercialism diluted any First Amendment protection to the salesperson.

Circumstances: Breard, a regional representative of a Pennsylvania subscription company, was arrested while going door-to-door in Alexandria, Louisiana, soliciting subscriptions for nationally known magazines. Arrest was on the basis for his not having first obtained consent of the owners of the residences solicited. He objected on grounds that the ordinance violated the due process clause of the 14th Amendment and the speech and press clauses of the First Amendment. Breard argued in his appeal that the ordinance was an unreasonable imposition on his right to earn a living, that it was an impermissible burden on interstate commerce, and that, because he was selling magazines, the ordinance violated the First Amendment guarantee of press freedom. The Louisiana Supreme Court affirmed the trial court's guilty verdict. The U.S. Supreme Court also affirmed.

Opinion: Justice Stanley F. Reed wrote the Court's 6-to-3 opinion, joined by Justices Felix Frankfurter, Robert H. Jackson, Harold H. Burton, Tom C. Clark, and Sherman Minton. Dissenting were Chief Justice Fred M. Vinson and Justices Hugo L. Black and William O. Douglas. Reed explained that the commercial aspect of Breard's situation—door-to-door sales of magazine subscriptions—rendered his activities more easily subject to state regulation than the press might ordinarily be. "The issue brings into collision the rights of the hospitable housewife, peering on Monday morning around her chained door, with those of Mr. Breard's courteous, well-trained but possibly persistent solicitor. . . . Behind the housewife are many housewives and home-owners in the towns where [such] ordinances offer their aid. Behind Mr. Breard [is his employer] with an annual business of $5,000,000 in subscriptions." Reed said there were other ways to sell magazines besides intruding upon the privacy of families through door-to-door sales techniques. "It would seem to be . . . a misuse of the great guarantees of free speech and free press to use those guarantees to force a community to admit the solicitors of publications to the home premises of its residents."

Chief Justice Vinson, joined by Douglas, dissented, noting that the ordinance was prohibitory rather than regulatory and discriminated against interstate commerce by favoring local merchants. Justice Black, joined by Douglas, dissented because the ordinance, as it applied to magazine solicitation, infringed the liberty of the press. "The constitutional sanctuary for the press must necessarily include liberty to publish and circulate. In view of our economic system, it must also include freedom to solicit paying subscribers." Black saw Breard and his sales force as "agents of the press."

Referenced Cases: *New State Ice Co. v. Liebmann,* 285 U.S. 262 (1932), *Adams v. Tanner,* 244 U.S. 590 (1917), *Gundling v. Chicago,* 177 U.S. 183 (1900), and *Williams v. Arkansas,* 217 U.S. 79 (1910), on relevance of the due process clause of the 14th Amendment; *Olsen v. Nebraska,* 313 U.S. 236 (1941), and *Lincoln Federal Labor Union AFL v. Northwestern Iron & Metal Co.,* 335 U.S. 525 (1949), on legislation that is regulatory or prohibitory; *Asbell v. Kansas,* 209 U.S. 251 (1908), *Savage v. Jones,* 225 U.S. 501 (1912), and *Hartford Acci. & Indem. Co. v. Illinois,* 298 U.S. 155 (1936), on relevance of the commerce clause; *H. P. Hood & Sons Inc. v. Du Mond,* 336 U.S. 525 (1949), and *Dean Milk Co. v. Madison,* 340 U.S. 349 (1951), on the Court not permitting local interests to self-protection against out-of-state competition by curtailing interstate business; *Martin v. Struthers,* 319 U.S. 141 (1943), a viable precedent but ordinance not aimed solely at commercial advertising; *Marsh v. Alabama,* 326 U.S. 501 (1946), and

Tucker v. Texas, 326 U.S. 517 (1946), on protection for the distribution of matter more religious than commercial; *Robbins v. Shelby County Taxing Dist.*, 120 U.S. 489 (1887), the first of cases regarding soliciting orders for goods to be shipped across state lines being interstate commerce; *Bunger v. Green River*, 300 U.S. 638 (1937), on sustaining a conviction under a similar ordinance.

Further Reading:

4 *Alabama L. Rev.* 107 (Fall 1951).
16 *Albany L. Rev.* 294 (June 1952).
1 *Buffalo L. Rev.* 189 (Winter 1951).
30 *Chicago-Kent L. Rev.* 164 (March 1952).
37 *Iowa L. Rev.* 261 (Winter 1952).
27 *No. Dakota L. Rev.* 416 (Oct. 1951).
3 *Syracuse L. Rev.* 202 (Fall 1951).
22 *Tenn. L. Rev.* 559 (June 1952).
26 *Tulane L. Rev.* 92 (Dec. 1951).
20 *Univ. Cincinnati L. Rev.* 509 (Nov. 1951).

1966   *John Mills v. Alabama*, 384 U.S. 214, 16 L.Ed.2d 484, 86 S.Ct. 1434

Argued: April 19, 1966.

Decided: May 23, 1966.

Summary: A state law banning editorials on election day held in violation of the First Amendment.

Circumstances: Mills, editor of the Birmingham *Post-Herald*, was charged with violating Alabama's Corrupt Practices Act for publishing on election day an editorial urging voters to adopt the mayor-council form of government. The statute made it a crime "to do any electioneering or to solicit any votes . . . in support of or in opposition to any proposition that is being voted on on the day on which the election affecting such candidates or propositions is being held." The trial court sustained demurrers on the grounds that the statute abridged freedom of speech and press in violation of the Alabama Constitution and the First and 14th Amendments to the U.S. Constitution. However, the state supreme court held that publication of the editorial on election day violated the law and did not abridge either constitution. It remanded, but the U.S. Supreme Court ruled its judgment final and appealable to the high court.

Opinion: Justice Hugo L. Black wrote for eight members of the Court in the unanimous decision. William O. Douglas, joined by William J. Brennan, Jr., filed a separate concurring opinion. John M. Harlan also wrote separately. In reversing the Alabama Supreme Court's determination that the restriction was "reasonable" because it was limited to election days, Black wrote: "Suppression of the right of the press to praise or criticize governmental agents and to clamor and contend for or against change . . . muzzles one of the very agencies the Framers of the Constitution thoughtfully and deliberately selected to improve our society and keep it free. The Alabama Corrupt Practices Act by providing criminal penalties for publishing editorials such as the one here silences the press at a time when it can be most effective. It is difficult to conceive of a more obvious and flagrant abridgment of the constitutionally guaranteed freedom of the press. We hold that no test of reasonableness can save a state law from invalidation as a violation of the First Amendment when that law makes it a crime for a newspaper editor to do no more than urge people to vote one way or another in a publicly held election." Justice Douglas, with Brennan, emphasized the finality of the judgment reversed, responding to Harlan's view, that "limitations on the jurisdiction of this Court . . . should be respected and not turned on and off at the pleasure of its members or to suit the convenience of litigants." Justice Harlan did not concur but rested reversal on the ground that the relevant statutory provision did not give the editor fair warning.

Referenced Cases: *Pope v. Atlantic Coast Line R. Co.*, 345 U.S. 379 (1953), *Construction Laborers v. Curry*, 371 U.S. 542 (1963), and *Richfield Oil Corp. v. State Board*, 329 U.S. 69 (1946), on the Court's jurisdiction where trial courts are bound by statute in defenseless cases; *Lovell v. Griffin*, 303 U.S. 444 (1938), holding that the press includes "humble leaflets and circulars"; *NAACP v. Button*, 371 U.S. 415 (1963), holding that the threat of sanctions are as detrimental as their actual application.

Further Reading:
28 *Ohio St. L. J.* 146 (Winter 1967).

1969   *Clarence Brandenburg v. Ohio*, 395 U.S. 444, 23 L.Ed.2d 430, 89 S.Ct. 1827

Argued: Feb. 27, 1969.

Decided: June 9, 1969.

Summary: A speaker could not be convicted under a statute that permitted punishment for "mere advocacy" of illegal action. To be constitutional a statute can only prohibit advocacy where it "is directed to inciting or producing imminent lawless action and is likely to incite or produce such actions."

Circumstances: Brandenburg, a leader of a Ku Klux Klan (KKK) group, had invited a Cincinnati television reporter and cameraman to a KKK rally at a farm in Hamilton County. Portions of the footage they took with KKK cooperation appeared on the local station and nationwide. Film footage, which became the prosecution's primary evidence, depicted a burning cross, and Brandenburg was identified as speaking of "niggers" and sending "Jews back to Israel." He was convicted under the Ohio Criminal Syndicalism statute for "advocating . . . the duty, necessity, or propriety of crime, sabotage, violence, or unlawful methods of terrorism as a means of accomplishing industrial or political reform." He was fined $1,000 and sentenced to one to ten years in prison. Brandenburg challenged the statute's constitutionality under the First and 14th Amendments. The Ohio intermediate appellate court affirmed without opinion. The state supreme court dismissed his appeal, sua sponte, "for the reason that no substantial constitutional question exists herein." The U.S. Supreme Court reversed.

Opinion: A per curiam decision, expressing the unanimous view of the Court and overruling *Whitney v. California* (1927). The Court said that *Whitney*, which sustained the constitutionality of a similar statute against syndicalism, had been thoroughly discredited by later decisions. The Court did not decide whether Brandenburg's hateful comments were protected speech. It overturned his conviction because the Ohio statute permitted convictions for advocacy, as had the California law, that did not present an imminent danger. The Court said that a statute which fails to distinguish between "mere abstract teaching" of force and violence and "preparing a group for violent action and steeling it to such action" intrudes upon the freedoms guaranteed by the First and 14th Amendments. "It sweeps within its condemnation speech which our Constitution has immunized from governmental control." Separately, Justices Hugo L. Black and William O. Douglas concurred with the judgment, but added that the clear-and-present-danger doctrine, replaced by "imminent danger" in *Brandenburg* and thus not totally ignored, "should have no place in the interpretation of the First Amendment." Douglas insisted that, "apart from rare instances . . . speech is . . . immune from prosecution."

Referenced Cases: *Dennis v. U.S.*, 341 U.S. 494 (1951), discrediting *Whitney v. California*, 272 U.S. 357 (1927), and fashioning the imminent lawless action principle; *Noto v. U.S.*, 367 U.S. 290 (1961), *Herndon v. Lowry*, 301 U.S. 242 (1937), and *Bond v. Floyd*, 385 U.S. 116 (1966), on mere abstract teaching compared to preparing for violent action; *Yates v. U.S.*, 354 U.S. 298 (1957), *De Jonge v. Oregon*, 299 U.S. 353 (1937), *Stromberg v. California*, 283 U.S. 359 (1931), *U.S. v. Robel*, 389 U.S. 258 (1967), *Keyishian v. Board of Regents*, 385 U.S. 589 (1967), *Elfbrandt v. Russell*, 384 U.S. 11 (1966), *Aptheker v. Secretary of State*, 378 U.S. 500 (1964), and *Baggett v. Bullitt*, 377 U.S. 360 (1964), on speech immunized from governmental control; *Schenck v. U.S.*, 249 U.S. 47 (1919), *Frohwerk v. U.S.*, 249 U.S. 204 (1919), *Debs v. U.S.*, 249 U.S. 211 (1919), *Abrams v. U.S.*, 250 U.S. 616 (1919), *Schaefer v. U.S.*, 251 U.S. 466 (1920), *Pierce v. U.S.*, 252 U.S. 239 (1920), and *Gitlow v. New York*, 268 U.S. 652 (1925), on the evolution of the clear-and-present-danger test, as established and interpreted by Justices Oliver Wendell Holmes and Louis D. Brandeis; *Bridges v. California*, 314 U.S. 252 (1941), on tightening and confining the test to a narrow category; *Speiser v. Randall*, 357 U.S. 513 (1958), on brigading speech with action, per Justice Douglas.

Further Reading:

55 *ABA J.* 875 (Sept. 1969).

22 *Stanford L. Rev.* 1163 (June 1970).

1969 *Supreme Ct. Rev.* 41 (1969).

39 *Univ. Cincinnati L. Rev.* 210 (Winter 1970).

72 *West Virginia L. Rev.* 117 (Dec.–Feb. 1969–70).

1974   *The Miami Herald Publishing Co., A Division of Knight Newspapers, Inc. v. Pat L. Tornillo, Jr.,* 418 U.S. 241, 41 L.Ed.2d 730, 94 S.Ct. 2831, 1 Med.L.Rptr. 1898

Argued: April 17, 1974.

Decided: June 25, 1974.

Summary: A state "right to reply" statute ruled in violation of the First Amendment.

Circumstances: A provision of the Florida Election Code, enacted in 1913, provided that where the publisher of a newspaper assails the personal character or official record of any political candidate, the candidate has the right to demand that the paper print, free of charge, any reply the candidate may make to the newspaper's allegations. In the fall of 1972, Tornillo, executive director of a teachers' union in Dade County, was the subject of two editorials critical of his candidacy for the House of Representatives. He demanded the right to reply to the attacks in the *Miami Herald*, which refused his request. Tornillo sought declaratory and injunctive relief and monetary damages in the Circuit Court, Dade County. The court held the statute unconstitutional, saying that the statute was subject to the infirmity of vagueness. The court complained that no editor could know in advance exactly what words would offend the statute or the scope of the reply required. The state supreme court, in a 6-to-1 per curiam ruling, reversed the lower court and upheld the constitutionality of the statute, emphasizing that there was a crucial difference between such legislation and direct restraints on content. The *Herald* appealed to the U.S. Supreme Court, which reversed Florida's top court and declared the state law unconstitutional.

Opinion: Chief Justice Warren E. Burger wrote the unanimous opinion. William J. Brennan, Jr., joined by William H. Rehnquist, concurred separately. Byron R. White, while concurring, wrote separately that he feared the people would be at the complete mercy of the press. Burger did not challenge the observation that the size and monopolistic aspects of the media may limit debate on public issues because the "marketplace of ideas" was controlled by a few owners. Though recognizing the validity of the arguments for access and the concerns over the power of the press, Burger said that a government-enforced right of reply for the print media violated the Constitution. After reviewing relevant prior cases, the chief justice said that, beginning with *Associated Press v. U.S.* (1945), compulsion exerted by government on a newspaper to print that which "reason tells them should not be published" is unconstitutional. "A responsible press is an undoubtedly desirable goal, but press responsibility is not mandated by the Constitution and like many other virtues it cannot be legislated." He said the Florida statute failed to clear the barriers of the First Amendment because of its intrusion into the function of editors. "A newspaper is more than a passive receptacle or conduit for news, comment, and advertising. The choice of material to go into a newspaper, and the decisions made as to limitations on the size and content of the paper, and treatment of public issues and public officials—whether fair or unfair—constitute the exercise of editorial control and judgment." Burger said that the Florida statute was an unconstitutional government restraint on publishing in the same way as a law forbidding publication. Editors, confronted with a reply requirement, "might well conclude that the safe course is to avoid controversy," thereby blunting or reducing political and electoral coverage in Florida.

Justice Brennan, joined by Rehnquist, added that the decision addressed only right of reply statutes, not the constitutionality of retraction laws in defamation action. Justice White, in concurring, warned that the decision, taken with *Gertz v. Welch*

(1974), announced the same day, may leave the people at the complete mercy of the press, "at least in this stage of our history when the press, as the majority in this case so well documents, is steadily becoming more powerful and much less likely to be deterred by threats of libel suits."

Referenced Cases: *North Dakota State Pharmacy Bd. v. Snyder's Stores*, 414 U.S. 156 (1973), enunciating the principles of final judgment; *Associated Press v. U.S.*, 326 U.S. 1 (1945), on freedom from governmental interference; *New York Times Co. v. Sullivan*, 376 U.S. 254 (1964), on the principle that debate on public issues should be uninhibited, robust, and wide-open; *Rosenbloom v. Metromedia Inc.*, 403 U.S. 29 (1971), on experimenting with right-to-access regulation; *Branzburg v. Hayes*, 408 U.S. 665 (1972), emphasizing no restriction on what the press may publish; *Columbia Broadcasting System Inc. v. Democratic National Committee*, 412 U.S. 94 (1973), on adversity to any attempt to extend a right of access to newspapers; *Pittsburgh Press Co. v. Human Relations Comm'n*, 413 U.S. 376 (1973), on limiting discriminatory advertising but endorsing unlimited editorial judgment; *Grosjean v. American Press Co.*, 297 U.S. 233 (1936), regarding constitutional limitations on governmental powers; *Mills v. Alabama*, 384 U.S. 214 (1966), on protecting press discussion of governmental affairs; *New York Times Co. v. U.S.*, 403 U.S. 713 (1971), on governmental tampering in advance of publication; *Rosenblatt v. Baer*, 383 U.S. 75 (1966), on preventing and redressing attacks on reputation; *Gertz v. Robert Welch Inc.*, 418 U.S. 323 (1974), on increasing the plaintiff's burden of proving liability and damages.

Further Reading:

60 *ABA J.* 1115 (Sept. 1974).
5 *Cumberland-Samford L. Rev.* 535 (Winter 1975).
24 *Emory L. J.* 217 (Winter 1975).
43 *Fordham L. Rev.* 223 (Nov. 1974).
88 *Harvard L. Rev.* 174 (Nov. 1974).
23 *Kansas L. Rev.* 300 (Winter 1975).
20 *NY L. Forum* 645 (Winter 1975).
35 *Ohio St. L. J.* 954 (1974).
28 *Southwestern L. J.* 1038 (Winter 1974).
28 *Stanford L. Rev.* 563 (Feb. 1976).
29 *Univ. Miami L. Rev.* 477 (Spring 1975).

1980   *Frank W. Snepp, III v. U.S. and U.S. v. Frank W. Snepp, 444 U.S. 507, 62 L.Ed.2d 704, 100 S.Ct. 763*

Decided: Feb. 19, 1980.

Summary: Restricted the speech of a government employee, an ex-Central Intelligence Agency (CIA) agent; publication of his book on Vietnam held in violation of prepublication employment agreement.

Circumstances: Snepp, a former CIA intelligence officer in Vietnam, published a book critical of the American evacuation of that country. It was published without Snepp first submitting it to the agency for prepublication review, a condition of his employment with the CIA in 1968. The District Court for the Eastern District of Virginia found that Snepp had "willfully, deliberately and surreptitiously breached his position of trust with the CIA and the secrecy agreement." Also finding that the book caused "irreparable harm and loss" to the United States, the court enjoined future breaches of Snepp's agreement and imposed the constructive trust on his royalties. The Court of Appeals for the Fourth Circuit agreed that Snepp had breached a valid contract, but ruled that the record did not support imposition of the trust. The court perceived that Snepp had a First Amendment right to publish unclassified information, which the government agreed had not been divulged. The Supreme Court reversed that part of the ruling and remanded to the court of appeals for reinstatement of the district court's judgment.

Opinion: A per curiam decision, expressing the view of Chief Justice Warren E. Burger and Justices Potter Stewart, Byron R. White, Harry A. Blackmun, Lewis F. Powell, Jr., and William H. Rehnquist. Dissenting were William J. Brennan, Jr., Thurgood Marshall, and John Paul Stevens. The Court held that the agent, who had entered a trust relationship when he signed the government employment contract, had breached his fiduciary obligation by publishing a book without submitting the manuscript to the CIA for review. Agency employees are required to sign a trust agreement that subjects them to lifetime censorship. The

Court said it made no difference whether the book actually contained classified information. The Court went on to say that the appropriate remedy was the imposition of a "constructive trust" on all earnings from the book, which revert to the government. The trust remedy, which "simply requires him to disgorge the benefits of his faithlessness," the Court said, is tailored to deter "those who would place sensitive information at risk." Even the former agent's publication of unclassified material relating to intelligence activities might be detrimental to national interests, the justices reasoned. Such publication might inadvertently reveal classified information and perhaps scare off sources fearful that the CIA was not able to guarantee confidentiality. In a footnote, the Court suggested that the CIA's censorship powers did not depend exclusively on the prepublication agreement. Even in the absence of an agreement, "the CIA could have acted to protect substantial government interests by imposing reasonable restrictions on employee activities that in other contexts might be protected by the First Amendment."

In dissent, Justice Stevens, joined by Brennan and Marshall, argued that the constructive trust was not authorized, noting that the book contained no classified, nonpublic material. "Like an ordinary employer, the CIA has a vital interest in protecting certain types of information; at the same time, the CIA employee has countervailing interest in preserving a wide range of work opportunities (including work as an author) and in protecting his First Amendment rights. The public interest lies in a proper accommodation that will preserve the intelligence mission of the Agency while not abridging the free flow of unclassified information." Stevens accused the Court of having fashioned a new remedy "to enforce a species of prior restraint on a citizen's right to criticize the government." In a strongly worded footnote, Stevens said that the mere fact that the CIA has the authority to review the text of a critical book in search of classified information before it is published "is bound to have an inhibiting effect on the author's writing." He said, moreover, that the right to delay publication until after the review is itself a form of prior restraint that would not be tolerated in other contexts.

Referenced Cases: None in the text of the opinion. Mentioned in footnotes: *CSC v. Letter Carriers*, 413 U.S. 548 (1973), *Buckley v. Valco*, 424 U.S. 1 (1976), *Greer v. Spock*, 424 U.S.

828 (1976), and *Cole v. Richardson*, 405 U.S. 676 (1972), on government interest in secrecy of information and appearance of confidentiality; *New York Times Co. v. U.S.*, 403 U.S. 713 (1971), and *Nebraska Press Asso. v. Stuart*, 427 U.S. 539 (1976), on prior restraint in other contexts.

Further Reading:
30 *Cleveland State L. Rev.* 247 (1981).
81 *Columbia L. Rev.* 662 (April 1981).
59 *No. Carolina L. Rev.* 417 (Jan. 1981).
21 *Santa Clara L. Rev.* 697 (Summer 1981).
49 *Univ. Cincinnati L. Rev.* 690 (1980).
130 *Univ. Pa. L. Rev.* 775 (April 1982).

Selected Bibliography

Abrams, Floyd, "The Press *Is* Different: Reflections on Justice Stewart and the Autonomous Press," 7 *Hofstra L. Rev.* 563 (1979).

Anderson, Alex J., "The Formative Period of First Amendment Theory, 1870–1915," 24 *American J. Legal History* 56 (1981).

Anderson, David A., "The Origins of the Press Clause," 30 *UCLA L. Rev.* 456 (1983).

"Barometer of Freedom of the Press: The Opinions of Mr. Justice White," 8 *Pepperdine L. Rev.* 157 (Dec. 1980).

BeVier, Lillian R., "An Informed Public, An Informing Press: The Search for a Constitutional Principle," 68 *California L. Rev.* 482 (May 1980).

Blanchard, Margaret A., "Institutional Press and Its First Amendment Privileges," 1978 *Supreme Ct. Rev.* 521 (1978).

Blasi, Vincent, "The Checking Value in First Amendment Theory," 1977 *American Bar Found. Res. J.* 521 (1977).

———. "The Pathological Perspective and the First Amendment," 85 *Columbia L. Rev.* 449 (1985).

Bogen, R. H., "Balancing Freedom of Speech," 38 *Maryland L. Rev.* 387 (1979).

Bork, R. H., "Neutral Principles and Some First Amendment Problems," 47 *Indiana L. J.* 1 (Fall 1971).

Brennan, William J., Jr., "Supreme Court and the Meiklejohn Interpretation of the First Amendment," 79 *Harvard L. Rev.* 1 (1965).

Cahn, Edmond, "The Firstness of the First Amendment," 65 *Yale L. J.* 464 (1956).

Carroll, Thomas F., "Freedom of Speech and of the Press in the Federalist Period: The Sedition Act," 18 *Michigan L. Rev.* 615 (1920).

Chafee, Zechariah, Jr., "Do Judges Make or Discover Law?" 91 *Proceedings of American Philosophical Soc.* 420 (1947).

Dale, Francis L., and Mitchell W. Dale, "Full Court Press: The Imperial Judiciary vs. the Paranoid Press," 7 *Pepperdine L. Rev.* 241 (Winter 1980).

Douglas, William O., "Press and First Amendment Rights," 7 *Idaho L. Rev.* 1 (Spring 1970).

Emerson, Thomas I., "First Amendment Doctrine and the Burger Court," 68 *California L. Rev.* 422 (1980).

Farber, D. A., and P. P. Frickey, "Practical Reason and the First Amendment," 34 *UCLA L. Rev.* 1615 (June/Aug. 1987).

Ferguson, A. F., "First Amendment Freedoms: Cornerstone of a Free Society," 30 *Maryland Bar J.* 2 (Oct. 1987).

"First Amendment Rights to Free Speech and a Free Press: Change and Continuity—A Symposium," 12 *Akron L. Rev.* 229 (Fall 1978).

Frankfurter, Felix, "Some Observations on the Nature of the Judicial Process of Supreme Court Litigation," 98 *Proc. American Philosophical Society* 233 (1954).

Gillmor, Donald M., "The Fragile First," 8 *Hamline L. Rev.* 277 (1985).

Gottlieb, Stephen E., "The Speech Clause and the Limits of Neutrality," 51 *Albany L. Rev.* 19 (Fall 1986).

Gunther, Gerald, "Learned Hand and the Origins of Modern First Amendment Doctrine: Some Fragments of History," 27 *Stanford L. Rev.* 752 (1975).

Hale, F. Dennis, "A Comparison Coverage of Speech and Press Verdicts of Supreme Court," 56 *Journalism Quarterly* 43 (Spring 1979).

Heck, Edward V., "Justice Brennan and Freedom of Expression Doctrine in the Burger Court," 24 *San Diego L. Rev.* 1153 (Sept.–Oct. 1987).

Hunter, Howard Owen, "Problems in Search of Principles: The First Amendment in the Supreme Court, 1791–1930," 35 *Emory L. J.* 59 (1986).

Kalven, Harry Jr., "Broadcasting, Public Policy, and the First Amendment," 10 *J. Law and Economics* 15 (Oct. 1967).

Kurland, Philip B., "The Original Understanding of the Freedom of the Press Provision of the First Amendment," 55 *Mississippi L. J.* 225 (June 1985).

Levy, Leonard, "On the Origins of the Free Press Clause," 32 *UCLA L. Rev.* 177 (1984).

Lewis, Anthony, "A Preferred Position for Journalism?" 7 *Hofstra L. Rev.* 595 (1979).

Lively, Donald E., "The Sometimes Relevant First Amendment," 60 *Temple L. Q.* 881 (Winter 1987).

MacKenzie, John P., "Warren Court and the Press," 67 *Michigan L. Rev.* 303 (Dec. 1968).

Meiklejohn, Alexander, "The First Amendment Is an Absolute," 1961 *Supreme Ct. Rev.* 257 (1961).

Monaghan, Henry P., "First Amendment 'Due Process,'" 83 *Harvard L. Rev.* 518 (Jan. 1970).

Nelson, Harold L., "Seditious Libel in Colonial America," 3 *American J. Legal History* 160 (1959).

Nimmer, M. B., "Does Copyright Abridge the First Amendment Guarantees of Free Speech and Press," 17 *UCLA L. Rev.* 1180 (June 1970).

Pember, Don R., "The Pentagon Papers Decision: More Questions Than Answers," 48 *Journalism Quarterly* 403 (1971).

Perry, Michael J., "Freedom of Expression: An Essay on Theory and Doctrine," 78 *Northwestern Univ. L. Rev.* 1137 (1983).

Pound, Roscoe, "The Scope and Purpose of Sociological Jurisprudence," 24 *Harvard L. Rev.* 591 (1911) and 25 *Harvard L. Rev.* 140 (1912).

Rabban, David M., "The First Amendment in Its Forgotten Years," 90 *Yale L. J.* 514 (1981).

Ragan, Fred D., "Justice Oliver Wendell Holmes, Jr., Zechariah Chafee, Jr., and the Clear and Present Danger Test for Free Speech: The First Year, 1919," 53 *J. American History* 24 (1971).

"Reconciling Red Lion and Tornillo: A Consistent Theory of Media Regulation," 28 *Stanford L. Rev.* 563 (1976).

Richards, B. A., "Historical Rationale of the Speech-and-Press Clause of the First Amendment," 21 *Univ. Florida L. Rev.* 203 (Fall 1968).

Richards, David A. J., "A Theory of Free Speech," 34 *UCLA L. Rev.* 1837 (June/Aug. 1987).

Richardson, Elliot L., "Freedom of Expression and the Function of the Courts," 65 *Harvard L. Rev.* 1 (Nov. 1951).

Sowle, Kathryn, "Defamation and the First Amendment: The Case for a Constitutional Privilege of Fair Report," 54 *NYU L. Rev.* 469 (June 1979).

Strong, F. R., "Fifty Years of 'Clear and Present Danger': From Schenck to Brandenburg—and Beyond," 1969 *Supreme Ct. Rev.* 41 (1969).

"Symposium on Press Clause," 7 *Hofstra L. Rev.* 3 (Spring 1979).

Tinder, Glenn, "Freedom of Expression, the Strange Imperative," 69 *Yale Review* 161 (Winter 1980).

Van Alstyne, William W., "Hazards to the Press of Claiming a 'Preferred Position,'" 28 *Hastings L. J.* 761 (Jan. 1977).

Yudof, Mark G., "When Governments Speak: Toward a Theory of Government Expression and the First Amendment," 57 *Texas L. Rev.* 863 (Aug. 1979).

Zacharias, Fred C., "Flowcharting the First Amendment," 72 *Cornell L. Rev.* 936 (July 1987).

Libel

1952   *Joseph Beauharnais v. Illinois*, **343 U.S. 250, 96 L.Ed. 919, 72 S.Ct. 725**

Argued: Nov. 28, 1951.

Decided: April 28, 1952.

Summary: Held that libelous utterances are not "within the area of constitutionally protected speech" and are outside the clear-and-present-danger test. A state criminal libel statute held not violative of the First and 14th Amendments.

Circumstances: Beauharnais was convicted for distributing anti-Negro leaflets on the streets of Chicago in violation of a 1917 Illinois statute that makes it a crime to exhibit in a public place any publication "which . . . portrays depravity, criminality, unchastity, or lack of virtue of a class of citizens, of any race, color, creed or religion which . . . exposes the citizens of any race, color, creed or religion to contempt, derision, or obloquy or which is productive of breach of the peace or riots." The defendant was fined $200, the maximum penalty under the law, for distributing handbills containing a petition to the mayor and aldermen of Chicago "to halt the further encroachment, harassment and invasion of white people, their property, neighborhoods and persons, by the Negro." Beauharnais's language throughout was especially strong at a time when officials had a difficult time keeping the peace. The trial judge instructed the jury to find the defendant guilty if they believed he had distributed the handbills. *Beauharnais* was the first conviction under a group libel statute to be upheld by an appellate court. The Supreme Court affirmed.

Opinion: Justice Felix Frankfurter wrote the 5-to-4 opinion, joined by Chief Justice Fred M. Vinson and Justices Harold H.

Burton, Tom C. Clark, and Sherman Minton. Dissenting were Hugo L. Black, Stanley F. Reed, William O. Douglas, and Robert H. Jackson. Frankfurter said that no constitutional problem was raised by limiting certain "narrowly limited" classes of speech, including the obscene, the lewd, and the libelous. He said that such utterances were not an essential part of any exposition of ideas. The justice noted that if a state may punish a libelous utterance directed at an individual, "we cannot deny to a State power to punish the same utterance directed at a defined group."

Justice Black, joined by Douglas, criticized the majority for the "expansive scope" it had accorded libel, making it punishable "to give publicity to any picture, play, drama, or any printed matter which a judge may find unduly offensive to any race, color, creed or religion." Black said that the same kind of state law that made Beauharnais a criminal for advocating segregation may send people to jail for promoting equality and integration. Justice Reed, with Douglas, turned his view on the vagueness of the words under question, noting that such words possess neither general nor special meanings "well enough known to apprise those within their reach as to limitations on speech." Justice Douglas, in a separate dissent, wrote that the "peril of speech" must be clear and present to override the "plain command of the First Amendment." He accorded speech a "preferred position" as contrasted to some other civil rights. To rule otherwise is to warn every minority that when the Constitution guarantees free speech it does not mean what it says. Justice Jackson, in a separate dissent, cited the 14th Amendment's safeguard of liberty for the accused, which he believed had not been applied by the Illinois courts. Regarding the majority's finding of group libel, Jackson opined: "No group interest in any particular prosecution should forget that the shoe may be on the other foot in some prosecution tomorrow."

Referenced Cases: *Nash v. United States*, 229 U.S. 373 (1913), *Cox v. New Hampshire*, 312 U.S. 569 (1941), and *Chaplinsky v. New Hampshire*, 315 U.S. 568 (1942), regarding the "animating context of well-defined usage" of language; *Cantwell v. Connecticut*, 310 U.S. 296 (1940), regarding the communication of information or opinion safeguarded by the Constitution, also incitable acts deemed punishable by states; *American Foundries v. Tri-City Council*, 257 U.S. 184 (1921), on group rights; *Bridges v. California*, 314 U.S. 252 (1941), regarding the 14th Amendment's impact on the First Amendment and on the states; *Rochin v. California*, 342 U.S. 165 (1952), on the Court's notions of "canons of decency"; *American Communications Assn. v. Douds*, 339 U.S. 382 (1950), *Herndon v. Lowry*, 301 U.S. 242 (1937), *Winters v. New York*, 333 U.S. 507 (1948), regarding the abridgment of speech that becomes an incitement to crime; *Schenck v. U.S.*, 249 U.S. 47 (1919), *Abrams v. U.S.*, 250 U.S. 616 (1919), *Schaefer v. U.S.*, 251 U.S. 466 (1920), formulating the clear-and-present-danger test as a "rule of reason"; *Gitlow v. New York*, 268 U.S. 652 (1925), *Palko v. Connecticut*, 302 U.S. 319 (1937), and *Near v. Minnesota*, 283 U.S. 697 (1931), regarding the relationship between "freedom" in the First Amendment and "liberty" in the 14th Amendment.

Further Reading:

38 *ABA J.* 762 (Sept. 1952).
5 *Alabama L. Rev.* 125 (Fall 1952).
19 *Brooklyn L. Rev.* 120 (Dec. 1952).
41 *California L. Rev.* 290 (Summer 1953).
38 *Cornell L. Q.* 240 (Winter 1953).
2 *DePaul L. Rev.* 93 (Autumn–Winter 1952).
15 *Georgia Bar J.* 366 (Feb. 1953).
66 *Harvard L. Rev.* 96, 112 (Nov. 1952).
41 *Kentucky L. J.* 436 (May 1953).
27 *St. John's L. Rev.* 135 (Dec. 1952).
31 *Texas L. Rev.* 330 (Feb. 1953).
1952 *Univ. Illinois L. Forum* 433 (Fall 1952).
101 *Univ. Pa. L. Rev.* 870 (April 1953).
14 *Univ. Pittsburgh L. Rev.* 118 (Fall 1952).
6 *Vanderbilt L. Rev.* 393 (Feb. 1953).

1964   *New York Times Co. v. L. B. Sullivan, and Ralph D. Abernathy et al. v. L. B. Sullivan,* **376 U.S. 254, 11 L.Ed.2d 686, 84 S.Ct. 710, 95 A.L.R.2d 1412, 1 Med.L. Rptr. 1527**

Argued: Jan. 6, 1964.

Decided: March 9, 1964.

Summary: Misstatements of fact about public officials constitutionally protected unless the false material is published with "actual malice"—with knowledge of its falsity or with reckless disregard of whether it was true or false. For the first time the Court determined the extent to which the Constitution limits state power in libel damages in action brought by public officials against critics of official conduct.

Circumstances: Sullivan, an elected city commissioner in Montgomery, Alabama, brought a libel action against the newspaper for its publication of a paid advertisement that appeared over the names of several individuals, four of whom Sullivan also sued in a separate action: *Ralph D. Abernathy et al. v. L. B. Sullivan*, argued and decided with *Times v. Sullivan*. As Montgomery commissioner of public affairs, Sullivan's duties included supervision of the police department. His name, as such, was not mentioned in the advertisement, which included statements, some of which were false, about police action directed allegedly against black students protesting segregation and against a leader of the civil rights movement. Sullivan said the statements referred to him because he was head of the police department. After being instructed by the trial judge that the statements were "libelous per se" (injury implied without proof of actual damages) and that malice was presumed regarding compensatory damages, the jury awarded Sullivan $500,000 in damages against all defendants. The Alabama Supreme Court affirmed the verdict. The Alabama high court rejected the defendants' constitutional objections on the ground that the First Amendment does not protect libelous publications. The U.S. Supreme Court reversed.

Opinion: Justice William J. Brennan, Jr. wrote for six members in the unanimous decision. They were Chief Justice Earl Warren and Justices Tom C. Clark, John M. Harlan, Potter Stewart, and Byron R. White. Hugo L. Black, joined by William O. Douglas, and Arthur Goldberg, also joined by Douglas, wrote separate concurring opinions. Brennan said the Court considered the case against the background of a "profound national commitment to the principle that debate on public issues should be uninhibited, robust, and wide-open, and that it may well include vehement, caustic, and sometimes unpleasantly sharp attacks on government and public officials." The Court held that the rule of law applied by the state courts was constitutionally deficient for failure to provide the safeguards for freedom of speech and press that are required by the constitution in libel action brought by a public official against critics of his official conduct—in particular, to provide a qualification for honest misstatements of fact defeasible only upon a showing of actual malice. Regarding the "commercial speech" aspect, Brennan noted that the publication was not a commercial advertisement in the sense that the Court had previously used that term in not granting constitutional privilege. "It communicated information, expressed opinion, recited grievances, protested claimed abuses, and sought financial support on behalf of a movement whose existence and objectives are matters of the highest public interest and concern."

Justices Black, Douglas, and Goldberg expressed the view that the Constitution's free speech and press guarantees afforded the defendants an absolute, unconditional privilege to publish their criticism of official conduct. "An unconditional right to say what one pleases about public affairs is what I consider to be the minimum guarantee of the First Amendment," said Black. Goldberg added that the First and 14th Amendments afforded an unconditional privilege to criticize official conduct "despite the harm which may flow from excesses and abuses." However, purely private defamation directed against the private conduct of a public official or private citizen may not realize the same protection because it has little to do with the political ends of a self-governing society, Goldberg said. All nine members agreed that damages should not have been awarded and that the news media needed greater protection against libel suits brought by public officials. Black, Douglas, and Goldberg argued that Brennan's opinion for the Court did not go far enough in insulating the press from the dangers of libel.

Referenced Cases: *Valentine v. Chrestensen*, 316 U.S. 52 (1942), *NAACP v. Button*, 371 U.S. 415 (1963), *Bantam Books v. Sullivan*, 372 U.S. 58 (1963), *Smith v. California*, 361 U.S. 147 (1959), *Lovell v. Griffin*, 303 U.S. 444 (1938), and *Associated Press v. U.S.*, 326 U.S. 1 (1945), regarding commercial speech and freedom of speech for those who do not have access to publishing facilities; *Pennekamp v. Florida*, 328 U.S. 331 (1946), and *Beauharnais v. Illinois*, 343 U.S. 250 (1952), regarding sanctions on expression critical of the official conduct of public officials; *Roth v. U.S.*, 354 U.S. 476 (1957), *Stromberg v. California*, 283 U.S. 359 (1931), *Bridges v. California*, 314 U.S. 252 (1941), *Whitney v. California*, 274 U.S. 357 (1927), *Terminiello v. Chicago*, 337 U.S. 1 (1949), and *DeJonge v. Oregon*, 299 U.S. 353 (1937), regarding the general proposition that freedom of expression on public questions is secured by the First Amendment; *Speiser v. Randall*, 357 U.S. 513 (1958), and *Cantwell v. Connecticut*, 310 U.S. 296 (1940), regarding truth as a defense, especially the burden of proof on the speaker; *Gitlow v. New York*, 268 U.S. 652 (1925), *Schneider v. State*, 308 U.S. 147 (1939), and *Edwards v. South Carolina*, 372 U.S. 229 (1963), regarding the 14th Amendment and the application to the states of First Amendment restrictions; *Barr v. Matteo*, 360 U.S. 564 (1959), regarding the privileged utterances of public officials.

Further Reading:

30 *Albany L. Rev.* 316 (June 1966).
14 *American Univ. L. Rev.* 71 (Dec. 1964).
44 *Boston Univ. L. Rev.* 563 (Fall 1964).
31 *Brooklyn L. Rev.* 191 (Dec. 1964).
83 *Columbia L. Rev.* 603 (1983).
52 *Cornell L. Q.* 419 (Winter 1967).
18 *Cumberland L. Rev.* 111 (87/88).
14 *DePaul L. Rev.* 181 (Autumn–Winter 1964).
15 *DePaul L. Rev.* 376 (Spring–Summer 1966).
78 *Harvard L. Rev.* 201 (Nov. 1964).
4 *Houston L. Rev.* 528 (Winter 1966).
50 *Iowa L. Rev.* 170 (Fall 1964).
48 *Marquette L. Rev.* 128 (Summer 1964).
30 *Missouri L. Rev.* 467 (Summer 1965).
26 *Montana L. Rev.* 110 (Fall 1964).
43 *No. Carolina L. Rev.* 315 (Feb. 1965).
10 *NY L. Forum* 249 (June–July 1964).
6 *Rutgers Camden L. J.* 471 (1975).
38 *So. Calif. L. Rev.* 349 (Spring 1965).
16 *Syracuse L. Rev.* 132 (Fall 1964).
31 *Tenn. L. Rev.* 504 (Summer 1964).
42 *Texas L. Rev.* 1080 (Oct. 1964).
14 *UCLA L. Rev.* 631 (Jan. 1967).
113 *Univ. Pa. L. Rev.* 284 (Dec. 1964).

114 *Univ. Pa. L. Rev.* 241 (Dec. 1965).
25 *Univ. Pittsburgh L. Rev.* 752 (June 1964).
18 *Vanderbilt L. Rev.* 1429 (June 1965).
51 *Virginia L. Rev.* 106 (Jan. 1965).
15 *Western Reserve L. Rev.* 803 (Sept. 1964).
7 *William & Mary L. Rev.* 215 (May 1966).

1964   *Jim Garrison v. Louisiana*, **379 U.S. 64, 13 L.Ed.2d 125, 85 S.Ct. 209, 1 Med.L.Rptr. 1548**

Reargued: Oct. 19, 1964.

Decided: Nov. 23, 1964.

Summary: Within nine months of its *New York Times Co. v. Sullivan* ruling, the Court held that the *Times* rule of "actual malice" for public officials applies not only to civil libel actions but "also limits state power to impose criminal sanctions for criticism of the official conduct of public officials." Two elements were added to "reckless disregard" in the Court's definition of "actual malice": "serious doubts" about the truth of the publication and "a high degree of awareness of probable falsity."

Circumstances: During a dispute with eight judges of the criminal district court of Orleans Parish, Louisiana, District Attorney Garrison, already known for his outspokenness, held a press conference and attributed a large backlog of pending cases to the "inefficiency, laziness, and excessive vacations" of the judges. He also accused them of hampering his enforcement of vice laws by refusing to authorize money for criminal investigations. Garrison was tried without a jury before a judge from another parish and convicted of criminal libel as defined in the state statute. The Supreme Court of Louisiana affirmed. The U.S. Supreme Court reversed.

Opinion: Justice William J. Brennan, Jr., in expressing the views of six members of the Court, said that not only did the *Times* rule limit state power in civil defamation action brought by a public official, but it also limits state power in criminal libel proceedings. "Only those false statements made with the high degree of awareness of their probable falsity demanded by *New York Times* may be the subject of either civil or criminal sanctions." The Court reversed the trial court's conviction of Garrison, who had been accused under Louisiana's criminal defamation statute permitting punishment of truthful criticism of public officials if made with actual malice, and punishment of false statements made with ill will. The justices who joined Brennan were Tom C. Clark, John M. Harlan, Potter Stewart, Byron R. White, and Chief Justice Earl Warren. Justice Hugo L. Black, joined by William O. Douglas, concurred, saying "that under our Constitution there is absolutely no place in this country for the old, discredited English Star Chamber law of seditious criminal libel." Douglas, joined by Black, added in a separate opinion that the constitutional guarantee of free speech prohibits prosecution for seditious libel even for a knowingly false statement or one made with reckless disregard of the truth. Justice Arthur J. Goldberg, in a separate addendum, wrote that libel on the official conduct of government officials, as well as libel on government, "has no place in our Constitution."

Referenced Cases: *New York Times Co. v. Sullivan*, 376 U.S. 254 (1964), on constitutional limits on civil "public official" libel and the "actual malice" standard; *Chaplinsky v. New Hampshire*, 315 U.S. 568 (1942), and *Beauharnais v. Illinois*, 343 U.S. 250 (1952), regarding narrowly drawn statutes designed to protect breach of peace; *Barr v. Matteo*, 360 U.S. 564 (1959), and *Howard v. Lyons*, 360 U.S. 593 (1959), on defamatory publication within the scope of official duty; *Roth v. U.S.*, 354 U.S. 476 (1957), on freedom of speech when "brigaded with illegal action."

Further Reading:
51 *ABA J.* 269 (March 1965).
14 *American Univ. L. Rev.* 220 (June 1965).
79 *Harvard L. Rev.* 157 (Nov. 1965).
19 *Southwestern L. J.* 399 (June 1965).
16 *Syracuse L. Rev.* 879 (1965).
39 *Tulane L. Rev.* 355 (Feb. 1965).
19 *Vanderbilt L. Rev.* 1429 (June 1965).
40 *Washington L. Rev.* 898 (Oct. 1965).

1966   *Alfred D. Rosenblatt v. Frank P. Baer,*
           383 U.S. 75, 15 L.Ed.2d 597, 86 S.Ct. 669,
           1 Med.L.Rptr. 1558

Argued: Oct. 20, 1965.

Decided: Feb. 21, 1966.

Summary: "Public official," as identified in *New York Times v. Sullivan* (1964), held to include government employees who have substantial responsibility for the conduct of government business. The Court questioned the validity of group libel under *Beauharnais v. Illinois* (1952) and supported the public's right to know of suspected mismanagement of public funds.

Circumstances: Baer, the former supervisor of a county recreation area, brought suit in a New Hampshire state court against an unpaid local newspaper columnist, who alleged "mismanagement and speculation" by the management of a ski resort after Baer's discharge as supervisor. Rosenblatt's column made no specific reference to Baer, but it stated that the recreation area was "doing literally hundreds of per cent BETTER than last year" and added: "What happened to all the money last year? and every other year?" The jury's award of damages was affirmed by the New Hampshire Supreme Court, which noted that recovery was not barred by *Times v. Sullivan,* decided after the trial. On certiorari, the U.S. Supreme Court reversed and remanded to the New Hampshire Supreme Court.

Opinion: Justice William J. Brennan, Jr., wrote for five members, including Chief Justice Earl Warren and Justices Tom C. Clark, Potter Stewart, and Byron R. White. William O. Douglas, Stewart, Hugo L. Black, and John M. Harlan also wrote separately. Abe Fortas dissented. Brennan said, "It is clear that the 'public official' designation applies at the very least to those among the hierarchy of government employees who have or appear to the public to have substantial responsibility for or control over the conduct of governmental affairs." Further, he said the trial court was in error in instructing the jury that "an imputation of impropriety or a crime to one or some of a small group that casts suspicion on all is actionable." Justice Douglas, separately, suggested that the constitutional question should be based on whether a public *issue*, not a public official, is involved. Justice Stewart, separately, noted that the *New York Times* rule requiring a showing of "actual malice" for defamed public officials "should not be applied except where a State's law of defamation has been unconstitutionally converted into a law of seditious libel." Justice Black, joined by Douglas, concurred in the reversal but dissented in the remand, believing that the libel judgment was constitutionally forbidden. "The only sure way to protect speech and press against these threats (i.e., press-destroying judgments) is to recognize that libel laws are abridgments of speech and press and therefore are barred in both federal and state courts by the First and Fourteenth Amendments." Justice Harlan, concurring in part and dissenting in part, questioned the Court's application of its own "impersonal" libel principle. *Times v. Sullivan* should have been read by the trial court as permitting "conventional tort law," which permits recovery when the group is small enough to include the plaintiff, he said. Justice Fortas dissented on the ground that the writ of certiorari was improvidently granted because the trial had occurred before *Times v. Sullivan.*

Referenced Cases: *New York Times Co. v. Sullivan,* 376 U.S. 254 (1964), establishing the "actual malice" standard; *Garrison v. Louisiana,* 379 U.S. 64 (1964), regarding "public official" status; *Pennekamp v. Florida,* 328 U.S. 331 (1946), discussing the problem of the variation among states of free expression; *Thornhill v. Alabama,* 310 U.S. 88 (1940), on the historical development of freedom of discussion; *Stromberg v. California,* 283 U.S. 359 (1931), when the Court "squarely held" that the First Amendment was applicable to the states by reason of the 14th Amendment; *Jackson v. Denno,* 378 U.S. 368 (1964), on the jury, not the judge, determining fact in libel cases.

Further Reading:
52 *ABA J.* 375 (April 1966).
34 *Fordham L. Rev.* 761 (May 1966).
80 *Harvard L. Rev.* 124 (Nov. 1966).
17 *Mercer L. Rev.* 476 (Summer 1966).
39 *Temple L. Q.* 510 (Summer 1966).
42 *Washington L. Rev.* 654 (1967).
7 *William & Mary L. Rev.* 215 (1966).

1967 *Curtis Publishing Co. v. Wallace Butts* and *Associated Press v. Edwin A. Walker,* 388 U.S. 130, 18 L.Ed.2d 1094, 87 S.Ct. 1975, 1 Med.L.Rptr. 1568

Argued: Feb. 23, 1967.

Decided: June 12, 1967.

Summary: Extended application of *New York Times* rule of "actual malice" to "public figures"—persons who thrust themselves "into the 'vortex' of an important public controversy."

Circumstances: Wally Butts, athletic director at the University of Georgia at the time of the alleged libel, sued the *Saturday Evening Post* (owned by Curtis) in the District Court for Northern Georgia for an article of March 23, 1963, charging him with having "fixed" the 1962 football game between Georgia and the University of Alabama. The article was based on information supplied by an Atlanta insurance salesman, George Burnett, who said he overheard a phone conversation between Butts and Paul Bryant, the Alabama coach. Evidence at trial cast serious doubt on the adequacy of the investigation conducted by the magazine. The jury awarded Butts $60,000 in general damages and $3 million in punitive damages. The judge reduced the total to $460,000. Curtis appealed to the Court of Appeals for the Fifth Circuit, which affirmed the judgment by a two-to-one vote, and the U.S. Supreme Court upheld the award. Bryant also filed suit against Curtis and, following the Butts decision, received an out-of-court settlement reportedly totaling $300,000.

Edwin Walker, a retired army general of "some political prominence," sued the Associated Press for libel on the basis of inaccuracies in an AP story filed on Walker's participation against the enrollment of James Meredith, a black, at the University of Mississippi. The AP dispatch reported that Walker, who in private life had actively opposed federal intervention in school desegregation, had taken command of a violent crowd and led a charge against federal marshalls seeking to effectuate a court decree integrating the university. Walker filed suit in the state courts in Texas, his home state, seeking a total of $2 million in compensatory and punitive damages. The jury awarded $500,000 compensatory damages and $300,000 punitive damages, but the judge, finding no evidence of malice, struck the punitive damages. The Texas Court of Civil Appeals affirmed the award and the judge's decision, and the state supreme court denied a writ of error.

In the plurality opinion of the U.S. Supreme Court, Justice John M. Harlan suggested a distinction between "hot news" and other kinds of news, the latter requiring more care on the part of reporters: "The evidence showed that the Butts story was in no sense 'hot news' and the editors of the magazine recognized the need for a thorough investigation of the serious charges. Elementary precautions were, nevertheless, ignored. In contrast . . . , the dispatch which concerns us in Walker was news which required immediate dissemination [and] nothing in this series of events gives the slightest hint of a severe departure from accepted publishing standards."

Opinion: Although the Court could not agree on an opinion, the justices managed to overturn the judgment for Walker and sustained the judgment for Butts by 5-to-4. Seven members—Chief Justice Earl Warren and Justices William J. Brennan, Jr., Tom C. Clark, Abe Fortas, John M. Harlan, and Potter Stewart, and Byron R. White—agreed that both plaintiffs were public figures for First Amendment purposes. Five—Warren, Brennan, Hugo L. Black, William O. Douglas, and White—agreed that the *Times* actual malice rule was applicable to public figures. Four—Clark, Fortas, Harlan, and Stewart—substituted a lesser standard for public figures based on "highly unreasonable conduct." In the *Butts* decision, five justices affirmed the judgment of the Court of Appeals for the Fifth Circuit on the ground that the relevant constitutional standard had been met. Clark, Fortas, Harlan, and Stewart applied their own standard for governing libel actions against public figures. Warren applied the *Times* standard. Brennan and White dissented, noting that the trial court's instructions to the jury did not comport with the *Times* standard. Black and Douglas, also in dissent, said that the Court should abandon the *Times* rule and "adopt the rule to the effect that the First Amendment was intended to leave the press free from the harassment of libel judgments." In the *Walker* decision, all justices voted to reverse the judgment of the Texas Court of Appeals. Warren,

Brennan, Black, Douglas, and White opined that the *Times* standard had not been met, whereas Clark, Fortas, Harlan, and Stewart based their view on the ground that their standard had also not been met.

Referenced Cases: *New York Times Co. v. Sullivan*, 376 U.S. 254 (1964), *Garrison v. Louisiana*, 379 U.S. 64 (1964), *Rosenblatt v. Baer*, 383 U.S. 75 (1966), and *Time, Inc. v. Hill*, 385 U.S. 374 (1967), on rule that prohibits a public official from recovering damages unless he proves "actual malice" and extension of rule to public figures, an issue not yet "fully settled"; *Michel v. Louisiana*, 350 U.S. 91 (1955), *Johnson v. Zerbst*, 304 U.S. 458 (1938), *Hormel v. Helvering*, 312 U.S. 552 (1941), and *Palko v. Connecticut*, 302 U.S. 319 (1937), on waiver of constitutional legal objections and protections; *Thornhill v. Alabama*, 310 U.S. 88 (1940), regarding freedom of discussion and the need to embrace all issues; *Adderley v. Florida*, 385 U.S. 39 (1966), on freedom of speech not inclusive of the freedom to trespass; *NAACP v. Button*, 371 U.S. 415 (1963), on "breathing space"; *Near v. Minnesota*, 283 U.S. 697 (1931), on prior restraint; *Associated Press v. NLRB*, 301 U.S. 103 (1937), regarding the press' lack of immunity from general laws; *Grosjean v. American Press Co., Inc.*, 297 U.S. 233 (1936), on special burden of the press; *Dennis v. U.S.*, 341 U.S. 494 (1951), regarding "free debate of ideas" resulting in the "wisest governmental policies"; *Whitney v. California*, 274 U.S. 357 (1927), on libel plaintiffs who can counterargue defamatory statements; *Seaboard Air Line R. Co. v. Padgett*, 236 U.S. 668 (1915), regarding isolated statements in jury instructions; and *Graver Tank & Mfg. Co. v. Linde Air Products Co.*, 336 U.S. 271 (1949), on trial evidence.

Further Reading:
53 *ABA J.* 853 (Sept. 1967).
32 *Albany L. Rev.* 207 (Fall 1967).
34 *Brooklyn L. Rev.* 290 (Winter 1968).
53 *Cornell L. Rev.* 649 (Nov. 1967).
81 *Harvard L. Rev.* 160 (Nov. 1967).
1967 *Sup. Ct. Rev.* 267 (1967).
44 *Washington L. Rev.* 461 (Winter 1969).

1967 *Beckley Newspapers Corp. v. C. Harold Hanks*, 389 U.S. 81, 19 L.Ed.2d 248, 88 S.Ct. 197, 1 Med.L.Rptr. 1585

Decided: Nov. 6, 1967.

Summary: Held that a public official, up for re-election, failed to show "actual malice" on the part of the newspaper with the "convincing clarity" required by *New York Times Co. v. Sullivan* (1964).

Circumstances: Hanks, a clerk of the Wyoming County criminal and circuit courts, charged that during his re-election campaign he was defamed by three editorials. The jury awarded him $5,000. One editorial in the Beckley *Post-Herald* said that "perhaps his blustering threats were able to intimidate" the head of the county board of health into opposing flouridation of the local water supply. Hanks argued that because the newspaper did not make an investigation into the threats its editorial was reckless, as the jury determined. But the U.S. Supreme Court found no "high degree of awareness of ... probable falsity demanded by *New York Times.*"

Opinion: In the per curiam opinion, expressing the views of Chief Justice Earl Warren and Justices William J. Brennan, Jr., John M. Harlan, Thurgood Marshall, Potter Stewart, and Byron R. White, the Court wrote that "it cannot be said on this record that any failure of petitioner to make a prior investigation constituted proof sufficient to present a jury question whether the statements were published with reckless disregard of whether they were false or not." The Court reversed the jury verdict for the plaintiff. The West Virginia Supreme Court of Appeals had denied the defendant's appeal for review. Justice Hugo L. Black, joined by William O. Douglas, concurred on the ground that the Constitution afforded an absolute, unconditional privilege to print criticism of official conduct. Justice Abe Fortas did not participate.

Referenced Cases: *New York Times Co. v. Sullivan,* 376 U.S. 254 (1964), *Garrison v. Louisiana,* 379 U.S. 64 (1964), *Henry v. Collins,* 380 U.S. 356 (1965), *Rosenblatt v. Baer,* 383 U.S.

75 (1966), *Curtis Publishing Co. v. Butts*, 388 U.S. 130 (1967), and *Time, Inc. v. Hill*, 385 U.S. 374 (1967), all on public official and public figure libel standards to ensure "reckless disregard" and guard against "forbidden intrusion on the field of free expression."

Further Reading:
None indexed.

1968   *Phil A. St. Amant v. Herman A. Thompson*, 390 U.S. 727, 20 L.Ed.2d 262, 88 S.Ct. 1323, 1 Med.L.Rptr. 1586

Argued: April 4, 1968.

Decided: April 29, 1968.

Summary: In a clear public-official defamation case, held that a plaintiff had to show that the defendant entertained serious doubts as to the truth of the libelous statement. Thus, the public official had the burden of proving that the false statements were made with "actual malice" as defined in *New York Times v. Sullivan* (1964).

Circumstances: In the course of a political speech over a Baton Rouge, Louisiana, television station, St. Amant, a candidate for public office, accused his opponent of accepting bribes. He went on to read a sworn statement from a Teamsters Union member, who described Thompson, a deputy sheriff, as a middleman in the activity. Thompson sued St. Amant for libel and won $5,000 in damages. The trial had taken place in 1962, two years before *Times v. Sullivan*. But the *Times* "actual malice" standard for public officials had become law at the time the Louisiana Court of Appeal reversed on the ground that the facts failed to show that St. Amant had acted with reckless disregard. The Supreme Court, "for purposes of this case," accepted the determinations.

Opinion: Justice Byron R. White wrote for six members in the 8-to-1 decision, including Chief Justice Earl Warren and

Justices John M. Harlan, William J. Brennan, Jr., Potter Stewart, and Thurgood Marshall. Hugo L. Black and William O. Douglas concurred separately. Abe Fortas dissented. The Court ruled that the plaintiff, a deputy sheriff, fell short of proving the defendant's "reckless disregard" for the accuracy of his statements. "There must be sufficient evidence to permit the conclusion that the defendant in fact entertained serious doubts as to the truth of his publication. Publishing with such doubts shows reckless disregard for truth or falsity and demonstrates actual malice." Justices Black and Douglas added that the Constitution affords an absolute, unconditional privilege to publish criticism of official conduct. Justice Fortas, in dissent, believed the libel was broadcast with actual malice. Even a public official, who should be subject to severe criticism, should have a remedy in law "if he is needlessly, heedlessly, falsely accused of crime. *New York Times* does not preclude this minimal standard of civilized living."

Referenced Cases: *New York Times Co. v. Sullivan,* 376 U.S. 254 (1964), establishing the "actual malice" standard for public officials; *Garrison v. Louisiana,* 379 U.S. 64 (1964), establishing the showing that a false publication was made with a "high degree of awareness of . . . probable falsity"; *Curtis Publishing Co. v. Butts,* 388 U.S. 130 (1967), regarding evidence of either deliberate falsification or reckless publication "despite the publisher's awareness of probable falsity" as essential to recovery by public officials.

Further Reading:
54 *ABA J.* 699 (July 1968).
17 *J. Public L.* 426 (1968).
15 *Loyola L. Rev.* 107 (1968–69).
47 *No. Carolina L. Rev.* 471 (Feb. 1969).
1969 *Utah L. Rev.* 118 (Jan. 1969).

1968   *Marvin L. Pickering v. Board of*
             Education of Township High School
             District 205, Will County, Illinois, **391**
             U.S. 563, 20 L.Ed.2d 811, 88 S.Ct. 1731

Argued: March 27, 1968.

Decided: June 3, 1968.

Summary: Invalidated the dismissal of a high school teacher for criticizing school administration. Public employment not a privilege to be conditioned on surrender of constitutional rights.

Circumstances: Pickering, a high school teacher, was fired by the Board of Education for a letter he had sent to a local newspaper in 1964 in response to a proposed tax increase. The letter attacked the board's handling of a 1961 bond issue and its subsequent allocation of monies between the schools' academic and athletic programs. Pickering also charged the superintendent of schools with attempting to prevent teachers in the district from opposing or criticizing the proposed bond issue. The board determined that the publication of the letter was detrimental to the efficient operation of the schools of the district and that the interests of the school required the dismissal. Upon noting false statements during a public hearing on the dismissal, the board further charged that the errors would be disruptive and foment "controversy, conflict and dissension" among teachers, administrators, the board, and the community. The circuit court upheld the dismissal and the Supreme Court of Illinois, two justices dissenting, affirmed the judgment and rejected Pickering's contention that his remarks and comments were protected by the First Amendment. The U.S. Supreme Court reversed.

Opinion: Justice Thurgood Marshall wrote the majority opinion, joined by Chief Justice Earl Warren and Justices John M. Harlan, William J. Brennan, Jr., Potter Stewart, and Abe Fortas. William O. Douglas and Hugo L. Black concurred separately. Byron R. White concurred in part and dissented in part. Marshall thought it neither "appropriate [n]or feasible to attempt to lay down a general standard against which all such statements may be judged," but he noted a "disinclination to make an across-the-board equation of dismissal from public employment for remarks critical of superiors with awarding damages in a libel suit by a public official for similar criticism." The standard used was a balancing of interests related to more than one constitutional

issue. "In these circumstances . . . the interest of the school administration in limiting teachers' opportunities to contribute to
public debate is not significantly greater than its interest in limiting a similar contribution by any member of the general public."
The Court also looked at the case in terms of defamation, "a
potent means of inhibiting speech," and concluded that the
teacher could not be dismissed for his letter, even with erroneous
information, "absent proof of false statements knowingly or reck-
lessly made by him." Justices Douglas and Black concurred on the
basis of their prior opinions in *Time, Inc. v. Hill, Rosenblatt v.
Baer, Garrison v. Louisiana, Curtis Publishing Co. v. Butts*, and
New York Times Co. v. Sullivan. Justice White, concurring in part
and dissenting in part, agreed with the application of the *Times v.
Sullivan* standard, but found it "wholly unsatisfactory for this
Court to make the initial determination of knowing or reckless
falsehood from the cold record now before us."

Referenced Cases: *Wieman v. Updegraff*, 344 U.S.
183 (1952), *Shelton v. Tucker*, 364 U.S. 479 (1960), and *Keyishian
v. Board of Regents*, 385 U.S. 589 (1967), regarding the Court's prior
rejection of compelling teachers to relinquish their First Amendment rights; *New York Times Co. v. Sullivan*, 376 U.S. 254 (1964),
Linn v. United Plant Guard Workers, 383 U.S. 53 (1966), *Time, Inc.
v. Hill*, 385 U.S. 374 (1967), and *St. Amant v. Thompson*, 390 U.S.
727 (1968), which established and developed the "actual malice"
standard for public officials; *Garrison v. Louisiana*, 379 U.S. 64
(1964), and *Wood v. Georgia*, 370 U.S. 375 (1962), on statements by
public officials on matters of public concern, even those directed
at their "nominal superiors."

Further Reading:
35 *Brooklyn L. Rev.* 270 (Winter 1969).
44 *Chicago-Kent L. Rev.* 194 (Fall (1967).
53 *Minnesota L. Rev.* 864 (March 1969).
20 *Syracuse L. Rev.* 72 (Fall 1968).

1970   *Greenbelt Cooperative Publishing
Assoc. v. Charles S. Bresler, 398 U.S. 6,*

26 L.Ed.2d 6, 90 S.Ct. 1537, 1 Med.L.Rptr. 1589

Argued: Feb. 24, 25, 1970.

Decided: May 18, 1970.

Summary: The word "blackmail" could not reasonably be understood as a criminal accusation, rather an invective uttered in the heat of public debate.

Circumstances: Bresler, a real estate developer in Greenbelt, Maryland, instituted a libel action against the publishers of a weekly newspaper, the *Greenbelt News Review*, for reporting in two news stories that at public meetings some citizens characterized Bresler's negotiating position as "blackmail." Bresler had sought zoning variances to build a high-rise apartment building. Residents opposed his effort. When he offered to donate land to the city for a badly needed school in exchange for the variance, an opponent said at a public meeting that the offer was blackmail. The word appeared several times in news accounts, both with and without quotation marks, and was used once as a subheadline. The jury awarded Bresler $5,000 in compensatory damages and $12,500 in punitive damages. The judge's instructions stated that the plaintiff could recover if the publications had been made with malice, defined as "spite, hostility, or deliberate intention to harm," and said that malice could be found in the "language" of the publication itself. The Maryland Court of Appeals affirmed. On certiorari, the U.S. Supreme Court reversed and remanded to the Maryland Court of Appeals.

Opinion: Justice Potter Stewart, writing for himself and Chief Justice Warren E. Burger and Justices John M. Harlan, William J. Brennan, Jr., Thurgood Marshall, and Harry A. Blackmun, held "clearly correct" plaintiff's concession that he was a "public figure" under *Curtis Publishing Co. v. Butts* (1967). Justices Byron R. White, Hugo L. Black, and William O. Douglas concurred separately. The Court was guided by the principle that newspapers enjoy the qualified privilege of fair comment when they report on public meetings concerned with local governmental issues. Stewart said the trial judge's instructions to the jury had erroneously permitted a finding of liability "merely on the basis of a combination of falsehood and general hostility." The Court also concluded that as a matter of constitutional law, the word "blackmail" in these circumstances was not slander when spoken, and not libel when reported in the newspaper. Justice White agreed that the jury instruction had been erroneous, but he disagreed with the majority's claim of "superior insight" as to how "blackmail" would be understood by the ordinary reader in Greenbelt. Justice Black, joined by Douglas, said that the First Amendment was intended to leave the press free from the harassment of libel suits. They concurred on the basis of their opinions in *New York Times v. Sullivan* (1964), *Curtis Publishing v. Butts* (1967), and *Garrison v. Louisiana* (1964).

Referenced Cases: *New York Times Co. v. Sullivan*, 376 U.S. 254 (1964), on the meaning of "public official" and "actual malice"; *Curtis Publishing Co. v. Butts*, 388 U.S. 130 (1967), on the definition of "public figure"; *Rosenblatt v. Baer*, 383 U.S. 75 (1966), regarding the discussion of public affairs; *Garrison v. Louisiana*, 379 U.S. 64 (1964), and *Beckley Newspapers Corp. v. Hanks*, 389 U.S. 81 (1967), on uninhibited debate on public issues; *Time, Inc. v. Hill*, 385 U.S. 374 (1967), and *Stromberg v. California*, 283 U.S. 359 (1931), regarding erroneous jury instructions and free political discussion; *Thornhill v. Alabama*, 310 U.S. 88 (1940), on the breadth of free expression.

Further Reading:
56 *ABA J.* (Sept. 1970).
32 *Univ. Pittsburgh L. Rev.* 450 (Spring 1970).

1971   *Monitor Patriot Co. v. Roselle A. Roy,*
          401 U.S. 265, 28 L.Ed.2d 35, 91 S.Ct. 621,
          1 Med.L.Rptr. 1619

Argued: Dec. 17, 1970.

Decided: Feb. 24, 1971.

Summary: Held that the First and 14th Amendments prohibit a "public official" from recovering damages for libel related to official conduct unless proven "actual malice."

Circumstances: On Sept. 10, 1960, three days before the New Hampshire Democratic primary for the U.S. Senate, the *Concord Monitor* published a syndicated "D.C. Merry-Go-Round" column that discussed the criminal records of several of the candidates, characterizing Alphonse Roy as a "former small-time bootlegger." Roy, unsuccessful in his bid, sued the Monitor Patriot Co. and the North American Newspaper Alliance, distributor of the column. The trial judge instructed the jury on its requirement of "actual malice," but only if the libel was in the "public sector" and concerned the plaintiff's fitness for office. Since the jury found that the libel was in the "private sector" and not related to fitness for office, judgment was entered against both the newspaper and the distributor. The New Hampshire Supreme Court affirmed, holding that the judge had properly instructed the jury on the question of the alleged libel's relevancy to Roy's fitness for office. On certiorari, the U.S. Supreme Court reversed and remanded.

Opinion: Justice Potter Stewart wrote for seven members in the unanimous decision, joined by Chief Justice Warren E. Burger and Justices John M. Harlan, William J. Brennan, Jr., Byron R. White, Thurgood Marshall, and Harry A. Blackmun. Hugo L. Black, joined by William O. Douglas, concurred separately. Stewart said that "publications concerning candidates must be accorded at least as much protection under the First and Fourteenth Amendments as those concerning occupants of public office." He said the jury had been improperly permitted to determine that the charge of prior criminal activity was not relevant to the plaintiff's fitness for office. On the question of whether the charges of criminal conduct related sufficiently to "official conduct" to apply *New York Times Co. v. Sullivan* (1964), Stewart said it was "a matter of constitutional law that a charge of criminal conduct, no matter how remote in time or place, can never be irrelevant to an official's or a candidate's fitness for office for purposes of application of the 'knowing falsehood or reckless disregard' rule." The Court also reversed on the ground that the jury was permitted to make its own "unguided determination" on the issue of relevancy. Justice Black, with Douglas, concurred on the basis of two other judgments of the same day—*Time Inc. v. Pape* and *Ocala Star-Banner v. Damron*—and for reasons set out in *New York Times v. Sullivan, Curtis Publishing v. Butts,* and *Garrison v. Louisiana.* Justice White's separate concurrence was in the form of a separate opinion in *Ocala.*

Referenced Cases: *New York Times Co. v. Sullivan,* 376 U.S. 254 (1964), on the "actual malice" standard for public officials; *Garrison v. Louisiana,* 379 U.S. 64 (1964), *Curtis Publishing Co. v. Butts,* 388 U.S. 130 (1967), and *Greenbelt Cooperative Publishing Assn. v. Bresler,* 398 U.S. 6 (1970), regarding the expense of this basic approach; *Roth v. U.S.,* 354 U.S. 476 (1957), on the "unfettered interchange of ideas" in political campaigns; *Abrams v. U.S.,* 250 U.S. 616 (1919), on the protection of "opinion that we loathe and believe to be fraught with death"; *Cantwell v. Connecticut,* 310 U.S. 296 (1940), on "the tenets of one man may seem the rankest error to his neighbor"; *Speiser v. Randall,* 357 U.S. 513 (1958), and *Smith v. California,* 361 U.S. 147 (1959), on the relevancy of a candidate's fitness for office; *St. Amant v. Thompson,* 390 U.S. 727 (1968), on protected and unprotected speech and "case-by-case adjudication."

Further Reading:
57 *ABA J.* 496 (May 1971).
21 *DePaul L. Rev.* 248 (Autumn 1971).
17 *NY L. Forum* 869 (1971).
2 *Texas So. Univ. L. Rev.* 173 (Fall 1971).

1971   *Ocala Star-Banner Co. v. Leonard Damron,* **401 U.S. 295, 28 L.Ed.2d 57, 91 S.Ct. 628, 1 Med.L.Rptr. 1624**

Argued: Dec. 17, 1970.

Decided: Feb. 24, 1971.

Summary: The constitutional rule of "actual malice" for a "public official" plaintiff ruled applicable on the ground that public discussion about the qualifications of a candidate for elective office presents "what is probably the strongest possible case" for application of the *New York Times* rule.

Circumstances: Damron, a mayor and candidate for county tax assessor, sued the *Star-Banner* for libel per se for reporting that he had been charged with perjury in a civil rights suit pending in federal court. The story was false. It was his brother, James, who had been charged, and one of the editors testified that he had "inadvertently" changed the name to Leonard Damron, the more well-known of the brothers, when a reporter telephoned in the story. The judge granted Damron's motion for a directed verdict and instructed the jury on the awarding of damages, which the jury determined as $22,000 in compensatory damages. The Florida District Court of Appeal affirmed the judgment and the state supreme court refused to review the decision. The appeals court had determined that the defamatory publication was not related to the manner in which Damron performed his duties and, hence, was not protected by the "actual malice" standard for public officials. On certiorari, the Supreme Court reversed and remanded.

Opinion: Justice Potter Stewart, expressing the view of seven members of the Court, as he had in a similar case decided the same day, *Monitor Patriot Co. v. Roy*, wrote: "In that case we held that a charge of criminal conduct against an official or a candidate, no matter how remote in time or place, is always 'relevant to his fitness for office' for purposes of applying the *New York Times* rule of knowing falsehood or reckless disregard of the truth." Stewart was joined by Chief Justice Warren E. Burger and Justices Harry A. Blackmun, William J. Brennan, John M. Harlan, Thurgood Marshall, and Byron R. White. In a separate opinion, White noted that, though the *Times* rule extends protection to lies and falsehoods, the sole basis for protecting publishers who spread false information is that otherwise the truth would too often be suppressed. Justice Hugo L. Black, joined by William O. Douglas, concurred but dissented from permitting the case to be retried under different jury instructions. He referred to his opinion in *Monitor*, which was also joined by Douglas.

Referenced Cases: *New York Times Co. v. Sullivan*, 376 U.S. 254 (1964), on the "actual malice" test; *Monitor Patriot*

Co. v. Roy, 401 U.S. 265 (1971), regarding candidates for public office as "public officials"; *Henry v. Collins,* 380 U.S. 356 (1965), *Curtis Publishing Co. v. Butts,* 388 U.S. 130 (1967), and *Greenbelt Cooperative Publishing Assn. v. Bresler,* 398 U.S. 6 (1970), on application of the *Times* rule; *Garrison v. Louisiana,* 379 U.S. 64 (1964), on "fitness for office"; *St. Amant v. Thompson,* 390 U.S. 727 (1968), and *Time, Inc. v. Pape,* 401 U.S. 279 (1971), on the protection of "innocent falsehoods."

Further Reading:
See under *Monitor Patriot Co. v. Roy* (1971), decided the same day.

1971   *Time, Inc. v. Frank Pape,* 401 U.S. 279, 28 L.Ed.2d 45, 91 S.Ct. 633, 1 Med.L.Rptr. 1627

Argued: Dec. 16, 1970.

Decided: Feb. 24, 1971.

Summary: The Court, for the first time explicitly, dealt with issues raised by the news media's publication of the defamatory allegations of others. It ruled that the magazine's conduct reflected "at most an error of judgment rather than reckless disregard of the truth" when it reported an instance of police brutality as published in a government study.

Circumstances: In Nov. 1961, the U.S. Commission on Civil Rights published a report, entitled *Justice,* a part of which was devoted to "police brutality and related private violence." In reporting on the publication's release, *Time* magazine cited Chicago police treatment of James Monroe and his family, but failed to note that Monroe's subsequent civil rights action against the deputy chief of detectives, Frank Pape, was not part of the commission's independent findings. Earlier, on Feb. 20 of the same year, the Court had permitted, in *Monroe v. Pape,* 365 U.S. 167 (1961), the plaintiff to sue several Chicago police officers for violation of the Federal Civil Rights Act in their handling of Monroe's detainment. Monroe won his suit against Pape in Jan. 1963 and was awarded $8,000 in damages. Detective Pape, meanwhile, sued *Time* for libel in the District Court for Northern Illinois, which granted the magazine's dismissal motion on the ground that the article was fair comment on a government report and therefore privileged under state law. The Court of Appeals for the Seventh Circuit reversed, but after remand the district court granted *Time*'s motion for summary judgment on the basis of *New York Times Co. v. Sullivan*, decided in the interim. Again, the court of appeals reversed, holding the need for a trial to determine whether *Time*'s failure to make clear that it was reporting no more than allegations showed "actual malice." The district court granted *Time*'s motion for a directed verdict and Pape appealed for a third time. The court of appeals again reversed and said that it was appropriate for the jury to decide whether omission of the word "alleged" showed "actual malice." On certiorari, the Supreme Court reinstated the directed verdict for *Time*.

Opinion: Justice Potter Stewart, expressing the view of Chief Justice Warren E. Burger and Justices Harry A. Blackmun, William J. Brennan, Jr., Thurgood Marshall, and Byron R. White, held that under the circumstances of the case, *Time* magazine had not itself created a "falsification" when it failed to note that a report by the U.S. Commission on Civil Rights was technically limited to the "allegations" of brutality in a private civil rights action against the police officer, Pape. Stewart wrote that "a vast amount of what is published in the daily and periodical press purports to be descriptive of what somebody *said* rather than of what anybody did." He also noted that the commission's report was "extravagantly ambiguous" regarding whether the facts were merely allegations or actual truth. In an important passage in the opinion, Stewart said: "Time's omission of the word 'alleged' amounted to the adoption of one of a number of possible rational interpretations of a document that bristled with ambiguities. The deliberate choice of such an interpretation, though arguably reflecting a misconception, was not enough to create a jury issue of 'malice' under *New York Times*. To permit the malice issue to go to the jury because of the omission of a word like 'alleged,' despite the context of that word in the Commission Report and the external evidence of the Report's overall meaning, would be to impose a much stricter standard of liability on errors of interpretation or judgment than on errors of historic fact." But he added that "alleged" remained an important word in published reports damaging to reputation. "Our decision . . . is based on the specific facts of this case." Justice Hugo L. Black, joined by William O. Douglas, concurred in their opinion of the same day in *Monitor Patriot Co. v. Roy*. Justice John M. Harlan, in dissent, departed from the Court's review of the factual record and said the court of appeals had applied the correct standard.

Referenced Cases: *New York Times Co. v. Sullivan*, 376 U.S. 254 (1964), on establishment of the "public official" standard of "actual malice"; *Niemotko v. Maryland*, 340 U.S. 268 (1951), on the Court's right to "reexamine the evidentiary"; *Beckley Newspapers v. Hanks*, 389 U.S. 81 (1967), *St. Amant v. Thompson*, 390 U.S. 727 (1968), and *Greenbelt Cooperative Publishing Assn. v. Bresler*, 398 U.S. 6 (1970), on the Court's review of tension between the Constitution and state libel laws; *Garrison v. Louisiana*, 379 U.S. 64 (1964), on the "high degree of awareness of . . . probable falsity" standard.

Further Reading:
See under *Monitor Patriot Co. v. Roy*, 401 U.S. 265 (1971), decided the same day.

1971   *George A. Rosenbloom v. Metromedia, Inc.*, 403 U.S. 29, 29 L.Ed.2d 296, 91 S.Ct. 1811, 1 Med.L.Rptr. 1597

Argued: Dec. 7, 8, 1970.

Decided: June 7, 1971.

Summary: Three justices, in the plurality holding, said the conditional First Amendment privilege should include all persons, public and private, who become involved in events of "public or general concern." Five said plaintiff could not recover under constitutional guarantees that restrict state libel laws.

Circumstances: The plaintiff, Rosenbloom, a distributor of nudist magazines in Philadelphia, was arrested in 1963 on criminal obscenity charges. He was later acquitted when the trial judge found that his magazines were, as a matter of law, not obscene. Radio station WIP, in reporting the arrest, stated that police had confiscated 1,000 "allegedly" obscene books at Rosenbloom's home and 3,000 more at his warehouse. Two weeks later, Rosenbloom sued to stop police from disrupting his business. When WIP reported on the suit and called Rosenbloom a "girlie-book peddler" engaged in the "smut literature racket," the plaintiff sued for libel in federal district court. The court held that *Times v. Sullivan* was not applicable, and the jury awarded $25,000 general damages and $725,000 punitive damages. The latter was reduced to $250,000 by the judge. The Court of Appeals for the Third Circuit reversed, citing *Times v. Sullivan* and concluding that "the fact that the plaintiff was not a public figure cannot be accorded decisive significance if the recognized important guarantees of the First Amendment are to be adequately implemented." The Supreme Court, in affirming the decision, adopted the same rationale. In sum, the eight justices who participated announced their views in five separate opinions, none of which commanded more than three votes.

Opinion: The case raised the question of whether the *New York Times*'s knowing-or-reckless-falsity standard applied in a state civil libel action brought not by a "public official" or a "public figure" but by a private individual for a defamatory falsehood about the individual's involvement in an event of public or general interest. Justice William J. Brennan, Jr., who wrote the Court's opinion in *New York Times v. Sullivan* (1964) setting the "actual malice" standard, said the standard applied when the defamation related to the plaintiff's involvement in a matter of public or general concern, not the public or private status of the individual. He was joined by Chief Justice Warren E. Burger and Justice Harry A. Blackmun. Hugo L. Black and Byron R. White concurred in separate opinions. Black wrote that the First Amendment does not permit the recovery of libel judgments against the news media even when statements are broadcast with knowledge they are false. White held that, absent "actual malice," the First Amendment gives the press and the broadcast media "a privilege to report and comment upon the official actions of public servants in full detail, with no requirement that the reputation or privacy of an individual involved in or affected by the official action be spared from public view."

Justices John M. Harlan, Thurgood Marshall, and Potter Stewart dissented. William O. Douglas did not participate. Harlan urged that punitive damages be allowed in cases where actual malice is proved and where the damages "bear a reasonable and purposeful relationship to the actual harm done." Justice Marshall, joined by Stewart, expressed the view that in private-plaintiff libel actions damages should be restricted to actual losses related to "some proved harm." He said the *Times* malice standard "offers inadequate protection" for private individuals. States should be left to determine their own fault standards, so long as absolute or strict liability was not used.

Referenced Cases: *New York Times Co. v. Sullivan*, 376 U.S. 254 (1964), on the limitations on state libel laws; *Time Inc. v. Hill*, 385 U.S. 374 (1967), and *Thornhill v. Alabama*, 310 U.S. 88 (1940), regarding protection needed for open discussion of societal issues; *Curtis Publishing Co. v. Butts* and *Associated Press v. Walker*, 388 U.S. 130 (1967), on uninhibited public debate on public issues and events; *Rosenblatt v. Baer*, 388 U.S. 75 (1966), regarding the functions of constitutional guarantees for freedom of expression; *Speiser v. Randall*, 357 U.S. 513 (1958), on the fear of guessing wrong and causing self-censorship; *Monitor Patriot Co. v. Roy*, 401 U.S. 265 (1971), on the reasonable-man standard of liability; *St. Amant v. Thompson*, 390 U.S. 727 (1968), on the need to protect some erroneous publications; *Garrison v. Louisiana*, 329 U.S. 64 (1964), regarding calculated falsehood being outside "fruitful exercise" of the right of free speech; *Pennekamp v. Florida*, 328 U.S. 331 (1946), *Jacobellis v. Ohio*, 378 U.S. 184 (1964), and *Edwards v. South Carolina*, 372 U.S. 229 (1963), on the Court's authority and responsibility; *NAACP v. Button*, 371 U.S. 415 (1963), on "breathing space" requirement in free debate; *Cohen v. California*, 403 U.S. 15 (1971), *Brandenburg v. Ohio*, 395 U.S. 444 (1969), and *Butler v. Michigan*, 352 U.S. 380 (1957), on speakers' presumptive rights before an audience regarding open, uninhibited, and robust speech.

Further Reading:
25 *Arkansas L. Rev.* 525 (1972).
40 *Fordham L. Rev.* 651 (1972).

40 *George Washington L. Rev.* 151 (1971).
7 *Gonzaga L. Rev.* 340, 344 (1972).
20 *Journal of Pub. L.* 601 (1971).
6 *Suffolk Univ. L. Rev.* 712 (1972).
39 *Univ. Cincinnati L. Rev.* 363 (1970).
31 *Univ. Pittsburgh L. Rev.* 734 (Summer 1970).

1974   *Elmer Gertz v. Robert Welch, Inc.,* **418 U.S. 323, 41 L.Ed.2d 789, 94 S.Ct. 2997, 1 Med.L.Rptr. 1633**

Argued: Nov. 14, 1973.

Decided: June 25, 1974.

Summary: Held that states may impose any standard of care, from actual malice to simple negligence, so long as they do not impose liability without fault. Nature of the plaintiff is critical, rather than public or general interest of defamatory statements. Punitive damages are to be based on "actual malice" standard.

Circumstances: Gertz, a prominent Chicago attorney, sued the publisher of *American Opinion*, the magazine of the ultraconservative John Birch Society, for an article accusing him of discrediting the police and being a "Leninist," a "Communist-fronter," and a member of the National Lawyers' Guild, "a Communist organization" that "probably did more than any other outfit to plan the Communist attack on the Chicago police during the 1968 Democratic Convention." Gertz caught the magazine's attention when he agreed to represent the parents of a youth who had been shot to death by a Chicago policeman, Richard Nuccio, whom they had sued for damages. Despite Gertz's remote connection to the prosecution of Nuccio, the article portrayed him as an architect of the "frame-up." There was little doubt that the magazine had published "serious inaccuracies"; for example, the writer said that Gertz's police file was voluminous, whereas the lawyer had no such record. The trial court ruled that the statements were libel per se under Illinois law and that Gertz was a private individual; thus, the only issue was damages. On further reflection, however, the court decided that the *New York Times* standard was applicable on the ground that the privilege protected discussion of any public issue regardless of the status of the defamed person, and the Court of Appeals for the Seventh Circuit agreed. In 1981, following the Supreme Court's reversal and remand, a Chicago jury found that *American Opinion* had acted with actual malice and awarded Gertz $100,000 in actual damages and $300,000 in punitive damages. On appeal, the Seventh Circuit Court of Appeals affirmed the award and the U.S. Supreme Court in 1983 declined to review, ending litigation begun in 1969.

Opinion: Justice Lewis F. Powell, Jr., wrote the 5-to-4 opinion, joined by Justices Harry A. Blackmun, Thurgood Marshall, William H. Rehnquist, and Potter Stewart. Blackmun also wrote a separate concurrence. Dissenting were Chief Justice Warren E. Burger and Justices William O. Douglas, William J. Brennan, Jr., and Byron R. White. Following a decade of decisions related to *New York Times Co. v. Sullivan* (1964), the Court returned much of evolving libel law back to the states whenever a "private individual" was involved. In reviewing that case and its progeny, including many *dicta* passages, Powell concluded that "the state interest in compensatory injury to the reputation of private individuals requires that a different rule should obtain with respect to them." The rationale expressed noted that "private individuals are . . . more vulnerable to injury, and the state interest in protecting them is correspondingly greater." Private individuals are also more deserving of recovery. In an opinion valuable for its elaborate, if not sometimes confusing, explanation and categorization of public officials, public figures, and private individuals, Powell asserted that so long as states do not impose "liability without fault"—a "new negligence standard," according to Chief Justice Burger in dissent—they may define "for themselves" the appropriate standard of liability for a defamatory falsehood injurious to a private person. Powell itemized three other requirements: (1) a state may not impose a standard that permits liability for mere factual misstatement, but rather such an error must signal "substantial danger to reputation"; (2) a state may permit recovery only for "actual injury," including not only out-of-pocket losses but also impairment of reputation and standing in the community, personal humiliation of reputation and standing in the community, personal humiliation, and mental suffering; and (3) punitive damages, usually awarded by juries to punish unpopular opinion, may be granted only on a showing of actual malice. "In short, the private defamation plaintiff who establishes liability under a less demanding standard than that stated by *New York Times v. Sullivan* may recover only such damages as are sufficient to compensate him for actual injury." In finding that Gertz was not a public figure, Powell further distinguished private individuals from public persons: "He plainly did not thrust himself into the vortex of this public issue, nor did he engage the public's attention in an attempt to influence its outcome."

Justice Blackmun wrote separately to explain his reluctance on the basis of the paramount need for a definitive ruling. "By removing the specters of presumed and punitive damages in the absence of *New York Times* malice, the Court eliminates significant and powerful motives for self-censorship that otherwise are present in the traditional libel action." Additionally, "I feel that it is of profound importance for the Court to come to rest in the defamation area and to have a clearly defined majority position that eliminates the unsureness engendered by Rosenbloom's [*Rosenbloom v. Metromedia, Inc.* (1971)] diversity."

Justice Burger, fearing too much diversity if states set the standards, wrote in dissent that he would prefer to allow the private-citizen area of libel law to continue to evolve rather than "embark on a new doctrinal theory which has no jurisprudential ancestry." He would reinstate the jury's verdict of $50,000 for Gertz. Justice Douglas dissented on the ground that the Constitution prohibits damages against a publisher for a discussion of public affairs. Justice Brennan, also in dissent, said that states are required to apply the *Times* standard in civil libel actions concerning media reports of private individuals involved in events of public or general interest, a standard that Gertz could not prove. He would affirm the judgment for Welch by the Court of Appeals for the Seventh Circuit.

Justice White, in a lengthy and strongly worded dissent also laced with *dicta*, would reinstate the jury's verdict on the ground that states should be free to impose strict liability in private plaintiff actions against the media. Such "sweeping changes," he said, though popular with the press, would deprecate the reputation interest of ordinary citizens and render them powerless to protect themselves. "Simply put, the First Amendment did not confer a 'license to defame the citizen.'" White took the opportunity to comment on the "communications industry," which he opined has become increasingly concentrated in a few powerful hands operating very lucrative businesses reaching across the nation and into almost every home. "Requiring them to pay for the occasional damage they do to private reputation will play no substantial part in their future performance or their existence." White found the Court's decision "a classic example of judicial overkill." He would reverse the court of appeals' judgment and reinstate the jury's verdict.

Referenced Cases: *New York Times Co. v. Sullivan*, 376 U.S. 254 (1964), regarding a constitutional privilege against liability for defamation; *Curtis Publishing Co. v. Butts* and *Associated Press v. Walker*, 388 U.S. 130 (1967), on the "public figure" category; *Rosenbloom v. Metromedia, Inc.*, 403 U.S. 29 (1971), on the "public issue" privilege; *St. Amant v. Thompson*, 390 U.S. 727 (1968), *Beckley Newspapers Corp. v. Hanks*, 389 U.S. 81 (1967), and *Garrison v. Louisiana*, 379 U.S. 64 (1964), on a "high degree of awareness of . . . probable falsity"; *Barr v. Matteo*, 360 U.S. 564 (1959), on public officials' immunity from their own libelous utterances; *Rosenblatt v. Baer*, 386 U.S. 75 (1966), on the protection of private personality; *NAACP v. Button*, 371 U.S. 415 (1963), regarding needed "breathing space" for the press; *Time, Inc. v. Hill*, 385 U.S. 374 (1967), on factual misstatement; *Thornhill v. Alabama*, 310 U.S. 88 (1940), on freedom of discussion as related to society's ability to cope with the "exigencies" of the time; *Griswold v. Connecticut*, 381 U.S. 479 (1965), regarding how some aspects of otherwise public lives may reside outside the area of public or general concern; *Speiser v. Randall*, 357 U.S. 513 (1958), on self-censorship as publishers "steer far wide of the unlawful zone"; *In re Winship*, 397 U.S. 358 (1970), on preponderance of evidence and the balance of interests; *Monitor Patriot Co. v. Roy*, 401 U.S. 265 (1971), regarding the constitutional protection of "vehement, caustic, and sometimes unpleasantly sharp attacks"; *Washington Post Co. v. Chaloner*, 250 U.S. 290 (1919), *Baker v. Warner* 231 U.S. 588 (1913), *Nalle v. Oyster*, 230 U.S. 165 (1913), *Dorr v. U.S.*, 195 U.S. 138 (1904), *Pollard v. Lyon*, 91 U.S. 225 (1876), and *White v. Nicholls*, 3 How. 266 (1845), for the history of the "classic law of libel," especially regarding federal law and defamatory utterances unprotected by the First Amendment; *Patterson v. Colorado ex rel. Attorney General*, 205 U.S. 454 (1907), and *Near v. Minnesota ex rel. Olson*, 283 U.S. 697 (1931), on the protection of speech contrary to the public welfare; *Chaplinsky v. New Hampshire*, 315 U.S. 568 (1942), and *Beauharnais v. Illinois*, 343 U.S. 250 (1952), on the abolishment of the crime of libel.

Further Reading:

1982 *Arizona L. J.* 1 (1983).
20 *Arizona L. Rev.* 797 (1978)
28 *Case Western Reserve L. Rev.* 306 (Winter 1978).
Newsletter, Inland Daily Press Assoc. (April 30, 1981).
8 *John Marshall L. J.* (Spring 1975).
10 *New England L. Rev.* 585 (Spring 1975).
28 *Southwestern L. J.* 1043 (Winter 1974).
48 *Temple L. Q.* 450 (Winter 1975).
54 *Texas L. Rev.* 199 (Jan. 1976).
61 *Virginia L. Rev.* 1249 (1975).
2 *Western St. Univ. L. Rev.* 227 (Spring 1975).

1976   *Time, Inc. v. Mary Alice Firestone*, 424 U.S. 448, 47 L.Ed.2d 154, 96 S.Ct. 958, 1 Med.L.Rptr. 1665

Argued: Oct. 14, 1975.

Decided: March 2, 1976.

Summary: Ruled that, because the plaintiff had not voluntarily "thrust herself to the forefront of any particular public controversy," she was a private individual and, therefore, state libel law should apply. In Florida, where the libel action was brought, the standard is negligence for private persons in defamation suits.

Circumstances: In *Time* magazine's "Milestones" column for Dec. 22, 1967, it was erroneously reported that Russell A. Firestone, Jr., heir to the tire fortune, had been granted a divorce from his wife, Mary Alice, on grounds of "extreme cruelty and adultery." The magazine also reported that the divorce trial had "produced enough testimony of extramarital adventures on both sides, said the judge, 'to make Dr. Freud's hair curl.'" As it turned out, the judge found "a gross lack of domestication" on both sides. There was no finding of adultery. When Ms. Firestone's request for a retraction failed, she sued the magazine for libel in the Florida Circuit Court. After the trial, she was awarded $100,000, which the state's Fourth Circuit Court of Appeals overturned, in part because it said *Time* had reported fairly the divorce judgment and because Ms. Firestone had not established any recoverable damages. Florida's supreme court, given shortly after *Gertz v. Robert Welch, Inc.* (1974), reinstated damages on the ground that the false report of adultery was clear and convincing evidence of negligence. A majority of the U.S. Supreme Court concluded that because Ms. Firestone was a private person Florida libel law should apply. But the Court remanded the case for a finding of fault as stipulated by *Gertz.*

Opinion: Justice William H. Rehnquist, joined by Chief Justice Warren E. Burger and Justices Harry A. Blackmun, Lewis F. Powell, Jr., and Potter Stewart, held that Firestone was not a public figure for purposes of the rule requiring a showing of actual malice and that the Florida courts properly found that the magazine article was false. On the question of "matters of general or public interest," as explored in *Rosenbloom v. Metromedia, Inc.* (1971) but later repudiated in *Gertz,* Rehnquist responded: "Dissolution of a marriage through judicial proceedings is not the sort of 'public controversy' referred to in *Gertz,* even though the marital difficulties of extremely wealthy individuals may be of interest to some portion of the reading public." Nor did Firestone freely choose to publicize her married life, but instead was compelled to go to court to obtain legal release "from the bonds of matrimony." The Court also rejected the argument, as presented by the publisher, that states are precluded from imposing civil liability based on the publication of truthful information contained in official court records open to public inspection. In *Gertz,* Rehnquist noted, the Court had eschewed a subject-matter test for one focusing on the character of the defamation plaintiff. "As to inaccurate and defamatory reports of facts, matters deserving no First Amendment protection, we think *Gertz* provides an adequate safeguard for the constitutionally protected interests of the press and affords it a tolerable margin for error by requiring some type of fault." Though not necessarily agreeing with the Rehnquist rationale, Justice Powell, joined by Stewart, noted that, because the divorce decree "invited misunderstanding," the jury or court should have weighed such factors before assessing liability in accordance with *Gertz*.

Justice William J. Brennan, Jr., in dissent, expressed concern over the degree of First Amendment protection for "erroneously reporting the results of a public judicial proceeding" and said that under such circumstances the actual malice standard was applicable. Justice Byron R. White, also in dissent, argued that *Gertz* was not applicable because the defamation had been published long before that decision, and therefore state law applied. Justice Thurgood Marshall, finding the Court's determination "baffling," dissented on essentially two grounds—he believed Firestone to be a public figure, and he felt there was insufficient basis for a finding of fault under *Gertz*. The latter will never be known, however, because Firestone decided in 1978, after ten years of litigation, to drop the libel suit. She said, according to her attorneys, that she "was completely vindicated by the jury verdict seven and a half years ago." Justice John Paul Stevens did not participate.

Referenced Cases: *New York Times Co. v. Sullivan*, 376 U.S. 254 (1964), on the "actual malice" standard; *Curtis Publishing Co. v. Butts*, 388 U.S. 130 (1967), extending the *Times* standard to "public figure" plaintiffs; *Gertz v. Robert Welch, Inc.*, 418 U.S. 323 (1974), on limiting the "public figure" category of plaintiffs and redefining libel liability; *Rosenbloom v. Metromedia, Inc.*, 403 U.S. 29 (1971), on private persons in matters of public and interest; *Boddie v. Connecticut*, 401 U.S. 371 (1971), on the involuntary nature of judicial proceedings; *Cox Broadcasting Corp. v. Cohn*, 420 U.S. 469 (1975), on the publication of information in official court records; *Lincoln v. Power*, 151 U.S. 436 (1894), on reexamining lower court determinations; *Lyons v. Oklahoma*, 322 U.S. 596 (1944), and *Gallegos v. Nebraska*, 342 U.S. 55 (1951), on deferring to state courts in the review of constitutional claims; *Rosenblatt v. Baer*, 383 U.S. 75 (1966), on balancing "human dignity" against the "system of free expression"; *St. Amant v. Thompson*, 390 U.S. 727 (1968), regarding protection of erroneous publications as well as true ones; *Craig v. Harney*, 331 U.S. 367 (1947), regarding the public nature of trials whose proceedings may be reported "with impunity"; *Sheppard v. Maxwell*, 384 U.S. 333 (1966), the press' role in subjecting the judicial process to public scrutiny; *Bridges v. California*, 314 U.S. 252 (1941), on public controversies, which are likely to get into court; *Williams v. U.S.*, 401 U.S. 646 (1971), regarding Supreme Court interference in state defamation policy.

Further Reading:

43 *Brooklyn L. Rev.* 123 (Summer 1976).
25 *Emory L. J.* 705 (Summer 1976).
5 *Florida St. Univ. L. Rev.* 446 (Summer 1977).
13 *Idaho L. Rev.* 53 (Winter 1976).
29 *Mercer L. Rev.* 841 (Spring 1978).
61 *Minnesota L. Rev.* 645 (April 1977).
8 *No. Carolina Central L. J.* 109 (Fall 1976).
4 *Ohio Northern L. Rev.* 91 (1977).
14 *San Diego L. Rev.* 435 (March 1977).
20 *St. Louis Univ. L. J.* 625 (1976).
31 *Univ. Miami L. Rev.* 216 (Fall 1976).

1979 *Anthony Herbert v. Barry Lando*, 441 U.S. 153, 60 L.Ed.2d 115, 99 S.Ct. 1635, 4 Med.L.Rptr. 2575, 46 U.S.L.W. 2251

Argued: Oct. 31, 1978.

Decided: April 18, 1979.

Summary: On the heels of a number of libel decisions that permitted "public official" and "public figure" plaintiffs to recover damages on a showing of "actual malice," the Court here allowed plaintiff's discovery inquiries into editorial processes and "state of mind" of defendant. Held that such efforts to show actual malice are not barred under the First Amendment.

Circumstances: The action resulted from a report on the CBS television program, "The Selling of Colonel Herbert," produced and edited by Barry Lando and narrated by Mike Wallace as part of a *60 Minutes* segment. The show was aired on Feb. 4, 1973, and Lt. Col. Herbert, who had served in Vietnam and who received widespread media attention in 1969–70 when he accused his superior officers of covering up reports of war crimes, alleged that the program and a magazine article written by Lando falsely portrayed him as a liar. Herbert's attorneys deposed Lando on 26 separate occasions over a year and filled 2,903 pages of transcript with an additional 240 exhibits. Lando, claiming a First Amendment privilege, refused to answer questions that he thought concerned the editorial process. District Court Judge Charles Haight, in New York, rejected the claim and held that Lando had to answer the questions because the defendant's state of mind was of "central importance" to the issue of malice. A panel of the Second Circuit Court of Appeals reversed, saying that such an "inquisition" would chill the editorial process. The Supreme Court, on certiorari, reversed by a 6-to-3 vote. The Court said that as long as the public-figure plaintiff has a special burden of proof in a defamation case, denial of "discovery of editorial state of mind would make that burden unduly onerous."

Opinion: Federal Rules of Civil Procedure 26(b) permits discovery of any matter "relevant to the subject matter involved" in a pending action if it would either be admissable in evidence or "appears reasonably calculated to lead to the discovery of admissible evidence." In an opinion written by Justice Byron R. White and joined by Chief Justice Warren E. Burger and Justices Harry A. Blackmun, Lewis F. Powell, Jr., William H. Rehnquist, and John Paul Stevens, the Court held that because the defendant's state of mind was central to the issue of actual malice, the plaintiff's questions were relevant to his efforts to learn whether the defendant had any reason to doubt the veracity of some sources or to prefer one source over another. The Court refused to construe the First and 14th Amendments as providing further protection for the press "than has hitherto been recognized," specifically the barring of inquiries into the editorial processes of those responsible for the publication of damaging falsehoods. White noted that "according an absolute privilege to the editorial process of a media defendant in a libel case is not required, authorized, or presaged by our prior cases. To erect an impenetrable barrier to the plaintiff's use of such evidence on his side . . . is a matter of some substance, particularly when defendants themselves are prone to assert their

good-faith belief in the truth of their publications, and libel plaintiffs are required to prove knowing or reckless falsehood with
'convincing clarity.'" Justice Powell, in a separate opinion, concurred that First Amendment rights "should not be expanded to
create an evidentiary privilege." He added that, in supervising
discovery in a libel suit by a public figure, a district court has a
duty to consider First Amendment interests as well as the private
interests of the plaintiff.

Justice William J. Brennan, Jr., dissenting in part, agreed that
the press had no "editorial privilege" shielding it from discovery,
but he said that the determination of privilege, when applicable,
should depend on the circumstances of a particular case. "If . . . a
public-figure plaintiff is able to establish, to the prima facie satis-
faction of a trial judge, that the publication at issue constitutes
defamatory falsehood, the claim of damaged reputation becomes
specific and demonstrable, and the editorial privilege must yield."
Justice Potter Stewart, in dissent, noted that, according to the
constitutional rule of *New York Times Co. v. Sullivan* (1964),
"inquiry into the broad 'editorial process' is simply not relevant in
a libel suit brought by a public figure against a publisher. And if
such an inquiry is not relevant, it is not permissible." Citing the
restrictions imposed by *New York Times* and its progeny, the
justice wrote: "The gravaman of such a lawsuit thus concerns that
which was in fact published. What was *not* published has nothing
to do with the case. And liability ultimately depends upon the
publisher's state of knowledge of the falsity of what he published,
not at all upon his motivation in publishing it—not at all, in other
words, upon actual malice as those words are ordinarily understood." Earlier in his dissent, Stewart had noted that in common
usage "malice" means "ill will" or "hostility" but that the constitutional standard of "actual malice" has nothing to do with hostility or
ill will. Justice Thurgood Marshall, also in dissent, expressed the
view that the press should be protected from unnecessarily protracted or tangential inquiry and that discovery requests should be
measured against a strict standard of relevance. Although no privilege was called for as to the discovery of an individual journalist's
state of mind, Marshall would foreclose discovery in defamation
cases as to the substance of editorial conversation. "To preserve a
climate of free interchange among journalists, the confidentiality of
their conversation must be guaranteed."

Referenced Cases: *New York Times Co. v. Sullivan,* 376 U.S. 254 (1964), *Rosenblatt v. Baer,* 383 U.S. 75 (1966), *Linn v. Plant Guard Workers,* 383 U.S. 53 (1966), *Beckley Newspapers Corp. v. Hanks,* 389 U.S. 81 (1967), *Curtis Publishing Co. v. Butts,* 388 U.S. 130 (1967), *Time, Inc. v. Hill,* 385 U.S. 374 (1967), *St. Amant v. Thompson,* 390 U.S. 727 (1968), *Greenbelt Cooperative Publishing Assn. v. Bresler,* 398 U.S. 6 (1970), *Monitor Patriot Co. v. Roy,* 401 U.S. 265 (1971), *Time, Inc. v. Pape,* 401 U.S. 279 (1971), *Ocala Star-Banner Co. v. Damron,* 401 U.S. 295 (1971), *Rosenbloom v. Metromedia, Inc.,* 403 U.S. 29 (1971), *Letter Carriers v. Austin,* 418 U.S. 264 (1974), *Gertz v. Robert Welch, Inc.,* 418 U.S. 323 (1974), and *Time, Inc. v. Firestone,* 424 U.S. 448 (1976), cases defining the elements of the constitutional restrictions imposed by *Times v. Sullivan* and its progeny, especially the "actual malice" threshold for public-official and public-figure plaintiffs; *Beauharnais v. Illinois,* 343 U.S. 250 (1952), and *Chaplinsky v. New Hampshire,* 315 U.S. 568 (1942), regarding libelous utterances as unprotected speech; *Miami Herald Publishing Co. v. Tornillo,* 418 U.S. 241 (1974), and *Columbia Broadcasting System, Inc. v. Democratic National Committee,* 412 U.S. 94 (1973), on "required" publication; *McCarthy v. Arndstein,* 266 U.S. 34 (1924), and *U.S. v. Nixon,* 418 U.S. 683 (1974), describing privilege against self-incrimination and executive privilege; *Schlagenhauf v. Holden,* 379 U.S. 104 (1964), and *Hickman v. Taylor,* 329 U.S. 495 (1947), on informing litigants about deposition-discovery rules; *First National Bank of Boston v. Belotti,* 435 U.S. 765 (1978), and *Saxbe v. Washington Post Co.,* 417 U.S. 843 (1974), on public interest in free flow of news and commentary; *Roviaro v. U.S.,* 353 U.S. 53 (1957), regarding qualified "informer's privilege" for the "furtherance and protection of the public interest in effective law enforcement"; *Whitney v. California,* 274 U.S. 357 (1927), on First Amendment serving self-government; *NAACP v. Button,* 371 U.S. 415 (1963), regarding overbroad statutes that prohibit constitutional rights; *Dombrowski v. Pfister,* 380 U.S. 479 (1965), and *Thornhill v. Alabama,* 310 U.S. 88 (1940), on "vindication of freedom of expression"; *Grosjean v. American Press Co.,* 297 U.S. 233 (1936), and *Red Lion Broadcasting Co. v. FCC,* 395 U.S. 367 (1969), on right of public to receive information; *Branzburg v. Hayes,* 408 U.S. 665 (1972), on preservation of the "informative function" of the press and broadcast media; *Pittsburgh Press Co. v. Pittsburgh Commission on Human Relations,* 413 U.S. 376 (1973), on regulation of the editorial process; *NLRB v. Sears, Roebuck & Co.*, 421 U.S. 132 (1975), on "predecisional communications" within Executive Branch.

Further Reading:
66 *California L. Rev.* 1127 (Sept. 1978).
78 *Columbia L. Rev.* 448 (March 1978).
9 *Cumberland L. Rev.* 277 (Spring 1978).
47 *George Washington L. Rev.* 286 (Nov. 1978).
1978 *Northwestern L. Rev.* 583 (Oct. 1978).
31 *Stanford L. Rev.* 1035 (July 1979).
13 *Tulsa L. J.* 837 (1978).
1978 *Univ. Illinois L. Forum* 605 (1978).
47 *Univ. Missouri-KC L. Rev.* 273 (Winter 1978).
31 *Vanderbilt L. Rev.* 375 (March 1978).

1979 *Ronald R. Hutchinson v. William Proxmire and Morton Schwartz*, 443 U.S. 111, 61 L.Ed.2d 411, 99 S.Ct. 2675, 5 Med.L.Rptr. 1279

Argued: April 17, 1979.

Decided: June 26, 1979.

Summary: A U.S. senator held not immune from defamation action, and a scientist, the plaintiff, held not a "public figure."

Circumstances: Proxmire, a senator from Wisconsin, initiated his "Golden Fleece of the Month Award" in March 1975 to publicize what he believed were the most egregious examples of wasteful government spending. The second award, in April 1975, went to the National Science Foundation, NASA, and the Office of Naval Research for spending nearly half a million dollars for seven years to support Hutchinson's research, most of it having to do with the emotional behavior of certain animals. Proxmire learned of Hutchinson's funded research from Schwartz, his legislative assistant, who helped prepare the senator's Senate speech on the subject, excerpts of which were sent in a press release to the news media. Comment also appeared in a newsletter from Proxmire's office. On April 16, 1976, Hutchinson filed suit in the District Court for the Western District of Wisconsin, alleging that he had suffered a loss of respect in his profession and loss of income and ability to earn income in the future. The court granted Proxmire summary judgment, ruling that the speech or debate clause afforded the senator absolute immunity, that Hutchinson was a public figure, and that the senator had not acted with actual malice. The Court of Appeals for the Seventh Circuit affirmed. On certiorari, the Supreme Court reversed and remanded to the Court of Appeals.

Opinion: Chief Justice Warren E. Burger wrote the 8-to-1 opinion, joined by Justices Byron R. White, Thurgood Marshall, Harry A. Blackmun, Lewis F. Powell, Jr., William H. Rehnquist, John Paul Stevens, and, in part, Potter Stewart. William J. Brennan, Jr., dissented. Research behavioral scientist Ronald Hutchinson was found not to be a public figure, despite lower court determinations. The fact that Hutchinson received substantial federal funds did not make him a public figure, nor did the fact that his research findings appeared in professional journals. "Neither of those factors," Burger wrote, "demonstrates that Hutchinson was a public figure prior to the controversy engendered by the Golden Fleece Award; his access, such as it was, came after the alleged libel." Burger said that Hutchinson had not thrust himself or his views into public controversy to influence others. Proxmire's concern about general public expenditures, which is shared by most and relates to most such expenditures, was not sufficient to make the researcher a public figure. "If it were, everyone who received or benefited from the myriad public grants for research could be classified a public figure—a conclusion that our previous opinions have rejected." Moreover, Burger said, Hutchinson at no time had assumed any role of public prominence in the broad question of concern about expenditures. Finally, Hutchinson's access to the media, a factor in determining public figure status, was limited to responding to the Golden Fleece Award. On the lower court's determination that Proxmire was protected by the speech or debate clause of the Constitution, Burger said that speech in the Senate would have been wholly immune and available to the public in the Congressional Record. "But neither the newsletters nor the press release was 'essential to the deliberations of the Senate' and neither was part of the deliberative process." Justice Stewart agreed in part by the *dicta* in Footnote 10, that "libelous remarks in the follow-up telephone calls to executive agencies . . . are not protected" by the speech or debate clause. Justice Brennan, in a brief dissent, said that public criticism by legislators of unnecessary governmental expenditures, "whatever its form," is a legislative act shielded by the speech or debate clause.

Referenced Cases: *New York Times v. Sullivan*, 376 U.S. 254 (1964), setting the standards of "actual malice," "public official," and "public figure"; *Doe v. McMillan*, 412 U.S. 306 (1973), *Dombrowski v. Eastland*, 387 U.S. 82 (1967), and *Eastland v. U.S. Servicemen's Fund*, 421 U.S. 491 (1975), *Gravel v. U.S.*, 408 U.S. 606 (1972), *U.S. v. Brewster*, 408 U.S. 501 (1972), and *Kilbourn v. Thompson*, 103 U.S. 168 (1881), on the speech or debate clause; *Time Inc. v. Firestone*, 424 U.S. 448 (1976), *Gertz v. Robert Welch, Inc.*, 418 U.S. 323 (1974), *Rosenbloom v. Metromedia*, 403 U.S. 29 (1971), *St. Amant v. Thompson*, 390 U.S. 727 (1968), *Curtis Publishing v. Butts*, 388 U.S. 130 (1967), and *Rosenblatt v. Baer*, 383 U.S. 75 (1966), on the Court's balancing of vigorous debate on public issues and protection to individual reputation.

Further Reading:
65 *ABA J.* 1230 (Aug. 1979).
9 *Capital Univ. L. Rev.* 729 (Summer 1980).
30 *DePaul L. Rev.* 1 (Fall 1980).
68 *Georgia L. J.* 783 (Feb. 1980).
93 *Harvard L. Rev.* 161 (Nov. 1979).
7 *Hastings Const. L. Q.* 325 (Winter 1980).
14 *John Marshall L. Rev.* 263 (Fall 1980).
26 *Loyola L. Rev.* 159 (Winter 1980).
4 *Oklahoma City Univ. L. Rev.* 17 (Fall 1979).
See also under *Wolston v. Reader's Digest*, 443 U.S. 157 (1979), decided the same day.

1979   *Ilya Wolston v. Reader's Digest Association, Inc. et al., 443 U.S. 157, 61*

L.Ed.2d 450, 99 S.Ct. 2701, 5 Med.L.Rptr. Supplement 5

Argued: April 17, 1979.

Decided: June 26, 1979.

Summary: Plaintiff, who refused to testify before a federal grand jury on Soviet spy activities, held not a "public figure" in defamation action, despite media attention.

Circumstances: In 1974, the Reader's Digest Association published a book, *KGB, the Secret Work of Soviet Agents*, by John Barron. Referring to disclosures by investigative bodies in Great Britain and the United States, Barron identified Wolston as a Soviet agent in the United States. Wolston sued in the District Court for the District of Columbia, claiming that the passages on his indictment for espionage were false and defamatory. In 1957–58, a special federal grand jury in New York City had conducted a major investigation into the activities of Soviet intelligence agents in the United States, resulting in the arrest and conviction of Wolston's aunt and uncle, Myra and Jack Soble. Wolston was interviewed on several occasions by FBI agents, but he failed to appear before the grand jury because of mental depression over the entire episode. The news media wrote of the events. Wolston pleaded guilty to having failed to respond to the grand jury subpoena. He received a one-year suspended sentence and was placed on probation for three years, conditioned on his cooperation with the grand jury in any further espionage inquiries. He eventually returned to private life. At no time was Wolston indicted for espionage, as indicated in Barron's book in 1974. Meanwhile, the district court granted Reader's Digest and Barron summary judgment, holding that Wolston was a public figure. The Court of Appeals for the District of Columbia affirmed. The Supreme Court reversed.

Opinion: Justice William H. Rehnquist wrote for six members in the 8-to-1 decision, including Chief Justice Warren E. Burger and Justices Potter Stewart, Byron R. White, Lewis F. Powell, Jr., and John Paul Stevens. Harry A. Blackmun, joined by Thurgood Marshall, concurred separately. William J. Brennan, Jr., dissented, as he had in *Hutchinson v. Proxmire* (1979), a similar case decided the same day. Rehnquist said the Court had provided constitutional protection for stories about public figures in large part because such people voluntarily risk injury caused by defamatory falsehoods. But this plaintiff had not thrust himself to the forefront of the public controversy involving the investigation of Soviet espionage in the United States. Wolston was "dragged unwillingly" into the spotlight. "The mere fact that [Wolston] voluntarily chose not to appear before the grand jury, knowing that his action might be attended by publicity, is not decisive on the question of public figure status." Rehnquist said Wolston never discussed the espionage investigation with the press and confined his involvement to what was necessary in defending himself in court. He played a minor role in the controversy, Rehnquist said. Nor had Wolston engaged the public's attention in order to influence the public issues involved. He did not "in any way seek to arouse public sentiment in his favor and against the investigation. A private individual is not automatically transformed into a public figure just by becoming involved in or associated with a matter that attracts public attention." Blackmun added that the lapse of 16 years between Wolston's participation in the espionage controversy and publication of the defamatory reference was sufficient to erase whatever public-figure attributes he may have once possessed. Justice Brennan, in dissent, said Wolston was a limited public figure. He urged remand on the ground of the existence of actual malice by the book's author.

Referenced Cases: See under *Hutchinson v. Proxmire*, 443 U.S. 111 (1979), decided by similar rationale the same day.

Further Reading:

65 *ABA J.* 1545 (Oct. 1979).
1980 *Brigham Young Univ. L. Rev.* 450 (1980).
13 *Loyola Univ., LA, L. Rev.* 179 (Dec. 1979).
58 *No. Carolina L. Rev.* 1042 (June 1980).
7 *Ohio Northern L. Rev.* 125 (Jan. 1980).
1980 *Wisconsin L. Rev.* 568 (1980).
See also under *Hutchinson v. Proxmire*, 443 U.S. 111 (1979), decided the same day.

1984 *Kathy Keeton v. Hustler Magazine, Inc., et al.,* 465 U.S. 770, 79 L.Ed.2d 790, 104 S.Ct. 1473, 10 Med.L.Rptr. 1405

Argued: Nov. 8, 1983.

Decided: March 20, 1984.

Summary: Regular circulation of a magazine in a "forum state" held sufficient for jurisdiction in a libel action based on the magazine's contents. A restatement of the legal theory of long-arm jurisdiction.

Circumstances: Keeton, a resident of New York, sued *Hustler* magazine, an Ohio corporation, for libel in the state of New Hampshire, which has a six-year statute of limitations. The District Court for New Hampshire dismissed her suit because it believed that the due process clause of the 14th Amendment forbade the application of the state's long-arm statute in order to acquire personal jurisdiction over *Hustler*. The Court of Appeals for the First Circuit affirmed, noting that "the New Hampshire tail is too small to wag so large an out-of-state dog." The Supreme Court reversed.

Opinion: Justice William H. Rehnquist wrote for eight members in the 9-to-0 opinion. He was joined by Chief Justice Warren E. Burger and Justices Byron R. White, Thurgood Marshall, Harry A. Blackmun, Lewis F. Powell, Jr., John Paul Stevens, and Sandra Day O'Connor. William J. Brennan, Jr., concurred separately. Rehnquist said that *Hustler*'s regular circulation in New Hampshire, 10,000–15,000 copies of the magazine each month, was sufficient to support an assertion of jurisdiction. "False statements of fact harm both the subject of the falsehood *and* the readers of the statement," Rehnquist wrote. "New Hampshire may rightly employ its libel laws to discourage the deception of its citizens." The state may extend its concern for the injury that in-state libel inflicts on a nonresident, he added. Justice Brennan, concurring on narrower grounds, said that an assertion of jurisdiction was valid irrespective of the state's interest in enforcing its libel laws or its unique statute of limitations. The same day, a unanimous Court ruled, in *Calder v. Jones* (1984), that California courts could assume jurisdiction in a case brought by a resident against a newspaper published in Florida but circulated in California.

Referenced Cases: *Klaxon Co. v. Stentor Co.*, 313 U.S. 487 (1941), on so-called single publication role; *World-Wide Volkswagen Corp. v. Woodson*, 444 U.S. 286 (1980), and *International Shoe Co. v. Washington*, 326 U.S. 310 (1945), on due process clause requirement of jurisdiction over nonresident defendant; *Shaffer v. Heitner*, 433 U.S. 186 (1977), and *Rush v. Savchuk*, 444 U.S. 320 (1980), regarding relationship among the defendant, the forum, and the litigation; *Gertz v. Robert Welch, Inc.*, 418 U.S. 323 (1974), holding that "there is no constitutional value in false statements of fact"; *Hanson v. Denckla*, 357 U.S. 235 (1958), on the issue as personal jurisdiction, not choice of law; *Perkins v. Benquet Mining Co.*, 342 U.S. 437 (1952), on jurisdiction despite lack of residency by either party.

Further Reading:
1984 *Arizona St. L. J.* 459 (1984).
34 *Catholic Univ. L. Rev.* 1125 (Summer 1985).
7 *Communication & Law* 27 (Aug. 1985).
18 *Creighton L. Rev.* 125 (1984/85).
98 *Harvard L. Rev.* 165 (Nov. 1984).
16 *St. Mary's L. J.* 513 (1985).
30 *Villanova L. Rev.* 193 (Feb. 1985).

Note: Also on that day the Court decided *Calder v. Jones*, 465 U.S. 783 (1984), ruling unanimously that the California court had personal jurisdiction over a Florida newspaper reporter and editor in a libel action brought by a California resident. Shirley Jones, the actress, sued Ian Calder and John South for an article they wrote and edited in Florida for the *National Enquirer*. The Superior Court had granted a motion to quash for lack of personal jurisdiction, ruling that First Amendment considerations weighed more heavily than an assertion of jurisdiction. It said, however, that Jones could sue the publisher, not the reporters, in California. The state court of appeals reversed. On certiorari, the U.S. Supreme Court affirmed that judgment. Justice Rehnquist, who also wrote the *Keeton v. Hustler* opinion, noted that material for the article was drawn from California sources and the brunt of the harm would be suffered in California. "An individual injured in California need not go to Florida to seek redress from persons who, though remaining in Florida, knowingly cause the injury in California."

1984 **Bose Corporation v. Consumers Union of United States, Inc., 466 U.S. 485, 80 L.Ed.2d 502, 104 S.Ct. 1949, 10 Med.L.Rptr. 1625**

Argued: Nov. 8, 1983.

Decided: April 30, 1984.

Summary: Held that federal appellate judges must independently review both the facts and the law in cases governed by *New York Times Co. v. Sullivan* (1964) to determine if "actual malice" has been established with "convincing clarity." A technical ruling, it means that media defendants who lose a libel trial because of a finding of actual malice can obtain an independent de novo review of the decision through appeal to a higher court.

Circumstances: Bose, a stereo loudspeaker manufacturer, brought a product disparagement suit against Consumers Union, publisher of *Consumer Reports* magazine, alleging that a statement about the Bose 901 speaker system was false and defamatory. The article said that the sound of individual musical instruments "tended to wander about the room." Following lengthy discovery, the District Court for Massachusetts refused to dismiss the suit and held that the manufacturer was a public figure within the meaning of the rule precluding recovery unless the plaintiff could prove by "clear and convincing evidence" that the publisher made a "false and disparaging statement" with actual malice. In his judgment for Bose, the judge said that the article contained a false statement of "fact," because the sound of instruments tended to wander "along the wall" between the speakers, rather than "about the room" as reported in the magazine. The judge found clear and convincing proof of actual malice in the author's choice of the word "about." After a 19-day trial, another court concluded in 1981 that Bose had lost $106,296 in sales because of the article and that Dr. Amar G. Bose, inventor and manufacturer of the 901 system, had spent $9,000 to offset the article's effect. Consumers Union was ordered to pay a total award of $115,296. The Court of Appeals for the First Circuit reversed, holding that its review of the "actual malice" determination was not limited to the clearly erroneous standard of Rule 52(a) of the Federal Rules of Civil Procedure, but that it must perform a de novo review of the facts. The Supreme Court affirmed.

Opinion: Justice John Paul Stevens, expressing the views of Justices Harry A. Blackmun, William J. Brennan, Jr., Thurgood Marshall, and Lewis F. Powell, Jr., held that the "clearly erroneous" requirement of Rule 52(a) of the Federal Rules of Civil Procedure does not prescribe the standard for reviewing a determination of actual malice. He said that *New York Times Co. v. Sullivan,* which set the actual malice standard for public-official and public-figure plaintiffs, imposed a special obligation on appeals courts considering libel judgments against the media. In such cases, courts must "'make an independent examination of the whole record' in order to make sure 'that the judgment does not constitute a forbidden intrusion on the field of free expression.'" Stevens explained that, in reviewing a libel judgment against the news media, the judges have "a constitutional responsibility that cannot be delegated to the trier of fact, whether the factfinding function be performed in the particular case by jury or by a trial judge." Chief Justice Warren E. Burger concurred. Justice Byron R. White dissented, noting that the question whether the defamatory statement was written with actual knowledge of its falsity was a matter of historical fact not subject to de novo review. Justice William H. Rehnquist, joined by Sandra Day O'Connor, dissented on the ground that the "clearly erroneous" standard of Rule 52(a) applies to actual malice determinations, which involve no more than findings about the mens rea of an author, "findings which appellate courts are simply ill-prepared to make in any context, including the First Amendment context."

Referenced Cases: *New York Times Co. v. Sullivan,* 376 U.S. 254 (1964), for the "actual malice" standard; *Gertz v.*

Welch, Inc., 418 U.S. 323 (1974), for a definition of "public figure" and the need for ideas to compete; *Inwood Laboratories, Inc. v. Ives Laboratories, Inc.*, 456 U.S. 844 (1982), *Pullman-Standard v. Swint*, 456 U.S. 273 (1982), and *U.S. v. U.S. Gypsum Co.* (1948), 333 U.S. 364, on the meaning of Rule 52(a); *NAACP v. Claiborne Hardware Co.*, 458 U.S. 886 (1982), *Greenbelt Cooperative Publishing Assn. v. Bresler*, 398 U.S. 6 (1970), and *St. Amant v. Thompson*, 390 U.S. 727 (1968), on appellate court obligation to make an independent judgment to ensure free expression; *Chaplinsky v. New Hampshire*, 315 U.S. 568 (1942), *Hess v. Indiana*, 414 U.S. 105 (1973), *Street v. New York*, 394 U.S. 576 (1969), *Beauharnais v. Illinois*, 343 U.S. 250 (1952), *Brandenburg v. Ohio*, 395 U.S. 444 (1964), *Roth v. U.S.*, 354 U.S. 476 (1957), and *New York v. Ferber*, 458 U.S. 747 (1982), regarding the limits of First Amendment protection, that is, fighting words, libelous speech, incitement to riot, obscenity, and child pornography; *Terminiello v. Chicago*, 337 U.S. 1 (1949), and *Police Department of Chicago v. Mosley*, 408 U.S. 92 (1972), on the principle of "viewpoint neutrality"; *Edwards v. South Carolina*, 372 U.S. 229 (1963), on the duty "to make an independent examination of the whole record"; *Pennekamp v. Florida*, 328 U.S. 331 (1946), regarding the examination of statements for "threat of clear and present danger"; *Miller v. California*, 413 U.S. 15 (1973), and *Jenkins v. Georgia*, 418 U.S. 153 (1974), on "essentially questions of fact" and independent examination of evidence regarding a motion picture; *Speiser v. Randall*, 357 U.S. 513 (1958), on "the line between speech unconditionally guaranteed and speech which may legitimately be regulated"; *One, Inc. v. Olesen*, 355 U.S. 371 (1958), and *Sunshine Book Co. v. Summerfield*, 355 U.S. 372 (1958), on the due process clause of the 14th Amendment; *Time, Inc. v. Pape*, 401 U.S. 279 (1971), on "actual malice" as a "constitutional rule"; *Monitor Patriot Co. v. Roy*, 401 U.S. 265 (1971), on, "as a matter of constitutional law," the jury not being allowed to determine the relevancy of a defamatory statement to plaintiff's status as a public figure; *Moore v. Chesapeake & Ohio R. Co.*, 340 U.S. 573 (1951), regarding the trier of fact and unbelieved testimony; *Herbert v. Lando*, 441 U.S. 153 (1979), on limiting liability to instances where some culpability is present to eliminate the risk of censorship and suppression of truthful matter; *Fiske v. Kansas*, 274 U.S. 380 (1927), on the intermingling of federal law and a finding of fact that necessitates review.

Further Reading:
71 *Cornell L. Rev.* 477 (Jan. 1986).
8 *Hamline L. Rev.* 105 (Jan. 1985).
19 *Suffolk Univ. L. Rev.* 94 (Spring 1985).
7 *Univ. Arkansas, Little Rock, L. J.* 741 (1984).
60 *Washington L. Rev.* 503 (1985).

1985 ***Dun & Bradstreet, Inc. v. Greenmoss Builders, Inc., 472 U.S. 749, 86 L.Ed.2d 593, 105 S.Ct. 2939, 11 Med.L.Rptr. 2417***

Reargued: Oct. 3, 1984.

Decided: June 26, 1985.

Summary: Not all plaintiffs involved in public issues should have to prove actual malice. *Gertz v. Robert Welch, Inc.* (1974) held not applicable against "nonmedia" libel defendants.

Circumstances: Greenmoss, a construction contractor, sued Dun & Bradstreet, a credit reporting agency, for libel for circulating a false report that the contractor had filed for bankruptcy. The Vermont courts held that because Dun & Bradstreet was not a news medium, the state's common law should prevail, permitting the jury to presume damages. The jury awarded Greenmoss $50,000 in compensatory damages and $300,000 in punitive damages. The Supreme Court upheld the verdict, 5-to-4. The trial court also granted Greenmoss' motion for a new trial on the ground that instructions to the jury permitted it to award damages on a lesser showing than actual malice, as believed required by the *Gertz* decision. The Supreme Court of Vermont reversed, saying *Gertz* did not apply to nonmedia libel actions. The U.S. Supreme Court affirmed.

Opinion: Justice Lewis F. Powell, Jr., joined by Justices William H. Rehnquist and Sandra Day O'Connor, said that the First Amendment interest in speech on matters of purely private concern is less than that for matters of public concern, and does not outweigh the state interest in awarding presumed and punitive damages. Chief Justice Warren E. Burger, in a separate concurring opinion, added that *Gertz* should be overruled and believed that that decision was limited to expressions of general public importance. Justice Byron R. White, who also concurred and agreed with Burger's view of *Gertz*, added that the First Amendment provides no more protection to the press in defamation suits than it does to others exercising their freedom of speech.

Justice William J. Brennan, Jr., joined by Justices Thurgood Marshall, Harry A. Blackmun, and John Paul Stevens in dissent, wrote that the *Gertz* rule applies to any false statements regardless of whether they implicate a matter of public importance. "The only question presented is whether a jury award of presumed and punitive damages based on less than a showing of actual malice is constitutionally permissible. *Gertz* provides a forthright negative answer." They accused Powell and White of cutting away "the protective mantle of *Gertz*."

Referenced Cases: *Gertz. v. Robert Welch, Inc.,* 418 U.S. 323 (1974), restricting damages that a private individual can secure for a libel that involves a matter of public concern; *New York Times Co. v. Sullivan,* 376 U.S. 254 (1964), limiting the reach of state libel laws, encouraging robust and wide-open debate on public issues, establishing the "actual malice" standard; *Curtis Publishing Co. v. Butts,* 388 U.S. 130 (1967), extending protection to public figures; *Rosenbloom v. Metromedia, Inc.,* 403 U.S. 29 (1971), extending rule to matters of public or general interest; *Garrison v. Louisiana,* 379 U.S. 64 (1964), citing public affairs speech as the essence of self-government; *Connick v. Myers,* 461 U.S. 138 (1983), on the necessity of determining "public concern" speech as revealed by the whole record; *Joseph Burstyn, Inc. v. Wilson,* 343 U.S. 495 (1952), rejecting the argument that protected speech is diminished because it concerns economic matters.

Further Reading:
50 *Albany L. Rev.* 845 (Summer 1986).
1986 *Brigham Young Univ. L. Rev.* 233 (1986).
6 *California Law* 38 (Jan. 1986).
62 *Chicago-Kent L. Rev.* 297 (1985).
98 *Harvard L. Rev.* 847 (1985).
20 *Indiana L. Rev.* 767 (1987).

19 *John Marshall L. Rev.* 929 (Summer 1986).
48 *Ohio State L. J.* 513 (1987).
60 *St. John's L. Rev.* 144 (Fall 1985).
54 *Univ. Cincinnati L. Rev.* 1375 (1986).

1986   *Philadelphia Newspapers, Inc., et al. v. Maurice S. Hepps et al.*, 475 U.S. 767, 89 L.Ed.2d 783, 106 S.Ct. 1558, 12 Med.L.Rptr. 1977

Argued: Dec. 3, 1985.

Decided: April 21, 1986.

Summary: A private person suing the media for libel in connection with a matter of "public concern" must prove the alleged defamation false.

Circumstances: The Philadelphia *Inquirer* published a series of investigative articles between May 1975 and May 1976 alleging that Hepps (a principal stockholder in General Programming Inc., which franchises "Thrifty" stores) and several franchisees had links to organized crime and had attempted to influence Pennsylvania's governmental process. They brought libel action in a state court, which concluded that the state libel law, giving the defendant the burden of proving the truth of the statements, violated the Constitution. The jury ruled for the newspaper. The Pennsylvania Supreme Court viewed *Gertz v. Robert Welch, Inc.* (1974) as simply requiring the plaintiff to show fault. It held that to place the burden of showing truth on the defendant did not unconstitutionally inhibit free debate, and remanded for a new trial. On certiorari, the U.S. Supreme Court reversed and remanded to the Pennsylvania Supreme Court.

Opinion: Justice Sandra Day O'Connor wrote for the 5-to-4 Court, joined by Justices William J. Brennan, Jr., Thurgood Marshall, Harry A. Blackmun, and Lewis J. Powell, Jr. Dissenting were Chief Justice Warren E. Burger and Justices Byron R. White,

William H. Rehnquist, and John Paul Stevens, who wrote the minority opinion. Courts in some few states, Pennsylvania foremost among them, took the position that the language in *Gertz* allowed them to assume falsity in libel suits brought against media by private individuals. The Court overruled that interpretation in *Hepps*, holding that the First Amendment requires anyone who sues the media for libel in connection with a matter of public concern to bear the burden of proving with clear and convincing evidence that the defamatory statements are false. State courts are not permitted to hold to the common law assumption of falsity in media libel cases. Strongly suggested is that such action, directed at news media treatment of a public issue, cannot survive unless the plaintiff has convincing evidence of a false and defamatory assertion of fact. However, *Hepps* appears to leave open the possibility that a private person could prevail on some lesser standard of proof if the alleged libel concerned a private matter. "We believe that the common law's rule on falsity—that the defendant must bear the burden of proving truth—must similarly fall here to a constitutional requirement that the plaintiff bear the burden of showing falsity, as well as fault, before recovering damages." Further, O'Connor stated that the fact that the plaintiff's burden is weightier because of a state "shield" law, which allows media employees to refuse to divulge their sources, does not require a different constitutional standard than would prevail in the absence of such a law. Justice Brennan, with Blackmun, added that the Court's rules were applicable to both media and nonmedia defendants.

Justice Stevens, writing for the four dissenters, said that the First Amendment does not require private-figure plaintiffs to bear the burden of proving falsity even where matters of public concern are involved. "I simply do not understand . . . why a character assassin should be given an absolute license to defame by means of statements that can be neither verified nor disproven," Stevens wrote. "The danger of deliberate defamation by reference to unprovable facts is not a merely speculative or hypothetical concern."

Referenced Cases: *New York Times v. Sullivan*, 376 U.S. 254 (1964), on the extent to which constitutional protections limit a state's power to award damages in a libel action brought by a public official; *NAACP v. Button*, 371 U.S. 415 (1963), on "breathing space" for freedoms of expression; *Curtis Publishing Co. v. Butts*, 388 U.S. 130 (1967), and *Wolston v. Reader's Digest Assn.*, 443 U.S. 157 (1979), on "public figure" suits; *Dun & Bradstreet v. Greenmoss Builders*, 472 U.S. 749 (1985), involving not only private-figure plaintiff but also speech of private concern; *Garrison v. Louisiana*, 379 U.S. 64 (1964), and *Herbert v. Lando*, 441 U.S. 153 (1979), on civil defamation remedy and culpability; *Consolidated Edison Co. v. Public Service Comm'n of NY*, 447 U.S. 530 (1980), *First National Bank v. Bellotti*, 435 U.S. 765 (1978), and *Renton v. Playtime Theatres*, 475 U.S. 41 (1986), regarding government restrictions based on content, speaker, and secondary effects; *Rosenbloom v. Metromedia*, 403 U.S. 29 (1971), on proving falsity on matters of public concern; *Time Inc. v. Firestone*, 424 U.S. 448 (1976), on society's "equally compelling" need for judicial redress on libelous utterances.

Further Reading:

72 *ABA J.* 71 (July 1986).
20 *Creighton L. Rev.* 271 (1986/87).
64 *Denver Univ. L. Rev.* 65 (1987).
1986 *Detroit College of Law Rev.* 1219 (Winter 1986).
25 *Duquesne L. Rev.* 1075 (Summer 1987).
20 *Indiana L. Rev.* 767 (1987).
38 *Mercer L. Rev.* 785 (Spring 1987).
61 *Notre Dame L. Rev.* 125 (1986).
18 *Rutgers L. J.* 687 (Spring 1987).
61 *St. John's L. Rev.* 143 (Fall 1986).
18 *St. Mary's L. J.* 581 (1986).
58 *Temple L. Q.* 409 (Summer 1985).
54 *Texas L. Rev.* 1221 (1976).
12 *Thurgood Marshall L. Rev.* 253 (Fall 1986).
55 *Univ. Missouri-KC L. Rev.* 526 (Spring 1987).
61 *Virginia L. Rev.* 1349 (1975).
25 *William & Mary L. Rev.* 825 (1984).

1986   ***Jack Anderson et al. v. Liberty Lobby, Inc., and Willis A. Carto***, **477 U.S. 242, 91 L.Ed.2d 202, 106 S.Ct. 2505, 12 Med.L.Rptr. 2297**

Argued: Dec. 3, 1985.

Decided: June 25, 1986.

Summary: Public figures and other well-known plain-tiffs must show "clear and convincing" proof of defamation to ward off dismissal of libel cases in pretrial rulings.

Circumstances: Liberty Lobby, a citizen's group, and Willis Carto, its founder, sued columnist Jack Anderson for two articles published in *The Investigator* that portrayed the Carto group as neo-Nazi, anti-Semitic, racist, and fascist. At a pretrial hearing, the district court judge threw out the suit and awarded summary judgment to Anderson. The judge determined Carto a "public figure" who would have to prove that the magazine state-ments were false and that Anderson had acted with actual malice. No such proof existed, the court said. The Court of Appeals for the District of Columbia disagreed with the application of these standards and reinstated the suit, ruling that a determination of actual malice may only come after the plaintiff had had an oppor-tunity to present evidence. The Supreme Court reversed.

Opinion: Justice Byron R. White wrote for the 6-to-3 Court, joined by Justices Thurgood Marshall, Harry A. Blackmun, Lewis F. Powell, Jr., John Paul Stevens, and Sandra Day O'Connor. Dissenting were Chief Justice Warren E. Burger and Justices Wil-liam J. Brennan, Jr., and William H. Rehnquist. The Court applied the "actual malice" standard of *New York Times v. Sullivan* (1964) to pretrial hearings on libel actions by public figures. White said that in order to avoid a summary judgment a plaintiff must show by "clear and convincing" evidence that the allegedly defamatory state-ments were printed or broadcast with actual malice—knowledge that the statements were untrue or were disseminated with reckless disregard of the truth or falsehood. "Where the factual dispute concerns actual malice," White said, "the appropriate summary judg-ment question will be whether the evidence in the record could support a reasonable jury finding either that the plaintiff has shown actual malice by clear and convincing evidence or that the plaintiff has not." He said the mere existence of a scintilla of evidence in support of the plaintiff's position will be insufficient in a motion for summary judgment or a directed verdict.

Justice Brennan, dissenting separately, said that if a plaintiff presents evidence that either directly or by permissible inference supports all of the elements he needs to prove in order to prevail, the plaintiff has made out a prima facie case. A defendant's motion for summary judgment must fail regardless of the burden of proof that the plaintiff must meet. Justice Rehnquist, joined by Burger in dissent, argued that trial courts should not be required to apply the "clear and convincing evidence" standard in deciding motions of summary judgment in libel suits.

Referenced Cases: *New York Times v. Sullivan,* 376 U.S. 254 (1964), establishing the actual malice standard for public officials; *Curtis Publishing Co. v. Butts,* 388 U.S. 130 (1967), extending that standard to libel suits brought by public figures; *First National Bank of Arizona v. Cities Service Co.,* 391 U.S. 253 (1968), *Adickes v. S. H. Kress & Co.,* 398 U.S. 144 (1970), and *Dombrowski v. Eastland,* 387 U.S. 82 (1967), on summary judgment turning of proper jury question; *Brady v. Southern R. Co.,* 320 U.S. 476 (1943), Wilkerson v. McCarthy, 336 U.S. 53 (1949), *Improvement Co. v. Munson,* 14 Wall. 442 (1872), *Pleasants v. Fant,* 22 Wall. 116 (1875), and *Pennsylvania R. Co. v. Chamberlain,* 288 U.S. 333 (1933), on directed verdicts where reasonable minds differ; *Sartor v. Arkansas Gas Corp.,* 321 U.S. 620 (1944), and *Bill Johnson's Restaurant v. NLRB,* 461 U.S. 731 (1983), on whether the evidence presents a sufficient disagreement to require jury submission or whether it is so one-sided that one party must prevail; *Jackson v. Virginia,* 443 U.S. 307 (1979), on beyond-a-reasonable-doubt standard applied to a motion for acquittal; *Poller v. CBS,* 368 U.S. 464 (1962), on state of mind as a factor in summary judgment; *Bose Corp. v. Consumers Union,* 466 U.S. 485 (1984), regarding discredited testimony not sufficient for drawing contrary conclusion.

Further Reading:

100 *Harvard L. Rev.* 250 (Nov. 1986).
32 *Loyola L. Rev.* 1071 (Winter 1987).
39 *Oklahoma L. Rev.* 559 (Fall 1986).
20 *Univ. Calif., Davis, L. Rev.* 955 (Summer 1987).

1988 *Hustler Magazine and Larry C. Flynt v. Jerry Falwell, 485 U.S. ___, 99 L.Ed.2d 41, 108 S.Ct.*

Argued: Dec. 2, 1987.

Decided: Feb. 24, 1988.

Summary: The Court, reaffirming and extending its rules protecting criticism of public figures, even "outrageous" and offensive criticism, held First Amendment prohibited such persons from recovering damages for intentional infliction of emotional distress as the result of parody absent falsity made with actual malice.

Circumstances: In 1983 and 1984, *Hustler* had published a parody advertisement in which the Rev. Falwell was depicted as having committed incest with his mother in an outhouse. The ad carried in small print at the bottom, "Ad parody— not to be taken seriously." Falwell sought damages for invasion of privacy, libel, and "intentional infliction of emotional distress." The trial court threw out the invasion-of-privacy claim and the jury found no grounds for libel because the parody had not been represented as factual or understood as such by readers. However, Falwell was awarded $200,000 compensatory damages for emotional distress. The Court of Appeals for the Fourth Circuit upheld the ruling, Judge J. Harvie Wilkinson III dissenting from the denial of rehearing en banc. The Supreme Court overturned the award.

Opinion: Chief Justice William H. Rehnquist wrote the 8-to-0 decision. Justice Byron R. White filed a separate opinion concurring in the judgment. Justice Anthony M. Kennedy did not participate in the case. Rehnquist said: "The sort of robust political debate encouraged by the First Amendment is bound to produce speech that is critical of those who hold public office or those public figures who are [in former Chief Justice Earl Warren's words] 'intimately involved in the resolution of important public questions or, by reason of their fame, shape events in areas of concern to society at large.'" False statements of fact are valueless, but nevertheless inevitable in free debate. Although a bad motive, as in this case, may be deemed controlling for purposes of tort liability in other areas of law, Rehnquist said the First Amendment prohibits such a result in the area of public debate about public figures. Falwell had argued that because the material was "outrageously false," it was intentional, but the Court held that outrageous was so subjective a standard and prone to jury misuse that it simply could not withstand First Amendment challenges. Rather than "emotional distress," the Court held that public figures must prove libel to collect damages, presuming the false material was knowingly presented as factual truth. Justice White said separately that *New York Times v. Sullivan* (1964) had little to do with the case because the jury found that the ad contained no assertion of fact.

Referenced Cases: *New York Times Co. v. Sullivan*, 376 U.S. 254 (1964), on the "actual malice" standard; *Bose Corp. v. Consumers Union of U.S. Inc.*, 466 U.S. 485 (1984), on the freedom to speak one's mind as essential to the quest for truth; *Gertz v. Robert Welch Inc.*, 418 U.S. 323 (1974), on no such thing as a "false" idea; *Associated Press v. Walker* and *Curtis Publishing Co. v. Butts*, 388 U.S. 130 (1967), on public figures as those involved in public questions and in areas of public concern generally; *Baumgartner v. U.S.*, 322 U.S. 665 (1944), regarding Justice Felix Frankfurter on the "right to criticize public men and measures"; *Monitor Patriot Co. v. Roy*, 401 U.S. 265 (1971), on political candidates who cry foul when an opponent or reporter attempts to demonstrate the contrary of what they are saying; *Philadelphia Newspapers Inc. v. Hepps*, 475 U.S. 767 (1986), on "breathing space" required in freedoms of expression; *Zacchini v. Scripps-Howard Broadcasting Co.*, 433 U.S. 562 (1977), ruling that the actual malice standard is not applicable to right of publicity tort of appropriation; *Garrison v. Louisiana*, 379 U.S. 64 (1964), holding that the First Amendment even protects evil motivations; *NAACP v. Clairborne Hardware Co.*, 458 U.S. 886 (1982), on speech that embarrasses is also protected; *FCC v. Pacifica Foundation*, 438 U.S. 726 (1978), on government neutrality in the marketplace of ideas; *Street v. New York*, 394 U.S. 576 (1969), on the protection of offensive ideas; *Chaplinsky v. New Hampshire*, 315 U.S. 568 (1942), on "fighting words" lawfully punishable; *Dun & Bradstreet Inc. v. Greenmoss Builders Inc.*, 472 U.S. 749 (1985), holding that not all speech is of equal First Amendment importance.

Further Reading:

21 *Akron L. Rev.* 113 (Summer 1987).

1987 *Brigham Young Univ. L. Rev.* 313 (1987).

20 *Indiana L. Rev.* 767 (Fall 1987).

81 *Northwestern Univ. L. Rev.* 993 (Summer 1987).

48 *Ohio State L. J.* 513 (1987).

19 *Rutgers L. J.* 157 (Fall 1987).

Selected Bibliography

Anderson, David A., "Libel and Press Self-Censorship," 53 *Texas L. Rev.* 422 (1975).

———, "Reputation, Compensation, and Proof," 25 *William & Mary L. Rev.* 747 (1984).

Ashdown, Gerald, "Gertz and Firestone: A Study in Constitutional Policy-Making," 61 *Minnesota L. Rev.* 645 (1977).

Barton, James C., Sr., "Federalism—'87 and Beyond—A Confrontation: New York Times v. Sullivan," 18 *Cumberland L. Rev.* 111 (1987–88).

Berney, Arthur L., "Libel and the First Amendment—A New Constitutional Privilege," 51 *Virginia L. Rev.* 1 (Jan. 1965).

Bertelsman, William O., "The First Amendment and Protection of Reputation and Privacy—New York Times v. Sullivan and How it Grew," 56 *Kentucky L. J.* 718 (1967).

Bow, James, and Ben Silver, "Effects of Herbert v. Lando on Small Newspapers and TV Stations," 61 *Journalism Quarterly* 414 (Summer 1984).

Christie, George, "Defamatory Opinions and the Restatement (Second) of Torts," 75 *Michigan L. Rev.* 1621 (1977).

Cross, H. L., "Some Twilight Zones in Newspaper Libel," 1 *Cornell L. Q.* 238 (1916).

"Defamation and the First Amendment: New Perspectives," 25 *William & Mary L. Rev.* Special Issue (1983–84).

Delgado, Richard, "Words That Wound: A Tort Action for Racial Insults, Epithets and Name-Calling," 17 *Harvard Civil Rights–Civil Liberties L. Rev.* 133 (1982).

Drechsel, Robert E., and Deborah Moon, "Libel and Business Executives: The Public Figure Problem," 60 *Journalism Quarterly* 709 (Winter 1983).

Eaton, Joel, "The American Law of Defamation Through Gertz v. Robert Welch, Inc. and Beyond: An Analytical Primer," 61 *Virginia L. Rev.* 1349 (1975).

Epstein, Richard A., "Was New York Times v. Sullivan Wrong?" 53 *Univ. Chicago L. Rev.* 782 (1986).

"Falwell v. Flint: Intentional Infliction of Emotional Distress as a Threat to Free Speech," 81 *Northwestern Univ. L. Rev.* 993 (Summer 1987).

Frakt, Arthur N., "Evolving Law of Defamation: New York Times Co. v. Sullivan to Gertz v. Welch, Inc., and Beyond," 6 *Rutgers Camden L. J.* 471 (1975).

Franklin, Marc A., "Winners and Losers and Why: A Study of Defamation Litigation," 1980 *American Bar Found. Res. J.* 795 (1980).

———, "Suing the Media for Libel: A Litigation Study," 1981 *American Bar Found. Res. J.* 455 (1981).

———, "Good Names and Bad Law: A Critique of Libel Law and a Proposal," 18 *Univ. San Francisco L. Rev.* 1 (1983).

Franklin, Marc A., and Daniel Bussel, "The Plaintiff's Burden in Defamation: Awareness and Falsity," 25 *William & Mary L. Rev.* 825 (1984).

"Further Limits on Libel Actions—Extension of the New York Times Rule to Libels Arising from Discussion of 'Public Issues,'" 16 *Villanova L. Rev.* 955 (May 1971).

Gertz, Elmer, "Greenmoss Builders Inc. v. Dun & Bradstreet Inc. Invites Controversy," 19 *John Marshall L. Rev.* 929 (1986).

Ingbar, Stanley, "Defamation: A Conflict Between Reason and Decency," 65 *Virginia L. Rev.* 785 (1979).

Kalven, Harry, Jr., "The New York Times Case: A Note on the Central Meaning of the First Amendment," 1964 *Supreme Ct. Rev.* 191 (1964).

Langvardt, Arlen W., "Meida Defendants, Public Concerns, and Public Plaintiffs: Toward Fashioning Order from Confusion in Defamation Law," 49 *Pittsburgh L. Rev.* 91 (Fall 1987).

Lewis, Anthony, "New York Times v. Sullivan Reconsidered: Time to Return to 'The Central Meaning of the First Amendment,'" 83 *Columbia L. Rev.* 603 (1983).

———, "Annals of Law: The Sullivan Case," *The New Yorker* (Nov. 5, 1984).

Magnetti, Donald L., "In the End, Truth Will Win Out . . . Or Will It?" 52 *Missouri L. Rev.* 299 (Spring 1987).

Magruder, Calvert, "Mental and Emotional Disturbance in the Law of Torts," 49 *Harvard L. Rev.* 1033 (1936).

Mead, Terrance C., "Suing Media for Emotional Distress: A Multi-Method Analysis of Tort Law Evolution," 23 *Washburn L. J.* 24 (1983).

Nimmer, Melville B., "The Right to Speak from Times to Time: First Amendment Theory Applied to Libel and Misapplied to Privacy," 56 *California L. Rev.* 935 (1968).

Pedrick, Willard H., "Freedom of the Press and the Law of Libel: The Modern Revised Translation," 49 *Cornell L. Q.* 581 (1964).

Pierce, Samuel R., Jr., "Anatomy of an Historic Decision: New York Times Co. v. Sullivan," 43 *North Carolina L. Rev.* 315 (1965).

"Private Lives and Public Concerns: The Decade Since Gertz v. Robert Welch, Inc.," 51 *Brooklyn L. Rev.* 425 (Winter 1985).

Probert, Walter, "Defamation, A Camouflage of Psychic Interests: The Beginning of a Behavioral Analysis," 15 *Vanderbilt L. Rev.* 1173 (1962).

Reisman, David, "Democracy and Defamation: Control of Group Libel," 42 *Columbia L. Rev.* 727 (1942).

Robertson, David W., "Defamation and the First Amendment: In Praise of Gertz v. Robert Welch, Inc.," 54 *Texas L. Rev.* 199 (1976).

Rosen, Mark L., "Media Lament—The Rise and Fall of Involuntary Public Figures," 54 *St. John's L. Rev.* 487 (1980).

Sack, R. D. and R. J. Tofel, "First Steps Down the Road Not Taken: Emerging Limitations on Libel Damages," 90 *Dickinson L. Rev.* 609 (1986).

Silver, Isidore, "Libel, the 'Higher Truths' of Art, and the First Amendment," 126 *Univ. Pa. L. Rev.* 1065 (May 1978).

Smolla, Rodney, "Let the Author Beware: The Rejuvenation of the American Law of Libel," 132 *Univ. Pa. L. Rev.* 1 (1983).

Spencer, Dale R., "Establishment of Fault in Post-Gertz Libel Cases," 21 *St. Louis Univ. L. J.* 21 (1977).

Stevens, George E., "Negligence in Defamation Before Gertz," 56 *Journalism Quarterly* 832 (Winter 1979).

Titus, Herbert W., "Statement of Fact Versus Statement of Opinion—A Spurious Dispute in Fair Comment," 15 *Vanderbilt L. Rev.* 1203 (1962).

Van Alstyne, William W., "First Amendment Limitations on Recovery from the Press—An Extended Comment on the 'Anderson Solution,'" 24 *William & Mary L. Rev.* 793 (1984).

Watkins, John J., and Charles W. Schwartz, "Gertz and the Common Law of Defamation: Of Fault, Nonmedia Defendants, and Conditional Privileges," 15 *Texas Tech L. Rev.* 823 (1984).

Weiler, Paul C., "Defamation, Enterprise Liability, and Freedom of Speech," 17 *Toronto L. J.* 278 (1967).

Wilson, Deborah, "The Law of Libel and the Art of Fiction," 44 *Law & Contemporary Problems* 29 (1981).

Newsgathering

1965   *Louis Zemel v. Dean Rusk, Secretary of State, 381 U.S. 1, 14 L.Ed.2d 179, 85 S.Ct. 1271*

Argued: March 1, 1965.

Decided: May 3, 1965.

Summary: Upheld the authority of the secretary of state, as part of the Executive, to refuse to validate passports of U.S. citizens for travel to certain restricted countries as embodied in the Passport Act of 1926. On the peripheral issue of freedom of speech, such refusal does not deny rights guaranteed by the First Amendment.

Circumstances: Prior to 1961 no passport was required for travel anywhere in the Western Hemisphere. On Jan. 3 of that year, the United States broke diplomatic and consular relations with Cuba. Subsequently, the Department of State eliminated Cuba from the area for which passports were not required and declared all outstanding U.S. passports (except those held by individuals already in Cuba) to be invalid for travel to and in Cuba "unless specifically endorsed for such travel under the authority of the Secretary of State." When Zemel's request for validation was denied, he sued the secretary of state and the attorney general in the District Court for the District of Connecticut, seeking, among other relief, a judgment saying that he was entitled under the Constitution and laws of the United States to travel to Cuba. A divided three-judge panel granted the secretary of state's motion for summary judgment and dismissed the action against the attorney general. The Supreme Court affirmed.

Opinion: In a ruling on direct appeal, Chief Justice Earl Warren, joined by Justices William J. Brennan, Jr., Tom C. Clark,

John M. Harlan, Potter Stewart, and Byron R. White, said that the language of the Passport Act "is surely broad enough to authorize area restrictions, and there is no legislative history indicating an intent to exclude such restrictions from the grant of authority" to the Executive. In distinguishing the case from others, where political beliefs or associations restricted travel, in *Zemel* denial came not because of any characteristic peculiar to Zemel but rather because of foreign policy considerations affecting all citizens. To the extent that the secretary's refusal to validate passports for U.S. reporters wishing to visit Cuba acts as an inhibition on newsgathering, it is an inhibition of action, according to Warren. "The right to speak and publish does not carry with it the unrestrained right to gather information." The chief justice noted that unauthorized entry to such places as the White House can be prohibited, "but that does not make entry into the White House a First Amendment right."

Justice Hugo L. Black dissented on the ground that the Passport Act violated the provision in Article 1 of the Constitution granting all legislative power to Congress. "[R]egulation of passports, just like regulation of steel companies, is a law-making—not an executive, law-enforcing—function," Black said, referring to the Court's decision in *Youngstown Sheet & Tube Co. v. Sawyer*, 343 U.S. 579 (1952). "Our Constitution has ordained that laws restricting the liberty of our people can be enacted by the Congress and by the Congress only." Justice William O. Douglas, also in dissent and joined by Arthur J. Goldberg, wrote that restrictions on the right to travel in times of peace should be so particularized that a First Amendment right is not precluded unless some clear countervailing national interest stands in the way of its assertion. Goldberg, in a separate dissent that questioned the Executive's "inherent power" to impose travel restrictions in peacetime, noted "the long history of freedom of movement which Americans have enjoyed." Goldberg guessed that even if Congress were to consider "a more discriminately fashioned statute" in light of our commitment to freedom of the press, it would consent under any circumstances to prohibiting newsmen from traveling to foreign countries.

Referenced Cases: *Phillips v. U.S.*, 312 U.S. 246 (1941), on appellate jurisdiction of the District Court for the District of Connecticut; *Kent v. Dulles*, 357 U.S. 116 (1958), and

Aptheker v. Secretary of State, 378 U.S. 500 (1964), on relevance of the Fifth Amendment; *William Jameson & Co. v. Morgenthau,* 307 U.S. 171 (1939), and *Schneider v. Rusk,* 372 U.S. 224 (1963), on the convening of a three-judge court; *Idlewild Liquor Corp. v. Epstein,* 370 U.S. 713 (1962), on constitutionality of federal statutes; *Udall v. Tallman,* 380 U.S. 1 (1965), and *Norwegian Nitrogen Co. v. U.S.,* 288 U.S. 294 (1933), holding that, while construing a statute, courts must weigh its administration; *Edwards v. California,* 314 U.S. 160 (1941), on the right to travel within the United States; *U.S. v. Curtiss-Wright Corp.,* 299 U.S. 304 (1936), regarding presidential action in foreign and domestic affairs; *Evers v. Dwyer,* 358 U.S. 202 (1958), and *Terrace v. Thompson,* 263 U.S. 197 (1923), on actions for injunction or declaratory relief in advance of criminal prosecution; *NAACP v. Alabama,* 377 U.S. 288 (1958), and *Cantwell v. Connecticut,* 310 U.S. 296 (1940), on standards for adjudicating First Amendment rights.

Further Reading:

51 *ABA J.* 772 (Aug. 1965).
30 *Albany L. Rev.* 154 (Jan. 1966).
59 *American J. International L.* 835 (Oct. 1965).
32 *Brooklyn L. J.* 181 (Dec. 1965).
43 *Denver L. J.* 204 (Spring 1966).
1966 *Duke L. J.* 244 (Winter 1966).
4 *Duquesne Univ. L. Rev.* 170 (Fall 1965).
34 *Fordham L. Rev.* 143 (Oct. 1965).
34 *George Washington L. Rev.* 167 (Oct. 1965).
79 *Harvard L. Rev.* 123 (Nov. 1965).
14 *Kansas L. Rev.* 523 (March 1966).
50 *Minnesota L. Rev.* 977 (April 1966).
40 *St. John's L. Rev.* 280 (May 1966).
2 *Texas Int'l L. Forum* 99 (Winter 1966).
13 *UCLA L. Rev.* 470 (Jan. 1966).

1971   *New York Times Co. v. U.S. and U.S. v. The Washington Post Co.,* **403 U.S. 713, 29 L.Ed.2d 822, 91 S.Ct. 2140**

Argued: June 26, 1971.

Decided: June 30, 1971.

Summary: In a per curiam opinion, expressing the view of six justices, the majority held that the government had not met its burden of showing justification for the imposition of a prior restraint of expression.

Circumstances: In the District Court for the Southern District of New York, the government sought an injunction against the publication by the *New York Times* of the contents of a classified study, "History of U.S. Decision-Making Process on Viet Nam Policy," and in a similar suit in the District Court for the District of Columbia the government sought an injunction against the *Washington Post*. Each court denied relief. The Court of Appeals for the District of Columbia affirmed the judgment of the district court, but the Court of Appeals for the Second Circuit remanded to the district court for further hearings. On certiorari, the Supreme Court affirmed the judgment of the Court of Appeals for the District of Columbia, but reversed the judgment of the Court of Appeals for the Second Circuit and remanded with instructions to affirm the judgment of the District Court for the Southern District of New York. The case had begun the day after the first article of a planned series appeared in the *Times*, when Attorney General John Mitchell asked the paper to stop publication. When the *Times* refused, the government sought an injunction, and a temporary restraining order was granted. This case is known popularly as "The Pentagon Papers Case."

Opinion: In response to the government's request for a permanent restraining order to prohibit the *Times* and the *Post* from publishing the contents of a classified study, the short per curiam opinion noted the Court's previous reliance on the "heavy burden" test and held that the government had failed to meet that burden. The chief justice and each associate justice filed separate opinions. Justice Hugo L. Black, joined by William O. Douglas, said that the enjoining of the publication of news "would make a shambles of the First Amendment." Rather than condemn the newspapers in the name of "national security," Black said they should be commended for "serving the purpose that the Founding

Fathers saw so clearly." Douglas, joined by Black, added that the First Amendment leaves no room for governmental restraint on the press and called for open and robust debate on public questions. Justice William J. Brennan, Jr., in another concurring opinion, said that the First Amendment stands as an absolute bar to judicial restraints in circumstances of the kind presented by these cases. "The error that has pervaded these cases from the outset was the granting of any injunctive relief whatsoever, interim or otherwise." Justice Potter Stewart, joined by Byron R. White, stated that the Court was asked to perform a function that the Constitution gave to the Executive, not the Judiciary, and disputed the government's position that disclosure in these cases would result in direct, immediate, and irreparable damage to the nation and its people. White, joined by Stewart, conceded the extraordinary protection against prior restraints, but warned that termination of the ban on publication does not mean that the law now invites newspapers and others to publish sensitive documents or that they would be immune from criminal action if they did so. Justice Thurgood Marshall, concurring, noted that under the concept of separation of power the Court did not have the authority to protect the national interest, "to use its power of contempt to prevent behavior that Congress has specifically declined to prohibit."

Chief Justice Warren E. Burger, dissenting, said that the First Amendment right is not absolute and that the cases had been decided in unseemly haste. "We all crave speedier judicial processes but when judges are pressured as in these cases the result is a parody of the judicial function." Justice John M. Harlan, joined by Harry A. Blackmun and Burger, thought that the Court was almost irresponsibly feverish in dealing with the cases and that the doctrine against prior restraints did not prevent courts from taking the time to act responsibly. Blackmun, in a separate dissent, said that he could not subscribe to unlimited absolutism for the First Amendment at the cost of other constitutional provisions. He said he believed that the publication of critical documents would result in the death of soldiers, the destruction of alliances, the increased difficulty of negotiations with the enemy, the prolongation of the war, and further delay in the freeing of American prisoners.

Referenced Cases: *Hirabayashi v. U.S.*, 320 U.S. 81 (1943), on the power to wage war; *Near v. Minnesota*, 283 U.S. 697

(1931), on prior restraint of the press; *Organization for a Better Austin v. Keefe*, 402 U.S. 415 (1971), on the "heavy presumption" against the constitutional validity of prior restraint on expression; *New York Times Co. v. Sullivan*, 376 U.S. 254 (1964), on "uninhibited, robust, and wide-open" debate on public questions; *Schenck v. U.S.*, 249 U.S. 47 (1919), regarding the narrow class of cases—for example, in wartime—when the First Amendment's ban may be overridden; *Gorin v. U.S.*, 312 U.S. 19 (1941), on prohibited activities consonant with due process; *Youngstown Sheet & Tube Co. v. Sawyer*, 343 U.S. 579 (1952), on national security vis-à-vis disclosure of potentially damaging information; *Chicago & Southern Air Lines v. Waterman S. S. Corp.*, 333 U.S. 103 (1948), on presidential responsibility in the conduct of foreign affairs; *Northern Securities Co. v. U.S.*, 193 U.S. 197 (1904), for Justice Oliver Wendell Holmes's admonition: "Great cases like hard cases make bad law. For great cases are called great, not by reason of their real importance in shaping the law of the future, but because of some accident of immediate overwhelming interest which appeals to the feelings and distorts the judgment."

Further Reading:

57 *ABA J.* 918 (Summer 1971).
23 *Case Western Reserve L. Rev.* 3 (Nov. 1971).
17 *Howard L. J.* 579 (1972).
18 *Loyola L. Rev.* 151 (1971–72).
4 *Loyola Univ., Chicago, L. J.* 227 (Winter 1973).
5 *Loyola-LA., L. Rev.* 392 (April 1972).
47 *Notre Dame Lawyer* 927 (April 1972).
6 *Suffolk Univ. L. Rev.* 184 (Fall 1971).

1972   *Paul M. Branzburg v. John P. Hayes, In the Matter of Paul Pappas, and U.S. v. Earl Caldwell*, 408 U.S. 665, 33 L.Ed.2d 626, 92 S.Ct. 2646, 1 Med.L.Rptr. 2617

Argued: Feb. 23, 1972.

Decided: June 29, 1972.

Summary: In its first decision on the claim of journalists to a constitutional privilege against revealing confidential sources of information or confidential information, the Court ruled that the First Amendment accords a newsperson no privilege against appearing before a grand jury and answering questions on either the identity of his or her news sources or information that the newsperson received in confidence.

Circumstances: Branzburg, a reporter for the Louisville, Kentucky, *Courier-Journal*, wrote an article on his observations of two young Jefferson County residents synthesizing hashish from marijuana. A photo showed a pair of hands preparing the substance at a laboratory table. In the article Branzburg said he had promised not to identify the two hashish makers. During his appearance before the grand jury, Branzburg refused to identify the two informants. A state trial judge, John P. Hayes, ordered the reporter to answer the questions and rejected Branzburg's contention that the Kentucky reporters' privilege statute authorized his refusal to answer. The state court of appeals denied his petition, arguing that, though the shield law afforded a newsperson the privilege of refusing to reveal the identity of an informant, the statute did not permit a reporter to refuse to testify on events he had seen firsthand, including the identities of the persons he had observed. In a second case, Branzburg sought to quash a summons to appear before a Franklin County grand jury regarding another firsthand article on drug use in the capital city. The court of appeals once again rejected his claim of a First Amendment privilege. Pappas, a television newsman for a New Bedford, Massachusetts, station, refused to answer a series of questions from a Bristol County grand jury on what he had seen and heard while inside a Black Panther headquarters. The trial judge, noting the absence of a statutory newsperson's privilege in Massachusetts, ruled that Pappas had no constitutional privilege. The supreme judicial court of the state concluded that newspeople, like all citizens, are obligated to appear when summoned and to answer relevant questions. Caldwell, assigned by the *New York Times* to cover the Black Panther Party in California, was more fortunate than the other two reporters in that, when he challenged a grand jury summons, the Court of Appeals for the Ninth Circuit reversed the contempt commitment. On certiorari, the Supreme Court affirmed the lower court rulings in *Branzburg* and *Pappas* and reversed the *Caldwell* decision.

Opinion: The Court split in its decision on the three related cases. Justice Byron R. White, who wrote the opinion of the 5-to-4 Court, was joined by Chief Justice Warren E. Burger and Justices Harry A. Blackmun and William H. Rehnquist in voting against the constitutional privilege. Lewis F. Powell, Jr., voting with the majority, favored the privilege in some circumstances, but not in these cases. In favor of the privilege were William O. Douglas, who supported an absolute right, and Potter Stewart, William J. Brennan, Jr., and Thurgood Marshall, who endorsed a qualified right. White disputed the reporters' claim that compelling newspersons to disclose confidential information seriously impedes the free flow of information protected by the First Amendment. "These cases involve no intrusions upon speech or assembly, no prior restraint or restriction on what the press may publish, and no express or implied command that the press publish what it prefers to withhold. The use of confidential sources by the press is not forbidden or restricted; reporters remain free to seek news from any source by means within the law." It has generally been held, according to White, that the First Amendment does not guarantee the press a constitutional right of special access to information not available to the public in general. The "great weight" of authority is that newspersons are not exempt from the normal duty of appearing before a grand jury and answering questions relevant to a criminal investigation. In response to the concern that *all* confidential news sources would be affected by the decision, White wrote that only where sources themselves are implicated in crime or possess information relevant to the grand jury's task need they or the reporter be concerned about grand jury subpoenas. "The crimes of news sources are no less reprehensible and threatening to the public interest when witnessed by a reporter than when they are not."

In dissent, Justices Stewart, Brennan, and Marshall said that before a newsperson is asked to appear before a grand jury and reveal confidences, the government must show: (1) probable cause to believe that the reporter has information clearly relevant to a specific probable violation of law; (2) that the information cannot be obtained by alternative means less destructive of First Amendment rights; and (3) a compelling and overriding interest in the information. Stewart asserted that the "probable cause" and "alternative means" tests would serve the vital function of mediating between the public interest in the administration of justice and the constitutional protection of the full flow of information. He agreed with the court of appeals' holding in the Caldwell case, that the government had not shown a "compelling and overriding national interest" in the reporter's confidential information. Douglas, also in dissent, said that the press holds a preferred position in the Constitution and that the decision would impede the wide-open and robust dissemination of ideas and counter-thought so essential to self-government. "Fear of exposure will cause dissidents to communicate less openly to trusted reporters. And, fear of accountability will cause editors and critics to write with more restrained pens."

Justice Powell, who cast the decisive vote, refused to accept the notion that the First Amendment might not afford the journalist a privilege in other instances. He said a balance must be struck between freedom of the press and the obligation of all citizens to give relevant testimony. In short, "The courts will be available to newsmen under circumstances where legitimate First Amendment interests require protection."

Referenced Cases: *Associated Press v. NLRB*, 301 U.S. 103 (1937), on no special immunity for newspapers from general laws; *Oklahoma Press Publishing Co. v. Walling*, 327 U.S. 186 (1946), holding that the Fair Labor Standards Act is not an abridgment of the First Amendment; *Mabee v. White Plains Publishing Co.*, 327 U.S. 178 (1946), and *Associated Press v. U.S.*, 326 U.S. 1 (1945), on application of Sherman Act to the press; *Grosjean v. American Press Co.*, 297 U.S. 233 (1936), and *Murdock v. Pennsylvania*, 319 U.S. 105 (1943), holding that newspapers may be subjected to nondiscriminatory forms of general taxation; *New York Times Co. v. Sullivan*, 376 U.S. 254 (1964), *Garrison v. Louisiana*, 379 U.S. 64 (1964), *Curtis Publishing Co. v. Butts*, 388 U.S. 130 (1967), and *Monitor Patriot Co. v. Roy*, 401 U.S. 265 (1971), on press not free to publish with impunity everything and anything it desires; *Craig v. Harney*, 331 U.S. 367 (1947), holding that the press may also be punished for contempt of court; *Zemel v. Rusk*, 381 U.S. 1 (1965), and *New York Times Co. v. U.S.*, 403 U.S. 713 (1971), on qualified constitutional right of special access to information; *Sheppard v. Maxwell*, 384 U.S. 333 (1966), *Estes v. Texas*, 381 U.S. 532 (1965), and *Rideau v. Louisiana*, 373 U.S. 723 (1963), on fair trial/free press conflict; *Hannah v. Larche*, 363 U.S. 420 (1960), *Costello v. U.S.*, 350 U.S. 359 (1956), and

Blair v. U.S., 250 U.S. 273 (1919), on constitutionally mandated grand jury proceedings and its authority to subpoena witnesses; *U.S. v. Bryan*, 339 U.S. 323 (1950), and *Blackmer v. U.S.*, 284 U.S. 421 (1932), on the public's right to evidence; *Toledo Newspaper Co. v. U.S.*, 247 U.S. 402 (1918), holding that the press is subject to restraints that separate right from wrong-doing; *Roviaro v. U.S.*, 353 U.S. 53 (1957), on the role of anonymity in reporting knowledge of crimes; *Watkins v. U.S.*, 354 U.S. 178 (1957), *DeGregory v. Attorney General of New Hampshire*, 383 U.S. 825 (1966), *NAACP v. Alabama*, 357 U.S. 449 (1958), *NAACP v. Button*, 371 U.S. 415 (1963), and *Bates v. Little Rock*, 361 U.S. 516 (1960), on grand jury exposure and protection; *Hale v. Henkel*, 201 U.S. 43 (1906), and *Hendricks v. U.S.*, 223 U.S. 178 (1912), on grand jury examinations and indictments; *Lovell v. Griffin*, 303 U.S. 444 (1938), and *Mills v. Alabama*, 384 U.S. 214 (1966), on press freedom as "fundamental personal right" not confined to newspapers and periodicals; *Gibson v. Florida Legislative Investigation Committee*, 372 U.S. 539 (1963), *Baird v. State Bar of Arizona*, 401 U.S. 1 (1917), and *In re Stolar*, 401 U.S. 23 (1971), on the extent to which the First Amendment must yield to government's need to know a journalist's unprinted information vis-à-vis needs of investigating committees; *Cantwell v. Connecticut*, 310 U.S. 296 (1940), on distinction between freedom to believe and freedom to act; *Abrams v. U.S.*, 250 U.S. 616 (1919), *Dennis v. U.S.*, 341 U.S. 494 (1951), and *Uphaus v. Wyman*, 360 U.S. 72 (1959), on clear-and-present-danger test and the compelling-interest test; *Feiner v. New York*, 340 U.S. 315 (1951), and *Terminiello v. Chicago*, 337 U.S. 1 (1949), on law and order versus free speech.

Further Reading:

37 *Brooklyn L. Rev.* 502 (Spring 1971).
58 *California L. Rev.* 1198 (1970).
71 *Columbia L. Rev.* 838 (1971).
8 *Harvard Civil Rights L. Rev.* 181 (Jan. 1973).
61 *Kentucky L. J.* 551 (1972–73).
56 *Massachusetts L. Q.* 155 (June 1971).
70 *Michigan L. Rev.* 229 (1971).
8 *New England L. Rev.* 336 (Spring 1973).
64 *Northwestern Univ. L. Rev.* 18 (1969).
47 *Oregon L. Rev.* 243 (1968).
44 *Popular Government* 18 (1978).

24 *Vanderbilt L. Rev.* 667 (1971).
8 *Wake Forest L. Rev.* 567 (Oct. 1972).
52 *Yale L. J.* 607 (1943).
80 *Yale L. J.* 317 (1970).

1974 *Eve Pell, Betty Segal, and Paul Jacobs v. Raymond K. Procunier, Director, California Department of Corrections and Raymond K. Procunier v. Booker T. Hillery, Jr., 417 U.S. 817, 41 L.Ed.2d 495, 94 S.Ct. 2800*

Argued: April 16, 17, 1974.

Decided: June 24, 1974.

Summary: In this, the first time the Court faced the issue of a First Amendment right of access to newsworthy information, the Court ruled that "newsmen have no constitutional right of access to prisons or their inmates beyond that afforded the general public."

Circumstances: In California before 1971, journalists could conduct face-to-face interviews with prisoners upon request. But prison officials believed that such attention given some famous prisoners turned them into celebrities and caused a breakdown in discipline. Thus, the California Department of Corrections Manual was revised to provide that "press and other media interviews with specific individual inmates will not be permitted." Four inmates and three journalists brought suit in the District Court for the Northern District of California challenging the constitutionality of the regulation. The inmates contended a violation of their rights of free speech, and the reporters alleged an infringement of their newsgathering activity, both guaranteed by the First and 14th Amendments. A three-judge panel granted the inmates' motion for summary judgment, but dismissed the action of the media reporters. On appeal, the Supreme Court reversed the ruling for the inmates and affirmed the ruling against the journalists.

Opinion: By a 5-to-4 vote, the Court, in an opinion written by Justice Potter Stewart, joined by Chief Justice Warren E. Burger and Justices Byron R. White, Harry A. Blackmun, and William H. Rehnquist, said that although the First and 14th Amendments prevent the government from interfering with a free press, the Constitution does not guarantee the press access to information not available to the general public. "It is one thing to say that a journalist is free to seek out sources of information not available to members of the general public," Stewart wrote. "It is quite another thing to suggest that the Constitution imposes upon government the affirmative duty to make available to journalists sources of information not available to members of the public generally." Accordingly, since a California prison regulation prohibiting media interviews with special individual inmates does not deny the press access to sources available to the public, the Court held that it did not abridge the protections of the First and 14th Amendments. Stewart said that in the absence of evidence that prison rules were adopted to control specific expression, the Court deferred to the judgment of corrections officials, who possess the expertise to determine which forms of inmate communication do not create a clear and present danger to prison security.

Justice William O. Douglas, in a dissent joined by William J. Brennan, Jr., and Thurgood Marshall, said that an absolute ban on interviews with specific inmates was far in excess of any legitimate government interest and was an infringement on the public's right to know. He said the average citizen is unlikely to inform himself about the operation of the prison system and, instead, relies on the media for information. Justice Lewis F. Powell, Jr., agreed with one majority ruling, that the regulation did not abridge inmate freedom of speech, but disagreed on the media issue, that restrictions on access were constitutional so long as the press was treated the same as the public. "California's absolute ban against prisoner-press interviews impermissibly restrains the ability of the press to perform its constitutionally established function of informing the people on the conduct of their government."

Referenced Cases: *Price v. Johnson*, 334 U.S. 266 (1948), and *Cruz v. Beto*, 405 U.S. 319 (1972), on privileges and rights while incarcerated; *Zemel v. Rusk*, 381 U.S. 1 (1965), regarding individualized requests to communicate; *Kleindienst v. Mandel*, 408 U.S. 753 (1972), on the pros and cons of face-to-face discussion and questioning; *Procunier v. Martinez*, 416 U.S. 396 (1974), on censorship of prisoner mail; *Preiser v. Rodriguez*, 411 U.S. 475 (1973), on state prison problems being within state authority and expertise; *Grayned v. City of Rockford*, 408 U.S. 104 (1972), *Cox v. New Hampshire*, 312 U.S. 569 (1941), *Poulos v. New Hampshire*, 345 U.S. 395 (1953), *Cox v. Louisiana*, 379 U.S. 536 (1965), and *Adderley v. Florida*, 385 U.S. 39 (1966), on time, place, and manner regulations; *Time, Inc. v. Hill*, 385 U.S. 374 (1967), *Garrison v. Louisiana*, 379 U.S. 64 (1964), *New York Times Co. v. Sullivan*, 376 U.S. 254 (1964), *New York Times Co. v. U.S.*, 403 U.S. 713 (1971), *Organization for a Better Austin v. Keefe*, 402 U.S. 415 (1971), *Bantam Books, Inc. v. Sullivan*, 372 U.S. 58 (1963), *Near v. Minnesota*, 283 U.S. 697 (1931), and *Stanley v. Georgia*, 394 U.S. 557 (1969), on free flow of information, public officials, and prior restraints; *Branzburg v. Hayes*, 408 U.S. 665 (1972), on newsgathering and confidentiality of sources; *Saxbe v. Washington Post Co.*, 417 U.S. 843 (1974), on ban against prisoner-press interviews; *Tinker v. Des Moines School District*, 393 U.S. 503 (1969), and *Healy v. James*, 408 U.S. 169 (1972), on application of First Amendment principles in light of special characteristics of environment; *NAACP v. Button*, 371 U.S. 415 (1963), and *Cantwell v. Connecticut*, 310 U.S. 296 (1940), on adjudication of substantive First Amendment rights; *NLRB v. Fruit Packers*, 377 U.S. 58 (1964), on erosion of First Amendment freedoms.

Further Reading:

60 *ABA J.* 1118 (Sept. 1974).
60 *Cornell L. Rev.* 446 (March 1975).
88 *Harvard L. Rev.* 165 (Nov. 1974).
2 *Hastings Const. L. Q.* 829 (Summer 1975).
70 *Northwestern Univ. L. Rev.* 352 (May–June 1975).
9 *San Francisco L. Rev.* 718 (Spring 1975).
11 *Suffolk Univ. L. Rev.* 1354 (Summer 1977).
43 *Univ. Cincinnati L. Rev.* 913 (1974).
124 *Univ. Pa. L. Rev.* 166 (Nov. 1975).
18 *Villanova L. Rev.* 165 (1972).

1974 *William B. Saxbe, Attorney General of the U.S. v. The Washington Post Co., 417 U.S. 843, 41 L.Ed.2d 514, 94 S.Ct. 2811*

Argued: April 17, 1974.

Decided: June 24, 1974.

Summary: Ruled that a regulation prohibiting interviews with inmates did not abridge freedom of the press nor deny press access to sources available to the general public.

Circumstances: Upon hearing that inmates who participated in strike negotiations had been punished once prisoners returned to work, Ben Bagdikian and his paper, the *Washington Post*, sought permission to interview inmates in the federal prisons at Lewisburg, Pennsylvania, and Danbury, Connecticut. They were denied on the basis of Policy Statement 1220.1A of the Federal Bureau of Prisons prohibiting personal interviews between newsmen and individually designated inmates of federal medium-security and maximum-security prisons. The District Court for the District of Columbia held that the policy statement, insofar as it totally prohibited all press interviews at the prisons involved, violated the First Amendment. The Court of Appeals for the District of Columbia Circuit ordered a remand for more findings, and when the district court reaffirmed its decision, the court of appeals also affirmed. On certiorari, the Supreme Court reversed and remanded to the district court.

Opinion: Justice Potter Stewart, who also wrote the *Pell v. Procunier* (1974) decision, said that the policies of the Federal Bureau of Prisons regarding visitations to prison inmates did not differ significantly from the California regulations the Court upheld in *Pell*. He said the visitation policy "does not place the press in any less advantageous position than the public generally. Indeed, the total access to federal prisons and prison inmates that the Bureau of Prisons accords to the press far surpasses that available to other members of the public." He also noted that the case was "constitutionally indistinguishable" from *Pell*, in which the Court held: "Newsmen have no constitutional right of access to prisons or their inmates beyond that afforded the general public." As in the earlier case, Stewart was joined by Chief Justice Warren E. Burger and Justices Byron R. White, Harry A. Blackmun, and William H. Rehnquist. William O. Douglas, joined by William J. Brennan, Jr., and Thurgood Marshall, applied their *Pell* dissent, noting that an absolute ban on interviews with specific inmates is far broader than necessary to protect governmental interests and is an infringement on the public's right to know as protected by the free press guarantee of the First Amendment. Justice Lewis F. Powell, Jr., dissented, as he had in *Pell*, on the ground that a ban on prisoner-press interviews hindered the press in its function of keeping the public abreast of government conduct.

Referenced Cases: *Pell v. Procunier* and *Procunier v. Hillery*, 417 U.S. 817 (1974), regarding concern over inmate discipline and prison administration; *Adderley v. Florida*, 385 U.S. 39 (1966), on public access generally limited at prisons; *Zemel v. Rusk*, 381 U.S. 1 (1965), and *Branzburg v. Hayes*, 408 U.S. 665 (1972), precedents limiting First Amendment rights; *U.S. v. O'Brien*, 391 U.S. 367 (1968), on determining which government regulations implicate First Amendment freedoms; *Kleindienst v. Mandel*, 408 U.S. 753 (1972), *Lamont v. Postmaster General*, 381 U.S. 301 (1965), and *Martin v. City of Struthers*, 319 U.S. 141 (1943), on the right to receive information and ideas; *Tinker v. Des Moines School District*, 393 U.S. 503 (1969), regarding the First Amendment applied in light of special characteristics of the environment.

Further Reading:
See under *Pell v. Procunier*, 417 U.S. 817 (1974), a similar case decided the same day.

1978   *Richard Nixon v. Warner Communications, Inc.*, **435 U.S. 589, 55 L.Ed.2d 570, 98 S.Ct. 1306, 46 U.S. L.W. 4321, 3 Med.L.Rptr. 2074**

Argued: Nov. 8, 1977.

Decided: April 18, 1978.

Summary: In denying the press the right of *physical* access to tapes used as evidence at the trials of presidential aides charged with obstructing justice during the Watergate investigation, the Court said that the common law right of access had been superceded by congressional action creating a procedure for processing and releasing the tapes to the public.

Circumstances: Some 22 hours of conversations taped at the White House were played for the jury and the public in the courtroom during the trial of seven presidential aides indicted for conspiring to obstruct justice in connection with the investigation of the 1972 burglary of the Democratic National Committee headquarters. Six weeks into the trial, Warner Communications asked the court for permission to copy, broadcast, and sell to the public those portions of the tapes played at the trial. Immediate access was denied because of possible prejudice to the rights of the convicted defendants, whose appeals were pending. The Court of Appeals for the District of Columbia reversed, ruling that the common law right of access to judicial records required the district court to release the tapes. On certiorari, the Supreme Court reversed and remanded to the court of appeals with instructions denying respondents' application with prejudice.

Opinion: In considering what he called "this concededly singular case," Justice Lewis F. Powell, Jr., joined by Chief Justice Warren E. Burger and Justices Potter Stewart, Harry A. Blackmun, and William H. Rehnquist, concluded that the First Amendment had not been violated because the press had been permitted to listen to the tapes during the trial and had been given transcripts. He pointed to the Presidential Recordings Act, which granted authority to the Administrator of General Services to take custody of presidential tapes and documents for historical preservation. Unlike the Court's decision in *Cox Broadcasting Corp. v. Cohn* (1975), Powell said that in this case there simply were no restrictions on press access to information in the public domain. "The issue presented . . . is not whether the press must be permitted access to public information to which the public generally is guaranteed access, but whether these copies of the White House tapes—to which the public has never had *physical* access—must be made available for copying. Our decision in *Cox Broadcasting* simply is not applicable." Justice Byron R. White, dissenting in part, joined by William J. Brennan, Jr., said that although the congressional procedure disposed of the matter, the case should be remanded with instructions to deliver the tapes to the Administrator of General Services "forthwith." Justice Thurgood Marshall, in dissent, said that the Presidential Recordings Act, to the degree that it provides assistance in deciding the case, strongly indicates that the tapes should be released to the public. Justice John Paul Stevens, also dissenting, said that any desire to protect the dignity of the presidency was largely eviscerated by the historic importance of the litigation and that the trial exhibits were already entirely in the public domain.

Referenced Cases: *Nixon v. Administrator of General Services*, 433 U.S. 425 (1977), on the constitutionality of the Presidential Recordings Act; *U.S. v. Nixon*, 418 U.S. 683 (1974), on the confidentiality of presidential conversations; *Cox Broadcasting Corp. v. Cohn*, 420 U.S. 469 (1975), on First Amendment protection for publication of information "in the public domain on official court records"; *Estes v. Texas*, 381 U.S. 532 (1965), *Saxbe v. Washington Post Co.*, 417 U.S. 843 (1974), *Pell v. Procunier*, 417 U.S. 817 (1974), and *Zemel v. Rusk*, 381 U.S. 1 (1965), on reporter's rights no greater than those of the public generally.

Further Reading:
64 *ABA J.* 891 (June 1978).

1978   *Landmark Communications, Inc. v. Commonwealth of Virginia*, 435 U.S. 829, 56 L.Ed.2d 1, 98 S.Ct. 1535

Argued: Jan. 11, 1978.

Decided: May 1, 1978.

Summary: The state could not sufficiently justify punishing a newspaper for accurately reporting information from a confidential judicial inquiry, such action being an encroachment on the First Amendment.

Circumstances: Early in Oct. 1975, the *Virginian Pilot*, a Landmark newspaper, published an article accurately depicting a pending inquiry by the Virginia Judicial Inquiry and Review Commission and identified the state judges whose conduct was being investigated. A month later a grand jury indicted Landmark for violating a state statute prohibiting the dissemination of information on the commission. The paper's managing editor testified at the trial in the Circuit Court of Norfolk that he printed the story because he believed the subject a matter of public importance. The court returned a guilty verdict and fined Landmark $500. The Virginia Supreme Court affirmed, rejecting a contention that the Virginia criminal statute violated the First Amendment. On appeal, the U.S. Supreme Court reversed and remanded to the Virginia Supreme Court.

Opinion: The Court voted 7-to-0, Justices William J. Brennan, Jr., and Lewis F. Powell, Jr., not participating. Chief Justice Warren E. Burger, joined by Justices Byron R. White, Thurgood Marshall, Harry A. Blackmun, William H. Rehnquist, and John Paul Stevens, said that the issue was whether confidentiality could be enforced by a fine levied for a truthful publication. He said that accurate reporting of the conduct of public officials, even untruthful expression, "lies near the core of the First Amendment." The article published by the *Virginian Pilot* provided accurate factual information on a pending inquiry by the Virginia Judicial Inquiry and Review Commission, and in so doing "clearly served those interests in public scrutiny and discussion of governmental affairs which the First Amendment was adopted to protect." Regarding the risk of injury to individual judges and to the operation of the review board, Burger said the danger "must be extremely serious and the degree of imminence extremely high before utterances can be punished." Justice Potter Stewart, in a separate concurring opinion, said that nothing in the Constitution prevented Virginia from punishing those who violated the confidentiality of its review commission, but that its statute could not be extended to punish a newspaper. "Though government may deny access to information and punish its theft, government may not prohibit or punish the publication of that information once it falls into the hands of the press, unless the need for secrecy is manifestly overwhelming."

Referenced Cases: *Nebraska Press Assn. v. Stuart,* 427 U.S. 539 (1976), *Wood v. Georgia,* 370 U.S. 375 (1962), *Saxbe v. Washington Post Co.,* 417 U.S. 843 (1974), and *Pell v. Procunier,* 417 U.S. 843 (1974), on illegal acquisition of information and compelled right of access; *New York Times Co. v. Sullivan,* 376 U.S. 254 (1964), regarding untruthful speech when public officials are involved; *Virginia State Board of Pharmacy v. Virginia Citizens' Consumer Council,* 425 U.S. 748 (1977), on truthful commercial information; *Buckley v. Valeo,* 424 U.S. 1 (1976), on criminal sanctions as potential encroachments; *Mills v. Alabama,* 384 U.S. 214 (1966), on protection for free discussion of governmental affairs; *Bridges v. California,* 314 U.S. 252 (1941), on judges not immune from criticism; *Cox Broadcasting Corp. v. Cohn,* 420 U.S. 469 (1975), on broadcasting information already in the public domain; *Pennekamp v. Florida,* 328 U.S. 331 (1946), on application of clear-and-present-danger test; *In re Sawyer,* 360 U.S. 622 (1959), regarding punishment for violating judicial confidentiality.

Further Reading:
64 *ABA J.* 892 (June 1978).
31 *Federal Communications L. J.* 85 (Winter 1978).
3 *Univ. San Francisco L. Rev.* 244 (1969).

1978 *James Zurcher v. The Stanford Daily and Louis P. Bergna, District Attorney, and Craig Brown v. The Stanford Daily,* **436 U.S. 547, 56 L.Ed.2d 525, 98 S.Ct. 1970, 3 Med.L.Rptr. 2377**

Argued: Jan. 17, 1978.

Decided: May 31, 1978.

Summary: Seeing the case as essentially a Fourth Amendment question, not a First Amendment matter, the Court ruled that under existing law a warrant may be issued to search any property, whether or not occupied by a third party, if there is reason to believe that evidence of a crime will be found.

Circumstances: In early April 1971, four policemen, representing the Santa Clara County (California) District Attorney's Office, which had secured the search warrant, conducted a search of the offices of the *Stanford Daily*, the student newspaper at Stanford University. They were looking for negatives, film, and pictures showing events at a demonstration at the university hospital, especially assaults on police officers at the scene. The warrant affidavit made no allegation that newspaper staff members were involved in unlawful acts at the hospital. In the presence of some members of the staff, police searched photo labs, filing cabinets, desks, and wastepaper baskets. Locked drawers and rooms were not opened. The search revealed only the photos that had already appeared in the newspaper. A month later the *Daily* and various staff members sought declaratory and injunctive relief in the District Court for the Northern District of California. They alleged denial of rights under the First, Fourth, and 14th Amendments. The court, in denying the injunction but granting declaratory relief, said that the Fourth and 14th Amendments forbade a warrant to search for materials in the possession of a person not suspected of crime unless there is reason to believe a subpoena impractical. The court also held that First Amendment issues are involved where the innocent object of the search is a newspaper. The search was declared illegal. The Court of Appeals for the Ninth Circuit affirmed. On certiorari, the Supreme Court reversed.

Opinion: Justice Byron R. White, writing the 5-to-3 opinion, joined by Chief Justice Warren E. Burger and Justices Harry A. Blackmun, Lewis F. Powell, Jr., and William H. Rehnquist, said that the Fourth Amendment has not been a barrier to warrants to search property on which there is probable cause to believe that "fruits, instrumentalities, or evidence of crime" is located, whether or not the owner or possessor of the premises is himself reasonably suspected of complicity in the crime under investigation. "The critical element in a reasonable search is not that the owner of the property is suspected of crime but that there is reasonable cause to believe that the specific 'things' to be searched for and seized are located on the property to which entry is sought." White noted that the amendment has struck the balance between privacy and public need, and said there is no justification for a court to strike a new balance by insisting on the use of a subpoena, which is a less intrusive alternative to a search warrant. The justice conceded that where the materials sought may be protected by the First Amendment, the requirements of the Fourth Amendment must be applied with "scrupulous exactitude." He rejected the notion that such unannounced searches threaten freedom of the press, reasoning that the framers of the Constitution were aware of the struggle between the Crown and the press during the 17th and 18th centuries but nevertheless did not forbid warrants involving the press. Justice Powell, in a separate concurring opinion that took issue with Justice Potter Stewart's dissent, said that the Fourth Amendment did not require a new exception, whereby any search of an entity protected by the press clause of the First Amendment is unreasonable so long as a subpoena could be used as a substitute procedure. He also noted that, in issuing a warrant to search a newspaper office, a magistrate should judge the reasonableness of the warrant in light of the particular circumstances.

Stewart, joined by Thurgood Marshall in dissent, said it is "self-evident that police searches of newspaper offices burden the freedom of the press," especially the possible disclosure of information received from confidential sources or identity of the sources themselves. Stewart preferred the subpoena to the search warrant on the ground that the former device allows a newspaper, through a motion to quash, an opportunity for an adversary hearing. Justice John Paul Stevens, also dissenting, opined that the only conceivable justification for an unannounced search of an innocent citizen is the fear that, if notice were given, he would conceal or destroy the object of the search. "But if nothing said under oath in the warrant application demonstrates the need for an unannounced search by force, the probable-cause requirement is not satisfied." Justice William J. Brennan, Jr., did not participate.

Referenced Cases: *Fisher v. U.S.*, 425 U.S. 391 (1976), and *Camara v. Municipal Court*, 387 U.S. 523 (1967), on invasion of privacy and "probable cause" in justifying search and seizure;

U.S. v. Kahn, 415 U.S. 143 (1974), holding that warrants need not name the person from whom things will be seized; *See v. Seattle*, 387 U.S. 541 (1967), and *Frank v. Maryland*, 359 U.S. 360 (1959), on security from intrusion into personal privacy; *Colonnade Catering Corp. v. U.S.*, 397 U.S. 72 (1970), and *U.S. v. Biswell*, 406 U.S. 311 (1972), which dispensed with warrant requirement in cases involving limited inspections and searches; *Carroll v. U.S.*, 267 U.S. 132 (1925), *Husty v. U.S.*, 282 U.S. 694 (1931), and *U.S. v. Ventresca*, 380 U.S. 102 (1965), on warrants to search versus entitlements to arrest; *Stanford v. Texas*, 379 U.S. 476 (1965), and *Marcus v. Search Warrant*, 367 U.S. 717 (1961), regarding search and seizure stifling expression; *A Quantity of Books v. Kansas*, 378 U.S. 205 (1964), *Lee Art Theatre Inc. v. Virginia*, 392 U.S. 636 (1968), and *Heller v. New York*, 413 U.S. 483 (1973), on seizure of obscene material; *Branzburg v. Hayes*, 408 U.S. 665 (1972), on confidential information and sources; *Carroll v. Princess Anne*, 393 U.S. 175 (1968), on a hearing prior to a restraining order; *Warden v. Hayden*, 387 U.S. 294 (1967), on "probable cause" history.

Further Reading:

20 *Boston College L. Rev.* 783 (May 1979).
28 *DePaul L. Rev.* 123 (Fall 1978).
17 *Harvard Journal on Legislation* 152 (Winter 1980).
13 *Indiana L. Rev.* 835 (June 1980).
9 *Pepperdine L. Rev.* 131 (1981).
28 *Stanford L. Rev.* 957 (May 1976).
36 *Washington & Lee L. Rev.* 1177 (Fall 1979).

1978   *Thomas L. Houchins, Sheriff of the County of Alameda, Calif., v. KQED, Inc.*, 438 U.S. 1, 57 L.Ed.2d 553, 98 S.Ct. 2588, 3 Med.L.Rptr. 2521

Argued: Nov. 29, 1977.

Decided: June 26, 1978.

Summary: Neither the First nor the 14th Amendment mandates a right of access to government information or sources of information within the government's control. Under the Constitution, the press does not enjoy a right of access to a jail "different from or greater than" that afforded the public in general.

Circumstances: On March 31, 1975, KQED, licensed operator of television and radio stations in the San Francisco Bay Area, reported the suicide of a prisoner in the Greystone portion of the Alameda County jail at Santa Rita. The program also carried a statement by a prison psychiatrist that conditions at the facility contributed to inmate illnesses. When Sheriff Houchins, who controlled access to the jail, denied KQED's request to inspect and take pictures in that portion of the jail where the suicide took place, the station and the Alameda and Oakland branches of the NAACP brought a civil rights action for equitable relief in the District Court for the Northern District of California. The court preliminarily enjoined the sheriff from denying media access, and the Ninth Circuit Court of Appeals affirmed. However, Justice William H. Rehnquist, as circuit justice, granted the sheriff's application for a stay of the injunction pending the outcome of a petition for certiorari to the Supreme Court. That Court reversed the district court's decision.

Opinion: Chief Justice Warren E. Burger, in a plurality opinion joined by Justices Byron R. White and William H. Rehnquist, with whom Potter Stewart concurred separately, said that the media are not a substitute for or an adjunct of government and, like the courts, are "ill equipped" to deal with problems of prison administration. "Unarticulated but implicit in the assertion that media access to the jail is essential for informed public debate on jail conditions is the assumption that media personnel are best qualified persons for the task of discovering malfeasance in public institutions. But that assumption finds no support in the decisions of this Court or the First Amendment." Burger said there were a number of other ways that reporters could learn of prison conditions, including letters from inmates, interviews with former inmates, prison visitors, public officials, institutional personnel, and the lawyers of prisoners. He said that the public interest in prisons was protected by inspections by the state Board of Corrections and health and fire officials. Justice Stewart, who disassociated himself from the plurality opinion, argued separately for a distinction between the right of access enjoyed by the public generally and the broader needs of reporters. Though agreeing "substantially" with the chief justice on the matter of "equal access once government has opened its doors," Stewart said that the concept of equal access must be accorded more flexibility in order to accommodate the practical distinctions between the press and the general public.

Justice John Paul Stevens, in a dissent joined by William J. Brennan, Jr., and Lewis F. Powell, Jr., said that restrictions on access to the jail in existence when litigation began abridged the public's right to be informed about jail conditions in violation of the First and 14th Amendments' protections. Justices Harry A. Blackmun, ill at the time, and Thurgood Marshall did not participate in the decision. (Presumably, Marshall withdrew because he once was general counsel for the National Association for the Advancement of Colored People, whose Alameda and Oakland branches had joined KQED in the suit against Sheriff Houchins.)

Referenced Cases: *Pell v. Procunier*, 417 U.S. 817 (1974), and *Saxbe v. Washington Post*, 417 U.S. 843 (1974), on the right of access to prisons and jails; *Branzburg v. Hayes*, 408 U.S. 665 (1972), regarding rights to gather news and receive information; *Grosjean v. American Press Co.*, 297 U.S. 233 (1936), and *Mills v. Alabama*, 384 U.S. 214 (1966), on the role of media in informing the public; *Virginia Pharmacy Board v. Virginia Citizens' Consumer Council*, 425 U.S. 748 (1976), *Procunier v. Martinez*, 416 U.S. 396 (1974), and *Kleindienst v. Mandel*, 408 U.S. 753 (1972), on the right to receive ideas and information; *Columbia Broadcasting System Inc. v. Democratic National Committee*, 412 U.S. 94 (1973), and *Miami Herald Publishing Co. v. Tornillo*, 418 U.S. 241 (1974), on the decision to publish or not to publish; *U.S. v. W. T. Grant Co.*, 345 U.S. 629 (1953), on Court's power regarding a previous course of action.

Further Reading:

64 *ABA J.* 1282 (Aug. 1978).
12 *Akron L. Rev.* 291 (Fall 1978).
87 *Harvard L. Rev.* 1505 (1974).
92 *Harvard L. Rev.* 174 (Nov. 1978).
6 *Hastings Const. L. Q.* 933 (Spring 1979).

26 *Hastings L. J.* 631 (1975).
39 *Louisiana L. Rev.* 1005 (Spring 1979).
54 *Notre Dame Lawyer* 288 (Dec. 1978).
19 *Santa Clara L. Rev.* 235 (Winter 1979).
53 *Tulane L. Rev.* 629 (Fall 1979).
33 *Univ. Miami L. Rev.* 680 (March 1979).

1979 *Robert K. Smith v. Daily Mail Publishing Co.*, **443 U.S. 97, 61 L.Ed.2d 399, 99 S.Ct. 2667, 5 Med.L.Rptr. 1305**

Argued: March 20, 1979.

Decided: June 26, 1979.

Summary: A West Virginia law making it a crime to publish, without the written approval of the juvenile court, lawfully acquired, truthful information on the identity of a juvenile offender, held violative of the First Amendment. The Court affirmed a state court ruling that the statute functioned as a prior restraint on speech.

Circumstances: In early 1978, a 15-year-old student was shot and killed in a junior high school near Charleston, West Virginia, and a 14-year-old classmate was identified by several eyewitnesses and arrested shortly after the incident. Reporters and photographers from the Charleston *Daily Mail* and *Gazette*, having learned of the shooting from a police radio, obtained the assailant's name from witnesses, the police, and an assistant prosecutor who were at the school. The first story in the *Daily Mail* did not include the alleged attacker's name, a decision based on the prohibition against publication without prior court approval. But, when the *Gazette* published the name and picture and three radio stations broadcast the information, the *Daily Mail*'s next account included the juvenile's name. A grand jury indicted both newspapers. The West Virginia Supreme Court of Appeals overturned the indictments, ruling that the statute abridged the First Amendment. The U.S. Supreme Court, on certiorari, affirmed the judgment.

Opinion: The vote was 8-to-0, Justice Lewis F. Powell, Jr.,
not participating. Chief Justice Warren E. Burger, joined by Justices William J. Brennan, Jr., Potter Stewart, Byron R. White, Thurgood Marshall, Harry A. Blackmun, and John Paul Stevens, held
that, whether or not the law operated as a prior restraint, a state
cannot punish truthful publication of information lawfully obtained "except when necessary to further an interest more substantial that is present" in this case. Even assuming that the law
served a state interest of the highest order, Burger said the statute's approach does not satisfy constitutional requirements, in
that it did not restrict the electronic media or any form of publication, except newspapers, from printing the names of youths
charged in a juvenile proceeding. The decision is narrow, Burger
pointed out, since there was no issue of unlawful press access to
confidential judicial proceedings, no privacy issue, and no issue of
prejudicial trial publicity. Justice William H. Rehnquist, concurring separately, agreed that the West Virginia statute "does not
accomplish its stated purpose," since it discriminates against
newspapers, but that a ban on all forms of mass communications
affecting juvenile offenders could pass muster under the First
Amendment.

Referenced Cases: *Nebraska Press Assn. v. Stuart*,
427 U.S. 539 (1976), *New York Times Co. v. U.S.*, 403 U.S. 713
(1971), *Organization for a Better Austin v. Keefe*, 402 U.S. 415
(1971), and *Near v. Minnesota*, 283 U.S. 697 (1931), on "prior
restraint" on speech; *Landmark Communications, Inc. v. Virginia*,
435 U.S. 829 (1978), and *Cox Broadcasting Corp. v. Cohn*, 420 U.S.
469 (1975), regarding the reach of First Amendment protection
beyond prior restraints; *Southeastern Promotions, Ltd. v. Conrad*,
420 U.S. 546 (1975), on the exacting scrutiny of prior restraints;
Oklahoma Publishing Co. v. District Court, 430 U.S. 308 (1977), on
the dissemination of truthful information once "publicly revealed" or "in the public domain"; *Houchins v. KQED, Inc.*, 438 U.S.
1 (1978), and *Branzburg v. Hayes*, 408 U.S. 665 (1972), on the press'
acquisition beyond government sufferance of information; *Davis
v. Alaska*, 415 U.S. 308 (1974), on reasons for protecting the anonymity of the juvenile offender; *American Communications Assn.
v. Douds*, 339 U.S. 382 (1950), on free speech and press versus
competing interests of the public; *Jones v. Opelika*, 316 U.S. 584
(1942), on the temptation to support any claim of interference

with speech or press; *In re Gault*, 387 U.S. 1 (1967), on confidentiality as a way of hiding youthful errors; *Kent v. U.S.*, 383 U.S. 541 (1966), regarding rehabilitative goals of juvenile justice system.

Further Reading:

65 *ABA J.* 1390 (Summer 1979).
11 *Clearinghouse Rev.* 203 (1977).
7 *Hastings Const. L. Q.* 352 (Winter 1980).
65 *Iowa L. Rev.* 1471 (July 1980).
17 *J. Missouri Bar* 66 (1961).
16 *Juvenile Court Judges J.* 21 (1965).
56 *No. Dakota L. Rev.* 279 (1980).
7 *Ohio Northern L. Rev.* 148 (Jan. 1980).
7 *Pepperdine L. Rev.* 801 (Summer 1980).
30 *Rocky Mtn. L. Rev.* 101 (1958).
20 *Santa Clara L. Rev.* 405 (Spring 1980).

1984 *Seattle Times Co. et al. v. Keith Milton Rhinehart et al.*, 467 U.S. 20, 81 L.Ed.2d 17, 104 S.Ct. 2199, 10 Med.L.Rptr. 1705

Argued: Feb. 21, 1984.

Decided: May 21, 1984.

Summary: Held constitutional a protective order against dissemination of discovery information, that newspapers could be restrained from publishing material acquired by them as defendants in a libel suit.

Circumstances: The Seattle *Times* and the Walla Walla *Union-Bulletin*, both in the state of Washington, were sued for $14 million by Rhinehart, head of the Aquarian Foundation, a religious group that believed in communication with the dead. The papers had reported, among other things about the foundation, that Rhinehart treated inmates at the Walla Walla State Penitentiary to a six-hour "extravaganza" that included "a chorus line of girls [who] shed their gowns and bikinis and sang." During discovery, the foundation was ordered to produce the names of its members and donors, and at the same time the papers were prohibited from publishing the information. Rhinehart and the foundation sued in Washington Superior Court for defamation and invasion of privacy, alleging that the stories contained "fictional and untrue" statements. The protective order pertained only to material gained in the discovery process. The Supreme Court of Washington affirmed both the production order and the protective order. On certiorari, the U.S. Supreme Court affirmed.

Opinion: Justice Lewis F. Powell, Jr., wrote the Court's unanimous opinion. Justice William J. Brennan, Jr., joined by Thurgood Marshall, joined the opinion but filed a separate opinion. Powell said the restraint on publication inherent in the trial court's protective order was not the "classic prior restraint that requires exacting First Amendment scrutiny." Although the order prohibited publication of information acquired through the "legislative grace" of the discovery process, the same information could be disseminated if obtained in another way. The Court said that the state of Washington had demonstrated a "substantial" government interest: the rules that allowed parties in civil suits to obtain information relevant to their cases. Those rules ensured that the newspapers could acquire information important to their defense, but they also protected against damages that might occur if the information was made available to the general public. "There is an opportunity . . . for litigants to obtain—incidentally or purposefully—information that not only is irrelevant but if publicly released could be damaging to reputation and privacy. The government clearly has a substantial interest in preventing this sort of abuse of its processes." Justices Brennan and Marshall added that the plaintiffs' interest in privacy and religious freedom were sufficient to justify the protective order and to overcome the protections afforded free expression by the First Amendment.

Referenced Cases: *American Communications Assn. v. Douds*, 339 U.S. 382 (1950), holding that freedom of speech does not comprehend the right to speak on any subject at any time; *Procunier v. Martinez*, 416 U.S. 396 (1974), holding that limitations be no greater than necessary to protect particular governmental interest; *Zemel v. Rusk*, 381 U.S. 1 (1965), on the right to speak and publish does not carry with it the unrestrained right to gather information; *Gannett Co. v. DePasquale,* 443 U.S. 368 (1979), regarding pretrial depositions and interrogatories not public components of a civil trial; *Herbert v. Lando,* 441 U.S. 153 (1979), and *Gumbel v. Pitkin,* 124 U.S. 131 (1888), on government interest in preventing abuse of the discovery process.

Further Reading:

71 *Minnesota L. Rev.* 171 (Oct. 1986).
47 *Univ. Pittsburgh L. Rev.* 547 (Winter 1986).
8 *Univ. Puget Sound L. Rev.* 123 (Fall 1984).
1985 *Wisconsin L. Rev.* 1055 (1985).

Selected Bibliography

Barron, Jerome A., "The Rise and Fall of a Doctrine of Editorial Privilege: Reflections on Herbert v. Lando," 47 *George Washington L. Rev.* 1002 (Aug. 1979).

Blasi, Vince, "Press Subpoenas: An Empirical and Legal Analysis," 70 *Michigan L. Rev.* 229 (1971).

Boyd, J. Kirk, "Legislative Response to Zurcher v. Stanford Daily," 9 *Pepperdine L. Rev.* 131 (1981).

Cairney, Roberta L., "Sunlight in the County Jail: Houchins v. KQED Inc. and Constitutional Protection for Newsgathering," 6 *Hastings L. Q.* 933 (Spring 1979).

Chamberlin, Bill, "Protection of Confidential News Sources: An Unresolved Issue," 44 *Popular Government* 18 (1978).

Cullen, Brian M., "Circumventing Branzburg: Absolute Protection for Confidential News Sources," 18 *Suffolk Univ. L. Rev.* 615 (1984).

Duckworth, Barton L., "Communications Law: The Decline of Press Privilege," 19 *Washburn L. J.* 54 (Fall 1979).

DuVal, B. S., Jr., "The Occasions of Secrecy," 47 *Univ. Pittsburgh L. Rev.* 579 (Spring 1986).

Emerson, Thomas I., "Legal Foundations of the Right to Know," 1976 *Washington Univ. L. Rev.* 1 (1976).

Frazer, Douglas H., "The Newsperson's Privilege in Grand Jury Proceedings: An Argument for Uniform Recognition and Application," 75 *J. Criminal Law and Criminology* 413 (1984).

Goodale, James, "Branzburg v. Hayes and the Developing Qualified Privilege for Newsmen," 26 *Hastings L. J.* 709 (1975).

————, "Legal Pitfalls in the Right to Know," 1976 *Washington Univ. L. Rev.* 29 (1976).

Gordon, David, "The Confidences Newsmen Must Keep," 10 *Columbia Journalism Rev.* 17 (Nov.–Dec. 1971).

Guest, James, and Alan Stanzler, "The Constitutional Argument for Newsmen Concealing Their Sources," 64 *Northwestern Univ. L. Rev.* 18 (1969).

Henkin, Louis, "The Right to Know and the Duty to Withhold: The Case of the Pentagon Papers," 120 *Univ. Pa. L. Rev.* 271 (1971).

Killenberg, George M., "Branzburg Revisited: The Struggle to Define Newsman's Privilege Goes On," 55 *Journalism Quarterly* 703 (Winter 1978).

Kutner, Louis, "Contempt Power: The Black Robe—A Proposal for Due Process," 39 *Tennessee L. Rev.* 27 (1971).

Lapham, Lewis, "The Temptations of a Sacred Cow," *Harpers* (Aug. 1973).

Mehra, Achal, "Newsmen's Privilege: An Empirical Study," 59 *Journalism Quarterly* 560 (Winter 1982).

————, "Sanctions for Reporters Who Refuse to Disclose Sources in Libel Cases," 60 *Journalism Quarterly* 437 (Autumn 1983).

Middleton, Kent R., "Journalists' Interference with Police: The First Amendment, Access to News and Official Discretion," 5 *Comm/Ent* 443 (Spring 1983).

Murasky, Donna M., "The Journalist's Privilege: Branzburg and Its Aftermath," 52 *Texas L. Rev.* 829 (1974).

"The Newsman's Privilege After Branzburg: The Case for a Federal Shield Law," 24 *UCLA L. Rev.* 160 (1976).

"The Right of the Press to Gather Information After Branzburg and Pell," 124 *Univ. Pa. L. Rev.* 166 (1975).

Shepard, Tate S., "Cameras in the Courtroom: Here to Stay," 10 *Univ. Toledo L. Rev.* 925 (Summer 1979).

Silver, Ben, and James Bow, "Effects of Herbert v. Lando on the News Process," 60 *Journalism Quarterly* 115 (Spring 1983).

Stewart, Potter, "Or of the Press," 26 *Hastings L. Rev.* 631 (1976).

Teeter, Dwight L., and S. Griffin Singer, "Search Warrants in Newsrooms: Some Aspects of the Impact of Zurcher v. The Stanford Daily," 67 *Kentucky L. J.* 847 (1978–79).

Trager, Robert, and Harry W. Stonecipher, "Gag Orders: An Unresolved Dilemma," 55 *Journalism Quarterly* 231 (Summer 1978).

White, Theodore, "Why the Jailing of Farber 'Terrifies Me,'" *New York Times Magazine* (Nov. 26, 1978).

Obscenity

1896 *Lew Rosen v. U.S.,* **161 U.S. 29, 16 S.Ct. 434, 40 L.Ed. 606**

Argued: Oct. 29, 1895.

Decided: Jan. 27, 1896.

Summary: Rejected the contention that a charge of mailing obscene material must be supported by evidence that a defendant knew the material to be obscene.

Circumstances: Rosen, owner and manager of the paper *Broadway,* was indicted under U.S. Rev. Stat. Section 3893 prohibiting the mailing of material deemed nonmailable. The copy of the paper read into evidence included pictures of women partially covered with lampblack that could be easily erased with a piece of bread. At trial Rosen presented a "clean" copy in which the pictures, with females in "different attitudes of indecency," were not obscured by lampblack. He was found guilty at trial. His motion to arrest the judgment was denied. The Circuit Court for the Southern District of New York affirmed the judgement. The Supreme Court, finding no error of law in the record, affirmed.

Opinion: Justice John M. Harlan wrote the Court's 7-to-2 opinion, joined by Chief Justice Melville W. Fuller and Justices Stephen J. Field, Horace Gray, David J. Brewer, Henry B. Brown, and Rufus W. Peckham. Dissenting were Edward D. White and George Shiras, Jr. Harlan wrote: "Undoubtedly the mere depositing in the mail of a writing, paper, or other publication of an obscene, lewd, or lascivious character, is not an offense under the statute if the person making the deposit was . . . without knowledge, information, or notice of its contents." But the justice went on to note that Rosen, owner and manager of the questionable newspaper, must have understood from the original indictment that the government imputed to him such knowledge. Further, Rosen went to trial without suggesting that he was not sufficiently informed of the nature and cause of the accusation against him. The defendant did not ask for a bill of particulars nor object to indictment as insufficient, Harlan wrote, "but made his defense on the broad ground that the paper that he caused to be deposited in the postoffice was not obscene, lewd, or lascivious." Harlan reiterated the trial court's test of obscenity as "whether the tendency of the material is to deprave and corrupt the morals of those whose minds are open to such influence and into whose hands a publication of this sort may fall." Justice White, joined by Shiras, dissented on the ground that, though the indictment identified the paper as an entirety, it failed to designate what specific matter was found to be obscene by the grand jury upon which its presentment was made. The grand jury indictment was flawed, they averred.

Referenced Cases: *Grimm v. U.S.*, 156 U.S. 604 (1895), and *Goode v. U.S.*, 159 U.S. 663 (1895), holding that response to a decoy letter no defense for mailing prohibited publications; *Pleasants v. Fant*, 22 Wall. 89 U.S. 116 (1875), *Montclair Twp. v. Dana*, 107 U.S. 162 (1883), *Marshall v. Hubbard*, 117 U.S. 415 (1886), and *Sparf v. U.S.*, 156 U.S. 51 (1895), on settled doctrine of instructing jury on applicable principles regarding evidence presented; *Montana R. Co. v. Warren*, 137 U.S. 348 (1890), on the Court's obligation to demand specific material; *Mackin v. U.S.*, 117 U.S. 348 (1886), *Ex parte Wilson*, 114 U.S. 417 (1885), and *In re Claasen*, 140 U.S. 200 (1891), on the infamous nature of the offense; *Ex parte Bain*, 121 U.S. 1 (1887), and *Hopt v. Utah*, 110 U.S. 574 (1884), holding that mere silence or acquiescence of accused cannot deprive him of his constitutional rights.

Further Reading:
12 *Albany L. J.* 37, 95 (1875).
16 *Albany L. J.* 220 (1877).
23 *Case & Comment* 16, 23 (1916).
44 *Chicago Legal News* 70 (1911).
25 *Medico-Legal J.* 195 (1907).
23 *Yale L. J.* 559 (1914).

1946   *Robert E. Hannegan, as Postmaster General of the U.S. v. Esquire Inc.*, 327 U.S. 146, 66 S.Ct. 456, 90 L.Ed. 586, 1 Med.L.Rptr. 2292

Argued: Jan. 1, 1946.

Decided: Feb. 4, 1946.

Summary: Rejected the postmaster's contention that second-class mailing privileges may be denied to a nonobscene publication because it does not "contribute to the public good and the public welfare."

Circumstances: *Esquire* magazine, which had been granted a second-class permit in 1933, was asked to show cause in 1943 why the permit should not be suspended or revoked. A hearing was held before a board designated by the then–postmaster general, and it recommended the permit not be revoked. Hannegan, the new postmaster general, felt differently and revoked because he believed it did not comply with a part of the Classification Act of 1879, which stipulated that a condition of acquiring the second-class permit is that the publication must be of a public character or devoted to literature, the sciences, arts, or some special industry, and have a legitimate list of subscribers. The Court of Appeals for the District of Columbia had reversed a dismissal by the district court of a suit to enjoin the postmaster general's revocation order. On writ of certiorari, the Supreme Court affirmed.

Opinion: Justice William O. Douglas wrote the Court's unanimous opinion, joined by Chief Justice Harlan F. Stone and Justices Hugo L. Black, Stanley F. Reed, Frank Murphy, Wiley B. Rutledge, and Harold H. Burton. Felix Frankfurter wrote a separate concurring opinion. Robert H. Jackson did not participate. Douglas said that the controversy was not whether the magazine publishes "information of a public character" or is devoted to "literature" or to the "arts," as the postmaster general stipulated. "It is whether the contents are 'good' or 'bad.' To uphold the order of revocation [of the magazine's second-class permit] would, therefore, grant the Postmaster General a power of censorship. Such a power is so abhorrent to our traditions that a purpose to grant it should not be easily inferred. It is difficult to imagine that the Congress . . . gave the Postmaster General . . . discretion to deny periodicals the second-class rate, if in his view they did not contribute to the public good." He concluded: "What is good literature, what has educational value, what is refined public information, what is good art, varies with individuals as it does from one generation to another. There doubtless should be contrariety of views concerning Cervantes's Don Quixote, Shakespeare's Venus & Adonis, or Zola's Nana. But a requirement that literature or art conform to some norm prescribed by an official smacks of an ideology foreign to our system." Justice Frankfurter added that, since the postmaster general had disavowed the nonmailability of the magazine and since Congress did not qualify literature, the sciences, and arts by any standard of taste, the postmaster general exceeded his powers.

Referenced Cases: *Ex parte Jackson,* 96 U.S. 727 (1878), that Congress can constitutionally make it a crime to send fraudulent or obscene material through the mails; *U.S. ex rel. Milwaukee S. D. Pub. Co. v. Burleson,* 255 U.S. 407 (1921), on the use of the mails as a privilege that may be extended or withheld on any grounds; *Houghton v. Payne,* 194 U.S. 88 (1904), *Bates & G. Co. v. Payne,* 194 U.S. 106 (1904), and *Smith v. Hitchcock,* 226 U.S. 53 (1912), on the postmaster general's duty to execute postal laws; *Leach v. Carlile,* 258 U.S. 138 (1922), on the First Amendment forbidding control of posted sealed letters.

Further Reading:
34 *California L. Rev.* 431 (June 1946).
9 *Georgia Bar J.* 101 (Aug. 1946).
45 *Michigan L. Rev.* 230 (Dec. 1946).
94 *Univ. Pa. L. Rev.* 325 (April 1946).

1952   *Joseph Burstyn, Inc. v. Lewis A. Wilson, Commissioner of Education of the State of New York, et al.,* **343 U.S. 495,**

96 L.Ed. 1098, 72 S.Ct. 777, 1 Med.L.Rptr. 1357

Argued: April 24, 1952.

Decided: May 26, 1952.

Summary: Commercial motion pictures were entitled to First Amendment protection even though "their production, distribution, and exhibition is a large-scale business conducted for private profit." The film medium cannot be censored by a state, except in cases of obscenity.

Circumstances: On Nov. 30, 1950, the motion picture division of the New York education department issued a license to Burstyn, a motion picture distributor, to exhibit "The Miracle," with English subtitles as one part of a trilogy, "Ways of Love." The film, lasting 40 minutes, was produced in Italy by Roberto Rossellini and starred Anna Magnani as a demented goat-tender. During an eight-week period of its showing, the state Board of Regents received hundreds of letters, telegrams, postcards, affidavits, and other communications protecting and defending the public exhibition of the film. An appointed three-member panel of the board determined that the film was "sacrilegious." The board later ordered the commissioner of education to rescind the license. The state appellate division upheld the regents' determination, holding that the banning of any motion picture "that may fairly be deemed sacrilegious to the adherents of any religious group . . . is directly related to public peace and order." On appeal the New York Court of Appeals, two judges dissenting, affirmed the order of the appellate division. The Supreme Court unanimously reversed, disapproving in the process its earlier theory in *Mutual Film Corp. v. Industrial Commission* (1915), that the basic principles of freedom of speech and press applied to motion pictures.

Opinion: Justice Tom C. Clark wrote for six members of the court, including Chief Justice Fred M. Vinson and Justices Hugo L. Black, William O. Douglas, Sherman Minton, and Harold H. Burton. Stanley F. Reed added a brief separate concurrence. Felix Frankfurter, joined by Robert H. Jackson and Burton, wrote a separate concurrence, making the judgment unanimous. At issue was the constitutionality, under the First and 14th Amendments, of a New York state statute banning "sacrilegious" films. The law instructed film distributors to submit their products to the director of the motion picture division of the state's education department for the granting of an exhibition license, "unless such film or a part thereof is obscene, indecent, immoral, inhuman, sacrilegious, or is of such a character that its exhibition would tend to corrupt morals or incite to crime." The case was the first "to present squarely" to the Court whether motion pictures were within the ambit of protection that the First Amendment, through the 14th, secures to any form of "speech" or "the press." Clark, in recognizing motion pictures as a "significant medium for the communication of ideas," said that their importance as an organ of public opinion is not lessened by the fact that they are designed to entertain as well as to inform. Comparing them to the print media, the justice said, "We fail to see why operation for profit should have any different effect in the case of motion pictures." On the matter of films having a greater capacity for evil, Clark responded, "If there be capacity for evil it may be relevant in determining the permissible scope of community control, but it does not authorize substantially unbridled censorship such as we have here." Justice Reed, though allowing that the Court's view did not foreclose a state's right to license films, added that the Court's duty was to examine closely each case to determine whether the First Amendment was honored. Justice Frankfurter, in a long concurrence, said that the term "sacrilegious," as used in the New York statute, was unconstitutionally vague. "To criticize or assail religious doctrine may wound to the quick those who are attached to the doctrine and profoundly cherish it. But to bar such pictorial discussion is to subject nonconformists to the rule of sects." Appended to Frankfurter's opinion are the etymological sources he consulted on the terms "blasphemy" and "sacrilege."

Referenced Cases: *Gitlow v. New York*, 268 U.S. 652 (1925), the first in a series of Court decisions on the Due Process Clause of the 14th Amendment as part of the First Amendment guarantee against state invasion; *Winters v. New York*, 333 U.S. 507 (1948), on informative entertainment, or "What is one man's amusement, teaches another's doctrine"; *Mutual Film Corp. v. In-*

dustrial Commission, 236 U.S. 230 (1915), identifying motion pictures as not intended to be part of the press or as organs of public opinion; Near v. Minnesota, 283 U.S. 697 (1931), reiterating the history of prior restraints on the press; Kunz v. New York, 340 U.S. 290 (1951), on vesting unlimited control in a censor; Ashwander v. TVA, 297 U.S. 288 (1936), on the polarizing effect of absolute and abstract arguments; Cantwell v. Connecticut, 310 U.S. 296 (1940), holding that, in the realms of religious faith and political belief, "the tenets of one man may seem the rankest error to his neighbor."

Further Reading:

38 ABA J. 760 (Sept. 1952).
32 Boston Univ. L. Rev. 451 (Nov. 1952).
19 Brooklyn L. Rev. 125 (Dec. 1952).
41 Georgia L. J. 94 (Nov. 1952).
66 Harvard L. Rev. 115 (Nov. 1952).
1 J. Public L. 519 (Fall 1952).
41 Kentucky L. J. 257 (Jan. 1953).
37 Minnesota L. Rev. 209 (Feb. 1953).
24 Mississippi L. J. 248 (March 1953).
31 No. Carolina L. Rev. 103 (Dec. 1952).
27 Notre Dame Lawyer 450 (Spring 1952).
27 NYU L. Rev. 699 (Oct. 1952).
25 Rocky Mtn. L. Rev. 253 (Feb. 1953).
26 So. Calif. L. Rev. 206 (Feb. 1953).
27 St. John's L. Rev. 131 (Dec. 1952).
3 Syracuse L. Rev. 365 (Spring 1952).
26 Temple L. Q. 192 (Fall 1952).
21 Univ. Cincinnati L. Rev. 475 (Nov. 1952).
6 Univ. Florida L. Rev. 131 (Spring 1953).
1952 Univ. Illinois L. Forum 439 (Fall 1952).
1953 Washington Univ. L. Q. 206 (April 1953).

1957   *Alfred E. Butler v. State of Michigan,* 352 U.S. 380, 1 L.Ed.2d 412, 77 S.Ct. 524

Argued: Oct. 16, 1956.

Decided: Feb. 25, 1957.

Summary: Invalidated a state obscenity statute because of the overbreadth of its definitional provision, that "[t]he incidence of this enactment is to reduce the adult population . . . to reading only what is fit for children."

Circumstances: Butler was charged with violating Section 343 of the Michigan Penal Code, for selling to a police officer what the trial judge characterized as "a book containing obscene, immoral, lewd, lascivious language, or descriptions, tending to incite minors to violent, or depraved or immoral acts, manifestly tending to the corruption of the morals of youth." The judge denied a motion for dismissal. Butler was fined $100. The Michigan Supreme Court denied his leave to appeal. On appeal from the judgment entered by the Recorder's Court of Detroit, the U.S. Supreme Court reversed the conviction.

Opinion: Justice Felix Frankfurter, writing for eight brethren, said that the Michigan Penal Code prohibiting the distribution of any material "tending to incite minors to violent or depraved or immoral acts" violated the due process clause of the 14th Amendment. Joining the opinion were Chief Justice Earl Warren and Justices Stanley F. Reed, William O. Douglas, Harold H. Burton, Tom C. Clark, John M. Harlan, and William J. Brennan, Jr. Hugo L. Black concurred in the result. Frankfurter wrote: "It is clear on the record that appellant was convicted because Michigan . . . made it an offense for him to make available for the general reading public (and he in fact sold to a police officer) a book that the trial judge found to have a potentially deleterious influence upon youth. The State insists that, by thus quarantining the general reading public against books not too rugged for grown men and women in order to shield juvenile innocence, it is exercising its power to promote the general welfare. Surely, this is to burn the house to roast the pig." He said the legislation was not reasonably restricted to the evil with which it was said to deal. "It thereby arbitrarily curtails one of those liberties of the individual, now enshrined in the Due Process Clause of the Fourteenth Amendment, that history has attested as the indispensable conditions for the maintenance and progress of a free society."

Referenced Case: *Winters v. New York*, 333 U.S. 507 (1948), on the doctrine that found a New York obscenity statute invalid.

Further Reading:
43 *ABA J.* 442 (May 1957).
71 *Harvard L. Rev.* 146 (Nov. 1957).
73 *Law Quarterly Review* 299 (July 1957).
11 *Miami L. Q.* 523 (Summer 1957).

1957 *Samuel Roth v. U.S. and David S. Alberts v. California*, 354 U.S. 476, 1 L.Ed.2d 1498, 77 S.Ct. 1304, 1 Med.L.Rptr. 1375

Argued: April 22, 1957.

Decided: June 24, 1957.

Summary: Obscenity, defined as "utterly without redeeming social importance," held not within the area of constitutionally protected speech or press. A work is obscene if, to the average person, applying contemporary community standards, the dominant theme of the material, taken as a whole, appeals to prurient interests.

Circumstances: Roth, a New York publisher and seller of books, photographs, and magazines, was convicted in the District Court for the Southern District of New York on four counts of a 26-count indictment charging him with sending obscene circulars, advertisements, and a book through the mails in violation of federal law. His conviction was affirmed by the Court of Appeals for the Second Circuit. Alberts, a Beverly Hills mail-order merchant, was found guilty in the municipal court, having waived a jury trial, for "lewdly keeping for sale obscene and indecent books, and with writing, composing and publishing an obscene advertisement of them" in violation of the California Penal Code. His conviction was affirmed by the Appellate Department of the Superior Court of California. On certiorari for Roth and on appeal for Alberts, the U.S. Supreme Court affirmed the convictions.

Opinion: Justice William J. Brennan, Jr., wrote for five members of the Court, including Harold H. Burton, Tom C. Clark, Stanley F. Reed, and Felix Frankfurter. Chief Justice Earl Warren concurred separately. John M. Harlan concurred in *Alberts* and dissented in *Roth*. William O. Douglas, joined by Hugo L. Black, dissented. Thus, a 7-to-2 Court upheld the conviction of Alberts and a 6-to-3 Court upheld the conviction of Roth. The Court, in addressing for the first time the question of whether obscenity falls within the area of protected speech and press, under either the First or the 14th Amendment, said that "numerous opinions" indicate that it does not. "The First Amendment was not intended to protect every utterance," Brennan wrote. It is not absolute. He concluded that the purpose of the amendment is to protect the unfettered interchange of ideas. "All ideas having even the slightest redeeming social importance—unorthodox ideas, controversial ideas, even ideas hateful to the prevailing climate of opinion—have the full protection of the guarantees, unless excludable because they encroach upon the limited area of more important interests." Brennan also said that sex and obscenity are not synonymous. "Obscene material . . . deals with sex in a manner appealing to prurient interest. The portrayal of sex, e.g., in art, literature and scientific works, is not itself sufficient reason to deny material the constitutional protection of freedom of speech and press." The Court also rejected the old Hicklin test, long used by courts as judging obscenity by the effect of isolated passages upon the most susceptible persons. Hence, the Court held that neither the federal statute, under which Roth was convicted, nor the state statute, under which Alberts was convicted, offended "constitutional safeguards against convictions based upon protected material, or fail[ed] to give men in acting adequate notice of what is prohibited." The federal obscenity statute, punishing the use of the mails for obscene material, was found a proper exercise of the postal power delegated to Congress. The California statute "in no way imposes a burden or interferes with the federal postal functions."

Chief Justice Warren, though concurring in the result, doubted the wisdom of the broad language used by the majority.

"The conduct of the defendant is the central issue, not the obscenity of a book or picture." He said it was proper in these cases for the state and federal governments to punish Roth and Alberts, who "were plainly engaged in the commercial exploitation of the morbid and shameful craving for materials with prurient effect. That is all that these cases present to us, and that is all we need to decide." Justice Harlan, who concurred in *Alberts*, dissented in *Roth*, fearing that the "broad brush" used by the majority may loosen the tight reins that he believed state and federal governments should hold on the enforcement of obscenity statutes. "In short, I do not understand how the Court can resolve the constitutional problems now before it without making its own independent judgment upon the character of the material upon which these convictions are based. I am very much afraid that the broad manner in which the Court has decided these cases will tend to obscure the peculiar responsibilities resting on state and federal courts in this field and encourage them to rely on easy labeling and jury verdicts as a substitute for facing up to the tough individual problems of constitutional judgment involved in every obscenity case." Harlan feared more the censorial powers of the federal government than the regulation of "human conduct" by the states. "Congress has no substantive power over sexual morality," but the states "bear direct responsibility for the protection of the local moral fabric."

In strong dissent, Justice Douglas, joined by Black, said that by sustaining the convictions, "we make the legality of a publication turn on the purity of thought which a book or tract instills in the mind of the reader. If we were certain that impurity of sexual thoughts impelled to action, we would be on less dangerous ground in punishing the distributors of this sex literature. Government should be concerned with antisocial conduct, not with utterances. Freedom of expression can be suppressed if, and to the extent that, it is so closely brigaded with illegal action as to be an inseparable part of it." He concluded: "I have the same confidence in the ability of our people to reject noxious literature as I have in their capacity to sort out the true from the false in theology, economics, politics, or any other field."

Referenced Cases: *Ex parte Jackson*, 96 U.S. 727 (1878), *U.S. v. Chase*, 135 U.S. 255 (1890), *Robertson v. Baldwin*, 165 U.S. 275 (1897), *Public Clearing House v. Coyne*, 194 U.S. 497

(1904), *Hoke v. U.S.*, 227 U.S. 308 (1913), *Near v. Minnesota*, 283 U.S. 697 (1931), *Chaplinsky v. New Hampshire*, 315 U.S. 568 (1942), *Hannegan v. Esquire*, 327 U.S. 146 (1946), *Winters v. New York*, 333 U.S. 507 (1948), and *Beauharnais v. Illinois*, 343 U.S. 250 (1952), Court opinions supporting assumption that obscenity is not protected speech; *Thornhill v. Alabama*, 310 U.S. 88 (1940), holding that protected speech includes "all matters of public concern . . . information and education with respect to the significant issues of the day . . . all issues about which information is needed or appropriate to enable the members of society to cope with the exigencies of their period"; *U.S. v. Harriss*, 347 U.S. 612 (1954), *Boyce Motor Lines v. U.S.*, 342 U.S. 337 (1952), *U.S. v. Ragen*, 314 U.S. 513 (1942), *U.S. v. Wurzbach*, 280 U.S. 396 (1930), *Hygrade Provision Co. v. Sherman*, 266 U.S. 497 (1925), *Fox v. Washington*, 236 U.S. 273 (1915), *Nash v. U.S.*, 229 U.S. 373 (1913), and *U.S. v. Petrillo*, 332 U.S. 1 (1947), on the ambiguous but not insufficient nature of legislative language; *United Pub. Workers v. Mitchell*, 330 U.S. 75 (1947), regarding "powers granted by the Constitution to the Federal Government are subtracted from the totality of sovereignty originally in the states and the people"; *Palko v. Connecticut*, 302 U.S. 319 (1937), on states' power confined by 14th Amendment if inconsistent with "ordered liberty"; *Gitlow v. New York*, 268 U.S. 652 (1925), regarding Justice Oliver Wendell Holmes's view on free speech as part of 14th Amendment; *Dennis v. U.S.*, 341 U.S. 494 (1951), holding that speech, to be punishable, must be related to action; *Giboney v. Empire Storage & Ice Co.*, 336 U.S. 490 (1949), and *NLRB v. Virginia Electric & P. Co.*, 314 U.S. 469 (1941).

Further Reading:

43 *ABA J.* 931 (Oct. 1957).

7 *American Univ. L. Rev.* 39 (Jan. 1958).

37 *Boston Univ. L. Rev.* 529 (Fall 1957).

7 *DePaul L. Rev.* 111 (Autumn–Winter 1957).

7 *Duke L. J.* 116 (Spring 1958).

26 *Fordham L. Rev.* 70 (Spring 1957).

71 *Harvard L. Rev.* 146 (Nov. 1957).

4 *Howard L. J.* 105 (Jan. 1958).

46 *Illinois Bar J.* 323 (Dec. 1957).

41 *Marquette L. Rev.* 320 (Winter 1957–58).

5 *New York Law Forum* 93 (Jan. 1959).

36 No. Carolina L. Rev. 189 (Feb. 1958).
19 *Ohio State L. J.* 137 (Winter 1958).
36 *Texas L. Rev.* 226 (Dec. 1957).
24 *Univ. Chicago L. Rev.* 769 (Summer 1957).
27 *Univ. Cincinnati L. Rev.* 61 (Winter 1958).
1957 *Univ. Illinois L. Forum* 499 (Fall 1957).
19 *Univ. Pittsburgh L. Rev.* 166 (Dec. 1957).
60 *West Virginia L. Rev.* 89 (Dec. 1957).

Note: Also on that day the Court decided *Kingsley Books Inc. v. Brown*, 354 U.S. 436 (1957), in which five members, in an opinion written by Justice Felix Frankfurter, upheld the constitutionality of a state statute permitting municipal injunctions against the sale or distribution of allegedly obscene books or magazines and which authorized seizure or destruction of such materials if found obscene at trial. The Court placed no restraint on matters not already, and not yet, found to be offensive. Frankfurter was joined by Justices Harold H. Burton, Tom C. Clark, John M. Harlan, and Charles E. Whittaker. Dissenting were Chief Justice Earl Warren and Justices William O. Douglas, Hugo L. Black, and William J. Brennan, Jr.

1959 *Eleazar Smith v. California*, 361 U.S. 147, 4 L.Ed.2d 205, 80 S.Ct. 215

Argued: Oct. 20, 1959.

Decided: Dec. 14, 1959.

Summary: Before a person can be convicted for selling obscene books, the state must prove scienter—that the seller had knowledge of the contents of the books.

Circumstances: Smith, the proprietor of a Los Angeles bookstore, was convicted in a municipal court under a city ordinance making it unlawful "for any person to have in his possession any obscene or indecent writing, [or] book . . . [i]n any place of business where . . . books . . . are sold or kept for sale." The

Appellate Division of the Superior Court for Los Angeles County affirmed the judgment, imposing a jail sentence. The offense, as defined by the municipal court, included no element of scienter, and thus the ordinance was construed as imposing a "strict" or "absolute" criminal liability. On appeal, the Supreme Court reversed.

Opinion: Justice William J. Brennan, Jr., wrote for five members of the Court, including Chief Justice Earl Warren and Justices Tom C. Clark, Charles E. Whittaker, and Potter Stewart. Justices Hugo L. Black, William O. Douglas, Felix Frankfurter, and John M. Harlan each concurred in separate opinions. Thus, a unanimous Court ruled that the city ordinance, though aimed at obscene matter, had such a tendency to inhibit constitutionally protected expression that it could not stand under the Constitution. The ordinance imposed criminal sanctions on a bookseller if an obscene book were found in his shop. "We think this ordinance's strict liability feature would tend seriously . . . to restrict the dissemination of books which are not obscene, by penalizing booksellers, even though they had not the slightest notice of the character of the books they sold." Elsewhere, Brennan said: "By dispensing with any requirement of knowledge of the contents of the book on the part of the seller, the ordinance tends to impose a severe limitation on the public's access to constitutionally protected matter."

Justice Black would have had the opinion more sweeping, noting separately that no government agency, including Congress and the Supreme Court, has the power to subordinate speech and press to what it thinks are more important interests. "If, as it seems, we are on the way to national censorship, I think it timely to suggest again that there are grave doubts in my mind as to the desirability or constitutionality of this Court's becoming a Supreme Board of censors—reading books and viewing television performances to determine whether, if permitted, they might adversely affect the morals of the people throughout the many diversified local communities in this vast country. Censorship is the deadly enemy of freedom and progress. The plain language of the Constitution forbids it. I protest against the Judiciary giving it a foothold here."

Justice Douglas, relying on his dissent in *Roth v. U.S.* (1957), added, "Neither we nor legislatures have power . . . to weigh the values of speech or utterance against silence. The only grounds for suppressing this book are very narrow. I have read it; and while it is repulsive to me, its publication or distribution can be constitutionally punished only on a showing not attempted here." Justice Frankfurter concurred because the trial court violated the 14th Amendment's due process clause by excluding the testimony of qualified witnesses regarding the prevailing literary standards and moral criteria by which books comparable to the one in question are deemed not obscene. Justice Harlan, concurring in part and dissenting in part, held the conviction defective because the trial judge denied every attempt to introduce evidence of community standards. He wanted the judgment reversed and remanded for a new trial.

Referenced Cases: *Near v. Minnesota*, 283 U.S. 697 (1931), on safeguarding press and speech via due process clause of the 14th Amendment; *Dennis v. U.S.*, 341 U.S. 494 (1951), and *Lambert v. California*, 355 U.S. 225 (1957), on the element of scienter in criminal jurisprudence; *Speiser v. Randall*, 357 U.S. 513 (1958), *Thornhill v. Alabama*, 310 U.S. 88 (1940), *Winters v. New York*, 333 U.S. 507 (1948), and *Wieman v. Updegraff*, 344 U.S. 183 (1952), on burden of proof, unconstitutional applications of statutes, and elimination of scienter; *Roth v. U.S.*, 354 U.S. 476 (1957), establishing obscene speech as unprotected; *U.S. v. Balint*, 258 U.S. 250 (1922), and *Morissette v. U.S.*, 342 U.S. 246 (1952), similar decisions on censorial role of merchants, comparing "what feeds the belly" to "what feeds the brain"; *American Communications Asso. v. Douds*, 339 U.S. 382 (1950), on exploring the state of a man's mind; *Dean Milk Co. v. Madison*, 340 U.S. 349 (1951), on the limits of state power; *Beauharnais v. Illinois*, 343 U.S. 250 (1952), on Justice Black's dissent, a "Pyrrhic victory" for speech and press; *Boyd v. U.S.*, 116 U.S. 616 (1886), regarding "stealthy encroachments" on citizens' rights; *Fox v. Washington*, 236 U.S. 273 (1915), holding that not all laws against defamation and inciting crime by speech are unconstitutional; *Giboney v. Empire Storage Co. v. U.S.*, 336 U.S. 490 (1949), and *NLRB v. Virginia Power Co.*, 314 U.S. 469 (1941), on the relationship between expression and illegal action.

Further Reading:
46 *ABA J.* 197 (Feb. 1960).
26 *Brooklyn L. Rev.* 289 (April 1960).

74 *Harvard L. Rev.* 126 (Nov. 1960).
38 *No. Carolina L. Rev.* 634 (June 1960).
35 *NYU L. Rev.* 1086 (May 1960).
21 *Ohio State L. J.* 242 (Spring 1960).
2 *William & Mary L. Rev.* 491 (1960).

1964   *Nico Jacobellis v. Ohio*, 378 U.S. 184, 12 L.Ed.2d 793, 84 S.Ct. 1676

Reargued: April 1, 1964.

Decided: June 22, 1964.

Summary: Obscenity must be determined on the basis of a "national" standard, and the primary test for measuring censurable material is whether it is "utterly without redeeming social importance."

Circumstances: Jacobellis, manager of a motion picture theater in Cleveland Heights, was convicted on two counts of possessing and exhibiting an obscene film in violation of Ohio law. *Les Amants* (The Lovers) depicted an unhappy marriage, the wife's falling in love with a younger man, and an explicit, but brief, love scene toward the end. Jacobellis was fined $500 on the first count and $2,000 on the second, and sentenced to the workhouse if the fines were not paid. His conviction by three judges in the Court of Common Pleas, Cuyahoga County, having waived trial by jury, was affirmed by an intermediate appellate court and by the state supreme court. On appeal, the U.S. Supreme Court reversed.

Opinion: Although six justices voted to reverse the Ohio courts, they were unable to agree on an opinion in support of the holding. Concurring in the reversal were Justices William J. Brennan, Jr., Arthur J. Goldberg, Hugo L. Black, William O. Douglas, Potter Stewart, and Byron R. White. Dissenting were Chief Justice Earl Warren and Justices Tom C. Clark and John M. Harlan. Brennan, joined by Goldberg, reiterated the constitutional test as first enunciated in *Roth-Alberts* (1957), that "whether to the average person, applying contemporary community standards, the dominant theme of the material taken as a whole appeals to prurient interest," and that obscenity is excluded from the constitutional protection only because it is "utterly without redeeming social importance." He also reaffirmed the position taken in *Roth-Alberts* to the effect that the protected status of an allegedly obscene work must be determined on the basis of a national standard. "It is, after all, a national Constitution we are expounding." Black, joined by Douglas, concurred on the broad ground that a conviction for exhibiting a motion picture abridges freedom of the press as safeguarded by the First Amendment, which is made obligatory on the states by the 14th. Stewart reached the conclusion that, under those amendments, criminal laws in the area are constitutionally limited to hard-core pornography. Although the justice did not attempt to define "hard-core," nor perhaps could he ever intelligibly do so, he said: "But I know it when I see it, and the motion picture involved in this case is not that."

Warren, joined by Clark, dissented, believing that the Court meant community, not national, in its reference to standards in *Roth-Alberts*. "This is the only reasonable way . . . to obviate the necessity of this Court's sitting as the Super Censor of all the obscenity purveyed throughout the Nation." Harlan, also in dissent, said that he would make the test one of "rationality" for the states and that they should not be prohibited from banning any material which, taken as a whole, has been found in state judicial proceedings "to treat sex in a fundamentally offensive manner."

Referenced Cases: *Joseph Burstyn Inc. v. Wilson*, 343 U.S. 495 (1952), on motion pictures within the ambit of the First Amendment; *Roth v. U.S.* and *Alberts v. California*, 354 U.S. 476 (1957), on obscenity not being subject to protection; *Bantam Books v. Sullivan*, 372 U.S. 58 (1963), and *Speiser v. Randall*, 357 U.S. 513 (1958), on the "dim and uncertain line" that often separates obscenity from protected expression; *Manual Enterprises v. Day*, 370 U.S. 478 (1962), on "facing up to the tough individual problems of constitutional judgment involved in every obscenity case"; *Watts v. Indiana*, 338 U.S. 49 (1949), *Norris v. Alabama*, 294 U.S. 587 (1935), and *Pennekamp v. Florida*, 328 U.S. 331 (1946), on the Court's duty to review facts of each case independently and according to the due process clause; *Kingsley Int'l Pictures v. Regents*, 360 U.S. 684 (1959), on sex as portrayed in nonobscene settings; *Butler v. Michigan*, 352 U.S. 380 (1957), and *Smith v. California*, 361 U.S. 147 (1959), on local community standards of decency; *Thompson v. Louisville*, 362 U.S. 199 (1960), and *Universal Camera Corp. v. Labor Board*, 340 U.S. 474 (1951), on establishing a standard of evidence for obscenity cases.

Further Reading:
51 *ABA J.* 173 (Feb. 1965).
78 *Harvard L. Rev.* 207 (Nov. 1964).
43 *No. Carolina L. Rev.* 172 (Dec. 1964).
40 *Notre Dame Lawyer* 1 (Dec. 1964).
16 *So. Carolina L. Rev.* 639 (1964).
16 *Western Reserve L. Rev.* 780 (May 1965).

1964　　*A Quantity of Copies of Books et al. v. Kansas*, 378 U.S. 205, 12 L.Ed.2d 809, 84 S.Ct. 1723

Argued: April 1, 2, 1964.

Decided: June 22, 1964.

Summary: Found constitutionally deficient a state statute allowing prosecutors to obtain warrants for the seizure of allegedly obscene materials prior to an adversary hearing to determine their obscenity.

Circumstances: Under a Kansas statute authorizing seizure of allegedly obscene books before an adversary determination of their obscenity—and, after determination, their destruction—the attorney general secured an order from the District Court of Geary County for the sheriff to seize certain paperback novels from the P-K News Service, Junction City. After the hearing, the court directed the sheriff to destroy 1,715 copies of 31 novels. The state supreme court upheld the procedures and affirmed the order. On appeal, the U.S. Supreme Court reversed.

Opinion: As with *Jacobellis v. Ohio* (1964), determined the same day, the seven justices voting to reverse the Kansas courts did not agree on an opinion. The warrant authorized the sheriff to seize all copies of specified titles, which were subsequently held obscene and ordered destroyed. Justice William J. Brennan, Jr., wrote for the plurality, including Chief Justice Earl Warren and Justices Byron R. White and Arthur J. Goldberg. They deemed the Kansas procedure unconstitutional for failure to afford "a hearing on the question of . . . obscenity . . . before the warrant issued. For if seizure of books precedes an adversary determination of their obscenity, there is danger of abridgment of the right of the public in a free society to unobstructed circulation of nonobscene books." The plurality drew upon the Court's first such case, *Marcus v. Search Warrant* (1961), reversing a Missouri judgment directing the destruction of copies of 100 obscene publications. In that case, the Court ruled that, even assuming obscenity, the procedures were deficient for lack of safeguards against suppression of nonobscene publications protected by the Constitution. Justice Hugo L. Black, joined by William O. Douglas, concurred on the ground that book-burning violates the First and 14th Amendments. They found the procedural questions irrelevant. Justice Potter Stewart found no fault with the procedures, unlike the "unlimited authority" deemed wanting in *Marcus*, but concurred because the books were not hard-core pornography, his rationale in *Jacobellis*. Justice John M. Harlan, joined by Tom C. Clark, dissented, as in *Jacobellis*, on the grounds that Kansas could find the books obscene and that the Constitution does not require an adversary hearing before seizure. Harlan said Brennan's opinion "straitjackets the legitimate attempt of Kansas to protect what it considers an important societal interest."

Referenced Cases: *Marcus v. Search Warrant,* 367 U.S. 717 (1961), on a "strikingly similar" Missouri search-and-seizure statute and implementing court rule; *Kingsley Books Inc. v. Brown,* 354 U.S. 436 (1957), permitting injunctions against distribution of obscene material and allowing seizure; *Bantam Books v. Sullivan,* 372 U.S. 58 (1963), on the constitutional requirement of a procedure "designed to focus searchingly on the question of obscenity"; *Speiser v. Randall,* 357 U.S. 513 (1958), and *Smith v. California,* 361 U.S. 147 (1959), on separation of legitimate from illegitimate speech; *Jacobellis v. Ohio,* 378 U.S. 197 (1964), Justice Stewart on hard-core pornography; *Times Film Corp. v. Chicago,* 365 U.S. 43 (1961), on prior restraint requiring "particularistic analysis."

Further Reading:
51 *ABA J.* 174 (Feb. 1965).
78 *Harvard L. Rev.* 207 (Nov. 1964).
1 *L. Ed. 2d* 2211
4 *L. Ed. 2d* 1821

1965   *Ronald L. Freedman v. Maryland,* **380 U.S. 51, 13 L.Ed.2d 649, 85 S.Ct. 734**

Argued: Nov. 19, 1964.

Decided: March 1, 1965.

Summary: Struck down procedures for determining whether a motion picture was obscene because the burden of proof was up to the exhibitor. Also, the statute provided no assurance of prompt judicial review of an adverse administrative ruling.

Circumstances: Freedman challenged the constitutionality of the Maryland motion picture censorship statute and showed the film *Revenge at Daybreak* at his Baltimore theater without first submitting the picture to the state Board of Censors as required by the law. The state conceded that the film was acceptable and Freedman would have received a license to show it. He was convicted on the violation, and the state court of appeals affirmed. The Supreme Court reversed, finding the statute unconstitutional.

Opinion: A unanimous Court found that the First Amendment had been violated by a Maryland motion picture censorship statute that requires film exhibitors to submit films they want to show to a board of censors prior to showing; the statute then bans unapproved films. Justice William J. Brennan, Jr., wrote for seven members, including Chief Justice Earl Warren and Justices Tom C. Clark, John M. Harlan, Potter Stewart, Byron R. White, and Arthur J. Goldberg. William O. Douglas, joined by Hugo L. Black, concurred separately. Brennan said that the administration of a censorship system for motion pictures presented peculiar dangers to constitutionally protected speech. Unlike a prosecution for obscenity, he said, a censorship proceeding puts the initial burden on the exhibitor or distributor. "Because the censor's business is to censor, there inheres the danger that he may well be less responsive than a court—part of an independent branch of government—to the constitutionally protected interests in free expression. And if it is made unduly onerous, by reason of delay or otherwise, to seek judicial review, the censor's determination may in practice be final." But the Court held that a noncriminal process can avoid "constitutional infirmity" only if the following safeguards are present: (1) the burden of proving that the film is unprotected expression rests on the censor; (2) the requirement of advance submission cannot be administered to lend finality to censor's determination; and (3) the procedure must ensure a prompt final judicial decision to minimize the deterrent effect of an interim and possibly erroneous denial of a license. "The Maryland scheme fails to provide adequate safeguards against undue inhibition of protected expression, and this renders the requirement of prior submission of films to the Board an invalid previous restraint." Justice Douglas said movies are entitled to the same degree and kind of protection under the First Amendment as other forms of expression. "I would put an end to all forms and types of censorship and give full literal meaning to the command of the First Amendment."

Referenced Cases: *Times Film Corp. v. Chicago*, 365 U.S. 43 (1961), and *Bantam Books v. Sullivan*, 372 U.S. 58 (1963), on upholding of submission of films prior to showing, but not "under all circumstances"; *Near v. Minnesota*, 283 U.S. 697 (1931), on "protection even as to previous restraint is not absolutely unlimited"; *Thornhill v. Alabama*, 310 U.S. 88 (1940), *Staub v. Baxley*, 355 U.S. 313 (1958), *Saia v. New York*, 334 U.S. 558 (1948), *Thomas v. Collins*, 323 U.S. 516 (1945), *Hague v. CIO*, 307 U.S. 496 (1939), *Lovell v. Griffin*, 303 U.S. 444 (1938), and *NAACP v. Button*, 371 U.S. 415 (1963), regarding "one who might have had a license for the asking may . . . call into question the whole scheme of licensing when he is prosecuted for failure to procure it"; *Marcus v. Search Warrant*, 367 U.S. 717 (1961), *Manual Enterprises v. Day*, 370 U.S. 478 (1962), and *A Quantity of Books v. Kansas*, 378 U.S. 205 (1964), on the need for judicial determination in freedom of expression cases; *Kingsley Books v. Brown,* 354 U.S. 436 (1957), on state injunctive procedure for preventing sale of obscene books.

Further Reading:
51 *ABA J.* 481 (May 1965).
17 *Baylor L. Rev.* 119 (Winter 1965).
54 *California L. Rev.* 1832 (Oct. 1966).
79 *Harvard L. Rev.* 149 (Nov. 1965).
20 *Law and Contemporary Prob.* 648 (1955).
10 *St. Louis Univ. L. J.* 142 (Fall 1965).
109 *Univ. Pa. L. Rev.* 67 (1960).

1966   *A Book Named "John Cleland's Memoirs of a Woman of Pleasure" et al. v. Attorney General of Massachusetts,* 383 U.S. 413, 16 L.Ed.2d 1, 86 S.Ct 975, 1 Med.L.Rptr. 1390

Argued: Dec. 7, 8, 1965.

Decided: March 21, 1966.

Summary: Reversing a determination in a state civil equity action that the book commonly known as *Fanny Hill* was obscene, the Court reaffirmed the three-part test of *Roth v. U.S.* (1957).

Circumstances: Cleland's book, commonly known as *Fanny Hill*, was written in about 1750. In a civil equity suit brought by the Massachusetts attorney general, it was judged obscene in a proceeding that put on trial the book, not its publisher, G. P. Putnam's Sons, or its distributor. Putnam's had reissued the book in 1963. A large number of orders were placed by universities and libraries, including the Library of Congress, which requested permission to translate the volume into Braille. "But the Commonwealth of Massachusetts instituted the suit that ultimately found its way here," according to Justice William O. Douglas, "praying that the book be declared obscene so that the citizens of Massachusetts might be spared the necessity of determining for themselves whether or not to read it." At a hearing before a judge of the state superior court, expert witnesses testified to the book's literary, cultural, or educational value. The judge found *Fanny Hill* obscene and not entitled to constitutional protection. The Massachusetts Supreme Court affirmed. On appeal to the U.S. Supreme Court, Justice William J. Brennan, Jr., noted that the sole question before the state courts was whether the book satisfied the test of obscenity established in *Roth*. The Court found the judgment based on an erroneous interpretation of the federal constitutional standard.

Opinion: There was no opinion of the Court, although six justices agreed on reversal. Justice William J. Brennan, Jr.'s plurality opinion, joined by Chief Justice Earl Warren and Justice Abe Fortas, argued that under *Roth* and its companion, *Alberts v. California* (1957), a work may not be deemed obscene "in the abstract" unless "three elements . . . coalesce: it must be established that (a) the dominant theme of the material taken as a whole appeals to a prurient interest in sex; (b) the material is patently offensive because it affronts contemporary community standards relating to the description or representation of sexual maters; and (c) the material is utterly without redeeming social value." The Supreme Judicial Court of Massachusetts had erred in holding the book obscene even though it found that "'the testimony may indicate this book has some minimal literary value.'" Brennan noted that for a book to be proscribed it must be found to be *utterly* without redeeming social value, even though it is found to possess the requisite prurient appeal and to be patently offensive.

Justices Hugo L. Black and Potter Stewart concurred for reasons stated in their dissents in *Ginzburg v. U.S.* and *Mishkin v. New York*, both decided the same day as *Memoirs*. Black said the Court was without constitutional power to censor regardless of the subject matter discussed. Stewart said the book was not "hardcore" pornography. Justice William O. Douglas concurred on the ground that "the First Amendment does not permit the censorship of expression not brigaded with illegal action." He questioned the Court's deciding the case on so "disingenuous" a basis as *Fanny Hill* having at least "some minimal literary value." Elaborating more than was his custom, Douglas instructed: "Every time an obscenity case is to be argued here, my office is flooded with letters and postal cards urging me to protect the community or the Nation by striking down the publication. The messages are often identical even down to commas and semicolons. The inference is irresistible that they were all copied from a school or church blackboard. Dozens of postal cards often are mailed from the same precinct. The drives are incessant and the pressures are great. Happily we do not bow to them. I mention them only to emphasize the lack of popular understanding of our constitutional system. Publications and utterances were made immune from majoritarian control by the First Amendment, applicable to the States by reason of the Fourteenth. No exceptions were made, not even for obscenity. The Court's contrary conclusion in *Roth*, where obscenity was found to be 'outside' the First Amendment, is without justification."

Justice Tom C. Clark, dissenting, wrote that he had "stomached" such cases for almost ten years and that "this book is too much even for me." He accused the publisher, G. P. Putnam's Sons, of "preying upon prurient and carnal proclivities for its own pecuniary advantage." Justice John M. Harlan, dissenting, said his premise was that, in the area of obscenity, the Constitution does not bind the states and the federal government in the same fashion: "The Fourteenth Amendment requires of a State only that it apply criteria rationally related to the accepted notion of obscenity and that it reach results not wholly out of step with current American standards." Justice Byron R. White dissented on the ground that if a state insists on treating *Fanny Hill* as obscene and forbidding its sale, the First Amendment does not prevent it from doing so. "Censure stems from a legislative act, and legislatures are constitutionally free to embrace such books whenever they wish to do so."

Referenced Cases: *Ginzburg v. U.S.*, 383 U.S. 463 (1966), and *Mishkin v. New York*, 383 U.S. 502 (1966), on purveyor's emphasis on sexually provocative aspects of publications, decided the same day; *Bridges v. California*, 314 U.S. 252 (1941), on the First Amendment and common law; *New York Times v. Sullivan*, 376 U.S. 254 (1964), on claiming no "talismanic immunity from constitutional limitations"; *Kingsley Int'l Pictures v. Regents*, 360 U.S. 684 (1959), and *Joseph Burstyn v. Wilson*, 343 U.S. 495 (1952), on First Amendment as absolute; *Roth v. U.S.* and

Alberts v. California, 354 U.S. 476 (1957), on *"utterly* without redeeming social value" as standard; *Chaplinsky v. New Hampshire*, 315 U.S. 568 (1942), on weighing social value against social order and morality; *Manual Enterprises v. Day*, 370 U.S. 478 (1962), and *Jacobellis v. Ohio*, 378 U.S. 184 (1964), on the evolving "social value" test; *Gitlow v. New York*, 268 U.S. 652 (1925), the Court's first indication that the 14th Amendment protects "free speech"; *Schneider v. State*, 308 U.S. 147 (1939), *Schenck v. U.S.*, 249 U.S. 47 (1919), *Dennis v. U.S.*, 341 U.S. 494 (1951), *Beauharnais v. Illinois*, 343 U.S. 250 (1952), and *Kovacs v. Cooper*, 336 U.S. 77 (1949), decisions regulating utterances.

Further Reading:
52 *Harvard L. Rev.* 40 (1938).
45 *Minnesota L. Rev.* 5 (1960).
46 *Minnesota L. Rev.* 1009 (1962).
25 *Univ. Pittsburgh L. Rev.* 469 (1964).
10 *Wayne L. Rev.* 655 (1964).
See also under *Ginzburg v. U.S.*, 383 U.S. 463 (1966), decided the same day.

1966   *Ralph Ginzburg et al. v. U.S.*, 383 U.S. 463, 16 L.Ed.2d 31, 86 S.Ct. 942, 1 Med.L.Rptr. 1409

Argued: Dec. 7, 1965.

Decided: March 21, 1966.

Summary: The manner in which material is marketed, advertised, and displayed is a factor in determining whether a work is obscene, called "pandering" or "the business of purveying textual or graphic matter openly advertised to appeal to the erotic interest of customers."

Circumstances: A judge sitting without a jury in the District Court for the Eastern District of Pennsylvania convicted Ginzburg and three of his corporations on all 28 counts of an indictment charging violation of the federal obscenity statute, 18 U.S.C. Section 1461. The three publications mailed were *Eros*, a hardcover expensive magazine; "Liaison," a biweekly newsletter; and *The Housewife's Handbook on Selective Promiscuity*. *Eros* had sought mailing privileges from the postmasters of Intercourse and Blue Ball, Pennsylvania, indicating to the trial court that the basis of appeal was salacious. Turned down, mailing privileges were obtained from Middlesex, New Jersey. The Court of Appeals for the Third Circuit affirmed the convictions, as did the Supreme Court.

Opinion: Justice William J. Brennan, Jr., wrote the Court's 5-to-4 decision, joined by Chief Justice Earl Warren and Justices Tom C. Clark, Byron R. White, and Abe Fortas. Dissenting were Hugo L. Black, William O. Douglas, John M. Harlan, and Potter Stewart, each of whom wrote separate opinions. The Court affirmed a federal conviction for mailing three publications: a hardcover magazine dealing with sex, a sexual newsletter, and a short book purporting to be a sexual autobiography. Brennan noted that "the prosecution charged the offense in the context of the circumstances of production, sale, and publicity and assumed that, standing alone, the publications themselves might not be obscene." Brennan, for the Court, found "abundant evidence to show that each of the accused publications was originated or sold as stock in trade of the sordid business of pandering" and that "this evidence . . . was relevant in determining the ultimate question of obscenity and . . . serves to resolve all ambiguity and doubt. . . . Where the purveyor's sole emphasis is on the sexually provocative aspects of his publications, that fact may be decisive in the determination of obscenity" although "in other contexts the material would escape such condemnation."

Justice Black, in dissent, argued simply that the federal government is without any power whatever under the Constitution to put any type of burden on speech and expression of ideas of any kind, as distinguished from conduct. "As bad and obnoxious as I believe governmental censorship is in a Nation that has accepted the First Amendment as its basic ideal for freedom, I am compelled to say that censorship that would stamp certain books and literature as illegal in advance of publication or conviction would in some ways be preferable to the unpredictable book-by-book censorship into which we have now drifted." Justice Douglas added: "A book should stand on its own, irrespective of the reasons why it was written or the wiles used in selling it. It is shocking to me for us to send to prison anyone for publishing anything, especially tracts so distant from any incitement to action as the ones before us." Justice Harlan dissented on the ground that the federal government is restricted to banning from the mails only "hard-core" pornography, which was not the narrow class of the publications involved. Stewart averred that, if the First Amendment means anything, it means that a man cannot be sent to prison merely for distributing publications that offend a judge's aesthetic sensibilities, "mine or any other's." Censorship, he said, reflects a society's lack of confidence in itself. "It is the hallmark of an authoritarian regime. In upholding and enforcing the Bill of Rights, this Court has no power to pick or to choose. When we lose sight of that fixed star of constitutional adjudication, we lose our way. For then we forsake a government of law and are left with government by Big Brother."

Referenced Cases: *Roth v. U.S.*, 354 U.S. 476 (1957), on the standards for judging obscenity; *Mishkin v. New York*, 383 U.S. 502 (1966), decided the same day as *Ginzberg*, regarding a background of the commercial exploitation of erotica solely for prurient appeal; *Cole v. Arkansas*, 333 U.S. 196 (1948), and *Shuttlesworth v. Birmingham*, 382 U.S. 87 (1969), on affirming a conviction and sentence on the basis of an amended statute not part of charge; *Dombrowski v. Pfister*, 380 U.S. 479 (1965), *Smith v. California*, 361 U.S. 147 (1959), and *Speiser v. Randall*, 357 U.S. 513 (1958), on vigilance in safeguarding First Amendment rights; *Memoirs v. Massachusetts*, 383 U.S. 413 (1966), decided the same day as *Mishkin* and *Ginzberg*, on the danger in courts sifting and choosing among conflicting versions of the "redeeming social importance" of a work; *One Inc. v. Olesen*, 355 U.S. 371 (1958), on appealing to specific tastes and interests, in this instance, homosexuals; *Manual Enterprises v. Day*, 370 U.S. 478 (1962), on focusing solely on the character of the material in question.

Further Reading:
52 *ABA J.* 478 (May 1966).
19 *Alabama L. Rev.* 187 (Fall 1966).
31 *Albany L. Rev.* 143 (Jan. 1967).
16 *American Univ. L. Rev.* 122 (Dec. 1966).

OBSCENITY

Colorado L. Rev. 152 (Fall 1966).
Connecticut Bar J. 670 (Dec. 1966).
Cornell L. Q. 785 (Summer 1966).
George Washington L. Rev. 85 (Oct. 1966).
Harvard L. Rev. 124 (Nov. 1966).
Louisiana L. Rev. 100 (Dec. 1966).
Missouri L. Rev. 127 (Winter 1967).
Rutgers L. Rev. 43, 497 (Fall 1966).
So. Carolina L. Rev. 497 (1966).
Tennessee L. Rev. 516 (Summer 1966).
Texas L. Rev. 1382 (July 1966).
Tulane L. Rev. 126 (Dec. 1966).
Univ. Florida L. Rev. 185 (Summer 1966).
Univ. Pittsburgh L. Rev. 1 (Oct. 1966).
Villanova L. Rev. 869 (Summer 1966).
Western Reserve L. Rev. 1325 (June 1966).

1966   *Edward Mishkin v. New York*, 383 U.S. 502, 16 L.Ed.2d 56, 86 S.Ct. 958

Argued: Dec. 7, 1965.

Decided: March 21, 1966.

Summary: Found scienter adequate and state statute constitutionally valid in affirming convictions for distributing obscene books appealing to "deviant" prurient interests and sexual practices.

Circumstances: A panel of three judges of the Court of Special Sessions of the City of New York found Mishkin guilty of violating Section 1141 of the New York Penal Law by hiring others to prepare, publish, and possess obscene books with the intent to sell them. He was sentenced to three years in prison and fined $12,000. The Appellate Division, First Department, affirmed, as did the state Court of Appeals. On appeal, the Supreme Court also affirmed.

MISHKIN v. NEW YORK

Opinion: Justice William J. Brennan, Jr., delivered the Court's 6-to-3 opinion, joined by Chief Justice Earl Warren and Justices Tom C. Clark, Byron R. White, and Abe Fortas, the same majority as in *Ginzburg v. U.S.* (1966), decided the same day. This time, however, John M. Harlan joined the Court's opinion but filed a separate concurrence. Dissenting in separate opinions, as each had also done in *Ginzburg*, were Hugo L. Black, William O. Douglas, and Potter Stewart. The Court affirmed convictions for distributing obscene books, most of which, Brennan said, "depict such deviations as sado-masochism, fetishism and homosexuality." Brennan rejected Mishkin's contention that books "depicting various deviant sexual practices . . . do not satisfy the prurient-appeal requirement because they do not appeal to a prurient interest of the 'average person' in sex." The Court held, rather, that "where the material is designed for and primarily disseminated to a clearly defined deviant sexual group, rather than the public at large, the prurient-appeal requirement of the *Roth* test is satisfied if the dominant theme of the material taken as a whole appeals to the prurient interest in sex of the members of that group." Justice Harlan concurred on the issue of obscenity, reiterating the view expressed in his dissent in *Memoirs v. Massachusetts* (1966), decided the same day as *Mishkin* and *Ginzburg*, that the 14th Amendment requires of a state only that it apply criteria rationally to the notion of obscenity. Justice Black announced in dissent that the First and 14th Amendments taken together command that neither Congress nor the states shall pass laws "which in any manner abridge freedom of speech and press—whatever the subjects discussed." Justice Stewart dissented because, "however tawdry those books may be, they are not hard-core pornography," and their publication is, therefore, protected by the First and 14th Amendments. Justice Douglas applied his *Ginzburg* dissent.

Referenced Cases: *Ginzburg v. U.S.*, 383 U.S. 463 (1966), involving, like *Mishkin*, convictions under a criminal obscenity statute; *Roth v. U.S.*, 354 U.S. 476 (1957), on the term "obscene"; *Smith v. California*, 361 U.S. 147 (1959), on the scienter requirement; *Flournoy v. Weiner*, 321 U.S. 253 (1944), and *Prudential Ins. Co. v. Cheek*, 259 U.S. 530 (1922), on the Court's probable jurisdiction; *A Quantity of Books v. Kansas*, 378 U.S. 205 (1964), and *Marcus v. Search Warrant*, 367 U.S. 717 (1961), on First Amendment aspect of search and seizure issue; *The Monrosa v.*

Carbon Black, 359 U.S. 180 (1959), on an improvidently granted writ of certiorari; *Memoirs v. Massachusetts*, 383 U.S. 413 (1966), regarding Justice Harlan's dissent.

Further Reading:
See under *Ginzburg v. U.S.*, 383 U.S. 463 (1966), decided the same day.

1967   *Robert Redrup v. New York, William L. Austin v. Kentucky, and Gent et al v. Arkansas*, 386 U.S. 767, 18 L.Ed.2d 515, 87 S.Ct. 1414

Argued: Oct. 10, 11, 1966.

Decided: May 8, 1967.

Summary: A per curiam opinion, reversing convictions for selling obscene books to willing adults.

Circumstances: Redrup, a clerk at a New York City newsstand, was arrested when he sold two paperback books, *Lust Pool* and *Shame Agent*, to plainclothes policemen. Total cost of the books was $1.65. He was convicted in the city criminal court. The Appellate Term of the Supreme Court of New York, First Judicial Department, affirmed. Austin, owner and operator of a bookstore and newsstand in Paducah, was convicted for violating Kentucky criminal law after one of his saleswomen sold two magazines, *High Heels* and *Spree*, to a woman resident of the town. In the third case, the prosecuting attorney of the 11th Judicial District of Arkansas brought civil proceedings under a state law to have certain issues of various magazines declared obscene, among them *Gent*, *Swank*, *Bachelor*, *Modern Man*, *Cavalcade*, *Gentleman*, *Ace*, and *Sir*. The County Chancery Court entered the requested judgment after a trial with an advisory jury. The Arkansas Supreme Court affirmed. The U.S. Supreme Court reversed in all cases.

Opinion: The three cases arose from a "recurring conflict" between state power to suppress the distribution of books and magazines through criminal or civil proceedings, and the guarantees of the First and 14th Amendments. The Court concluded that distribution in each case was protected from suppression, whether criminal or civil, in personam, "against the person," or in rem, "against the thing." Justices Hugo L. Black and William O. Douglas consistently held that a state is utterly without power to suppress, control, or punish the distribution of any writings or pictures upon the ground of their "obscenity." Justice Potter Stewart held that a state's power is narrowly limited to a distinct and clearly identifiable class of material, described as "hard-core" pornography. Other members of the Court subscribed to a "not dissimilar standard," holding to the three-part standard enunciated in *Roth v. U.S.*, 354 U.S. 476 (1957), and in *Memoirs v. Massachusetts* (1966), known as the Roth-Memoirs Test, a coalescent definition of obscenity. Justice John M. Harlan did not view the "social value" element as an independent factor in judging obscenity. "Whichever of these constitutional views is brought to bear upon the cases before us, it is clear that the judgments cannot stand." Harlan and Tom C. Clark dissented, arguing that the Court failed to address specific questions raised by each case. The dispositions do not reflect well on the processes of the Court, Harlan said.

Referenced Cases: *Prince v. Massachusetts*, 321 U.S. 158 (1944), and *Butler v. Michigan*, 352 U.S. 380 (1957), on state concern for juveniles; *Beard v. Alexandria*, 341 U.S. 622 (1951), and *Public Utilities Comm'n v. Pollak*, 343 U.S. 451 (1952), on invading individual privacy; *Ginzburg v. U.S.*, 383 U.S. 463 (1966), on pandering; *Memoirs v. Massachusetts*, 383 U.S. 413 (1966), on "obscene in the constitutional sense"; *Smith v. California*, 361 U.S. 147 (1959), on the scienter requirement.

Further Reading:
53 *ABA J.* 657 (July 1967).
21 *Hastings L. J.* 175 (1969).

1968 *Interstate Circuit, Inc. v. Dallas* and *United Artists Corp. v. Dallas*, 390 U.S. 676, 20 L.Ed.2d 225, 88 S.Ct. 1298

Argued: Jan. 15, 16, 1968.

Decided: April 22, 1968.

Summary: Voided for vagueness a city ordinance designed to classify films as suitable or not suitable for persons under age 16.

Circumstances: An exhibitor and distributor of a film, *Viva Maria*, deemed "not suitable for young persons," was enjoined from exhibiting it without acceptance of the requirements imposed by the restricted classification. The Texas Court of Civil Appeals, Fifth Supreme Judicial District, affirmed and the Texas Supreme Court denied discretionary review. On appeal, the U.S. Supreme Court reversed the court of civil appeals.

Opinion: Justice Thurgood Marshall wrote for six members in the 8-to-1 decision, including Chief Justice Earl Warren and Justices Tom C. Clark, William J. Brennan, Jr., Potter Stewart, and Byron R. White. William O. Douglas, joined by Hugo L. Black, concurred separately. John M. Harlan dissented. A film was unsuitable in Dallas if, inter alia, it portrayed "sexual promiscuity" so as to "create the impression on young persons that such conduct is profitable, desirable, acceptable, respectable, praiseworthy or commonly accepted," of if "its calculated or dominant effect on young persons is substantially to arouse sexual desire." Marshall noted that vagueness and its "attendant evils" are not rendered less objectionable because the regulation of expression is one of classification rather than direct suppression. Such vague ordinances, if allowed to spread to other localities, could inhibit filmmakers, distributors, and exhibitors. Local exhibitors, who cannot afford to risk losing the youthful audience when a film may be of marginal interest to adults, may contract to show only the totally inane, Marshall said. "The vast wasteland that some have described in reference to another medium might be a verdant paradise in comparison." The Court held the ordinance unconstitutionally vague because it failed to provide sufficiently narrow standards and definitions for the classification board to employ. Justice Douglas, joined by Black, said that even obscene material was protected by the First Amendment.

Justice Harlan, dissenting and noting the Court had entered a new phase of the "intractable obscenity problem," said that, in all except rare instances, no substantial free-speech interest is at stake, given the right of the states to control obscenity. "From the standpoint of the Court itself the current approach has required us to spend an inordinate amount of time in the absurd business of perusing and viewing the miserable stuff that pours into the Court, mostly in state cases, all to no better end than second-guessing state judges."

Referenced Cases: *Joseph Burstyn v. Wilson*, 343 U.S. 495 (1952), on First Amendment protection of motion pictures; *NAACP v. Button*, 371 U.S. 415 (1963), on the necessary "precision of regulation"; *Freedman v. Maryland*, 380 U.S. 51 (1965), and *Times Film Corp. v. Chicago*, 365 U.S. 43 (1961), on procedural safeguards and judicial superintendence of censor's action; *Winters v. New York*, 333 U.S. 507 (1948), regarding vague and indefinite statutory standards; *Gelling v. Texas*, 343 U.S. 960 (1952), *Superior Films Inc. v. Dept. of Education*, 346 U.S. 587 (1954), *Commercial Pictures v. Regents*, 346 U.S. 587 (1954), *Holmby Productions v. Vaughn*, 350 U.S. 870 (1955), and *Kingsley Int'l Pictures v. Regents*, 360 U.S. 684 (1959), on film licensing standards judged unconstitutionally vague; *Roth v. U.S.*, 354 U.S. 476 (1957), on the Court's obscenity standards; *Bantam Books v. Sullivan*, 372 U.S. 58 (1963), on classification as opposed to direct suppression; *Ginsberg v. New York*, 390 U.S. 629 (1968), on regulating dissemination to juveniles; *Niemotko v. Maryland*, 340 U.S. 268 (1951), on narrowly drawn, reasonable, and definite standards; *Memoirs v. Massachusetts*, 383 U.S. 413 (1966), and *Ginzburg v. U.S.*, 383 U.S. 463 (1966), on refinement of standards developed in *Roth*; *Manual Enterprises v. Day*, 370 U.S. 478 (1962), and *Jacobellis v. Ohio*, 378 U.S. 184 (1964), for Justice Harlan on hardcore pornography and prudish overzealousness as standards.

Further Reading:
54 *ABA J.* 702 (July 1968).
33 *Albany L. Rev.* 173 (Fall 1968).

55 *California L. Rev.* 926 (Aug. 1967).
37 *Univ. Missouri-KC L. Rev.* 127 (Winter 1969).

1969   *Robert Eli Stanley v. Georgia,* 394 U.S. 557, 22 L.Ed.2d 542, 89 S.Ct. 1243

Argued: Jan. 14, 15, 1969.

Decided: April 7, 1969.

Summary: Ruled that First and 14th Amendments prohibit making private possession of obscene material a crime.

Circumstances: Police, suspecting Stanley of conducting a betting operation from his home, obtained a search warrant authorizing them to enter his home to look for evidence of gambling. They found no such evidence, but in a desk drawer in Stanley's bedroom an officer found three reels of eight-millimeter film, which, upon viewing in the living room, police deemed obscene. Stanley was tried and convicted in the Supreme Court of Fulton County of knowingly having possession of obscene matter in violation of Georgia law. The Supreme Court of Georgia affirmed. On appeal, the U.S. Supreme Court reversed and remanded to the state high court.

Opinion: Justice Thurgood Marshall wrote for six justices in the unanimous decision, including Justices William O. Douglas, John M. Harlan, William J. Brennan, Jr., Byron R. White, and Abe Fortas. Hugo L. Black concurred separately, as did Potter Stewart, who was joined by Brennan and White. Chief Justice Earl Warren, replaced by Warren E. Burger in 1969, did not participate. Prohibitions on private possession, said Marshall, interfere with a person's First Amendment "right to read or observe what he pleases—the right to satisfy his intellectual and emotional needs in the privacy of his own home." Mere categorization of the films as "obscene" was deemed insufficient justification for such an invasion. "Whatever may be the justifications for other statutes regulating obscenity, we do not think they reach into the privacy of one's own home." In the Court's view, the state's asserted interest in protecting "the individual's mind from the effects of obscenity . . . to control the moral content of a person's thoughts" was "wholly inconsistent with the philosophy of the First Amendment." The Court said that "little empirical basis" supported the state's contention that exposure to obscene materials might lead to deviant sexual behavior or crimes of sexual violence. Justice Black agreed separately that mere possession of reading matter or movie films, whether obscene or not, could not be made a crime without violating the Constitution. Justice Stewart, joined by Brennan and White, concurred, but would have reversed the conviction on the ground that seizure of the films was unwarranted and unconstitutional and, hence, inadmissible evidence at trial.

Referenced Cases: *Roth v. U.S.*, 354 U.S. 476 (1957), and *Ginsberg v. New York*, 390 U.S. 629 (1968), on states' rights to limit unprotected obscenity; *Smith v. California*, 361 U.S. 147 (1959), and *Jacobellis v. Ohio*, 378 U.S. 184 (1964), regarding obscenity as unprotected by the First Amendment; *Alberts v. California*, 354 U.S. 476 (1957), companion to *Roth*, on conviction for keeping, advertising, and selling obscene and indecent books; *Martin v. Struthers*, 319 U.S. 141 (1943), *Griswold v. Connecticut*, 381 U.S. 479 (1965), *Lamont v. Postmaster General*, 381 U.S. 301 (1965), and *Pierce v. Society of Sisters*, 268 U.S. 510 (1925), on the right to receive information and ideas; *Olmstead v. U.S.*, 277 U.S. 438 (1928), Justice Louis D. Brandeis, in dissent, on "the right to be let alone—the most comprehensive of rights and the right most valued by civilized man"; *Kingsley Int'l Pictures v. Regents*, 360 U.S. 684 (1959), and *Joseph Burstyn v. Wilson*, 343 U.S. 495 (1952), on constitutional protection of "expression which is eloquent no less than that which is unconvincing"; *Whitney v. California*, 274 U.S. 357 (1927), on education as deterrent to crime; *Redrup v. New York*, 386 U.S. 767 (1967), on obscene material intruding on the sensibilities or privacy of the general public; *Stanford v. Texas*, 379 U.S. 476 (1965), on search warrant validity; *Mapp v. Ohio*, 367 U.S. 643 (1961), on inadmissible evidence.

Further Reading:
55 *ABA J.* 583 (June 1969).
11 *Arizona L. Rev.* 731 (Winter 1969).
21 *Baylor L. Rev.* 502 (Fall 1969).

57 *California L. Rev.* 1257 (Nov. 1969).
83 *Harvard L. Rev.* 147 (Nov. 1969).
21 *Mercer L. Rev.* 337 (Winter 1970).
49 *Nebraska L. Rev.* 660 (March 1970).
31 *Ohio St. L. J.* 364 (Spring 1970).
7 *San Diego L. Rev.* 111 (Jan. 1970).
1969 *Supreme Ct. Rev.* 203 (1969).
43 *Temple L. Q.* 89 (Fall 1969).
48 *Texas L. Rev.* 646 (Fall 1970).
22 *Univ. Florida L. Rev.* 138 (Summer 1969).
24 *Univ. Miami L. Rev.* 179 (Fall 1969).
23 *Vanderbilt L. Rev.* 369 (March 1970).
11 *William & Mary L. Rev.* 261 (Fall 1969).

1973   *Marvin Miller v. California*, 413 U.S. 15, 37 L.Ed.2d 419, 93 S.Ct. 2607, 1 Med.L.Rptr. 1441

Reargued: Nov. 7, 1972.

Decided: June 21, 1973.

Summary: Rejected prior test that censored material be "utterly without redeeming social value" and substituted "does not have serious literary, artistic, political or scientific value"; also redefined community standards as those of the state or local community in determining obscene matter.

Circumstances: Miller was convicted of violating the California Penal Code for mailing five unsolicited brochures to a restaurant in Newport Beach. The brochures, which contained pictures and drawings of men and women engaged in a variety of sexual activities, advertised four erotic books and a film. The young manager of the restaurant had opened the mail in the presence of his mother, and together they reported the incident to police, who arrested Miller. He was convicted by a trial court. The Appellate Division, Superior Court, Orange County, affirmed. On appeal, the Supreme Court vacated and remanded to the Orange

County Superior Court. Though sympathetic to the California determination, the Court nevertheless found the conviction improper because the state courts had applied the wrong standard to determine obscenity. However, for the first time in 16 years—since *Roth v. U.S.* (1957)—five justices managed to agree on a definition of obscenity.

Opinion: The first of five obscenity cases decided on June 21, 1973, the same 5-to-4 vote in each, and the majority opinion in each written by Chief Justice Warren E. Burger, joined by Byron R. White, Harry A. Blackmun, Lewis F. Powell, Jr., and William H. Rehnquist. Dissenting in each decision were William O. Douglas, William J. Brennan, Jr., Potter Stewart, and Thurgood Marshall. Most important are Burger's opinion for the Court in *Miller*, outlining the new standards, and Brennan's review of 16 years of "disharmony of views" in his *Paris Adult Theatre* dissent.

Burger focused on *Miller's* origins, that sexually explicit materials had been thrust by "aggressive sales action upon unwilling recipients who had in no way indicated any desire to receive such materials." He said that the Court had recognized that states have a legitimate interest in prohibiting dissemination or exhibition of obscene material "when the mode of dissemination carries with it a significant danger of offending the sensibilities of unwilling recipients or of exposure to juveniles." This was in reference to *Redrup v. New York* (1967), in which the Court per curiam reversed convictions for selling obscene books to willing adults. In a review of *Roth* and *Memoirs v. Massachusetts* (1966), Burger said that they had imposed an almost impossible burden of proof on prosecutors, requiring them to prove a negative, that the material was "utterly without" redeeming social value. That concept has never commanded the adherence of more than three justices at one time, said the chief justice, who then noted that the author of the Roth-Memoirs test, Justice Brennan, had abandoned his former position, moving, ironically, closer to the absolute position of Justices Black and Douglas. Burger went on to say that states could control the traffic in pornography if they acted under statutes specifically defining obscenity, "carefully limited" and confined to "works which depict or describe sexual conduct." A state offense must also be limited to works that, "taken as a whole, appeal to the prurient interest in sex, which portray sexual conduct in a patently offensive way, and which, taken as a whole, do

not have serious literary, artistic, political, or scientific value." On
the matter of community standards, Burger said that nothing in
the First Amendment requires that a jury must consider hypothetical and unascertainable "national standards" when attempting to
determine obscenity. "It is neither realistic nor constitutionally
sound to read the First Amendment as requiring that the people of
Maine or Mississippi accept public depiction of conduct found
tolerable in Las Vegas, or New York City."

Douglas, in dissent, protested that the majority had given
juries of lay citizens a task that even the Court had shown little
talent for doing—deciding what is obscene. The new test, he
thought, "would make it possible to ban any paper or any journal
or magazine in some benighted place." Brennan, in dissent and
joined by Stewart and Marshall, said that the California statute
was overbroad and therefore invalid on its face. He deferred to his
dissent in *Paris Adult Theatre*.

Referenced Cases: *Interstate Circuit v. Dallas*, 390
U.S. 676 (1968), on what Justice John M. Harlan called "the intrac-
table obscenity problem"; *Stanley v. Georgia*, 394 U.S. 557 (1969),
Ginsberg v. New York, 390 U.S. 629 (1968), *Redrup v. New York*,
386 U.S. 767 (1967), *Jacobellis v. Ohio*, 378 U.S. 184 (1964), *Rabe v.
Washington*, 405 U.S. 313 (1972), *U.S. v. Reidel*, 402 U.S. 351
(1971), *Joseph Burstyn v. Wilson*, 343 U.S. 495 (1952), *Breard v.
Alexandria*, 341 U.S. 622 (1951), *Kovacs v. Cooper*, 336 U.S. 77
(1949), *Prince v. Massachusetts*, 321 U.S. 158 (1944), *Butler v.
Michigan*, 352 U.S. 380 (1957), and *Public Utilities Comm'n v.
Pollak*, 343 U.S. 451 (1952), on state interest in controlling obscenity directed at unwilling recipients or juveniles; *Roth v. U.S.*, 354
U.S. 476 (1957), on standards for judging obscenity and rejection of
claim that obscene materials are protected by First Amendment;
Memoirs v. Massachusetts, 383 U.S. 413 (1966), on Court's new
test of obscenity; *Kois v. Wisconsin*, 408 U.S. 229 (1972), on
applying contemporary community standards; *Ginzburg v. U.S.*,
383 U.S. 463 (1966), and *Mishkin v. New York*, 383 U.S. 502 (1966),
on Court's standards until *Miller*; *Paris Adult Theatre I v. Slaton*,
413 U.S. 49 (1973), on Justice Brennan's departure from former
position; *Hoyt v. Minnesota*, 399 U.S. 524 (1970), *Walker v. Ohio*,
398 U.S. 434 (1970), and *Cain v. Kentucky*, 397 U.S. 319 (1970), on
the value of diversity of tastes and attitudes; *Gooding v. Wilson*,
405 U.S. 518 (1972), *Dombrowski v. Pfister*, 380 U.S. 479 (1965),

Baggett v. Bullitt, 377 U.S. 360 (1964), *Coates v. Cincinnati*, 402 U.S. 611 (1971), *U.S. v. Raines*, 362 U.S. 17 (1960), and *NAACP v. Button*, 371 U.S. 415 (1963), on protecting attacks on overly broad statutes.

Further Reading:

59 *ABA J.* 890 (Aug. 1973).
40 *Brooklyn L. Rev.* 442 (Fall 1973).
4 *Capital Univ. L. Rev.* 315 (1975).
6 *Columbia Human Rights L. Rev.* 219 (Spring 1974).
7 *Columbia Human Rights L. Rev.* 349 (Spring–Summer 1975).
6 *Connecticut L. Rev.* 165 (Fall 1973).
23 *Emory L. J.* 551 (Spring 1974).
10 *Georgia State Bar J.* 327 (Nov. 1973).
87 *Harvard L. Rev.* 160 (Nov. 1973).
88 *Harvard L. Rev.* 1838 (June 1975).
24 *Hastings L. J.* 1303 (May 1973).
11 *Houston L. Rev.* 224 (Oct. 1973).
10 *Idaho L. Rev.* 193 (Spring 1974).
62 *Illinois Bar J.* 218 (Dec. 1973).
49 *Indiana L. J.* 320 (Winter 1974).
42 *J. Bar Assoc. Kansas* 317 (Winter 1973).
51 *J. Urban L.* 314 (Nov. 1973).
45 *Mississippi L. J.* 435 (April 1974).
36 *Montana L. Rev.* 285 (Summer 1975).
1 *Ohio Northern L. Rev.* 97 (1973).
48 *St. John's L. Rev.* 568 (March 1974).
18 *St. Louis Univ. L. J.* 297 (Winter 1973).
26 *Univ. Florida L. Rev.* 324 (Winter 1974).
28 *Univ. Miami L. Rev.* 238 (Fall 1973).
8 *Univ. Richmond L. Rev.* 325 (Winter 1974).
5 *Univ. West LA Rev.* 63 (Fall 1973).
8 *Valparaiso L. Rev.* 166 (Fall 1973).

1973 *Paris Adult Theatre I et al. v. Lewis R. Slaton, District Attorney, Atlanta Judicial Circuit, et al.*, 413 U.S. 49, 37

L.Ed.2d 445, 93 S.Ct. 2628, 1 Med.L.Rptr. 1454

Argued: Oct. 19, 1972.

Decided: June 21, 1973.

Summary: Adults-only movie theaters may be banned, even if they do not invade the privacy of others and even if patrons are properly warned, reasoning "that a sensitive, key relationship of human existence, central to family life, community welfare, and the development of human personality, can be debased and distorted by crass commercial exploitation of sex."

Circumstances: Local Atlanta officials filed complaints against two "adult" movie theaters and their owners for exhibiting to the public for money two obscene films in violation of Georgia law. The films, *Magic Mirror* and *It All Comes Out in the End*, depicted sexual conduct characterized as "hard-core pornography" leaving "little to the imagination." The theaters, Paris I and II, are linked by a common lobby on Peachtree Street. On Dec. 28, 1970, investigators employed by the Criminal Court of Fulton County entered as paying customers and viewed the films. Following a nonjury trial, the court concluded that, even if the films were "obscene," their exhibition was permissible since they were shown only to consenting adults who knew beforehand what they would see. The Georgia Supreme Court reversed, holding the movies obscene and constitutionally prohibited even though shown only to consenting adults. The U.S. Supreme Court, having just "clarified" via *Miller v. California* (1973) the constitutional definition of obscene material subject to state regulation, vacated and remanded to the Georgia Supreme Court for reconsideration in the light of *Miller*.

Opinion: The second of five obscenity cases decided this day, the same 5-to-4 vote in each, and the majority opinion in each delivered by Chief Justice Warren E. Burger, joined by Byron R. White, Harry A. Blackmun, Lewis F. Powell, Jr., and William H. Rehnquist. Dissenting in each decision were William O. Douglas, William J. Brennan, Jr., Potter Stewart, and Thurgood

Marshall. In upholding the judgment of the Georgia Supreme Court that two "adult" movie houses were constitutionally unprotected, Burger said the justification was "the interest of the public in the quality of life and the total community environment, the tone of commerce in the great city centers and, possibly, the public safety itself." Despite a full adversary proceeding, there was no judicial error in failing to require "expert" evidence that the material was obscene. "The films, obviously," he said, "are the best evidence of what they represent." The justices rejected the consenting adults standard, as announced in *Redrup v. New York* (1967), and said that the state had a legitimate interest in regulating the use of obscene material in local commerce and in all places of accommodation, as long as the regulations do not run afoul of specific constitutional prohibitions, such as the revised obscenity test Burger described in *Miller*, decided the same day. Citing the Hill-Link Minority Report of the Commission on Obscenity and Pornography, which found an arguable correlation between obscene material and crime, Burger nevertheless said it was not for the Court to resolve "empirical uncertainties" in legislation unless constitutional rights were being impinged upon. "Although there is no conclusive proof of a connection between antisocial behavior and obscene material, the legislature of Georgia could quite reasonably determine that such a connection does or might exist." He chastised his "absolutist" brethren, who find it uncomfortable to explain why rights of association, speech, and press should be severely restrained in the marketplace of goods and money, but not in the marketplace of pornography. Observing that "free will" is not a governing concept in human affairs, Burger, with assistance from the sociologist Irving Kristol, noted inconsistency in the liberal position: "States are told by some that they must await a 'laissez faire' market solution to the obscenity-pornography problem, paradoxically 'by people who have never otherwise had a kind word to say for laissez-faire,' particularly in solving urban, commercial, and environmental pollution problems." Privacy, he added, though encompassing the personal intimacies of the home, the family, marriage, motherhood, procreation, and child rearing, does not perforce include the right to watch obscene movies in places of public accommodation. "Where communication of ideas, protected by the First Amendment, is not involved, or the particular privacy of the home protected by *Stanley* [*v. Georgia* (1969)], or any of the other 'areas or zones' of constitutionally protected privacy, the mere fact that, as a consequence, some human 'utterances' or 'thoughts' may be incidentally affected does not bar the State from acting to protect legitimate state interests."

Justice Douglas, in a separate dissent, said that, since obscenity was protected by the First Amendment, any regime of censorship and punishment required a constitutional amendment. The creation of the "obscenity" exception to the amendment was a "legislative and judicial tour de force," he opined, and he applauded the effort of Brennan "to forsake the low road." Brennan, who had authored the Roth-Memoirs standard, admitted that the efforts over 16 years had not been without serious problems. He therefore reluctantly concluded "that none of the available formulas, including the one announced today, can reduce the vagueness to a tolerable level while . . . striking an acceptable balance between the protections of the First and Fourteenth Amendments, on the one hand, and on the other the asserted state interest in regulating the dissemination of certain sexually oriented materials." In an effort to draw a new line between protected and unprotected speech, Brennan urged, after reviewing the long history of American obscenity laws, that at least in the absence of distribution to juveniles or obtrusive exposure to unconsenting adults, the two amendments prohibit the state and federal government from attempting "wholly to suppress sexually oriented materials on the basis of their allegedly 'obscene' contents."

Referenced Cases: *U.S. v. Reidel*, 402 U.S. 351 (1971), and *Stanley v. Georgia*, 394 U.S. 557 (1969), on distribution to willing adults for private home viewing; *Miller v. California*, 413 U.S. 15 (1973), *Kois v. Wisconsin*, 408 U.S. 229 (1972), and *Roth v. U.S.*, 354 U.S. 476 (1957), holding that obscene material is unprotected; *Kingsley Books v. Brown*, 354 U.S. 436 (1957), on warning procedures; *Blount v. Rizzi*, 400 U.S. 410 (1971), *Teitel Film Corp. v. Cusack*, 390 U.S. 139 (1968), *Freedman v. Maryland*, 380 U.S. 51 (1965), and *U.S. v. Thirty-Seven Photographs*, 402 U.S. 363 (1971), on standards for adversary proceedings; *Amato v. Wisconsin*, 404 U.S. 1063 (1972), *Smith v. California*, 361 U.S. 147 (1959), and *Ginzburg v. U.S.*, 383 U.S. 463 (1966), regarding the requirement of "expert" affirmative evidence; *Redrup v. New York*, 486 U.S. 767 (1967), on regulating materials to juveniles and uncon-

senting adults; *Breard v. Alexandria*, 341 U.S. 622 (1951), on rights
other than those of the advocates; *Jacobellis v. Ohio*, 378 U.S. 184
(1964), *Memoirs v. Massachusetts*, 383 U.S. 413 (1966),
Beauharnais v. Illinois, 343 U.S. 250 (1952), and *Kovacs v. Cooper*,
336 U.S. 77 (1949), on the right of the nation and the states to
maintain a decent society; *Chaplinsky v. New Hampshire*, 315
U.S. 568 (1942), on protecting "the social interest in order and
morality"; *Ferguson v. Skrupa*, 372 U.S. 726 (1963), *Lincoln Federal
Labor Union v. Northwestern Iron & Metal Co.*, 335 U.S. 525
(1949), *SEC v. Capital Gains Research Bureau*, 375 U.S. 180 (1963),
American Power & Light v. SEC, 329 U.S. 90 (1946), *Brooks v. U.S.*,
267 U.S. 432 (1925), *Hoke v. U.S.*, 227 U.S. 308 (1913), *Sugar Institute v. U.S.*, 297 U.S. 553 (1936), *Merrick v. N. W. Halsey & Co.*,
242 U.S. 568 (1917), *Caldwell v. Sioux Falls Stock Yards*, 242 U.S.
559 (1917), *Hall v. Geiger-Jones Co.*, 242 U.S. 539 (1917), *Tanner v.
Little*, 240 U.S. 369 (1916), and *Rast v. Van Deman & Lewis Co.*,
240 U.S. 342 (1916), on lawful state regulation of commercial and
business affairs; *Citizens to Preserve Overton Park v. Volpe*, 401
U.S. 402 (1971), on how imponderables impact legislatures and
administrators in preserving the environment; *Board of Education v. Allen*, 392 U.S. 236 (1968), on the "unprovable assumption"
that books relate to a complete education; *Griswold v. Connecticut*, 381 U.S. 479 (1965), *Day-Brite Lighting v. Missouri*, 342 U.S.
421 (1952), *Sullivan v. Little Hunting Park*, 396 U.S. 229 (1969),
Daniel v. Paul, 395 U.S. 298 (1969), *Blow v. North Carolina*, 379
U.S. 684 (1965), *Hamm v. Rock Hill*, 379 U.S. 306 (1964), *Heart of
Atlanta Motel v. U.S.*, 379 U.S. 241 (1964), on "private" for the
purpose of civil rights litigation and statutes; *Palko v. Connecti-
cut*, 302 U.S. 319 (1937), *Roe v. Wade*, 410 U.S. 113 (1973),
Eisenstadt v. Baird, 405 U.S. 438 (1972), *Loving v. Virginia*, 388
U.S. 1 (1967), *Prince v. Massachusetts*, 321 U.S. 158 (1944),
Skinner v. Oklahoma, 316 U.S. 535 (1942), *Pierce v. Society of
Sisters*, 268 U.S. 510 (1925), and *Meyer v. Nebraska*, 262 U.S. 390
(1923), on privacy of home, family, marriage, motherhood, procreation, and child rearing; *U.S. v. Orito*, 413 U.S. 139 (1973), and
U.S. v. 12 200-Ft. Reels of Film, 413 U.S. 123 (1973), decided the
same day as *Miller* and *Paris Adult Theatre*, on home privacy not
the same as commercial, or public, privacy; *Interstate Circuit v.
Dallas*, 390 U.S. 676 (1968), regarding Justice John M. Harlan on
"variety of views . . . unmatched in any other course of constitu-

tional adjudication"; *Papachristou v. Jacksonville*, 405 U.S. 156
(1972), *Gregory v. Chicago*, 394 U.S. 111 (1969), *Niemotko v.
Maryland*, 340 U.S. 268 (1951), *Cantwell v. Connecticut*, 310 U.S.
296 (1940), and *Thornhill v. Alabama*, 310 U.S. 88 (1940), on arbitrary and erratic enforcement of the law; *Gooding v. Wilson*, 405
U.S. 518 (1972), *Cohen v. California*, 403 U.S. 15 (1971), and
Terminiello v. Chicago, 337 U.S. 1 (1949), on limiting expression
to *serious* literary or political value; *Herndon v. Lowry*, 301 U.S.
242 (1937), regarding the vagaries of jury determinations.

Further Reading:
26 *Stanford L. Rev.* 1161 (May 1974).
See also under *Miller v. California*, 413 U.S. 15 (1973), decided the
same day.

Note: Also on that day the Court decided *Kaplan v. California*, 413 U.S. 115 (1973), on the proprietor of an "adult" bookstore selling an unillustrated book containing repetitively descriptive material of an explicitly sexual nature. The Court ruled
that states could constitutionally prohibit the sale of obscene
books "to any one, including consenting adults."
     U.S. v. 12 200-Ft. Reels of Super 8mm Film, 413 U.S. 123
(1973), on the importation of obscene matter for personal use and
possession. The Court upheld a federal statute prohibiting the
importation of any obscene material, whether for private or commercial purposes.
     U.S. v. Orito, 413 U.S. 139 (1973), on interstate transporta-
tion of lewd, lascivious, and filthy materials. The Court upheld a
federal statute prohibiting transportation in commerce of obscene
materials by common carrier, whether for private or commercial
purposes. Chief Justice Burger wrote the Court's opinion in all
three cases, as he had in *Miller* and *Paris Adult Theater*. All five
were vacated and remanded in the light of the new obscenity
definition established in *Miller*.

1974   *William L. Hamling et al. v. U.S.*, **418 U.S. 87, 41 L.Ed.2d 590, 94 S.Ct. 2887, 1 Med.L.Rptr. 1479**

Argued: April 15, 1974.

Decided: June 24, 1974.

Summary: Federal court jurors may determine a "community standard" for obscenity. Expert testimony deemed irrelevant. Prosecution need only show defendant had knowledge of contents, not that defendant knew materials to be obscene.

Circumstances: On March 5, 1971, a grand jury in the District Court for the Southern District of California indicted Hamling, Earl Kemp, Shirley R. Wright, David L. Thomas, Reed Enterprises Inc., and Library Service Inc. on 21 counts of an indictment charging them with use of the mails to carry an obscene book, *The Illustrated Presidential Report of the Commission on Obscenity and Pornography*, plus an obscene brochure advertising where to buy the book, violating 18 U.S.C. Sections 2, 371, and 1461. After a jury trial, they were convicted on 12 counts of mailing and conspiring to mail the obscene advertisement, a single-sheet brochure mailed to approximately 55,000 persons around the country. The advertisement carried photos depicting heterosexual and homosexual intercourse, sodomy, and "a variety of deviate sexual acts." The jury conviction came on Dec. 23, 1971, and the Court of Appeals for the Ninth Circuit affirmed on June 7, 1973, 14 days before the Supreme Court's *Miller v. California* decision, on June 21. On writ of certiorari, the Supreme Court affirmed.

Opinion: Justice William H. Rehnquist wrote the 5-to-4 opinion, joined by Chief Justice Warren E. Burger and Justices Byron R. White, Harry A. Blackmun, and Lewis F. Powell, Jr. Dissenting were William O. Douglas, William J. Brennan, Jr., Potter Stewart, and Thurgood Marshall. Rehnquist first identified the principal question: What rules of law shall govern obscenity convictions accrued prior to *Miller*? Where judgments were not final, tried cases would be examined in the light of *Miller*. Rehnquist noted that *Miller* and its companion, *Paris Adult Theatre*, permit a juror to draw upon knowledge of the community or vicinage in deciding what conclusion "the average person, applying contemporary community standards" would reach in a given case. He added: "The legal definition of obscenity does not change with each indictment; it is a term sufficiently definite in legal meaning to give a defendant notice of the charge against him." The Court said that application of the federal statute, 18 U.S.C.S. Section 1461, had not violated the First Amendment and was not unconstitutionally vague for failing to give fair notice of the types of material proscribed. The brochure mailed to advertise *The Illustrated Presidential Report of the Commission on Obscenity and Pornography* was deemed a form of hard-core pornography. Further on community standards, the Court said that jurors were not required to pay any attention to experts who testify, but that the jurors themselves are, in effect, the experts.

Justice Douglas, in dissent, said: "If officials may constitutionally report on obscenity, I see nothing in the First Amendment that allows us to bar the use of a glossary factually to illustrate what the report discusses." Justice Brennan, joined in dissent by Stewart and Marshall, argued, as he had in dissent in *Paris Adult Theatre*, that absent distribution to juveniles or obtrusive exposure to unconsenting adults, the First and 14th Amendments prohibit suppressing sexually oriented materials on the basis of their allegedly "obscene contents." He said community or local standards would force self-censorship by national distributors.

Referenced Cases: *Miller v. California*, 413 U.S. 15 (1973), *Memoirs v. Massachusetts*, 383 U.S. 413 (1966), and *Roth v. U.S.*, 354 U.S. 476 (1957), on standards for judging obscene materials; *U.S. v. Reidel*, 402 U.S. 351 (1971), *Manual Enterprises v. Day*, 370 U.S. 478 (1962), and *Ginzburg v. U.S.*, 383 U.S. 463 (1966), cases reaffirming *Roth*; *Paris Adult Theatre I v. Slaton*, 413 U.S. 49 (1973), and *Kaplan v. California*, 413 U.S. 115 (1973), regarding the possible irrelevance of expert testimony; *U.S. v. Dotterweich*, 320 U.S. 277 (1943), and *Dunn v. U.S.*, 284 U.S. 390 (1932), on consistency not required in verdicts or judgments; *U.S. v. Schooner Peggy*, 1 Cranch. 103 (1801), *Linkletter v. Walker*, 381 U.S. 618 (1965), and *Bradley v. School Board of Richmond*, 416 U.S. 696 (1974), on change in law occurring after a relevant event will be given effect while case is on direct review; *Stone v. New York, C. & St. L. R. Co.*, 344 U.S. 407 (1953), and *Schulz v. Pennsylvania R. Co.*, 350 U.S. 523 (1956), precedents for juror drawing on knowledge of propensities of a "reasonable" person in determining community views; *Boyd v. U.S.*, 271 U.S. 104 (1926), *Namet v. U.S.*,

373 U.S. 179 (1963), and *Lopez v. U.S.*, 373 U.S. 427 (1963), on judging jury instructions as a whole rather than isolated phrases; *Stillwell v. Phelps*, 130 U.S. 520 (1889), on discretion in determining admissible evidence; *Jenkins v. Georgia*, 418 U.S. 153 (1974), decided the same day as *Hamling*, regarding proscribing material in terms of substantive constitutional law; *Hagner v. U.S.*, 285 U.S. 427 (1932), *U.S. v. Debrow*, 346 U.S. 374 (1953), and *U.S. v. Carll*, 105 U.S. 611 (1882), on indictment sufficiency; *Glasser v. U.S.*, 315 U.S. 60 (1942), and *Blumenthal v. U.S.*, 332 U.S. 539 (1947), on evidence sufficiency; *NLRB v. Donnelly Co.*, 330 U.S. 219 (1947), *Michelson v. U.S.*, 335 U.S. 469 (1948), and *Salem v. U.S. Lines*, 370 U.S. 31 (1962), on evidentiary rulings; *Hannegan v. Esquire*, 327 U.S. 146 (1946), regarding second-class mailing privilege and presumption of kind of material mailed; *California v. Pinkus*, 400 U.S. 922 (1971), and *Burgin v. South Carolina*, 404 U.S. 806 (1971), on relevance of nonobscene to obscene materials in determining admissibility; *Mishkin v. New York*, 383 U.S. 502 (1966), on prurient interest directed at "clearly defined deviant group"; *Rowan v. U.S. Post Office Dept.*, 397 U.S. 728 (1970), on Post Office authorization to refrain sender from further mailings; *Thiel v. Southern Pacific Co.*, 328 U.S. 217 (1946), and *Smith v. Texas*, 311 U.S. 128 (1940), on ensuring "an impartial jury drawn from a cross-section of the community"; *White v. Georgia*, 385 U.S. 545 (1967), *Avery v. Georgia*, 345 U.S. 559 (1953), and *Alexander v. Louisiana*, 405 U.S. 625 (1972), on eligibility for jury service; *Jacobellis v. Ohio*, 378 U.S. 184 (1964), on Justice Brennan on local versus national standards affecting First Amendment; *Cole v. Arkansas*, 333 U.S. 196 (1948), and *Eaton v. Tulsa*, 415 U.S. 697 (1974), on treating a conviction as a conviction upon a charge not made.

Further Reading:
60 *ABA J.* 1114 (Sept. 1974).
7 *Columbia Human Rights L. Rev.* 349 (Spring–Summer 1975).

Note: Also on that day the Court decided *Jenkins v. Georgia*, 418 U.S. 153 (1974), ruling unanimously that local standards were appropriate, but that juries did not have "unbridled discretion" in deciding what is obscene. The Court also ruled that the film *Carnal Knowledge* did not portray "patently offensive 'hard-core' sexual conduct" and was thus protected by the First and

14th Amendments. Justice Rehnquist wrote the Court's opinion, joined by Chief Justice Burger and Justices White, Blackmun, and Powell. Justice Douglas concurred separately, as did Brennan, who was joined by Stewart and Marshall. Brennan said the Georgia obscenity statutes were overbroad, especially in the absence of distribution to juveniles or unconsenting adults.

1982   *New York v. Paul Ira Ferber*, 458 U.S. 747, 73 L.Ed.2d 1113, 102 S.Ct. 3348, 8 Med.L.Rptr. 1809

Argued: April 27, 1982.

Decided: July 2, 1982.

Summary: Held constitutional a state criminal statute prohibiting knowing promotion of portrayals of specifically described sex acts by children under age 16.

Circumstances: Ferber, proprietor of a Manhattan store specializing in sexually oriented products, sold two films to an undercover policeman. The films were devoted almost exclusively to young boys masturbating. Ferber was indicted on four counts of violating New York state's laws controlling dissemination of child pornography. He was convicted on two counts in the Supreme Court, New York County, affirmed without opinion by the Appellate Division, New York State Supreme Court. The New York Court of Appeals reversed on First Amendment grounds. Although the court recognized the state's "legitimate interest in protecting the welfare of minors," it found flaws in the statute, saying it was underinclusive and overbroad. On certiorari, the U.S. Supreme Court reversed and remanded to the New York Court of Appeals.

Opinion: Justice Byron R. White, writing for six members, said that child pornography, like obscenity, is not protected by the First Amendment if it involves scienter and a visual depiction of sexual conduct by children without serious literary, political, or scientific value. He was joined by Chief Justice Warren E. Burger and Justices Lewis F. Powell, Jr., William H. Rehnquist, and Sandra Day O'Connor. O'Connor also wrote a separate opinion, as did William J. Brennan, Jr., joined by Thurgood Marshall, and John Paul Stevens. Harry A. Blackmun concurred in the result. This was the Court's first examination of a statute directed at and limited to depictions of sexual activity involving children. Noting that 47 states had enacted statutes to combat the "exploitive use of children in the production of pornography," White said the Court could find no value whatsoever in encouraging children to engage in sex and that states could go beyond the limits imposed by *Miller v. California* (1973) in the regulation of pornographic depictions of children. "The prevention of sexual exploitation and abuse of children constitutes a government objective of surpassing importance." He cited, in a footnote, what one state study group declared: "The act of selling these materials is guaranteeing that there will be additional abuse of children." And, he said, the value of permitting live performances and photographic reproductions of children engaged in lewd conduct is "exceedingly modest," seldom constituting an important and necessary part of a literary performance or scientific or educational work. But, as with obscenity laws generally, criminal responsibility may not be imposed without some element of scienter on the part of the defendant. On the issue of overbreadth, White said that the New York law was not "substantially overbroad" and that, in any event, it properly reflected a legitimate state interest. O'Connor added that New York need not except from its law material with serious literary, scientific, or educational value, for a child photographed while masturbating surely suffers the same psychological harm whether the community labels the photo "edifying" or "tasteless."

Justice Brennan, with Marshall, stated that absent particular harm to children or unconsenting adults, states lack power to suppress sexually oriented materials. The First Amendment protects depictions of children that have serious literary, artistic, scientific, or medical value. Justice Stevens added: "While I disagree with the Court's position that such speech is totally without First Amendment protection, I agree that generally marginal speech does not warrant the extraordinary protection afforded by the overbreadth doctrine." Justice Blackmun concurred without opinion.

Referenced Cases: *Miller v. California*, 413 U.S. 15 (1973), on the Court's guidelines for judging unprotected obscene speech; *Chaplinsky v. New Hampshire*, 315 U.S. 568 (1942), the foundation for exclusion of obscenity from the realm of protected expression; *Roth v. U.S.*, 354 U.S. 476 (1957), holding that "obscenity is not within the area of constitutionally protected speech or press"; *Interstate Circuit v. Dallas*, 390 U.S. 676 (1968), and *Redrup v. New York*, 386 U.S. 767 (1967), on "the intractable obscenity problem" and its Court history; *Stanley v. Georgia*, 394 U.S. 557 (1969), *Ginsberg v. New York*, 390 U.S. 629 (1968), and *Jacobellis v. Ohio*, 378 U.S. 184 (1964), on offending the sensibilities of unwilling recipients or of exposure to juveniles; *Globe Newspapers v. Superior Court*, 457 U.S. 596 (1982), *Prince v. Massachusetts*, 321 U.S. 158 (1944), and *FCC v. Pacifica Foundation*, 438 U.S. 726 (1978), on safeguarding minors and the well-being of youth; *U.S. v. Darby*, 312 U.S. 100 (1941), upholding federal restrictions on sale of goods manufactured in violation of the Fair Labor Standards Act; *Young v. American Mini Theatres*, 427 U.S. 50 (1976), on "whether speech is, or is not, protected . . . often depends on the content of the speech"; *New York Times v. Sullivan*, 376 U.S. 254 (1964), and *Beauharnais v. Illinois*, 343 U.S. 250 (1952), on libel as unprotected except when public officials are the target; *Smith v. California*, 361 U.S. 147 (1959), and *Hamling v. U.S.*, 418 U.S. 87 (1974), on the element of scienter; *Broadrick v. Oklahoma*, 413 U.S. 601 (1973), on overbreadth scrutiny and conduct-related regulation; *Wainwright v. Stone*, 414 U.S. 21 (1973), and *Gooding v. Wilson*, 405 U.S. 518 (1972), on the Court as final arbiter between state laws and the Constitution; *McGowan v. Maryland*, 366 U.S. 420 (1961), regarding prudential limitations on constitutional adjudication; *Village of Schaumburg v. Citizens for a Better Environment*, 444 U.S. 620 (1980), *Dombrowski v. Pfister*, 380 U.S. 479 (1965), *U.S. v. Raines*, 362 U.S. 17 (1960), and *Thornhill v. Alabama*, 310 U.S. 88 (1940), on the overbreadth doctrine.

Further Reading:
68 *ABA J.* 1153 (Sept. 1982).
16 *Creighton L. Rev.* 509 (1982/83).
10 *Florida St. Univ. L. Rev.* 684 (Winter 1983).
96 *Harvard L. Rev.* 141 (Nov. 1982).
73 *J. Criminal L. and Criminology* 1337 (Winter 1982).

1982 *Supreme Ct. Rev.* 285 (1982).
19 *Wake Forest L. Rev.* 95 (Feb. 1983).

1986 *City of Renton et al. v. Playtime Theatres, Inc., et al.,* 475 U.S. 41, 89 L.Ed.2d 29, 106 S.Ct. 925, 54 U.S.L.W. 4160

Argued: Nov. 12, 1985.

Decided: Feb. 25, 1986.

Summary: An ordinance, restricting the display of non-obscene sexual plays, films, and printed materials to certain zones within the city, held a valid response to problem of adult theaters and nonviolative of the First Amendment.

Circumstances: Playtime Theatres and Sea-First Properties bought two theaters in Renton, Washington, near Seattle, and at the same time sought a declaratory judgment in the District Court for the Western District of Washington that the city's zoning regulation against adult movie houses violated the First and 14th Amendments. The District Court entered summary judgment in the city's favor, but the Court of Appeals for the Ninth Circuit reversed and remanded for reconsideration, declaring the ordinance a substantial restriction on First Amendment interests. It wanted the city to show substantial interests to support the ordinance. The U.S. Supreme Court reversed the appellate court's judgment.

Opinion: Justice William H. Rehnquist wrote for the 7-to-2 Court, joined by Chief Justice Warren E. Burger and Justices Byron R. White, Lewis F. Powell, Jr., John Paul Stevens, and Sandra Day O'Connor. Harry A. Blackmun concurred separately. William J. Brennan, Jr., joined by Thurgood Marshall, dissented. The Court relied on *Young v. American Mini Theatres Inc.,* 427 U.S. 50 (1976), in which it held that Detroit's zoning ordinance, which prohibited locating an adult theater within 1,000 feet of any two other "regulated uses" or within 500 feet of any residential zone, did not violate the First and 14th Amendments. Rehnquist said that the Renton ordinance, like the one in Detroit, did not ban adult theaters altogether, but provided that such theaters could not be situated within 1,000 feet of any residential zone, single or multiple family dwelling, church, park, or school. "The ordinance is therefore properly analyzed as a form of time, place, and manner regulation." Further, the Renton ordinance was completely consistent with the Court's definition of "content-neutral" speech regulations as those that "are *justified* without reference to the content of the regulated speech," as determined in *Virginia Pharmacy Board v. Virginia Citizens' Consumer Council*, 425 U.S. 748 (1976), *Clark v. Community for Creative Non-Violence*, 468 U.S. 288 (1984), *City Council of Los Angeles v. Taxpayers for Vincent*, 466 U.S. 789 (1984), and *Heffron v. International Society for Krishna Consciousness*, 452 U.S. 640 (1981). In sum, the Court found the ordinance a valid governmental response to the "admittedly serious problems" created by adult theaters. Justice Blackmun concurred separately but without opinion.

Justice Brennan, with Marshall, dissented on the ground that the ordinance selectively imposed limitations on the location of a movie theater based exclusively on the content of the films shown. "The constitutionality of the ordinance is . . . not correctly analyzed under standards applied to content-neutral time, place, and manner restrictions." He also found the ordinance invalid because it did not provide for reasonable alternative avenues of communication, unlike the freedom enjoyed by other establishments.

Referenced Cases: See under "Opinion" above. Also: *Carey v. Brown*, 447 U.S. 455 (1980), and *Police Dept. of Chicago v. Mosley*, 408 U.S. 455 (1972), on restraining speech on the basis of its content; *Schad v. Mount Ephraim*, 452 U.S. 61 (1981), and *Erznoznik v. City of Jacksonville*, 422 U.S. 205 (1975), on regulations not tailored narrowly enough; *Williamson v. Lee Optical Co.*, 348 U.S. 483 (1955), on "secondary effects" of adult businesses; *Consolidated Edison Co. v. Public Service Comm'n of N.Y.*, 447 U.S. 530 (1980), holding that time, place, and manner restrictions may not be based on content or subject matter; *Metromedia Inc. v. San Diego*, 453 U.S. 490 (1981), regarding Justice Brennan on the city's need to address seriously secondary land-use effects associated with adult movie theaters; *Terminiello v. Chicago*, 337 U.S. 1 (1949), holding that because some residents may be offended is no reason for regulation of speech.

Further Reading:

20 *Akron L. Rev.* 187 (Fall 1986).
87 *Columbia L. Rev.* 344 (March 1987).
100 *Harvard L. Rev.* 190 (Nov. 1986).
56 *Mississippi L. J.* 401 (Aug. 1986).
7 *Pace L. Rev.* 251 (Fall 1986).
18 *Pacific L. J.* 351 (Jan. 1987).
22 *Wake Forest L. Rev.* 673 (1987).
14 *Western St. Univ. L. Rev.* 287 (Fall 1987).

1986   *Richard Arcara, District Attorney of Erie County v. Cloud Books, Inc., etc., et al.*, 478 U.S. 697, 92 L.Ed.2d 568, 106 S.Ct.

Argued: April 29, 1986.

Decided: July 7, 1986.

Summary: A state statute permitting closure of an adult bookstore used for prostitution and lewdness held not in violation of First Amendment.

Circumstances: During the fall of 1982, the Erie County Sheriff's Department conducted an undercover investigation into reported illicit sex activities at the Village Books and News Store in Kenmore, New York. A deputy said he personally observed patrons masturbating, fondling, and engaged in fellatio, plus instances of prostitute solicitation. The Supreme Court of New York, Special Term, denied the owners' motion for summary judgment. The Supreme Court, Appellate Division, affirmed, but the Court of Appeals of New York modified the order and granted partial summary judgment on the closure claim. On certiorari, the U.S. Supreme Court reversed.

Opinion: Chief Justice Warren E. Burger wrote for six members, including Justices Byron R. White, Lewis F. Powell, Jr., William H. Rehnquist, John Paul Stevens, and Sandra Day O'Connor. O'Connor wrote a separate concurrence, joined by Stevens. Dissenting were Justices Harry A. Blackmun, joined by William J. Brennan, Jr., and Thurgood Marshall. The Court applied, as had the New York Court of Appeals, the standards set down in *U.S. v. O'Brien* (1968) for analyzing regulations aimed at nonspeech activity but which have an incidental effect on speech, such as, in that case, the burning of draft cards. However, the New York high court found closure of the bookstore an unconstitutional restraint on the owners' First Amendment rights because it was not essential to the purposes of the law. Even though in *O'Brien* the Court found draft card burning not ordinarily expressive conduct, Burger said it had some semblance of expression not apparent in this case. "[U]nlike . . . symbolic draft card burning . . . , the sexual activity carried on in this case manifests absolutely no element of protected expression." He also pointed out that, since every civil and criminal remedy imposes some burden on First Amendment protected activities, no one would claim that all such liability gives rise to a valid First Amendment claim. "The legislation providing the closure sanction was directed at unlawful conduct having nothing to do with books or other expressive activity." Justice O'Connor, with Stevens, argued that the First Amendment standard of review was not applicable, since the government was regulating neither speech nor an incidental nonexpressive effect of speech. Justice Blackmun, with Brennan and Marshall, dissented on the ground that when the state impairs First Amendment activity by shutting down a bookstore it must show, at a minimum, that it has chosen the least restrictive means of pursuing its legitimate objectives. "An obvious method of eliminating such acts is to arrest the patron committing them." Instead, the statute imposes absolute liability on the store simply because the activity occurs on the premises.

Referenced Cases: *U.S. v. O'Brien*, 391 U.S. 367 (1968), on draft card burning as symbolic expression; *Clark v. Community for Creative Non-Violence*, 468 U.S. 288 (1984), and *U.S. v. Albertini*, 472 U.S. 675 (1985), applying *O'Brien* to a ban on camping and sleeping in public places and re-entering a military base after being barred; *Minneapolis Star v. Minnesota Comm'r of*

Revenue, 460 U.S. 575 (1983), on a tax effecting expressive activity; *Paris Adult Theatre I v. Slaton*, 413 U.S. 49 (1973), on using the First Amendment as a cloak for unlawful conduct; *Buckley v. Valeo*, 424 U.S. 1 (1976), *Pell v. Procunier*, 417 U.S. 817 (1974), and *Jones v. North Carolina Prisoners' Union*, 433 U.S. 119 (1977), on some First Amendment restrictions; *Smith v. California*, 361 U.S. 147 (1959), on bookstores facilitating free expression; *Near v. Minnesota*, 283 U.S. 697 (1931), *Schad v. Mount Ephraim*, 452 U.S. 61 (1981), and *Southeastern Promotions Inc. v. Conrad*, 420 U.S. 546 (1975), holding that a statutory challenge to the First Amendment "must be tested by its operation and effect"; *Marsh v. Alabama*, 326 U.S. 501 (1946), *Cantwell v. Connecticut*, 310 U.S. 296 (1940), *Schneider v. State*, 308 U.S. 147 (1939), and *Grayned v. Rockport*, 408 U.S. 104 (1972), on trespass, breach of peace, littering, and anti-noise ordinances found violative; *Young v. American Mini Theatres Inc.*, 427 U.S. 50 (1976), and *Renton v. Playtime Theatres*, 475 U.S. 41 (1986), on balancing the state's interests against a fundamental right; *Speiser v. Randall*, 357 U.S. 513 (1958), First Amendment interests require use of "sensitive tools"; *Marcus v. Search Warrant*, 367 U.S. 717 (1961), *Freedman v. Maryland*, 380 U.S. 51 (1965), and *Vance v. Universal Amusement*, 445 U.S. 308 (1980), on the need for narrowly drawn procedures for abatement of an ordinary nuisance.

Further Reading:
20 *Creighton L. Rev.* 893 (1986/87).

1987   *Richard Pope and Charles G. Morrison v. Illinois*, **481 U.S. ___ , 95 L.Ed.2d 439, 107 S.Ct. 1918**

Argued: Feb. 24, 1987.

Decided: May 4, 1987.

Summary: Community standards not applicable in jury determination of "whether the work, taken as a whole, lacks serious literary, artistic, political, or scientific value."

Circumstances: On July 21, 1983, detectives in Rockford, Illinois, purchased certain magazines from Pope and Morrison, attendants at an adult bookstore. Each, charged with violating an Illinois obscenity statute, moved for dismissal on the
ground that the law failed to require an objective analysis of the
value question. Upon conviction, they appealed to the Illinois
Court of Appeals, Second District, which affirmed the trial courts.
The Illinois Supreme Court denied review. On certiorari, the U.S.
Supreme Court vacated and remanded to the Illinois Court of
Appeals for consideration of the harmless-error issue.

Opinion: Justice Byron R. White wrote the Court's opinion, joined by Chief Justice William H. Rehnquist, Lewis F. Powell,
Jr., Sandra Day O'Connor, and Antonin Scalia. Harry A. Blackmun
concurred in part and dissented in part. Dissenting were William
J. Brennan, Jr., Thurgood Marshall, and John Paul Stevens. At issue
was the third prong of the tripartite test for judging whether
material is obscene, as delineated in *Miller v. California* (1973).
White reiterated that the Court never meant for the value question to be settled by community standards. In *Smith v. U.S.*, 431
U.S. 291 (1977), the Court held that, in a federal prosecution for
mailing obscene materials, the first and second prongs of *Miller*—
appeal to prurient interest and patent offensiveness—are issues of
fact for the jury to determine by applying contemporary community standards. White pointed out that the ideas a work represents
need not obtain majority approval to merit First Amendment
protection. Neither, he said, does the value of the work vary from
community to community based on the degree of local acceptance
it has won. "The proper inquiry is not whether an ordinary
member of any given community would find serious literary,
artistic, political, or scientific value in allegedly obscene material,
but whether a reasonable person would find such value in the
material, taken as a whole." Thus, the jury instruction, that jurors
must apply a statewide community standard in deciding if the
magazines were without "value," violated the First and 14th
Amendments. The trial judge had instructed the respective juries
to determine whether the material was obscene on how it would
be viewed by ordinary adults in the entire state. White also said,
however, that the convictions may stand if on remand, but without retrial, it could be decided "beyond a reasonable doubt" that
the verdict was not affected by the erroneous instruction.

Justice Scalia, separately, found the instructions a "harmless error" because a "reasonable person" standard would just as likely convict as would a "community" standard embracing all of Illinois. The justice questioned the wisdom of applying an "objective" test, as the defendants had argued, since, at least in the case of literary or artistic value, many people have found literature in Dada and art in the replication of a soup can. He advised a legal maxim founded on ancient wisdom: "De gustibus non est disputandum. Just as there is no use arguing about taste, there is no use litigating about it. For the law courts to decide 'What is Beauty' is a novelty even by today's standards."

Justice Blackmun, in dissent, agreed with Stevens, who found the "harmless error" analysis inappropriately applied, but concurred with White on the value question. Justice Brennan, too, agreed with Stevens on the unconstitutionality of criminalizing possession or sale of obscene materials to consenting adults. Stevens, with Marshall, said: "A juror asked to create 'a reasonable person' in order to apply the standard the Court announces today, might well believe that the majority of the population who find no value in such a book are more reasonable than the minority who do find value. First Amendment protection surely must not be contingent on this type of subjective determination." Brennan and Blackmun joined parts of Stevens' dissent.

Referenced Cases: *Miller v. California*, 413 U.S. 15 (1973), the ruling case for judging whether material is obscene; *Secretary of State Maryland v. Joseph H. Munson Co.*, 467 U.S. 947 (1984), on invalidating a repealed statute to avoid future prosecutions; *Dombrowski v. Pfister*, 380 U.S. 479 (1965), and *U.S. v. Thirty-Seven Photographs*, 402 U.S. 363 (1971), on giving notice that sale of obscene materials would be prosecuted; *Rose v. Clark*, 478 U.S. 570 (1986), regarding the appropriateness of a harmless error inquiry; *Connecticut v. Johnson*, 460 U.S. 73 (1983), on finding facts beyond reasonable doubt; *Chapman v. California*, 386 U.S. 18 (1967), the standard for determining harmless error; *Paris Adult Theatre I v. Slaton*, 413 U.S. 49 (1973), on eroding protected speech in an effort to suppress unprotected speech; *U.S. v. Martin Linen Supply Co.*, 430 U.S. 564 (1977), on the constitutional right to jury trial forbids directing a verdict for the prosecution; *Cohen v. California*, 403 U.S. 15 (1971), on Justice John M. Harlan's view that the Constitution "leaves matters of taste and style largely to the individual"; *U.S. v. Cardiff*, 344 U.S. 174 (1952), on ill-defined legislation that may lead to criminal prosecution, "as much of a trap for the innocent as the ancient laws of Caligula"; *Stanley v. Georgia*, 394 U.S. 557 (1969), *U.S. v. Reidel*, 402 U.S. 351 (1971), and *U.S. v. 12 200-Ft. Reels of Film*, 413 U.S. 123 (1973), on the criminalization of mere possession of obscene matter.

Further Reading:

21 *Creighton L. Rev.* 379 (1987–88).
78 *J. Criminal L. and Criminology* 735 (Winter 1988).

Selected Bibliography

"Arcara v. Cloud Books, Inc.: Locking Out Prostitution," 15 *Hastings Const. L. Q.* 181 (Fall 1987).

Barton, Richard L., "The Lingering Legacy of Pacifica: Broadcasters' Freedom of Silence," 53 *Journalism Quarterly* 429 (1976).

Berns, Walter, "Pornography vs. Democracy: The Case for Censorship," 22 *The Public Interest* 3 (Winter 1971).

Bonnicksen, Andrea L., "Obscenity Reconsidered: Bringing Broadcasting into the Mainstream Commentary," 14 *Valparaiso L. Rev.* 261 (1981).

Catlett, Steven T., "Enjoining Obscenity as Public Nuisance and the Prior Restraint Doctrine," 84 *Columbia L. Rev.* 1616 (1984).

"The Civil Rights Pornography Ordinances—An Examination Under the First Amendment," 73 *Kentucky L. J.* 1081 (1984/85).

Cushman, Robert E., "National Police Power Under the Postal Clause of the Constitution," 4 *Minnesota L. Rev.* 402 (1920).

Dunlap, Mary C., "Sexual Speech and the State: Putting Pornography in Its Place," 17 *Golden Gate Univ. L. Rev.* 359 (Fall 1987).

Dworkin, Andrea, "Against the Male Flood: Censorship, Pornography and Equality," 8 *Harvard Women's L. J.* 1 (1985).

Eades, R. W., "Control of Seditious Libel as a Basis for the Development of the Law of Obscenity," 11 *Akron L. Rev.* 29 (Summer 1977).

Emerson, Thomas I., "Pornography and the First Amendment: A Reply to Professor MacKinnon," 3 *Yale L. and Policy Rev.* 130 (Fall 1984).

"Falwell and Flynt: First Amendment Protection of Satirical Speech," 39 *Baylor L. Rev.* 313 (Winter 1987).

"Filthy Words, the FCC, and the First Amendment: Regulating Broadcast Obscenity," 61 *Virginia L. Rev.* 579 (1975).

"The First Amendment Becomes a Nuisance: Arcara v. Cloud Books, Inc.," 37 *Catholic Univ. L. Rev..* 191 (Fall 1987).

Glassman, Marc B., "Community Standards of Patent Offensiveness: Public Opinion Data and Obscenity Law," 42 *Public Opinion Q.* 161 (1978).

Grant, S. S., and S. E. Angoff, "Massachusetts and Censorship," 10 *Boston Univ. L. Rev.* 147 (Jan. 1930).

Grunes, Rodney, "Obscenity Law and the Justices: Reversing Policy on the Supreme Court," 9 *Seton Hall L. Rev.* 403 (1978).

Henkin, Louis, "Morals and the Constitution: The Sins of Obscenity," 63 *Columbia L. Rev.* 391 (1963).

Hoffman, Eric, "Feminism, Pornography, and the Law," 133 *Univ. Pa. L. Rev.* 497 (1985).

Leventhal, Harold, et al., "An Impirical Inquiry into the Effects of Miller v. California on the Control of Obscenity," 52 *NYU L. Rev.* 810 (Oct. 1977).

Levine, G. D., "Sexual Sensationalism and the First Amendment: The Supreme Court's Questionable Regime of Obscenity Adjudication," 42 *NY State Bar J.* 193 (April–June 1970).

Loewy, A. H., "Free Speech: The 'Missing Link' in the Law of Obscenity," 16 *J. Public Law* 81 (1967).

Maag, Marilyn J., "The Indianapolis Pornography Ordinance: Does the Right to Free Speech Outweigh Pornography's Harm to Women?" 54 *Univ. Cincinnati L. Rev.* 249 (1985).

MacKinnon, Catherine A., "Discussion of Not a Moral Issue," 2 *Yale L. and Policy Rev.* 321 (Spring 1983).

———, "Pornography, Civil Rights, and Speech," 20 *Harvard Civil Rights–Civil Liberties L. Rev.* 1 (1985).

Main, E. J., "The Neglected Prong of the Miller Test for Obscenity: Serious Literary, Artistic, Political, or Scientific Value," 11 *So. Illinois Univ. L. J.* 1159 (Summer 1987).

Mott, Kenneth, and Christine Kellett, "Obscenity, Community Standards, and the Burger Court: From Deterrence to Disarray," 13 *Suffolk Univ. L. Rev.* 14 (1979).

"Much Ado About Dirty Books," 75 *Yale L. J.* 1364 (1966).

Potuto, J. R., "Stanley + Ferber = The Constitutional Crime of At-Home Child Pornography Possession," 76 *Kentucky L. J.* 15 (1987/88).

"Project: An Empirical Inquiry into the Effects of Miller v. California on the Control of Obscenity," 52 *NYU L. Rev.* 810 (1977).

"Regulation of Pornography: Is Erotica Self-Expression Deserving of Protection?" 23 *Loyola L. Rev.* 445 (Summer 1987).

Richards, D. A. J., "Pornography Commissions and the First Amendment: On Constitutional Values and Constitutional Facts," 39 *Maine L. Rev.* 275 (1987).

Shogue, Richard, "An Atlas for Obscenity: Exploring Community Standard," 7 *Creighton L. Rev.* 157 (1974).

"Stanley v. Georgia: A First Amendment Approach to Obscenity Control," 31 *Ohio State L. J.* 364 (Spring 1970).

Stone, G. R., "Anti-Pornography Legislation as Viewpoint-Discrimination," 9 *Harvard J. L. and Public Policy* 461 (Spring 1986).

Strosser, Nadine, "The Convergence of Feminist and Civil Liberties Principles in the Pornography Debate," 62 *NYU L. Rev.* 201 (April 1987).

Sunstein, C. R., "Pornography and the First Amendment," 1986 *Duke L. J.* 589 (Sept. 1986).

"Symposium on Pornography," 20 *New England L. Rev.* (1984–85).

"Symposium on the 1986 Commission on Pornography: The Attorney General's Commission and the New Politics of Pornography," 1987 *American Bar Found. Res. J.* 641 (Fall 1987).

Teeter, Dwight L., and Don R. Pember, "The Retreat from Obscenity: Redrup v. New York," 21 *Hastings L. J.* 175 (1969).

Wright, George R., "Defining Obscenity: The Criterion of Value," 22 *New England L. Rev.* 315 (Dec. 1987).

Yen, Alfred C., "Judicial Reviews of the Zoning of Adult Entertainment: A Search for the Purposeful Suppression of Protected Speech," 12 *Pepperdine L. Rev.* 651 (1985).

Privacy

1878   *Ex Parte Jackson,* **96 U.S. 727, 24 L.Ed. 877**

Argued: No oral argument.

Decided: May 13, 1878.

Summary: Letters deposited in the post office are protected from examination by federal statute. But Congress may exclude from the mail certain matter deemed injurious to public morals. The Postal Act of 1874 found constitutionally valid.

Circumstances: Jackson was indicted in the Circuit Court for the Southern District of New York for "knowingly and unlawfully" mailing on Feb. 23, 1877, a lottery circular. He was convicted, fined $100, and jailed until the fine was paid. The Supreme Court ruled this procedure appropriate. Finding Jackson's imprisonment legal, the Court also found the postal act constitutional.

Opinion: Justice Stephen J. Field delivered the Court's unanimous opinion, joined by Chief Justice Morrison R. Waite and Justices Nathan Clifford, Noah H. Swayne, Samuel F. Miller, William Strong, Joseph P. Bradley, Ward Hunt, and John M. Harlan. Field pointed out that Congress possessed the power to regulate the entire postal system, including the right to determine what shall be excluded. But Congress also meant for certain matter, such as personal letters and sealed packages, to be fully guarded from examination. "The constitutional guaranty of the right of the people to be secure in their papers against unreasonable searches and seizures extends to their papers, thus closed against inspection, wherever they may be." No law allowed postal officials the authority to "invade the secrecy of letters and . . .

sealed packages," and all regulations must be subordinated to the "great principle embodied in the fourth amendment of the Constitution." Field referred to President Andrew Jackson's annual message to Congress of 1835, urging passage of a law prohibiting circulation of "incendiary publications" in the South. In response, according to Field, Senator John Calhoun reported that it was up to the states, not Congress, to determine "what is and what is not calculated to disturb their security." While condemning the circulation of incendiary publications, Calhoun insisted that Congress was without power to ban their transmission through the mail on the ground that such would abridge liberty of the press. "It would in fact, in some respects, more effectually control the freedom of the press than any sedition law, however severe its penalties." However, though Congress could not ban such use of the postal system, it could prevent delivery by the postmasters in those states where their circulation was forbidden. The Court then decided: "Whilst regulations excluding matter from the mail cannot be enforced in a way which would require or permit an examination into letters, or sealed packages subject to letter postage, without warrant, issued upon oath or affirmation, in the search for prohibited matter, they may be enforced upon competent evidence of their violation obtained in other ways; as from the parties receiving the letters or packages, or from agents depositing them in the post-office, or others cognizant of the facts." Known objectionable printed matter, which is open to examination, is regulated and the regulations enforced through the courts. Congress had declared information on lotteries unmailable in an amendment to its postal law passed March 3, 1873, which targeted "obscene, lewd, or lascivious" matter. Lotteries, Field said, are supposed to have a demoralizing influence on the people. Although certain printed matter may be excluded from the mails, its transportation in any other way could not be forbidden. "Liberty of circulation is as essential to that freedom [of the press] as liberty of publishing; indeed, without the circulation, the publication would be of little value."

Referenced Cases: *McCullough v. Maryland*, 4 Wheat. 316 (1819), on congressional right to protect the mails by legislation; *Kohl v. U.S.*, 91 U.S. 367 (1876), on Congress' "sovereign control" over post offices and post roads.

Further Reading:
36 *Michigan L. Rev.* 703 (March 1938).

1967 *Time, Inc. v. James J. Hill*, 385 U.S. 374, 17 L.Ed.2d 456, 87 S.Ct. 534, 1 Med.L. Rptr. 1791

Reargued: Oct. 18, 19, 1966.

Decided: Jan. 9, 1967.

Summary: Applying the actual-malice test of libel to false-light privacy, ruled that First Amendment precludes redress of false reports on matters of public interest absent knowing falsity or reckless disregard of the truth.

Circumstances: In 1952 the Hill family had been held hostage in their suburban Philadelphia home by three escaped convicts, two of whom were later killed in a shoot-out with police. Media attention soon died down, but was revived less than a year later when novelist Joseph Hayes published *The Desperate Hours*, a story remarkably similar to the Hills' experience. The book was eventually made into a successful Broadway play and a Hollywood film. It was the play, as reviewed by *Life* magazine, that incited the legal action. James Hill sued for invasion of privacy after the appearance of the magazine article, which included photos taken of the Philadelphia tryout cast in front of the Hills' former home. Hill sought damages on grounds that the article was inaccurate and constituted "fictionalization," as forbidden under the New York state privacy statute. He also said *Life* had used the family's name for trade purposes, also illegal without consent, and that the piece put the family in a false light. A state jury awarded Hill $50,000 compensatory and $25,000 punitive damages, which, on appeal to the Appellate Division of the New York Supreme Court, was reduced to $30,000 compensatory damages, no punitive damages. The New York Court of Appeals affirmed, two judges dissenting. On appeal, the U.S. Supreme Court set aside the judgment and remanded to the Court of Appeals. Hill, who had subsequently moved his family from the Philadelphia area to resume their private life, dropped the case after 11 years of litigation.

Opinion: Justice William J. Brennan, Jr., wrote for five members, including John M. Harlan, Potter Stewart, Byron R. White, and Hugo L. Black. Black also wrote a separate concurrence, joined by William O. Douglas, who also wrote separately. Dissenting were Chief Justice Earl Warren and Justices Abe Fortas and Tom C. Clark. Richard M. Nixon, then in private law practice in New York City, represented Hill in oral argument before the Court. In this, the first suit before the Court involving privacy and the press, Brennan stated: "Exposure of the self to others in varying degrees is a concomitant of life in a civilized community. The risk of this exposure is an essential incident of life in a society which places a primary value on freedom of speech and of press." Brennan argued for an extension of the conditional privilege in *New York Times v. Sullivan* (1964), a majority opinion that he also wrote, which held that the Constitution delimits a state's power to award damages for libel in actions brought by public officials against critics of their official conduct. "Factual error, content defamatory of official reputation, or both, are insufficient for an award of damages for false statements unless actual malice—knowledge that the statements are false or in reckless disregard of the truth—is alleged and proved." On the case at bar, Brennan said that the subject of the *Life* article, the opening of a new play linked to an actual incident, is a matter of public interest. The Court refused to "saddle the press with the impossible burden of verifying [the facts] to a certainty," which would "create a grave risk of serious impairment of the indispensable service of a free press in a free society." Further, "even negligence would be a most elusive standard, especially when the content of the speech itself affords no warning of prospective harm to another through falsity. A negligence test would place on the press the intolerable burden of guessing how a jury might assess the reasonableness of steps taken by it to verify the accuracy of every reference to a name, picture, or portrait." But he added that constitutional guarantees can tolerate sanctions against *calculated* falsehood without significant impairment of the essential function.

Justice Black, with Douglas, concurred "in order for the Court to be able to agree on an opinion . . . [but did] not recede from any of the views I have previously expressed about the much wider press and speech freedoms I think the First and Fourteenth Amendments were designed to grant to the people of the Nation." Douglas, separately, said that it was "irrelevant to talk of any right of privacy in this context," that a "fictionalized treatment of the event is . . . as much in the public domain as would be a water-color of the assassination of a public official." Justice Harlan concurred in the ruling but dissented from the Court's "view of the proper standard of liability to be applied on remand. Were the jury on retrial to find negligent rather than, as the Court requires, reckless or knowing 'fictionalization,' I think that federal consti-tutional requirements would be met." Harlan said that, because Hill came to public attention through an unfortunate circum-stance not of his making, he in no sense waived any protection afforded him from irresponsible publicity. "A constitutional doc-trine which relieves the press of even . . . minimal responsibility in cases of this sort seems to me unnecessary and ultimately harmful to the permanent good health of the press itself." Justice Fortas, with Warren and Clark, believed that the jury instructions, "although . . . not a textbook model," satisfied the *Times v. Sulli-van* standard of knowing or reckless falsity.

Referenced Cases: *Valentine v. Chrestensen*, 316 U.S. 52 (1942), and *New York Times v. Sullivan*, 376 U.S. 254 (1964), on the commercial and noncommercial aspects of pro-tected speech; *Garrison v. Louisiana*, 379 U.S. 64 (1964), on truth as a defense; *Thornhill v. Alabama*, 310 U.S. 88 (1940), on freedom to discuss "all issues . . . to cope with the exigencies of [the] period"; *Bridges v. California*, 314 U.S. 252 (1941), on "timeliness and importance of the ideas seeking expression"; *Winters v. New York*, 333 U.S. 507 (1948), on the "elusive" line between informing and entertaining; *Speiser v. Randall*, 357 U.S. 513 (1958), and *Smith v. California*, 361 U.S. 147 (1959), on the danger of penaliz-ing legitimate utterance; *Chaplinsky v. New Hampshire*, 315 U.S. 568 (1942), on knowing falsehood being beyond protection; *Rosenblatt v. Baer*, 383 U.S. 75 (1966), on state interest in protect-ing individual reputation; *Joseph Burstyn v. Wilson*, 343 U.S. 495 (1952), *Ex parte Jackson*, 96 U.S. 727 (1878), *Grosjean v. American Press Co.*, 297 U.S. 233 (1936), and *Lovell v. Griffin*, 303 U.S. 444 (1938), on breadth of expression safeguarded by First Amendment; *Betts v. Brady*, 316 U.S. 455 (1942), and *Gideon v. Wainwright*,

372 U.S. 335 (1963), on Sixth Amendment guarantee of right to counsel; *Drombrowski v. Pfister*, 380 U.S. 479 (1965), regarding the "chilling effect" on free expression; *Mapp v. Ohio*, 367 U.S. 643 (1961), on power of state to control intrusion by newsgatherers; *Brown v. Louisiana*, 383 U.S. 131 (1966), and *NAACP v. Button*, 371 U.S. 415 (1963), on fundamental nature of First Amendment, its "delicate" and "vulnerable" freedoms; *Olmstead v. U.S.*, 277 U.S. 438 (1928), on Justice Louis D. Brandeis, in dissent, on the right of privacy as "the most comprehensive of rights and the right most valued by civilized men."

Further Reading:

53 *ABA J.* 360 (April 1967).
31 *Albany L. Rev.* 364 (June 1967).
16 *American Univ. L. Rev.* 442 (June 1967).
33 *Brooklyn L. Rev.* 318 (Winter 1967).
56 *California L. Rev.* 935 (Aug. 1968).
44 *Chicago-Kent L. Rev.* 58 (Spring 1967).
81 *Harvard L. Rev.* 160 (Nov. 1967).
28 *Montana L. Rev.* 243 (Spring 1967).
45 *No. Carolina L. Rev.* 740 (April 1967).
19 *So. Carolina L. Rev.* 249 (1967).
1967 *Supreme Ct. Rev.* 267 (1967).
18 *Syracuse L. Rev.* 661 (Spring 1967).
45 *Texas L. Rev.* 758 (March 1967).
20 *Vanderbilt L. Rev.* 1171 (Oct. 1967).
8 *William & Mary L. Rev.* 683 (Summer 1967).

1974 *Margaret Mae Cantrell et al. v. Forest City Publishing Co. et al.*, 419 U.S. 245, 42 L.Ed.2d 419, 95 S.Ct. 465, 1 Med.L.Rptr. 1815

Argued: Nov. 13, 1974.

Decided: Dec. 18, 1974.

Summary: A private-person plaintiff, showing that the newspaper had acted with reckless disregard for the truth, satisfied the "actual malice" standard of *New York Times v. Sullivan* (1965).

Circumstances: The false light occurred in a follow-up story that a Cleveland *Plain-Dealer* reporter, Joseph Eszterhas, wrote about the death of Mrs. Cantrell's husband, Melvin, when the Silver Bridge at Point Pleasant, West Virginia, collapsed into the Ohio River ten days before Christmas in 1967. Eszterhas requested of his editor permission to do the follow-up piece on some of the survivors. In his earlier story, the reporter had written about the funeral and the impact of Cantrell's death on his family. Five months later Eszterhas returned with a photographer and interviewed Cantrell's children. His widow was not home. The story, which appeared in the paper's Sunday magazine section in Aug. 1968, said that Margaret Cantrell "will talk neither about what happened nor about how they are doing. She wears the same mask of nonexpression she wore at the funeral." The extensive embellishments led Mrs. Cantrell to sue the reporter and the newspaper. In a diversity of citizenship action, the jury in the District Court for the Northern District of Ohio found each of the defendants liable for compensatory damages. The Court of Appeals for the Sixth Circuit reversed, finding that there was no proof that the newspaper had printed the story with knowledge of its falsities and remanded with judgment in favor of the defendants. On certiorari, the Supreme Court reversed and remanded with directions that the District Court judgment be affirmed.

Opinion: Justice Potter Stewart wrote for the 8-to-1 Court, joined by Chief Justice Warren E. Burger and Justices William J. Brennan, Jr., Byron R. White, Thurgood Marshall, Harry A. Blackmun, Lewis F. Powell, Jr., and William H. Rehnquist. William O. Douglas dissented. Unlike its first false-light privacy decision, *Time Inc. v. Hill*, 385 U.S. 374 (1967), this time a clear majority reiterated the actual malice standard as established by *New York Times v. Sullivan*, 376 U.S. 254 (1965), and said that evidence of "calculated falsehoods" was sufficient proof of actual malice. The reporter must have known, Stewart said, that his story contained a number of untrue statements. The Court took note of *Gertz v. Robert Welch*, 418 U.S. 323 (1974), but saw no reason to decide whether its rationale with respect to private individuals should be applied to Mrs. Cantrell, since she was clearly a private person. Stewart said the reporter exaggerated the poverty of the family and fabricated quotes and descriptions attributed to Mrs. Cantrell, whom the writer had not interviewed on a second trip to her home. Although the Court said the fabrications were calculated falsehoods, the photographer, whose pictures appeared with the story, were accurate and did not contribute to the falsehood.

Justice Douglas dissented on the ground that the Court's decision against the reporter and publisher abridged freedom of the press in violation of the First and 14th Amendments. "To make the First Amendment freedom to report the news turn on subtle differences between common-law malice and actual malice is to stand the Amendment on its head." He concluded that, in matters of public import such as the present news reporting, there must be freedom from damages lest the press be frightened into playing a more ignoble role than the framers of the Constitution visualized.

Referenced Cases: See under "Opinion" above.

Further Reading:
61 *ABA J.* 348 (March 1975).
64 *Iowa L. Rev.* 1061 (July 1979).
59 *Marquette L. Rev.* 573 (1976).

1975   *Cox Broadcasting Corp. et al. v. Martin Cohn*, **420 U.S. 469, 43 L.Ed.2d 328, 95 S.Ct. 1029, 1 Med.L.Rptr. 1819**

Argued: Nov. 11, 1974.

Decided: March 3, 1975.

Summary: The press cannot be held liable for invasion of privacy when reporting facts already part of the public record. A state can neither prevent such publication or broadcast nor define such activity as invasion of privacy.

Circumstances: In Aug. 1971, Cohn's 17-year-old daughter, Cynthia, was raped and murdered. In compliance with a

Georgia law making it a crime to broadcast or publish the name of a rape victim, the news media did not identify her. Some eight months later, during the trial of six youths indicted for the crime, a reporter for WSB-TV learned the victim's name from the indictments made available to him and later that day identified her in a newscast on the proceedings. In May 1972, the father brought an action for money damages, claiming his privacy had been invaded by the broadcasts revealing the name of his deceased daughter. The Superior Court of Fulton County rejected a claim of privilege under the First and 14th Amendments and granted summary judgment to the father. The Georgia Supreme Court ruled that liability did not follow as a matter of law, that summary judgment was improper, but that the First and 14th Amendments did not require judgment for the station. The state high court thus held that the name of a rape victim was not a matter of public concern and that the state statute was a legitimate limitation on press freedom. On appeal, the U.S. Supreme Court reversed.

Opinion:　Justice Byron R. White wrote for six members in the 8-to-1 decision. He was joined by Justices William J. Brennan, Jr., Potter Stewart, Thurgood Marshall, Harry A. Blackmun, and Lewis F. Powell, Jr. William O. Douglas concurred separately, as did Powell. Chief Justice Warren E. Burger concurred without opinion. William H. Rehnquist dissented. After reviewing the history of the right of privacy, its "impressive credentials," White noted that the case did not involve the appropriation of one's name or photograph, "a physical or other tangible intrusion into a private area," or a publication of otherwise private information that is also false although perhaps not defamatory. "The developing law surrounding the tort of invasion of privacy recognizes a privilege to the press to report the events of judicial proceedings." Even the prevailing law recognizes that the interests in privacy fade when the information involved already appears on the public record, White said. By placing the information in the public domain on official court records, the state must have concluded that the public interest was thereby being served. "The freedom of the press to publish that information appears to us to be of critical importance to our type of government in which the citizenry is the final judge of the proper conduct of public business." White concluded: "We are reluctant to embark on a course that would make public records generally available to the media but forbid their publication if offensive to the sensibilities of the supposed reasonable man. Such a rule would make it very difficult for the media to inform citizens about the public business and yet stay within the law. The rule would invite timidity and self-censorship and very likely lead to the suppression of many items that would otherwise be published and that should be made available to the public." But he also said that, if privacy interests are to be protected, states may seek means to avoid public documentation or other exposure of private information. However, once true information is disclosed in public court documents open to public inspection, the press cannot be sanctioned for publishing it.

Justice Powell added separately that truth was a complete defense in a defamation action brought by a private person as distinguished from a public official or public person. Justice Douglas argued simply that the government could not suppress or penalize publication of "news of the day" and that the First and 14th Amendments prohibited the use of state law to impose damages for the mere discussion of public affairs. Justice Rehnquist, in dissent, was of the opinion that the decision of the state court was not a final judgment and that the appeal should be dismissed for want of jurisdiction.

Referenced Cases: *Garrity v. New Jersey*, 385 U.S. 493 (1967), on constitutional validity invoking the Court's appellate jurisdiction; *Radio Station WOW v. Johnson*, 326 U.S. 120 (1945), *Carondelet Canal & Nav. Co. v. Louisiana*, 233 U.S. 362 (1914), and *Forgay v. Conrad*, 6 How. 201 (1848), on the final-judgment rule normally precluding higher review; *Mills v. Alabama*, 384 U.S. 214 (1966), regarding the Court's jurisdiction when an appellant has no defense other than a federal claim; *California v. Stewart*, 384 U.S. 436 (1966), *North Dakota State Board of Pharmacy v. Snyder's Drug Stores*, 414 U.S. 156 (1973), *Construction Laborers v. Curry*, 371 U.S. 542 (1963), *Mercantile National Bank v. Langdeau*, 371 U.S. 555 (1963), and *Miami Herald Publishing Co. v. Tornillo*, 418 U.S. 241 (1974), further on the matter of judicial jurisdiction; *Time Inc. v. Hill*, 385 U.S. 374 (1967), on right of privacy at common law in 30 states, plus the District of Columbia, and by statute in four states; *New York Times Co. v. Sullivan*, 376 U.S. 254 (1964), *Garrison v. Louisiana*, 379 U.S. 64 (1964), and *Curtis Publishing Co. v. Butts*, 388 U.S. 130 (1967), on truth as a defense in defamation action; *Sheppard v.*

Maxwell, 384 U.S. 333 (1966), on the press as guarantee to fairness of trials and administration of justice; *Estes v. Texas*, 381 U.S. 532 (1965), *Pennekamp v. Florida*, 328 U.S. 331 (1946), and *Bridges v. California*, 314 U.S. 252 (1941), regarding the special protected nature of reporting judicial proceedings; *U.S. v. O'Brien*, 391 U.S. 367 (1968), and *Chaplinsky v. New Hampshire*, 315 U.S. 568 (1942), on publication of truthful information; *Gertz v. Robert Welch*, 418 U.S. 323 (1974), on truth as a defense in defamation action brought by private person as distinguished from public official or public person; *Younger v. Harris*, 401 U.S. 37 (1971), and *Samuels v. Mackell*, 401 U.S. 66 (1971), on state-federal harmony and district court interference with ongoing state judicial proceedings.

Further Reading:

5 *Capital Univ. L. Rev.* 267 (1976).
14 *Duquesne L. Rev.* 507 (Spring 1976).
24 *Emory L. J.* 1205 (Fall 1975).
9 *Georgia L. Rev.* 963 (Summer 1975).
43 *Tennessee L. Rev.* 689 (Summer 1976).
45 *Univ. Chicago L. Rev.* 180 (Fall 1977).
124 *Univ. Pa. L. Rev.* 1385 (June 1976).
15 *Washburn L. J.* 163 (Winter 1976).

1977   *Hugo Zacchini v. Scripps-Howard Broadcasting Co.,* 433 U.S. 562, 53 L.Ed.2d 965, 97 S.Ct. 2849, 2 Med.L.Rptr. 1199

Argued: April 25, 1977.

Decided: June 28, 1977.

Summary: Recognized a performer's right to the publicity value of his performance, as an aspect of right to privacy, and held a broadcaster not immune constitutionally from liability for televising an entire act.

Circumstances: Zacchini, a human cannonball, was performing at a county fair in northeastern Ohio, when, over his objections, a reporter from a Cleveland television station filmed his act. A general admission fee was charged to the entire fairgrounds, but there was no additional cost for Zacchini's performance. Reporters were admitted to the grounds without charge, and the reporter in question visited the fair on two occasions. On the first, Zacchini requested that his act not be filmed; but the next time the reporter filmed the performance anyway. A 15-second film clip of the stunt was broadcast on WEWS during its 11 P.M. news program. The clip was accompanied by favorable commentary that even urged people to see the "thriller . . . *in person.*" Zacchini sued for invasion of privacy, alleging that the broadcast was an unlawful appropriation of his *professional* privacy. The trial court granted Scripps-Howard's motion for summary judgment, but the Ohio Court of Appeals reversed, holding that "total appropriation" of the act was an invasion of the property right "which will give rise to a cause of action . . . based either on conversion [of property] or [on] the invasion of the performer's common law copyright." Two of the judges relied on the doctrines of conversion and copyright, the third on Zacchini's right of publicity. All agreed that the First Amendment did not protect the broadcast. The Ohio Supreme Court reinstated the trial-court determination, saying that, even though Zacchini enjoyed a performer's right to the publicity value of his performance, his act was nevertheless a matter of legitimate public interest, which the station was privileged to report. The court said that "freedom of the press inevitably imposes certain limits upon an individual's right of privacy." The U.S. Supreme Court, in yet another reversal, said that the First and 14th Amendments did not immunize the broadcasting company from liability for televising Zacchini's entire act.

Opinion: Justice Byron R. White wrote the 5-to-4 opinion, joined by Chief Justice Warren E. Burger and Justices Potter Stewart, Harry A. Blackmun, and William H. Rehnquist. Dissenting were Lewis F. Powell, Jr., joined by William J. Brennan, Jr., Thurgood Marshall, and John Paul Stevens. The Court reversed the Ohio Supreme Court, which, relying on *Time Inc. v. Hill* (1967), had held that the challenged invasion was privileged, saying that the press "must be accorded broad latitude in its choice of how much it presents of each story or incident, and of the emphasis to be given to such presentation." But White said that the 1967 case involved an entirely different tort from the "right of publicity" in *Zacchini*. "The broadcast of a film of petitioner's entire act poses a substantial threat to the economic value of that performance," White said. Comparing Zacchini's right, under Ohio law, "to the publicity value of his performance" to patent and copyright laws, White said that the right of publicity rests on more than a desire to compensate the performer for the time and effort invested in his act. "The protection provides an economic incentive for him to make the investment required to produce a performance of interest to the public." In this case, he said, Ohio has recognized what may be the strongest case for a "right of publicity"—involving, not the appropriation of an entertainer's reputation to enhance the attractiveness of a commercial product, but the appropriation of the very activity by which the entertainer acquired his reputation in the first place.

Justice Powell, with Brennan and Marshall, dissented, saying that the First Amendment protects the station from a "right of publicity" or "appropriation" suit, absent a strong showing by the plaintiff that the news broadcast was subterfuge or cover for private or commercial exploitation. Justice Stevens, also in dissent, added that the basis of the state court's action was sufficiently doubtful to warrant remand for clarification.

Referenced Cases: *Wilson v. Loew's Inc.*, 355 U.S. 597 (1958), and *Herb v. Pitcairn*, 324 U.S. 117 (1945), on the Court's power over state judgments if having incorrectly adjudged federal rights; *Perkins v. Benguet Consolidated Mining*, 342 U.S. 437 (1952), on emerging right of publicity under Ohio law; *Time Inc. v. Hill*, 385 U.S. 374 (1967), and *New York Times v. Sullivan*, 376 U.S. 254 (1964), regarding First Amendment limitations on state tort actions; *Fox Film Corp v. Muller*, 296 U.S. 207 (1935), and *Enterprise Irrigation Dist. v. Farmers Mutual Canal Co.*, 243 U.S. 157 (1917), on the combination of state and federal dispositive grounds; *Steele v. Louisville & Nashville R. Co.*, 323 U.S. 192 (1944), and *Indiana ex rel. Anderson v. Brand*, 303 U.S. 95 (1938), cases invoking state law; *Rosenbloom v. Metromedia*, 403 U.S. 29 (1971), *Gertz v. Robert Welch*, 418 U.S. 323 (1974), and *Time Inc. v. Firestone*, 424 U.S. 448 (1976), on defamation suits brought by public officials and public figures; *Kalem Co. v. Harper Bros.*, 222

U.S. 55 (1911), *Manners v. Morosco*, 252 U.S. 317 (1920), *U.S. v. Paramount Pictures*, 334 U.S. 131 (1948), *Washingtonian Publishing Co. v. Pearson*, 306 U.S. 30 (1939), *Goldstein v. California*, 412 U.S. 546 (1973), and *Kewanee Oil Co. Bicron Corp.*, 416 U.S. 470 (1974), on copyright law.

Further Reading:

63 *ABA J.* 1448 (Oct. 1977).
7 *Capital Univ. L. Rev.* 439 (1978).
26 *Cleveland State L. Rev.* 587 (1977).
1978 *Detroit College L. Rev.* 339 (Summer 1978).
1978 *Duke L. J.* 1198 (Dec. 1978).
91 *Harvard L. Rev.* 208 (Nov. 1977).
6 *Human Rights* 335 (Spring 1977).
38 *Louisiana L. Rev.* 619 (Winter 1978).
24 *Loyola L. Rev.* 111 (Winter 1978).
29 *Mercer L. Rev.* 861 (Spring 1978).
31 *Rutgers L. Rev.* 269 (July 1978).
30 *Stanford L. Rev.* 1185 (July 1978).
39 *Univ. Pittsburgh L. Rev.* 561 (Spring 1978).
1977 *Utah L. Rev.* 817 (1977).

Other Cases Briefly Noted

Boyd v. U.S., 116 U.S. 616 (1886). The Court, in an opinion written by Justice Joseph P. Bradley, held that federal subpoenas for certain business records in customs forfeiture proceedings are violative of the Fourth and Fifth Amendments. Bradley said that the doctrines of these amendments "apply to all invasions on the part of the government and its employees of the sanctity of a man's home and the privacies of life. It is not the breaking of his doors, and the rummaging of his drawers, that constitutes the essence of the offense; but it is the invasion of his indefeasible right of personal security, personal liberty, and private property."

Union Pacific Railway v. Botsford, 141 U.S. 250 (1891). The Court, in an opinion written by Justice Horace Gray, restrained a court's authority to order revelation of private information in a civil suit, favoring the right of self-control over government intervention. Gray noted that "no right is held more sacred, or is more carefully guarded by the common law, than the right of every individual to the possession and control of his own person, free from all restraint or interference of others, unless by clear and unquestionable authority of law. The right to one's person may be said to be a right of complete immunity: to be let alone."

Meyer v. Nebraska, 262 U.S. 390 (1923). Relying on the 14th Amendment's due process clause, the Court found unconstitutional a state law prohibiting the teaching of any modern language other than English in any private, denominational, parochial, or public elementary school. In an opinion written by Justice James C. McReynolds, the Court said that the statute, as applied to instruction in German in a parochial school, "unreasonably infringes the liberty guaranteed . . . by the Fourteenth Amendment," which states that the government shall not deprive any person "of life, liberty, or property, without due process of law." Extending privacy protection to education, the Court endorsed generally "those privileges long recognized at common law as essential to the orderly pursuit of happiness by free men."

Pierce v. Society of Sisters, 268 U.S. 510 (1925). In an opinion written by Justice James C. McReynolds, the Court struck down an Oregon statute that required children to attend public rather than private or parochial elementary schools. In upholding parental right to educational privacy, the Court preferred individual freedom over a community goal. Echoling his earlier opinion in *Meyer v. Nebraska* (1923), McReynolds said that the statute "unreasonably interferes with the liberty of parents and guardians to direct the upbringing and education of children under their control." One way, the Court concluded, to help ensure the realization of "liberty" for the parents and "destiny" for the child is through a right to privacy. "The child is not the mere creature of the state; those who nurture him and direct his destiny have the right, coupled with the high duty, to recognize and prepare him for additional obligations."

Buck v. Bell, 274 U.S. 200 (1927). In its opinion, written by Justice Oliver Wendell Holmes, the Court upheld a Virginia statute permitting the sexual sterilization of mentally defective institutionalized persons suffering from hereditary types of insanity or imbecility when believed to be in the best interest of the patient and society. Implying that such persons have less privacy rights than other members of society, Holmes reasoned: "We have seen more than once that the public welfare may call upon the best citizens for their lives. It would be strange if it could not call upon those who already sap the strength of the State for these lesser sacrifices . . . in order to prevent our being swamped with incompetence. It is better for all the world, if instead of waiting to execute degenerate offspring for crime, or to let them starve for this imbecility, society can prevent those who are manifestly unfit from continuing their kind. The principle that sustains compulsory vaccination is broad enough to cover cutting the Fallopian tubes."

Olmstead v. U.S., 277 U.S. 438 (1928). The seven-member majority ruled that obtaining information by wiretapping was not a search or seizure within the meaning of the Fourth Amendment and, thus, not subject to constitutional restrictions. But the case is most famous for the dissents it provoked by Justices Louis D. Brandeis and Oliver Wendell Holmes. Disputing the Court's refusal to treat wiretapping as an invasion of privacy as protected by the Fourth Amendment, Brandeis wrote: "The makers of our Constitution undertook to secure conditions favorable to the pursuit of happiness. They recognized the significance of man's spiritual nature, of his feelings and of his intellect. They sought to protect Americans in their beliefs, their thoughts, their emotions and their sensations. They conferred, as against the Government, the right to be let alone—the most comprehensive of rights and the right most valued by civilized men."

Goldman v. U.S., 316 U.S. 129 (1942). Justice Owen J. Roberts, for the Court, said that listening in an adjoining room to the words of another on the telephone did not violate the FCC's provision forbidding anyone to "interrupt" any "communication." Federal agents had used an electronic detectaphone to listen in on phone conversations regarding a bankruptcy conspiracy. In finding that the agents did not violate the Fourth Amendment, the Court refused to overrule *Olmstead v. U.S.* (1928). Roberts wrote: "The listening in the next room to the words of [Joseph P.] Shulman as he talked into the telephone receiver was no more the interception of a wire communication within the meaning of the [Communications] Act, than would have been the overhearing of the conversation by one sitting in the same room." Chief Justice Harlan F. Stone and Justice Felix Frankfurter dissented on the ground that *Olmstead* should have been overruled. Justice Frank Murphy, also in dissent, said the use of the detectaphone constituted "unreasonable search and seizure." He said: "One of the great boons secured to the inhabitants of this country by the Bill of Rights is the right of personal privacy guaranteed by the Fourth Amendment." Justice Robert H. Jackson did not participate.

Skinner v. Oklahoma, 316 U.S. 535 (1942). In its opinion, written by Justice William O. Douglas, the Court ruled against a state statute that provided for the sterilization of persons convicted three or more times of felonies involving moral turpitude but that excepted those convicted of "offenses arising out of the violation of the prohibitory laws, revenue acts, embezzlement, or political offenses." Douglas noted: "We are dealing here with legislation which involves one of the basic civil rights of man. Marriage and procreation are fundamental to the very existence and survival of the race."

Prince v. Massachusetts, 321 U.S. 158 (1944). The Court, in its opinion by Justice Wiley B. Rutledge, upheld a state statute prohibiting children under specified ages from selling or exercising any trade in any street or public place. In this case, the law had been applied to the legal guardian of a child attempting to sell religious pamphlets of the Jehovah's Witnesses. Rutledge wrote: "It is cardinal with us that the custody, care and nurture of the child reside first in the parents," in recognition of which "decisions have respected the private realm of family life which the state cannot enter."

NAACP v. Alabama, 357 U.S. 449 (1958). Justice John M. Harlan's opinion for a unanimous Court held unconstitutional a state court order requiring the NAACP to produce membership lists. Harlan wrote: "The immunity from state scrutiny of membership lists which the Association claims on behalf of its members is here so related to the right of the members to pursue their lawful private interest privately and to associate freely with others in so doing as to come within the protection of the Fourteenth Amendment." The Court thus extended the right of privacy to include anonymity while participating in public expression. This case, the Court's first dealing directly with informational privacy, protects private information largely in order to guarantee the free exercise of associational rights under the First Amendment.

Poe v. Ullman, 367 U.S. 497 (1961). The case dealt with two married women and a doctor who had sought judgments declaring unconstitutional Connecticut statutes prohibiting physicians from giving contraceptive advice. The Court, in dismissing their appeal, noted that the state's history of failure to enforce its ban did not indicate a serious threat to prosecution. Justice Felix Frankfurter wrote the opinion, joined by Chief Justice Earl Warren and Justices Tom C. Clark and Charles E. Whittaker. William J. Brennan, Jr., concurred separately. John M. Harlan, in a dissent that has had a major influence on subsequent privacy decisions, objected to the Court's refusal to deal with the broader constitutional issues. He said the statute violated the 14th Amendment. "I believe that a statute making it a criminal offense for *married couples* to use contraceptives is an intolerable and unjustifiable invasion of privacy in the conduct of the most intimate concerns of an individual's private life." Also dissenting were Justices Hugo L. Black, William O. Douglas, and Potter Stewart.

Mapp v. Ohio, 367 U.S. 643 (1961). Justice Tom C. Clark, for the Court, said that evidence obtained by searches and seizures was inadmissible in a criminal trial in a state. In holding that the exclusionary rule was an essential part of both the Fourth and 14th Amendments, Clark wrote: "Having once recognized that the right of privacy embodied in the Fourth Amendment is enforceable against the States, and that the right to be secure against rude invasions of privacy by state officers is ... constitutional in origin, we can no longer permit that right to remain an empty promise." Justices Hugo L. Black and William O. Douglas concurred. John M. Harlan, with Felix Frankfurter and Charles E. Whittaker, dissented, as did Potter Stewart in part.

Griswold v. Connecticut, 381 U.S. 479 (1965). The decision invalidated a Connecticut law, upheld in *Poe v. Ullman* (1961), forbidding the dissemination of birth control information as a violation of a right to marital privacy. Justice William O. Douglas, writing for the seven-member majority, said that any important liberty not safeguarded by the Bill of Rights can be found in the "penumbra," or shadow, of a specific guarantee. "Various guarantees create zones of privacy," he wrote, and cited the right of association, for example, as part of the First Amendment. He noted other facets of privacy contained in the Third, Fourth, and Fifth Amendments, and included the Ninth for good measure. Justice John M. Harlan, though concurring, found the penumbra approach sufficient to strike down the Connecticut law, but said it did not go far enough. The decision need not depend on "radiations" from the Bill of Rights, he said. "The Due Process Clause of the Fourteenth Amendment stands ... on its own." Justice Hugo L.

Black, in dissent, said he could find no *specific* language in the Constitution protecting a "broad, abstract and ambiguous" right of privacy. Justice Potter Stewart, also in dissent, said he could find no *general* rights of privacy in the Bill of Rights or in any part of the Constitution.

Katz v. U.S., 389 U.S. 347 (1967). Here the Court introduced the element of legitimate "expectation of privacy" and attempted to define further what it has since called "constitutionally pro-tected areas" for private behavior. Justice John M. Harlan said that the Fourth Amendment protects people, not places, explaining that "there is a twofold requirement, first, that a person have exhibited an actual (subjective) expectation of privacy and, second, that the expectation be one that society is prepared to recognize as 'reasonable.'" Overturning in effect *Olmstead v. U.S.* (1928), the Court held that electronic listening in on a telephone conversation in a public telephone booth violated privacy as protected by the 14th Amendment's search and seizure provision. Harlan likened the phone booth, albeit a public facility, to a house, where there is more expectation of privacy than in, for example, a motor vehicle. Justices Hugo L. Black and Potter Stewart dissented, as they had in *Griswold v. Connecticut* (1965), on the extent to which the privacy right can be covered by the Constitution.

Stanley v. Georgia, 394 U.S. 557 (1969). The Court, in its opinion written by Justice Thurgood Marshall, held that the First and 14th Amendments prohibited making the private possession of obscene material a crime. See more under *Obscenity*.

Eisenstadt v. Baird, 405 U.S. 438 (1972). Justice William J. Brennan, Jr., writing for the Court, held that a Massachusetts statute forbidding distribution of contraceptives to be used for preventing conception violated the Equal Protection Clause. Appearing to extend *Griswold v. Connecticut* (1965) to unmarried persons, the Court said that no "ground of difference . . . rationally explains the different treatment accorded married and unmarried persons." Baird had been convicted for giving a young woman a package of vaginal foam at the end of a lecture on contraception that he had delivered on a Massachusetts campus. State statutes made it a crime to distribute contraceptives for preventing conception, but allowed for distribution to married persons on prescription by doctors or druggists. Nor was distribution to prevent disease prohibited. Brennan wrote: "It is true that in *Griswold* the right of privacy in question inhered in the marital relationship.

Yet the marital couple is not an independent entity with a mind and heart of its own, but an association of two individuals each with a separate intellectual and emotional makeup. If the right of privacy means anything, it is the right of the *individual*, married or single, to be free from unwarranted governmental intrusion into matters so fundamentally affecting a person as the decision whether to bear or beget a child." Chief Justice Warren E. Burger, in dissent, said: "I simply cannot believe that the limitation on the class of lawful distributors has significantly impaired the right to use contraceptives in Massachusetts."

Roe v. Wade, 410 U.S. 113 (1973). Justice Harry A. Blackmun, writing for the Court, concluded that the right of privacy includes the abortion decision, "but that this right is not unqualified and must be considered against important state interests in regulation." In its 7-to-2 decision, the Court ruled unconstitutional the restrictive abortion laws of Texas, Georgia (*Doe v. Bolton*, 410 U.S. 179, decided the same day), and those of virtually every other state. After noting that the Constitution does not explicitly mention any right of privacy, Blackmun reviewed the line of decisions from which had evolved a right of personal privacy. Justices William H. Rehnquist and Byron R. White dissented, the latter accusing the Court of exercising "raw judicial power."

California Bankers' Assoc. v. Shultz, 416 U.S. 21 (1974). In a key informational privacy case, the Court upheld the Bank Secrecy Act (BSA) of 1970, which required banks to keep records and to file certain reports that have "a high degree of usefulness in criminal, tax, or regular investigations or proceedings." In this case, the plaintiffs included several bank customers and the American Civil Liberties Union. They argued unsuccessfully that the BSA violated the Fourth Amendment's protection against unreasonable search and seizure. They said the act also violated the First, Fifth, Ninth, Tenth, and 14th Amendments. The banks objected to the extra work involved, but also opined that the law made them agents of the government in the surveillance of citizens. Justice William O. Douglas, in a vigorous dissent, said: "It would be highly useful to governmental espionage to have like reports from all our bookstores, all our hardware and retail stores, all our drug stores. These records might be 'useful' in criminal investigations."

Bowers v. Hardwick, 478 U.S. 186 (1986). Justice Byron R. White wrote for the 5-to-4 Court, holding that the due process clause of the 14th Amendment did not confer a fundamental right on homosexuals to engage in consensual sodomy, even in the privacy of the home. A practicing homosexual was charged with violating a Georgia statute criminalizing sodomy, described as any sexual act involving the sex organs of one person and the mouth or anus of another. The "act" took place with an adult male in Hardwick's bedroom, to which police had access after entering his home on a warrant for another matter. The Court of Appeals for the 11th Circuit reversed the district court's dismissal and remand, holding that the statute violated Hardwick's right to privacy as protected by the Ninth Amendment and by the due process clause of the 14th. The Supreme Court reversed that judgment, Justice White saying that past Court formulations did not extend such a right to homosexuals. "Proscriptions against that conduct have ancient roots," he wrote. Justice Harry A. Blackmun, for the minority, said that *Bowers* was more than a case about homosexual rights; rather, it was about "the most comprehensive of rights and the right most valued by civilized men, namely the right to be let alone," quoting Justice Louis D. Brandeis in *Olmstead v. U.S.* (1928). What the Court failed to endorse, Blackmun said, was the fundamental interest individuals have in controlling the nature of their intimate associations with others.

See also under *Freedom of Information Act* for decisions in which personal privacy, as defined in Exemption 6, has been a factor.

Selected Bibliography

Allen, Anita L., "Rethinking the Rule Against Corporate Privacy Rights: Some Conceptual Quandries for the Common Law," 20 *John Marshall L. Rev.* 607 (Summer 1987).

Arnold, Marc, and Andrew Kisseloff, "An Introduction to the Federal Privacy Act of 1974 and Its Effect on the Freedom of Information Act," 11 *New England L. Rev.* 463 (1976).

Ashdown, Gerald G., "Media Reporting and Privacy Claims—Decline in Constitutional Protection for the Press," 66 *Kentucky L. J.* 759 (1977–78).

Bezanson, Randall, et al., "Symposium: Toward a Resolution of the Expanding Conflict Between the Press and Privacy Interests," 64 *Iowa L. Rev.* 1061 (July 1979).

Bloustein, Edward J., "Privacy as an Aspect of Human Dignity: An Answer to Dean Prosser," 39 *NYU L. Rev.* 962 (1964).

Bostwick, Gary L., "A Taxonomy of Privacy: Repose, Sanctuary and Intimate Decision," 64 *California L. Rev.* 1447 (1976).

Burgoon, Judee K., "Privacy and Communication," 6 *Communication Yearbook* 206 (1982).

Davis, Frederick, "What Do We Mean by Right to Privacy?" 4 *So. Dakota L. Rev.* 1 (1959).

Emerson, Thomas I., "The Right of Privacy and Freedom of the Press," 14 *Harvard Civil Rights–Civil Liberties L. Rev.* 329 (Summer 1979).

"False Light Invasion of Privacy: False Tort?" 17 *Southwestern Univ. L. Rev.* 135 (1987).

Glasser, Theodore, "Resolving the Press-Privacy Conflict: Approaches to the Newsworthiness Defense," 4 *Communication and Law* 23 (Spring 1982).

Hixson, Richard F., "Whose Life Is It, Anyway? Information as Property," 1 *Information and Behavior* 76 (1985).

——, "Privacy, Pornography, and the Supreme Court," 21 *John Marshall L. Rev.* (1988).

Konvitz, Milton R., "Privacy and the Law: A Philosophical Prelude," 31 *Law and Contemporary Problems* 272 (1966).

Lashner, Marilyn A., "Privacy and the Public's Right to Know," 53 *Journalism Quarterly* 679 (1976).

Lazar, Erik D., "Towards a Right of Biography: Controlling Commercial Exploitation of Personal History," 2 *Comm/Ent* 489 (Spring 1980).

Lee, William E., "The Supreme Court on Privacy and the Press," 12 *Georgia L. Rev.* 215 (Winter 1978).

Levine, Marla E., "The Right of Publicity as a Means of Protecting Performers' Style," 14 *Loyola-LA L. Rev.* 129 (1980).

Ludlow, Warren, "Zacchini v. Scripps-Howard Broadcasting Company: Media Appropriation, the First Amendment and State Regulation," 1977 *Utah L. Rev.* 817 (1977).

Marks, Kevin, "An Assessment of the Copyright Model in Right of Publicity Cases," 70 *California L. Rev.* 786 (1982).

Nimmer, Melville B., "The Right to Speak from Times to Time: First Amendment Theory Applied to Libel and Misapplied to Privacy," 56 *California L. Rev.* 935 (1968).

O'Brien, Denis, "The Right of Privacy," 2 *Columbia L. Rev.* 437 (1902).

O'Connor, Thomas H., "The Right of Privacy in Historical Perspective," 53 *Massachusetts L. Q.* 101 (1968).

Pember, Don R., "The Burgeoning Scope of Access Privacy and the Portent for a Free Press," 64 *Iowa L. Rev.* 1155 (1979).

Pember, Don R., and Dwight L. Teeter, "Privacy and the Press Since Time, Inc. v. Hill," 50 *Washington L. Rev.* 57 (1974).

Posner, Richard, "The Right to Privacy," 12 *Georgia L. Rev.* 393 (1978).

Pound, Roscoe, "The Fourteenth Amendment and the Right of Privacy," 13 *Western Reserve L. Rev.* 34 (1961).

"Privacy, Computers, and the Commercial Dissemination of Personal Information," 65 *Texas L. Rev.* 1395 (June 1987).

"The Privacy Interests of AIDS-Infected Blood Donors," 18 *Cumberland L. Rev.* 267 (1987–88).

"Process, Privacy, and the Supreme Court," 28 *Boston College L. Rev.* 691 (July 1987).

Prosser, William L., "Privacy," 48 *California L. Rev.* 383 (1960).

Rovere, Richard H., "The Invasion of Privacy (1): Technology and the Claims of Community," 27 *American Scholar* 413 (1958).

Schadrack, Mark, "Privacy and the Press: A Necessary Tension," 18 *Loyola-LA L. Rev.* 949 (1985).

Schoeman, Ferdinand, "Adolescent Confidentiality and Family Privacy," 20 *John Marshall L. Rev.* 641 (Summer 1987).

Sims, Andrew B., "Right to Publicity: Survivability Reconsidered," 49 *Fordham L. Rev.* 453 (1981).

Trubow, George B., and Kenneth A. Michaels, Jr., "False Light Privacy Actions: Constitutional Constraints and Standards of Proof of Fault," 20 *John Marshall L. Rev.* 854 (Summer 1987).

Wacks, Raymond, "The Poverty of Privacy," 96 *Law Quarterly Rev.* 73 (1980).

Warren, Samuel D., and Louis D. Brandeis, "The Right to Privacy," 4 *Harvard L. Rev.* 193 (1890).

Wilkins, Richard G., "Defining the 'Reasonable Expectations of Privacy': An Emerging Tripartite Analysis," 40 *Vanderbilt L. Rev.* 1077 (Oct. 1987).

Wright, J. Skelly, "Defamation, Privacy, and the Public's Right to Know: A National Problem and a New Approach," 46 *Texas L. Rev.* 630 (1968).

Zimmerman, Diane L., "Requiem for a Heavyweight: A Farewell to Warren and Brandeis Privacy Tort," 68 *Cornell L. Rev.* 291 (1983).

INDEX OF DECISIONS

NOTE: Decisions fully summarized appear in **bold** and the first page on which the decision is discussed appears in *italics*.

SUBJECT INDEX